Felix Meyer and Anne C. Shreffler

Elliott Carter

A Centennial Portrait in Letters and Documents

A Publication of the Paul Sacher Foundation

The Boydell Press
Woodbridge, Suffolk

2008

Imprint

A Publication of the Paul Sacher Foundation, Basel

Translations from German: J. Bradford Robinson
Copy editing: Kathryn Bailey Puffett
Index: Heidy Zimmermann

Cover illustration:
Elliott Carter working at his desk (New York, February 1966),
photograph by William Gedney
© William Gedney photographs, Duke University Rare Book,
Manuscript, and Special Collections Library

Design: Sibylle Ryser, Basel, www.sibylleryser.ch
Typesetting: Sibylle Ryser
Setting of musical notation: ngb | notengrafik berlin
Fonts: Sabon Next, Akkurat
Paper: Tatami White
Reproduction: Photolitho Sturm AG, Muttenz/Basel
Printed by Kreis Druck AG, Basel
Bound by Buchbinderei Grollimund AG, Reinach/Basel
Printed in Switzerland

First published 2008

The Boydell Press, an imprint of Boydell & Brewer Ltd
PO Box 9, Woodbridge, Suffolk IP12 3DF, UK
and of Boydell & Brewer Inc.
668 Mt Hope Avenue, Rochester, NY 14620, USA
Website: www.boydell.co.uk

ISBN-13: 978 1 84383 404 5
ISBN-10: 1 84383 404 9

Table of Contents

Acknowledgements

A book of this kind is best served by collaborative effort. Original documents preserve undiluted but only partial truths; without the help of many people and institutions we could not have collected the multitude of details and points of fact that were neessary to make the documents "speak." Our thanks first and foremost are owed to Elliott Carter, who gave generously of his time, shared his memories with us, and granted permission for the use of all the documents gathered together in this book. His serene good humor was contagious and gave us the energy and the will to persevere when the task seemed daunting. Virgil Blackwell's active engagement with the whole project was likewise essential. He worked tirelessly to provide us with recent scores, photos, and other material; as a musician who has played Carter's music since the mid-1970s, he also drew from his encyclopedic knowledge to give us rich insights about Carter's music and about New York's musical life.

We are grateful for the extensive support from the staff of the Paul Sacher Foundation, which has made it possible to complete this publication in a relatively short time. In particular, we would like to thank Henrike Hoffmann, the librarian in charge of the Elliott Carter Collection, who checked all the original documents and prepared them for reproduction as well as providing valuable assistance with the work list. Special thanks are also due to Sabine Hänggi, who tracked down innumerable pieces of information from the four corners of the earth, and in general provided indispensable help. We would further like to thank Carlos Chanfón, Evelyne Diendorf, Tina Kilvio Tüscher, and Johanna Blask for their assistance in matters large and small. Robert Piencikowski gave us valuable advice on the documents in French. Matthias Kassel kept track of permissions and copyright issues and, in his capacity as coordinator of publications, gave us valuable guidance on the book's layout and presentation. Finally, Heidy Zimmermann was graciously willing to prepare the index, a thankless job in a book with so many names and titles. At Harvard University, research funds from the Faculty of Arts and Sciences made it possible to support a research assistant: Louis Epstein prepared a preliminary version of the work list and handled the correspondence relating to permissions.

One peculiar aspect of this transatlantic cooperation was that the commentary texts and introduction were written originally in a mixture of German and English. Since we conceived this volume together (and both take full responsibility for all parts of it), we are especially grateful to J. Bradford Robinson, whose excellent translations finally unified the language of the manuscript, and to Kathryn Bailey Puffett, whose sharp editorial eye helped to smooth over the stylistic differences that remained.

Many others helped us by generously sharing their expertise, memories, and materials. We would like especially to thank Emily Abrams Ansari, Irvine Arditti, Amy Beal, Gianmario Borio, Martin Brody, David Carter, Angela De Benedictis, Laurel Fay, David Gable, Dorothea Gail, Paul Griffiths, Doris Lanz, John Link, Lewis Lockwood, Drew Massey, Dominique Nabokov, Carol Oja, Charles Rosen, Claudia Vincis, Roman Vlad, Christoph Wolff, Susan Davenny Wyner, and Yehudi Wyner. We are also grateful to Arion Scheifele (President, Cadillac Club of Switzerland, Waldenburg, Switzerland) for sharing his knowledge of historical automobiles.

Many libraries and archives generously provided material for this book. Among the librarians and archivists who searched for information and expeditiously sent along documents and copies, we are grateful to Bethany Alexander (Office Administrator, Bath Festival, Bath UK), George Boziwick (Chief, Music Division, New York Public Library for the Performing Arts), Riccardo Cerocchi (President, Campus Internazionale di Musica, Latina), Hugh Cobbe (former Head of Manuscripts and Music, British Library, London), Rob Hudson (Associate Archivist, Carnegie Hall), Kendall L. Crilly (Director, Irving S. Gilmore Music Library, Yale University), Virginia Danielson (Richard F. French Librarian, Eda Kuhn Loeb Music Library, Harvard University); Linda Edgerly (Consulting Archivist, American Academy in Rome), David Gollon (Pitkin County Library, Aspen, CO), Dell Hollingsworth (former Music Specialist, Harry Ransom Humanities Research Center, University of Texas, Austin), Jennifer B. Lee (Librarian for Public Services and Programs, Rare Book and Manuscript Library, Columbia University), Luca Logi (Archivio Musicale, Teatro del Maggio Musicale Fiorentino), Catherine Massip (Director, Music Division, Bibliothèque Nationale de France, Paris), Kerry Masteller (Eda Kuhn Loeb Music Library, Harvard University), Andreas Maul (Musikproduktion/Dramaturgie, Hessischer Rundfunk, Frankfurt am Main), Lize Musch (Production Manager, Stichting Comité voor het Concertgebouw, Amsterdam), Louise North (Archives Researcher, BBC Written Archives Centre, Reading), Barbara Perkel (Boston Symphony Orchestra Archives), Robin Rausch (Music Specialist, Library of Congress, Washington, D.C.), Astrid Schirmer (Secretary to Pierre Boulez), Melissa Tacke (Project Archivist, Bennington College), Liza Vick (Eda Kuhn Loeb Music Library, Harvard University), László Vikárius (Director, Bartók Archívum, Budapest), Frank Villella (Archivist, Rosenthal Archives of the Chicago Symphony Orchestra), Richard Wandel (Associate Archivist, New York Philharmonic Archives), Antje Werkmeister (Berliner Staatsoper Unter den Linden), and Yvonne Widger (Administrator, The Dartington Hall Trust).

We have made every effort to locate and obtain permission from all copyright holders, and would welcome any information about those few we have not been able to identify.

Musical Examples

The facsimiles of Elliott Carter's music manuscripts are reproduced by permission of the publishers listed below.

Boston Concerto
© Copyright 2002 by Hendon Music, Inc., a Boosey & Hawkes Company

Canon for 3: Igor Stravinsky in Memoriam
Copyright © 1972 (Renewed) by Associated Music Publishers, Inc. (BMI). International Copyright Secured. All Rights Reserved.

Clarinet Concerto
© Copyright 1996 by Hendon Music, Inc., a Boosey & Hawkes Company

Concerto for Orchestra
Copyright © 1972 (Renewed) by Associated Music Publishers, Inc. (BMI). International Copyright Secured. All Rights Reserved.

The Defense of Corinth
© 1950 by Mercury Music Corp. Theodore Presser Company, Sole Representative. All Rights Reserved. Used by Permission.

Eight Pieces for Four Timpani
Copyright © 1968 (Renewed) by Associated Music Publishers, Inc. (BMI). International Copyright Secured. All Rights Reserved.

Emblems
© 1949 by Mercury Music Corp. Theodore Presser Company, Sole Representative. All Rights Reserved. Used by Permission.

Esprit rude/Esprit doux I
© Copyright 1985 by Hendon Music, Inc., a Boosey & Hawkes Company

Esprit rude/Esprit doux II
© Copyright 1994 by Hendon Music, Inc., a Boosey & Hawkes Company

The Harmony of Morning
Copyright © 1955 (Renewed) by Associated Music Publishers, Inc. (BMI). International Copyright Secured. All Rights Reserved

Heart Not so Heavy As Mine
Copyright © 1939 (Renewed) by Associated Music Publishers, Inc. (BMI). International Copyright Secured. All Rights Reserved.

Holiday Overture
Copyright © 1946 (Renewed) by Associated Music Publishers, Inc. (BMI). International Copyright Secured. All Rights Reserved.

In Sleep, in Thunder
© Copyright 1982 by Hendon Music, Inc., a Boosey & Hawkes Company

In the Distances of Sleep
© Copyright 2006 by Hendon Music, Inc., a Boosey & Hawkes Company

Mad Regales
© Copyright 2008 by Hendon Music, Inc., a Boosey & Hawkes Company

Mosaic
© Copyright 2005 by Hendon Music, Inc., a Boosey & Hawkes Company

Night Fantasies
Copyright © 1982 (Renewed) by Associated Music Publishers, Inc. (BMI). International Copyright Secured. All Rights Reserved.

Oboe Concerto
© Copyright 1998 by Hendon Music, Inc., a Boosey & Hawkes Company

Oboe Quartet
© Copyright 2002 by Hendon Music, Inc., a Boosey & Hawkes Company

Piano Concerto
Copyright © 1967 (Renewed) by Associated Music Publishers, Inc. (BMI). International Copyright Secured. All Rights Reserved.

Piano Sonata
© 1948 by Mercury Music Corp. Theodore Presser Company, Sole Representative. All Rights Reserved. Used by Permission.

Pocahontas
Copyright © 1941 (Renewed) by Associated Music Publishers, Inc. (BMI). International Copyright Secured. All Rights Reserved.

Sonata for Flute, Oboe, Cello, and Harpsichord
Copyright © 1960 (Renewed) by Associated Music Publishers, Inc. (BMI). International Copyright Secured. All Rights Reserved.

Sonata for Violoncello and Piano
Copyright © 1951 (Renewed) by Associated Music Publishers, Inc. (BMI). International Copyright Secured. All Rights Reserved.

Sound Fields
© Copyright 2007 by Hendon Music, Inc., a Boosey & Hawkes Company

Soundings
© Copyright 2006 by Hendon Music, Inc., a Boosey & Hawkes Company

Steep Steps
© Copyright 2000 by Hendon Music, Inc., a Boosey & Hawkes Company

String Quartet No. 1
Copyright © 1956 (Renewed) by Associated Music Publishers, Inc. (BMI). International Copyright Secured. All Rights Reserved.

String Quartet No. 2
Copyright © 1961 (Renewed) by Associated Music Publishers, Inc. (BMI). International Copyright Secured. All Rights Reserved.

String Quartet No. 3
Copyright © 1973 (Renewed) by Associated Music Publishers, Inc. (BMI). International Copyright Secured. All Rights Reserved.

String Quartet No. 4
© Copyright 1986 by Hendon Music, Inc., a Boosey & Hawkes Company

String Quartet No. 5
© Copyright 1998 by Hendon Music, Inc., a Boosey & Hawkes Company

Symphonia: Sum Fluxae Pretium Spei
© Copyright 2002 by Hendon Music, Inc., a Boosey & Hawkes Company

Symphony No. 1
Copyright © 1961 (Renewed) by Associated Music Publishers, Inc. (BMI). International Copyright Secured. All Rights Reserved.

A Symphony of Three Orchestras
Copyright © 1978 (Renewed) by Associated Music Publishers, Inc. (BMI). International Copyright Secured. All Rights Reserved.

Syringa
Copyright © 1980 (Renewed) by Associated Music Publishers, Inc. (BMI). International Copyright Secured. All Rights Reserved.

Tempo e tempi
© Copyright 1999 by Hendon Music, Inc., a Boosey & Hawkes Company

Three Occasions
© Copyright 1989 by Hendon Music, Inc., a Boosey & Hawkes Company

Trilogy
© Copyright 1992 by Hendon Music, Inc., a Boosey & Hawkes Company

Triple Duo
© Copyright 1983 by Hendon Music, Inc., a Boosey & Hawkes Company

Variations for Orchestra
Copyright © 1958 (Renewed) by Associated Music Publishers, Inc. (BMI). International Copyright Secured. All Rights Reserved.

Violin Concerto
© Copyright 1990 by Hendon Music, Inc., a Boosey & Hawkes Company

Voyage
Copyright © 1973 (Renewed) by Associated Music Publishers, Inc. (BMI). International Copyright Secured. All Rights Reserved.

What Next?
© Copyright 1999 by Hendon Music, Inc., a Boosey & Hawkes Company

Woodwind Quintet
Copyright © 1952 (Renewed) by Associated Music Publishers, Inc. (BMI). International Copyright Secured. All Rights Reserved.

Note on Transcriptions

In transcribing the letters and text documents we have kept editorial changes to a minimum. For example, even though Carter generally follows American spelling and usage, we did not change the occasional words he spelled in British English ("theatre," "labour," etc.). We have also preserved the original spellings of proper names, particularly Russian ones that were in common usage at the time ("Prokofieff," "Shostakovitch," etc.), and all shorthand references to generically titled works, such as "cello sonata," or "Second String Quartet." (In the commentaries, such works are always referred to by their publication titles: *Sonata for Violoncello and Piano, String Quartet No. 2,* etc.) In contrast, specific work titles (*A Mirror on Which to Dwell, Syringa,* etc.) as well as titles of books and periodicals are consistently italicized; this is the case even when they are emphasized in other ways in the documents (for example, by all-capitals, underlining, or quotes). Throughout, we have tacitly corrected the occasional misspelling of the composer's first name. For the sake of readability and to ensure a certain consistency, we have discreetly regularized the punctuation, especially in the lectures and interviews, as well as the capitalization of words. Except for a few misspellings, which we have tacitly corrected, all other editorial changes are marked by square brackets, which are also used for written-out abbreviations.

Bibliographical Abbreviations

CC
Elliott Carter: In Conversation with Enzo Restagno for Settembre Musica 1989, I.S.A.M. Monographs 32, trans. Katherine Silberblatt Wolfthal (Brooklyn New York: Institute for Studies in American Music, 1991)

CEL
Elliott Carter, *Collected Essays and Lectures, 1937–1995,* ed. Jonathan W. Bernard (Rochester: University of Rochester Press, 1997)

FW
Allen Edwards, *Flawed Words and Stubborn Sounds: A Conversation with Elliott Carter* (New York: W.W. Norton, 1971)

ML
The Musical Languages of Elliott Carter, ed. Jon Newsom (Washington, D.C.: Library of Congress, 1984)

SS
Elliott Carter: Sketches and Scores in Manuscript (New York: New York Public Library and Readex Books, 1973)

WEC
The Writings of Elliott Carter: An American Composer Looks at Modern Music, ed. Else Stone and Kurt Stone (Bloomington, IN, and London: Indiana University Press, 1977)

Link 2000
John F. Link, *Elliott Carter: A Guide to Research* (New York and London: Garland, 2000)

Noubel 2000
Max Noubel, *Elliott Carter ou le temps fertile* (Geneva: Editions Contrechamps, 2000)

Schiff 1983
David Schiff, *The Music of Elliott Carter* (London: Eulenburg, 1983)

Schiff 1998
David Schiff, *The Music of Elliott Carter,* new edition (London: Faber; Ithaca: Cornell University Press, 1998)

Introduction

In the course of music history many composers have reached a very advanced age, and several have succeeded in maintaining their creative powers well into their seventies and eighties. Yet the case of Elliott Carter, who will celebrate his one-hundredth birthday in December 2008, is seemingly unprecedented: not only has he remained miraculously active, producing more new compositions in recent years than ever before, he has also had the good fortune of being able to take part personally in some of the many concerts, festivals, and events mounted this year in his honor. But the great attention bestowed on Carter this year is only partly attributable to the rituals of an anniversary-obsessed culture. This wave has long been visible from afar, and seems to be the natural, almost inevitable culmination of his steady rise to international recognition and esteem. This fact, too – that a centenarian composer, far from having to be "recalled to mind," has been accompanied by growing success for years and even decades – is wholly extraordinary, especially when the composer is, like Carter, a creator of contemporary music who has consistently forged his own path and paid so little heed to the prevailing taste of the public.

With this publication, the Paul Sacher Foundation joins the large host of well-wishers paying tribute to the composer on his one-hundredth birthday. A good twenty years ago Carter entrusted to the Foundation the bulk of his music manuscripts and other papers relating to his creative activity. In response, our book presents a generous selection of documents on his life and work, almost all of which have not been published before. While most of Carter's articles and lectures are available in carefully edited collections[1] and his compositions, both singly and as a whole, have been the subject of many studies,[2] the handwritten documents, especially his letters and music manuscripts, have until now been accessible to only a small circle of specialists. Our volume is intended to remedy this situation. Its letters and other writings, as well as the photographs and music manuscripts, cast spotlights on Carter's life and the major way stations in his artistic career, and its extensive annotations provide context and commentary. For all its many gaps, it is our hope that the resulting portrait in letters and documents will add new facets to existing knowledge about the composer, and that the material gathered together in this book will stimulate further engagement with Carter's music and his artistic ideas as well as with his life – there is much more to be said, for example, about the relationship between technique and aesthetics in Carter's music, and a full-scale biography still remains to be written.

Making a selection from the huge body of extant documents was no easy matter. But it was clear to us from the outset that the book should include a relatively large number of letters, especially considering that so little of Carter's correspondence has been published.[3] And we were also convinced that Carter's letters should be complemented as often as possible by those of his correspondents, in order to illuminate his exchange of ideas and experiences with other musicians, colleagues, and friends. Some eighty-five letters to and from Carter (the former from the holdings of the Paul Sacher Foundation, the latter from various libraries and collections in Europe and the United States) ultimately found their way into our volume. Granted, this is a small

1 *The Writings of Elliott Carter: An American Composer Looks at Modern Music,* ed. Else Stone and Kurt Stone (Bloomington, IN, and London: University of Indiana Press, 1977; hereafter *WEC*) and Elliott Carter, *Collected Essays and Lectures, 1937–1995,* ed. Jonathan W. Bernard (Rochester: University of Rochester Press, 1997; hereafter *CEL*).

2 The most important full-length studies are David Schiff, *The Music of Elliott Carter* (London: Eulenburg, 1983; hereafter Schiff 1983), new edition (London:

Faber; Ithaca: Cornell University Press, 1998; hereafter Schiff 1998), and Max Noubel, *Elliott Carter ou le temps fertile* (Geneva: Editions Contrechamps, 2000; hereafter Noubel 2000). Most of his writings until 1993 and 2000, respectively, are listed in William T. Doering, *Elliott Carter: A Bio-Bibliography,* Bio-Bibliographies in Music 51 (Westport, CT, and London: Greenwood Press, 1993) and John Link, *Elliott Carter: A Guide to Research* (New York and London: Garland, 2000; hereafter Link 2000).

3 One exception is the correspondence with Charles Ives, which was published by Carter himself in "Documents of a Friendship with Ives," *Parnassus* 3/2 (Summer 1975), pp. 300–315, and reprinted many times, most recently in *CEL,* pp. 107–118. We have therefore refrained from including items from this correspondence in our volume, apart from the letter of recommendation that Ives wrote in 1926.

number, given the roughly 10,000 letters preserved in the Foundation's Elliott Carter Collection alone,[4] but the letters we have selected cover the whole of the composer's career and provide insight into his artistic ties and friendships with figures as diverse as Charles Ives, Nadia Boulanger, Aaron Copland, Conlon Nancarrow, Nicolas Nabokov, William Glock, Goffredo Petrassi, Pierre Boulez, Oliver Knussen, Heinz Holliger, Daniel Barenboim, and James Levine, to mention only some of the most celebrated names. Several of these exchanges (the correspondence with Copland, Nabokov, and Glock, for example) are not only very extensive but so interesting that we regret not being able to present them here more fully. However, given our goal of a multifaceted portrait, our combination of single letters and letter exchanges with diverse correspondents has the advantage of covering a larger span of time and a greater range of topics than if we had concentrated more fully on fewer correspondents. It also shows how subtly Carter calibrated the tone of his letters to the specific relationships he maintained with his correspondents. To sense his subtlety, however, it is necessary to read the letters closely, for on the surface most of these documents seem to adopt a rather straightforward style of writing concerned mainly with precision and clarity. Indeed, for Carter, letter writing was never so much a matter of subjective self-expression as it was a means of organizing and reporting on his professional life and intellectual work. Accordingly, he always chose his wording with great circumspection and often prepared drafts of his letters before writing them out in fair copy, even when corresponding with friends. (Several of these drafts, which reveal the composer's more impulsive and sometimes belligerent side, are preserved in the Paul Sacher Foundation's holdings.)

The letters are complemented by several lengthier texts in which Carter addresses subjects relating to aesthetics, compositional technique, and the music of other composers. Particularly interesting are some of his lectures and essays which either remained unpublished or never appeared in their original language: "The Need for New Choral Music" (1953), "Music in the United States" (1954), "Sound and Silence in Time: A Contemporary Approach to the Elements of Music" (1957), and "France – America Ltd." (1976). These writings are, in their own way, no less substantial and revealing of Carter's longstanding engagement with historical or theoretical questions of musical creativity than the texts published in the two existing anthologies (*WEC* and *CEL*), and the same is true of his radio lecture "Arnold Schönberg: Variations for Orchestra" (1957) and his conference paper "Extending the Classical Syntax" (1961). Here, too, we might easily have included other complete lectures and essays from the Foundation's holdings. Instead, we decided to augment the texts mentioned above with several items existing only as sketches or in unfinished form (such as his notes for a planned essay of 1945 on "Music in America at War" and his 1946 preface, co-written with Paul Rosenfeld, for a prospective book on Charles Ives), as well as two interviews from the 1970s and 1980s and several tributes to musically-minded friends. For in recent years the interview (often subsequently revised) and the eulogy have become his preferred modes of verbal expression. While Carter frequently used to give lectures and write lengthy essays, he has now, in his old age, expressed his thoughts more often in the informal framework of interviews and conversations. And if his earlier texts tended to deal mainly with professional issues, in recent years he has taken up

---

4 In many cases the Foundation's correspondence archive also contains carbon copies of Carter's own letters. However, we refer to these in our volume only when it has proved impossible to locate the originals, some of which contain addenda by the author.

his pen especially when an occasion arose to pay tribute to his friends. (The parallel with the many compositional homages he has recently written is obvious.)

In addition to the handwritten letters and texts, all of which are reproduced in diplomatic transcription, our volume also presents a small selection of photographs and more than fifty facsimiles of music manuscripts. The latter are intended to illuminate Carter's creative process on the basis of selected works. The selection is fairly generous until well into the 1980s and less so thereafter, given the remarkable increase in his productivity over the last two decades. The reasons behind our selection were pragmatic: rather than trying to single out the most important pieces, we were mainly intent on representing the full spectrum of Carter's compositional work. Obviously a few sporadic pages of score can convey only a patchy impression of his compositional techniques or the conceptions behind his works. Taken as a whole, however, we hope that these samples of Carter's music will clearly illustrate his considerable changes of style over the years – changes that continue to this very day – while projecting something of the constants and variables of his compositional technique. At the same time the manuscripts reproduced in facsimile are intended to shed light on the various forms of notation that Carter has used in his work. We therefore present not only fair copies, but also sketches and drafts. All the handwritten material we have drawn on (and few composers have produced such a huge amount, especially with regard to sketches) is taken from the Foundation's own holdings. This decision was likewise pragmatic: a full examination of the Carter documents preserved in other libraries – especially the Library of Congress, which holds, among many other documents, important sketches for some of his major works from the 1940s to the 1960s[5] – would have been impossible within the available time frame. As it happened, this was hardly a drawback, for the Basel holdings contain primary sources for virtually all of his works, and the object of our book was not so much to present a deep examination of his creative process as to illustrate some typical features of his working methods.

The source materials we have compiled are arranged in chronological order in eight chapters, each of which is headed with a quotation drawn either from the documents or from the titles of Carter's musical works. The dates marking these chapters are intended less to imply major junctures in Carter's life and artistic evolution than to indicate thematic points of emphasis. Within the chapters, the documents are often gathered into small groups. This is especially so in the case of the letters, whereas most of the music manuscripts stand on their own (unless a letter refers directly to a piece reproduced in manuscript). Finally, each group of documents or each work is preceded by an introductory text, and all the illustrations (facsimiles and photographs) are accompanied by brief commentaries. These introductory texts and commentaries are designed not only to highlight the immediate context of the documents presented, but also to suggest points of contact between them and to provide further information on Carter's life and works. Wherever possible, we have drawn on primary sources, augmented by reminiscences that the composer has conveyed to us in several interviews. This made it possible not only to deduce some new dates and facts, but to correct a number of minor inaccuracies in the existing literature – which unfortunately does not preclude the possibility that new errors may have slipped unawares into our text. The purpose of our book,

---

5 See the chapter "Elliott Carter's Compositions" in Link 2000, pp. 13–63, entries nos. 19, 45, 49, 50, 51, 53–56, 67, 71, 77, 79–81, 86–90, 94, 98, 106, 109, and 111.

however, is not just to provide factual details, but rather to present an overall picture of Carter as a composer, of his artistic impact and his position in the music of the twentieth and twenty-first centuries – a picture which is sketched in the discussion below.

To Be a Composer in America – and the World

It has never been easy to define what is "American." A large, relatively young, ethnically diverse, and loosely-regulated society is not well suited to forging a sense of national unity among its inhabitants. Dvořák's famous suggestion to American composers (in 1893) that they express authentic national sentiments by appropriating the music of African-American former slaves and decimated populations of American Indians, clearly based on Central European concepts of nationalism, was so incompatible with American realities that it seemed faintly ridiculous even at the time.[6] At the beginning of the twentieth century, the waves of immigration from Eastern and Southern Europe were seen as the main challenge to an American national identity; the country's new diversity threatened to break apart the fragile unity that had been achieved after the Civil War. But, for some, the presence of different nationalities that refused to consign themselves to the "melting pot" was a source of strength rather than a weakness. Randolph Bourne, writing during the First World War, believed that the patchwork quilt of immigrants gave the United States an immeasurable advantage over the more homogeneous nationalisms of Europe: "America is coming to be, not a nationality but a transnationality, a weaving back and forth, with the other lands, of many threads of all sizes and colors."[7] In 1918, Van Wyck Brooks, who also embraced Bourne's "cosmopolitan vision" in principle, saw both positive and negative effects of the American situation for fostering an indigenous literature, concluding: "There is a kind of anarchy that fosters growth and there is another anarchy that prevents growth, because it lays too great a strain upon the individual."[8] Indeed, openness to new ideas and individualism are perhaps the most typically American traits, but, as Brooks maintained, precisely these features often hinder the establishment of traditions and inhibit the development of historical continuity. Individual regions, ethnic groups, or subcultures may develop traditions, but – ever since the cultural dominance of the settlers of English descent was called into question – no single culture or region has had the authority to impose its tradition on the country as a whole. As a result, an artist in America does not automatically inherit a pre-existing "American tradition" or an "American identity," but must work to establish these for him- or herself; constantly reinventing the present means it is necessary to reinvent the past as well.

Throughout Carter's life – and his conscious awareness of the issue spans from about 1920, when he was twelve years old, to his hundredth year in 2008 and beyond – he has constantly thought about what it means to be an American composer. He has done this during a time when Americans looked across national boundaries and became aware of the internationalism within their own population to a degree unprecedented in their history. Whether the encounters were antagonistic (as in both world wars and in the Cold War) or peaceable (as in the countless exchanges engaged in

---

6 See Jack Sullivan, *New World Symphonies: How American Culture Changed European Music* (New Haven: Yale University Press, 1999), pp. 1–17.

7 Randolph Bourne, "Trans-National America," *The Atlantic Monthly*, no. 118 (July 1916), pp. 86–97; quoted from the online version at http://www.theatlantic.com/issues/16jul/bourne.htm, accessed 3 March 2008.

8 Van Wyck Brooks, "On Creating a Usable Past" (1918), in *Van Wyck Brooks: The Early Years: A Selection from His Works, 1908–1925*, ed. Claire Sprague, revised edition (Boston: Northeastern University Press, 1993), pp. 219–226, esp. 219.

by individuals and institutions), the "American century" was characterized above all by its transnational spirit. Like that of many of his contemporaries, Carter's identity as an American composer emerged from continuing dialogues with his American past and an international present. Less overtly Americanist than Copland's or Roy Harris's, Carter's American identity emphasized the integration of America in the world rather than its separation from it.

Coming of age in the heady atmosphere of 1920s New York modernism, Carter was shaped by the rich cultural life of the city. In his youth an avid reader of journals, including *The Seven Arts, The Dial,* and *Partisan Review,* Carter responded to the new ideas emerging from the circle that came to be known as the New York Intellectuals. Chief among those was the embrace of what was called cosmopolitan values, which Terry A. Cooney describes as a desire for a mature and sophisticated American culture "that could measure up to the traditions of Europe."[9] By blending the American spirit – decentralized, diverse, anarchic – with the advances of European high modernism, a new art could be created, more powerful than any before. Americans were uniquely suited to create this new art, because they were already masters of synthesis owing to their experience of living in a diverse society and their geographic and psychic distance from Europe. Edmund Wilson claimed in 1931, for example, that contemporary art must reject false dualisms like the European categories of classicism and romanticism, naturalism and symbolism; superseding and combining these would result in an art that could "provide us with a vision of human life and its universe, richer, more subtle, more complex and more complete than any man has yet known."[10] Both aspects of this vision became leading ideas for Carter: first, that American art should be every bit as sophisticated as that of the masterpieces of European modernism; and, second, that American artists were in a unique position to find new forms of expression that would reflect the complexities of modern American urban life.

The young Carter systematically created his own "usable past" by learning as much contemporary music as he could. (He said he did not like "old music" – the music of the standard classical repertory – in his youth.) He attended concerts of the League of Composers and became acquainted with Aaron Copland, Israel Citkowitz, Marc Blitzstein, Theodore Chanler, and other members of New York's modern music scene. He also admired the music of the American "ultra-moderns" – Varèse, Cowell, Copland, Ruth Crawford Seeger, and Ruggles – which proved to be a major influence. Regular attendance at Koussevitzky's concerts with the Boston Symphony Orchestra while he was a student at Harvard between 1926 and 1930 (Carter claims he never missed a concert during these years) gave him a wide exposure to contemporary and earlier American music. In an article on the Boston composer Henry F. Gilbert (1868–1928) written for *Modern Music* in 1943, Carter expresses admiration for this forgotten figure and, like Van Wyck Brooks almost thirty years earlier, puts his finger on the Achilles' heel of American culture: its tendency to forget. "It has been characteristic of musical life in America to neglect the composers of its own past," Carter wrote, articulating a recurring sense of frustration with the lack of continuous traditions in American musical life. The young Harvard graduate, alienated from the conservative Music Department, sympathized with Gilbert's role as Cambridge outsider: "From his barn, near Harvard, which was

9 Terry A. Cooney, *The Rise of the New York Intellectuals: Partisan Review and Its Circle, 1934–1945* (Madison: University of Wisconsin Press, 1986), pp. 5–25, esp. 7.

10 Edmund Wilson, *Axel's Castle: A Study in the Imaginative Literature of 1870–1930* (1931), quoted in Cooney, *The Rise of the New York Intellectuals* (see note 9), p. 29. See also Van Wyck Brooks's plea for the

artist to reconcile the "'Highbrow' and 'Lowbrow'," in *America's Coming of Age* (1915), in *Van Wyck Brooks: The Early Years* (see note 8), pp. 81–96.

then educating such erudite composers as John Knowles Paine, Arthur Foote, Walter Spalding, and Edward Burlingame Hill, Gilbert threw down the challenge. American serious music was too imitative 'not only of the methods of Europe but of its spirit [...]'"[11]

Carter's relationship with Charles Ives, who was born only six years later than Gilbert, was considerably more complex. In addition to psychological factors – Ives served as a kind of musical father-figure to the young Carter, and his later ambivalence surely comes in part from a kind of distancing associated with his coming of age – Ives's music challenged and confounded Carter's assumptions about how American musical history had developed.[12] According to this narrative, the use of popular songs and hymns, while common to an older generation of composers, including Gilbert, was supposed to have been superseded by a new, more abstract, American modernism. Yet Ives extravagantly combined hymn tunes and Civil War marching songs with the most daring tonal, formal, and rhythmic experiments. Ives had built his music precisely on the fault line between an older model of small-town "Americanism" and the utopia of a progressive, urban modernism, which Carter's understanding had put into two separate compartments. Given that Ives's unwieldy, sprawling works and his withdrawal from public musical life contradicted much of the young Carter's carefully constructed aesthetic of cosmopolitan modernism, his earlier difficulties with Ives are not surprising; more remarkable is the fact that Carter was able to come to terms with Ives as soon and as thoroughly as he did.[13] Already by 1946, Carter was planning to collaborate on a book on Ives with the critic Paul Rosenfeld, in which they were to position the older composer as an "American Moussorgsky": an outsider genius (see below, pp. 71–72). More significantly (whether consciously or not), throughout his life Carter the composer continued to find solutions for the same musical problems that Ives had posed: the combination of different groups of instruments moving at different speeds, new formal concepts, new ways to control the flow of time, and ways of orchestrating so that complex polyphonic textures could be clearly heard.

Carter's cosmopolitan American aesthetic, as we have seen, was not incompatible with a familiarity with European culture. He traveled to Europe throughout his childhood with his parents (often in connection with his father's business trips), and learned French at the same time as his mother tongue. After his studies at Harvard, he followed the example of Copland and his teacher Walter Piston and went to France to study with Nadia Boulanger. Carter and his wife Helen spent increasing amounts of time in Europe after World War II: four year-long residencies at the American Academy in Rome, a year in Berlin on a Ford Foundation grant, a trip to the Far East, as well as participation in countless music festivals, ISCM meetings, and prize juries throughout Western and Eastern Europe. In 1981 he won the prestigious Ernst von Siemens Music Prize (see below, pp. 241–243), and in 1982 he chose the London-based firm Boosey and Hawkes as his publisher; after this, his reputation in Europe grew exponentially. His travels continued: Paris, Rome, and London are especially close to his heart (he has never felt particularly comfortable in Germany). He has enjoyed close friendships with many Europeans, including William Glock, Goffredo Petrassi, Pierre Boulez, Oliver Knussen, and Heinz Holliger.

11 Elliott Carter, "American Figure, with Landscape," *Modern Music* 20/4 (May–June 1943), pp. 219–225, esp. 219 and 222; most recently reprinted in *CEL*, pp. 134–138, esp. 134 and 136.

12 See Elliott Carter, "The Case of Mr. Ives," *Modern Music* 16/3 (March 1939), pp. 172–176; most recently reprinted in *CEL*, pp. 87–90. This was a review of John Kirkpatrick's New York première of the *Concord Sonata* in 1939.

13 See Elliott Carter, "Charles Ives Remembered," in *Charles Ives Remembered: An Oral History*, ed. Vivian Perlis (New Haven: Yale University Press, 1974), pp. 131–145 (most recently reprinted in *CEL*, pp. 98–107); and "Documents of a Friendship with Ives" (see above, p. 1, note 3).

His earlier relationship with Europe, however, was primarily musical. The American première of Stravinsky's *Le Sacre du printemps* in 1924, which was a pivotal event for Carter as well as for many others, set the stage for a lifelong passion for the music of Stravinsky. The young Carter also sought out of scores of Schoenberg, Berg, Webern, and Bartók and consumed them voraciously. While studying with Boulanger, he encountered a wide range of contemporary and earlier repertory. Through her he finally made his peace with traditional concert music and grew to love much of it, including early music.

Yet other American composers have spent more time than Carter outside the United States. He never had a second residence, like Virgil Thomson, nor did he emigrate to another country, like Frederic Rzewski. (In this sense, too, Carter is more like Wallace Stevens than Henry James or T. S. Eliot.[14]) In all his travels, Carter has always considered himself to be a representative of American music. Two of the texts included in this volume are essays about American music that were intended for foreign audiences: "Music in America at War" points out the basic differences between the structure of musical life in America and that in France (see below, pp. 67–70); "Music in the United States," originally published in French translation in a Belgian journal, emphasizes the diversity of approaches within American music, reflecting the typically American "rapidly changing, unpredictable situation in which little remains fixed for very long" (see below, p. 111). Neither text has any hint of the intense frustration with American musical life that Carter developed during the 1960s and expressed most forcefully in a book-length interview, *Flawed Words and Stubborn Sounds* (1971).[15] The failure of American society adequately to support its artists has been a constant theme in his later writings and interviews.

But in spite of the undeniable difficulties that Carter experienced within a largely conservative American musical mainstream, he has never gone unrecognized in the US. The numerous signs of American recognition that Carter received during the 1960s, 70s, and 80s include Pulitzer Prizes in 1960 and 1973, a major exhibition of his music manuscripts (accompanied by a book publication) in 1973 at the New York Public Library (see below, p. 220), a collection of his writings published in 1977, and substantial celebrations of his seventieth and eightieth birthdays (in 1978 and 1988, respectively). His Elson Lecture at the Library of Congress in 1978 led to the book, *The Musical Languages of Elliott Carter* (1984).[16] Few contemporary composers in any country have received major book-length studies of their music, as Carter did with David Schiff's *The Music of Elliott Carter* in 1983 (revised and expanded in 1998). Carter's first honorary doctorate was awarded by the New England Conservatory in 1961 (at the age of 52), and others have followed in a steady stream.

Even as his music became increasingly performed in Europe after 1980, it has not been neglected by American musicians. Leading American ensembles such as the Juilliard String Quartet, Speculum Musicae, and soloists including Charles Rosen, Ursula Oppens, Paul Jacobs, and Gilbert Kalish have regularly performed and recorded his music. (Leonard Bernstein had recorded his *Concerto for Orchestra* with the New York Philharmonic for Columbia Records already in 1970.) Carter's music, though out of step with the polystylistic and neotonal trends of the 1980s and 1990s, continued to be commissioned by American ensembles and performed in the United States during

---

14 Although comparisons with these writers can be productive and illuminating. David Schiff, for example, compares Carter with Henry James and Wallace Stevens, pointing out their shared "midatlantic perspective on Europe and America"; see Schiff 1998, p. 3.

15 Allen Edwards, *Flawed Words and Stubborn Sounds: A Conversation with Elliott Carter* (New York: W.W. Norton, 1971; hereafter *FW*).

16 *The Musical Languages of Elliott Carter*, ed. Jon Newsom (Washington, D.C.: Library of Congress, 1984; hereafter *ML*).

these years. In the twenty-first century, because an expert performing tradition has developed, and perhaps also because the composer has continuously refined his notation, Carter's music does not seem to pose extraordinary difficulties anymore. The number of performances on both sides of the Atlantic commemorating his one-hundredth year is astounding by any measure.[17]

A curiosity of recent criticism is that Carter's music is considered by many Europeans to be typically American, and by many Americans to be Eurocentric.[18] Both are off the mark, as they fail to recognize the American model of international modernism embraced by many artists of Carter's generation. Carter's American identity was formed in dialogue with the American and European traditions of literature and music from his life experience as a cosmopolitan New Yorker on both continents. Carter has never envisioned American identity as something isolated from the rest of the world. Like the poet Hart Crane, Carter forged his aesthetic out of many impulses. By answering Bourne's call for the "enterprise of integration […] a spiritual welding which should make us […] not weaker, but infinitely strong," he achieved a synthesis that shaped his basic artistic outlook in a manner that is quintessentially American.[19]

A Good Citizen of Contemporary Music: Carter's Involvement with Musical Institutions

Carter is no iconoclast. Throughout his life, he has participated in musical institutions, locally and internationally, working tirelessly to improve conditions for composers and to support performances in a cultural environment that was not always supportive of complex post-tonal music. To these ends, he has written music journalism, organized concerts, taught at universities and conservatories, and served on the boards of new music societies, prize committees, and foundations. The nature of his involvement with musical institutions has changed over the course of his life, starting with active participation and culminating in positions of authority, particularly in the 1960s and 1970s. But while Carter did exert considerable influence in new music circles (and still does), those groups – in America at least – are themselves so fragmented and marginal in terms of the society at large that it does not seem appropriate to speak in terms of power and control. Compared with Heinrich Strobel, who ran the Südwestfunk Baden-Baden, one of Germany's largest radio stations, the Donaueschingen music festival, and the music journal *Melos*, or William Glock, who directed the influential Third Programme of the BBC and edited *The Score*, Carter's hard-won clout seems rather limited.

Given the high costs and meager rewards of such activity, why did he participate in the institutions of contemporary music to the extent he did? Part of the answer can be found in his roots in the intellectual environment of New York in the 1920s and 1930s, in which there was a sense of a public discourse and collective ownership of culture. If politics, literature, and art were debated in "little magazines" like *The Dial* and *Partisan Review*, then music should be part of this debate – and Minna Lederman's *Modern Music* saw to that. Concerts being just as important for composers as publishing is for authors, organizations like the Franco-American Musical Society, the International Compos-

17 See the lists of performances in Boosey & Hawkes's monthly brochures, "Elliott Carter Centenary 2008."

18 The latter viewpoint has been expressed by Richard Taruskin: "He [Carter] strenuously opposed stylistic eclecticism, and deliberately rejected a national (or 'Americanist') creative identity in favor of a 'universal' (that is, generally Eurocentric) one." (Richard Taruskin, *The Late Twen-*

tieth Century, The Oxford History of Western Music 5 [Oxford and New York: Oxford University Press, 2005], p. 225.) Along similar lines, Kyle Gann has written: "Just as Elliott Carter came from neoclassicism and became Europeanized, [Roger] Reynolds became Europeanized from the direction of experimentalism." (Kyle Gann, *American Music in the Twentieth Century* [New York: Schirmer, 1997], p. 170.) Gann

discusses Carter in a chapter entitled "Atonality and European Influence," pp. 113–118 (Gann equates the two nouns in the title).

19 Bourne, "Trans-National America" (see above, p. 4, note 7).

20 For a detailed discussion of the origins, goals, and historical contexts of these organizations, see Carol J. Oja, *Making Music Modern: New York in the 1920s*

ers' Guild, the League of Composers, the Copland-Sessions Concerts, and the Pan-American Association created a healthy and highly competitive brew of musical activity.[20] New scores were published by the Composers' Music Corporation, Alma Morgenthau Wertheim's Cos Cob Press, and Henry Cowell's *New Music Quarterly*, which also put out a few highly influential recordings.[21] While hardly unanimous in its aesthetic aims – one should even take the degree of public debate and controversy as an index of cultural vitality – the New York musical scene of the 1920s and early 30s was much more coherent than it would become after the war. Because of New York City's artistic and intellectual preeminence during the 1920s and early 30s, its cultural élite then set the standards for the musical life of the whole country. Carter's concert-organizing and administrative activities were inspired by his early experiences in New York; these efforts may have been in part an attempt to compensate for the gradual dissolution and fragmentation of this cohesive intellectual scene after 1945, which was a major disappointment to him. "It seems to me," he told Allen Edwards in the late 1960s, "that an élite patterned on that of Europe (without, of course, a similar historical and cultural basis) did exist in America up until the depression of the thirties. Since then, however, this group, if it still exists, has lost much of its power to give a single cultural style to American society – if it ever really had it."[22] Carter's lifelong participation in the "civic life" of new music can be explained by his conviction that cultural life does not come from the random coalescence of individual efforts, but rather from people working together to mold tastes and to give direction to musical life.

Carter has devoted a remarkable amount of energy to presenting contemporary music to the public, an activity which, he has said, absorbed a great deal of his time in the late 1930s, 40s, and 50s.[23] Early on he became a member of the New York based League of Composers, which had broken off from Varèse's International Composers' Guild in 1923. Carter's work in the League with Aaron Copland, Minna Lederman (who edited the League's journal, *Modern Music*), and its president Claire Reis gave him the opportunity to meet many composers – American and European – and to hear dozens of important premières. Two of his own works, *Voyage* and *Warble for Lilac Time*, were premièred in a League concert in 1947.

The more forward-looking International Society for Contemporary Music (ISCM), founded in 1922 in Salzburg, made an even greater impact on his life and his career. During World War II, when the official ISCM had ceased its activities (and the sections in German-controlled Europe had been closed down as "culturally bolshevist"), the US section formed a kind of "government in exile" by holding international ISCM festivals in 1941 and 1942 in the United States (in New York and Berkeley, respectively).[24] In 1943 Carter was a co-founder of the ISCM's Forum Group for young composers; his *Pastoral* for viola and piano was played at a Forum concert in 1943 (see below, p. 54, note 42). But Carter's main motivation for being active in the ISCM was the opportunity to present the music of composers he admired (as relatively few of his own works were played at ISCM concerts). His wife Helen collaborated closely with him in these activities. For example, after Bartók died, he, Helen, and Edward Steuermann organized a memorial concert, an especially notable event in light of the general lack of interest in Bartók's music at that time.[25]

(Oxford, New York, etc.: Oxford University Press, 2000), especially Chapter 11 ("Organizing the Moderns"), pp. 177–200.

21 Ibid., pp. 158–159.

22 *FW*, p. 14.

23 Elliott Carter, "Documents of a Friendship with Ives" (1975), in *CEL*, p. 109.

24 For a history of the US chapter of the ISCM, see David Gresham, "The International Society for Contemporary Music,

United States Section: 1923–1961" (DMA thesis, Juilliard School, 1999).

25 This concert, which featured the *Second Sonata for Violin and Piano, Out of Doors*, and the *Sonata for Two Pianos and Percussion*, took place on 4 February 1946 in New York Times Hall. Steuermann played with Bronislaw Gimpel (violin), Fritz Jahoda (piano), George Gaber (timpani), and Ben Silver and Morris

Tilkin (percussion). The inference that Steuermann was involved in the orga-nization is based on Carter's account, "Edward Steuermann" (1966), in *CEL*, p. 157. Carter remembered the lack of interest in Bartók's music in his interview with Felix Meyer and Anne Shreffler, 13 June 2007.

Carter served the American section of the ISCM in various capacities: as a member of the board of directors (1946–52), as vice-president (1951–52 and 1955–56), and as president (1950–51 and 1952–53). In September 1950, he described to his friend William Glock the circumstances that led him to take on the ISCM presidency: "This year has seen a gradual revolution in contemporary music circles; the two rival organizations, the League of Composers and the ISCM, both were faced with the resignation of their chairmen, Aaron Copland of the League and Mark Brunswick of the ISCM. Since I am the only one on both boards and never say a word at any meeting, I was nominated to succeed both of the presidents – I provisionally accepted the ISCM, mostly devoted to 12-tone music which I can stand in small doses, but a little less cliquish than the League." (See below, p. 95). A high point of his ISCM presidency was the first all-Webern concert in New York City, on 28 December 1952 at the Lexington Avenue YM and YWHA.[26] Carter remembers that, although the hall was almost empty, Stravinsky and Robert Craft had come and brought the scores.[27]

Carter's genuine dedication to the mission of both the League and the ISCM – which he underplayed in his somewhat disingenuous account to Glock – comes through again and again in his letters and essays. In his 1953 lecture "The Need for New Choral Music" he recalled: "What a struggle it was to keep these groups going – I refer to the League of Composers and the International Society for Contemporary Music – in the face of public apathy [and] small attendance. It was done by a continual effort of a small group mostly of composers during times when our efforts seemed fruitless and often worthy of the severe criticism which no one hesitated to pile on us." (See below, p. 106).

In the years to come, Carter would attend most international ISCM festivals and serve on the jury for the ones in Haifa (1954), Cologne (1960), and Amsterdam (1963). The ISCM festival in Baden-Baden in 1955, during Carter's vice-presidency, gave him the opportunity to hear a performance of Schoenberg's *Variations for Orchestra* with the Südwestfunk Orchestra conducted by Hans Rosbaud, which spurred on an intensive re-examination of the piece and of the twelve-tone method, which Carter never adopted himself (see his radio lecture about the piece, below, pp. 141–147). The same festival featured Rosbaud conducting a new work of Boulez, *Le Marteau sans maître*. Carter's activities in the ISCM also led to some important friendships, for example with Goffredo Petrassi and Roman Vlad (Carter was able to meet these and other Italian friends during the 1959 ISCM festival in Rome). By observing the ISCM at close hand, Carter became acutely aware of the structural disadvantages that American composers suffered in comparison with their European colleagues, whose new music networks were generously subsidized by their governments.[28] This theme was to become a leitmotif in all of his future writings. In the context of minimal state support for new music in the US, Carter believed the role of composer-organized groups was especially crucial. As he wrote in 1953: "Though some have found it fashionable to scoff at organizations such as the League and the ISCM for being too special and sheltered, developing music written only for other composers, the importance of their role cannot be underestimated."[29]

26 Bethany Beardslee sang the *Four Songs*, op. 12; *Three Songs*, op. 23; *Five Canons*, op. 16; and *Six Songs*, op. 14. The New Music String Quartet performed the *Five Movements*, op. 5, and *Six Bagatelles*, op. 9. The program also featured the *Four Pieces for Violin and Piano*, op. 7, and *Three Little Pieces for 'Cello and Piano*, op. 11. The pianist was Jacques Monod (who accompanied the songs from memory), and the clarinettists were Luigi Cancellieri and Sidney Keil.

27 See *Elliott Carter: In Conversation with Enzo Restagno for Settembre Musica 1989*, ISAM Monographs 32, trans. Katherine Silberblatt Wolfthal (New York: Institute for Studies in American Music and Brooklyn College of the City University of New York, 1991; hereafter CC), p. 35.

28 Carter addresses this topic in "The Agony of Modern Music in America," which was probably intended as a report to the ISCM for the international festival in Baden-Baden (1955), but which remained

unpublished at the time (see *CEL*, pp. 53–57, esp. 56).

29 Carter, "To Be A Composer in America" (1953), in *CEL*, pp. 201–210, esp. 204.

30 Igor Stravinsky and Robert Craft, *Conversations with Igor Stravinsky* [1958] (Berkeley and Los Angeles: University of California Press, 1980), p. 132.

31 Carter had been under the impression that the position at Columbia was a permanent one, but after two years he was told that he had been hired to fill a temporary vacancy left by Otto Luening. He

Whereas Carter saw his work administering contemporary music organizations as a necessary burden whose results were clearly worth whatever effort they cost, his relationship to his teaching duties was more ambivalent. In the late 1950s Stravinsky warned young composers against university teaching, because the academic environment "may not be the right contrast for a composer's non-composing time. The real composer thinks about his work the whole time; he is not always conscious of this, but he is aware of it later when he suddenly knows what he will do."[30] These well-known words probably circulate guiltily in the subconscious mind of many an American composer. For unlike Europe, where there have been many different forms of support for composers, America provides little in the way of support for musical life outside of university or conservatory teaching.

Carter, too, has taught for most of his career, although in spite of more than four decades of activity as a teacher, he has never been identified as a "university composer" like Milton Babbitt or Roger Sessions. One reason was that he changed institutions often. After a two-year stint at St. John's College in Annapolis, MD (1940–42), where he taught music, Greek, and mathematics according to the interdisciplinary "tutorial" model of the college, Carter left the College in order to have more time to compose. The year after the war ended he was offered the position of professor of music at Peabody Conservatory, where he stayed two years (from 1946 to 1948). He moved directly from this position to one with the same title at Columbia University, which he again left after two years.[31] In 1951, Douglas Moore, the chairman of the music department at Columbia, suggested he apply for the chairmanship of the Princeton University Music Department (to succeed Roy Welch), but Carter was not interested in taking on such a time-intensive administrative position (see Carter's letter to Copland, 23 February 1951, below, pp. 99–100).[32] For the next five years, he did not teach, but devoted himself to composition and his activities with the ISCM, the American Academy in Rome (1953–54), and Nicolas Nabokov's Congress for Cultural Freedom. These years of international activity were followed by a year-long stint as professor of composition at Queens College in New York (1955–56). Four years after leaving this position he took on another professorship, this time at Yale University, where he again remained two years; his students here included Joel Chadabe and Alvin Curran. In the fall of 1963, Carter was offered a position at Princeton University which, according to his wife, "many consider the very best job for a composer in the country. That is, if one wants to teach. Roger Sessions will retire next year, and Princeton has asked if E[lliott] will take his place. All things considered, if he ever intends to teach again this would be ideal, since he thinks that music department the best in the country."[33] This he turned down, again for fear that it would impinge upon his composing time. Finally, in 1964, Carter found a position that was compatible with his creative life, at the Juilliard School, where he remained until his retirement twenty years later at the age of seventy-five.[34]

In addition to his regular positions at universities and conservatories, Carter also taught for shorter periods of time as visiting professor or composer-in-residence at various institutions. After returning from a year as composer-in-residence at the American Academy in Rome in 1963, he embarked on a

---

was disappointed at having to leave, because he liked the job and thought he had done well. (Elliott Carter, video-taped conversation with Virgil Blackwell, April 2008; Elliott Carter Collection, Paul Sacher Foundation.)

32 He told us in January 2008: "It would have been a very important job, but I didn't want to spend the rest of my life sitting in a little room answering the phone." Roy Dickinson Welch chaired the Princeton University Music Department from 1934 until his death in 1951. His

appointment of a stellar faculty, including Oliver Strunk, Roger Sessions, Milton Babbitt, and Edward T. Cone, established Princeton as one of the leading music departments in the country for decades to come. Welch was succeeded in 1952 by the musicologist Arthur Mendel.

33 Letter from Helen Carter to Nicolas Nabokov, 9 November 1963; Elliott Carter Collection, Paul Sacher Foundation. Sessions retired in 1965. He had no single successor; in subsequent years, Peter Westergaard and Claudio Spies joined the

composition faculty, and J. K. Randall received tenure. Milton Babbitt, the senior figure in the department, had become Conant Professor of Music in 1960.

34 Since he was in Berlin on a Ford Foundation grant until the end of November 1964, Carter must have started teaching only in the spring semester of 1965.

two-week residency at Dartmouth College from 5 to 18 August 1963. This ended unsatisfactorily, as Helen Carter reported: "After several days he called and said he was ready to go back to Rome. I really don't know if that is [his] first impression of academic life, after being away for so long, or if it is genuine disgust."[35] Immediately afterwards Carter threw himself into planning his residency in Berlin (under the auspices of the Ford Foundation), where he stayed from January to November 1964. The Ford Foundation had offered Carter four generous stipends for students; Chadabe and Curran, plus the Korean composer Isang Yun and the American expatriate Frederic Rzewski (both of whom Carter took on as "students" to fill the available stipends) were able to join Carter in Berlin.[36]

One teaching stint was cut short by external events, as he described to Stravinsky during the turbulent months of spring 1968: "I was professor-(not dog-)-at-large for my annual month at Cornell – very much at large as the students, etc. demonstrated over the M[artin] L[uther] King assassination during a good part of my stay." (Letter of 7 June 1968, see below, p. 193.) Carter also served as visiting professor at Carleton College and at MIT (both in 1966). In addition to his college teaching, he also taught regularly at summer music schools, including the Dartington School (where Peter Maxwell Davies was one of his students), the Salzburg Seminars, and the Aspen Festival. His most noted students, in addition to Chadabe, Curran, and Davies, include Tod Machover, Jeffrey Mumford, Tobias Picker, David Schiff, and Ellen Taafe Zwilich. Carter's sporadic teaching career is indicative of the high priority he always put on his creative work and of the means he had at his disposal that gave him the freedom to do this. (In his early years, a small independent income allowed him to live for certain periods of time without teaching, and after a while he began to earn enough from commissions and performances to support himself.)

But Carter kept his distance from academia not just for practical reasons; he also feared that a composer-professor "[...] could lose the sense of writing for the outer society which he should be helping to develop."[37] For a composer who worked his whole life to propagate and support contemporary music, this was a large drawback indeed. Carter's articles and lectures were generally meant for a wider readership than those of many of his colleagues, who embraced the university environment as an opportunity to pursue specialized research (witness the highly specialized articles on music theory written by composers during the 1960s and 1970s). His ambivalence about teaching ultimately comes from a clash between his belief that new music is part of a broader cultural dialogue – a belief he acted upon in his indefatigable work on behalf of contemporary music organizations – and the inertia and hermeticism that can be found in large institutions, including universities.

Carter the Composer: A Radical Traditionalist

In the late 1940s and early 1950s the populist ideals that had emerged during the Great Depression and had been rechanneled to nationalistic ends in the Second World War seemed utterly depleted, and new networks arose for the support of contemporary music. At this time Carter began thoroughly to rethink the foundations of his composing. As a result of this self-critical inquiry, he in-

---

35 Letter from Helen Carter to Nicolas Nabokov, 13 August 1963; Nicolas Nabokov Papers, Harry Ransom Humanities Research Center, University of Austin at Texas.

36 In a conversation with the authors, Carter described how Curran and Chadabe had been actual students, and how he had taken on Rzewski and Yun so that they

could each get the $3000 that the Ford Foundation offered. (Interview with Felix Meyer and Anne Shreffler, 11 June 2007.)

37 Elliott Carter, "The Composer is a University Commodity," *College Music Symposium*, no. 10 (Fall 1970), pp. 68–70, esp. 68; most recently reprinted in *CEL*, pp. 83–85, esp. 83.

creasingly detached himself, not only from functional harmony (with its concomitant regularity of rhythm and syntax), but from thematic and motivic development and the traditional formal canon that had until then, if only subliminally, undergirded his musical language. Like many other composers, he thereby parted ways with neoclassicism[38] and situated himself in the vicinity of the postwar avant-garde.

Still, Carter was disinclined to adopt the experimental trends in contemporary music that rocked the foundations of the art music tradition in the 1950s. For example, he adhered entirely to an aesthetic centered on the work of art: the self-contained artifact produced by the composer, with its rich skein of relations and maximum sophistication, remained the focal point of his interest, as it still does today. Accordingly, he also adhered to the traditional distribution of roles between the composer (the creator of the work of art), the performer (its transmitter), and the listener (its recipient). It was not least such basic convictions that prevented him from, say, entering the realm of electronics, concept art, or aleatoric music. Granted, as we know from his lecture "Sound and Silence in Time" (1957), his main reason for distancing himself from electronic music was that the limitless potential of the new sonic material left composers hopelessly unmoored or drove them to use arbitrary procedures, namely "the method of utter random choice and the method of imposing some arbitrary outside order pattern" (see below, p. 132). But he was probably no less bothered by the fact that electronic music, by placing the compositional result once and for all in an unalterable acoustical form, rendered the performer superfluous and thus cast doubt on the work's status as text, as well as on the institution of the concert as a vehicle of presentation. Yet Carter was even more skeptical towards concept art and aleatoric music for loosening the notion of the finished work, for he felt that blurring the musical text and shifting the act of creation more and more towards the performer and the listener inevitably entailed a lowering of artistic stature. Consequently, he once mockingly described the more radical experiments in "open-ended forms" as "blank pieces of paper with the direction to the performer at the foot: 'Play anything you like but be sure to put the title and my name as composer on the program.'" He even rejected more moderate essays along these lines (e.g. compositions in which a single element such as pitch, rhythm, or the order of sections is "left open"), arguing that the only way to achieve a sonically satisfying result in all performances was through methodological simplification: "In a way such works receive many first performances and have to be conceived in a very different way from other music: since to be worthwhile they must be immediately intelligible and effective, the methods must be very simple and definite although in a different but equally effective way at each performance."[39]

Instead, Carter channeled his drive towards innovation primarily in the direction of maximum sophistication and a systematic employment of the traditional twelve-tone chromatic material, combined with a corresponding range and variety in the shaping of musical time. In this very general sense, the goals he pursued were similar to those of the composers of the "Darmstadt School." But, unlike many of the European composers whose work he encountered in the 1950s (and whom he also met personally during his many trips to Italy, France, England, and Germany), he never submitted to the serialist mentality. Accordingly, his attitude towards the music of the Second

38 Although in Carter's case the term has no overtones of backward-looking nostalgia or academic formalism and is best viewed in the sense of an innovative "classicist modernism" employing novel techniques. On the concept of "classicist modernism," see Hermann Danuser, "Einleitung," *Die klassizistische Moderne in der Musik des 20. Jahrhunderts: Internationales*

Symposium der Paul Sacher Stiftung 1996, Veröffentlichungen der Paul Sacher Stiftung 5, ed. Hermann Danuser (Winterthur, 1997), pp. 11–20, esp. 12–16.

39 Elliott Carter, "Letter from Europe" (1962), *Perspectives of New Music* 1/2 (Spring 1963), pp. 195–205, esp. 199; most recently reprinted in *CEL*, pp. 31–40, esp. 34–35 and 35, respectively.

Viennese School, with which he had been familiar for years, even if his thorough study of its theoretical foundations had to wait until the mid-1950s, differed markedly from that of his younger (European) colleagues: if Boulez, Stockhausen, and Maderna, among others, used the music of Schoenberg, Berg, and especially Webern as an immediate point of departure for their own music and were primarily interested in its dodecaphonic aspects (or in its latent evolutionary potential), Carter judged this music mainly for its expressive content without considering its technical "applicability." Particularly revealing is his view of Webern as expressed in a letter of 3 May 1957 to William Glock: "[...] frankly I find the rather Mendelssohnian charm of W[ebern] delightful and touching, but as an analyzer of music I must say I find the part you can't explain the best part of any piece." (See below, p. 149.) Consequently, he had no objections in principle towards the use of "classical" twelve-tone technique, at least insofar as it produced what he considered convincing acoustical results. But by the same token he was all the more disconcerted with the further evolution of the serial principle in the form of total serialism, towards which he indeed raised an objection in principle: "Each of the 'parameters' has a different way of being perceived and hence cannot be organized according to the same system of serialization and have any similar effect."[40]

Like the pronouncements on electronic and aleatoric music quoted above, this statement bears witness to the high priority that Carter attaches to the perceivability of musical structures: indeed, throughout his life he has always viewed music primarily as a sonic event whose meaning should be immediately intelligible to a trained listener, if not in every facet, then at least in rough outline. To do justice to this claim without limiting his pursuit of new material resources, he increasingly sought, beginning in the late 1940s, a stratification of the compositional fabric in which the separate parts or layers sharply contrast in harmony and rhythm. Typically these parts or layers are assigned particular intervals or types of motion that complement each other to create a whole. By thinking in terms of independent compositional layers, each using only one segment of the overall rhythmic and harmonic vocabulary he meticulously defines for each work, Carter followed a specifically American tradition, drawing on Charles Ives's layering techniques, the concept of "dissonant counterpoint" exemplified in the music of Ruth Crawford Seeger (and theoretically elaborated in the writings of her husband Charles Seeger),[41] and the ideas of Henry Cowell, who, in his *New Musical Resources* (1930), presented new, rationally argued possibilities for handling musical time, including the successive and simultaneous use of precisely interlocking tempos.[42] The "centrifugal" compositional principle applied by these composers was designed to achieve maximum "dissonance," not only in pitch but in other musical dimensions, and it left clear traces in Carter's thought and music. This was especially true of Cowell's suggestions in the field of rhythm, which had repercussions not only in Carter's technique of "metrical modulation," but in his later use of polyrhythms extending across an entire movement or work. (That said, Carter never adopted Cowell's proposed correlation between rhythmic proportions and overtone ratios).

The stratification of the compositional fabric makes it easier for the listener to follow Carter's music, not least by virtue of its metaphorical potential: because each instrument or instrumental group assigned to a strand of continuity has a distinctive rhythmic and harmonic profile, it func-

---

40 Ibid., pp. 200 and 35–36, respectively.

41 The most extensive presentation of Seeger's theories is found in his treatise "Tradition and Experiment in (the New) Music," which was published posthumously in Charles Seeger, *Studies in Musicology II, 1929–1979*, ed. Ann M. Pescatello (Berkeley, Los Angeles, etc.: University of California Press, 1994), pp. 43–266.

42 Henry Cowell, *New Musical Resources* (New York and London: Alfred A. Knopf, 1930); reprint, with notes and an accompanying essay by David Nicholls (Cambridge: Cambridge University Press, 1996), chapter 2 ("Rhythm"), pp. 45–108.

tions like a character in an imaginary play. Cowell had already pointed to certain operatic prec-
edents in the simultaneous use of multiple tempos, specifically recalling "the famous quartet from
Rigoletto, in which each of the characters is expressing a different emotion."[43] This quasi-dramatic
conception reaches full fruition with Carter; it is no accident that he has spoken of the "character-
continuities" in his music and cited scenes from Mozart (the first-act finale of *Don Giovanni*) and
Verdi (the second-act finale of *Falstaff*) as historical models for his superposition of contrasting pro-
cedural layers.[44] Thus a large part of his music can be heard, in a quite concrete sense, as a "discourse" among human individuals. This is especially evident in the case of his chamber music, as in
his *String Quartet No. 2*, to which Carter, in a letter of 11 May 1959 to Goffredo Petrassi, applied the
Pirandello phrase "four instrumentalists in search of an author" (see below, p. 158). But it is also true
in the orchestral works, particularly the concertos, where the personification of the instruments he
employs (often in the form of a confrontation between an individual and the collective) is highly
developed.

That such "ties to reality" are far less specific than those, say, of program music is only to be
expected in a composer who developed his own musical language in the anti-Romantic 1940s and
1950s. (Even in those works inspired by literary models, such as the *Double Concerto, Concerto for
Orchestra*, or *Symphony of Three Orchestras*, Carter transformed his models irreversibly into musical
ideas and images at an early stage of the creative process.) Yet it is equally clear that Carter never
proceeds from an abstract material starting point, but invariably employs his compositional devices for the purpose of expressing fundamental human experience. If the expressive contents of his
imaginary "scenarios" resist precise definition, in the final analysis his music unmistakably evokes
humans agents and their perceptions, modes of behavior, and experience in the world. Both his
penchant for conceiving instruments as characters, putting them through every imaginable form
of interaction and conflict, and his projection of contrasting forms of temporal perception (as inspired by forerunners in literature, film, and dance) reflect central facts of human experience that
became especially relevant in the psychologically "aware" twentieth century.[45]

Finally, Carter's "personification" of the instrumental ensemble gives performers particularly
propitious opportunities to identify with the music. To be sure, his scores pose considerable challenges in execution, demanding from the instrumentalists not only great virtuoso agility but maximum rhythmic independence. But these challenges emerge so closely with the specific nature of
the instruments employed that they never seem recherché. Nor is it surprising that the choice of
instruments regularly forms the conceptual starting point of his compositional work – an aspect
that Carter once tersely summarized in a panel discussion with Pierre Boulez at the University of
California at Los Angeles (see below, p. 259): "My pieces derive directly from instruments. I write
specifically for instruments." (Boulez, in contrast, admitted in the same discussion to a more flexible approach – "[...] sometimes I begin with instruments, sometimes with an idea" – and pointed
out that the idea may at times alter the instrumentation or vice versa.)[46] But most of all Carter takes
his bearings less from an abstract sonic and executive potential than from the idiosyncrasies and
special strengths of the particular musicians for whom he writes.

---

43 Ibid., pp. 93–94.
44 *FW*, pp. 101–102.
45 See especially Jonathan W. Bernard,
"Elliott Carter and the Modern Meaning
of Time," *The Musical Quarterly* 79/4
(Winter 1995), pp. 644–682.
46 Quoted in Daniel Cariaga, "Boulez,
Carter Discuss their Art(s)," *Los Angeles
Times*, 17 May 1984.

This was by no means the case in the early decades of Carter's professional career. The *String Quartet No. 1* (1950–51), for example, was written without a commission, and hence without prospects of performance. (Carter is fond of interpreting the unexpected success of this unusually long and demanding work, which led to his breakthrough in the United States, as paradoxical proof of the need to align himself more with his own expressive urges than with the exigencies of musical life.[47] Perhaps, however, it merely reflects the fact that the string quartet, unlike orchestral or choral music, has long been supported by a performance tradition in which the challenges of modernism are approached with special openness and competence.) But at least since the late 1950s, when Carter increasingly found himself wooed by first-class ensembles, soloists, and conductors, his relation with his performers has taken on the cooperative character of a close exchange of ideas both during the final stages of the compositional process and during rehearsals. This collaboration, which has ultimately led to the writing of a large number of short birthday pieces and other musical presents for his musical friends, is essentially related to technical details, not to underlying conceptual issues. Still, it has had an important impact on the work of all concerned. First of all, it has sensitized performers to the special demands posed by Carter's music. But by the same token it has sharpened Carter's already heightened awareness of the executive and expressive potential of instruments and voices, enabling him to exploit them efficiently and to set down his ideas in such precise notation that even performers personally unacquainted with him can play his music well. Indeed, while earlier in his career he often had to wait many years for an adequate performance of his works, he now feels that the gap has been bridged: "My music gets played practically at once the way I intended it to be."[48]

Although Carter radically reformulates the expectations of the traditional genres that he uses (in part by dividing the instruments in large ensembles into unconventional, heterogeneous groupings), he does not usually require the creation of completely new types of ensembles. It is the symphony, concerto, string quartet, sonata, and song cycle – all of which originated in the seventeenth and eighteenth centuries – and not modern hybrids such as Stravinsky's *Histoire du Soldat* that are at the core of Carter's production. (Even the *Sonata for Flute, Oboe, Cello and Harpsichord*, an unorthodox ensemble for the time, uses the same instruments as a baroque trio sonata). *Triple Duo* is his only work for that most ubiquitous of twentieth-century configurations, the *Pierrot* ensemble with percussion, and even here Carter has regrouped the traditional mixed quartet plus piano into three duos of similar instruments. (Not at all traditional on the other hand is his intensive and extended use of percussion throughout his career.) Writing for existing ensembles has given Carter a musical framework that spurs on his creativity; it has also allowed him to have his music featured in mainstream institutions instead of being confined to marginalized new music circles.

In short, Carter has drawn on existing traditions for key points of his creative process and his artistic philosophy, preferring to prolong and rejuvenate them rather than to call them into question. This applies to his preservation of the idea of a self-contained work of art, set down in writing with maximum precision, and to his focus on working with conventional tonal material (for example, precluding electronic sounds and largely avoiding experimental performance techniques on conven-

---

47 John Tusa, interview with Elliott Carter, n. d. [2000], http://bbc.co.uk/radio3/john tusainterview/carter_transcript.shtml.

48 Ibid.

49 See, for example, Andy Carvin, "American Gothic: An Interview with Elliott Carter," 17 February 1994, at http://edwebproject.org/carter.html.

50 Especially revealing in this light are the headlines of two early articles from *Time* magazine: "Elite Composer," *Time*, 28 May 1956, pp. 48, and "Composer for Professionals," *Time*, 26 May 1961, pp. 80–81.

51 Richard Taruskin, in his *Oxford History of Western Music*, described Carter's evolution since *String Quartet No. 1* as follows: "From now on he [Carter]

tional instruments). It applies equally to his understanding of the role of the performer, whom he employs primarily as an interpreter of his ideas and not, as in aleatoric music, as a "co-author." And finally it is no less applicable, at least in intention, to his understanding of listeners: although Carter has often said that he never thinks of the audience while composing, but only of the performers,[49] his efforts to make the musical events audible, and his penchant for casting his musical discourse in quasi-dramatic roles, doubtless spring from a desire to make statements of maximum concision and urgency and to communicate them to his listeners. At the same time, however, Carter is a "radical" in that he has fully explored, in the wake of early modernism, the potential of music liberated from traditional harmonic and rhythmic fetters, in particular the superposition of contrasting textural layers to a point of extreme complexity. This may explain why the communicative link he intended to build with audiences has ultimately fallen short of the link to his performers. Whatever the case, it is obvious that Carter's music poses severe demands on his listeners and presupposes an increased willingness on their part to engage with it both intellectually and emotionally. To be sure, as its growing acceptance in the concert hall demonstrates, it is by no means an elitist "music for experts" (a tag frequently attached to it by conservative critics since the 1950s[50]); nor is it, with its manifold expressive subtexts, as abstract as Richard Taruskin, for example, has recently claimed.[51] But neither has it fully reached the wider public (at least for the time being), assuming that such a thing exists in an age in which the culture of classical art music seems to have disintegrated into an increasing number of subcultures, and listeners' tastes have become more eclectic.

Carter's move in the late 1940s and early 1950s towards a fully chromatic pitch vocabulary has often been interpreted as an abandonment of an "anonymous" style that he had shared with Copland and other American composers, and as the discovery of his distinctive, mature voice.[52] Still, no matter how striking this stylistic about face, his mature compositions did not entirely break with the past. The same may be said of other composers who took part in the postwar shift of artistic paradigms. But many of these composers definitively turned their backs on their earlier music: György Ligeti, for example, spoke in retrospect of the "prehistoric Ligeti" and long opposed the performance and publication of his "pre-avantgarde" compositions antedating his flight from Hungary in 1956. Carter, in contrast, had a much more accepting relation to his earlier works. True, he was quick to cast a gimlet eye on his juvenile and student works, many of which he either destroyed or withdrew, and to this day he will have nothing to do with the performance or publication of the few surviving works antedating the *Tarantella* of 1937 (his first acknowledged composition), such as the incidental music to *Philoctetes* (1931) or the *String Quartet in C* (1937?). But he has always stood behind his published works of the late 1930s and 1940s – the ballet *Pocahontas*, *Symphony No. 1*, and the many choral pieces from these years – without casting doubt on their value in light of his later evolution. Even in the late 1950s, having long formulated his new compositional style, he expressly thanked William Glock for considering a BBC performance of his *Symphony No. 1*, adding that "[it is] a work for which I have a great deal of affection, although my friends all feel that it is completely uncharacteristic. I even had to restrain Goldman from condemning it in his article."[53] (Letter of 3 May 1957 to William Glock; see below, p. 149.)

---

would identify with the romantic, asocial concept of artistry in its priestliest form [...]. He was now an *artifex*, as unconcerned with edifying the public as he was with shocking it. Henceforth his reference would be to his art alone, and to its history – both the history he had inherited and the history he would make." (Richard Taruskin, *Oxford History of Western Music 5* [see above, p. 8, note 18], p. 281.)

52 Boulez, for example, said in an interview: "Carter, on the other hand [unlike Messaien], began almost anonymously. I read through his ballet *Pocahontas* once and if I had not already known it was by Carter, I would never have guessed he was the composer: it is more like Copland than Carter now!" (Philippe Albèra, "Pierre Boulez in Interview [2]: On Elliott Carter, 'a composer

who spurs me on'," *Tempo* no. 217 (July 2001), pp. 2–6, esp. 4.)

53 Richard [Franko] Goldman, "The Music of Elliott Carter," *The Musical Quarterly* 43/2 (April 1957), pp. 151–170.

Far from repudiating his "early" works – a doubtful label in any case for music that Carter composed into his forties – the composer went to great lengths to get many of them published and performed even after 1950. In a letter to Nicolas Nabokov of 9 July 1956, for example, Carter wrote: "I am very happy that you are hoping to give something of mine next year – my Louisville piece [the *Variations for Orchestra*] [...] is a very hard nut to crack – I am not sure how it would sound in an open-air concert with not many rehearsals – perhaps the *Minotaur* might go better." (See below, p. 128.) Carter was sufficiently proud of his 1947 ballet to urge Kurt Stone, his editor at Associated Music Publishers, to "please be sure that some of my scores, esp[ecially] the quartet and *Minotaur*, will be on sale at Donauesch[ingen]."[54] He revised an even earlier ballet score, the *Suite from "Pocahontas"* (1939), in 1960 and published it in 1969, the same year in which he completed the *Concerto for Orchestra*. Again and again he engaged creatively with his earlier works, revising or arranging them for new instrumental combinations while always preserving their harmonic language. He arranged the *Elegy* (1943), originally for cello (or viola) and piano, for string quartet in 1946 and for string orchestra in 1952, and revised the viola and piano version in 1961; he revised the *Symphony No. 1* (1942) before its publication in 1961, and orchestrated the *Three Poems of Robert Frost* (1942) and *Voyage* (1942–43) more than thirty years after their composition. In 1987 Carter made a new version of *Pastoral* (1940) for English horn, marimba, and string orchestra for Heinz Holliger to perform. And as late as 2007 the long compositional history of the *Elegy* came full circle as the composer arranged the quartet version for cello and piano – the very combination of instruments for which he had originally written this work more than sixty-five years earlier (under the title *Adagio for Violoncello and Piano*).[55] While some of these arrangements may have been simply a way for a composer to keep his hand in, they also attest to Carter's belief in the validity and musical quality of the original works. Moreover, they provided him a welcome opportunity to keep up his formidable technique in tonal composition, an area in which he has always held himself and his students to the very highest standards.

In spite of the wide stylistic range, Carter's œuvre – which is still growing as this book goes to press – has ultimately been quite consistent, in terms of both compositional technique and aesthetic principles. Both the "early" and the "mature" Carter share a constant preoccupation with time and rhythm; a formal ideal that depends more on the continual transformation of material than on themes, periodicity, or discrete formal units; a fundamentally polyphonic conception of texture; and, finally, careful attention to notation as a means of communicating with the performer in ever more precise ways. The result has been music that requires – and rewards – repeated listening. (Even *Pocahontas*, which seems very accessible today, sounded difficult and inaccessible when it was premièred next to Copland's *Billy the Kid*; see below pp. 41/44.) Nor has Carter's basic aesthetic position changed: for him, music reflects and reenacts the situation of human beings in modern life rather than abstract metaphysical ideals.

In addition to indicating a personal artistic consistency, Carter's refusal to repudiate his earlier, tonal music can also be understood as part of the musical context common to American composers of his generation. (It is much less common for European composers; it would be difficult to imag-

---

54 Letter from Elliott Carter to Kurt Stone, 6 October [1957]; Irving S. Gilmore Music Library, Yale University.

55 In a program note on this arrangement Carter has written that he was under the impression that the original version had been lost; see program booklet for the Tanglewood Festival of Contemporary Music, 20–24 July 2008, p. 78. However, a photostat of the score of the *Adagio* is preserved in the Paul Sacher Foundation.

ine Boulez taking the same position with regard to his early works, and Ligeti's attitude has already been mentioned.) The US has never had a central, predominant artistic leadership that adjudicated what was to be included or excluded; centralized government support for the arts is also lacking. Instead, American musical life is socially, geographically, and aesthetically highly diverse; cultivated and vernacular traditions have always existed side by side, and within each of these, multiple styles compete for attention in a decentralized musical landscape. Even between 1950 and 1970, when avant-garde music enjoyed a certain prestige in American new music circles, contemporary tonal music never fell out of fashion or ceased being performed.[56] In this context, Carter had every reason to expect that his earlier music would find a place in the repertoire; he may even have assumed that it would have a better chance than his more complex recent music, or that it might pave the way for it.

Carter's long life has spanned most of the twentieth century and part of the twenty-first; one of his earliest memories is seeing English battleships in the Hudson River during World War I, and many years later he watched the twin towers of the World Trade Center crumble from his living-room window. During that time he has crossed paths with many of the most influential musicians and musical institutions of his time, in the US and in Europe; his letters and writings give us a sense of these encounters and of the historical contexts in which they occurred. But Carter's main path has always been his composition. A portrait of a composer, like the one sketched in this book, has to contend with the fact that, unlike a political figure, whose deeds are visible and whose every thought leaves a trace within his or her sphere of influence, a composer works in silence and isolation. The parts of the life that can be shown in letters and documents are necessarily peripheral to the central activity of composition, which in Carter's case probably took up most of his waking hours. This is why we have chosen to include pages from his music manuscripts as well as verbal documents. It is the music, after all, that will be Carter's main legacy to the future.

Felix Meyer and Anne Shreffler

---

56 Tonal composers whose works enjoyed prominence in this period include Samuel Barber, Gian Carlo Menotti, Carlisle Floyd, Dominick Argento, Douglas Moore, Ned Rorem, and Jack Beeson.

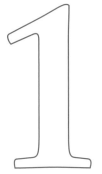

"Rather an Exceptional Boy"

1908–1935

Childhood and Youth (1908–26)

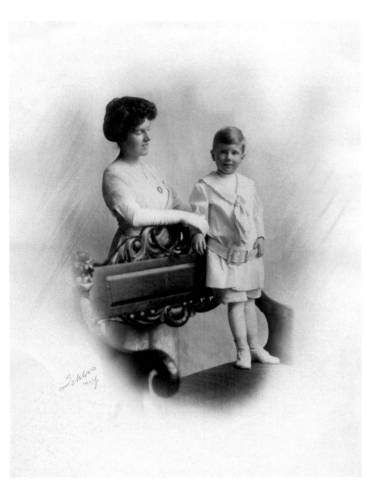

1   Elliott Carter with his mother (1912),
    photo by J. Schloss

When Elliott Carter was born in New York City on 11 December 1908, no one would have predicted that he would have a musical career, much less become an internationally renowned composer. His course in life – to follow in the footsteps of his father, after whom he was named – seemed clearly plotted. Elliott Cook Carter, Sr. (1886–1955), was a prosperous lace importer and civic leader; president and owner of the firm E. C. Carter & Son, he also served as president of the Westport (CT) Country Club and was a member of the New York Athletic Club.[1] The latter membership must have been mainly for social purposes, as he had had polio as a child and walked with a severe limp; this meant that, as Carter told us, "the son never played baseball or soccer."[2] His mother, Florence Chambers Carter (1887–1970), was born in Brooklyn of Northern Irish descent, fiercely Protestant, and was very concerned to provide the right social and family environment that would support her husband's career.

Carter's paternal grandfather, Eli C. Carter, was a Civil War veteran from upstate New York who had launched and built up the lace importing company. He had married Marion Levy, a daughter of a large Jewish immigrant family from Silesia. Carter's grandmother was not observant and evidently did not raise her son, Carter's father, in the Jewish tradition, but was nonetheless very proud of her family and her heritage.[3] Carter's father left school at the age of thirteen to go to work in his father's business, where he was trained to deal directly with the Belgian, French, and Swiss farmers who made lace during the winter. When Eli Carter retired, he did not simply let his son, Carter's father, take over "the best lace curtain business in New York at that time," but sold it to him, putting him at a distinct financial disadvantage that took years to overcome.

Carter was born on 95th Street between Riverside Drive and Westend Avenue; later the family moved to another apartment on 97th Street and Amsterdam Avenue. Then "my father thought we should be out in the country, so we moved to Flatbush," to a house with a porch. "We moved back [to the city] when I started to go to school." The composer remembers moving from an apartment on the ground floor of 420 Riverside Drive up to the 11th floor of the same building as the family's fortunes improved. At their home on 420 Riverside

1 "Elliott C. Carter" (obituary), *The New York Times*, 30 December 1955.

2 Much of the information and all of the direct quotations in these paragraphs come from our interviews with Carter, 11–16 June 2007. We have made every effort to corroborate the statements and confirm dates whenever possible.

3 Carter recalls how his father seemed completely uninterested in religion, but when Elliott was a child the family attended the Presbyterian church.

Drive on the Upper West Side of Manhattan the family led a comfortable existence, even though Carter's father lacked his grandfather's business sense and often struggled to keep his head above water, especially after the lace curtain trade collapsed during the mid-1920s.[4]

The Carters made sure that their only child (a daughter had died shortly after birth) received the best education possible in order to prepare him for the family business. Carter recalls: "When I was about seven years old [...] I had a governess who taught me French. There was a period in my life when I spoke French much better than English." Carter was sent to the expensive and well-regarded Horace Mann School, which when he started was on 120th Street and Broadway. He continued to attend the Horace Mann School when the Boys School moved to the Riverdale section of the Bronx in 1914 and graduated from high school there in 1926.

As part of his duties in the business (which was still owned and run by Eli Carter), Carter's father traveled to Europe about four times a year to buy lace in Belgium, Switzerland, and France, and he continued these trips even during World War I. Carter remembers his mother's anxieties about the U-boats during his father's absences;[5] he also remembers "the Hudson River full of English battleships." After the war Carter's father, who was a pacifist, took him to Europe to see the battlefields. Carter says he never forgot the scenes of destruction (including the Reims cathedral in ruins) and the human misery. He remembers the hyperinflation in Germany – "there were a million marks per dollar one day and two million the next day" – on a trip when they stayed at the old Hotel Adlon in Berlin and "the waiters stole food off the tables." On later trips to Europe with his father Carter bought books and scores. Well-worn copies of early editions of

2   Elliott Carter in the family car, a Cadillac, with his mother (driver's seat), grandmother Marion Levy Carter (back seat, dark suit), and other family members (ca. 1916)

3   Elliott Carter on his bicycle (1918)

4   Carter's account is corroborated by a history of lace curtain production offered on the website of the company Queen Anne's Lace Curtains: "The weaving trade expanded in leaps and bounds, and it reached its height of development in or around 1910, and continued a very high level of activity up to the middle of the 1920's – the principal market for the product by that time being the United States of America. Around the mid 1920's, the market for the products started to decline." (See http://www.queenanneslace-curtains.com/madras lace curtain trade. html, consulted 28 April 2008.)

5   These fears were not unfounded, as German submarines struck U.S. merchant and passenger ships with great regularity during World War I. The *Lusitania*, for example, was sunk on 7 May 1915, claiming 1198 lives.

Proust, Joyce, books on the Bauhaus, and French poetry are still in his library today. On one trip to Vienna and Paris in 1925 he was able to buy a number of scores of music by Schoenberg and his school (up to and including Schoenberg's *Suite for Piano*, op. 25) as well as the orchestration treatise of Rimsky-Korsakov.[6] He spent the summer of 1926 working at his father's perfume factory in Binghamton, New York – with the declining demand for lace curtains, his father had branched out into selling cheap perfume to five-and-ten-cent stores – and studying orchestration at night.[7]

Elliott Cook Carter, Sr., expected his son to join him in business and was disappointed at his choice of an artistic career. Even though Carter's parents did not approve of their son's musical ambitions, they provided him with piano lessons (which he admits he didn't like very much) and did not overtly oppose his efforts to study music. Already in his early teens Carter was rebelling against his parents by showing a lack of interest in business and by his passionate engagement with the most controversial modern literature and music: "[Material success] was what they were concerned with. They came from poor families, both of them, so [...] they were naturally concerned with that. I don't hold it against them. Obviously my life is a revolt against all of this." In high school Carter fell in with a group of like-minded young people who were interested in modernism in literature, art, and music. They went to concerts and exhibitions, and had heated discussions of the latest books. Carter remembers hearing the Philadelphia Orchestra under Stokowski playing music by Varèse. He also attended concerts of the Franco-American Music Society (later Pro Musica), the International Composers' Guild, and the League of Composers. A concert given on 31 January 1924 by Pierre Monteux and the Boston Symphony Orchestra in Carnegie Hall with Stravinsky's *Rite of Spring* was a revelation; it was this experience that made Carter decide to become a composer.[8]

This concert also influenced his decision to attend Harvard University, which of course also pleased his parents. Carter remembers that he was attracted to Harvard not only because of the university, but also "because the Boston Symphony was directed by [Serge] Koussevitzky, and they played a great deal of contemporary music. [...]

When I went to Harvard, I began to realize that I really ought to know older music, and I think I went to every single concert that the Boston Symphony gave for the six years that I was there."

During his father's lifetime Carter received a modest allowance of somewhat less than $500 per year, which, although not nearly enough to live on, helped to supplement his income during his studies and early career. When his father died in 1955, the estate, which consisted at this time of stocks and some small real estate investments, was divided between Carter and his mother, and the busy composer found himself saddled with managing his mother's portion as well as his own. Upon his mother's death in 1970 the full inheritance was distributed among Carter, his son, and his grandson.

---

6 Nikolay Rimsky-Korsakov, *Principes d'orchestration, avec exemples notés tirés de ses propres œuvres*, trans. from the Russian by M.-D. Calvocoressi, ed. Maximilian Steinberg (Berlin: Edition Russe de Musique; Paris: Max Eschig, 1914).

7 As demand for handmade lace declined, Carter's father switched to drapes, then established a perfume business. When these did not do well, he branched out into other business ventures, including the manufacture of heartshaped breath sweeteners called "sweethearts," for which he hoped to receive the endorsement of "America's sweetheart," the movie star Mary Pickford.

8 For an account of the furor caused by this performance, see Carol J. Oja, *Making Music Modern: New York in the 1920s* (Oxford, New York etc.: Oxford University Press, 2000), pp. 286–287.

Support from Charles Ives (1926)

In 1924 Carter's music teacher at the Horace Mann School, Clifton J. Furness, introduced him to Charles Ives, who became a sort of musical mentor to the young man, taking him to concerts and sending the following letter of recommendation to the Dean of the Faculty of Arts and Sciences at Harvard University. Carter remained in contact with Ives and Furness even after enrolling at Harvard as an undergraduate in 1926. It was thanks to Ives, for example, that he became acquainted with the first issues of Henry Cowell's newly launched *New Music Quarterly* in 1928 and was able to enjoy a subscription. Furness, who had by then likewise enrolled at Harvard to obtain a doctorate in English literature, joined the young Carter in two recitals sponsored by the newly founded Friends and Enemies of Modern Music in Hartford, CT, on 12 December 1928 and 15 May 1929. In the first recital, Carter played several piano duos with Furness as well as a few solo items. (The printed program lists the titles of the works but leaves open the question of which musician played which piece.[9] Later, in a letter to John Kirkpatrick, Carter could only recall having played the Minuet from Schoenberg's *Suite for Piano*, op. 25,[10] but could not confirm having performed the "Thoreau" movement from Ives's *Concord Sonata:* "My meagre pianism allowed me only to play the Alcotts [movement] and I can't remember if I ever wandered through it in public or not."[11]) At the second recital, of which all that survives is an invitation card, the two men wanted to play a movement from a violin sonata by Ives, either with a violinist or in an arrangement for two pianos.[12] Unfortunately, nothing more is known about this.

4   Charles Ives, letter of recommendation for Elliott Carter [1926]

Letter to Harvard Dean in re Elliott Carter

Carter strikes me as rather an exceptional boy. He has an instinctive interest in literature, and especially music, that is somewhat unusual. He writes well – an essay in his school paper, "Symbolism in Art," shows an interesting mind. I don't know him intimately, but his teacher in Horace Mann School, Mr. Clifton J. Furness, and a friend of mine, always speaks well of him – that he's a boy of good character and does well in his studies. I am sure his reliability, industry, and sense of honor are what they should be – also his sense of humor, which you do not ask me about.

[Typed letter draft, carbon copy with handwritten heading; Charles Ives Papers, Irving S. Gilmore Music Library, Yale University; photocopy in the Elliott Carter Collection, Paul Sacher Foundation. Reprinted by permission of the American Academy of Arts and Letters, copyright owner.]

---

9   The works listed (more probably excerpts) are by Stravinsky, Milhaud, Schoenberg, Poulenc, Casella, Malipiero, Henry F. Gilbert, Ives, Satie, Hindemith, and Antheil; some of them were performed from pianola rolls. The program is reproduced in Schiff 1983, p. 15. See also Donald Harris's "Elliott Carter in Hartford" in the program booklet for "An Elliott Carter Retrospective on the Composer's 70th Birthday," Hartford, CT, 1 and 3 February 1979, pp. [2]–[3] and [6]–[7].

10 The "Six Pieces" by Schoenberg listed in the program are thus probably not the *Six Little Piano Pieces,* op. 19 (nor the six movements of the *Suite,* op. 25), but a combination of pieces of varying provenance.

11 Letter from Elliott Carter to John Kirkpatrick, 25 November 1959; John Kirkpatrick Papers, Irving S. Gilmore Music Library, Yale University.

12 See letter from Clifton Furness to Charles Ives, 23 April [1929]; Charles Ives Papers, Irving S. Gilmore Music Library, Yale University.

My Love is in a Light Attire (1928)

Only a handful of works written before Carter's studies with Boulanger have survived. Carter destroyed many of his student works in the late 1930s, and others have been lost.[13] The song *My Love is in a Light Attire*, his earliest extant composition, survived only because Carter sent the manuscript to Henry Cowell in the hope that it would be published in *New Music*. This did not happen, but Cowell saved the score and returned it in 1958.[14] Carter was probably referring to this song, originally part of a group of settings of Joyce's *Chamber Music*, in his letter to Ives from January (or February) 1928: "[...] I wrote two more songs and planned partly another movement of that string quartet."[15] Joyce's *Chamber Music*, a collection of delicate but conventional lyric poems suitable for musical setting, was never controversial like *Ulysses* (which had been banned in the U.S. in 1920 after excerpts had been published serially in *The Little Review;* it was published in its entirety in Paris by Sylvia Beach in 1922).[16] Still, for an American college sophomore in the 1920s, setting Joyce would have been a declaration of modernist allegiance. The poem uses the metaphor of the wind in leaves to describe the loved one as she moves among the apple trees, holding up her dress. Whether the word "light" refers to weight or to color is left open; the poem captures a moment of fleeting, sun-drenched joy. The poem's three quatrains alternate iambic tetrameter with trimeter and employ a rhyme scheme of alternating lines in which no rhymes are repeated. Carter does not set the seventh and eighth lines of the poem ("My love goes slowly, bending to / Her shadow on the grass"); his version therefore de-emphasizes the image of the loved one, who now makes an appearance only in the last two lines ("My love goes lightly, holding up / Her dress with dainty hand").

5   *My Love is in a Light Attire,* for voice and piano (1928, unpublished), on a text by James Joyce, autograph full score in ink, p. [1]

The song shows Carter's obvious modernist ambitions. The outer parts of the ABA form, which set the first and third quatrains, are in 5/8 meter and are notated with the polytonal key signature of four sharps in the piano's right hand only. This voice presents an ostinato which runs through the outer sections, made up of the two black-key fourths, G♯–C♯ and D♯–G♯, at first played separately, then together. Both the voice's predominantly "white-key" vocabulary and its register are shared by the piano's melodic left hand. The endings of the first two phrases ("apple trees" and "companies"), on B♭ and E♭, respectively, converge with the ostinato to create a quasi-pentatonic sonority. As David Schiff has noted, the brief middle section uses Debussyan harmonies and introduces the G-major tonality that will end the piece (as in the fourth system) (see Schiff 1983, p. 73). The accentuation of the text's weak syllables ("My love is in a light attire / Among the...") might have been intended as yet another unconventional modern feature, or was perhaps a reference to Stravinsky's often unorthodox text accentuation. Carter's song resembles Israel Citkowitz's setting of the same poem in its irregular meter (Citkowitz's is in 10/8), its predominantly high register, and the registral proximity of the piano left hand's line to the vocal part. Citkowitz's *Five Songs for Voice and Piano*, of which *My Love is in a Light Attire* is the last, were published in 1930 by Cos Cob Press and performed in April of that year at a Copland-Sessions concert in New York.[17] Since Carter's setting was probably composed first, it is possible that his piece influenced Citkowitz's. But since Citkowitz was away from New York in 1928 (he was studying with Nadia Boulanger in Paris from 1927 to 1931), it seems more likely that both young composers were reacting to the same models of polytonality and irregular meters found in contemporary works of Ives, Bartók, and Milhaud.

---

13   The list of Carter's works given in Claire Reis's *Composers in America: Biographical Sketches of Living Composers, with a Record of Their Works, 1912–1937* (New York: Macmillan, 1938), p. 57, contains many that are unknown today. David Schiff reproduced this page in his first book, with Carter's added comments on the status of each work (as far as he could recollect in the late 1970s). According to this annotated list, many works, including a symphony, a collection of madrigals, two string quartets, a flute sonata, and a one-act opera, were destroyed by the composer in the late 1930s; see Schiff 1983, p. 72.

14   See letter from Henry Cowell to Elliott Carter, 24 May 1958; Elliott Carter Collection, Paul Sacher Foundation.

15   Elliott Carter, "Documents of a Friendship with Ives," *Parnassus* 3/2 (Summer 1975), pp. 300–315, esp. 303. Most recently reprinted in *CEL*, pp. 107–118, esp. 110. The quoted letter is also reprinted in *Selected Correspondence of Charles Ives*, ed. Tom C. Owens (Berkeley etc.: University of California Press, 2007), p. 147.

16   *Chamber Music* was published in London in 1907. Carter might also have consulted the editions printed in Boston in 1918 or New York in 1923.

17   The concert took place on 13 April 1930 at the President Theatre, and included works by Roy Harris, István Szélenyi, Pál Kadosa, Imre Weisshaus, Citkowitz, Jean Binet, and Jerzy Fitelberg. The Citkowitz songs were performed by Ethel Codd Luening (soprano) and Aaron Copland (piano).

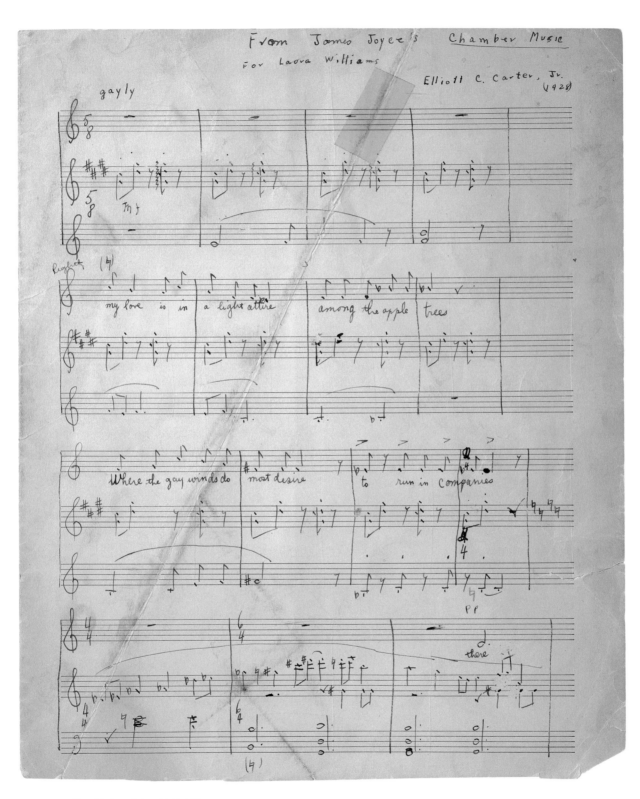

5   *My Love is in a Light Attire*

Student at Harvard University (1926–32)

6 Elliott Carter in his student years (ca. 1932)

As an undergraduate at Harvard (1926–30), Carter studied English literature rather than music. He later explained this decision: "[…] I found that no one could understand why I wrote what I did when I tried doing harmony exercises, just as I couldn't understand why I should write harmony exercises at all. […] Certainly, I would have been glad if somebody at Harvard had explained to me what went on in the music of Stravinsky, Bartók, and Schoenberg, and had tried somehow to develop in me the sense of harmony and counterpoint that these composers had, without going through all that traditional stuff, which I didn't like. But this was the order of the day, and finally I got very angry and decided not to study music as an undergraduate."[18] Consequently the bulk of his musical training took place initially at the Longy School of Music, where he studied theory as well as oboe (with Louis Speyer, the English horn player of the Boston Symphony Orchestra). After obtaining his A.B. degree in English literature, however, Carter remained at Harvard to concentrate on music. During these graduate studies (1930–32), which led to an A.M. degree, he studied harmony and counterpoint with Walter Piston and composition with Gustav Holst, who was a visiting professor at that time. Carter has fondly recalled his years at Harvard, where he came into contact with such fellow-students as James Agee, Ralph Kirkpatrick, and Lincoln Kirstein: "It was an exciting time to be at Harvard, although it was the period of prohibition, bathtub gin, and speakeasies, which led to odd adventures at times." Not least of all he has recalled his formative experiences as a member of the Harvard Glee Club under the direction of the Harvard professor Archibald Davison: "Modernism made its way into the Harvard Glee Club, and I remember as a singer [performing] beautiful works by Darius Milhaud and Holst and, especially, Stravinsky's *Oedipus Rex*, which we sang with the Boston Symphony."[19] The student orchestra at Harvard, the Pierian Sodality, also played more adventurous repertory than that taught in the Music Department. During Carter's first two years at Harvard the orchestra was conducted by Nicolas Slonimsky, who led the group into an "orgy of First Performances that rocked the Yard with works such as [Pancho] Vladigerov's *Caresses* and [Leo] Ornstein's *Prélude tragique*."[20]

18 *FW*, pp. 45–66.
19 Carter, in *Colloquy* (Alumni Quarterly, Graduate School of Arts and Sciences, Harvard University), no. 9 (Summer 2001), pp. 13 and 21, esp. 21. Milhaud's *Psaume 121* (1921), Poulenc's *Chanson à boire* (1922), and Holst's "How Mighty Are the Sabbaths" (no. 3 from *Six Choruses*, op. 53, 1932) were written for the Harvard Glee Club. The performances of *Oedipus*

Rex with the Boston Symphony Orchestra conducted by Serge Koussevitzky took place on 24–25 February 1928; they were the first concert performances of this work in America.
20 Elliot Forbes, *A History of Music at Harvard to 1972* (Cambridge, MA: Department of Music, Harvard University, 1988), p. 62.

Between his freshman and sophomore years at Harvard (1927), in spite of his parents' objections,[21] Carter got a summer job in Tunisia transcribing Arabic music for the Baron Rudolphe d'Erlanger. The Baron, who had built a magnificent palace, *Nejma Ezzohara* (Arabic for "Star of Venus"), in Sidi-bou-Said, about twenty kilometers northeast of Tunis, was a pioneering scholar of Arabic history and culture. He was an artist of considerable skill – his painting *Street in Cairo* is in the Tate Collection in London – but his true passion was Arabic music. "D'Erlanger believed that with the decline of traditional patronage and the increasing lure of Western influences, the very survival of the *ma'luf* [a genre of Arabic-Andalusian music] depended on providing the fragile oral tradition with a foundation of music theory and notation."[22] His life's work was his six-volume study *La musique arabe*, which contains four medieval Arabic treatises on music in French translation and two volumes on modern Arabic music: one on mode and melodic organization, and one on rhythm. The Baron's collaborators included his secretary, Manoubi Snoussi, an expert on Tunisian music, and the Scottish musician and orientalist Henry George Farmer. Some of the hundreds of pages of transcriptions in this treatise may have been done by Carter (see music example below).

The composer stayed at the home of Laura Williams, who studied and performed Arabic music, and later dedicated *My Love is in a Light Attire* to her (see above, pp. 26–27).[23] Working entirely without recording equipment (magnetic tape, of course, did not yet exist), Carter transcribed the playing of the Arabic musicians from their live performances, approximating the non-Western pitches and rhythms as best he could. He acquired and learned to play the darabukka (an Arabic drum), which is still a treasured possession.

Rodolphe d'Erlanger, *La musique arabe* (Paris: Geuthner, 1930); reprint (Paris: Geuthner, Institut du Monde Arabe, 2001). Vol. 6: *Essai de codification des règles usuelles de la musique arabe moderne: Le système rythmique; Les diverses formes de composition artistique*, p. 206.

---

21 Interview with Felix Meyer and Anne Shreffler, 13 June 2007.
22 Ruth Davis, "Al-Andalus in Tunis: Sketches of the Ma'luf in the 1990s," *Music and Anthropology*, no. 7 (2002), http://www.fondazionelevi.org/ma/index/number7/davis/dav_03.htm, accessed 14 January 2008.
23 *FW*, p. 41.

Incidental Music for *Philoctetes* (1932)

It is tempting to see Carter's encounter with Arabic drumming as one of the sources of his lifelong exploration of new means of rhythmic organization. But whether the musical experiences of that Tunisian summer had such long-range effects or not, they did have an immediate impact on one of his early compositions: the incidental music that he wrote for the Harvard Classical Club's production of Sophocles's play *Philoctetes*. Carter's music, which sets the choruses of the original Greek text, is scored for male chorus, oboe, and Arabic darabukka (though he allows the substitution of "a large sized affair like a tambourine without the metal jingles" if the Arabic drum is not available). The play was performed on 15 and 17 March 1933 in the Lowell House Dining Hall, in Carter's absence, as he had graduated with his master's degree in the spring of 1932 and had already left for Paris. The young Harvard assistant professor and later noted Homer scholar Milman Parry – Carter's Greek teacher – directed the production; the musicians were Louis Speyer (oboe), C. T. Murphy (drum), and the chorus of the Classical Club, led by E. C. Weist. The student newspaper, the *Harvard Crimson*, reported: "The work of the chorus, involving the memorization of a long and difficult score, was almost impeccable. In the score, the composition of Elliott Carter '29 [*sic*], no attempt was made to adhere pedantically to the canons of Greek music, but its general nature and effect were skillfully copied by using a modal scale, keeping the range well within three octaves and by introducing few harmonies, of fourths or fifths, between chorus and actor, and chorus and instrument. As a result, the chanting never became tiresome, and it rose to several heights of extreme beauty, particularly in the scene with Philoctetes, after the exit of Odysseus and Neoptolemus. The difficulties of reproducing the authentic singing too scrupulously were thus happily avoided; they were successfully met in the case of the instrumentation by using an oboe and tabor."[24] Another review, anticipating a lasting trope in Carter criticism, found the choral chanting to be quite modern, "a song-speech that might have been [a] stripped prototype of that twentieth-century invention of Herr Schönberg."[25] Carter's interest in Greek classical literature has continued throughout his life.

As late as 1977 he consulted his old Harvard textbook, *Greek Lyric Poets* by M. H. Morgan (Cambridge, MA: Harvard University Press, 1929), for the Greek texts for his polytextual cantata *Syringa* (see Schiff 1998, p. 188).

7   *Incidental Music for Sophocles's Play "Philoctetes",* for oboe, drum (Arabic darabukka), and men's chorus (1932, unpublished), autograph full score in ink, p. 2

Philoctetes was one of Sophocles's last plays, written three years before he died at the age of ninety. It concerns the noble warrior Philoctetes, who on account of a painful wound in his foot that would not heal had been abandoned by Odysseus fifteen years earlier on the deserted island of Lemnos. When Odysseus learns that he will need the assistance of Philoctetes and his magic bow, which had been given to him by Heracles, in order to defeat the Trojans, Odysseus persuades Neoptolemos, the young son of Achilles, to help him trick Philoctetes into accompanying them to Troy. But Philoctetes does not want to offer any aid to those who have treated him so abominably. Neoptolemos, because of his noble heritage and innate moral sense, is ultimately incapable of deceiving Philoctetes, with whom he sympathizes. In the end, the dead Heracles appears as a god and instructs Philoctetes to go to Troy, where he will be cured and achieve great victories. Carter wrote an overture for solo oboe and set the choral passages of the drama for men's voices, oboe, and drum. The passage shown is the beginning of the "parodos," or opening chorus (verses 135–218). Here the chorus articulates Neoptolemos's subconscious thoughts: his fear and loneliness on the foreign island and his pity for the wretched Philoctetes. Neoptolemos is already deeply uneasy about his moral quandary. Carter uses modal pitch material (such as the C-Lydian in the page shown), and the rhythmic patterns reflect the accentuation of the Greek text. Carter carefully tailored the score to the abilities of amateur performers: the choral part, carried by seven singers, is often in unison and doubled by the oboe, and the rhythms are uncharacteristically simple, even for this phase in Carter's development. He indicates the precise placement of the hand on the drum: "[quarter note on middle line] means beat in the center of the head,

---

24   [Anon.], "'Philoctetes': Enthusiastic Lowell House Audience Applauds Classical Club's Staging of Tragedy," [clipping from *The Harvard Crimson*], in Harvard University Archives file "Carter, Philoctetes": HUD 2933.70.2PF.

25   Press clipping [unidentified]: "A First Time For Sophocles at Cambridge: The Harvard Classical Club Produces Remarkably His 'Philoctetes,'" in Harvard University Archives file "Carter, Philoctetes": HUD 2933.70.2PF.

[quarter note on second line from top] means beat at the edge," just as he had learned on the darabukka. He also instructs the drummer to sit on the stage, where he could "conduct the chorus as well as beat his drum." The oboe player sits offstage in the wings.

7 *Incidental Music for Sophocles's Play "Philoctetes"*

The Paris Years (1932–35)

After completing his studies at Harvard, Carter decided, at the suggestion of Walter Piston, to continue his musical training with Nadia Boulanger in Paris. His mentor Charles Ives advised him against it; Carter remembers a long walk with Ives in which the older man admonished him to uphold his duties towards America.[26] But the young composer was not to be dissuaded, preferring to follow the footsteps of Aaron Copland, Virgil Thomson, Roy Harris, and Walter Piston, all of whom had studied with the legendary teacher in Paris. Accordingly, in 1932 he moved to Paris, where he remained until the spring of 1935, at times under straightened circumstances,[27] and spent two years studying with Boulanger. Here he deepened both his theoretical and his practical knowledge of ancient and early music (among other things, Boulanger's students regularly sang Bach cantatas), and considerably widened his outlook on contemporary music, although his teacher tended to favor the neoclassical music associated with Stravinsky, whom Carter met personally in these years. Most of all, he could polish his craftsmanship with Boulanger, who demanded great discipline from her students in harmony, counterpoint, and analysis. Although Carter felt he could not put the technical skills he had acquired in Paris to immediate use, he was deeply influenced by the artistic integrity with which Boulanger approached music. It comes as no surprise that in his later recollections, he maintains that the most important things she imparted to him were "a deep devotion to music, a sense of responsibility, an ability to pay careful attention to each note."[28] This is not the least reason for his lifelong gratitude towards his teacher, with whom he remained in contact both in person and by letter after finishing his studies. Boulanger, as we learn from her letter of recommendation of 1935, found not only Carter's musical gifts, but also his personality, winning. Even in later years, when Carter gradually drew away from her neoclassical ideals, she followed his artistic evolution with interest. There is, however, no disguising that his post-1950 compositions remained alien to her (see below, p. 151).

8 Counterpoint exercises (early 1930s), photocopy with annotations by Elliott Carter, p. [4]

A relatively large number of counterpoint exercises survive from Carter's years of study with Nadia Boulanger. Today most of them are preserved in the holdings of the Library of Congress, from which the two exercises shown here are taken. In 1993 Carter had photocopies of this and three other pages sent to him; he then annotated the copies, numbering the exercises and commenting on Boulanger's inscriptions on pages [1] and [3], and forwarded them to Frank Scheffer for use in his film project on Carter (see below, p. 291, note 18). The page shown here contains two exercises (numbered 8 and 9) in seven-voice florid counterpoint, with the cantus firmus first in the bass (no. 8) and then in the soprano (no. 9). No. 8, where Carter experimented with hidden entrances (each of the voices 3 through 7 begins on the pitch that is sounding in the preceding voice), also contains two inscriptions from Boulanger, who found fault with the augmented fourth in the melodic progression of the fifth voice (mm. 4–5) and the hidden parallel fifths that follow between voices 5 and 6. Yet Boulanger found little to object to in the other exercises found on these photocopies, and in one case (no. 1), she even wrote "à copier," instructing her student to write out this example in a fair hand for future reference in her lessons. Carter commented on this in his cover letter to Scheffer: "From what I can remember it took me about 100 counterpoint lessons (meeting once a week, except in summer) to arrive at the skill it took to write the examples included. I went on, then, to double choruses and canons, and invertible counterpoint. Then to fugue."[29]

26 Interview with Felix Meyer and Anne Shreffler, 27 January 2008.

27 Carter remembers that his mother gave him $1000 per year while he was studying in Paris. Upon hearing how much his allowance was, Boulanger apparently asked for half of that ($500) as her fee for teaching him, which left him so little money that he had to take on odd jobs teaching English and copying music to support himself. But Carter recalls that "after the first year she said, 'don't pay me any more, and when you start to make some money you can give me a payback.' She was a wonderful person."

28 Elliott Carter, "'Elle est la musique en personne': A Reminiscence of Nadia Boulanger," in CEL, pp 281–292, esp. 292.

29 Letter from Elliott Carter to Frank Scheffer, 20 February 1993; photocopy in the Elliott Carter Collection, Paul Sacher Foundation.

9 Nadia Boulanger, letter of recommendation for Elliott Carter, 11 May 1935

Les Maisonnettes / Hanneucourt / par Gargenville
(S. & O.) PTH 28
– May 11th, 1935 –

– To whom it may concern –
Having had Elliott Cook Carter as pupil for two years, I consider [it] a duty as well as a privilege to recognise his talent, his gifts, & his fine personality.

Excellent musician, he is a thorough worker, with a high intellectual viewpoint. His culture, acquired but also [the] result of his interest in life, is of an unusual quality; it is not something built & finished but always increasing, evolving, & extremely "true." His personality, so serious & loyal, so deeply sincere & understanding, so discreet & tactful, will help the others to solve the problems that he is ready to face, to discuss, to admit. And I consider Elliott Cook Carter as one who will, in teaching, in acting as a musician, as a teacher, as an open-minded man, bring a great inspiration, a fine direction.

If any other informations are wanted, I will be too glad to answer at any questions, having for E. C. Carter a great esteem.

Nadia Boulanger

[Autograph letter; Elliott Carter Collection, Paul Sacher Foundation. Reprinted by permission of the Fondation Internationale Nadia et Lili Boulanger.]

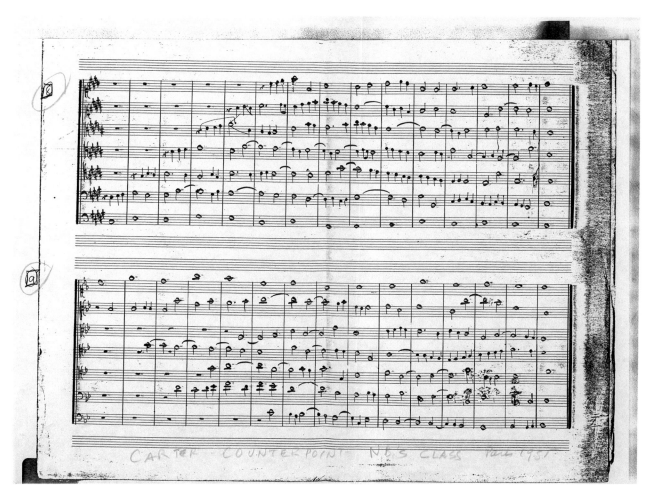

8 Counterpoint exercises

"A Kinetic
Projection of Ideas"

1935–1947

Return to America – *String Quartet in C* (1937)

In May 1935 Carter returned to the US. Initially he settled in Cambridge, where he renewed his contacts with
Harvard and wrote incidental music for a performance
of Plautus's *Mostellaria* scheduled for the spring of 1936.[1]
The renewal of his contact with Lincoln Kirstein proved
especially momentous: not only did Kirstein ask him, in
the summer of 1936, to compose the ballet *Pocahontas* for
his newly founded Ballet Caravan (see below, pp. 41–44),[2]
he also made Carter the music director of his dance company in 1937. By this time the composer had moved to
New York (in the fall of 1936) and had begun to write
reviews for Minna Lederman's journal *Modern Music*.
In these same years he also met such fellow-composers
as Aaron Copland and Nicolas Nabokov, both of whom
would become lifelong comrades-in-arms. This was especially true of Nabokov, with whom Carter maintained
a close friendship unclouded by professional rivalry, as
was not always the case with Copland. (The two men met
through Kirstein, and deepened their contact in early
1937, when Carter asked the more experienced Nabokov
for advice in orchestrating his *Tarantella*.) Not least, it
was then that Carter met his future wife, the sculptress
and art critic Helen Frost-Jones (b. Jersey City, 1907). At
that time he was living in George Antheil's apartment
on 55th Street (Antheil had left New York in May 1936
and settled permanently in Hollywood the following
August). Carter later recalled: "So I lived there and somebody brought Helen to the apartment and I thought she
was pretty nice. She came [...] and I will never forget the
night when we left a cigarette burning in a chair and finally the fire department came. By the time they came
we had put water on the chair. That's how we became
friends."[3] They married on 6 July 1939, in Chatham, MA
(on Cape Cod), after they had lived together "for quite a
long time," the composer remembers. In the small, private ceremony, Nicolas Nabokov served as Carter's best
man.[4] During this time Carter composed prolifically,
completing a symphony, a concerto for English horn and
orchestra, two string quartets, a flute sonata, a ballet, and
other works (all those named here were later destroyed
by the composer).

10 *String Quartet in C* (1937?, unpublished), autograph
full score in ink with annotations in pencil in
another hand, p. 16 (second movement, mm. 49–64)

One "pre-first" string quartet – a complete three-movement work in ink fair copy – has survived. This could be
either the "First String Quartet" from 1935 or the "Second String Quartet" from 1937, although given the re-
semblance between the unison beginning of the finale
and Bartók's *String Quartet No. 5*, which was first published in 1936, the latter is more likely. The mastery of invertible counterpoint, the neoclassical style, the mature
handwriting, and the performance indications in French
(for example, on this page, "Un peu détaché") suggest a
date of composition during or after Carter's studies with
Boulanger. The page shown is from the slow middle
movement ("Largo e tranquillo"), which is not divided
into contrasting sections, but continuously develops a
primary motive (here for example in the cello at letter F;
elsewhere on the page, the rhythm alone is heard). The
expanded tonality and contrapuntal texture of the passage are characteristic of the piece as a whole. The score
contains pencil markings (in another hand) indicating
corrections and suggestions. It would have made sense
for the young Carter, after his return to the US, to have
shown his scores to a colleague or a former teacher for
advice. The colloquial English used – "must begin greater
climax / real stuff", "make big climax" – would certainly
exclude Boulanger; nor does the handwriting resemble
Copland's. Carter remembers discussing his music with
his slightly older contemporaries Theodore Chanler and
Marc Blitzstein, and thinks it likely that the remarks on
this score were written by one of them.[5] In 1937 David
Diamond planned to include a recent string quartet by
Carter in a concert that he was planning in Paris; it is
possible that this is the work mentioned.[6]

1   This performance never took place, as
    we can see from a notice in the *Harvard
    Crimson* of 5 March 1937, which
    commented on a performance of Carter's
    Tarantella (the prologue to the incidental
    music) given on the same day: "The
    play was never performed and so Carter's
    piece remained unknown and unsung
    until it was rediscovered by G. Wallace
    Woodworth '24, conductor of the

Glee Club." For Woodworth's performances of the *Tarantella*, see below,
p. 47, note 21.
2   Carter remembers that Kirstein com-
    missioned the ballet because he had been
    favorably impressed with the *Tarantella*
    (videotaped conversation with Virgil
    Blackwell, April 2008).
3   Film interview with Frank Scheffer,
    November 1994; transcription in the

Elliott Carter Collection, Paul Sacher
Foundation, p. 68.
4   Interviews with Felix Meyer and Anne
    Shreffler, 12 and 15 June 2007.
5   Interview with Felix Meyer and Anne
    Shreffler, 26 January 2008.
6   See letter from David Diamond to Elliott
    Carter, 22 July 1937; Elliott Carter
    Collection, Paul Sacher Foundation.

Heart Not so Heavy as Mine (1938)

It was natural for a composer of Carter's generation and background to devote much energy to the composition of choral music. Choral singing was (and still is) an integral part of musical life at Harvard, and Carter remembers his years in the Glee Club with great fondness. During his studies with Boulanger, he sang a wide range of choral music from all periods, in addition to the weekly sessions of Bach cantatas, and while in Paris he also studied choral conducting with Henri Expert and sang in his chorus as well. After returning to the US, Carter put his experience to good use in his own composition. His *Tarantella* for men's chorus and piano four hands or chamber orchestra remained one of the most popular Harvard Glee Club numbers for many years. In New York he organized and led a madrigal group. He also had plans to compose a book of madrigals, of which only two works survive: *Harvest Home* and *To Music* (both composed in 1937 on texts by Robert Herrick). During the same year he composed *Let's Be Gay* for women's chorus and two pianos for the Glee Club of Wells College, where his friend Nicolas Nabokov taught.[7] Composing for chorus was therefore a kind of native language for Carter during the 1930s and 1940s, and the works indeed display intimate familiarity with the idioms of choral writing.[8] The *a cappella* chorus *Heart Not so Heavy as Mine*, on a poem by Emily Dickinson, was commissioned in 1938 by the Congregation Emanu-El of New York (on Fifth Avenue at 65th Street) and its music director, Lazare Saminsky, who was also a composer and a founding member of the League of Composers. Completed in December 1938, the work was premièred on 31 March 1939. The published score – the very first work of Carter's to be printed – appeared the same year with Arrow Music Press (AMP A-273), a small firm which had inherited Alma Wertheim's innovative Cos Cob catalogue. Arrow Music Press was a composer-initiated venture, with Lehman Engel as president, Marc Blitzstein and Virgil Thomson as vice-presidents, and Aaron Copland as secretary-treasurer.[9] All were close acquaintances of Carter, and all but Engel were Boulanger graduates.

11 *Heart Not so Heavy as Mine,* **for mixed chorus** *a cappella* **(1938), on a text by Emily Dickinson, proofs of the first edition with autograph corrections, p. 2**

The first page of this score is uncharacteristically diatonic – there is not a single accidental to disturb the B♭ minor. In its division of the choral texture into layers, though, the work is more typical of Carter's later music. Against a three-voice choral block setting the words "Heart not so heavy as mine" moving in halves and quarters, another more rhythmically active line interweaves among the others. The slower music reflects the first of the poem's two actors – the observer with a heavy heart – while the dotted rhythms evoke the careless tune, "a ditty of the street," sung by an oblivious passer-by. Except for correcting one inaccurately notated rhythm in the second system, Carter's corrections in the proofs are concerned entirely with the text. The version of the poem Carter set, taken from a 1937 edition of Emily Dickinson's poems, diverges considerably from the one given in a modern scholarly edition.[10] Dickinson's early editors often regularized her punctuation, replacing the poet's ubiquitous dashes with more ordinary periods and commas. There are also several variants in the wording:

Carter (1938)	*Complete Poems (1955)*
"Carolled and mused"	"Carolled and paused"
"Upon a toilsome way"	"Upon a dusty way"
"Weary, perhaps, and sore"	"Perhaps weary and sore"
"I pray you stroll once more"	"I pray you pass once more"

---

7   This work remained unpublished until Boosey and Hawkes brought it out in 1997.

8   As Carter said in an interview with Charles Rosen (in connection with the *Piano Sonata*): "I was very concerned with giving singers the kind of lines they were accustomed to and which would express the various feelings that I wanted to present by using the human voice." (*ML*, 33.)

9   See Carol J. Oja, "Cos Cob Press and the American Composer," *Notes* 4/2 (December 1988), pp. 227–252.

10   [Emily Dickinson,] *The Poems of Emily Dickinson*, ed. Martha Dickinson Bianchi and Alfred Leete Hampson (Boston: Little, Brown, 1937), pp. 34–35; [Emily Dickinson,] *The Complete Poems of Emily Dickinson*, ed. Thomas H. Johnson (Cambridge, MA: The Belknap Press, 1955), vol. 1, p. 67.

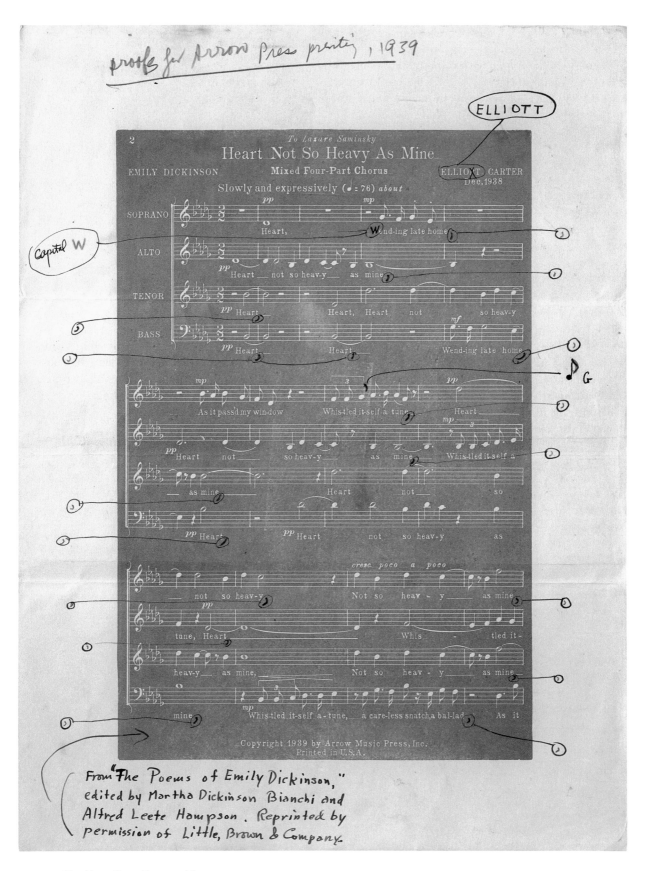

12   Helen Carter in her sculpture studio (1938)

Helen Frost-Jones, Carter's future wife, took a degree in art in the late 1920s from the Art Students League in New York, an independent school founded in 1875 with an emphasis on modernist art. Among her teachers were the sculptor Alexander Archipenko (1887–1964), who had exhibited his work at the Armory Show in 1913. Thereafter she worked both as a sculptress and as a director of the WPA art program in New York. Several of her works have found their way into museums, including a bust of Marcel Duchamp preserved in the Wadsworth Athenaeum Museum of Art in Hartford, and another of her husband, on display in the New York Public Library. She abandoned sculpture after marrying Carter in the summer of 1939. This photograph from 1938 shows the young artist working in her studio at 57th Street and Lexington Avenue.

12

Pocahontas (1936–39)

In the early 1930s Lincoln Kirstein, inspired by "Powhatan's Daughter," the second section of Hart Crane's cycle of poems *The Bridge* (1923–30), and by the works of the Flemish engraver Theodor de Bry, lit on the plan of choreographing the Pocahontas legend. He first sought the collaboration of the composer Virgil Thomson in 1933, but it was not until three years later, after he had asked Carter for a piece for his newly founded Ballet Caravan in June 1936, that the project materialized. An initial short version of Carter's score (for piano), choreographed by Lew Christensen, was mounted in Keene, NH, on 17 August 1936 and repeated by the Ballet Caravan various times on tour. Later Carter thoroughly reworked this original version, more than doubling the length of its music and removing a passage that was out of place in the dissonant, highly chromatic context. (It later formed the basis of the finale of his *Symphony No. 1*.) Kirstein was surprised by the assurance with which his former fellow-student at Harvard, whom he recalled "more as a classical scholar and mathematician than composer," solved the task at hand. He was especially taken with Carter's realization of his wish that "the marriage-finale, in which Powhatan's daughter appeared in an Elizabethan wedding dress, should sound like an 'American Indian' version of *Apollon Musagète*."[11] Carter's score indeed contains obvious echoes of Stravinsky, but equally of Prokofiev and Copland. More important, however, are the elements that point unmistakably to Carter's own later music: the dense contrapuntal manipulation of the melodic material, the thematic elisions and spacious development, and the gradual fade-out of the work's explosive opening bars. Equally important is the fact that Carter worked with a juxtaposition of primitivist and neoclassical stylistic elements derived directly from the plot – the conflict between the native Americans and the English adventurers intruding into the forests of Virginia.

13 *Pocahontas,* ballet legend in one act (1936-39), autograph piano reduction in ink, pp. 26-27 (mm. 303-331)

Here, in Carter's autograph piano reduction, we see the passage from the definitive version of *Pocahontas* in which the Indian chief Powhatan makes his entrance. (Powhatan is the father of Pocahontas, who later – "less out of pity than from her naïve curiosity," as Kirstein put it in a program note[12] – prevents the killing of the adventurer John Smith and ultimately meets an untimely death in the land of her conquerors as the wife of Smith's protégé, John Rolfe.) Powhatan's appearance, which ushers in the fourth movement of the better-known concert suite ("Torture of John Smith"), introduces a march with martial undertones to follow the gentle, playful music of the preceding section ("Princess Pocahontas and Her Ladies"). To conjure up a primitive musical ambience, Carter uses such modern devices as the gradual buildup of abrasively dissonant chords (e.g. in mm. 2–3 of system 3 on p. 27) and the rhythmic-metric displacement of thematic shapes. For example, the main theme, upon its return on p. 27 (second measure in system 4), is not only transposed up a semitone from its original form, but shortened to two bars and consequently placed on a downbeat rather than an upbeat. (Initially the second part of this twofold restatement matched the more expansive opening version, only to be crossed out and made to agree with the adjoining first part by means of repeat marks; see the correction in system 5.) Characteristically, Carter has made no overt use of native American themes. His music is more intent on abstraction than on folk-like illustration, as befitted a choreography and *mise-en-scène* described as follows in Kirstein's above-mentioned program note: "The ballet is probably as far from original Indian dancing as the first maps of America are from our roadmaps."

The première of the definitive version of *Pocahontas* (with Lew Christensen's choreography) took place in New York's Martin Beck Theatre on 24 May 1939 under the direction of Fritz Kitzinger, along with *Air and Variations* (a ballet by William Dollar with music taken from Bach's *Goldberg Variations* and orchestrated by Nicolas Nabokov) and Copland's *Billy the Kid* (choreographed by Eugene

---

11 [Lincoln Kirstein,] *Thirty Years: Lincoln Kirstein's The New York City Ballet,* expanded to include the years 1973–1978, in celebration of the company's thirtieth anniversary (New York: Alfred A. Knopf, 1978), pp. 73–74.

12 Lincoln Kirstein, "Pocahontas," introduction to an early performance of *Pocahontas* [1937]; photocopy in the Elliott Carter Collection, Paul Sacher Foundation.

National Blue Print Co.
New York City

Loring).[13] Although the response of audience and critics alike to *Billy the Kid* far surpassed the reception of the other two works (Copland's catchy, readily intelligible score exactly struck the taste of the times), Carter was not about to be deterred. Perhaps sensing that it would be a long time before his ballet would be performed again, he soon reworked it into a five-movement suite for concert performance.[14] On 23 September 1939, he sent the new score to Serge Koussevitzky, accompanied by a somewhat lukewarm letter of recommendation from Copland: "He [Carter] has never been played as yet by any major orchestra, and this is his first important orchestral work. I need not tell you about the quality of the piece as you can see that for yourself."[15] But once again, success eluded him: on 4 December 1939, Carter having inquired about the piece on 1 December, the maestro of the Boston Symphony Orchestra informed him via his secretary (and future second wife) Olga Naoumoff that the work would not be accepted, adding the surprising reasoning that it was too "light" to introduce the composer's music in the orchestra's concert programs. It must have been all the more satisfying to Carter, therefore, that in early 1940 the *Suite from "Pocahontas"* was chosen from eighty-nine applicants as the winner of the annual Juilliard School competition for the publication of American orchestral music. The score was duly published by Kalmus in 1941 in its *Juilliard Editions* series, albeit in a version so fraught with mistakes that it had to be replaced by a usable revised edition decades later.

14 Elliott Carter to Serge Koussevitzky, 23 September 1939

51 East 55th Street / New York City, N.Y.
September 23rd, 1939

Dear Dr. Koussevitzky:
At the suggestion of Mr. Aaron Copland, whose letter I enclose, I am sending Mr. Rogers, your librarian, my score, "Suite from *Pocahontas*." If you should find the music worthy of being performed by the Boston Symphony, I shall be only too glad to send the parts which are now complete.

My "Suite from *Pocahontas*" has not as yet been performed anywhere. As its title implies, it is a selection of pieces from my ballet, *Pocahontas*, which was commissioned by Mr. Lincoln Kirstein for his Ballet Caravan. The ballet was performed by this troupe last spring in New York. It tells the familiar American story of Pocahontas, an Indian princess, who saved Captain John Smith from sacrifice by the Indians and who finally went to England with another English explorer, John Rolfe. The score is in symphonic style and reflects the feelings of the characters. Actual Indian themes are only suggested, for the emphasis is more on the human feelings portrayed than on the picturesqueness of Indian music.

It would be too obvious for me to say that I would deeply appreciate, as any contemporary composer might, a performance of my music by the great Boston Symphony Orchestra.

Yours sincerely,
Elliott Carter

[Typed letter with autograph signature; Serge Koussevitzky Archive, Music Division, Library of Congress, Washington, D.C. Reprinted by permission.]

15 Olga Naoumoff to Elliott Carter, 4 December 1939

Boston Symphony Orchestra / Dr. Serge Koussevitzky, Conductor / G. E. Judd, Manager / C. W. Spalding, Assistant Manager / Symphony Hall, Boston

Mr. Elliott Carter
December 4, 1939

My dear Mr. Carter,
Dr. Koussevitzky has had an opportunity to examine your "Suite from *Pocahontas*" which you sent some time ago.

He wishes to compliment you on the score but finds that the piece – brilliant as it is – is too light for introducing your name for the first time in the Boston Symphony programs. Therefore, I am now returning you the score.

Yours sincerely,
Olga Naoumoff
Secretary to Dr. Koussevitzky

[Autograph letter; Elliott Carter Collection, Paul Sacher Foundation. Reprinted by permission.]

---

13 Two performances of the ballet with piano accompaniment had already taken place earlier, in York, PA, and Hampton, VA, on 16 and 17 January 1939.
14 Indeed, *Pocahontas* has not been produced again on stage to the present day, perhaps partly because, as Carter noted on a copy of the handwritten score, "[the] original parts were destroyed by a fire which burnt the costumes and scenery as well." (Elliott Carter Collection, Paul Sacher Foundation.)
15 Quoted from Aaron Copland and Vivian Perlis, *Copland: 1900 Through 1942* (London and Boston: Faber and Faber, 1984), p. 283.

Teaching at St. John's College –
The Defense of Corinth (1940–41)

After Carter's association with Kirstein's Ballet Caravan ended in 1939, he started looking for an academic position. On Copland's advice, he applied to Cornell University in the spring of 1940. The following summer, he was offered a job at St. John's College in Annapolis, MD. As Cornell had not yet made its decision, Carter accepted the offer from St. John's, where he taught music, Greek, and mathematics until the summer of 1942. The college's unique philosophy holds that each student should study the great primary texts of human civilization and discuss them in small groups; there are no majors, lecture courses, or electives. Together with Nabokov, who had left Wells College and had come to St. John's in the fall of 1941, Carter developed an ambitious music curriculum for the school, which included close study of major works of the Western canon as well as music notation, ear training, and elementary music theory.[16] Carter exerted considerable effort in conveying basic musical knowledge to his students, as can be seen in the manuals he prepared on "Musical Notation," "Musical Intervals and Scales," "The Greek Diatonic Scale," and "The Just Scale and Its Uses."[17] However, his heavy teaching load meant that he had little time to compose; in fact he produced only one major piece, *The Defense of Corinth*, during his time at St. John's.

The Defense of Corinth was the second work, after *Tarantella* (1936), that Carter wrote for the Harvard Glee Club and its conductor, G. Wallace ("Woody") Woodworth (1902–1969). Planned for a performance at St. John's during the Glee Club's spring tour of 1941, it proved to be too difficult (Carter had sent the score only in mid-February). The première finally took place on 12 March 1942 in Sanders Theatre at Harvard and was followed by a second performance on 4 April at Town Hall in New York. The fifteen-minute melodrama for speaker, men's chorus, and piano four hands certainly exceeded Woodworth's rather modest expectations when he commissioned the piece: "[...] I should want something not more than four or five minutes long, certainly not a cappella, and surely gay and brilliant."[18] In spite of the performance difficulties, Woodworth found Carter's work "brilliant and original" and clearly worth the wait; though ambitious and difficult, *The Defense of Corinth* fits well within the Glee Club tradition of comic and lighthearted works. The use of reciters and speaking choruses was more common in the first half of the twentieth century than it is today; Milhaud's *Choéphores*, *La mort d'un tyran*, and *Salade* – and above all, Stravinsky's *Oedipus Rex*, which had become a kind of signature piece for the Glee Club – were probably in Carter's ear when he was composing *The Defense of Corinth*.

16 *The Defense of Corinth,* for speaker, men's chorus, and piano four hands (1940–41), on a text by François Rabelais, photostat full score with autograph addition of the original, p. 8 (mm. 35-38)

Carter extracted the text of this piece from the "Author's Prologue" to the third book of Rabelais's *Gargantua et Pantagruel*, using a seventeenth-century English translation.[19] The text, analogous perhaps to today's rap poetry, is a virtuosic monologue delivered by a happily drunken narrator, full of tongue twisters and alliterative word play. Carter exploits the musical potential of the language sounds, always precisely notating the rhythm of the speaking parts and sometimes indicating that the consonant sounds "sh" or "s" should be sustained. He employs the full range of possibilities offered by the combination of a speaker with chorus, including that of the divided chorus singing and speaking (as in the page shown). The words are always understandable, even if the meaning of the archaic expressions is not always clear, as terms relating to fortifications like "ravelins," "gabions," "casemates," and "barbacans" are no longer part of everyday English usage. The piano music in this section satirizes military music with its distorted fanfares and dissonant "drum beats" in the second piano's left hand. Carter wrote the original French text above certain passages in this score, perhaps in anticipation of a performance in France. The frantic preparations for war undertaken by the Corinthians and the intentionally ridiculous mimicry of these preparations by the philosopher Diogenes, who beats, rubs, and polishes his bathtub, then pushes it repeatedly down the mountain, offer suggestive parallels to the situation of the US at that time. Although not

16 See Elliott Carter, "Music as a Liberal Art," *Modern Music* 22/1 (November 1944), pp. 12–16, esp. 14–16; most recently reprinted in *CEL*, pp. 309–313, esp. 312. Carter's and Nabokov's insistence on teaching music notation led to friction with the university administration; see Nicolas Nabokov, *Bagázh* (London: Secker & Warburg, 1975), p. 207.

17 Elliott Carter Collection, Paul Sacher Foundation.

18 Letter from G. Wallace Woodworth to Elliott Carter, 17 September 1940; Elliott Carter Collection, Paul Sacher Foundation.

19 The most widely available source for the text would have been the "World's Classics" series: François Rabelais, *Gargantua and Pantagruel,* trans. Thomas Urquhart and Peter Le Motteaux, World's Classics 111–113 (London: Oxford University Press, 1934).

yet a belligerent, the US was subject to internal and international pressure because of the precarious position of Great Britain after the fall of France in June 1940. There was considerable controversy at that time between isolationists and those who advocated a more active involvement in the war. While Diogenes's energetic but ultimately useless actions could represent a cynical view of the value of an artist's production in a time of war, the text has also been read as a "protest against American neutrality" (Schiff 1983, p. 83). As a Francophile, Carter probably did share the views of other prominent interventionists.[20] But perhaps the extravagant "busyness" of the Corinthians as they adjust their fortifications is just as meaningless as Diogenes beating, whirling, tumbling, or overturning his tub; as in a Jean Tinguely sculpture, the actions are as vigorous as they are pointless.

17   G. Wallace Woodworth to Elliott Carter, 15 February 1941

Harvard University / Department of Music / Cambridge, Massachusetts
February 15, 1941

Dear Elliott:

The Defense of Corinth arrived a week ago today and I find it enormously interesting. But do you realize that you have written a very difficult work indeed, and one which would involve long and arduous rehearsing for any chorus? As things go in the Harvard Glee Club, I should estimate that no matter what the performing length, it would take a good deal longer to learn than your *Tarantella*.[21] Much as I regret it, for as you know I was especially eager to do something of yours at the concert in Annapolis, it is just simply out of the question for us to prepare it.

When I wrote you in the autumn[22] my thought was to go to work right after Christmas and do the first performance in Sanders Theatre in March and take the piece all around on the spring trip, including New York as well as the special, shall we say "gala," performance at St. John's College. When you found yourself unable to get it to Cambridge by January first I thought we must abandon learning it with the whole Club, but I hoped to

run in a few special rehearsals, learn it with the picked group which goes on the spring trip, and do it at Annapolis. Even that plan is humanly impossible.

I trust you will understand and not hold it up against us. Certainly I don't hold the delay against you. The whole conception of the piece is brilliant and original, and the fact that it outgrew the original specifications of my "choral economy," especially as to the calendar, we shall just have to charge off to the expanding imagination.

I should guess that I have your only fair copy and I am, therefore, sending it back to you. When summer comes and I can turn my thoughts to plans for the next year I hope very much that I can have it back for detailed consideration.

With renewed regrets and all good wishes.
Sincerely yours,
Woody

Elliott Carter, Esq. / 10 Taney Avenue / Annapolis, Maryland

[Typed letter with autograph signature; Elliott Carter Collection, Paul Sacher Foundation. Reprinted by permission of Harriet Woodworth Koch.]

---

20   For example, the writer Archibald MacLeish was a vocal advocate of intervention, making radio addresses and appearances before Congress; see his influential book, *The American Cause* (New York: Duell, Sloan and Pearce, 1941).

21   Woodworth had performed Carter's *Tarantella* relatively often with the Harvard Glee Club, both in its version for men's chorus and piano four hands and the version for men's chorus and orchestra. His first performance of the former took place at Milton Academy, Boston, on 5 March 1937 (the piano parts were played by two distinguished future Harvard graduates, Irving Fine and William Austin). He first conducted the latter version in Boston's Symphony Hall on 17 May 1937 during a concert of the Boston Pops Orchestra.

22   In this letter Woodworth asked Carter for a new work for the Harvard Glee Club and described the conditions. (Letter from G. Wallace Woodworth to Elliott Carter, 17 September 1940; Elliott Carter Collection, Paul Sacher Foundation.)

18   Elliott Carter in St. Margaret, Annapolis (1942)

This photo from 1942, showing the composer with his two dachshunds Noodle and Suzy, was taken towards the end of Carter's two-year tenure in Annapolis. (The Carters were seldom without a dog; in later years they even took their pets with them during extended stays in Europe.) A short while later he left his job at St. John's College, out of the wish to devote more time to composing, but also from disappointment that the interdisciplinary curriculum left too little space for a deeper technical study of music. When he again accepted a teaching

18

Symphony No. 1 (1942)

position in 1946 (at Peabody Conservatory in Baltimore), he was all the more appreciative to find himself in specialized professional surroundings and able to focus on teaching composition. We can see this in a draft letter of summer 1948 to Douglas Moore, in which he responds very coolly to an offer to move to the Humanities Department at Columbia University: "[...] I am primarily interested in composing and can no longer afford the time and effort for excursions into other fields, no matter how alluring, as I once did at St. John's."[23] (It was not until Moore had given him the requisite assurances that he finally accepted the position.)

Having left his position at St. John's College in Annapolis, Carter found time again in 1942 to write a large-scale composition: the *Symphony No. 1*. He sketched the work during his summer holidays on Cape Cod and completed it, with a dedication to his wife, on 19 December 1942 in Santa Fe, NM, where he had withdrawn for a few months in the fall. In retrospect, Carter claimed that, following the failure of *Pocahontas,* he sought to write "in a deliberately restricted idiom" in order to reach a larger audience (*FW,* p. 58). Indeed, this three-movement piece for small orchestra is noteworthy for its transparent textures, predominantly diatonic materials, and a largely lyrical and cheerful demeanor. In a program note for the première, Carter related these qualities to the work's place of composition: "[...] I tried to suggest the Cape's characteristic beauties and something of the extraordinary cultural background of New England."[24] But it would be wrong to view this "pastoral symphony" (Schiff 1983/1998, pp. 115 and 274, respectively) merely as a concession to the populist taste of the day, for hidden behind the simple façade are many rhythmic and compositional subtleties. This applies in particular to the opening movement, which was the last to be written. It was designed as a combination of sonata and variation form oscillating between two rhythmic pulses in a ratio of 2:3 and is equally unconventional in its handling of tonality. In any event, the work is as far removed from the accessibilty of many other American symphonies of the 1940s as it is from their heroic and patriotic impulse. The *Symphony No. 1* was successfully premièred by the Eastman-Rochester Symphony Orchestra under Howard Hanson on 27 April 1944, but when Copland recommended the score in July 1944 to Richard Burgin, Koussevitzky's concertmaster and assistant, the Russian conductor showed no more interest than he had towards the *Suite from "Pocahontas."* Thereafter the work languished for several years, apart from a trial run-through with the New York Philharmonic under Ignace Strasfogel (2 January 1945), attended by, among others, Edgard Varèse.

---

23 Letter from Elliott Carter to Douglas Moore, August 1948; draft in the Elliott Carter Collection, Paul Sacher Foundation.

24 Program of the première, 27 April 1944, Fourteenth Annual Festival of American Music, Eastman-Rochester Symphony Orchestra, Rochester, NY.

Service in the OWI (1943–44)

19 *Symphony No. 1,* for orchestra (1942), photostat full score with autograph corrections, p. 131

Hoping for further performances and a possible publication (which had to wait until 1961), Carter subjected his *Symphony No. 1* to several stages of revision in the 1940s and 1950s. Among his later alterations (1953) is the insertion of two atmospheric string chords at the opening of the first movement.[25] More decisive, however, was an earlier cut made in the finale shortly after the première. In the final version this movement, based on material from the original version of *Pocahontas* (a madcap Haydnesque finale with square dance allusions and a jazzy clarinet solo), is wholly permeated by the quick quarter-note motion of the main theme, whereas in the original version the movement's drive is slowed down by a lengthy chorale-like passage towards the end. This passage, mentioned specifically in Carter's program notes for the première ("Towards the end, a recollection of the first movement interrupts the rapid pace"[26]), was later withdrawn at Copland's suggestion. The corrected copy shown here reveals that the cut was made in at least two stages. First, Carter deleted a few isolated details, such as the quarter-note string figure derived from the main theme, which interrupts or complements the woodwind and brass chorale several times (rehearsal no. 103). Then he discarded the entire page – and several other pages along with it. (A total of seventy-two bars are crossed out in this score.) Then, in a final stage, he added the finishing touches by scrapping the next twenty-six bars and reinstating the first five bars of the cut in slightly revised form. All in all, this led to a cut of ninety-three bars originally located just before m. 1184 in the definitive score (AMP 06145-146).

By 1943 Carter was looking for ways to get involved in the war effort. At the start of the war, a doctor had assigned him 4F status because of various physical ailments, but soon Carter came to feel guilty about this, because, "from the time of the Spanish Civil War, we all felt that Fascism was a real horror."[27] Back in New York after having spent the autumn of 1942 in Santa Fe, the thirty-four-year-old composer wrote to Copland on 10 May 1943: "I had hoped that I could join the war effort actively, but so far my luck has not been good." (See below, p. 54). Armed with the following letters of recommendation from such eminent cultural figures as Lincoln Kirstein (who at that time was serving as Consultant on Latin-American Art at the Museum of Modern Art) and the composer and professor at Columbia University Douglas Moore, Carter applied to government intelligence organizations, hoping to put his knowledge of foreign languages to good use. But this came to nothing, as entrance examinations deemed him unsuitable for decoding or other intelligence work. One agency – Carter does not remember which one – asked him to inform on German shopkeepers in New York City, but he was unwilling to do this. Carter was finally hired by the New York branch of the Office of War Information (OWI), where he worked until D-Day (6 June 1944) as Musical Advisor.[28] He was in charge of radio broadcasts for use in Europe and North Africa, which combined news and music (see *CC*, p. 32). In a letter written in April 1944 Carter explained: "We have been furiously turning out Greek, Albanian, Belgian, French, Roumanian, German, Hungarian, Norwegian, Danish, Dutch, and other musics, making records, sending them to far-away places, finding old recordings, digging up native singers and instrumentalists, and doing research, [so] that all my nights and days are dizzied with strange sounds, alas too often heard."[29] One of his duties was to produce a recording of Schoenberg's *Piano Concerto* to be broadcast over European radio.[30] As D-Day approached, Carter and other composers were put to work orchestrating national anthems: "Sam Barber did the *Marseillaise*, and I did *La Brabançonne*, the Belgian national anthem." At the time Carter joined in 1943 the Overseas Branch was in high gear: "the staff worked twenty-four hours a day on hundreds of productions in scores of different

---

25 These revisions were made with an eye to the New York première, which was given by the orchestra of the American Federation of Musicians under David Broekman on 16 January 1954. The program expressly calls it the "first performance in revised version."
26 Ibid.
27 Interview with Felix Meyer and Anne Shreffler, 12 June 2007. Much of the

information in this paragraph, and all otherwise unattributed quotations, come from this interview.
28 Schiff's assumption that Carter was away from New York during the war ("New York [...] may have thought that Carter was now out of the running, but he was just playing possum") can now be corrected (Schiff 1998, p. 18).

29 Letter from Elliott Carter to John Kirkpatrick, 1 April 1944; Elliott Carter Collection, Paul Sacher Foundation.
30 This was a recording of the work's première, given on 6 February 1944 by Edward Steuermann (piano) and the NBC Symphony Orchestra under Leopold Stokowski.

languages."[31] Copland, Cowell, Roy Harris, and Virgil Thomson were also actively involved with the agency, composing music for documentaries or war-themed works.[32] The international radio network Voice of America was the OWI's most successful venture. Political pressure led to a gradual decrease in funding for the OWI, which was dissolved in September 1945 after the end of the war.

20 Lincoln Kirstein, letter of recommendation for Elliott Carter, 21 January 1943

The Museum of Modern Art / New York / Lincoln Kirstein / Consultant on Latin-American Art
January 21, 1943

To whom it may concern:
I have known Elliott Carter for the past eleven years. I saw him in Paris in 1933 and know that he speaks French perfectly and reads and writes it nearly as well. From 1937 until 1939 Mr. Carter worked for me in the capacity of music director for a theatrical company of which I was director. He was at all times efficient, extremely capable, resourceful, as well as extremely honest. Since leaving my employ, Mr. Carter has been teaching with considerable distinction at St. John's College, Annapolis, Maryland. Mr. Carter is an excellent mathematician as well as an extremely talented composer of music.

Lincoln Kirstein

[Typed letter with autograph signature; Elliott Carter Collection, Paul Sacher Foundation. Writing by Lincoln Kirstein © 1943, renewed 2008 by the New York Public Library (Astor, Lenox, and Tilden Foundations).]

21 Douglas Moore, letter of recommendation for Elliott Carter, 1 February 1943

Columbia University / in the City of New York / Department of Music
February 1, 1943

To whom it may concern:
I have known Elliott Carter for six years. Among the younger men who have achieved prominence in the profession of music, he is one of the most outstanding. He has an extensive scholarly background and is able to organize and present his information with clarity and understanding, whether as teacher or writer. I have been much impressed by his ability to adapt himself to unusual situations which arise in connection with his teaching, such as, for instance, his organization of a course for the special needs of St. John's College. In this work he was able to interpret the ordinary material in the most unconventional and resourceful manner. In addition to music, he has had experience in the teaching of other academic subjects and his knowledge of French is extensive. He had three years' study in France and has an excellent conversational facility.

As a man he has integrity of character and an attractive personality. His loyalty to the United States is unquestionable.

Douglas Moore
Executive Officer

[Typed letter, carbon copy with autograph signature; Elliott Carter Collection, Paul Sacher Foundation.]

---

31 See Allan M. Winkler, *The Politics of Propaganda: The Office of War Information 1942–1945* (New Haven and London: Yale University Press, 1978), p. 78. In 1943 the Overseas Branch received over 90 percent of the OWI's total appropriation (p. 105). The director of the Overseas Branch in New York, the playwright Robert E. Sherwood (best known for his screenplay for the 1946 film, *The Best Years of Our Lives*), recruited a group of idealistic and talented writers, artists, filmmakers, musicians, and intellectuals, but the liberal, left-leaning world view of

the Overseas Branch brought it into constant conflict with the military, the State Department, President Roosevelt, and even with the OWI's Domestic Branch in Washington (pp. 73ff.).

32 Neil Lerner names Copland, Harris, and Thomson in "Aaron Copland, Norman Rockwell, and the 'Four Freedoms': The Office of War Information's Vision and Sound in The Cummington Story (1945)," in *Aaron Copland and His World*, ed. Carol J. Oja and Judith Tick (Princeton and Oxford: Princeton University Press, 2005), pp. 351–377. Carter remembers that Cowell was also involved with the OWI

33 As early as the mid-1980s, Carter toyed with the idea of writing a piece for unaccompanied violin to honor Copland on his eighty-fifth birthday in 1985. But it was not until February 1999, a good eighteen years after Copland's death, that the composition finally took shape. *Statement – Remembering Aaron* was united with one earlier and two later dedicatory pieces for solo violin – *Riconoscenza per Goffredo Petrassi* (1984), *Fantasy – Remembering Roger [Sessions]* (1999) and *Rhapsodic Musings (For Robert Mann)* (2000) – to create a four-movement dedicatory cycle entitled *Four Lauds*.

A Summary of Concerts for Aaron Copland (1943)

Though only eight years his senior, Aaron Copland (1900–1990) was already a highly successful composer when Carter first met him in the 1920s. When Copland gave the première of his *Piano Concerto* in Boston on 28–29 January 1927, the young Harvard student introduced himself in the artist's dressing room. Later he attended several lectures that Copland held at the New School for Social Research. He was also present on 1 May 1932 when Copland introduced his *Piano Variations* and a group of Ives songs at the first Festival of Contemporary American Music in Yaddo (near Saratoga Springs, NY). After Carter's return from Paris (where Copland had been Nadia Boulanger's first American pupil ten years earlier), these initial contacts developed into a lifelong friendship that found expression in Copland's dedication of the song "There Came a Wind like a Bugle" (no. 2 from *Twelve Poems of Emily Dickinson*, 1949–50) to Carter, as well as in the latter's memorial composition *Statement – Remembering Aaron*.[33] But for all their mutual esteem, the relationship between the two composers was artistically ambivalent. Carter neither could nor wanted to commit himself wholly to Copland's populist ideals: though admitting that Copland's success served him well (for the moment), he felt that his own need for expression pointed him in the direction of continuing in the early European modernist and American experimental traditions (as embodied for example by Ives, Cowell, and Crawford). Copland, in turn, was much slower to take Carter's music seriously than that of other younger composers, though he acknowledged its high-quality workmanship. The fact that he failed to mention Carter in his writings on American music was a thorn in the younger man's side as late as 1960, when Carter stood at the threshold of his international fame and began to outstrip Copland in the eyes of the postwar avant-garde (see below, p. 162). That said, the following exchange of letters from 1943 betrays nothing of this ambivalence and projects a tone of friendly camaraderie. From February to September 1943 Copland was staying in Hollywood to write the film score for Lewis Milestone's *The North Star*

(on a screenplay by Lillian Hellman). On 10 May 1943, Carter brought him up to date with a summary of important events on the New York scene and reported on his own work, his uncertain prospects of being accepted into the Army or the Navy, and his family life, which had entered a new dimension with the birth of his son, David Chambers Carter, on 4 January 1943. Copland seems not to have answered the letter, but on 5 October 1943, shortly before returning to New York, he responded to another letter written in early September. With wonted amiability, he not only gave Carter a brief résumé of his activities in Hollywood, but evinced curiosity about Carter's most recent compositions.

22   Elliott Carter to Aaron Copland, 10 May 1943

Dear Aaron,

It was swell to hear from you. We accept your congratulations on our babe with great pleasure.[34] Your letter deserved a more prompt answer, but what with changing diapers, having physical exams, doing articles for Minna,[35] and writing music, we have only just settled down to an organized life.

Lots of things have been going on in New York, as you know, but the concert of your music was the high point of the season for me.[36] I thought your sonata simply superb and enjoyed the movie-score piece too, though it was not very well played. Bernstein certainly did a fine job of putting the sonata across. The Abraham Lincoln piece under Koussy was also beautiful, but somehow not played in the proper mood.[37] The beginning did not catch the subdued power and mystery it should have, probably because of K[oussevitzky]'s nervous beat, likewise the scherzo seemed too brilliant and not easy-going enough, [and] Will Geer was a bit too folksy. Nevertheless the work could not help but make a wonderful effect. I was happy to hear it under better conditions than last summer's radio-plus-thunderstorm performance.[38] I did not

---

34   Copland's letter of congratulations has not survived.

35   Minna Lederman commissioned Carter to write the following three articles in the early part of 1943: "Films and Theatre, 1943," *Modern Music* 20/3 (March–April 1943), pp. 205–207 (partially reprinted in *WEC*, pp. 86–87); "American Figure, with Landscape," *Modern Music* 20/4 (May–June 1943), pp. 219–225 (most recently reprinted in *CEL*, pp. 134–138); and "Theatre and Films, 1943," *Modern Music* 20/4 (May–June 1943), pp. 282–284 (reprinted in *WEC*, pp. 93–95).

36   On 17 February 1943 the Composers Forum-Laboratory mounted a concert

entitled "The Music of Aaron Copland" in New York's Town Hall, including a performance by Leonard Bernstein of the *Piano Sonata*, the première of *Music for Movies* (a five-movement suite for small orchestra that Copland had compiled from the film scores for *The City*, *Of Mice and Men*, and *Our Town*) conducted by Daniel Saidenberg, and a "Discussion of Mr. Copland's Music" headed by Kenneth Klein. The panelists in the discussion were Virgil Thomson (representing the music critics), Israel Citkowitz (representing Copland), Daniel Saidenberg and Leonard Bernstein (the evening's two performers), and the dramatist and screenwriter

Clifford Odets ("representing a layman's viewpoint").

37   Serge Koussevitzky and the Boston Symphony Orchestra made a guest appearance in New York on 3 April 1943. The program included, besides the *Lincoln Portrait* (1942) with Will Geer as speaker, William Schuman's cantata *A Free Song* (1942), premièred eight days earlier in Boston. The choral part was sung by the Harvard Glee Club and the Radcliffe Choral Society.

38   Carter refers to a radio broadcast of 16 August 1942 in which André Kostelanetz conducted the CBS Symphony Orchestra and Carl Sandburg was the speaker.

get to hear your *Lark,* but the news of it was good.[39] After a season of awful movie scores to very fine pictures – we are looking forward to yours with great expectations.

The other music I have heard was almost entirely disappointing. Bill Schuman's *Prayer 1943* and his *Free Song* seemed well-intentioned enough but not convincingly realized.[40] Paul B[owles]'s *[The] Wind Remains* suffered from a poor choice of libretto and only half came off. His music was his usual.[41]

My viola and piano *Pastoral* was not very well played and was placed first on a program which should have begun with a more forceful piece.[42] I liked the work very much myself and so did Helen, but I don't think many people did. I guess it is a little strange, but I like chamber music that sounds that way.

In Santa Fe, I finished my Symphony in 3 movements for w[ood]w[ind] by twos, two trumpets, two horns and trombone, timpani, and strings. It turned out to be about twenty-three minutes and has a simple and what seems to me straightforward mood about it. I have not any plan of campaign for having it played yet, but as soon as I have the parts copied I will get busy. At present I am working on some Whitman songs which will be finished in a month or so.[43]

Helen and I have been leading a quiet private life with our baby. He appears to us to grow so fast that we are already after three months wishing he were small again. Almost each day reveals another sign of approaching maturity – finger wiggling, laughing, cooing, and all the other things that babies do and which excite parents and bore everybody else.

No news from my navy application for a commission, but my army one has kept me busy with physical exams. They found that I walk on my toes more than most and don't know whether to attribute it to, of all things, infantile paralysis. Papers mislaid also account for

the delay. My draft board is silent, except that I am in 1A, which keeps me from getting a defense job. I had hoped that I could join the war effort actively, but so far my luck has not been good.

We have missed you very much this year and are hoping that I will still be around when you return. Helen certainly will be. It is good news that you are writing a violin sonata – good luck.[44]

We would love to know how Hollywood strikes you in war time. Our best to Victor.[45]

Elliott

P. S. Helen and I left our car in Santa Fe and are now sorry that we did. We got enough gas coupons from the local board to get the car back here. We have been wondering if, by chance, you and Victor, or either one of you would be interested in driving the car back here when you return (if you do). The tires are almost new and the car in good condition. We would be glad to defray the cost of any repairs that might be necessary en route. Let us know so that we can send you the new license plates in time.

529 East 85 Street / New York, N. Y.
May 10, 1943

[Typed letter with autograph signature; Aaron Copland Collection, Music Division, Library of Congress, Washington, D.C. Reprinted by permission of the Aaron Copland Fund for Music, Inc., copyright owner.]

39   Copland's *Lark* for baritone and chorus (1938), on a text by Genevieve Taggard, was premièred in the Museum of Modern Art on 13 April 1943, with the Collegiate Chorale conducted by Robert Shaw.

40   William Schuman's orchestra piece *Prayer 1943*, later renamed *Prayer in Time of War* (1943), was performed on 25, 26, and 28 March 1943 by the New York Philharmonic Orchestra under the baton of Fritz Reiner. The cantata *A Free Song* was on the program of the Boston Symphony Orchestra's guest appearance on 3 April 1943 (see above, p. 53, note 37). This work received the first Pulitzer Prize in music; see Steve Swayne, "William Schuman, World War II, and the Pulitzer Prize," *The Musical Quarterly* 89/2–3 (Fall 2006), pp. 273–320.

41   The première of Paul Bowles's *The Wind Remains,* a kind of *zarzuela* on a text

by Federico García Lorca, took place in the Museum of Modern Art on 30 March 1943, conducted by Leonard Bernstein and choreographed by Merce Cunningham, who also danced a solo part. Carter reported in depth on this production in the column "Theatre and Films, 1943" in *Modern Music* 20/4 (May–June 1943), see above, p. 53, note 35.

42   Carter's *Pastoral* of 1940 was performed in the New York Public Library during the second Young Composers' Concert of the League of Composers on 14 March 1943. The performers were Ralph Hersh (viola) and Harrison Potter (piano). The program also included works by Vincent Persichetti, Beatrice Laufer, Lukas Foss, and Leonard Bernstein.

43   Of these Whitman settings only the song *Warble for Lilac Time* has survived. It exists in a version for soprano (or tenor) and

piano and in another for soprano and chamber orchestra.

44   Later Copland remarked of this passage in the letter, as in other reactions from his colleagues, that he sensed concern "about my possible defection to Hollywood." However, there was no real cause for concern, he continued, for during the breaks in his Hollywood schedule he regularly composed "serious music," including the initial sketches for a ballet (*Appalachian Spring*) and a larger concert piece (a piano concerto or symphony). See Aaron Copland and Vivian Perlis, *Aaron Copland: Since 1943* (New York: St. Martin's Press, 1989), p. 19. Copland's *Violin Sonata* is mentioned in his letter of 5 October 1943 to Carter; see below, p. 55.

45   Copland's companion Victor Kraft (1915–1976), who had initially studied

23   Elliott Carter to Aaron Copland [early September 1943]

529 E. 85 St. / New York, 28, N.Y.

Dear Aaron,

For a very long time I have been expecting a letter from you – but why should you write me, for I am indeed a poor correspondent, having taken so long to answer your letter before.

We have been having a quiet summer in the city, with occasional weeks in Connecticut, where we are at the moment. The baby grows fast, has his first tooth, and is learning to creep.

I have been writing a bunch of songs, 4 of which are finished with more on the way,[46] and copying the parts of my symphony. If I were sure of your present address and was not afraid of burdening you with extra luggage I would send you copies of these new works – Rumour has it that you are in Mexico.

If this is true, it means that you have finished work on your movie score, which I hope turned out the way you wanted it. We are looking forward to the time when we can hear it. How is your violin sonata coming along? Were you able to finish it before you left Hollywood?

Minna L[ederman] tells me that you liked my Gilbert article[47] and suggested that I write a book on American music.[48] It is something which, as you know, I have had in mind for a long time but which I have put off continually, wanting to spend all the time I could on composing, which interests me more, and I would like to get much more music written before I give myself to such a strenuous effort. Besides, there are many issues in the American scene which are not clearly formulated in [my] mind as yet.

Last Sunday we heard the voice of Corporal Blitzstein on the radio from England, interviewed on cultural subjects in London.[49]

He mentioned your name as one of the American composers that the English musical public are very interested in.

I keep reading references to a piece of yours on Cuban themes – I have never heard it – when was it played? Is it for orchestra?

Helen sends her best to you & Victor, as do I.
Elliott

[Autograph letter; Aaron Copland Collection, Music Division, Library of Congress, Washington, D.C. Reprinted by permission of the Aaron Copland Fund for Music, Inc., copyright owner.]

24   Aaron Copland to Elliott Carter, 5 October 1943

Mark Twain Hotel / Hannibal / Missouri
Oct 5 '43

Dear Elliott:

I don't quite dare make my reentrance into New York without first making a hasty reply to your letter of some weeks back. It arrived just at the time when I was in the thick of the movie score, with not a moment for myself.[50] Now it's hardly worth answering at length, because Victor and I are driving home – and will be there any minute now.

I look forward to seeing the new songs and the Symphony. But I don't see why they are put on evidence as reasons for not writing a book on American music! If I manage to do both, why not you?[51]

Most of my news is probably stale. The picture is done and will be released in November. I managed to finish two movements of the Violin Sonata, and a third of a new ballet for Martha Graham.[52]

---

music in New York, was later primarily a photographer.

46   See note 43.

47   Elliott Carter, "American Figure, with Landscape," *Modern Music* 20/4 (May–June 1943), pp. 219–225; most recently reprinted in *CEL*, pp. 134–138.

48   The project never materialized. Nor did a survey of "Music in America at War" planned a year and a half later at the behest of the OWI, though an outline survives in Carter's hand (see below, pp. 67–70).

49   Marc Blitzstein (1905–1964) served in the Eighth Air Force in London from August 1942 to the summer of 1945. He was released from duty in early 1943, which enabled him to compose a large-scale patriotic work, the so-called *Airborne Symphony*. From the fall of 1943 he was

musical director of the American Broadcasting Station in Europe.

50   The music to *The North Star* was recorded in early September 1943; the film was released the following October.

51   Besides his many compositional activities, Copland also published two books – *What to Listen for in Music* (New York: McGraw-Hill, 1939) and *Our New Music* (New York: McGraw-Hill, 1941) – which admittedly drew to a large extent on pre-existing articles and lectures. If the first is a sort of musical primer, *Our New Music* is a far-ranging overview of the European and American musical scenes in the first four decades of the twentieth century.

52   Copland finished his *Violin Sonata* shortly after returning to New York. Before the première, which he gave with the violinist Ruth Posselt on 17 January 1944, Copland

played the piece in his loft with David Diamond for a small circle of friends, including Carter. The ballet *Appalachian Spring*, in contrast, occupied him until July 1944. The delays in the project, which Copland was commissioned to compose by Elizabeth Sprague Coolidge in 1942, resulted from the fact that the choreographer and dancer Martha Graham was late in submitting the scenario, which was then subjected to much revision. Originally scheduled for performance on 30 October 1943 (Coolidge's birthday), *Appalachian Spring* was finally premièred at the Library of Congress on 30 October 1944 (after two postponements) with Martha Graham, Erick Hawkins, May O'Donnell, and Merce Cunningham in the main roles and Louis Horst conducting.

Voyage (1943)

The Cuban piece you refer to is called a Danzón Cubano. It's for 2 pianos and I wrote it last Dec[ember] for the League's 20th anniversary. B[oosey] & H[awkes] just issued it, if you're curious. It's a light number which amuses me – and I hope to orchestrate it someday.[53]

The picture lasted so long that I never did get to Mexico. We have just spent a week in Colorado, where I gave lectures on the South Americans in 3 towns: Colorado Springs, Denver, and Boulder. Took a side trip to visit the Central City Opry House – very echt, or so it seemed to me.

It will be grand to be back. I missed N[ew] Y[ork] and all the friends sumpin' awful.

Till soon – and our very best [to] Helen and the magnum opus.
Aaron

[Autograph letter; Elliott Carter Collection, Paul Sacher Foundation. Reprinted by permission of the Aaron Copland Fund for Music, Inc., copyright owner.]

While later New York composers such as John Cage and Morton Feldman were to find inspiration in abstract expressionist painting, Carter, the former English major, was a serious reader of contemporary poetry. The work of the American visionary poet Hart Crane stimulated three of Carter's compositions and arguably the development of his musical technique in general. The first, the ballet *Pocahontas*, is loosely based on "Powhatan's Daughter" from *The Bridge*. Carter was so taken with this poem, a vast modernist epic of American histories, landscapes, and images, that he originally planned to make it the subject of an oratorio.[54] These plans were ultimately realized thirty years later in a purely instrumental work, *A Symphony of Three Orchestras*. Carter's only vocal setting of Crane's poetry is the song *Voyage* (1943), whose text is the third of a group of six poems entitled "Voyages," Crane's gently erotic meditations on the sea and on love.[55] For the publication of this song in 1945 with Valley Music Press, the pianist and editor John Kirkpatrick had evidently asked the composer for an explanatory note on the somewhat obscure poem. In preparation for his remarks, Carter subjected the poem to another round of intense scrutiny that went far beyond what he had done while composing it. Kirkpatrick then returned Carter's first draft of the commentary (which has not survived) for revision. The text given below is the second draft, which Kirkpatrick again edited thoroughly before including it opposite the poem's text in the published score. While Carter arrived at an original reading of the poem through close study, his understanding of Crane's symbolism may also have been inspired by Waldo Frank's introduction to the volume, as for example when Frank writes: "Crane is using the symbol of the Sea as a principle of unity and release from the contradictions of personal existence."[56] Carter's commentary seeks to clarify the poem's dense language. He outlines three "protagonists" – love, the sea, and the poet – and in doing so idealizes and neutralizes its frankly erotic content. The somewhat unusual inclusion of a literary commentary in an edition of music was possible because Valley Music Press was a non-profit company, founded by the composers Ross Lee Finney and John Verrall and supported jointly by the women's colleges at which they were employed, Mount Holyoke and Smith, respectively. Kirkpatrick was also teaching at Mount Holyoke at this time. He had asked Carter in early summer 1944

---

53 Copland orchestrated *Danzón Cubano* in 1946. Its original version for two pianos was premièred by the composer and Leonard Bernstein in New York's Town Hall on 9 December 1942.

54 The first mention of this project occurs in a list of Carter's compositions published in Claire Reis, *Composers in America* (see above, p.26, note 13), p. 57, where it bears the date 1937. However, Carter clung to the plan for years, as we know from his comments in the lecture "The Need for New Choral Music" (1953); see below, pp. 107–108.

55 According to the acknowledgment in the Valley Music Press edition of "Voyage," the song's text was drawn from *The Collected Poems of Hart Crane*, edited with an introduction by Waldo Frank (New York: Liveright Publishing, 1933), p. [104]. Carter may have first read "Voyages" in Hart Crane, *White Buildings*, with a foreword by Allen Tate ([New York]: Horace Liveright, 1926), p. 52.

56 Waldo Frank, "An Introduction," in *The Collected Poems of Hart Crane* (see note 55), p. xvii.

about the possibility of publishing either *Warble for Lilac Time* or *Voyage* (the former was not published until 1956, with Peer Music).[57] In gratitude for Kirkpatrick's interest in his music and for his careful editing of this song, Carter dedicated *Voyage* to Kirkpatrick and his wife, Hope.

25   Elliott Carter to John Kirkpatrick, 6 October 1944

529 East 85 Street / New York, 28, N.Y.
October 6, 1944

Dear John,
I still feel powerless to thank you for the day you spent helping me with the score of my symphony.[58] Your help was invaluable and should result in a vastly improved performance.

[E]nclosed you will find rather a long analysis of the Crane poem. Maybe it is too long for your purpose, but, of course, I feel that I have only begun to say all there is to say. Beside[s] this explanation, I think the poem ought to appear as it is printed in the book, just for the sake of clarity.

Poetry still presents a terrible problem to me. I have been spending the last week in the Public Library trying to find new texts of songs and choruses. I guess I must be very fussy and have strange preconceived notions but my reading is singularly unrewarding.

We have been house-hunting in Redding and have seen some perfectly beautiful places, but we can't make up our minds and so continue to look.

By next summer we might be neighbours, which we would love after having had such pleasant times with Hope and you in Georgetown and Fire Island.

At present the common and mysterious cold has put Helen and David in bed, not too sick but sneezy. Helen asks me to write Hope and say that she would love to have a couple of quarts of applesauce, and that she would be glad to pick them up at your mother's, if it is not too much trouble for her. She says that David loves home-made sauce and that she is grateful.

Helen joins me in sending our best to you both,
Elliott

[Typed letter with autograph signature; John Kirkpatrick Papers, Irving S. Gilmore Music Library, Yale University. Reprinted by permission of Daisy Kirkpatrick.]

26   John Kirkpatrick to Elliott Carter, 3 November [1944]

21 Woodbridge St. / South Hadley Mass.
Nov. 3.

Dear Elliott,
Please forgive my not acknowledging the Crane commentary before this. The combination of recitals & teaching week is apt to bring on indigestion in the flow of events.

You certainly throw a great deal of light, both on the poem and on its relation to the music. I feel too, though, what you write about, that you "have only begun to say all there is to say." I think the occasion could stand still more. Do you think the material could be grouped as well according to its unfolding in the poem as by planes of interpretation? – or, if the latter, could each phrase receive some sort of comment? – just so the imaginary voice student or singer (with perhaps average obtuseness) could have something to hang on to in practically all of it?

We'd like to announce it on the card as:

... ELLIOTT CARTER Voyage (Hart Crane).   .60
Voice and piano
(with a commentary on the poem by the composer)
(to be ready in January)

Is that OK by you? We'd like to print up the cards pretty soon. Yes, the poem must be included as was. About other poetry – have you looked into the rest of Frost – or might you tie up with Emily Dickinson? Many have tried but none succeeded.

All best things from us both.
Hastily,
John

Hope to see you on the 13th.[59]

[Autograph letter; Elliott Carter Collection, Paul Sacher Foundation. Reprinted by permission of Daisy Kirkpatrick.]

---

[57] See undated letter from John Kirkpatrick to Elliott Carter, [June 1944]; Elliott Carter Collection, Paul Sacher Foundation.

[58] Kirkpatrick had helped the composer with the performance markings for his *Symphony No.1*, which was given a trial run-through by the New York Philharmonic under Ignace Strasfogel on 2 January 1945; see above, p. 49.

[59] On 13 November 1944, John Kirkpatrick presented a piano recital at New York Times Hall in which he played, in addition to works by Philippe de Vitry, François Couperin, Jean-Philippe Rameau, and Stephen Foster, the première of Ross Lee Finney's *Piano Sonata No. 3* (1942) and the first complete performance of Carl Ruggles's *Evocations* (1935–37 and 1943).

27 **Elliott Carter, commentary on Hart Crane's poem *Voyage* (as sent to John Kirkpatrick on 27 November 1944)**

To help the singer (and possibly the listener) in forming an interpretation of the text of this song (the third in a series of six "Voyages" by Hart Crane), it would perhaps be pertinent to describe something of what I have thought about it. As with most poetry, this poem can be read in several different ways. I neither venture to deal with them exhaustively nor least of all to construct a definitive interpretation. In the music I have tried to reflect the poetic meaning and the beauties of the piece by Crane. Without going into the psychological and emotional implications which every line challenges, I would like to give a short account below of the prose meaning as I see it on the most matter-of-fact level.

There are three protagonists: the sea, which is the medium through which everything in the poem moves and changes and to which every idea is referred; "love," to whom the poet addresses himself; and the poet. In two sections, the argument, stripped of symbols and connotations, runs something like this: since "love" is never far from his thoughts and represents the most desirable of conditions (first eight lines), the poet entreats "love" to allow him to go safely through an ordeal which will bring him under "love's" power. Of the protagonists, the sea is thought of under several aspects. In the first section the relation of sea to sky suggests the unifying, harmonizing power of love; while in the second the sea forms an obstacle to be voyaged through to reach love. At the end of each part the transforming power of the sea, with the peril of loss of identity, looms up as a danger which, by implication, is like that of love. This transforming power is given exemplification in the ordering of images and ideas in the poem itself, which uses many metaphors and moves rapidly from one level of meaning to another. "Love," another protagonist, for instance, to whom the poem is addressed, is in one place an actual person and in another seems transformed into the principle or power under whose spell the poet wishes to come. In the following analysis, for purposes of simplicity, I assume that the poem is addressed to the power, love, although it can just as well be explained in terms of a particular person. In this respect the poem has a double meaning.

After these general points, here is a line-by-line comment: the sea bears a relationship infinite in time, in space as well as in proximity to all things. It is like the mother of all, like a great bloodstream uniting all in a common bond ("Infinite consanguinity it bears"). Considered from this point of view, which is exhibited in the close relationship of sea and sky that the light of day reveals, the sea is comparable to love ("This tendered theme of you that light / Retrieves from sea plains where the sky / Resigns a breast that every wave enthrones"). Coming down to the particular scene or experience that may have suggested the poem, the poet then describes his beloved and himself swimming in the sea, he not following any path far removed from his beloved. Maintaining the level of meaning taken for the first four lines, these would naturally imply that the poet's thoughts often return to love ("While ribboned water lanes I wind / Are laved and scattered with no stroke / Wide from your side"). The section closes with a hint of the dangers lurking in the sea pictured as grasping at both swimmers with hand-like waves that could transform them into relics by disintegrating their bodies. In another poem, Crane wrote: "The dice of drowned men's bones," which suggests the meaning implied here ("whereto this hour / The sea lifts, also, reliquary hands").

The second section, which is one long sentence beginning and ending "And so ... Permit me voyage, love, into your hands...," turns to consider the ordeal the poet must undergo in order to come under the spell of love. Using other elements of the swimming scene mentioned above, the ordeal is represented metaphorically as a voyage into the depths, a rise to the surface, and a swim over the waves to reach the floating body of his love. The different depths of the sea suggest a turbulent architectural façade before which the poet rises, with gates at the bottom, pillars and pediments above them, and on top a roof of waves reflecting glittering lights and stars ("And so, admitted through black swollen gates / That must arrest all distance otherwise, – / Past whirling pillars and lithe pediments, / Light wrestling there incessantly with light, / Star kissing star through wave on wave unto / Your body rocking!"). Then once again the poet turns to the danger involved in the voyage. Death at sea is not bloody but a disintegration into relics scattered over the bottom from one end of the world to the other. It is like the transformation of a poet's experience that suffers disintegration and reorganization into word-relics made into a poem by the subtle poetic art ("and where death, if shed, / Presumes no carnage, but this single change,– / Upon the steep floor flung from dawn to dawn / The silken skilled transmemberment of song"). In the final line the poet asks permission of love to be allowed to complete his ordeal or voyage safely and to come under its power, wishing to surrender himself wholly to it.

I have purposely avoided an attempt to explain the ordeal described metaphorically in the poem, for that would involve a much lengthier discussion than there is room for here. Certainly the tragic career of Hart Crane himself throws one kind of light on the matter. In fact, viewed autobiographically, this particular work can be considered as a prophecy of his own personal voyage through life, which met its end when he wilfully extinguished himself in the hands of the sea.

Elliott Carter

[Typescript, with handwritten editorial annotations (not included in the transcription given here) by John Kirkpatrick; John Kirkpatrick Papers, Irving S. Gilmore Music Library, Yale University. Reprinted by permission of Daisy Kirkpatrick. The final version of the "Commentary" was published in Schiff 1983/1998, pp. 326–327 and 328–329, respectively.]

Infinite consanguinity it bears –
This tendered theme of you that light
Retrieves from sea plains where the sky
Resigns a breast that every wave enthrones;
While ribboned water lanes I wind
Are laved and scattered with no stroke
Wide from your side, whereto this hour
The sea lifts, also, reliquary hands.

And so, admitted through black swollen gates
That must arrest all distance otherwise,–
Past whirling pillars and lithe pediments,
Light wrestling there incessantly with light,
Star kissing star through wave on wave unto
Your body rocking!
          and where death, if shed,
Presumes no carnage, but this single change, –
Upon the steep floor flung from dawn to dawn
The silken skilled transmemberment of song;

Permit me voyage, love, into your hands...

28 Elliott Carter to John Kirkpatrick, [28 November 1944]

Dear John,

Yesterday, I sent you my new, rather lengthy, and detailed comment on the Crane. I think quoting the poem in the body of the text makes reading easier, though it does seem funny to be printing it once this way, once as a poem, and once as the text of the song, as if it were an idée fixe, which by now it truly has become for me. If I had worked on it as much as I have now, I don't know whether I would have written the song, or maybe it would have been a better song. Anyhow, I followed your suggestion about getting down to details for the singer's sake. I hope the dead serious tone and rather formal presentation won't frighten her away. By the way, I really do think that this song goes better for a gal than a man, but I don't suppose it is necessary to say this.

Since sending the new MS. of the song, which has a few notes lengthened in the voice part, I have been deliberating with a metronome and have decided definitely that I have marked it all too fast. MM. 104 is the fastest possible speed, and 96 on the slow side, so 100 is about right for the beginning, and about 108 for the two middle sections, returning to 100 at "Upon the steep floor." On the last page, I would like to make a note that the F major secondary ninth chord should not be rolled. I noted the way it should be played if the player can't hit all the notes together. I suspect that printing these notes as a footnote will complicate your printing problem, while a little sentence or two could serve just as well. I started to write what I thought should be said, but did not get very far, in any case it was sent off before I fully made up my mind how to explain. Do what you like with it. By the way, if you wish to edit the song, and call it "edited by J. K.," please do.[60]

By the way an important matter, I think of this song as being dedicated to Hope and John Kirkpatrick, and would like to have it appear somewhere near the title.

If you have any questions, changes, etc. to make – I will even be glad to change my commentary, if you think it needs it – please don't hesitate to write.

I recently met Charles Mills[61] and am quite impressed with his music, though it is perhaps not very appetizing to performers as being rather dull in sonority. But it is partly this that I like and partly the sobriety of it, with a very genuine seriousness of purpose.

Our best to you both. Will we see you during the Christmas season?
Elliott

[Typed letter with autograph signature; John Kirkpatrick Papers, Irving S. Gilmore Music Library, Yale University. Reprinted by permission of Daisy Kirkpatrick.]

29 *Voyage,* for voice and piano (1943), on a text by Hart Crane, printed edition (South Hadley, MA, and Northampton, MA: Valley Music Press, 1945), p. [1]

Carter's setting of *Voyage* reflects his verbal commentary: the opening line, with its suggestion of the broad expanse of the sea, is set apart from the rest of the text.[62] The rocking motive of the first measure saturates the piece, and, with its clear distinction between upbeats and downbeats, allows for subtle rhythmic inflections (see for example "from sea plains where the sky / Resigns a breast"). (Kirkpatrick had very astutely recognized that the piece was really in 2/2 and 3/2 rather than in Carter's original 4/4 and 6/4.[63]) The vocal line's diatonicism and clear melodic arch (reaching its first high point, rather conventionally, on "sky") draws on motives of fourths and fifths, which lend clarity and a firm sense of direction to the complex polytonal harmonies in the piano part. There is even an enharmonic shift from B♯ to C marking the shift in perspective from the sea to the sky ("Retrieves from sea plains"). Just as Crane's poem achieves modernist complexity with conventional, even archaic, language (for example, "While ribboned water lanes I wind / Are laved and scattered with no stroke"; "whereto this hour / The sea lifts," etc.), Carter's setting also combines advanced harmonies with a tonal, distinctively American vocabulary. Crane's poetry, unlike T. S. Eliot's, for example, would have been especially attractive to Carter because it provided him with a model of modernist expression that was also essentially American.

---

60 In the edition, Kirkpatrick followed every one of Carter's wishes and added a music example to the requested footnote to the ninth chord in m. 119. However, he declined to mention his own name as the editor of *Voyage.*

61 Charles Mills (1914–1982) began his musical career as a member of various jazz bands before studying composition with Copland, Sessions, and Harris.

He wrote the radio column "Over the Air" in *Modern Music* from spring 1941 to fall 1946, when the journal was discontinued.

62 Carter commented on this line in his lecture "The Need for New Choral Music" (1953); see below, pp. 107–108.

63 See letter from John Kirkpatrick to Elliott Carter, 3 December 1944; Elliott Carter Collection, Paul Sacher Foundation.

Holiday Overture (1944)

Shortly after D-Day (6 June 1944) Carter left his position at the OWI in New York and rented a summer house in Saltaire, Fire Island, for himself and his family. Among his guests at this time was Aaron Copland, who was then completing the orchestration of his ballet *Appalachian Spring*. Here, encouraged by the impending change of fortunes on the Western front and finally by the news of the liberation of Paris (late August 1944), Carter wrote the decidedly extroverted and optimistic *Holiday Overture*. No less than Carter's other works of the period, however, it is marked by a certain stylistic ambivalence. On the one hand, its syncopated diatonic themes point to the style of Piston and Copland, while on the other the complexity of its contrapuntal workmanship, culminating in a multi-voiced, harshly discordant final climax, announces a *volte face* from the stylistic ideals of neoclassicism. No less ambivalent was Copland's reaction to the *Holiday Overture*: although, as Carter later recalled, he found the work to be "just another one of those 'typical, complicated Carter scores'" (*FW*, p. 58), he soon recommended it for the first prize ($ 500) at the Independent Music Publishers Contest in 1945. (In the 1960s, Copland also included this work in his conductor's repertoire – the only Carter composition to enjoy this honor.) Connected with the prize was the assurance that it would be performed by Koussevitzky and the Boston Symphony Orchestra, but, as with the *Suite from "Pocahontas"* and the *Symphony No. 1*, the Boston performance never materialized. In the end Carter himself had to smuggle the orchestral parts out of the orchestra's library in order to have them copied and made available for performance elsewhere. (The première is generally assumed to have taken place in Frankfurt in 1946 under the baton of Hans Blümer [see Schiff 1983/1998, pp. 113 and 277, respectively, and Link 200, p. 36], but there is no record of either this performance or a later one in Berlin, both mentioned by Carter in his essay "The Orchestral Composer's Point of View."[64]) It was not until four years later that Koussevitzky returned the original orchestral material to the composer.

30 *Holiday Overture*, for orchestra (1944), photostat full score with autograph corrections, p. 59 (mm. 293–298)

Even though the quick eighth-note motion of the main theme pervades virtually the entire piece, the kinetic pulse of the *Holiday Overture* is offset early in the score by a slow, chorale-like theme first heard in the trumpets at rehearsal no. 7 (mm. 58ff.). As the piece progresses, these two tempo levels – plus a third level dominated by rapid sixteenths – constantly overlap as separate, individually homogeneous compositional layers. It is not until just before the end of the piece that Carter elevates the slow tempo to the "principal tempo" for a mighty climax comprising three sections. Each of these three sections leads to a sustained *tutti* chord at *forte* or *fortissimo*, as is visible in the second section shown in this example from the score, where, however, it is crossed out. (Here we see the final three bars, ending in an abrasive eleven-note chord.) Moreover, each section opens with a contrapuntal *tour de force*. For example, at the opening of the third section, where Carter restores the eighth-note pulse for two bars, one of the main themes is subjected to an eight-fold *stretto*, with the voices entering at eighth-note intervals. (The theme, beginning at the fourth quarter-note of the fourth bar [m. 296], appears in various instrumental groups in the following order: bassoon 1 / horn 2 / trombone 1 – English horn / horn 1 / horn 3 – bass clarinet / trombone 2 – oboe 2 / trumpet 3 – bassoon 2 / bass trombone – oboe 1 / trumpet 2 – contrabassoon / tuba – clarinet 1 / trumpet 1.) Carter introduced the option of omitting the second section (mm. 287–295) of the three-part climax both in this handwritten copy of the score and in an annotated copy of the first edition (a facsimile issued by Arrow Music Press in 1946). This may have resulted from his experiences in performance: the complex contrapuntal structure of this section, in which the above-mentioned theme is heard simultaneously at five conflicting tempos (and which almost resembles an Ivesian collage in effect, if not in technique), is difficult to present with the requisite clarity. By contrast, the revised new edition of 1968 (AMP 06119-68) has no indication of such an optional cut.

---

64 "[...] the work got its first performance in Frankfurt, Germany, and later in Berlin with Serg[iu] Celibidache conducting." (Elliott Carter, "The Orchestral Composer's Point of View," in *The Orchestral Point of View: Essays on Twentieth-Century Music by Those Who Wrote It*, ed. Robert Stephan Hines [Norman, OK: University of Oklahoma Press, 1970], pp. 39–61, esp. 42; most recently reprinted in *CEL*, pp. 235–250, esp. 237.) Carter may have been informed of planned performances that never took place. As the Frankfurt Radio Symphony Orchestra had given William Schuman's *American Festival Overture* on 7 July 1946 (for the opening of the Contemporary Music Week in Bad Nauheim), it is conceivable that the conductor of the concert, Hans Blümer, originally intended to perform the *Holiday Overture*, only to replace it with the Schuman piece, which is far less demanding technically.

The Harmony of Morning (1944)

Besides the *Holiday Overture*, Carter also wrote two vocal pieces in 1944, both on poems by Mark Van Doren (1894–1972), a writer and literary critic who taught at Columbia University. The first is the unpublished duet *The Difference* for soprano, baritone, and piano, the second *The Harmony of Morning* for women's chorus and chamber orchestra. This latter work, which was not published until 1955, was written in response to a commission from Lazare Saminsky, who had asked Carter in July 1944 for a setting of an American text, to be performed at a concert celebrating the first centennial of Temple Emanu-El. Carter turned to "Another Music,"[65] a poem published in 1935 and dealing in three stanzas with the harmony of nature, the harmony of music, and the harmony of thought. He adhered to the poem's form by producing a tripartite, heavily contrapuntal set of variations on a cantus firmus. The piece, completed in November 1944, received its première under the title of the poem, *Another Music*, at Temple Emanu-El on 25 February 1945. It was conducted by Saminsky, who later wrote that it was distinguished by "the same charm and transparency as the Dickinson piece [*Heart Not so Heavy as Mine*]."[66] The critic Virgil Thomson was equally taken with the new work, finding the orchestral writing so successful that he expressed the wish "to hear more of Carter's orchestral music."[67] The piece found favor not least with the poet himself. In a letter of 18 March 1945, Van Doren expressed his approval at renaming it *The Harmony of Morning* and looked forward to receiving an extra copy of the recording of the première, as Carter had promised. He also proposed a joint opera project based on his poem *The Mayfield Deer* – an idea that Carter, in his cautious reply of 24 March 1945, promised to take into consideration if the text appealed to him and if a "propitious occasion" should arise for such a time-consuming task. However, nothing came of the project; as is well known, it was more than half a century later, in 1997, that Carter embarked on his first and only opera. In later years he often received similar requests. In 1961, for example, the San Francisco Opera tried to interest him in an opera project, only to be turned down in view of what Carter considered the completely unsatisfactory circumstances on America's theatrical scene and the expectations of its audience.[68]

31 *The Harmony of Morning*, for women's chorus and chamber orchestra (1944), on a text by Mark Van Doren, photostat full score with autograph corrections, p. 36 (mm. 188–194)

This page shows part of a fugue setting of the poem's last lines: "[…] but in the chambers of a brain / Are bells that clap an answer when the words / Move orderly, with truth among the train." In this piece Carter draws upon two different historical techniques: baroque fugue and polyphonic fourteenth-century music. Carter had sung medieval music during his studies with Boulanger, and copied out a number of pieces, including the Machaut rondeau *Rose, Lys*, which was one of the sources of inspiration for *The Harmony of Morning*. In the passage shown the fugue subject is presented in *stretto* in the first and second soprano parts, but the voice-leading and harmonies are derived from a kind of contemporary re-hearing of medieval music. (Note the parallel fifths between the two vocal parts throughout the first three measures, and the frequent simultaneous octaves, fifths, and fourths between the same voices, which echo Machaut's rondeau.) As the first entrance of the chorus also features a sonority saturated with parallel fifths and octaves (the sonority recurs several times later), there is a high degree of harmonic coherence. This is reinforced by the prominent melodic fifths and octaves in the cantus firmus that runs through the piece. The resulting "open" harmonies do not sound archaic, but reflect sonorities typical of modern American music at this time. Carter took advantage of the fact that players from the New York Philharmonic would perform the five solo wind parts in the chamber orchestra by writing complex and idiomatic music for them. As he wrote to John Kirkpatrick: "The Philharmonic men had brilliant little concertino parts which they did very well, though the oboe was a bit rambunctious."[69] Here Carter has added extra contrapuntal parts for the clarinet and oboe in ink.

---

65 Mark Van Doren, "Another Music," in *A Winter Diary and Other Poems* (New York: Macmillan, 1935), p. 111; reprinted in idem, *Collected Poems: 1922–1938* (New York: Henry Holt, 1939), pp. 249–250.

66 Lazare Saminsky, *Living Music of the Americas* (New York: Howell, Soskind, and Crown, 1949), p. 93.

67 Virgil Thomson, "Music: Centenary Novelties," *New York Herald-Tribune*, 27 February 1945.

68 See letter from Elliott Carter to Kurt Herbert Adler, 26 June 1961; quoted below, p. 302.

69 Letter from Elliott Carter to John Kirkpatrick, 28 February 1945; Elliott Carter Collection, Paul Sacher Foundation.

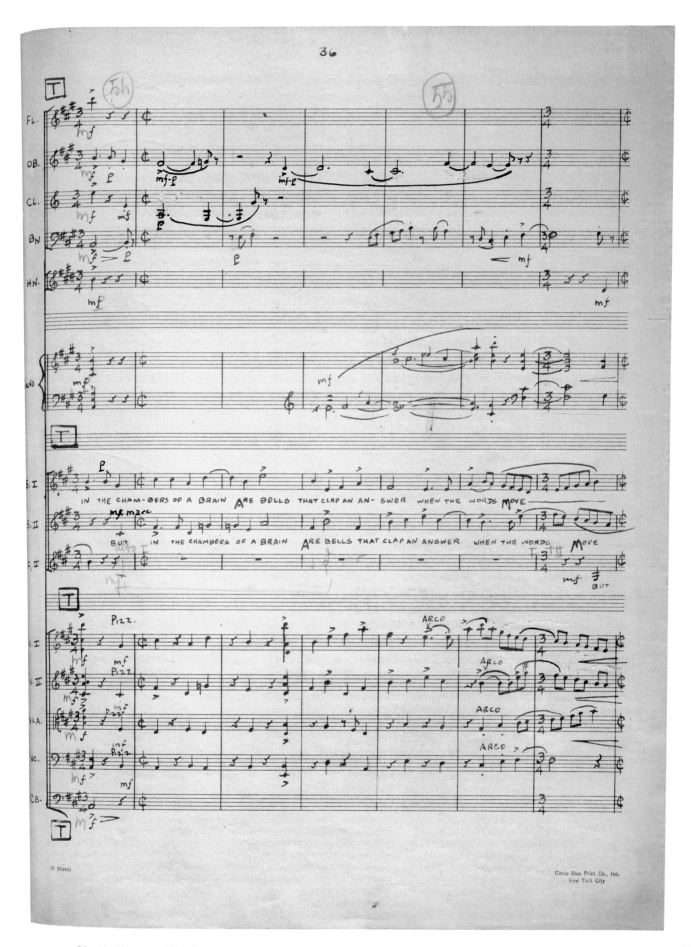

32   Mark Van Doren to Elliott Carter, 18 March 1945

393 Bleecker Street / New York 14
3/18/45

Dear Mr. Carter:

This is for the recording – for which many thanks, both because you had an extra copy made and because you will go to the trouble of carrying it to my wife. The favor in all this has been to me. Thanks are to you, for finding that poem and for doing such grand things to it – and, of course, for sending me the blueprint. When the record comes I'll read *and* listen, with the greatest fascination and suspense. The first hearing, at the Temple, was, like all such things, incomplete. I admired, but I have still to understand.

The Harmony of Morning is right for a title. *Music and Poetry,* while more comprehensive, is perhaps too much so. In any case, please suit yourself.

You spoke of wanting to write an opera. I hesitate to mention it, but a long narrative poem I published in 1941, *The Mayfield Deer,* seems to have possibilities – it has been made into a choral speaking drama at Brookline, Mass. And the story – frontier American – involves not only murders but gods![70]

If you are interested in considering this I'll be delighted to send you a copy of the book. Of course you can hardly say you're not interested! But you really can – that is, you can say nothing at all.

Sincerely,
Mark Van Doren

[Autograph letter; Elliott Carter Collection, Paul Sacher Foundation.]

33   Elliott Carter to Mark Van Doren, 24 March 1945

Dear Mr. Van Doren:

Forgive me for packing the record so carelessly that the needles wrapped in it should have fallen out. As you will see from the few enclosed, they are "red shanked 'transcription' needles" and under this name can be bought from any large record store.

I appreciate your eagerness to hear the record, I only hope closer acquaintance won't disappoint you.

Your *Mayfield Deer* has never crossed my path. I certainly would like to read it and think it over as an opera subject. But please don't get too high hopes over this. A friend of mine, Normand Lockwood, has just finished an opera for the Columbia Workshop, 750 pages of score, for 2 hours of music.[71] You can imagine the amount of merely calligraphic time such a project takes, and how carefully it must be considered by a composer before he decides to spend so much time and effort. But I would like to have such a project up my sleeve in case a propitious occasion should arise.

Sincerely,
Elliott Carter

529 East 85 Street, / New York, 28, N.Y.
March 24, 1945

[Typed letter with autograph signature; Mark Van Doren Papers, Rare Book and Manuscript Library, Columbia University. Reprinted by permission.]

---

70   Mark Van Doren, *The Mayfield Deer,* decorations by Armin Landeck (New York: Henry Holt, 1941).

71   The composer Normand Lockwood (1906–2002) had studied with Ottorino Respighi and Nadia Boulanger, among others, and was currently teaching at Columbia University. The Lockwood work mentioned by Carter is the opera *The Scarecrow* (1944–45) on a libretto written by Lockwood himself and his wife Dorothy after the play of the same title by Percy MacKaye (a stage adaptation of Nathaniel Hawthorne's story *Feathertop*). The opera premièred at Brander Matthews Theater at Columbia University on 9–12 May 1945, directed by Milton Smith and conducted by Otto Luening.

"Music in America at War" (1945)

Carter drafted the following text in connection with a festival of American music that was to have taken place in liberated Paris in June 1945, sponsored by the US Office of War Information. The festival's goal, according to its organizer Aaron Copland, was to "reflect current musical contemporary life in the U.S.A."[72] Apparently the composers Marcelle de Manziarly, Vittorio Rieti, Nicolas Nabokov, and Bohuslav Martinů (who had been living in the US during the war) had also been involved, although their exact roles in the project are unclear.[73] By 14 April 1945 the plans had been called off, much to Copland's disappointment. He wrote to Boulanger: "Just between ourselves I felt the O.W.I. made something of a mess of its own plans. They were venturing into what was a new field for them – concert giving – and unforeseen and serious financial complications arose. Since I am not a member of the OWI I have been able to do nothing but watch our plans go wrong. There is still some chance for the Fall – so I shall wait and see."[74] Carter had been commissioned to write an article – possibly a long essay for the festival's program book – by Carlos Moseley, who worked for the OWI at that time (he later became managing director and finally president of the New York Philharmonic). About fifty years later, Moseley reminisced to Carter: "One of our first meetings was toward the end of the war (WW II) when I commissioned you to write a piece on US music for the Festival of American Music being planned for Paris just after its liberation. Aaron was to have been the chairman, or mastermind. The idea began and ended in Paris, at high levels, and since it came to naught, your article never got used."[75] Carter drafted a four-page outline, but never completed the text, probably because of the very short time that elapsed between the hatching of the plan in late March 1945 and its cancellation in early April.[76] Carter did send a carbon copy of the typescript to Copland; this is the only copy known today. The text shows many signs of having been conceived for a French audience, starting with the title: American audiences would not have wanted or needed to hear about "Music in America at War" in the spring of 1945, when the war in Europe was clearly almost over. Carter mentions French institutions, such as Fontainebleau, and intends to discuss the "stimulating intellectual atmosphere of Paris for Americans between the wars." The strong emphasis on dance also seems aimed at French interests; in a text that does not name any American orchestras, Carter specifically names several ballet companies, including some that were offshoots of Diaghilev's Ballets Russes. The text was clearly intended for a non-specialist audience, as the avoidance of any reference to musical styles or techniques (such as neoclassicism or twelve-tone technique) indicates. Carter's goal is to portray music and musical life in America as diverse, democratic, and multicultural, but still rooted in tradition and comparable with European new music in terms of quality. By pointing out the decentralized nature of American musical life ("No élite or clique has been able to dominate the country and dictate the trends. No single musical center from which everything emanates"), Carter perceptively identifies and seeks to explain the most significant difference between American and French musical life. As befitting an OWI document, the tenor of the text is uniformly positive.

34 Elliott Carter, outline for a planned essay on "Music in America at War" (1945)

MUSIC IN AMERICA AT WAR

General Remarks.

Great ferment of ideas and interest on an increasingly wide scale.

Things to be borne in mind in any consideration of American mus[ic].

A. Shortness of our music history.

I. Only 200 years, and only during last 100 have we attained professional status.
    1. Americans of talent have often been extremely well trained in Europe and more recently here. Audiences have been educated to love the best of Europe.
    2. Only very recently has an American tradition begun to take shape.

72 In addition to works by American composers, Stravinsky's *Symphony in C* was also to have been included. See letter from Aaron Copland to Nadia Boulanger, 28 March 1945; Aaron Copland Collection, Music Division, Library of Congress.

73 See Letter from Aaron Copland to Marcelle de Manziarly, 24 April 1945: "I suppose you've heard – it's all off. [...] I console myself with composing. But how to console you, and Vittorio, and Nicky N., and Martinů for all the false

hopes raised. Well, you will do it for me better than I can myself [...] [*sic*]." (Aaron Copland Collection, Music Division, Library of Congress; quoted from the online version at "Aaron Copland Collection ca. 1900–1990, American Memory from the Library of Congress," http://memory.loc.gov./ammem/collections/copland/index.htm/, consulted 29 October 2007.)

74 Letter from Aaron Copland to Nadia Boulanger, 14 April 1945; Aaron Copland Collection, Music Division, Library of

Congress, quoted from the online version cited above (see note 73).

75 Letter from Carlos Moseley to Elliott Carter, 27 September 1994; Elliott Carter Collection, Paul Sacher Foundation.

76 In a letter to Carter of 29 March 1945, Mark Van Doren wished him "best luck to your piece on American music." (Elliott Carter Collection, Paul Sacher Foundation.) Copland's letter to Boulanger describing the festival's purpose was also written at the end of March.

B. Variety of cultural groups that have come to America. Little pressure put on them to conform to any preconceived idea of American culture. Been allowed to develop in its own way.

I. Local differences in cultural minorites not obliterated.
    1. People in America free to continue their previous native traditions or to join with majority.
        a. Chinese theatres, American Indian, Negro, foreign language radio programs, etc.
    2. General trends that have gained approval of majority.
        a. Jazz
        b. Among a smaller audience, Western European music, and American concert music.

C. Size of country and predominance of different cultural groups in various parts of US.
    1. In the past various localities favored the kinds of music most familiar to them. (New Orleans home of French opera, middle West-Central European, etc.)
    2. Recently a much wider acceptance of all types of serious music, with a resultant wide eclecticism.

These 3 factors (A. B. C.) have resulted in:

A. Lack of a firmly fixed, widely accepted musical tradition or consciousness of what "American" stands for musically. This is beginning to develop.

B. No élite or clique has been able to dominate the country and dictate the trends. No single musical center from which everything emanates.

C. Position of American music in concert repertoire.
    I. No American work has gained the recognition that is given to works of Beethoven, Franck, Verdi, Bizet, etc.
    II. Some are as popular as the works of important European contemporaries.
    III. Present widespread demand for more American music.

* * *

America is a musical nation, large and responsive audiences and intelligent support of all kinds of professional institutions and professional musicians.

THE AMERICAN MUSICAL PUBLIC

A. Audiences expect high quality from musicians and dancers, and eagerly support them.

1)   a) Excellence of concert repertory.
    b) Excellence of performers – Toscanini etc.
    c) Enthusiasm for this shown in the eager support of orchestras and performers by private individuals. Little support by state – musicians are on their own and have to be good in order to exist.
    d) Music for all income groups. Winter concerts for regular subscribers, often broadcast so that they can be heard by anyone. Summer concerts which often fill football stadiums with audiences at popular prices.

2)   How we got that way.
    a) Excellence of musical training in public schools, music schools, and in colleges all over country. Amateur choruses, orchestras, opera companies, and dance groups.
    b) Frequent broadcasts of best orchestras in country. (WQXR[77])
    c) Wide distribution of recordings.
    d) Use of good music in film. Modern composers – also "Fantasia".[78]

B. The size of the audience.

I.   Number of symphony orchestras and cities supporting concert series, touring dance companies, and operas.
II.   Spread of radio hook-ups and of films.

---

77 WQXR-FM is one of the oldest and best-known classical music radio stations in the United States. It has broadcast from the top of the Empire State Building since 1939.

78 The animated Walt Disney film featuring the Philadelphia Orchestra conducted by Leopold Stokowski was released in 1940.

79 Even though Carter certainly did not intend to provide a complete list of emigrants here, the omission of Krenek, of Wolpe, and especially of Bartók, may have been a memory slip in notes clearly written in haste. In his 1954 essay, "Music in the United States" (see below,

pp. 111–115), Carter includes a similar list of influential immigrants, adding Bartók and Krenek to these names, but Martinů is omitted. Wolpe, who is not mentioned in either list, may not have been sufficiently well-known in the mid-1950s to warrant inclusion.

80 The Ballet Russe de Monte Carlo, directed by Massine, was an offshoot of Colonel de Basil's Ballets Russes de Monte Carlo. (Both companies had been founded to capitalize on the popularity of Diaghilev's original Ballets Russes.) The Ballet Russe de Monte Carlo began in 1938 in the city of its name, then in the following year,

because of the war, moved to New York, where it was active until 1962. The company's heyday was in the mid-1940s, with productions including Copland's *Rodeo* (Agnes de Mille) and Stravinsky's *Danses concertantes* (Balanchine).

81 The Ballet Theatre, founded in 1940 in New York, later became the American Ballet Theatre.

82 Ballet Theatre productions in the early 1940s include *Pillar of Fire*, set to Schoenberg's *Verklärte Nacht* and choreographed by Anthony Tudor in 1942; *Fancy Free* (Bernstein, Robbins, 1944); and *Undertow* (William Schuman, Tudor, 1945).

THE PROFESSION OF MUSIC IN U.S.

A. Composition

I. Very great and ever increasing activity in past 30 or 40 years.

    1. Much of this activity stimulated by 2 organizations founded directly after last war.
        a. Fontainebleau School, founded by Damrosch. Fame of Nadia Boulanger started there, became the teacher of as many as 60 active composers and many performers and teachers. (Digression on the stimulating intellectual atmosphere of Paris for Americans between the wars.)
        b. Eastman School in Rochester, its festivals, Hanson.

    2. As part of our past several interesting composers had paved the way toward the use of native folk music in composition – Ives, Gilbert, Farwell, Chadwick.

    3. Present trends in American composition.
        a. Use of native American materials, early American hymns, dance tunes, jazz, and various kinds of music of the people.
            a'. Combination of these with the contemporary idiom – Copland
            b'. Reconstruction of an American style Trend toward simplicity – Thomson Avoidance of European procedures – Cowell
            c'. Use of various phases of romantic idioms – Hanson, Gershwin, and Harris.
        b. Proponents of an international style: Sessions, Piston, Barber.

    4. Activities of European composers living here during the war. Stravinsky, Milhaud, Schoenberg, Hindemith, Martinů, Eisler, and Weill.[79]

B. Performers and scholars.

I. American performers and scholars – used to go to Europe to study and probably will continue to do so after the war. But many excellent and popular ones have been trained here.

II. The public has always welcomed foreign artists.

III. Universities have developed excellent music departments and have contributed much excellent research.

C. Ballet and Modern Dance.

I. The various groups that emerged from the Diaghileff Ballet. The Ballet Russe de Monte Carlo[80] and the Ballet Theatre,[81] which incorporated many of the Russian dancers with some Americans, have been very active and toured the country many times with growing success.
    1. Emergence of some new American ballets in Monte Carlo troup[e] and the success of Balanchine.
    2. New ballets in Ballet Theatre repertoire.[82]

II. Several groups of ballet companies have emerged here. American Ballet, Ballet Caravan, and the Ballet International.[83]

III. The American Modern Dance.
    1. Martha Graham,[84] adherence to American ideals, new works.
    2. Humphrey, Weidman,[85] and others.
    3. Their influence on education throughout country.

D. Publications.

    1. American works have found more opportunities despite paper shortage.
    2. Works of resident Europeans also published.

---

83 The American Ballet was founded by Lincoln Kirstein and George Balanchine in 1933. In 1937, while the company was in residence at the Metropolitan Opera, Balanchine choreographed productions of Stravinsky's *Baiser de la fée, Jeu de cartes* (première), and *Apollon musagète*, with the composer conducting. Between 1936 and 1939 Kirstein organized the smaller Ballet Caravan, a touring group made up of several of the American Ballet's dancers, for which Carter served as music director (see above, pp. 37 and 41). In 1941 the two companies were amalgamated under the name American Ballet Caravan. Ballet International was founded in New York in the fall of 1944 by the Marquis George de Cuevas, a Chilean-American aristocrat who was married to Margaret Strong, a granddaughter of John D. Rockefeller; in spite of limitless funds, the company lasted only three years.

84 Martha Graham (1894–1991), the most influential figure in American modern dance, founded her ballet school and company in 1929, and both still flourish today. One of her most celebrated ballets was *Appalachian Spring*, to a score by Aaron Copland, which premièred on 30 October 1944 in Washington, D.C.

85 In 1928 the dancers and choreographers Doris Humphrey and Charles Weidman founded a ballet school and company in New York, which lasted until 1945. Humphrey and Weidman's ballets to American scores include the trilogy *New Dance* (*New Dance, Theatre Piece,* and *With My Red Fires*), with music by Wallingford Riegger (1935–36).

E. Criticism and books about music.

  1. [E]normous number of books published on every phase of music and musical history.
  2. The influence of critics in bringing American music to the attention of the public.

* * *

Summary.

The widespread interest and activity in various fields of music. (The fact that with England America was able to keep the traditions of music alive during the war?) America becoming one of the important cultural centers of the West.

[Typescript, carbon copy; Aaron Copland Collection, Music Division, Library of Congress, Washington, D.C. Reprinted by permission of the Aaron Copland Fund for Music, Inc., copyright holder.]

A Book Project on Charles Ives (1946)

Although Carter had been familiar with the writings of Paul Rosenfeld (1890–1946) since the mid-1920s, it was not until the fall of 1937 that he met this highly versatile critic of music, art, and literature. The two men exchanged thoughts on a regular basis in the years that followed. As their conversations often turned on Charles Ives, Carter finally suggested that Rosenfeld, an Ives enthusiast, should write a study of the composer. Carter himself, now in the "neoclassical" phase of his artistic evolution, had misgivings about his earlier mentor, finding in his music a considerable discrepancy between musical vision and compositional realization. (These misgivings found forthright expression in his famous review of John Kirkpatrick's New York première of the *Concord Sonata* on 20 January 1939.[86]) At first Rosenfeld hesitated, being preoccupied with preparations for his (never-to-be-completed) book on literary genres. He finally agreed on condition that Carter, in whom he had rekindled a certain amount of interest in Ives, should take charge of the analytical and technical part of the study. "So during Paul's last winter, after a decade of acquaintance and merging consonance – over innumerable cups of coffee and tea, during late dark afternoons – we talked and planned. It seemed to us vitally important to think through the age-old problem of the artist's relation to tradition, and the question of distinguishing a living tradition from sterile conventionality. Also, there was America's relation to European tradition, and the relation of experiment to creative imagination and expression. All this seemed to stand in vital need of redefinition in the light of our contemporary world."[87] The joint project was thwarted by Rosenfeld's sudden death in July 1946, and Carter was unwilling to carry on alone with the book, which had meanwhile caught the interest of the Prentice Hall publishing house. The project thus passed to Henry Cowell, who, together with his wife, wrote the first comprehensive monograph on Ives, beginning in 1947.[88] All that survives of Rosenfeld's and Carter's efforts is the previously unpublished preface given below, in which the authors emphasize the twin careers of their protagonist without labeling him a businessman who composed on the side. Their discussion therefore has nothing to say about possible technical limitations in Ives's music; nor is this

---

86 Elliott Carter, "The Case of Mr. Ives," *Modern Music* 16/3 (March–April 1939), pp. 172–176, most recently reprinted in *CEL*, pp. 87–90. A comparison of this critique with Rosenfeld's review of the première of the *Concord Sonata* in the preceding issue of *Modern Music* clearly reveals the contrary views of these two critics; see Paul Rosenfeld, "Ives' Concord Sonata," *Modern Music* 16/2 (January–February 1939),

pp. 109–112. Here Rosenfeld reviewed Kirkpatrick's first complete public performance of the *Concord Sonata* in Cos Cob, CT, on 28 November 1938. (Kirkpatrick had already performed the work privately at a lecture-recital in Stamford, CT, on 21 June 1938.)

87 Elliott Carter, "The Genial Sage," in *Paul Rosenfeld, Voyager in the Arts*, ed. Jerome Mellquist and Lucie Wiese (New York: Creative Age Press, 1948),

pp. 163–165, esp. 164–165; reprinted in *CEL*, pp. 306–307, esp. 307.

88 The book was published only after Ives's death and by a different publisher: Henry and Sidney Cowell, *Charles Ives and His Music* (New York: Oxford University Press, 1955). The genesis of this publication is discussed in Sidney Cowell, "The Cowells and the Written Word," in *A Celebration of American Music: Words and Music in Honor of H. Wiley Hitchcock*, ed. Richard

implicit in their comparison of Ives with Moussorgsky, Ives serving as his American equivalent. Instead, Rosenfeld and Carter, without entirely avoiding the gendered language almost obsessively favored by Ives himself ("one of the few virile composers born in America"), stress the visionary and forward-looking elements in Ives's music: his rejection of sclerotic academicisms, his inclusion of sounds from his local surroundings, and not least his development of a musical "inflection" that lent expression to a specifically national sensibility.

Carter's renewed interest in Ives also found expression in an essay that he wrote for the composer's seventieth birthday in 1944[89] and in his many efforts on behalf of the performance and publication of Ives's music. In particular, he actively co-founded the Charles Ives Society in 1944 (which the publicity-shy composer refused to support) and was instrumental in arranging an all-Ives concert at Columbia University in the spring of 1946, during which two ensemble pieces, *The Unanswered Question* and *Central Park in the Dark,* received their world premières.[90]

35 Paul Rosenfeld and Elliott Carter, preface to a planned book on Charles Ives (1946)

Future musical histories will have at least one more picturesque tale to tell about a creator of music and the conditions under which he brought his work to birth. This one will concern a reality whose scene was neither Vienna, Moscow [n]or Paris, but New York with its seven million inhabitants. It will concern the figure and work of the composer Charles E. Ives, who but a short while since was elected – a man over seventy years of age – to membership in the American Academy of Arts and [Letters].[91] By this election the Academy may be thought not so much to have distinguished Ives as to have distinguished itself, for Ives is a composer whom numbers of musicians and critics consider one of the few virile composers born in America; and pieces by him have been played and recorded by live musicians and ensembles here and abroad.

The picturesque tales hitherto told by musical histories have concerned composers many of whom, like Mozart, Schubert and Moussorgsky, lived in neglect and met the response and affection which should have been theirs only after their death. The tale which future histories will tell about Ives will not mention physical distress, though it cannot but mention the fact that the great musical public knew almost nothing of his work during the major part of his life, indeed was not even familiar with his name. What the future however will mention, probably not without wonder, is that this work was composed by a business man, an insurance man, the senior partner of a well-known firm of Wall Street insurance men, Ives and Myrick. Doubtless it will speculate how it came to be that two earnest souls, one an insurance man's, another a composer's, came to live together within one breast. Perhaps it will regret that a composer as inventive and talented as Ives was did not devote all his energies to music, for music is one of those things which do not die. Yet the future will not be able to say that the spirit of it suffered because he devoted his evenings and not his days to composing it. He plainly gave his best to it; and he will probably be thought of as a pure artist who loved his art for its own sake but did not think it had a right to constitute his sole concern. If the future does speak disparagingly of "business-men composers," it will probably not mean Ives by the term, but people very different from himself – composers like Richard Strauss and some 20th-century American composers [who] compromised their art in the effort to make it yield them a comfortable living.

Ives, who was born in Danbury, Conn[ecticut] in 1874, grew up in an atmosphere of aesthetic radicalism, for his father, who conducted a band, incessantly experimented with acoustic effects. While he was at Yale Ives conducted the little orchestra in the Hyperion Theatre and made similar experiments in acoustics. It is said that one day he presented [to] his teacher, Professor Horatio Parker, an organ composition which astoundingly began simultaneously in two keys. And in the subsequent decades he became one of the most original and inventive of modern composers – surely the most original and inventive one produced by America. He is the American equivalent of the great Russian composer Moussorgsky.

Crawford, R. Allen Lott, and Carol J. Oja (Ann Arbor: University of Michigan Press, 1990), pp. 79–91, esp. 85–90, and David C. Paul, "From American Ethnographer to Cold War Icon: Charles Ives through the Eyes of Henry and Sidney Cowell," *Journal of the American Musicological Society* 59/2 (Summer 2006), pp. 399–457, esp. 430–439.

89 Elliott Carter, "Ives Today: His Vision and His Challenge," *Modern Music* 21/4

(May–June 1944), pp. 199–202; most recently reprinted in *CEL,* pp. 90–93.

90 The concert was held on 11 May 1946 in McMillin Theatre as part of the Second Annual Festival of Contemporary American Music. In addition to the two works mentioned, the program included parts of the *String Quartet No. 2,* the recently premièred *Symphony No. 3,* the *Sonata for Violin and Piano No. 2,* and several songs. The pieces for instrumental ensemble

or orchestra were played by a student orchestra from the Juilliard Graduate School, conducted by Edgar Schenkman, with Theodore Bloomfeld serving as assistant conductor of the small offstage ensemble in *The Unanswered Question* and *Central Park.*

91 The typescript has "American Academy of Arts and Sciences." In fact, however, Ives was inducted into the American Academy of Arts and Letters on 25 December 1945.

Precisely as Moussorgsky revolted against what was not so much tradition among Russian composers as stale custom, so Ives revolted against stale custom in American composition. To find the true form for the emotions and states of consciousness welling within him, Ives – like Moussorgsky – studied the rhythms and idiom of the folk music, and based his style on the style of old country fiddlers and village choirs and other naive musicians and ensembles. However, Ives's innovations took him far further than Moussorgsky's ever took him, for Ives finally anticipated the most modern European techniques – polytonality and polyrhythmicality. He plays melodies in two different keys against each other, and melodies in different rhythms, so that some of his compositions sound like clashing brass bands. The difficulty of beating these complex rhythms is one of the factors standing between Ives and the average conductors. But they have been beaten here and abroad by certain conductors and probably will come to seem less difficult as the years pass.

Ives also is the American equivalent for Moussorgsky insomuch as he, too, in the form of magnificent music, has produced an interpretation of the vivacities and reactions peculiar to his own compatriots, just as Moussorgsky produced an interpretation of the vivacities and reactions of the Russian *moujik*. Ives's music emotionally connects us with facets of the American temperament – its humorousness and its nervousness, and its mysticism. For he too is a mystic, a kinsman of the transcendental New Englanders, whose student he has always been, and his music is pervaded with the contemplative moods and ecstasies of the Emersons and the Thoreaus. Not only the pastness of the American past, but its presence no less, becomes an experience in Ives, and his music offers to restore a sense of its own identity to America. In part this connection of Ives's music is a result of the American titles he has given to his compositions, but in far greater part it is due to the special spirit and moods of the music itself.

Ives has never neglected his music and has managed to get a part of it published, but he has devoted as much of his effort to assist other musicians as to advance his own compositions. About 1924 his work began attracting attention, and it is curious to remark that no matter how infrequently it has been performed it has usually called out favorable critical comments, often from such influential critics as Olin Downes and Lawrence Gilman. Ives's long illness and the recent loss of his eyesight ha[ve] prevented him from completing the editing of many of his larger works, and there is no doubt that his younger confrères will have to give him a hand. But a movement to do so already is under way, and the truth that we have really had a magnificent figure in American music will become plain.

[Typescript, carbon copy; Elliott Carter Collection, Paul Sacher Foundation.]

Piano Sonata (1945–46)

Carter began composing his *Piano Sonata* during the summer of 1945, with the support of a Guggenheim fellowship (his first), and finished it in January 1946. He wrote the piece for John Kirkpatrick, who, however, found the first movement "awfully intellectualized"[92] and never played the sonata. (Webster Aitken premièred it at the Frick Museum on 16 February 1947, in a concert that was broadcast by the Municipal Broadcasting System; James Sykes played the concert première on 5 March 1947 at Times Hall.) Like Samuel Barber's *Piano Sonata* (1947–49), Carter's explores the sonic and textural possiblities of the grand piano, including a large-scale Beethovenian fugue. The material of Carter's sonata is derived from the piano's paradoxical nature as percussion instrument on the one hand and lyrical melodic and chordal instrument on the other: he makes ample use of harmonics, resonance tones, different kinds of attacks, chords of different densities and spacing, and a variety of pedal techniques. Carter even modified the ending of the piece in order better to bring out the piano's resonance.[93] Creating instrumental "characters" who express themselves both with and against their natural idioms was to become a major concern in his future works, and the *Piano Sonata* marks an important step in this process (see *FW*, pp. 68–69). The *Piano Sonata* is also the first of many of Carter's works to exhibit a formal design in which movements are interrupted and resumed. Although Carter notated the work in two numbered movements (and all the published versions follow this), the fugal third movement is clearly embedded within the slow second movement, as Carter explains in an analysis he wrote for Edgard Varèse (see below, pp. 77–79). As David Schiff has pointed out, there are echoes of Debussy, Stravinsky, and particularly Copland in the *Piano Sonata* (Schiff 1983, p. 123). The work's complex textures, its mercurial shifts in mood and character, and above all its elevated tone, attest to a substantial engagement with the music of Ives as well.

36 *Piano Sonata* (1945–46)
a photostat score with autograph corrections, p. [1]
b proofs of the first edition with autograph corrections, p. 3

The main difference between Carter's original version of the *Piano Sonata* and the published version (issued in 1948 by Music Press and by Mercury Music Corporation) is a matter of notation, not sounding result: at some point, Carter decided to remove all the time signatures in the first movement.[94] The main effect of this decision is to simplify the appearance of the music. It also facilitates performance, since the pianist simply groups the beats into units of two or three instead of being forced to think about the measure as a unit (and, as in so much of Carter's music, it is the beat, not the measure, which is musically relevant here). The second movement preserves the conventional time signatures, causing Conlon Nancarrow to remark: "I think I understand why you didn't mark the measure units in the first movement and I think it is a good idea. [B]ut what I don't understand is why you marked them in the last movement where the note groupings are much easier to grasp."[95] Perhaps in spite of their redundancy, the time signatures in the second movement are a help to the performer rather than a distraction. The first page of the autograph score (here seen in photostat) contains much of the material for the piece: the opening octaves, designated as "a" in Carter's analysis of the piece for Varèse (see below, pp. 77–79); a brief figure in parallel thirds ("b"); a sixteenth-note motive in fourths and fifths ("c," fourth system, m. 1); a descending whole-step figure in dotted rhythm ("d," third system, m. 1); a melody based on fourths and thirds ("e," second system, m. 3); a virtuosic figure in sixteenth notes and cross rhythms, based on "c" ("f," fourth system, m. 2); and an ascending whole-tone scale fragment (with upbeat) in the left hand ("g", last system, m. 3). Practically all of the material for the entire work is heard already on the first page; only "h," which Carter designates as the actual first theme, and "i," which belongs to the second theme group, appear later. The published score also contains the first use of the Carterian term "scorrevole" to indicate the character of the faster music, instead of simply "flowing and expressive," as in the original manuscript.

92 Letter from John Kirkpatrick to Elliott Carter, [January 1946]; Elliott Carter Collection, Paul Sacher Foundation.

93 A photostat of the autograph shows the original ending; another photostat, marked "Truro & New York, Jan[uary] 1946," contains the changes. (Elliott Carter Collection, Paul Sacher Foundation.)

94 Schiff 1983, p. 128, names Kurt Stone as the editor responsible for this decision, but there is no evidence that Carter's association with Stone began before the early 1950s, when his music started to be published by Associated Music Publishers.

95 Letter from Conlon Nancarrow to Elliott Carter, 13 June [1951]; Elliott Carter Collection, Paul Sacher Foundation.

36 a *Piano Sonata*, photostat score

36 b *Piano Sonata,* proofs of the first edition

Among the composers with whom Carter maintained friendly relations was Edgard Varèse, who had achieved considerable successes in New York during the 1920s and early 1930s. In the 1940s, however, he was at the nadir of his career: his works were rarely played, if at all, and his utopian *Espace* project had come to a standstill. Because of these professional problems and others of a personal nature, Varèse focused his attention increasingly on his work as a choral director and lecturer. He therefore gratefully agreed when Otto Luening, in early 1948, invited him to take charge of a lecture course at Columbia University. In July and August of 1948 Varèse delivered a series of some thirty lectures entitled "Twentieth-Century Tendencies in Music," offering a broad survey of recent composition, subdivided more by style than by chronology.[96] To give proper attention to the most recent trends, he wrote to many fellow-composers while preparing the series, asking them for information on their work, for scores and recordings, and for a statement of their artistic credo. Among these composers was Carter, who quickly agreed. A few months later he sent Varèse some analytical notes on his *Piano Sonata*, along with a brief account of his artistic goals. Varèse used this material on 12 July 1948 in his fifth lecture, which also discussed the music of the New York composer Beatrice Laufer.[97]

Carter's analysis is interesting above all for its emphasis on small thematic cells, their relationships to each other, and their infinite capacity for transformation. This kind of material, which, as Carter tells Varèse, is inspired by the sonorous possiblities of the grand piano, has implications for the form of the piece. Rather than developing "blocks" of material sequentially, the piece takes on a fluid form in which motivic cells are transformed, combined, recalled, and foreshadowed. Even the work's most outwardly conventional feature, the fugue at the center of the second movement, plays with the notion of malleability in that the fugue subject itself is shortened and lengthened. The fugue also features an unorthodox "reverse exposition," in which the number of voices gradually decreases. Carter takes care to point out in his analysis all the fugue's arcane contrapuntal effects (including the medieval technique of isorhythm), which he evidently does not associate with historicist or classicist impulses, but rather with modernist invention. Carter's aesthetic

"credo," in which he states that his "music is essentially a kinetic projection of ideas, using perspectives in time," articulates a basic position that applies not only to the *Piano Sonata*, but also to all his later compositions.

37 Edgard Varèse to Elliott Carter, 8 January 1948

Edgard Varèse / 188 Sullivan Street, / New York 12, N.Y.
January 8, 1948

Dear E. C.
I have been invited to give a series of lectures on 20th-century music at Columbia University during the summer session of 1948. In such a course, covering all phases of contemporary music, it is possible to speak only of a limited number of composers individually. Among these I should like to include you.

I shall illustrate the lectures with records, and should also like to have a statement ... a sort of credo ... from each composer. Please send me whatever you would care to have me quote, including your musical aims, both aesthetically and technically.

Would you also answer the following: (1) Which one of your recorded works do you consider most representative? (2) Will you kindly furnish me with a score and your own analysis of this work?

Due to other commitments early in the spring I must complete the outline of my lectures as soon as possible and should appreciate a prompt reply.

Sincerely,
Edgard Varèse

[Typed letter with autograph signature; Elliott Carter Collection, Paul Sacher Foundation. Reprinted by permission of Marylin Vespier.]

---

96 See *Edgard Varèse: Composer, Sound Sculptor, Visionary*, A Publication of the Paul Sacher Foundation, ed. Felix Meyer and Heidy Zimmermann (Woodbridge, UK: The Boydell Press, 2006), pp. 282–283.

97 Beatrice Laufer (b. 1923) studied composition at the Juilliard School with Marion Bauer and Roger Sessions. Her opera *Ile*, based on Eugene O'Neill's play of the same name, was performed at the Royal Opera House in Stockholm in 1958 and has enjoyed several revivals.

38 Elliott Carter to Edgard Varèse, [June 1948]

Dear Varèse,

Forgive me about being so long answering you. I thought I had, and then I found the letter unmailed in my desk last week.

My piano sonata has been recorded privately by Webster Aitken – and I shall be only too glad to lend you the records for your class. However, Beveridge Webster will be here in New York during the summer and is going to play it then at the Juilliard School and will doubtless be glad to play it for your class if you ask him to. It would be much more interesting. The work takes 20 minutes, 10 for each movement.

The score is going to be printed soon but, I think, not soon enough for you to show it to your class. I am sending you the analysis and other information herewith and am asking the American Music Center to send you a copy of the score. I shall be glad to furnish you with anything more you wish, and in a few weeks, after I am through correcting exams, I would like to come over and discuss the music with you and bring you the records.

I am very happy to hear that you are feeling better.[98]

Cordially,
Elliott

Elliott Carter / 31 West 12 Street / New York, N.Y.

[Enclosures: (1) Analysis of the *Piano Sonata*; (2) Artistic credo]

(1) [Analysis of the *Piano Sonata*]

PIANO SONATA

Elliott Carter

My Piano Sonata was written while I held the Guggenheim Fellowship during the summer of 1945 and was completed in January 1946. It was first performed by Webster Aitken in February 1947 at a concert at the Frick Museum in N[ew] Y[ork]. Since then it has been performed by James Sykes at the N[ew] Y[ork] Times Hall, by Aitken at Town Hall, and by Beveridge Webster at an ISCM concert in May 1948.[99]

The work is conceived in a style that is purely idiomatic for the modern concert grand piano and employs a large range of techniques that are peculiar to that instrument. It carries out in this medium my interest in the plastic flow of music and in contrasting rates of change. I am especially interested in the time plan of music, and in the modelling of phrases and sections and their interconnections, rather than in the discovery of novel momentary effects, and I think that this work exhibits this phase of my musical thought rather clearly.

The whole sonata is in three movements – the second movement is interrupted by the third movement and then resumes at the end. There is a pause between the first and second.

The first movement begins with an introduction that contains material which is used throughout the work: the jump of the octave (a) reappears in the bass alternating between B and A♯, which sound the two conflicting tonalities of the work. For, all through the work, there is a conflict between keys a semitone apart. Motives (b) and (d) recur throughout both movements. The opening theme of the second movement uses an inversion of (d) and a suggestion of (b).

The material of the first movement, beside[s] this material, also consists of two arpeggio figures (c) and (f) and a motive (g), the phrase (e), which suggests the first part of the second theme, and the actual first theme (h), which is used in many different variations throughout the first movement.

---

98 Varèse was recovering from a gallstone operation which he had undergone in late October 1947.

99 The performances of the *Piano Sonata* mentioned by Carter were given by Webster Aitken in the Frick Museum (première, 16 February 1947), James Sykes in Times Hall (5 March 1947), Webster Aitken in Town Hall (12 March 1948), and Beveridge Webster at the ISCM concert, Hunter College Playhouse (2 May 1948).

FIRST MOVEMENT

Introduction: pages 1 & 2 to end of 4th brace.

First theme: page 2, 5th & 6th braces, to page 4, 4th brace, featuring (g) and (h).

Transition: page 4, brace 5, to page 5, brace 5. Note return of (a) at end, also (i).

Second themes: page 5, brace 5, last measure, to page 6, brace 4: first idea. Note (i) at end.
- page 6, brace 5, to page 7, 1st measure. Note three-part canon bottom of page 6.
- page 7, second measure to 5th brace: development of (i) with new phrases.

Development: return of (b) in harmonics, page 7, last brace
- page 8, top to 5th brace: development of (c) with fragments of (b) and (h).
- page 8, last brace, to page 9, 4th brace, last 2 meas: variations of (h).
- page 9, 4th brace, last measure, to bottom: part of second theme in bass.
- page 10, top to 5th brace: variation of (h) with (a) jump of octave which becomes repeated notes.
- page 10, last brace, to bottom of page 11: repeated notes and development of (f), amplification of intervals of (h) last two braces.

- page 12: interruption of development of (f) by statement of part of second theme which is derived from (e), top two braces.
- page 12, braces 3, 4, 5, and first part of 6: continuation of development of (f)

Recapitulation: begins with statement of (f), page 12, bottom, to page 13, bottom. Return of (h) and (g).
- page 14: return of introduction in varied form.
- page 14, last brace, to page 15, brace 3: return of second phrase of second theme.

Coda: page 15, brace 2 to end: from (c), (e), and later (i).

SECOND MOVEMENT

1st idea, page 17 to last two measures

2nd idea, page 17, last measure, to page 18, third brace. This idea furnishes accompaniment to

3rd idea, page 18, 3rd brace, last measure, to p. 18, 5th brace, end.

4th idea, p. 18, brace 5, last measure, to p. 19, brace 3, last 2 measures.

Return of part of first idea: p. 19, brace 3, last 2 meas., to p. 19, brace 5, last 2 meas.

Analysis of the *Piano Sonata:*
autograph music examples

Transition to third movement:
p. 19, brace 5, last meas., to p. 20, brace 2, last meas.: statement of (d), (c) in augmentation, and (g).

Introduction to movement 3, p. 20, brace 2, to p. 21, brace 3: phrases that combine motives from fugue subject and from (c).

THIRD MOVEMENT

Fugue with exposition in four parts and episodes made up from various contractions and lengthenings of the subject, and changes of character.

Exposition: p. 21, brace 3, last 2 meas., to p. 23, brace 5, last m.

Episode 1: from head of subject p. 23, brace 5, last meas., to page 24, brace 1, last meas.
- Stretto of contracted theme: p. 24, brace 1, last meas., to p. 24, brace 4, first meas.
- Stretto of another contraction of theme: p. 24, brace 4.
- Stretto in 2 parts of theme at full length: [p. 24,] brace 5, to p. 25, brace 1, meas. 2

Episode 2: from parts of fugue subject; p. 25, meas. 2, to p. 25, brace 5, last meas.
- New melody based on note values of fugue subject (starts in right hand), accompanied by fragments of fugue subject. New melody only uses 5 tones of scale: p. 25, brace 5, to p. 26, brace 3.

Episode 3: p. 26, brace 3, second measure, to end of brace 3, p. 27: fragments of subject.
- Fugue subject: in middle voice p. 27, braces 4 and 5.

Episode 4: Transition to restatement of subject: p. 27, brace 6, [to] top of p. 28
- Statement of shortened subject: p. 28, first 3 meas.

Reverse exposition: more and more voices drop out.
- Subject in B♭ – p. 28, brace 1, last 2 meas., to brace 2, end.
- "New melody" in augmentation in bass – p. 28, brace 3.
- Subject in B – p. 28, brace 5, last 2 meas.
- Repeated in four octaves – p. 29, top.

Coda and stretto on shortened subject four-parts p. 29

RETURN OF SECOND MOVEMENT

Transition – p. 30 to last brace.

3rd idea of second movement – p. 30, bottom, to top of p. 31.

4th idea – p. 31, brace 1, last meas., to top of p. 32.

1st idea – p. 32, brace 2, to p. 33, last brace. This idea begins to reveal its connection with (b), (d), and (e).

Coda: p. 33, last 2 meas., to end. From (b), (d), and (e). Note (d) in last measure between top note and bass.

(2) [Artistic credo]

As a composer I am primarily concerned with the contrasts and changes of character in music, in plastic flow, in motion from one point to another, and with the expression of feelings as they change smoothly or abruptly, one commenting, amplifying, or denying the other. The interesting operation of cause and effect, of transformation in time, of the whole sense of flow reveals itself in changes of harmony, of rhythm and texture rather than in static repetitions. My music is essentially a kinetic projection of ideas, using perspectives in time. Since I work primarily with this dimension, the actual details of harmony, texture, and tone color are chosen more for their suggestions of motion than for any intrinsic character they may have. On the whole I prefer to use the usual vocabulary of contemporary music and to view it in new temporal sequences.

[Typed letter with autograph signature; (analysis and artistic credo:) typescript with autograph corrections (p. 1 with later annotations by Edgard Varèse, not included in the transcription given here); (music examples:) autograph manuscript. Edgard Varèse Collection, Paul Sacher Foundation. Reprinted by permission of Marylin Vespier.]

Domestic Matters (1946)

The Carters spent the summer of 1946 at the country estate of Sidney Lanier (a grandson of the writer and musician Sidney Lanier) in Eliot, ME, where the string quartet of which their host's sister-in-law was a member, the Lanier String Quartet, also happened to be staying. In July, Carter reworked his *Adagio for Cello (Viola) and Piano* (1944) for this ensemble, consisting of members of the Boston Symphony Orchestra. The new version, retitled *Elegy*, received its première on 21 and 22 August 1946. He then turned to new compositional plans. (A letter to John Kirkpatrick informs us that he was busy with no fewer than four projects at this time: a ballet for Lincoln Kirstein's Ballet Society [*The Minotaur*], another choral piece for the Harvard Glee Club [*Emblems*], a cello sonata, and a sonatina for oboe and harpsichord.)[100]

From his summer holiday in Maine, Carter finally returned to New York before setting out for the Yaddo Festival, where his *Warble for Lilac Time*, composed three years earlier, was premièred on 14 September 1946. His wife, however, remained in New England and kept an eye out for a suitable summer house in Vermont. On 11 September she sent her impressions to her husband, who in turn, in the evening of the same day, wrote about his daily life in New York and his tedious labors on the choral piece *Emblems*. Few such letters between Elliott and Helen Carter have survived. Their interest lies not least of all in the light they shed on the couple's *modus vivendi* and the image they project of their respective roles. All in all, we can make out a traditional distribution of tasks, in which the husband concentrates primarily on the artistic work and the wife deals with the parenting of their son and the practical side of their life together. (Incidentally, Helen Carter's search for a summer house remained unsuccessful for the time being. It was not until 1950 that the Carters finally bought a house in Dorset, VT.) Yet Helen Carter did not limit her energy entirely to non-musical matters. On the contrary, she was actively involved in the planning of her husband's career and served for all practical purposes as his manager, supporting him not least by handling his extensive business correspondence.

39   Helen to Elliott Carter, [11 September 1946]

West Road / Dorset, Vermont
Wednesday

Dearest Elliott,
Your letter arrived yesterday, as I didn't go to the P[ost] O[ffice] on Monday. I went over to Wilmington to look for a house, no luck whatever. The Kochs have decided to move out of N[ew] Y[ork] to the suburbs so John can have a more quiet life for painting.[101] So yesterday (Tue[sday]) they were going to S[outh] Orange to look at a house that was for sale there, droll indeed!

I've been over to see the Armstrong house again, really it has everything but "atmosphere" – wonderfully built, good location, view, and easy to care for. Do write me what you think! You needn't come up here to go home with us – I think we will drive down Sunday.

In the meantime I've been over to see Mr. Mackey (the R[eal] E[state] agent in Manchester) about the 2 houses we saw together. He thinks if we leave the tenants stay until next May 1st, they will sell, they took it off the market now as they didn't have another place to go to. Anyway don't think too much about all this, but try to have a good time at Yaddo – I only hope they will do your piece and do it well.

The weather here since last Sunday has been too dreadful, raining and foggy – it's worse here than Maine in the rain – besides I have a dreadful cold, but David's has almost disappeared, mine will too by tomorrow I'm sure. I'm so sorry that you too have one & only hope by now it has quietly left you.

Love to you always
H.

[Autograph letter; Elliott Carter Collection, Paul Sacher Foundation.]

---

100 Letter from Elliott Carter to John Kirkpatrick [4 or 5 August 1946]; John Kirkpatrick Papers, Irving S. Gilmore Music Library, Yale University.

101 John Koch (1909–1978) was an American realist painter; see the exhibition catalogue *John Koch: Painting a New York Life*, ed. Jennifer N. Thompson and Miranda Hamson (London: New York Historical Society, 2001).

102 Carter's *Warble for Lilac Time* (on words by Walt Whitman), in its version for voice and chamber orchestra, was premièred at the Yaddo Festival in an evening concert on 14 September 1946. The performers were Helen Boatwright (soprano) and the Yaddo Chamber Orchestra, conducted by Frederick Fennell. A good six months later, on 16 March 1947, Helen Boatwright sang the première of the piano version, with Helmut Baerwald, at a concert of the League of Composers in New York.

103 In fall 1946 Carter had been commissioned by the Harvard Glee Club to write a choral work, for which he chose three poems by Allen Tate. His setting, *Emblems*, reached completion only a year later in September 1947.

40 Elliott to Helen Carter [11 September 1946]

Wednesday Night

Dear Helen,

How busy you are, going to Wilmington again – I feel desperately that I ought to put the whole matter of the house entirely in your hands and let you decide about it – but I know that you would not want it that way.

When I see what a mess I have made in the apartment! But at least I am off to Yaddo tomorrow afternoon and so won't make any more.[102] There is a little mouse in the kitchen and some roaches but not many – at least I'll clean that up.

Life goes on very quietly here – I got part of an idea for my chorus,[103] a sort of crystallization of one of the kinds of lonely mournful sounds that I have been looking for, and so I worked out a couple of phrases. I always start with the idea that I won't repeat any words in a song or a choral number – but it isn't long before I have to give that idea up – particularly in this queer piece which is going to be awful bleak and sad.

The truck strike does not affect anything except the size of newspaper as far as you can notice around here. In our back yard there is rather a noisy machine that gets turned on for the night shift in some factory at 1 AM and goes until morning, but it only kept me awake night before last – I hope it won't bother you.

I look forward to seeing John [Kirkpatrick] at Yaddo – he has such a pleasant strangeness – perhaps we could bring him back to Dorset with us.[104]

A very comforting article by Stephen Spender in the *Partisan Review* on how hard a time he has in writing poetry & how he hates to do it.[105] Writes everything over plenty of times. Mr. James told me what awful neurotics writers & dancers [are –] "in fact musicians seem to be the only healthy lot".[106] Spender seems in this to be far more sane & sensible than Ralph Kirkpatrick described him as being, and his essay is one of the best I have ever read on the mad artist.

I didn't get any word from you today, and how I miss [it]. Just a note, as mother used to say, to let me know you are all right helps a lot for me to imagine that you are here and that I might relieve certain morose hours with an imagining of what you might say or do if you were here. For know – you are missed, I do think of you, my love, in my subjective way, and know too that you are loved just as faithfully if not as madly as poor Suzy loved you.[107] I always remember your returns when those little black eyes rolled and she shrieked a[nd] carried on and licked your hand as if you were her only joy in life.

But I must rush to Benny Herrmann – who is broadcasting Ives tonight.[108]

Love to you all and a hug for David,
Elliott

[Typed letter with autograph signature; Elliott Carter Collection, Paul Sacher Foundation.]

---

104 John Kirkpatrick and Helen Boatwright (soprano) presented a matinée concert of piano and vocal works at the Yaddo Festival on 14 September 1946. One of the pieces on the program was Carl Ruggles's *Evocations*.

105 Stephen Spender, "The Making of a Poem," *Partisan Review* 13/3 (Summer 1946), pp. 294–308.

106 Carter had just met with Henry James of Prentice Hall, who urged him to proceed alone with the Ives book he had originally planned to write with Paul Rosenfeld. Carter turned him down and instead recommended Waldo Frank, whom he had met in summer 1945 and whose novel *Island in the Atlantic* (New York: Duell, Sloan and Pearce, 1946) he had just read. Ultimately the project was carried out by Henry and Sidney Cowell; see above, p. 70.

107 For Suzy, see above, p. 48.

108 On this evening Bernard Herrmann conducted the Columbia Broadcasting Symphony Orchestra in a performance of Ives's *Symphony No 3* that was broadast by WABC in its program "Invitation to Music" half an hour before midnight (11.30 pm to 0.00 am).

The Minotaur (1946–47)

In 1946, just before setting out for his summer holiday in Eliot, ME, Carter received a commission from Lincoln Kirstein to write a ballet on the Minotaur legend. The commission was intended for Kirstein's newly founded Ballet Society, the successor to his artistically successful but financially disastrous American Ballet Caravan. (Two years later, in 1948, the Ballet Society was transformed into the New York City Ballet.) Carter seized the opportunity all the more willingly in that it gave him a chance to work with the Russian-American choreographer George Balanchine (1904–1983), whose work he had admired during his student years in Paris and who was now associated with the Ballet Society. One thing that interested him in the ballet's subject was its timely relevance to current history: at the time, as Carter later emphasized in a memoir for Balanchine, the story of the man-eating Minotaur seemed like a parable for the atrocities perpetrated in the Nazi concentration camps.[109] But he was also taken with the narrative structure of the legend, whose complex thematic links and transformations favored his own compositional proclivities. It is therefore unsurprising that the idea of transformation plays an important role in the score. An especially telling use of this idea occurs at the transition between scenes 1 and 2, where Pasiphaë's heartbeats metamorphose into hammering sounds in the building of the Labyrinth. (The suggestion for this, according to the composer, came from Balanchine.[110]) Although Carter and the choreographer exchanged thoughts in preparation for the project, the collaboration came to naught: in early 1947, just before Carter completed the score, Balanchine received an appointment as ballet master at the Paris Opéra to replace Serge Lifar, who was suspected of having been a *collaborateur*. His place was taken by his assistant John Taras, and the ballet, with Taras's choreography, was premièred at the Central High School of Needle Trades in New York on 26 March 1947, conducted by Leon Barzin. On the same program were the ballets *Zodiac* by Rudi Revil (music) and Todd Bolender (choreography) and *Highland Fling* by Stanley Bate (music) and William Dollar (choreography).

41 *The Minotaur,* ballet in one act and two scenes (1946–47), early sketches in pencil in sketchbook, p. [38]

These early sketches for *The Minotaur* come from a sketchbook that also contains a number of compositional exercises, including fugues and canons. The remaining sketches, mainly preserved today in the Library of Congress, reveal that Carter later withdrew some of the ideas written down here, but others he retained and elaborated when he came to work out the score. Among these are the fanfare on page [30] (it accompanies King Minos' entrance at rehearsal no. 51ff. in the full score) and the theme in sarabande rhythm sketched on page [37], which is used to open and end the ballet and also occurs at the end of part 1. Another is the idea, written down on the bottom half of the page shown here (p. [38]), of presenting Theseus's return from the Labyrinth as a chaconne or passacaglia ("with bass in irregular time"). Later, however, Carter heavily altered the melodic shape of the predominantly whole-tone bass theme. By resorting to the formal model of the chaconne, Carter was able to present an obvious structural parallel to the ballet's plot: just as Ariadne's thread serves Theseus as a guide, the basso ostinato forms a backbone for the series of variations constructed above it. Moreover, it also has a deeper aesthetic and symbolic meaning, for it appears exactly at the spot where Theseus conquers the embodiment of irrationality – the Minotaur. Considering that Carter equated the Minotaur's depredations with Nazi barbarity and related the latter to the "German cult of hypertrophic emotion," the chaconne can be interpreted as that "return to reason" which the composer, at that time, found embodied in neoclassicism.[111] But in this work, too, the classicist references are combined with a modernist idiom, and once again an important role is given to the superposition of contrasting textural layers so typical of Carter's music. The score is noteworthy not least for its high degree of thematic coherence, resulting in part from the fact that Carter derived much of its thematic material from a fragment of ancient Greek music known as the Seikilos Song (see Schiff 1983/1998, pp. 106–107 and 231–232, respectively). He consequently reworked the chaconne theme, which proceeds mainly in seconds and thirds in this early sketch, by giving it a striking upward leap of a fifth in bars 1 and 5 – the same leap found at the opening of the Seikilos Song.

109 Elliott Carter, untitled article in *I Remember Balanchine: Recollections of the Ballet Master by Those Who Knew Him*, ed. Francis Mason (New York: Doubleday, 1991), pp. 163–169, esp. 166; reprinted in revised form under the title "Remembering Balanchine" in *CEL*, pp. 299–304, esp. 301.
110 Ibid., and *CC*, p. 32.

111 *FW*, p. 61. See Felix Meyer, "Klassizistische Tendenzen in der amerikanischen Musik der zwanziger bis vierziger Jahre," in *Die klassizistische Moderne in der Musik des 20. Jahrhunderts, Internationales Symposion der Paul Sacher Stiftung, Basel 1996*, ed. Hermann Danuser, Veröffentlichungen der Paul Sacher Stiftung 5 (Winterthur: Amadeus, 1997), pp. 187–200, esp. 198–200.

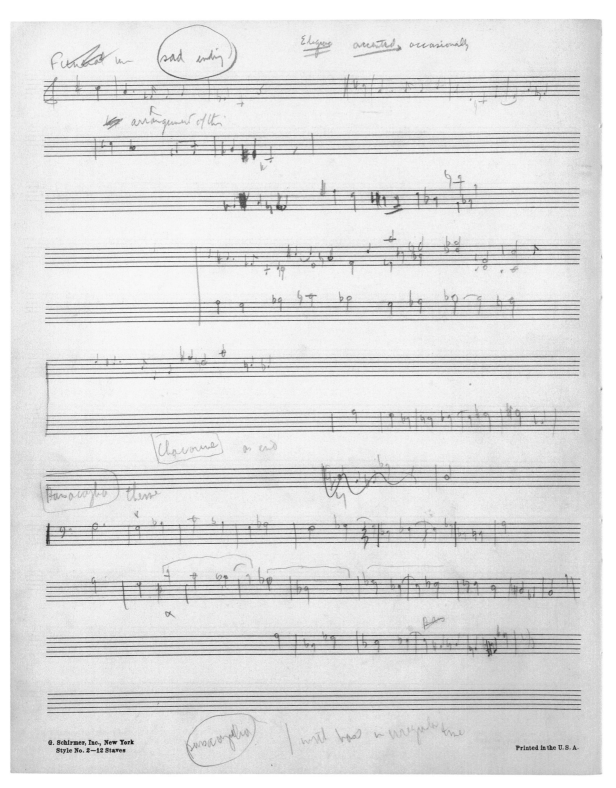

41 *The Minotaur*

42 *Sonatina for Oboe and Harpsichord*

Sonatina for Oboe and Harpsichord (1947)

Little is known about the circumstances behind Carter's unfinished *Sonatina for Oboe and Harpsichord.* We only know for certain that he was thinking about such a piece as early as summer 1946,[112] and that it was intended for the New York harpsichordist Sylvia Marlowe (1908–1981), a pioneer of the modern harpsichord who had studied with Nadia Boulanger and Wanda Landowska and continued the Landowska legacy by initiating and performing a large number of contemporary works for harpsichord.[113] Carter recalls working on the *Sonatina* in summer 1947 while staying in the French village of Èze on the Côte d'Azur, where he and his family were lodging in the Maison des Riquiers owned by the composer Samuel Barlow.[114] (The house was available because the tenant James V. Forrestal, the Secretary of the Navy and later Secretary of Defense in the Truman Administration, had cancelled his planned visit.) The unusual living conditions in this huge, venerable twelfth-century building (the Carters were besieged with visitors and, among other things, had to accommodate a Ferragosto celebration with the villagers) were not conducive to creative work, which may partly explain why the piece was left unfinished. (It was not until six years later, under quite different technical preconditions, that he completed a work for Sylvia Marlowe, namely, the *Sonata for Flute, Oboe, Cello, and Harpsichord* of 1952.) However, his first attempt to compose for the harpsichord left behind a number of sketches and drafts that shed much light on the project. Especially interesting is a more or less complete draft of the first movement. The other two movements, in contrast, survive only in fragments: the draft of the second movement breaks off after sixty-five bars, and all that remains of the rondo-finale are a few jottings in a sketchbook that Carter later used to work out the final movement of his *Woodwind Quintet* of 1948 (see below, pp. 90–92).

42 *Sonatina for Oboe and Harpsichord* (1947), first movement, full score draft in pencil, p. [1]

As in the *Sonatina for Violin and Harpsichord* of 1945 by his former teacher Walter Piston, to whom Carter devoted a long article the following year,[115] the harpsichord in Carter's *Sonatina* is employed primarily as a two-voice melody instrument. This is especially true of the passage shown here, the opening of the first movement, which is laid out as a three-part invention. There is no denying the neoclassical slant to this heavily linear, 228-bar contrapuntal movement in a freely handled sonata-allegro form. Equally obvious, however, are Carter's efforts to enliven the rhythm with syncopations and changes of meter and to explore the possibilities of modern, expanded tonality. As in the opening movement of *Symphony No. 1* or the *Piano Sonata*, the music is anchored on the pitches B and B♭, whose gravitational force becomes especially apparent at the ends of the main sectional divisions. (The exposition leads to an ostinato on B, the recapitulation resolves into B♭ major.) But the opening in particular reveals how purposefully Carter exploited the total chromatic: by the end of the second bar the single-voice melodic line of the harpsichord has presented eleven pitch classes, omitting only the B, which then becomes all the more prominent in bar 3, where it forms the first note of the oboe part (albeit *pianissimo*). As we can see here, the dynamics and articulation of the opening bars are meticulously specified. As the manuscript progresses, however, the level of detail decreases, though there are practically no gaps in the compositional fabric. Even the instruction written above the first bar ("restatement of theme: make this consequent of antecedent") is taken into account, as is a truncated version of the beginning of the recapitulation, making it far shorter than the original deleted passage.

112 See letter from Elliott Carter to John Kirkpatrick [4 or 5 August 1946]; John Kirkpatrick Papers, Irving S. Gilmore Music Library, Yale University.

113 Among the composers besides Carter who wrote pieces for Sylvia Marlowe are Vittorio Rieti, Virgil Thomson, Ned Rorem, Henry Cowell, and Henry Brant; see Larry Palmer, "Lavender and New Lace: Sylvia Marlowe and the 20th-Century Harpsichord Repertoire," *Contemporary Music Review*, no. 20, pt. 1 (2001), pp. 117–124.

114 Interview with Felix Meyer and Anne Shreffler, 15 June 2007. His memories of this summer in Èze were also put down in writing in a long letter of 7 June 2007 to James Levine; photocopy in the Elliott Carter Collection, Paul Sacher Foundation.

115 Elliott Carter, "Walter Piston," *The Musical Quarterly* 32/2 (July 1946), pp. 354–375; most recently reprinted (minus the original list of works) in *CEL*, pp. 158–175.

Emblems (1946–47)

Carter began to compose *Emblems*, the last of his three works for the Harvard Glee Club and his last choral piece for several decades, in September 1946 and completed it one year later. It represents the culmination of his choral writing and exploits the full sonic potential of the genre. The fifteen-minute long three-movement work includes chordal textures of varying densities – from eight-part harmonies to unisons –, madrigal-like imitation, and a high degree of rhythmic complexity. The work's expanded tonality and often complex harmonies (comprising fourths, thirds, and seconds) require highly skilled singers, particularly in the *a cappella* first movement. The second movement, which introduces a virtuosic piano part, is practically a piano concerto with chorus (see Schiff, 1983/1998, pp. 87 and 159, respectively). The work's difficulty and perhaps also its "awful bleak and sad" tone (see Carter's letter to Helen, [11 September 1946], above, p. 81) are hardly typical of traditional Glee Club music. For whatever reason, G. Wallace Woodworth waited four years after the piece's completion to program it, and then conducted only the second movement (at Harvard on 18 March 1951 and at Times Hall in New York on 3 April 1951).[116] The seemingly unlikely conjunction of the cosmopolitan and left-leaning Carter with the conservative Southern Agrarian Allen Tate (1899–1979) can be explained by Tate's involvement with the New York intellectual scene of that time. Tate was friend and mentor to Hart Crane, Robert Lowell, John Berryman, and Mark Van Doren, all of whom were part of Carter's poetic pantheon. When Carter wrote *Emblems*, Tate was at the height of his renown: during the 1940s he served as poet-in-residence at Princeton, consultant in poetry at the Library of Congress (a position that was later renamed poet laureate), poetry editor at Henry Holt publishers, and professor at New York University; he also contributed regularly to the flagship journal of the New York intellectuals, *The Partisan Review*.[117] Both Carter and Tate recognized the potential for artistic renewal within traditional forms; the elaborate but subtle rhyme scheme in the poem *Emblems* has its counterpart in the madrigalisms and fugal choral writing in Carter's setting.[118] Both artists also engaged fully with aesthetic modernism; Tate's significant early encounter with the poetry of T. S. Eliot is comparable to Carter's fascination with modern music in his youth. Moreover, the role of the American artist was of vital concern to both Tate and Carter: *Emblems* can be read as an elegy for the places and people left behind as Americans move westwards, and Carter's setting captures the poem's elegiac tone exactly. *Emblems* is an ambitious work, and its failure to reach its intended audience of New York intellectuals may have contributed to Carter's change of direction shortly afterwards, as he gave up his illusions about the possibility of a coherent American artistic and intellectual élite.

43 *Emblems*, for men's chorus and piano (1946–47), on a text by Allen Tate, photostat full score with editorial annotations in another hand, p. 2

The opening of the *a cappella* first movement shows Carter's recitative-like setting of the names of the Southern states "Maryland, Virginia, Caroline" (North and South Carolina). At first Carter struggled with finding a way to do justice to the poem's complexity: "[the] problem [of Tate's poems] is that they have quite intricate grammar and string along on a thread of thinking that is of many simultaneous different strands. It makes it very hard to find a general line without repeating phrases, and if you do that the grammatical structure is lost, and so I am doing lots of sketching and rejecting."[119] He finally gave up his resistance to repetition, however, as can be seen from this page, where the words "Pent images in sleep" are repeated. Carter also brought back the opening line ("Maryland, Virginia, Caroline") at the end of the movement, and rounded off the entire piece by returning to the *a cappella* texture and the harmonies (though not the words) of the beginning. Considerations of musical form – including large-scale recapitulation of material as well as local repetition of phrases – took priority over a literal setting of the text, yet Carter's setting also responded to the rhythms of the words and their meanings. The editorial annotations on this page show Kurt Stone's habitual close attention to every detail of the musical notation. He changed Carter's conventional choral notation (with each rhythmic value flagged separately) to an "instrumental" rhythmic notation with the notes beamed together, which makes it much easier to read (and to play on the piano during rehearsals).

---

116 The date of the première usually given – 3 April 1951 – can now be corrected. (See Schiff 1983/1998, p. 331 in both editions; and Link 2000, p. 32.)

117 On Tate's involvement with the *Partisan Review*, see Cooney, *The Rise of the New York Intellectuals* (see above, p. 5, note 9), pp. 208–209.

118 The second movement sets an earlier version of Tate's second stanza, which ends with the line, later deleted: "whose heart with memory shakes." The version of "Emblems" that Carter

consulted was probably either Allen Tate, *Poems 1928–1931* (New York and London: Charles Scribner's Sons, 1932), pp.21–23, or *Selected Poems by Allen Tate* (New York and London: Charles Scribner's Sons, 1937), pp. 106–108.

119 Letter from Elliott to Helen Carter, [10 September 1946]; Elliott Carter Collection, Paul Sacher Foundation.

"The Freedoms
of Instrumental Music"

1948–1956

Woodwind Quintet (1948)

Compared with the ballet *The Minotaur* and the chorus *Emblems*, the idiom of Carter's next work, the two-movement *Woodwind Quintet* of 1948, is simpler. The absence of experimentation in this piece, which nonetheless displays all the features typical of his style, is surely related to the lighter, more accessible nature of the wind quintet genre that Carter drew on. Yet it probably also resulted from his need to accommodate the technical skills of the musicians associated with the man who had asked him for the piece, the flutist Carleton Sprague Smith, at that time Chief of the Music Division of the New York Public Library. Even so, the *Woodwind Quintet*, like most of Carter's works of this period, was greeted with incomprehension. Some, including the players of Smith's ensemble, who were out of their depth and unable to play the music, considered it overly complex and too difficult to perform. The work was ultimately premièred on 21 February 1949 by Martin Orenstein (flute), David Abosch (oboe), Louis Paul (clarinet), Mark Popkin (bassoon), and Pinson Bobo (horn) during a radio broadcast concert organized in New York Times Hall by the National Association for American Composers and Conductors. In contrast, the composer Carl Ruggles, a radical musical individualist, seems to have found the piece far too conventional, judging from the derogatory remark he sent to John Kirkpatrick after the première: "As for Carter, I fail to find the slightest indication of anything that would make me think it was music."[1] And Carter himself? He found the piece "written in the kind of style [Nadia Boulanger] encouraged students during the middle 1930s to use, which, at the time I was a student, I did not like."[2] Accordingly he dedicated the piece to his former teacher, though only after the fact. The following exchange of letters shows that he told her of the dedication on 31 August 1949, and she thanked him – warmly, if belatedly – on 30 October 1949.

44 *Woodwind Quintet* (1948), photostat full score, p. [1]

In a program note for the *Woodwind Quintet* Carter wrote: "On looking over some earlier quintet works, I found the composers were in the habit of overlooking the fact that each of these instruments has a different sound. I, on the other hand, was particularly struck by this and so decided to write a work that would emphasize the individuality of each instrument and that made a virtue of their inability to blend completely."[3] In short, as in his other works of this period (and even more in his later music), Carter placed a premium on the distinctive features of each instrument and very clearly emphasized them at the beginning of the opening Allegretto. Thus in the first five bars the instruments are assigned highly contrasting materials: the flute states the melodious, rhythmically variable main theme (note the five different durations of its first five notes: 1 + 5 + 2 + 4 + 6 sixteenths) while the oboe, in staccato, strikes a mechanical eighth-note pulse; similarly, the clarinet adds arabesque-like dashes of color (before brusquely interrupting the preceding constellation and introducing a new order in m. 6) while the horn and bassoon are united in a drone-like fifth (mm. 1–2). On the other hand, this first page of the score only hints at the fact that the *Woodwind Quintet* is likewise based on the same B♭/B polarity that Carter had used in several other works (most recently in *Emblems* and the *Sonata for Violoncello and Piano*). Here we find it in the general movement away from the initial (expanded) B minor in the direction of the flat keys.

45 **Elliott Carter to Nadia Boulanger, 31 August [1949]**
(English translation in Appendix 1, p. 347)

Paris, le 31 août

Chère Mademoiselle,
Je suis bien navré de vous avoir manquée à Paris, mais il nous a fallu brusquement rentrer en Amérique à cause d'un changement ennuyeux de date au Cunard [Steamship Company] et je n'ai pas pu arranger de vous voir comme il aurait fallu. J'espère que la prochaine fois on pourrait vraiment se voir et se causer comme j'ai si longtemps souhaité.

Notre visite en France, si courte, pourtant a été remplie de charme et de plaisir. Les cathédrales, les châteaux et le paysage nous ont profondément émus de nouveau et nous aurions voulu partager avec vous nos impressions.

---

1   Letter from Carl Ruggles to John Kirkpatrick, 8 March 1949; quoted from Marilyn Ziffrin, *Carl Ruggles: Composer, Painter, and Storyteller* (Urbana and Chicago: University of Illinois Press, 1994), p. 195. Ruggles was present at the première of Carter's *Woodwind Quintet* because his *Angels* was performed at the same concert, conducted by Lou Harrison.

2   Program note for the *Woodwind Quintet*, 21 October 1981; carbon copy in the Elliott Carter Collection, Paul Sacher Foundation.

3   Undated program note for the *Woodwind Quintet*; carbon copy in the Elliott Carter Collection, Paul Sacher Foundation.

Sonata for Violoncello and Piano (1947–48)

Comme petit souvenir je vous envoie une copie de mon quintette que j'ai osé vous dédier et que j'espère vous donnera autant de plaisir à lire qu'il m'a donné de composer. Si je [pouvais] avoir la bonne chance de le faire jouer ici, ce serait un grand plaisir, car j'ai toujours admiré le jeu si fin des exécutants français.

Nous vous souhaitons une très bonne année ici – et comment cela ne pourrait-il pas être? Hélène me joint en vous envoyant nos vœux très affectueux,
Elliott

[Autograph letter; Fonds Nadia Boulanger, Bibliothèque Nationale de France. Reprinted by permission of the Fondation Internationale Nadia et Lili Boulanger.]

46   Nadia Boulanger to Elliott Carter, 30 October 1949
(in English, except for the postscript)

36, Rue Ballu, Paris IX / Trinité 90-17

Dear Elliott,
Not as awful as I seem. Received the letter, the quintet, the dedication – & ... well, I answered innerly – for it touched me so much. I am really happy with the whole matter: music, thought, affection. It makes the heart happy when everything blends so well. Can't write decently – not *a* minute of leisure but you will understand all what is implied in my profound appreciation.

We are most sad – what do I say, struck, discouraged, with Ginette Neveu's tragic end[4] – not only such a great artist, but a noble, loyal human being – it is really terrible!

So goes life – & it is the young who suddenly, when they are so needed, who precede us!

Give my love to your wife – receive *all* my thanks – et croyez toujours, cher Elliott, à la vieille solide affection de
N. B.

30 oct 1949

Moi aussi, je souhaite une exécution ici. Vous tiendrai au courant. [I, too, hope for a performance over here. I'll keep you posted.]

[Autograph letter; Elliott Carter Collection, Paul Sacher Foundation. Reprinted by permission of the Fondation Internationale Nadia et Lili Boulanger.]

Carter had begun thinking about writing a cello sonata in the summer of 1946[5] but started work on the piece only in the summer of 1948 and completed it on 11 December of that year, his fortieth birthday. He wrote the second movement (which contains the last key signature in Carter's music) first, followed by the third, fourth, and first movements. Written for the young cellist Bernard Greenhouse, who would later become a founding member of the Beaux Arts Trio, the work was premièred (in Town Hall on 27 February 1950) and later recorded by him with the pianist Anthony Makas.[6] It was one of Carter's first widely-acknowledged successes, and marked a major compositional breakthrough as well. Although Carter had long been interested in proportional tempo relationships and the metrical flexibility that results from additive rhythms, it was in the *Sonata for Violoncello and Piano* that he first worked out the technique that Richard Franko Goldman later called "metrical modulation."[7] In a letter to William Glock of 9 May 1955, Carter described noticing that the ordinary groupings of eighth notes into twos (for example, in 3/4 time) or threes (for example, in 6/8 time) could be manipulated to shift the speed of the pulse, and that these different tempo relationships could be employed analogously to key relationships: "[...] and then suddenly the whole idea came to me with its many arithmetical possibilities, which I worked out on paper as an amusement." (See below, p. 118.) Carter has ascribed the origins of his thinking about the structural possibilities of tempo relationships variously to medieval music, non-Western music, and the music of Stravinsky, Scriabin, Ives, and even Chopin, but Cowell's book *New Musical Resources* was probably the most significant influence.[8] He also acknowledges the impact of Rudolf Kolisch's article on tempo and character in Beethoven's music, in which the importance of tempo as a structural factor is emphasized (see Schiff 1983, p. 50).[9]

---

4   Two days earlier, on 28 October 1949, the French violinist Ginette Neveu (b. 1919) and her brother and accompanist Jean had died in an airplane crash over the Azores *en route* to a tour of the United States.

5   See letter from Elliott Carter to John Kirkpatrick, [4 or 5 August 1946]; John Kirkpatrick Papers, Irving S. Gilmore Music Library, Yale University.

6   American Recording Society, ARS-25 (recorded in 1951, issued in early 1952). The *Piano Sonata*, performed by Beveridge Webster, was on the same record.

7   Richard Franko Goldman, "Current Chronicle," *Musical Quarterly* 37/1 (January 1951), pp. 83–89.

8   Cowell, *New Musical Resources* (see above, p. 14, note 42). See Elliott Carter, liner notes to the recording Nonesuch H-71243 (1969); most recently reprinted in *CEL*, pp. 228–231, esp. 228–229, and *CC*, p. 41.

9   Rudolf Kolisch, "Tempo and Character in Beethoven's Music," *Musical Quarterly* 29/2 (April 1943), pp. 169–187. Joseph Schillinger's discussion of rhythm in *The Schillinger System of Musical Composition* (New York: Carl Fischer, 1946) was also

evidently a factor, even though Carter had given the book a largely negative review (Elliott Carter, "The Fallacy of the Mechanistic Approach," *Modern Music* 23/3 [Summer 1946], pp. 228–230; most recently reprinted in *CEL*, pp. 15–16). In retrospect, Carter acknowledged the stimulus received from Schillinger's book. In his interview with Enzo Restagno, for example, he admitted that "I probably got a push [...] also from that book by Schillinger I mentioned earlier, where he maintains that a four-beat measure can be accented as if it were in three, and vice versa, resulting in a sort of polyrhythm." (*CC*, p. 41.)

Dialogue with William Glock (1950)

47 *Sonata for Violoncello and Piano* (1947–48),
photostat full score with autograph corrections, p. 31
(fourth movement, mm. 40–54)

The Allegro final movement of the *Cello Sonata* (the third of the four to be composed) links with the tempos and material of previous movements, ending with the cello in "percussive" pizzicato quarter notes while the piano, cello-like, sustains long notes in the low register. (Carter restored this exchange of the two instruments' characteristic roles to "normalcy" when he composed the beginning of the first movement, creating a kind of circular form in which the end refers to, and reverses, the beginning.) This page shows the end of the first metrical modulation, which starts with the basic tempo of the movement, quarter = 120, accelerates to quarter = 140, then decelerates to the original tempo. At the top of the page, the fastest tempo, quarter = 140, has just been established. The deceleration occurs in two stages: first, as the sixteenth-note values remain constant, the pulse shifts from every fourth to every seventh sixteenth, resulting in quarter = 80 (m. 46). The sixteenths then slow as the quarter stays constant and is subdivided into six instead of seven sixteenths (m. 47) (slowing from an actual speed of 560 to 480). The groups of six sixteenths (which stay at the same speed) are then notated in 6/8 time: the dotted quarter, instead of the quarter, now moves at 80 (m. 48). The modulation is now essentially complete: all Carter has to do is to keep the sixteenths at the same speed and group them into fours rather than sixes, as he does in the 3/4 of m. 50. This brings us back to the original speed of quarter = 120 (480/4). It should be noted that metrical modulations are generally more difficult to describe than they are to perform; since the tempo shifts occur incrementally, and always on the basis on a constant note value, they are instinctively logical to the musician.

One of Carter's closest friends was the English musician, critic, and musical administrator William Glock (1908–2000). When the two men met in the late 1940s, Glock had just taken charge of the Summer Music School in Bryanston (Dorset). A few years later, in 1953, it relocated to Dartington (Devon), where it became one of Europe's most interesting summer festivals devoted to both early and contemporary music. From 1949 on Glock also edited the periodical *The Score*, whose contents, as he put it, were noted for a "preoccupation with contemporary music, with ideas rather than facts, and with practice rather than theory."[10] Preferring to let composers speak for themselves, he asked Carter on 12 January 1950 to write an article on American music for his journal. On 6 September 1950, after a delay of almost eight months, Carter declined, pointing out that any such article he would write on the subject would be too negative. (It was not until several years later that he was finally persuaded to write a piece for this journal, which was read closely and appreciatively from its very inception; see below, p. 115.) To illustrate his argument, he presented an account of the main events on America's current music scene – with a critical undertone, as in several later letters. Glock championed Carter's music time and again in the further course of his career: not only did he invite the composer to Dartington several times, he found a permanent place for his music in the concerts of the BBC, of which he was Controller of Music from 1959 to 1972. Carter, for his part, paid tribute to his friend by dedicating three compositions to him in the 1970s and 1980s: *Birthday Fanfare* for three trumpets, vibraphone, and chimes (1978); the song cycle *Syringa* (1977–78); and *Canon for 4* for flute, bass clarinet, violin, and cello (1984) to mark Glock's retirement as musical director of the Bath Festival.

---

10 William Glock, *Notes in Advance* (Oxford and New York: Oxford University Press, 1991), p. 87.

11 From 1944 William Glock was married to Clement Davenport, from whom he had a daughter, Oriel. After their divorce he married Anne Geoffroy-Dechaume in 1952.

12 Elliott Carter, "Music of the 20th Century," in *Encyclopaedia Britannica* 16 (Chicago: Encyclopaedia Britannica, 1953), pp. 16–18.

13 Carter held a professorship in composition at Columbia University from 1948 to 1950.

14 The Sixth Annual Festival of Contemporary Music took place at Columbia University (McMillin Theatre) from 18 to 21 May 1950. Copland's *Twelve Poems of Emily Dickinson* (1949–50), the second of which is dedicated to Carter, were premièred on 18 May 1950 by Alice

48 William Glock to Elliott Carter, 12 January 1950

The Score / 21 Well Walk / Hampstead / N.W. 3
January 12, 1950

Dear Elliott,

It was very nice of you to send all those chocolates; I'm sure Clement will be writing to thank you properly, in a day or two.[11] Meanwhile I'd like to ask you if you'd care to do a longish article for *The Score*, on American music; whatever aspect you may think worth while. The rate of pay is unfortunately poor: about £10 for 3,000 w[or]ds; it might be better, if you contemplate coming to Europe again in the near future, to let us deposit it here for you – you can then change it into French francs and have a few days of civilized life near the Mediterranean.

I was so sorry not to see more of you when you last came; we'll manage better next time.

If you agree to writing an article, do please let me know fairly soon. If you let me have it by February 20 it could go in the next number; otherwise April 20 will do. I'll send you a copy of No. 2, which appears in a week's time. The magazine has a long way to go yet, but I hope it will be decent one day.

Very best wishes to you both,
William

Could one make an interesting article out of American *opera*?

[Autograph letter; Elliott Carter Collection, Paul Sacher Foundation. Reprinted by permission of Sebastian Balfour and David Drew (William Glock Estate).]

49 Elliott Carter to William Glock, 6 September 1950

Elliott C. Carter Jr. / 31 West 12th Street / New York 11, N.Y.
September, 6th, 1950

Dear William,

Forgive me for not answering your kind letter sooner. When I received it in the middle of the winter, I was in the midst of writing a piece on 20th-century music for the *Encyclopaedia Britannica* to supplant that of Mr. Tovey and was up to my neck in the effort to match the urbanity and wisdom of my august predecessor.[12] Since that time teaching, a persistent and recurring virus infection, and several performances of my music have kept me in a state of exhaustion. Now Columbia University, where I have been teaching,[13] has closed down, ending with its annual music festival on which Aaron Copland's new song cycle was performed (and severely roasted by the press, although it contained some very fine music) and my *Holiday Overture*, which was received with indifference by the press but compliments on the part of my younger and less successful colleagues and hostility on the part of those more successful than I.[14] This next year, I shall be free from work as I have received both the Guggenheim Fellowship and the Award from the National Academy of Arts and Letters, and although I have been elected president of the American Section of the International Society for Contemporary Music, we are going to be on the move and I shall resign, so as to have some leasure to write.

As for an article on recent American music, I am too disheartened by most of the works of my colleagues to write with any enthusiasm. My article would sound like those letters of Mr. Lockspeiser printed in the *N[ew] Y[ork] Herald Tribune* that rip English music to pieces. Only, such an article written by a composer might sound like sour grapes and so I would prefer not to write it. I can suggest an excellent writer, Richard [Franko] Goldman (First Avenue, N.Y.), whose articles you may have read in *Musical Quarterly*.[15] He, apparently, feels more hope than I do.

This year has seen a gradual revolution in contemporary music circles; the two rival organizations, the League of Composers and the ISCM, both were faced with the resignation of their chairmen, Aaron Copland of the League and Mark Brunswick of the ISCM. Since I am the only one on both boards and never say a word at any meeting, I was nominated to succeed both of the presidents – I provisionally accepted the ISCM, mostly devoted to 12-tone music which I can stand in small doses, but a little less cliquish than the League. The season has been unexciting except for some revivals of Webern.[16] The operas – Blitzstein's unsuccessful *Regina* (with a fair amount of good music) and Menotti's *Consul* (successful in a Grand Guignol way with a purely "effect" score) were

Howland (soprano) and Aaron Copland (piano). Carter's *Holiday Overture* was placed on the program of the final orchestral concert, given on 21 May 1950 with Izler Solomon conducting the CBS Symphony Orchestra.

15 The conductor, bandleader, and music journalist Richard Franko Goldman (1910–1980) wrote a large number of articles for the "Current Chronicle" column of the *Musical Quarterly* as well as a study of the music of his former teacher at the Juilliard School, Wallingford Riegger ("The Music of Wallingford Riegger," *The Musical Quarterly* 36/1 [January 1950], pp. 39–61). A selection of his writings was reissued in Richard Franko Goldman, *Selected Essays and Reviews, 1948–1968*, ed. Dorothy Klotzman (Brooklyn: Institute for Studies in American Music, 1980).

16 The following works by Webern were performed in the 1949-50 season: the *Symphony*, op. 21 (New York Philharmonic, cond. Dimitri Mitropoulos, Carnegie Hall, 26 and 27 January 1950), the *Concerto*, op. 24 (Chamber Arts Society, cond. Robert Craft, Town Hall, 29 April 1950), and the *Quartet* for violin, clarinet, tenor saxophone, and piano, op. 22 (ISCM concert, McMillin Theatre at Columbia University, 5 May 1950).

Six Pieces for Kettledrums (1950)

not much fun.[17] Roger Sessions's Second Symphony – complex, chromatic, full of enigmatic gloom – was perhaps the best American work performed.[18] The young aren't very well trained and fall easily into the dodecaphonic trap, with its ready-made expression and its Viennese grimaces.

I liked the three copies of *[The] Score* which you so kindly sent me. The idea of not specializing in any particular field of music is excellent. The article on Petrassi, whose music is virtually unknown here, was a revelation.[19] The article on metrical experiments, on the other hand, did not go any further than those frequently met with in Bartók's music and in that of Tippett and some American composers.[20] I felt that I wanted to add the whole field of artificial divisions (triplets etc.) and to describe the more inclusive and varied methods that I have been using for a number of years, but I decided that it was presumptuous of a composer to describe his own technical methods when his music should really be the medium by which his technique is justified. Although the recent publication of *French Secular Music of the Late Fourteenth Century*, edited by Willi Apel and printed by the Medieval Academy of America,[21] reveals a whole new field of rhythmic technique which I find I have been trying to explore in my own music, and has been extremely illuminating to me. Still I do not feel that I should write about this.

After a great deal of thought this summer, we have decided to spend the year in Arizona rather than Rome[22] and so will not be passing through London – much to our regret. But Helen has decided for us that after a winter in the wild west we will be ready for some civilization again and will spend next summer again on the continent if we can scrape the money together.

Helen joins me in sending Clement and you our best. We would also like to be remembered to Robin and David and the Estes. We think of our short stay in England with great delight.

Yours,
Elliott

[Typed letter with autograph signature; William Glock Estate, British Library. Reprinted by permission of Sebastian Balfour and David Drew (William Glock Estate).]

In 1949–50 Carter wrote a series of compositional studies: *Eight Etudes and a Fantasy* for flute, oboe, clarinet, and bassoon, which he sketched in 1949 for demonstration purposes during an orchestration course at Columbia University and later elaborated, and *Six Pieces for Kettledrums* (1950). Both sets of studies explore the problem of obtaining a maximum of expressive variety from extremely limited material. In the *Six Pieces*, Carter focused mainly on the parameter of rhythm, but surely he was equally enticed by the (very restricted) possibilities of two-part texture inherent in four kettledrums played by one player. Like the *Eight Etudes*, the kettledrum pieces were not originally intended for publication. Rather, Carter viewed them as preliminary studies for his *String Quartet No. 1* and was anything but convinced of their viability on the concert platform, even after Al Howard premièred them at the Museum of Modern Art on 6 May 1952: "I couldn't distinguish the pitches of the drums and they all seemed very boring because there was all this unclear, swimming sound."[23] It was not until 1960 that he decided, after several players expressed interest, to publish two of them in revised form (*Recitative and Improvisation*, AMP 9601-6). And it was not until 1966, with the help of the percussionist Jan Williams, that he finally undertook to rework all six pieces – aiming, in particular, to heighten their timbral variety by using different drumsticks, varying the place of attack, and so forth – and to add two new ones: "Adagio" and "Canto," both dedicated to Williams. However, he did not consider that these addenda moulded the work into a unified whole: even in their definitive form, the pieces remained more of a loose gathering of isolated studies than a suite. This explains why Carter, in the printed edition of *Eight Pieces for Timpani* (AMP 6820, 1968), expressly asked that they not be performed complete, but in combinations of a maximum of four pieces.

17 Marc Blitzstein's musical *Regina* (1946–49), commissioned by Serge Koussevitzky and the Koussevitzky Music Foundation, was first heard in New York at the 46th Street Theatre on 31 October 1949. Another Broadway production was Gian Carlo Menotti's opera *The Consul* (1949–50), which received its New York première in the Ethel Barrymore Theatre on 15 March 1950.

18 The performances of Sessions's *Symphony No. 2* took place in Carnegie Hall on 12–15 January 1950, with Dimitri Mitropoulos conducting the New York Philharmonic.

19 John Weissmann, "Goffredo Petrassi," *The Score*, no. 3 (June 1950), pp. 49–62.

20 Daniel Jones, "Some Metrical Experiments," ibid., pp. 32–48.

21 *French Secular Music of the Late Fourteenth Century*, ed. Willi Apel (Cambridge, MA: Medieval Academy of America, 1950).

22 See below, p. 98.

23 "Elliott Carter: Eight Pieces for Timpani," [interview with Patrick Wilson], *Percussive Notes* 23/1 (October 1984), pp. 63–65, esp. 65.

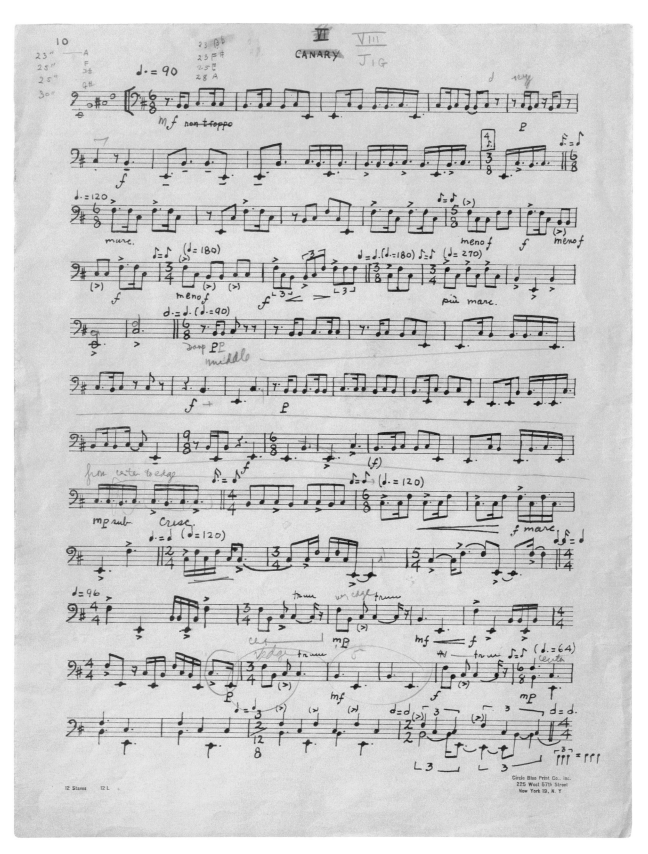

A Report on Conlon Nancarrow (1951)

50 *Six Pieces for Kettledrums* (1950), photostat score with autograph annotations, p. 10

Unlike the two added pieces "Adagio" and "Canto," which require pedal timpani, the *Six Pieces* are intended for kettledrums without tuning mechanisms, and each piece is thus limited to four pitches. In what was originally the final piece, "Canary," these pitches were E, B, C♯, and F, representing the all-interval tetrachord 0146 also employed a short while later in the *String Quartet No. 1*. The annotated fair copy shown here contains the first half of the piece, illustrating Carter's later efforts in timbral differentiation. The title "Canary," sometimes found in the plural (and changed accordingly in the printed edition), derives from a lively baroque triple-meter dance whose similarity with the gigue (or jig) is underscored by the variant title in Carter's hand. The original fair copy does not specify any particular types of drumstroke. However, when Carter later revised the piece after adding the two new items in 1966 (hence the provisional new number "VIII"), he supplied precise instructions on where to strike the drum head, e.g. "middle" (third measure of staff 5 [m. 25]) or "from center to edge" (beginning of staff 8 [m. 42]). Later he rigorously applied such instructions to the printed edition, with N standing for "normal striking position," C for "center of drum head," and R for "as close as possible to rim, still sounding pitch." He also added the pitches B and F in the first two measures of staff 5 (mm. 23–24) to form dyads, thereby interrupting the originally monophonic texture of the opening section. This section is now followed by a still more "polyphonic" two-voice section with a constant tempo in the left hand and an accelerating tempo in the right (beginning in the last measure of the second-last staff [m. 60]). Carter later included this passage in his lecture "Music and the Time Screen" to illustrate the technique of metrical modulation.[24]

In 1950 Carter received a Guggenheim Fellowship and a grant from the National Academy of Arts and Letters. In order to compose in peace, he withdrew between September 1950 and early June 1951 to the vicinity of Tucson, AZ, where he and his wife lived in one of two guest houses owned by the philanthropist Helen d'Autremont. (The other was occupied for a while by the literary critic, natural scientist, and Columbia University teacher Joseph Wood Krutch [1893–1970] and his wife Marcelle, with whom the Carters were on friendly terms: "Our almost daily meetings led to fascinating talks about the ecology of the region – how birds, animals, insects, and plants had adapted to the heat and the limited water supply, which consists of infrequent, spectacular but brief cloudbursts that for an hour seem about to wash everything away, and then very long droughts."[25]) Here, in the solitude of the Sonoran Desert, Carter completed *Six Pieces for Kettledrums* in November 1950 before immersing himself in his large-scale, roughly forty-minute *String Quartet No. 1*. From Arizona, Carter also renewed his friendship with Conlon Nancarrow during a side trip to Mexico City in January 1951. He vividly recounted his visit in the following letter to Copland, who had been living at the American Academy in Rome from January 1951 as a Fulbright scholar, causing Copland to remark: "Your Nancarrow story read like a novel."[26] In his letter Carter also refers to his last trip to Mexico City in June 1947, when the Carters met up with Copland to pay a joint visit to Nancarrow.[27] The renewed contact with Nancarrow, whom he had met in New York in 1939 and who now wrote highly complex polyrhythmic and polytemporal music for player piano, had a stimulating effect on Carter, causing him to champion Nancarrow's music in the coming years and leaving traces in his own *String Quartet No. 1*, which contains a direct reference to Nancarrow's *Rhythm Study No. 1* (mm. 167 ff. of movement 2).

24 Elliott Carter, "Music and the Time Screen," in *Current Thought in Musicology*, Symposia in the Arts and the Humanities 4, ed. John W. Grubbs (Austin and London: University of Texas Press, 1976), pp. 63–88, esp. 70–71; most recently reprinted in *CEL*, pp. 262–280, esp. 268.

25 Elliott Carter, liner notes to the recording Nonesuch H 71249 (1970); most recently reprinted under the title "String Quartets Nos. 1, 1951, and 2, 1959" in *CEL*, pp. 231–235, esp. 232.

26 Letter from Aaron Copland to Elliott Carter, 23 April 1951; published in *The Selected Correspondence of Aaron Copland*, ed. Elizabeth B. Crist and Wayne

Shirley (New Haven and London: Yale University Press, 2006), p. 205.

27 This visit had taken place on 19 June 1947. Copland also took the couple to the popular dance hall "El Salón Mexico," which he had immortalized some ten years earlier in his orchestral piece *El Salón Mexico* (1932–36); see Copland and Perlis, *Copland: Since 1943* (see above, p. 54, note 44), pp. 71 and 73.

28 Copland's thank-you note has not survived.

29 Nancarrow did not formally divorce his second wife, the sculptress Annette Margolis, until 20 July 1953. They had married in New York in 1947.

30 Nancarrow's former teacher, Nicolas Slonimsky, reported on this project in an article a short while later: "He [Nancarrow] has already started on the construction of mechanical drums, with hammers hitting different parts of the drumhead, thus securing a variety of timbres, like those employed by Stravinsky (in his 'History of a Soldier'); Bartók (in his Music for Strings, Percussion and Celesta); and particularly Varèse (in his all-percussion work, 'Ionization'). Later, there will follow similar applications for string and wind instruments. When, many years hence, Nancarrow completes his project – and he is fully

51 Elliott Carter to Aaron Copland, 23 February 1951

Dear Aaron,

We were very much touched by your birthday thank-you note.[28] Helen and I both hope that you are having a fine time in Rome. We are doing quite well in Tucson, thank you.

Last month Helen & I flew to Mexico City for a week's stay with some friends. We were able to be quite blasé indeed about many things they suggested doing because of your able guidance the last time. This time we really liked Mexico much more, though, because we got around in the country. We went to Paricutin and to Puebla. In fact the only thing we repeated from the last was a visit to Conlon [Nancarrow]. And let me tell you it was quite an undertaking as we had lost his address. But by going from house to house in San Angel Inn we finally struck a little bilingual girl who very uncertainly explained where he had moved to. By much exploring we found his house. It was a large estate quite in the country, with a big house built by Conlon & his wife, and quite far from it a huge studio all in heavy cement. When we arrived Conlon was in the midst of having a wall built, separating his studio from the house and from his wife. For they are now separated.[29]

Conlon, surrounded by workmen building a pool and piles of rubbish and dismantled bathrooms, led me to his studio, which has no windows and is shut in by two heavy doors almost like those on a safe deposit vault. In the clutter of the studio is a huge array of all sorts of drums, marimbas, mechanical pianos, and a two-story library built just like the stacks in Widener Library. He is at work on a mechanical percussion orchestra.[30]

Since you last saw him he has composed only a Boogie-Woogie Suite in 3 moderately long m[o]v[emen]ts and 5 Rhythm Studies which exploit the polyrhythmic capacity of his piano rolls to the full. The music is much more transparent and better made than before and constantly fascinating in rhythm, if not always in tune. All of it is now quite jazzy, almost popular in tone, as well as quite dissonant. He tells me that he has about 2 hours of music on rolls, which represents millions of carefully punched holes. He wants to issue the lot on some LP discs. But I could see that he is very slow at such practical matters and also very fussy about the acoustics of his studio. You see, he has taken to preparing his piano by hardening the hammers so that it sounds a little harpsichordy. This means that the recordings have to be done on the spot, and while he seems to have some money he apparently does not have enough to buy a very good tape recorder. It also means that he will not allow a "live" performance of his music with the rolls anywhere else. – By now the music is so tricky rhythmically that it could not be played by human means.

He seems a little bewildered by all these problems and I felt very strongly his isolation and his remoteness and his lack of experience with the musical world. Oddly enough his music has grown more accessible in general character.

Added to his other problems is the fact that the US won't issue him a passport because, although no communist, he was mixed up in the Spanish war. He is becoming a Mexican citizen so that he can travel – outside the US.[31]

I worked hard on him and persuaded him to lend me 2 scores – the only two he has made, of his two easiest pieces – the others are scarcely notatable [–] and have sent them to *New Music* in the hope of getting them printed.[32] Of course, the notes give very little idea of the music. But better than that – I got him to lend me some tape recordings that he had made on a borrowed machine just to test how it would sound. I have had some dubbings made of pieces whose titles I do not know but which I must say I find very interesting indeed.

If you were in N[ew] Y[ork] I would send them to you. Since you are not I would like to send them to someone that might take an interest in the music and possibly get in touch with Conlon and help to stimulate him to record commercially. I think he needs prodding – especially after all these years of being out of contact with music. Maybe you could suggest what I ought to do – at long distance – and to whom I could turn.[33]

We are having a lovely time here – living with no thought of next year. Douglas [Moore] thinks I ought to

determined to see it through – he will have at his service an orchestra of rhythmic and dynamic precision and technical perfection that would justify the wildest dreams of musical alchemists." (Nicolas Slonimsky, "Complicated Problem – Drastic Solution," *The Christian Science Monitor*, 10 November 1951.) Nancarrow himself downplayed the significance of his experiment: owing to technical problems, he said, the project had failed at the very beginning, and he therefore regretted all the more that several photos showing him at work on his "percussion orchestra" had entered circulation. See William Duckworth, *Talking Music:*

Conversations with John Cage, Philip Glass, Laurie Anderson, and Five Generations of American Experimental Composers (New York: Schirmer, 1995), pp. 43–44.

31 In 1937–38 Nancarrow had fought in the Spanish Civil War as a member of the Abraham Lincoln Brigade. Thereafter he was denied his American passport, and he emigrated to Mexico City in 1940. His efforts to obtain Mexican citizenship, mentioned in Carter's letter, dragged on for several years; see below, p. 138.

32 One of these compositions, *Rhythm Study No. 1*, was finally published in *New Music* as vol. 25, no. 1; see below, p. 138, note 33.

33 In his reply of 23 April 1951 Copland recommended Vladimir Cherniavsky, who in 1950 had published the first installment of a recording project entitled "The Music of Charles Ives" (Polymusic Records PRLP 1001). The project never proceeded beyond this album. Nor did anything come of the plan to interest Cherniavsky in a recording of Nancarrow's music. The first commercial Nancarrow recording had to wait until 1969, when "Conlon Nancarrow: Studies for Player Piano" was issued by Columbia Masterworks (MS 7222).

52

try to get the late Roy Welch's job,[34] but the prospect of being the head of a college music dep[artmen]t fills me with awful boredom. You see, I don't want too good a job, and to be so fussy is a great luxury. I am having a hard time getting my 'cello piece printed and may turn to Arrow in spite of the nasty cold shoulder I got on my choral piece.[35] It is going to be commercially recorded, and maybe printing is not so important as that.[36]

The University of Illinois is giving me an evening concert in May and on it is going to be played my new pieces for kettledrums because my quartet will not be finished in time.[37]

We went to Los Angeles and met Ingolf Dahl, whom we liked very much, and saw the Kirchners and heard parts of his very complicated new orchestral piece. It looks quite interesting.[38]

We don't miss being in New York so much this year, partly because of the weather, which is so pleasant and warm here, and partly because of the calm and the chance to spend long stretches of time doing what we like to do. I get lots of time to work and Helen to learn Spanish – she

was bitten by the Mexican bug. But we do miss not seeing our friends. Even though we have not seen you so much in the past years as we would have liked, still the few times ha[ve] meant a great deal to us. I hope that you will be in Tanglewood this summer. We have bought a house in Dorset, Vermont, and will come down to see you, if you are there. Or perhaps you could come up & see us.

Will you give my greetings to whatever friends I have in Rome, and I hope that you have a very productive winter –

Affectionately,
Elliott

Elliott Carter / Box 650, Route 4 / Tucson, Arizona.
February 23, 1951
Conlon Nancarrow / Apartado 31550 / Guadalupe Inn, / Mexico, 20, D. F.

Best to you, dear Aaron
Helen

[Typed letter with autograph signature and handwritten addendum by Helen Carter; Aaron Copland Collection, Library of Congress, Washington, D.C. Reprinted by permission of the Aaron Copland Fund for Music, Inc., copyright holder.]

---

34 The recently deceased Roy Dickinson Welch (1885–1951) had built up and headed the Music Department at Princeton University from 1935.

35 The *Sonata for Violoncello and Piano* was ultimately issued in 1953 by the Society for the Publication of American Music. The comment about Arrow

giving him a "nasty cold shoulder" refers to his setting of Robert Herrick, *To Music* (1937), which was published only in 1955 by Peer International.

36 Carter is referring to the recording made by Bernard Greenhouse and Anthony Makas in March 1951 and released by the American Recording Society together with Beveridge Webster's recording of the *Piano Sonata*; see above, p. 92, note 6.

37 This performance of the *Six Pieces for Kettledrums* at the University of Illinois failed to come about. The première took place only a year later in New York on 6 May 1952; see above, p. 96.

38 Leon Kirchner (b. 1919) taught at the University of Southern California from 1950 to 1954. At the time of Carter's visit he was working on his orchestral work *Sinfonia in Two Parts*. It received its

String Quartet No. 1 (1950–51)

52 Elliott and Helen Carter on a boat in the Floating Gardens of Xochimilco (1951)

During their short vacation in Mexico in January 1951, when among other things they visited Conlon Nancarrow, the Carters made a trip to the Floating Gardens of Xochimilco, a spot then located outside the city limits south of Mexico City but long since engulfed by urban sprawl. Carter sent this photo of the occasion to his son in Tucson, adding the following lines on the back: "Dear David, / Today we got up early and took the surface car for a very long ride way out into the country until we got to a little town called Xochimilco where there are floating gardens. We took a little boat with a man to paddle it (you can see him in the background) and we rowed around the canals where there are lots of flowers growing and lots of people in boats selling flowers, tortillas, all sorts of pictures and pepsi-cola. Also there were little orchestras of musicians that came and played for us in boats. We later went to the fair in the town and saw people selling cakes shaped like roosters. / *Dad*."[39]

The *String Quartet No. 1*, completed in September 1951 after almost a year of uninterrupted work, builds on techniques that Carter had developed over the last decade, yet the scope and ambition of the resulting synthesis has no precedent in his output. The innovative formal design of the forty-minute work divides the four movements – Fantasia, Scherzo, Adagio, and Variations – into three parts; the non-congruence of movement and part first seen in the *Piano Sonata* is here carried much further. Metrical modulation is used to govern much larger time frames and more contrapuntal voices than before. Carter's quartet shares with Schoenberg's *First String Quartet* its length, extensively contrapuntal texture, and wide expressive range; Carter's formal design even recalls the continuous, interlocking four movements of Schoenberg's quartet. If Schoenberg, Berg (especially his *Lyric Suite*), and Bartók were the quartet's European ancestors, its American grandfather was Ives, whose influence Carter explicitly acknowledged by using the head motive from Ives's *First Violin Sonata* as one of the main themes of the first movement. The quartet's innovation lies less in its specific techniques (which had all been used in earlier works) than in its open acknowledgment of the American "ultramodern" tradition of Ives, Ruggles, Cowell, Ruth Crawford Seeger, and Nancarrow, whose music Carter quotes, as noted above.[40] The quartet sent a clear signal that Carter's shift away from neoclassicism, which had begun some time before, was finally complete. In this work, he successfully merged the European traditions that had shaped his music until then with the "dissonant, 'advanced' music [of the American ultramoderns], the kind that I'd first liked and that had first attracted me to music."[41] The quartet was premièred by the Walden Quartet on 26 February 1953 at the McMillin Theatre of Columbia University, but the subsequent performance by the Parrenin Quartet on 11 April 1954 during the festival "Music in the Twentieth Century" in Rome attracted far more attention. Buoyed by the first prize of the Concours International de Composition pour Quatuor à Cordes in Liège and thrust into the limelight of an international festival, Carter's quartet received wide exposure but mixed reviews.[42] Perhaps not surprisingly, Carter's friend William Glock, in the journal *Encounter*, a publication of the Congress for Cultural Freedom (which had also sponsored the festival) praised

first performance on 31 January and 1 February 1952, with Dimitri Mitropoulos conducting the New York Philharmonic.

39 Elliott Carter, postcard to David Carter, [January 1951]; photocopy in the Elliott Carter Collection, Paul Sacher Foundation.

40 See Anne C. Shreffler, "Elliott Carter and His America," *Sonus* 14/2 (Spring 1994), pp. 38–66, esp. 50–51 and 61–62.

41 Jonathan W. Bernard, "An Interview with Elliott Carter," *Perspectives of New Music* 28/2 (Summer 1990), pp. 180–214, esp. 192.

42 One critic found the quartet impenetrable (Fedele d'Amico, "Current Chronicle," *The Musical Quarterly* 40/4 [October 1954], pp. 587–594, esp. 589); another wrote that it "showed exceptionally virile writing, but a fantasy so uncontrolled that it

abandoned musical coherence" (Reginald Smith Brindle, "Notes from Abroad," *The Musical Times* 95, no. 1336 [June 1954], pp. 328–329, esp. 328); and an Austrian critic did not mention it at all (Helmuth A. Fiechtner, "Tonkunst und Debatten beim Römischen Musikkongreß," *Österreichische Musikzeitschrift* 9/5 [May 1954], pp. 159–160).

the work's "tough[ness]," "strength and grandeur," in contrast to Henze's *Boulevard Solitude*, which combined "trite rhythms and dreary harmonies" and "drove the Italian audience quite mad."[43] The recording by the Walden Quartet probably did even more than these early performances to make the work known during the late 1950s and early 1960s.[44] In the meantime it has lost its shock value, though not its effectiveness, and is now considered to be one of Carter's most powerful and communicative works.

53 *String Quartet No. 1* (1950–51), photostat full score with autograph annotations, p. 41

This page shows the beginning of the work's notated second part, a scherzo here marked "Allegro scorrevole," although the scherzo movement is actually almost over, having already started some hundred bars earlier. The almost literal repetition in mm. 1–8 of part II of the last eight bars of part I (visible here in the correspondence of mm. 540–544 with mm. 4–8) creates an audible overlap, as if the work were a tape or film that has been momentarily rewound. Part II contains the entire third movement, Adagio, as well as the beginning of the final variations movement. The scherzo's fast tempo, the high degree of similarity among the four instruments, the conjunct motion, and the rhythmic uniformity contrast in almost every respect to the first movement. Small cells of three to five notes are freely circulated among the instruments in a homogeneous texture; the contrapuntal layers so often found in Carter's music are absent here. The small melodic intervals and quicksilver speed recall the fourth piece from *Eight Etudes and a Fantasy* for woodwind quartet, which is alluded to earlier in the movement (part I / mm. 472–475). The beginning of part II also displays a marked similarity to the scherzo of Ruth Crawford Seeger's *String Quartet 1931,* which Carter knew well.[45] Like the better-known references to Ives and Nancarrow, the unmistakable allusion to Crawford's quartet was a sign of respect for a work highly esteemed in American ultramodern circles, even if Carter did not acknowledge it explicitly at the time.[46]

Sonata for Flute, Oboe, Cello, and Harpsichord (1952)

Although the scoring of Carter's next large-scale work, the *Sonata for Flute, Oboe, Cello, and Harpsichord,* may kindle associations with neoclassicism, the composer stayed firmly on his modernist course. The three-movement work, composed for the harpsichordist Sylvia Marlowe and her Harpsichord Quartet, is far removed from the (neo-)baroque trio sonata not only in its compositional fabric, but also in the balance of the instruments. The harpsichord is treated with complete independence, framed by the flute, oboe, and cello. Moreover, the instrument Carter had in mind was not the historical harpsichord but its mid-twentieth-century descendant, with its powerful volume of sound and great variety of stops. Carter himself tested the dynamic and timbral potential of just such an instrument on a borrowed Challis harpsichord. Rather than referring directly to the music of the baroque masters, he followed in the footsteps of Claude Debussy, who reinterpreted and transformed eighteenth-century principles of musical design in a modernist spirit in his final three sonatas, which, as is well known, were originally meant to be augmented by another for oboe, horn, and harpsichord. "I put myself in his [Debussy's] position, a little, when I began to write my sonata," Carter said in retrospect, pointing out that he was interested not least in Debussy's conception of form, particularly his avoidance of "expositions and developments" in favor of a "free succession of episodes" (*CC,* p. 60). The *Sonata for Flute, Oboe, Cello, and Harpsichord* was premièred in Carnegie Recital Hall on 10 November 1953,[47] with Sylvia Marlowe accompanied by Claude Monteux (flute), Harry Shulman (oboe), and Bernard Greenhouse (cello).

43 William Glock, "Music Festival in Rome," *Encounter* 2/6 (June 1954), pp. 60–63, esp. 63. On the Congress for Cultural Freedom, see below, p. 126.

44 Elliott Carter, *String Quartet [No. 1]*; Walden Quartet. Columbia ML 5104 (recorded on 2 February 1955, released in June 1956).

45 See Nancy Yunhwa Rao, "Ruth Crawford's Imprint on Contemporary Composition,"

in *Ruth Crawford Seeger's Worlds: Innovation and Tradition in Twentieth-Century American Music,* ed. Ray Allen and Ellie M. Hisama (Rochester, NY: University of Rochester Press, 2007), pp. 110–147, esp. 120–125.

46 Carter discusses Crawford's quartet in his 1965 article, "Expressionism in American Music" (*Perspectives of New Music* 4/1 [Fall–Winter 1965], pp. 1–13, esp. 9; most

recently reprinted in *CEL,* pp. 72–83, esp. 79), and has often expressed his esteem for Crawford's music, but he never drew attention to the Crawford connection in his *String Quartet No. 1* as he had done with the Ives and Nancarrow references.

47 The date is incomplete in Link 2000, p. 48 ("November 1953") and incorrect in Schiff 1983/1998, pp. 164 and 111, respectively ("19 November 1953").

54 *Sonata for Flute, Oboe, Cello, and Harpsichord*

54 *Sonata for Flute, Oboe, Cello, and Harpsichord* (1952), autograph full score in ink, p. [1]

Unlike his first work for Sylvia Marlowe, the unfinished *Sonatina for Oboe and Harpsichord* of 1947 (see above, pp. 84–85), the *Sonata for Flute, Oboe, Cello, and Harpsichord* no longer resorts to traditional formal models such as sonata-allegro form. This is patently evident in the opening movement, which is conceived as a single large arc of tension beginning with a "splashing dramatic gesture whose subsiding ripples form the rest of the movement."[48] Notwithstanding the vividness of Carter's aqueous metaphor, the movement's formal design can be related equally well to a purely musical phenomenon – namely, the typical sound production of the harpsichord, in which a sharp plucked attack is followed by a rapid decay. The sound-curve produced by striking a key on the harpsichord is, one might say, projected macroscopically onto the large-scale form: it is replicated in slow motion in a sixty-eight-bar process during which an initial jolt of energy gradually dissipates. Here we see the first eight measures of Carter's fair copy of the full score, showing the movement's dramatic opening impetus. A harpsichord figure enters with striking chords and subsequent tremors, triggering a violent response from the other three instruments in which the buoyant gestures of flute, oboe, and cello blend into a densely woven, continuous skein of sound. As always, Carter has meticulously marked the dynamics and articulation in the musical text. This time he has also added symbols for *Hauptstimme* (in square brackets) and suggestions for the harpsichord stops. At the same time he has conceded a certain licence to the performer, especially with regard to rhythm: the entire opening section, unlike the later section in strict "Tempo giusto" (mm. 30ff.), is meant to be played "un poco rubato," that is, with a certain agogic flexibility. This manuscript is also the first to show the subsequent dedication to Kurt Stone, who accepted the work for Associated Music Publishers in 1957 after rejecting it in 1955.[49] At the time of the première, however, the sonata still bore a dedication to the woman who commissioned it, Sylvia Marlowe.

"The Need for New Choral Music" (1953)

On 10–11 August 1953 Carter took part in a symposium organized by the Harvard Summer School under the title "The American Composer and Choral Music" and consisting of round-table discussions and concerts. For this event he prepared the following lecture, which is published here for the first time. He delivered it on 11 August 1953 during an afternoon panel discussion led by Virgil Thomson on "The Need for New Choral Music." (Another lecture was delivered by Irving Fine.) The symposium ended on the same evening with a concert in which the Harvard Summer School Chorus, conducted by Harold C. Schmidt, sang works by Randall Thompson (*The Last Words of David*), Carter (*Musicians Wrestle Everywhere*), and Fine (*Choruses from "The Hour Glass"*) as well as Virgil Thomson's *Hymns from the Old South* and excerpts from Act III of *Four Saints in Three Acts*, conducted by the composer. A few days later Thomson reported on the event in the *New York Herald Tribune*. He began by stating the widespread opinion (also shared by the symposium's organizers) that American choral music as a whole fell short of the high level reached by its European counterpart. He then continued: "The choral conductors present were all for changing this situation by a program of commissioning choral works and of collaborating technically with composers. The composers [however] showed small enthusiasm for the prospect, harped continually on the musical and textual limits of the choral medium, on its compromising associations with musical amateurism, and its hopeless involvement with all that is most basic in American life."[50] This was precisely the view maintained by Carter, who, in his lecture, emphasized the limits of the medium itself and those of existing choral societies, concluding that "for me at least the time for writing deliberately simplified music has come to an end." Indeed, for decades he wrote no further choral or unaccompanied vocal music. It was not until 2007, exactly sixty years after *Emblems* (1947), that he finally returned to the medium with his John Ashbery settings *Mad Regales* for six solo voices, thereby acknowledging the fact that, in the intervening years, several vocal ensembles on the contemporary music scene had reached a level of skill and virtuosity barely imaginable in the 1950s.

48 Elliott Carter, liner notes for the recording Nonesuch Records H-71234, reprinted under the title "Two Sonatas, 1948 and 1952" in *CEL*, pp. 228–231, esp. 231.

49 See letters from Kurt Stone to Elliott Carter, 5 May 1955 and 8 August 1957; Elliott Carter Collection, Paul Sacher Foundation.

50 Virgil Thomson, "Choral Conference," *The New York Herald Tribune*, 16 August 1953; quoted from idem, *Music Reviewed, 1940–1954* (New York: Vintage Books [Random House], 1966), pp. 373–375, esp. 374.

55   Elliott Carter, "The Need for New Choral Music" (1953)

[Ladies and gentlemen,]
That there is a need for new choral music on the part of performers as well as of the listening public, although they may not always be aware of if, seems to me to be obvious. But why three composers of choral music should stand up here and bring this matter to your attention is not so clear to me, since whatever we may say will lose its force because it will inevitably be suspected of special pleading. Composers are hardly the ones to emphasize the need for new music, since the very existence of their works should be demonstration enough that they believe such a need exists. In fact, I, for one, would feel much more comfortable if I were sitting where you are, being persuaded by one of you, a music lover, a singer, or a conductor, up here that there is a need for new choral music. For after writing a number of choral works and having them seldom performed and even more seldom performed in an understanding way, I have often felt that there was no need at all for new choral music, especially as I have also noticed that many excellent works of my colleagues, both those here present and others, do not have a very much happier fate. Really, you know, it should be your turn to explain to us that there is a need and not expect us to do a salemanship job. There are men who devote their whole effort to selling and know how to do it better than we. Indeed, from what I have noticed, most of us composers, at least as far as our own works are concerned, still live back in that old-fashioned era when it was assumed that quality would eventually win recognition, and that to promote one's wares too intensively might very well bring one under the suspicion that one was not too sure of their intrinsic merit, that too much was being sacrificed for advertising and too little devoted to improving the product. We "benighted composers" believe in our products and often assume that they will make their own way, and on the whole our experience shows this to be true if we have enough patience.

In spite of these considerations it is not at all surprising really that composers have been asked to deal with this subject. For one thing, it is the composer's notes collected over many generations that have made choruses, indeed most performing organizations, what they are. These scores have not only set the standard of what choral singing is to be but have made choral singing the exciting and meaningful thing it is. And it is the scores of more recent composers that will cause choruses to develop and change and not get stuck in ruts. But another, probably more immediate, reason for our presence is that ever since the decline of aristocratic patronage, composers have had to further their own cause and to fight for their proper due of recognition. Indeed ever since about 1925 composers in this country, under the double impetus of fighting for two causes, the cause of so-called "modern music" and the cause of American music, have made a vigorous effort to bring themselves as a group before the public. They have sought all sorts of positions – in teaching, on newspapers, on boards of foundations – from which they could exercise power and educate (some have called it "condition") the musical world and the public at large to recognize and respect the newer points of view.

Today those of us who have been active in various ways in furthering these two causes are beginning to witness the acceptance of the music which we have made such a fuss about for so many years. Last night, at Sanders Theatre, I could not help thinking that all three of the works presented[51] were given their American premieres by organizations with which I have been connected. What a struggle it was to keep these groups going – I refer to the League of Composers and the International Society for Contemporary Music – in the face of public apathy [and] small attendance. It was done by a continual effort of a small group mostly of composers during times when our efforts seemed fruitless and often worthy of the severe criticism which no one hesitated to pile on us. I remembered, too, how at a reception for Bartók when he first came to live in this country before the war, the League gave this very 2-piano sonata played by the composer and his wife, and how perplexed many of us were by the first movement, which today holds no problems. How later, because of this bewilderment, we arranged for another performance at ISCM concerts. As a result of our hard work such music as this became known to an ever wider circle until today it is quite generally enjoyed.[52]

Such efforts as ours in New York, which had their like all over this country, started at a time when the eminent composers of today were quite generally disliked,

---

51   On the evening of 10 August 1953 the piano duo of Karl and Margaret Kohn, joined by two percussionists, had presented Stravinsky's *Sonata* and *Concerto for two pianos* as well as Bartók's *Sonata for Two Pianos and Percussion.*

52   The League of Composers concert at which Bartók and his wife Ditta Bartók-Pásztory (together with the percussionists Saul Goodman and Henry Denecke, Jr.) played the *Sonata for Two Pianos and Percussion* took place in New York's Town Hall on 3 November 1940. The performance at which the ISCM was involved may have been the CBS radio broadcast given on 10 November 1940 before a select audience with the percussionists Henry J. Baker and Edward J. Rubsam. Bartók and his wife are not known to have given another performance of the original version of this work before the American première of the version with orchestral accompaniment, performed in Carnegie Hall on 21–22 January 1943 with the New York Philharmonic conducted by Fritz Reiner.

and finally resulted not only in their acceptance but, more importantly, in their being surrounded by a small group of understanding musicians whose encouragement helped them to follow their own direction. It is indeed hard to imagine the fate of Stravinsky and Bartók in this country if they had had to face as hostile a public, a press, and a musical profession as the League of Composers did in the 20s and 30s when it first began to present their works.

Having gone through many such experiences and having noticed that many who received almost immediate acceptance, such as, for instance, Sibelius and Shostakovich, have gradually lost out while interest in the more adventurous composers continues to grow, many composers tend to feel that too direct a contact with the public taste can have its drawbacks. It ought to be evident to you that none of the works you heard last night could have been written at the time they were in response either to public or even to any but the most special demands of an unusually advanced musical group. That part of their quality resides in the fact that they were the logical continuation of the composer's development at the time he wrote [them] and each has a kind of force which it would not have had if it had not grown up under rather sheltered conditions. Following along this train of thought, many composers have felt that most choral organizations have been less receptive to new trends than almost any other type of musical performing group, and this has hindered them from devoting their best energies to compositions for such groups. Certainly the kind of choral music which generally is performed depends in its point of view and expression clearly on older music. More and more today, composers are losing interest in following older methods and hence quickly run up against difficulties with choral conductors and singers.

On the debit side, too, many feel the great limitations of writing for chorus, which next to the freedoms of instrumental music seem unbearably constricting. Each step in writing a chorus is beset with problems. For beside[s] writing coherent, expressive, well-composed music, a composer has to be very careful of a host of problems revolving around the text and around the limitations of choral performers. Many of us, for instance, are enthusiastic readers of contemporary poetry, but how few of us dare to set the poems we like because of their compressed, difficult meanings. I find that no one minds a difficult text in a foreign language, such texts of Paul Eluard as Poulenc has set,[53] but a similar thing in English becomes a major deterrent to performance. Another big question in choral writing which each composer has to decide for himself is the degree to which the text should be projected to the audience. If the musical texture is contrapuntal, as much contemporary music is, it becomes impossible for the hearer to catch the words. Personally, I have always tried to leave one moment in each phrase of a work where the words can be clearly heard, but I find that most older composers, especially during the great choral periods, did not bother much about this. Also, of course, there is the question of diction, of writing lines which follow the rhythm and inflection of a poetic reading of the text, and so on. If you add all this together and combine it with the limitations of range, of intonation, of breathing, you end up by shutting the book of poetry and turning to some other, less thorny, kind of music.

As a practical example of what I say, I would like to tell you about a project of mine. Ever since I began to compose, I have had the idea of writing a large choral work based on Hart Crane's poem *The Bridge*. It is, as you know, a difficult, rather incoherent long poem filled with passages of great beauty that contain the kind of impassioned vision which many readers find very moving. Over the years I have gradually attempted to develop a style which would allow me the particular degree of flexibility [and] fancifulness combined with logic that would be suitable for this poem. I have also written a few trial pieces, one of which [is] a setting of the poet's piece called *Voyage* for soprano and piano which occasionally gets performed.[54] This text, speaking of the all-embracing character of the ocean, starts out with the words "Infinite consanguinity it bears" and goes on from there to words, if somewhat shorter, not any less compact in meaning. You can imagine, as I did before I started, what a curious situation it could be for a singer to stand up before the ordinary concert audience and start singing these long words so full of "i" sounds and to realize that the more precisely they are pronounced, the more puzzling they would be for the audience. At the insistence of some friends, I finally set the poem and find that at every performance

---

53 Carter was probably thinking primarily of Poulenc's choral cantata *La figure humaine* (1943), though he may also have been familiar with the cantata *Un soir de neige* (1944).

54 See above, pp. 56–61.

there are always a great many who are infuriated because they can't understand a word, particularly if the text is put in front of them. The effect of this song nearly made me give up the idea of setting *The Bridge,* doubting whether such elaborate language needed music. But each year the idea comes back to me, and at times I am on the verge of throwing all discretion to the winds and writing a piece just for myself. But so far I have not been able to get up the courage to devote the enormous time and effort it would take for such a composition and, since no publisher would probably touch it, to face the enormous outlay of money for copying parts for chorus & orchestra. It is for reasons such as this that I would like to hear from someone else that there is a need for really new choral music.

To approach this from another point of view: during the long period of propagandist effort for new music, which seems now to be drawing to a close, it was stimulating, indeed very tempting, to write choral music which embodied as many of the new musical techniques of our time as were consistent with the limitations of choral singing. It was a way of familiarizing singers with new idioms and a way of using these idioms for very direct expression. Many composers did just this, some of them tricking out in modern dress essentially conventional moods and methods, while others tried to go farther, almost always with far less acceptance.

An outsider always feels about choral organizations that they have their own special inner problems. Either they are amateur groups recruited from educational institutions, groups that are quick to understand but not so proficient technically, or else vice versa. Most professional choruses stick to the tried and true for obvious economic reasons. Therefore, in most cases recent American composers have written for college or music school groups, in which there is more receptiveness to the new, but because of their rather limited vocal resources they have been very hesitant to violate the familiar practices of choral writing and to employ bolder imaginative methods which they might if they were writing for more highly trained voices. Efforts in this latter direction usually lead to bewilderment and rejection. However, as time goes on, fewer and fewer composers seem to be able to adapt their ideas to the college level of competence with any zest, and so they take chances and try other methods.

For instance, for my choral piece *Emblems* for men's voices and piano, I wrote an *a cappella* introduction in a recitative style that used a technique of contrasting very thick and very thin textures in rather quick succession – in a way not too uncommon in instrumental music but rare in choral. Two conductors, whose opinions I respect, assured me that they could not make head or tail of it. Later, however, unknown to me, an American college group learned the work and performed [it] widely on a tour of Europe and later recorded it commercially.[55] On questioning them, I found that neither the singers nor the conductor found anything in the work which puzzled them once they got to know it. Having made many similar misjudgements myself on other composers' works, I was amused to have this happen to me. In fact, I must say that I am always a bit concerned when a piece of mine is accepted too easily, for then it never seems to gain very enthusiastic friends, everybody is just a little too lukewarm. To bear this out, my *Emblems* became the favorite piece of this particular college group in spite of the fact that the text is obscure and the music not easy to sing.

Experiences such as I have mentioned, as well as others, have led me to believe that for me at least the time for writing deliberately simplified music has come to an end. Naturally it is in the temperament of some composers [to] write simply, but there are others of us who are beginning to see new possibilities of musical expression which excite our imaginations, and while these may provoke us to do what may seem surprising and curious, these newer trends may eventually lead music to something valuable and interesting.

In such a spirit, a composer is tempted to dismiss choral music as being too constricting, too conventionalized in spirit to offer many new aspects. But those of us who love the sound of the human voice, both alone & in groups, will try somehow to use it in some personal and imaginative way which justifies the need for a new choral music that is not just a palimpsest, a rewriting of old music in modern script. This takes, as I have tried to point out, a large amount of courage, effort, and imagination, and since the choral world is not so progressive one has to expect misunderstanding, dislike, and lack of performance as a matter of course. But the fact that in choral

55 These were the Colgate College Singers, who toured Europe in summer 1952. Their recording of Carter's *Emblems* with the pianist Bernard Weiser, conducted by James Sykes, was announced as "in preparation" in Abraham Skulsky's 1953 list of Carter's works (*ACA Bulletin* 3/2 [summer 1953], pp. 12–16, esp. 15), but seems not to have been released.

music there is a chance for greater directness and power may encourage some of us, if we are lucky, to use these resources in our own ways.

For it ought to be apparent that the vast apparatus of musical performance is put into motion by the composer's imaginings. You might almost say that, if they were not always brought into being by the composer's thoughts, instruments were made what they are, new mechanisms added, new bows invented, new hammers, to carry out more perfectly what the composer was trying to express. Being neglected by him, sackbuts, sarrusophones and serpents have fallen into oblivion, while strings to meet his demands have risen to the ninth and eleventh positions. Whether composers can create a condition in which a sixth finger will grow on a performer and in which basses will be able to sing down to the lower Russian depths and sopranos reach the shrill shriek of the piccolo, is a matter of conjecture – no doubt they will try with the help of magnetic tape. Even choruses have developed new techniques, new methods of tone production, accuracy of intonation and, what is more important, a new understanding of music, through the stimulating efforts of new composers. For composers have taught performers new thoughts, new feelings, and a new freedom which is invigorating the whole musical world. Without him the elaborate apparatus would lose its power, its reason for being; without the leavening of his new imaginings the whole musical world, ever more meaninglessly repeating its Bach, Beethoven, & Brahms, would wither and fade. Freedom, fantasy, discipline, surprise, and delight would be gone, people would lose interest in singing, playing and listening, reeds would no longer be carved with loving care, strings tuned with precision, voices would die, and music would be silenced.

[Typescript with autograph corrections (annotation at the top of p 1: "*final* draft" [ending missing]"); Elliott Carter Collection, Paul Sacher Foundation.]

Getting Settled at the American Academy in Rome (1953)

In 1953 Carter won the American Prix de Rome, which enabled him to spend a year as a fellow of the American Academy in Rome.[56] Founded in 1894, this venerable institution had built up a music program after the First World War and offered its fellows a pleasant and stimulating working atmosphere amidst an interdisciplinary artists' colony. Carter's stay lasted from mid-September 1953 to mid-September 1954. Here he not only renewed his acquaintance with his colleagues and "co-fellows" Frank Wigglesworth and Yehudi Wyner, he also met his old friend Nicolas Nabokov, who at that time was composer-in-residence at the American Academy. In April 1954 Nabokov also organized a large-scale festival conference ("Music in the XXth Century") mounted by the Congress for Cultural Freedom in cooperation with the European Center of Culture in Geneva and the Italian Radio. (The Congress for Cultural Freedom and Nabokov's festivals are discussed below, p. 126.) Carter took advantage of his time in the Italian capital to work on his *Variations for Orchestra*, commissioned a short while earlier (June 1953) by the Louisville Orchestra. Finally, he made important contacts with such fellow-artists as the novelist Ignazio Silone and the musicians Goffredo Petrassi, Luigi Dallapiccola, and Roman Vlad, with all of whom he forged long friendships. The following letter to Aaron Copland, written shortly after he moved to Rome, recounts Carter's living conditions and asks for Copland's help in obtaining an extension of his stay in Italy. He also tells him about the success of his *String Quartet No. 1* at the Concours International de Composition pour Quatuor à Cordes in Liège, a competition sponsored by the Koussevitzky Music Foundation. This work, submitted in late September under the fitting pseudonym "XPONO–METPOΣ" (Chronometros), was selected from 117 compositions and awarded the first prize. Carter unquestionably profited from the prestige associated with this award. However, he was ultimately forced to turn down the prize money of 40,000 Belgian francs, because the piece had already been played by the Walden Quartet in several places. Not having heard from the competition for months, Carter had released the work for performance on the assumption that it had met with disapproval.

---

56 The jury that chose composers for that year was chaired by Randall Thompson and also included Copland, Normand Lockwood, Nicolas Nabokov, and Walter Piston. See letter from Mary T. Williams, Executive Secretary, American Academy in Rome, to Nicolas Nabokov, 22 December 1952; Harry Ransom Humanities Research Center, University of Texas at Austin, Nicolas Nabokov Papers: Box 1, folder 7.

56 Elliott Carter to Aaron Copland, 11 October 1953

American Academy in Rome / Via Angelo Masina,
5 (Porta S. Pancrazio) / Rome
October 11, 1953

Dear Aaron,

Life is gradually getting over the comedy-of-errors stage for us here and we are beginning to be able to look around. It seems that if you are a tourist you can look around, but if you live in a place you hardly have time to see anything, and this is as true here as it is in New York. Finding an apartment, getting a maid, getting meals started have made us feel as if we were in a Mack Sennett silent movie, except that there were no subtitles to help us understand. Helen knows the past of verbs and I the future, and between us things are gradually getting done – with lots spilling out of the purse. Allen Tate is the poet in residence here and Nicolas [Nabokov] with his pretty wife and daughter is the composer, and we look with envying eye at the ease (or comparative ease) with which things get done in the Villa Aurelia.[57]

Next year, if nothing more interesting turns up in the US, we would like to stay here so as to get a little more use out of our long winter underwear and to really settle down to enjoying ourselves. After a considerable amount of struggle I have gotten a piano that works in a studio overlooking the vegetable garden which I enjoy and would like to continue to use. Hence the enclosed, which I hate to burden you with, especially in view of all the kindnesses you have done for me in the past.[58] It will mean a lot for me to be able to stay on, for I have just only begun to do the kind of work in which I can be useful. I shall be on the ISCM international jury to choose the festival programs in Jerusalem this year,[59] and hope to be active in other ISCM affairs all year.

Again I want to thank you and the others of the Koussevitzky Foundation for the commission; I will try and finish it this spring.[60] As you may have heard, that Foundation is also going to give me $800 because that string quartet of mine won the first prize in the Liège

international competition. Apparently the performers found it so hard they had to have a conductor. They tried to get William Walton, who was there, but he refused, although rather impressed.[61] Five out of seven judges were for the work. Paul Collaer, Jean Absil, Fernand Quinet, and the heads of various Belgian conservatories were the judges.[62]

Helen and David join me in sending you our best, with the hope that you had a fine trip to Mexico.[63]

Affectionately, and thanks,
Elliott

57 David Carter at the age of eleven (Christmas 1954)

---

57 As they were unable to live on the Academy's premises, the Carters initially took rooms in the Hotel Inghilterra, at that time still modest, and spent several weeks looking for a suitable apartment. They finally settled on a flat in Via Trebbia no. 3, near the Piazza Fiume, where David could attend the American school in the north of Rome while his father did his work in a studio of the Academy's Casa Rustica, half an hour away by bus. The composer-in-residence, Nabokov, had much more comfortable accommodation in Apartment A of the Villa Aurelia, located next to the Academy building on

the Janiculum. Later this apartment was placed at Carter's disposal during his own stays in Rome as composer-in-residence in 1962–63, 1968–69, and 1979–80.

58 Copland acceded to Carter's request for help in extending his stay in Rome by sending, as we know from Carter's letter of thanks, a "very nice letter" which is no longer extant; see letter from Elliott Carter to Aaron Copland, 26 November 1953 (carbon copy in the Elliott Carter Collection, Paul Sacher Foundation). After some discussion, Carter received such an extension but ultimately turned it down. Years later, he recalled that his

decision was based not only on the inconvenient living situation, but also on financial considerations: "[...] the Fellowship money I received from the Academy did not even cover the rent, not to mention the cost of the American school for my son, where he was not too happy." (Elliott Carter, "Reminiscence of Italy" (1988), *CEL*, pp. 292–284, esp. 294).

59 The jury for the 1954 ISCM festival did not convene until January 1954 (in Rome), and the festival itself did not take place in Jerusalem but in Haifa from 30 June to 10 July 1954.

"Music in the United States" (1954)

While in residence at the American Academy in Rome during the academic year 1953–54, Carter wrote the following essay on the current state of music in the U.S. The exact purpose is still unclear: it could have been a lecture given at the Rome festival in April 1954, in which he participated as a panelist, or possibly a talk at an American Academy event.[64] (Carter typically did not write such texts without a specific occasion.) It appeared in French in the Belgian journal *Synthèses*, a multidisciplinary journal founded in 1946. Featuring articles on literature, the arts, politics, technology, and business, the journal was politically non-aligned, but in its dedication to humanistic values and individual liberty also staked out an emphatically non-Communist position.[65] It was probably Nabokov who recommended to Carter that he send his text to *Synthèses*; although this was not one of the Congress for Cultural Freedom's "house" journals, Nabokov evidently did have some connection with its editors.[66] Nabokov probably also had something to do with the (uncredited) French translation of Carter's text: first, a sentence describing general characteristics of American intellectual and artistic life is tweaked to highlight that favorite Cold War word "freedom." Another indicator of Nabokov's involvement is a list of European immigrant composers who had exerted "enormous influence" on American musical life, in which "Nabokov" [!] was substituted for the politically unpalatable "Eisler." As in his "Music in America at War" outline (see above, pp. 67–70), Carter describes here for a foreign readership the decentralized structures of American musical life and the extreme variety of approaches on the composition scene. However, this text is much more detailed than the earlier one, discussing individual composers and their works, as well as pointing out the importance of institutions such as the Boston Symphony Orchestra under Koussevitzky, Howard Hanson's role at the Eastman School of Music, and the Louisville Orchestra's commissioning project. Carter continues to divide American music into two large categories, nationally-oriented (Americanist) and international, with both groups spanning the spectrum from conservative to avant-garde. A historiography that places Douglas Moore and Harry Partch in the same category (the Americanist one), or Samuel Barber and John Cage (in the internationalist one) may seem strange today but reflects ongoing debates of the time about the role of national identity in a postwar international environment. Carter emphasizes that American music had already become independent of Europe by the 1930s, and had maintained its character and identity despite the influence of the European exile composers. He even makes a stab at describing what "general, undefinable characteristics" distinguish American music from European music – these are primarily kinetic and rhythmic features – but acknowledges that these "are too intuitive to be discussed." To counter possible European perceptions of the United States as a cultural backwater, Carter points out the high standards of musical performance and the expanding audience for classical and new music. The tone is optimistic about the state of American music, in marked contrast to views that Carter would express elsewhere. The original version of this essay, in English, is printed here for the first time.

58 Elliott Carter, "Music in the United States" (1954)

To form an adequate idea of the present state of music in the United States, it is necessary to conceive of a rapidly changing, unpredictable situation in which little remains fixed for very long except the desire to hear and to produce excellent performances of the standard repertory of classics. Popular music ["la musique de jazz"], of course, changes style from year to year, sometimes striking out on astonishing new paths, and the growing understanding and enjoyment of contemporary music varies greatly from group to group. Each year more people join the large audience of intelligent listeners spread out over the country and more good performers and composers achieve reputations. Only the group of amateur musicians who read music for their own enjoyment does not

60 The work commissioned for the Koussevitzky Foundation in the Library of Congress – a sonata for two pianos – was never carried out, though a number of sketches for it have survived; see below, pp. 122–123.

61 The presentation of the award-winning work lay in the hands of the Quatuor Municipal de Liège; Carter's piece was conducted by the composer René Defossez.

62 Besides the journalist Paul Collaer and the composers Fernand Quinet and Jean Absil (head of the Liège Conservatoire), the jury also included René Defossez, Léon Jongen (head of the Brussels

Conservatoire), and two members of the Quatuor Municipal de Liège, Henri Koch and Eric Feldbusch.

63 Copland had traveled to Mexico in September 1953 to conduct a series of concerts with the Orquesta Sinfónica Nacional.

64 Nabokov had invited Carter to participate in a panel called "Aesthetics and Technique" (see his letter to Carter, 4 February 1954; Elliott Carter Collection, Paul Sacher Foundation). A lecture on music in the United States would not have fit in this panel, but may have been presented at another time during the conference.

65 See "Esprit de Synthèse," foreword to the issue of May 1954.

66 Frances Stonor Saunders writes: "Soon after [May 1950], Nabokov, accompanied by Denis de Rougemont, went to Brussels to address a dinner sponsored by the magazine *Synthèses*." (Frances Stonor Saunders, *Who Paid the Piper? The CIA and the Cultural Cold War* [London: Granta Books, 1999], p. 100.) The issue in which Carter's essay appeared also featured an advertisement for the Congress of Cultural Freedom's journal *Preuves*.

seem to be increasing as fast because their place seems to have been taken by the widely scattered group of record collectors. Because of the variety, the size, and the complexity of this development, this article proposes to limit itself to sketching the broad outlines of the schools of American composition against the background of the musical activity from which they emerged.

During the past fifty years the United States has shared with Europe in a rapid broadening out of the musical horizon to all levels of society through education and through the effects of mechanical reproduction of music and its radio transmission. The results of these popularizing efforts have been especially marked in America because half a century ago very few were interested in music. Since then this number has grown greatly, not only through widespread diffusion of music, but also because of the increase in population. This expansion of interest has caused such a change in musical life that even someone living in its midst can hardly form an idea of it. Today those occupied with the various commercial branches of the art like to point out that music is the third largest industry in the country. This does not convey the level of quality, nor which branch makes the most money. But it does suggest how numerous are symphony orchestras, music schools, performers, conductors, composers, publishers, and especially listeners. To many the number of competent composers of concert music (which is thought to be about 1,500) seems small for a country of this size by comparison with the vast number of performers.

It is always as difficult to assess the quality of music in one's own country as it is that in another. Perhaps some indication can be had from the fact that many American-trained instrumentalists and singers are replacing European musicians in orchestras and opera houses, which still maintain the same high standards. At the same time more native soloists make their appearances side by side with their foreign colleagues, often receiving equal acclaim. The day is past when an American had to study a long time in Europe, achieve a reputation there, and even in some cases continentalize his name before he could be successful at home.

Public taste itself has developed to the point where the masterpieces of new and old European music are demanded of performers. Beethoven and Brahms are rivals in popularity over the radio, while Bartók, Stravinsky, and Copland are often asked for. In this American audiences are like European audiences; however, in most parts of the country concerts attract an ever increasing new audience still unfamiliar with the classic repertoire. In the larger cities, there [are] audiences now quite familiar with these standard works who wish to hear unusual music, both new and old.

Since this development has taken place over such a wide area in such a short time, no single national musical style either of performance or of composition has emerged. Instead there are many, depending on the individual's teacher, his education, and his personal contacts. For this reason, the United States presents, perhaps, a more varied and complex picture than almost any European country, and it is nearly impossible to make any significant generalization except the obvious one that, taken as a whole, its music reflects the freedom, the adventurousness, the enthusiasm, the seriousness of purpose, and the diversity which characterize all American intellectual and artistic efforts at the present time.

A closer consideration of musical composition brings to light at once the special cultural problems faced by a new country. American music was awakened from its provincial lethargy by the impact of the revolution initiated by Bartók, Schoenberg, and Stravinsky just before World War I, and by the jazz of the same period. The effect of these two influences did not stimulate composers to imitate but to be inspired by the remarkable liberty toward tradition which these new iconoclasts revealed. Previously European influences such as German romanticism, Italian opera, and French impressionism had only evoked poor imitations. This new influence stirred musicians to life and helped them to create a series of original compositions so convincing and well-written that the foundations were laid for a truly native but varied school. After around 1935, when a number of these works had been written, no American composer could create without taking some aspect of this school into account, for a climate had been established in which American music could grow. And since each of the composers participating in this sudden birth had a style of his own, several different directions which American music was to follow were established.

These different directions developed under quite different conditions from those which exist in Europe. American music is still in the position of having to prove its worth to the general public. There are practically no state subventions of orchestras, opera houses, radio stations, and conservatories. Each of the first three of these has to appeal incessantly to a very large section of the public; otherwise its economic support disappears and, as occasionally happens, the institution fails. There is, therefore, a great deal of hesitation over playing new music and especially new American orchestral music by relatively unknown composers. American musicians who come to Europe with the aid of government grants and private fellowships (most of which require residence in Europe) look with envy on the number of opera and radio performances which contemporary European works receive, realizing such opportunities are unavailable at home. Actually the first encouragement for American composers came from small societies dedicated to presenting contemporary music. Later, during the depression, they had a brief taste of government support when orchestras of unemployed musicians were formed especially to play American music. But very soon this ceased and most composers returned to their chamber music societies for performances.

Only two outstanding efforts were made in these early years to encourage orchestral composition. One by the successful and popular conductor of the Boston Symphony, Serge Koussevitzky, who commissioned and played works by Copland, Roy Harris, Roger Sessions, Walter Piston, William Schuman, Samuel Barber, and David Diamond. The other effort was made by Howard Hanson in his annual American Music Festivals at the Eastman School of Music in Rochester, New York, who has played orchestral works of almost all American composers. Aside from these two isolated efforts, which have had no successors, little of this kind was accomplished until recently, when the symphony orchestra of Louisville, Kentucky, received a large sum of money from the Rockefeller Foundation to commission and play many European and American orchestral scores.[67] Nevertheless, the great majority of works are for chamber combinations, as there is a demand for these by recitalists and the small ensembles that play in universities. For it is in universities, such as the University of Illinois, where professional string quartets and other ensembles are appointed members of the music faculty, that contemporary music is most appreciated and encouraged.

To consider now the present direction of musical composition, one must first examine its relationship to Europe. There is a very natural tendency for Europeans to prefer that works of art produced outside their culture should emphasize what they think of as national charac-

teristics of the country of origin. The success of certain nationalist composers like Moussorgsky, Sibelius, and Vaughan Williams in creating a serious and human musical language out of folklore has impressed many Americans. Yet it must be remembered that the United States does not have this rich folklore tradition of Russia, England, etc., and to follow the philosophy of these composers is nearly impossible there. Twenty or thirty years ago this question was thought about a great deal by composers who made a determined effort not only to find a personal style but also one that was strikingly national. At present this is a matter of little concern, since it is becoming clear that a work of high inspiration and quality often confounds preconceived programs, and that American music will be established by good works, not by following a nationalistic dogma.

By nature the American musical world is essentially eclectic, as both the music and the musicians or their ancestors came from other countries of established traditions. The concert hall and opera house are the symbol of this, and musicians are brought up in their shadow. Thus in many respects the art adheres to international standards, and techniques travel from one country to another, so that it is no more surprising that an American composer should be influenced, for instance, by Viennese dodecaphonic technique than that a French or an Italian one should be. The fact that nowadays Americans feel free to absorb many foreign influences, indeed, may be a sign of maturity. For, as was pointed out, the works written around 1930 have furnished a climate, a basis for comparison, a clearly defined school which seems to have been so strongly established that in spite of the enormous influence which Bartók, Stravinsky, Schoenberg, Krenek, Hindemith, Toch, Weill, Eisler,[68] and Milhaud exerted while they inhabited the United States during the war, no serious young composer wishes to write in the style of any of these, and their former students make great efforts to throw off their teachers' influence. For American musicians do feel that certain general, undefinable characteristics now distinguish their music from that of Europe. Some have tried to relate them to the simple difference in habits of muscular tension and relaxation which causes Americans to stand, walk, act, and use their voices in a distinctly native way. Others maintain that Americans adhere to a strict regularity of pulse even when the music they perform or write grows more or less excited, louder or softer, and that this is what makes American

---

67 See below, p. 121.
68 In the French translation, Eisler's name is
replaced with Nabokov's.

music difficult for foreigners to play effectively. So far, however, these qualities, if they exist, are not generally agreed upon and are too intuitive to be discussed.

A helpful way of clarifying general tendencies is to divide American composition into two large categories: one which evokes a native spirit by the use of folklore or by some other means, and the other, which is more international in attitude. In each of these categories can be found many styles: conservative, advanced, and extreme. The problem of the first is complicated by the fact that folk music in America is as eclectic as its population which, once transplanted and cross-bred, took on a new character, such as the crossing of Spanish, Irish, and English melodies that produced cowboy songs. Overcoming this eclecticism, by focusing on these newer manifestations, Roy Harris and Aaron Copland evolved styles which captured and intensified, each in his own way, [their] feelings about the American milieux in which these newer songs were born. Of the two, Harris's music is the more romantic, while Copland's is the more nervous, rhythmic, and subtle. Their earliest compositions, more advanced than their more recent works, immediately attracted musicians in the late 1920s.

A little later a curious figure appeared: Virgil Thomson, who not only had been influenced by Erik Satie, but who also assumed the role of the Satie of American music. He preached simplicity, the avoidance of "academic" methods, and the poetry of naive and humble origins. In his surprising opera *Four Saints in Three Acts*, to an almost dadaist text by Gertrude Stein, this composer dealt with the American scene in a new way, by reassembling in new contexts all the elements of simple, uncultivated, popular American religious music and producing an unexpectedly sophisticated result, much as Satie did with circus music in *Parade*.[69] Like Satie, Thomson influenced the thinking of a whole group of composers no longer interested in the experimental side of contemporary music and eager to reach a wider audience. With Copland, this influence led to that serene idealization of America with its gentle touches of humor and its moving nobility which now marks all of his work.

In this very large folklorist field, there are conservatives like Howard Hanson, Douglas Moore, and the re-

cent works of Henry Cowell, and extremists like Charles Ives and Harry Partch, whose music employs 43 and more divisions of the octave, with many composers of different styles in between.

The same range of conservative to extreme marks those not concerned with "Americanizing." For instance, examples of the former, which are well-known and respected in Europe, are the works of Samuel Barber and Randall Thompson, while the extreme style was established about twenty-five years ago by Edgard Varèse, and today the experimentalists John Cage, Morton Feldman, Otto Luening, [and] Vladimir Ussachevsky work with *musique concrète* and other media.

In the midst of this international category stand its two most outstanding and individual exponents, Walter Piston and Roger Sessions. Piston, in a number of elegantly written works of neoclassic stamp, has developed a school of composers at Harvard University who, also influenced by Copland and Stravinsky (both lecturers there for a year), are becoming known by their leaders Harold Shapero, Lukas Foss, Irving Fine, and Arthur Berger.[70] Pursuing a different, more difficult, path, the music of Roger Sessions is being more and more admired today, now that musicians have begun to like Schoenberg and Berg. Previously Sessions's music was better known in Europe than at home, and it took a great deal of conviction for him to develop his complex, highly organized, and advanced style in the face of American disregard. Now his seriousness of purpose and his devotion to the tradition of music have not only won him many listeners but many interesting younger followers like Leon Kirchner, Andrew Imbrie, and Milton Babbitt, each of whom uses a more involved technique than has been customary in American music. Apart from the Sessions style, Wallingford Riegger has been writing in a personal type of dodecaphony for a number of years, and recently a new, more expressive way of using this method has been developed by Ben Weber.

The composition of concert music has been much more cultivated [than] that of opera in the United States. For, until recently, there has been very little opportunity for new operas to be produced. Large opera houses were and still are concerned almost entirely with the standard repertory. Quite recently, however, many universities with

---

69 Carter and Virgil Thomson were closer at this time than they would be later: in nominating Carter to the National Institute of Arts and Letters in 1956, Thomson referred to him "as the 'world's leading composer of contemporary chamber music'" (letter from Elliott Carter to Kurt Stone; Kurt Stone Collection, Irving S. Gilmore Music Library, Yale University). Thomson was also on the executive and the artistic committees of the Congress for Cultural Freedom. A fully-staged performance of *Four Saints in Three Acts* had been featured at the Congress's Paris festival in 1952, and Thomson had been involved in the planning of the 1954 Rome festival. Like Carter, Thomson was a close friend of Nabokov's. In retrospect Carter said of this work: "Nobody liked *Four Saints*. People thought the music not very interesting musically, though the Stein text was interesting." (Interview with Anthony Tommasini, 23 February 1994; quoted in idem, *Virgil Thomson: Composer in the Aisle* [New York and London: W.W. Norton, 1997], p. 201.)

70 At that time these composers, plus Alexei Haieff and Ingolf Dahl, were frequently grouped together under the label "Stravinsky school"; see Arthur Berger, "Stravinsky and the Younger American Composers," *The Score and I.C.A. Magazine*, no. 12 (June 1955), pp. 38–46.

Ideas for *The Score* (1954–55)

large music schools, theaters, and well-equipped faculties have turned to the production of new works. A number of operas designed for these small performances, such as Gian Carlo Menotti's *The Medium* and Virgil Thomson's *The Mother of Us All*, were commissioned by the Opera Workshop of Columbia University in New York City and were so successfully received that they made the tour of the country, and now many composers are writing with this university organization in mind.[71] At the same time Marc Blitzstein and Kurt Weill developed an operatic style similar enough to American musical comedy to attract Broadway theatergoers and were followed by Menotti and Jerome Moross. Operas were also commissioned for television programs. None of these reached the large opera-house stages in the United States, except that of the New York City Center, now partly subventioned by city taxes. Here Copland's new opera *The Tender Land* has just received its première.[72]

It is impossible within the scope of this article to discuss popular music. It is perhaps enough to remark that today there is a great deal of influence of contemporary concert music in this domain. Many popular pieces are being recorded of such extreme dissonance and originality of orchestration that concert musicians are very surprised that the public likes them.

To sum up, the newness of America's musical growth, since it has lacked the firm support of a tradition, has resulted in much unevenness of standards and of approach. Without the guidance of respected native examples, composers have sometimes wandered up trivial bypaths, sometimes been involved with fruitless theories. But the most attractive result that this youthfulness has had is to surround American music with an atmosphere of freshness, of excited enthusiasm. To many listeners, performers, and composers, the art of music emerged suddenly as an unexpected source of pleasure and inspiration, and this discovery of a new and infinitely rewarding art world provided a moving experience which is reflected in all the best manifestations of American music.

[Typescript, carbon copy with title in French ("La Musique aux Etats-Unis / par / Elliott Carter") and autograph corrections; Elliott Carter Collection, Paul Sacher Foundation. Published in French as "La Musique aux Etats-Unis," *Synthèses*, no. 96 (May 1954), pp. 206–211.]

In the 1950s Carter deepened his contact with William Glock, who had become so interested in American music that he decided to make it the subject of an entire issue of *The Score*. He thus turned to Carter in a letter of 18 September 1954, seeking his advice on possible topics and authors. In his reply of 5 November 1954 Carter granted his request in great detail, pointing out some peculiarities and problems in American's current musical scene – with tangible concern about what he perceived to be its conservative and commercial trends. An exchange of further letters ensued, and half a year later, on 5 May 1955, Glock informed him that the America issue of *The Score* was making good progress. It finally appeared in June 1955 and contained articles by, among others, Arthur Berger, Milton Babbitt, John Cage, Henry Cowell, Richard Franko Goldman, Lou Harrison, and Virgil Thomson.[73] Glock had indeed adopted some of Carter's suggestions when designing the issue, and in April 1955 he received from him an article on "The Rhythmic Basis of American Music" – the very subject that Glock had proposed in his letter of 18 September 1954 in reference to Copland.[74] At the same time Glock asked for information on metrical modulation for his own article on Carter[75] – a request that Carter granted by return of post (on 9 May 1955). In retrospect, Carter called the issue "very interesting" and thought it represented "a quite different picture of our music than would appear in an American magazine." But he also expressed regret that the music of such composers as Stefan Wolpe, Ross Lee Finney, Leon Kirchner, Theodore Chanler, and Milton Babbitt had not been discussed.[76]

---

71 Menotti's *The Medium* (on a libretto by the composer) was premièred in Brander Matthews Theater of Columbia University on 8 May 1946, as was Thomson's *The Mother of Us All* (on a text by Gertrude Stein) on 7 May 1947. Both works were commissioned and financed by the Alice M. Ditson Fund, and both productions were conducted by Otto Luening.

72 The original two-act version of Copland's opera *The Tender Land* (on a libretto by Horace Everett a.k.a. Erik Johns) was premièred at the New York City Opera on 1 April 1954, conducted by Thomas Schippers. Copland later produced a longer three-act version of the piece.

73 *The Score and I.M.A. Magazine*, no. 12 (June 1955).

74 Elliott Carter, "The Rhythmic Basis of American Music," ibid., pp. 27–32; most recently reprinted in *CEL*, pp. 57–62.

75 William Glock, "A Note on Elliott Carter," ibid., pp. 47–52.

76 See letter from Elliott Carter to William Glock, 6 September 1955; William Glock Estate, British Library.

59 William Glock to Elliott Carter, 18 September 1954

The Score / 32B Cornwall Gardens / [London] S.W. 7
September 18, 1954

Dear Elliott,
It was very kind of you to send the L. P. recording of the Quartet,[77] and to give me the score of the 'cello sonata. Next year at Summer School we're going to have quite a Carter festival – with the piano and 'cello sonatas, and the string quartet, which the Juilliard (who will be giving six concerts) have agreed to learn for the occasion.[78] I gave a long talk on your things, and Racine Fricker was among many who said afterwards how impressed they were with the Quartet.

What I now want to do is to have an American issue of *The Score*. I'm thinking of asking Richard [Franko] Goldman for something (perhaps on yourself). Do you think you could help at all with this issue? Perhaps by suggesting the best critics (and subjects). I'd like to have something on the younger generation; also something on the "rhythmic basis" of American music that Aaron is always talking about. Also, perhaps, an article on American schools of music. What other composers? Is it possible to get a fresh and interesting article on Copland? I might perhaps look for that over here. As you see, I'm hardly ready yet to ask for clear and intelligible subjects. But I'll write again presently, and meanwhile if you have any striking thoughts on the matter I'd be most grateful to hear them. Awful to bother you with this immediately after your return. My idea is [to] bring out this American issue in June; i.e., the articles would all have to be finished by March 10 or 15. It would be very pleasant if you and two others (say) would compose short pieces for the occasion (in the same way as Stravinsky's *Symphonies* began in the *Revue musicale*).[79] (About 3 pages each!?) Please consider this.

Love to you both,
William

[Autograph letter; Elliott Carter Collection, Paul Sacher Foundation. Reprinted by permission of Sebastian Balfour and David Drew (William Glock Estate).]

60 Elliott Carter to William Glock, 5 November 1954

Dear William,
Thank you for your letter of September 18. I am sorry that I could not answer it sooner, especially as you are making such an effort on my behalf, for which I am extremely grateful.

I was of course very agreeably surprised that the Juilliard Quartet has been engaged for next summer to play my Quartet. I remember that the last time we talked of this you mentioned the Parrenin, but I guess that fell through. Anyway the Juilliard has already asked for the parts of the Quartet and is beginning to learn the work. They ought to give it a wonderful performance as they have become increasingly better each year and now play in an absolutely extraordinary way – even classical music.

As for your American issue of *The Score*, what a fine idea for us. It is very hard, at the moment, however, to think of excellent critics who write of more recent music than that of Copland's generation. For some reason, we younger people have not engaged the attention of articulate apologists and, as far as I know, no one has attempted to write a large comprehensive article about the more recent composers except Aaron himself. There [is], to be sure, Richard [Franko] Goldman, who now edits the *Juilliard Review* [but] who has been busy and ill. Consequently I have not been able to discuss your project with him. There is also Arthur Berger, who now teaches at Brandeis University in Waltham, Massachusetts, giving a graduate course in music criticism in the music department, and who is no doubt the most intelligent, if not the most lively, of younger critics. There is the Webernish 12-tone Milton Babbitt, who wrote a very intelligent article on the Bartók quartets in the *Musical Quarterly* a number of years ago.[80] There is also Arthur Cohn, who has been writing a large work on chamber music with special emphasis on contemporary works[81]– I do not know how good a writer he is, but he will visit me with some of his writings in the next few weeks.

I think Copland might write a good article on the younger generation, as he sees more of it than the others – or an article on the "rhythmic basis" of American music. Certainly an article on music schools would be very inter-

---

77 This was probably a privately pressed LP, as the first commercial LP of the *String Quartet No. 1* was recorded only in early 1955 by the Walden Quartet; see below, p. 119.

78 The planned performance of the *Piano Sonata* at the Dartington Summer School did not come about until two years later, on 19 August 1957; see below, p. 147, note 55. Instead, Carter's *Sonata for Violoncello and Piano* was played twice, on 9 and 18 August 1955, by Christopher Bunting (cello) and Noel Lee (piano). *The String*

Quartet No.1 appeared on the program of the last of six Juilliard Quartet recitals on 26 August 1955, alongside two quartets by Joseph Haydn (op. 54, no. 1, and op. 77, no. 2); the other five recitals took place on 11, 13, 15, 20, and 22 August 1955.

79 Stravinsky's *Symphonies of Wind Instruments* originated in a short chorale for piano that he wrote in 1920 for a special commemorative issue of the *Revue musicale* in honor of Claude Debussy, who had died in March 1918 (*Tombeau de Claude Debussy*, supplement to *Revue*

musicale 1/2 [December 1920]). Stravinsky's work on this commissioned piece sparked a need to explore further certain musical ideas he had used in it. In this way the chorale, scored for winds, became the conclusion and final goal of his *Symphonies of Wind Instruments*, completed on 30 November 1920.

80 Milton Babbitt, "The String Quartets of Bartók," *The Musical Quarterly* 35/3 (July 1949), pp. 377–385.

81 Arthur Cohn (1910–1998) wrote two well-regarded books on twentieth-century

esting, but not by one of the Juilliard staff, as they all have an axe to grind (but also not by one who is anti-Juilliard). Arthur Berger might do this.

There are many subjects, of course – the role of "foundations" in contemporary music – the Guggenheim Foundation and more particularly the Rockefeller Foundation with its financing of the innumerable Louisville Symphony commissions – the Koussevitzky Foundation and its commissions – for ultimately the foundations are becoming the only patrons of music here. This might be a subject for Dr. Harold Spivacke of the Library of Congress in Washington (D.C.). As you know, the whole question of financing music here is quite different from that of England or anywhere else, and it is in the teeth of a widely apathetic public that contemporary music has flourished. I don't believe that even Copland is able to live on the proceeds of his music, although it is rather widely performed. There is also a subject, perhaps, in the growth of interest in contemporary music – how this was brought about, and how contemporary music flourishes or does not flourish at the present time. We in the ISCM, right at this moment, are faced with a debt of $ 400 from last year and everyone is thinking that it will be impossible to give our usual concerts. This is a chronic state and each year it seems to become worse. Much modern music is given by chamber music groups, chosen in a rather arbitrary way. Very little modern music is given by orchestras – less last year than ever before. Mitropoulos, who played all the Schoenberg et al. scores a few years ago, has been threatened with the loss of his position at the Philharmonic unless he stops. He is very disgruntled but toeing the line, and so it is most everywhere. Since the orchestras depend on private patrons not always amateurs of new music, and since the public tends to stay away from new works, the patrons do not wish the orchestra to incur any more of a deficit than usual and hence try to get the conductor to perform works which fill the house. This same thing obtains at the Metropolitan Opera, where the *Rake's Progress* was so poorly attended. It was dropped, therefore, and the director announced that for the present he would do no more experimenting.

The N[ew] Y[ork] City Center, too, has financial troubles of the same sort. Von Einem's *The Trial* was a disaster last year and lost so much money that nothing new will be done this year.[82] The new opera of Menotti, *The Saint of Bleecker Street*, therefore (although commissioned by the City Center), will have its performance on Broadway, where it is hoped that it will be possible to repay the cost of mounting it before it is finally taken over [by] the Center.[83] *Wozzeck*, a couple of years ago, played to full houses at the Center, but had finally to be dropped from the repertory because of its expense.[84]

On the other hand, everywhere there are young composers writing operas and concert works. Far more is produced than could ever be played, even far more of worth. There is such competition in this field that no one of recent vintage has been able to achieve the kind of reputation that many an older American composer had. There are local composers all over the country, each fighting to be heard and trying to keep the works of men from other localities from being played (this is how it seems here in New York). When they are played, the local critics don't like them. All of this, I think, comes from the basic fact that since contemporary music is not a paying proposition, very little effort is spent on considering it seriously – the way, for instance, modern painting or architecture are considered here.

Please forgive these random thoughts. I am sure that they are all familiar to you, but just in case they are not, they might help you to formulate some ideas. I should certainly be very glad to help you on your American issue, if I can. The next time I will be more prompt in answering.

We are all well, hope you both are the same.
Love, Elliott

P. S. When you have the time, would you please return the tape of my Quartet, if you don't need it?

[P.]P. S. An article by Ernst Krenek on the European musicians in the U. S. might be interesting.[85]

Elliott Carter / 31 West 12th Street / New York, 11, New York
November 5, 1954

[Typed letter with autograph signature; William Glock Estate, British Library. Reprinted by permission of Sebastian Balfour and David Drew (William Glock Estate).]

---

music, *The Collector's Twentieth-Century Music in the Western Hemisphere* (Philadelphia: Lippencott, 1961) and *Twentieth-Century Music in Western Europe: The Compositions and Recordings* (Philadelphia: Lippencott, 1965). His life's work, the four-volume, 3,000-page *Literature of Chamber Music*, was published only in 1997 (Chapel Hill, NC: Hinshaw Music).

82 Gottfried von Einem's opera *Der Prozess* [The Trial] after Kafka (1950–52) had been premièred at the Salzburg Festival on 17 August 1953. The production that followed at the New York City Opera (conducted by Joseph Rosenstock, staged by Otto Preminger) was first heard at New York City Center on 22 October 1953.

83 The première of Gian Carlo Menotti's opera *The Saint of Bleecker Street* (1953–54) took place at the Broadway Theater on 27 December 1954, conducted by Thomas Schippers. It was not until a decade later, on 18 March 1965, that the work was mounted at the New York City Opera, conducted by Vincent la Selva.

84 The New York City Opera's production of *Wozzeck* was premièred on 3 April 1952 under the baton of the house's new director, Joseph Rosenstock. The failure of this production, staged by Theodore Komisarjevsky, stood in glaring contrast to the triumph that the work had witnessed a year earlier in a concert performances in Carnegie Hall, with Dimitri Mitropoulos conducting the New York Philharmonic (12, 13, and 15 April 1951).

85 Handwritten postscriptum in the margin.

61 William Glock to Elliott Carter, 5 May 1955

The Score and I. M. A. Magazine / 32B Cornwall Gardens / [London] S.W. 7
May 5, 1955

My dear Elliott,

I think the American issue is working out fairly well; it is rather better balanced than I imagined earlier on, though I've had to leave 2 or 3 items over till September. Meanwhile, during the period whilst almost everything is at the printer's, I'd be most grateful if you could give me any guidance as to *how* you came to try out metrical modulation. I wish I'd seen more of your music than three choral pieces and the three larger works: piano sonata, 'cello sonata and string quartet. Still, I've tackled this subject ("m[etrical] mod[ulation]"), but shall probably rewrite my article to some extent, and you might say something that would help.

Incidentally, I believe the Juilliard will be playing the Quartet in London, too.[86]

Very best wishes to you both,
Y[ou]rs ever,
William

[Autograph letter; Elliott Carter Collection, Paul Sacher Foundation. Reprinted by permission of Sebastian Balfour and David Drew (William Glock Estate).]

62 Elliott Carter to William Glock, 9 May 1955

Elliott C. Carter, Jr. / 31 West 12th Street / New York City 11, N.Y.
May 9, 1955

Dear William,

I really have no real idea of how the notion of "metrical modulation" came to me. I only remember that one day while writing the second movement of my 'cello sonata (which was written first) I realized that the groupings of ⅛ notes often seemed to fall into threes and that it might be interesting to shift to another speed [–] and then suddenly the whole idea came to me with its many arithmetical possibilities, which I worked out on paper as an amusement. Then I decided to see if I could apply various uses of the notion to this 'cello sonata, using the analogy of key relationships as a guide. The whole notion of metric change began to fascinate me and I decided to write a first movement (the last one to be thought of) which presented the problem in its most extreme or most crystallised form. I worked out all the movements together bit by bit – for I could imagine how one movement would join to the next – picking up ideas first stated previously.

After the 'cello sonata was completed, I thought a great deal about this metrical modulation idea and decided that the 'cello sonata used it too schematically – "modulating" from one speed to another with each phrase – at times – or each large section, like the keys in a classic work. And I decided to try and write a work which was in constant change – in which each phrase modulated metrically so that the shifts of speed would be embedded into the very material of the work. Since the whole method involves continual change, it seemed to me that the main ideas of this work were ideas of change of character – this affected its whole plan.[87] I did not succeed in doing this in the quartet as completely as I wished – but in it I did the next best thing, which was to deal with the principle contrapuntally – having layers of different speeds emerge and disappear. The problem of planning a large-scale work full of different tempi was one that interested me also in the quartet. In general, as you must have noticed, the "modulations" usually do not take place at the point where the type of unit changes. These changes of unit are written at places where the performer can grasp the continuity of rhythm and often not where the meter sounds different. It is a system of gradual change, usually, composed directly into the music – arising from thematic and contrapuntal ideas – and takes a ridiculous amount of planning and thought.

Hope this answers your questions.[88]

Very best to both of you,
Elliott

[Autograph letter; William Glock Estate, British Library. Reprinted by permission of Sebastian Balfour and David Drew (William Glock Estate).]

---

86 This performance of the *String Quartet No. 1* took place in Wigmore Hall on 18 November 1955. The Juilliard Quartet also played Béla Bartók's *String Quartet No. 4* (1928) and Fartein Valen's *String Quartet No. 2* (1930–31) in the same concert.

87 This last sentence is a later insertion, written down the left margin of the page.

88 In his article "A Note on Elliott Carter" (see above, p. 115, notes 73 and 74), Glock finally drew in several passages on the wording of Carter's explanations. He also followed the reference in Carter's letter of 6 September 1950 (see above, p. 96) by pointing to Willi Apel's *French Secular Music of the Late Fourteenth Century* to illustrate the parallels between Carter's rhythmic techniques and certain procedures of the late Middle Ages.

63   Elliott Carter and the Walden Quartet during the
recording session for the *String Quartet No. 1* (1955),
photo by Fred Plaut.

In this photo, taken during the recording session for the *String Quartet No. 1* on 2 February 1955, Carter is shown with the members of the quartet, Homer Schmitt and Bernard Goodman (violins), John Garvey (viola), and Robert Swenson (cello). The Walden Quartet, in residence at the University of Illinois (Urbana-Champaign) from 1948 until 1957, specialized in contemporary repertoire and was a strong advocate of American music.[89] Carter's quartet was issued in Columbia Records' "Modern American Music Series," whose selection committee at this time was chaired by Virgil Thomson; other members included Aaron Copland, Henry Cowell, William Schuman, and Goddard Lieberson, then the executive vice-president of Columbia Records (and after 1956 its president).[90] Thom-

son described the project as coming out of the following conversation between himself and an official of Columbia Records: "American music gets published and performed all over the world nowadays, but the recording companies pretend it doesn't exist. [...] The business man replied to the composer, 'I'll change all that if you will show me how to do it.'"[91] The plan was to focus on chamber music, releasing at least six records a year. Carter's *String Quartet No. 2, String Quartet No. 3, Brass Quintet, Eight Pieces for Four Timpani*, and *A Fantasy about Purcell's "Fantasia upon One Note"* were later also recorded in this series, which began in the early 1950s and ended in 1978.

[MSS 52, Frederick and Rose Plaut Papers, Irving S. Gilmore Music Library, Yale University. Reprinted by permission.]

---

89   The quartet's world premières include, in addition to Carter's *String Quartet No. 1*, Ives's *String Quartet No. 2* and Schoenberg's *String Trio*, op. 45.

90   These are the committee members named in the liner notes to the Carter recording, Columbia ML 5104. In 1954, Samuel Barber was apparently also a member; see *Selected Letters of Virgil Thomson*, ed. Tim Page and Vanessa Weeks Page

(New York, London, etc.: Summit Books, 1988), p. 275 (editors' footnote).

91   [Virgil Thomson,] liner notes to Columbia ML 5104.

Variations for Orchestra (1953–55)

Although the Louisville Orchestra had already launched a program for the advancement and performance of contemporary music in 1948, the project only began to make headlines in 1953 when it received generous financial backing from the Rockefeller Foundation. This support enabled the orchestra, and its founder and conductor Robert Whitney (1904–1986), to commission works on a large scale from American and foreign composers – within certain political limits, for in the final analysis the Rockefeller Foundation, supported by the State Department, viewed this subsidy project as a prestige object of the "free world," and thus as a cultural instrument in the Cold War.[92] Among the first beneficiaries was Carter, who in July 1953 (shortly before his stay at the American Academy in Rome) was invited to contribute an orchestral piece tailored to the small, fifty-piece Louisville Orchestra. His thank-you letter to the orchestra's managing director, Richard H. Wangerin, reveals that he initially took three plans into consideration (in order of preference and "with a distinct emphasis on the first [idea]"): 1) a roughly twenty-minute piano concerto for Beveridge Webster or Webster Aitken, 2) a cello concerto (likewise roughly twenty minutes long) for Bernard Greenhouse, and 3) a ten- to fifteen-minute orchestral piece ("Variations?").[93] However, the commissioning institution disapproved of a piano concerto and would accept a cello concerto only for the orchestra's solo cellist, whom Carter did not know (it was Robert Whitney's sister), and the decision ultimately fell on a purely orchestral set of variations. Carter originally wanted the *Variations for Orchestra* performed within the space of a year, but his work on the score far outlasted his stay in Rome and was only finished on 14 November 1955. Moreover, the results were of such compositional complexity that, knowing the technical limitations of the conductor and his orchestra, he wrote to Robert Whitney shortly after finishing the piece: "If you would prefer not to perform the work on the basis of its demands on the orchestra, I would be disappointed but understanding [...]."[94] But Whitney rose to the challenge and gave the work its first performance on 21 April 1956. Like most of the pieces premièred in the Louisville commissioning project, the *Variations for Orchestra* were recorded a few weeks after the première for the orchestra's LP series.[95]

64 *Variations for Orchestra* (1953–55), photostat full score with autograph annotations and conductor's markings by Robert Whitney, p. 46 (mm. 213–228)

In his *Variations for Orchestra* Carter confronted the grand tradition of variation form, probing the full spectrum of variation techniques on the basis of a long melodic line and two so-called ritornellos. Especially important are his various procedures of acceleration and deceleration. For example, one of the ritornellos continually accelerates as the piece progresses, whereas the other becomes progressively slower. Accordingly, the momentum in the middle three of the nine variations slows down at first (variation 4), then reaches a standstill (variation 5), and finally picks up speed again (variation 6). Here we see the first sixteen bars of variation 4. The continuous change of tempo occurs in the form of a ritardando in which the opening tempo is halved in each of the four-bar units, only to leap back to the original tempo. To state his intentions with maximum clarity, Carter not only entered the corresponding expression marks in the score ("Ritardando molto," "Subito Tempo I") and added metronome marks at the beginning of each bar, he also supplied a "Conductor's Note" at the end of the page which, among other things, stresses that the change from sixteenths to eighth-notes after the double barline must remain inaudible because of the doubling of the tempo (i.e. the return to the opening tempo). Besides a few markings by the conductor of the première, Robert Whitney, this sample page of the score also contains annotations in Carter's hand. The faster metronome markings in dark blue and red crayon (quarter = 156 or 160 instead of quarter = 144) were made even faster in the printed edition (quarter = 200), and the markings for leading and subsidiary voices (in light blue and pink crayon, respectively) were ultimately refined into a three-tiered notational system: A = "principal voice," B = "secondary voice," C = "tertiary voice."

92 This topic is discussed in Jeanne Marie Belfy, "The Commissioning Project of the Louisville Orchestra, 1948–1958: A Study of the History and Music" (Ph.D. Diss., University of Kentucky, 1986), esp. chap. 5 ("Politics and Music: Commissioning as a Propaganda Tool"), pp. 180–205. See also Sandra Lee Fralin, "The Role of the Louisville Orchestra in the Fostering of New Music, 1947–1997"

(D.M.A. dissertation, Southern Baptist Theological Seminary, 2000).

93 Letter from Elliott Carter to Richard H. Wangerin, 13 August 1953; carbon copy in the Elliott Carter Collection, Paul Sacher Foundation.

94 Letter from Elliott Carter to Robert Whitney [ca. early December 1953]; Elliott Carter Collection, Paul Sacher Foundation.

95 Elliott Carter, *Variations for Orchestra*; Everett Helm, *Second Piano Concerto*. The Louisville Orchestra, cond. Robert Whitney (LP LOU-58-3), recorded on 20 May 1956, released in 1958; reissued in the CD series First Edition (FECD-0001) along with works by Aaron Copland, Luigi Dallapiccola, and William Schuman (2001).

Sonata for Two Pianos (ca. 1955–56)

Owing to the success of the *String Quartet No. 1* and several later works, Carter received several important commissions in the 1950s. He was unable to satisfy all of them, however, as his breakthrough into a highly personal and innovative musical language required meticulous planning and extensive sketching. As early as the summer of 1952, before the première of the *String Quartet No. 1,* he had been invited by the League of Composers to write an orchestral work: the "Symphony No. 2." Yet the piece never reached completion. Much the same happened in the case of at least three other projects: a piece for two pianos commissioned by the Serge Koussevitzky Music Foundation in the Library of Congress, a choral composition requested by an unidentified group in early 1956,[96] and a piece for violin and piano ordered from him by the Elizabeth Sprague Coolidge Foundation in the Library of Congress in summer 1957.[97] Nonetheless, some of these projects left behind various-sized bundles of sketches. Among these is the *Sonata for Two Pianos* that Carter essayed at the request of the Koussevitzky Foundation. As we know from his letter to Copland of 11 October 1953 (see above, p. 110), he planned to write this piece during the first half of his stay in Rome and to complete it in spring 1954. However, work on the *Variations for Orchestra* (commissioned just a few weeks before the piano piece) took so much of his attention that he put the project aside and did not return to it until winter 1955–56.

65 *Sonata for Two Pianos* (ca. 1955–56), verbal notes, 1 p.

Carter's work on the "Double Piano Sonata" – thus the title of the draft outline shown here – is documented in two folders of sketches. One folder mainly contains verbal and rhythmic notes written down on light brown carbon paper (22 pp.), whereas the other consists of drafts written in musical notation on normal manuscript paper (ca. 20 pp.). At that time Carter did not apply a date stamp to his sketches, as he began to do a short while later (to the great benefit of inquisitive musicologists!), so we cannot say exactly when these sketches arose. However, given that Carter told William Glock in late 1955 that he had started work on the *Sonata for Two Pianos,* it is safe to assume that most if not all of the sketches date from the winter of 1955–56.[98] This may also apply to the leaf shown here, which appears at the beginning of a twenty-two-page folder of sketches notated on carbon paper and offers insight into Carter's underlying conceptual ideas. The typewritten text in the upper half of the leaf reveals that the work was meant to be antiphonal, with the two pianos contrasting with each other and representing antithetical expressive characters (see e.g. piano I: "showy, unstable, very emotional" etc.; piano II: "quiet, sober, serious" etc.). The handwritten notes in the lower half, in contrast, shed light on the intended four-movement design. Especially noteworthy is the diagram of movement 3 ("Variations"), in which the conflicting lengths of the piano parts (three variations in piano I, four in piano II) are meshed in a quasi polyrhythmic way. Although Carter abandoned this project, he drew directly on the antiphonal conception of the *Sonata for Two Pianos* when he came to write his *Double Concerto* (1959–61).

---

96 See letter from Elliott Carter to William Glock, 5 February 1956; William Glock Estate, British Library.

97 See letter from Harold Spivacke (Library of Congress) to Elliott Carter, 5 August 1957; Elliott Carter Collection, Paul Sacher Foundation. Fifteen years later this commission finally resulted in Carter's *Duo for Violin and Piano* (1972–74).

98 See letter from Elliott Carter to William Glock, 4 December 1955; William Glock Estate, British Library.

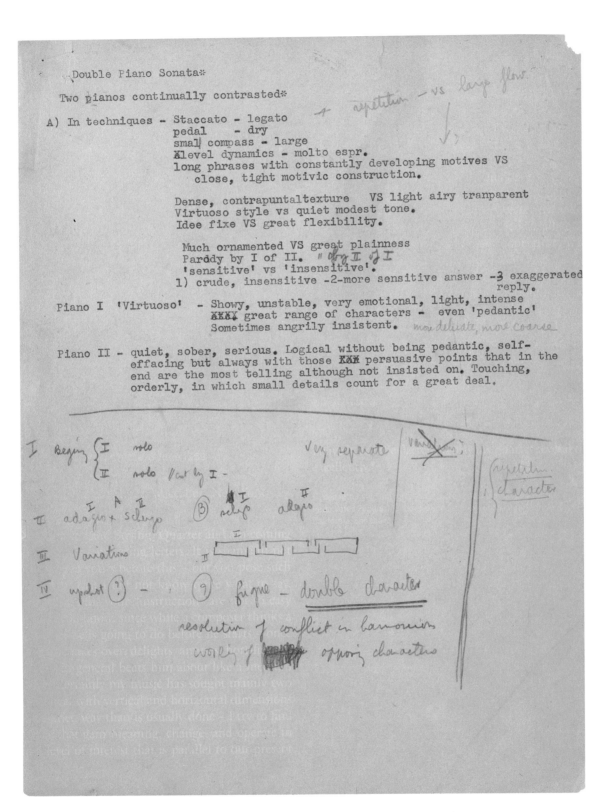

Double Piano Sonata*

Two pianos continually contrasted*

A) In techniques - Staccato - legato
               pedal   - dry
               small compass - large
               Xlevel dynamics - molto espr.
               long phrases with constantly developing motives VS
                    close, tight motivic construction.

               Dense, contrapuntaltexture   VS light airy tranparent
               Virtuoso style vs quiet modest tone.
               Idee fixe VS great flexibility.

               Much ornamented VS great plainness
               Parody by I of II. " dry II I
               'sensitive' vs 'insensitive'.
               1) crude, insensitive -2-more sensitive answer -3 exaggerated
                                                   reply.

Piano I 'Virtuoso' - Showy, unstable, very emotional, light, intense
                    XXXX great range of characters - even 'pedantic'
                    Sometimes angrily insistent. more delicate, more coarse

Piano II - quiet, sober, serious. Logical without being pedantic, self-
               effacing but always with those XXX persuasive points that in the
               end are the most telling although not insisted on. Touching,
               orderly, in which small details count for a great deal.

"Oppositions
and Cooperations"

1956–1962

Talking (Music) Politics with
Nicolas Nabokov (1956)

Nicolas Nabokov (1903–1978) was one of Carter's closest friends; they shared a reverence for Stravinsky and his music, a love of travel and good food, and a sense of humor (with Carter as the "straight man" to Nabokov's comic monologues and impersonations). But most of all they were both acutely aware of the artist's place in society and worked actively to improve the situation of the modern composer. Nabokov, a cousin of the famous author, did this out of strong political convictions. He held cultural freedom, as a product of freedom of thought and expression more generally, to be the most important feature of a democracy, and the one that most distinguished Western countries from communist ones. Nabokov's anti-communism, which was always of the liberal-democratic and not the McCarthyite sort, was bred in the bone of his White Russian heritage and nurtured during the Cold War. Shortly after moving to the Washington area Nabokov became part of an informal "Dumbarton Avenue Circle" led by the diplomat and later CIA agent Charles "Chip" Bohlen (at whose home on Dumbarton Avenue the group met), the British diplomat and philosopher Isaiah Berlin, and the diplomat and later influential Cold Warrior George F. Kennan. These contacts paved the way for Nabokov's later political career.[1] A founding member of the Congress for Cultural Freedom (CCF), Nabokov served as Secretary-General of this Paris-based but American (CIA)-financed organization until its demise in 1967. The aim of the CCF was to promote and display the products of the West's artistic freedom, spreading its political message through culture. Active in thirty-five countries, the CCF published journals, organized conferences, and supported the emigré orchestra Philharmonia Hungarica. In accordance with Nabokov's own interests, the CCF also invested considerable resources in ambitious music festivals, such as "Music of the Twentieth Century" in Rome in 1954, which had helped to establish Carter's international reputation.[2] Two years earlier Stravinsky – who shared Nabokov's political views and was,

like Carter, a close friend – had lent his luster to Nabokov's festival "L'Œuvre du XXème Siècle / Masterpieces of the XXth Century" (Paris 1952); the Venice festival "Tradition and Change in Music" (1958) featured the world première of his *Threni*.[3] Nabokov organized other major festivals in Tokyo (1961) and New Delhi (1963).[4] (On the "East-West Music Encounter" in Tokyo, see below, p. 163.) Although they included contemporary music, Nabokov's festivals centered around mainstream works that would attract large audiences. Carter was certainly sympathetic to Nabokov's politicized support for artistic freedom (as can be seen, for example, in Carter's correspondence with the State Department; see below, pp. 159–161), and he must have been grateful for the opportunities that the friendship with such an effective organizer provided. But his activism confined itself to organizations dedicated to promoting new music, such as the ISCM, whose future plans for a large-scale festival he confided to his friend. Carter's single-minded dedication to his composition and to the promotion of new American music should not be read as an apolitical stance, however, since the belief that art and politics should be separate was at the core of the Congress for Cultural Freedom's message.

---

1   See Ian Wellens, *Music on the Frontline: Nicolas Nabokov's Struggle against Communism and Middlebrow Culture* (Aldershot: Ashgate, 2002), pp. 4–5.

2   For a detailed account of the Congress for Cultural Freedom's activities, see Saunders, *Who Paid the Piper?* (see above, p. 111, note 66).

3   See Anne C. Shreffler, "Ideologies of Serialism: Stravinsky's *Threni* and the Congress for Cultural Freedom," in *Music and the Aesthetics of Modernity* [Festschrift for Reinhold Brinkmann], ed. Karol Berger and Anthony Newcomb (Cambridge, MA: Harvard University Department of Music, 2005), pp. 217–245.

4   The music festivals were only a small part of the Congress's activities, which included dozens of festivals worldwide on a wide variety of topics. In Peter Coleman's "Selective List of Conferences Sponsored by the Congress for Cultural Freedom" there are thirty-seven; see Coleman, *The Liberal Conspiracy: The Congress for Cultural Freedom and the Struggle for the Mind of Postwar Europe* (New York: The Free Press; London: Collier Macmillan, 1989), pp. 253–257.

5   The Belgian-born Marie-Claire Brot (b. 1921) became Nabokov's fourth wife in 1953; they divorced in 1970. Their son Alexandre (b. 1954) is mentioned later in the letter.

6   The Russian-American composer Alexei Haieff (1914–1994) was Nabokov's immediate predecessor as composer-in-residence at the American Academy in Rome (1952–53) and belonged to his circle of friends from an early date. Alain Daniélou (1907–1994) was a renowned specialist in Indian music who, among other things, took part in the conferences that Nabokov organized in Venice ("Tradition and Change in Music," 1958) and Tokyo ("East-West Music Encounter," 1961). From 1963 he also taught at the International Institute for Comparative Music Studies in Berlin, an institution co-founded by the Congress for Cultural Freedom.

66   Nicolas Nabokov to Elliott Carter, 28 June [1956]

Congrès pour la Liberté de la Culture /
104, Boulevard Haussmann, Paris VIIIe – Europe 55-15 /
Le Secrétaire général
Rome. 28. VI.

Dearest Elliott,
– Here we are in Rome for a tiny bit of a vacation. Marie-Claire and I miss you both here.[5] It is somehow incongruous to be here while Hellen [sic] and Elliottovitch aren't "Romans." The tempo is beautiful and yesterday Alexis Haieff, Alain Daniélou and ourselves drove out to the Abruzzi through the most wonderful countryside and visited Subiaco, Casamarini, and an old lovely castle which we discovered perched high above a grey-blue mountain.[6]

I am going back to Paris on the 4th of July, the day after the Academy concert, which I helped (a bit) to organize.[7] Petrassi, whom, I am sure, you will see in N[ew] Y[ork], will explain to you the reason why we could not have a piece of yours performed. First of all we only have a rump orchestra (1 t[ru]mp[e]t, 1 tr[om]b[o]ne, w[ood]-w[inds] all per one), and secondly Scaglia only had 2½ rehearsals for the concert. Under those conditions it would have been impossible to play any of your music properly and do it justice. But this 4th of July concert business (if it goes well this year again) might become an institution (so long as Labroca and I are around[8]) at the Academy and for next year we can plan *definitely* to play a piece of yours. By planning it long in advance and getting the parts several months ahead of time we could have the musicians prepare it well and perform it in a proper way. But which piece do you want to be played? The last one you wrote for Louisville?

This year's programme was made by Petrassi and contains Barber (*Capricorn*), Turchi (some new piece I do not know), and a 35-min.-long radio opera by Hollingsworth… The concert is held right outside of the villino in front of the Villa and I hope that the acoustics will be better than last year.

– There is little news on our side of the water: – Alexander is growing up beautifully and looks indecently blond, round, and gay. I have just been in Vienna and heard Frank Martin's *Tempest* (in German).[9] An excellent piece. Full of ingenious writing and honest craftsmanship. I also heard one of the best orchestras I have ever heard… the Leningrad Symphony…[10]

Now I am going back to Verderonne and will sit down and write some music. I will write you again from Parigi, where, I think, I will have more time to myself.

Love to you and Hellen [sic], dear Elliott, from us both,
Yours ever
Nicolas

P.S. Marg[herita] Rospigliosi told me that you wrote her about your music.[11] I told her that I will reply to you.

PP.SS. Thank you for sending me the string quartet score. It looks very well in print.[12]

[Autograph letter; Elliott Carter Collection, Paul Sacher Foundation. Reprinted by permission of Dominique Nabokov.]

67   Elliott Carter to Nicolas Nabokov, 9 July 1956

Elliott C. Carter, Jr., / (31 West 12th Street, /
New York City 11, N.Y.)
Meade [sic] Street, / Waccabuc / New York
July 9, 1956

Dear Nicolas,
Thanks for your letter, I got it after a more than complicated weekend moving to the above address. It was good to hear about Subiaco and the Abruzzi and your motor trip through such pleasant places with such pleasant friends – especially at the end of a trip from Dorset, Vermont, to Waccabuc through Sunday traffic with only a folding bed and a tarragon plant as companions. However, I did stop at Tanglefood [sic] for lunch with Petrassi and reheard (Yehudi Weiner[13] had been here a few days

7   The concert of 3 July 1956 at the American Academy in Rome was given by the Orchestra Sinfonica di Roma della Radio-televisione Italiana under the direction of Ferruccio Scaglia. The program included Barber's *Capricorn Concerto* for flute, oboe, trumpet, and strings, op. 21 (1944), Guido Turchi's *Piccolo concerto notturno* (1950), and a concert performance of Stanley Hollingsworth's opera *The Mother* after a fairy-tale by Hans Christian Andersen (1949).

8   The composer and critic Mario Labroca (1896–1973) was then head of the music department at Italian radio. He switched to the Venice Biennale in 1959.

9   Frank Martin's opera *Der Sturm* [The Tempest] was premièred at the Vienna State Opera on 17 June 1956, conducted

by Ernest Ansermet and staged by Heinz Arnold.

10   In June 1956 the Leningrad Philharmonic, led by its principal conductor Evgeny Mravinsky, made a concert tour of East Germany, West Germany, Switzerland, and Austria. The final stop on the tour was Vienna, where the orchestra gave three concerts in the Great Musikverein Hall (21–23 June 1956), followed by several LP recordings. The concerts of 21 and 23 June (with works by Mozart, Shostakovich, and Tchaikovsky) were conducted by Mravinsky, that on 22 June (with works by Berlioz, Mozart, and Rakhmaninov) by Kurt Sanderling. All three concerts featured solo performances by the violinist David Oistrakh.

11   Principessa Margherita Rospigliosi was the assistant of Laurance P. Roberts, the then director of the American Academy in Rome.

12   Carter's *String Quartet* (No.1) had appeared in print in late 1955 (AMP 95544-119).

13   The composer Yehudi Wyner (b. 1929) is the son of the composer and choral conductor Lazar Weiner, who was for many years Director of Music of the Central Synagogue in New York City. Wyner, who has used the Americanized spelling of his name since his first concert appearances in the early 1940s, won the Rome Prize in 1953 – the same year as Carter – and lived in Italy until 1956. In later years he taught at Yale, Brandeis, and other universities, and won the Pulitzer Prize in 2006.

ago) about the Rome concert. I understand and understood even when I first wrote to Petrassi how things were there, and I am not in the least annoyed or surprised. I am very happy that you are hoping to give something of mine next year – my Louisville piece (I played it to Stravinsky & Craft, who seemed both of them very impressed) is a very hard nut to crack – I am not sure how it would sound in an open-air concert with not many rehearsals – perhaps the *Minotaur* might go better.[14]

Anyhow Helen (who drove another car yesterday with Mexican dishes and Stendhal down from Vermont) and I would have been far happier if we had been with you in Rome travelling about with Marie-Claire – now Helen has learned a great deal of French – we speak it about the house more & more so that even David will be able to soon – and we could combine families without remaining on too primitive a level.

I don't know if you heard from Alexei Haieff about the League-ISCM's US plan for a festival here in 1958 (in mid-June). I suspect this project was got going by Betty Bean & Dick French and others[15] and will entail (naturally) quite large sums to be raised, since not only will the music be costly but more importantly it is planned to pay the trips of 25 or more delegates from Europe. I have pointed out to Dick French & Betty Bean that this might conflict with your planned Tokyo festival & suggested that it be put off. It might conflict since a) I suppose certain sources of money might be the same, [and] b) the delegates being in many cases probably the same might be occupied in Japan at the same time. Of course, it could be that a round-the-world trip could be worked out if these two were planned together –

Anyhow – I have no news from you about Tokyo – and so I cannot take any kind of a firm stand about an ISCM festival here. However, if you are interested and have some kind of a concrete proposal or plan for the future – perhaps these two things could be coordinated.

Perhaps Japan could give the ISCM 1958 festival as part of your plan & the US the following year – Mr. Strobel is the president of the whole thing now (Dick French is the US president) – but something should be done to coordinate the efforts of the US section & the Congrès about the various plans, or there may be trouble for one or the other –

I understood you were to conduct your Louisville piece with the Zurich radio – How did it go? I still have to hear it on a record – perhaps I can get permission from David Oppenheim at Columbia.[16]

Have you a machine of micro-sillon? If so – I will send you a copy of the records of the *Minotaur* & my string quartet.[17]

Mitropoulos has been acting strangely again. He made a speech at a Providence meeting of orchestral people & composers that the League-ISCM arranged, and it sounded [like a] purely brain-washed confession like the Moscow trials – Mr. Judson & Zirato sat nearby while Mitropoulos confessed to his terrible mistakes at having played so much contemporary music & hurt the Philharmonic, etc. etc.[18] Oddly enough all the other conductors understood the brain-washing aspect and were contemptuous of the whole proceeding, and Mitropoulos's speech reinforced our contention that more contemporary music should be played –

David grows apace – his voice changes – he is full of adolescent languour – loves to dance (ballroom) and will fit in with the gray-flannel-suit advertising-man atmosphere of Waccabuc – perhaps he will be the saviour of the family. I am still mad that I did not get a look at Alexandre as a babe – now the next time I see him he will be all grown up. We are heading for the Zurich ISCM festival next spring & England for the summer (1956–57) [and] maybe a trip through Spain in the spring.[19] By then Alexandre will be grown up and be able to walk.

14 The American Academy's 1957 summer concert, which again took place on 3 July, did not ultimately include a work by Carter. Instead the Orchestra Sinfonica della Radiotelevisione Italiana under the direction of Bruno Maderna performed music by Billy Jim Layton (*American Portrait*), Luigi Nono (*Composizione [No. 1] per orchestra*), Salvatore Martirano (*Contrasto*), and Richard Willis (*Symphony No. 1*).

15 Betty Randolph Bean (d. 2002) served as vice-president of the Boosey & Hawkes New York office, secretary of the American Soviet Music Society, and director of press and public relations for the New York Philharmonic. Richard F. French (1916–2001), Harvard class of '37, was vice-president and director of publications at Associated Music Publishers; in later years he served as president of Pro Musica

Antiqua (later New York Pro Musica), Tangeman Professor of Sacred Music at Union Theological Seminary, director of the Institute of Sacred Music at Yale University, and, from 1987 to 1993, director of Juilliard's Doctor of Musical Arts program. He was also an important patron of music performance, publishing, and libraries; see Christoph Wolff, "The Spirit of Richard F. French '37," in *The Golden Music: The Loeb Music Library at 50*, ed. Sarah Adams, Virginia Danielson, and Robert J. Dennis (= *Harvard Library Bulletin* 18/1–2 [2007], pp. 25–28).

16 Carter is referring to Nabokov's cantata *Symboli Chrestiani* for baritone and orchestra, written in 1955 for the Louisville Orchestra, which premièred the piece on 15 February 1956 under the baton of Robert Whitney. An LP recording of the

work, with the baritone soloist William Pickett, was released on the orchestra's own label (LOU-58-1). The Swiss radio recording mentioned by Carter was not made until 1 October 1956; Nabokov conducted Heinz Rehfuss (baritone) and the Beromünster Radio Orchestra. The clarinettist and record producer David J. Oppenheim was then head of the classical division at Columbia Records.

17 The *Suite from "The Minotaur"* had been recorded by the Eastman-Rochester Symphony Orchestra under Howard Hanson in January 1956, the *String Quartet No. 1* by the Walden Quartet in February 1955. Both recordings (Mercury MG 50103 and Columbia ML 5104, respectively) had just been released at the time of Carter's letter.

"Sound and Silence in Time" (1957)

We are keeping our apartamento in New York for the winter because we are not so sure about Waccabuc for all year round – although we will be about 15 miles from Sam B[arber] & 30 from Aaron [Copland].[20] I have been so busy buying and selling houses, getting lawyers and the rest, that life does not seem to be the same old thing at all.[21] It will certainly be altogether different with David off at Brooks School next winter – We might even take a trip in the spring – as I say – to Spain.

I understand Martinů will be the composer-in-residence at the Accademia next year – I thought that it was a good idea to have Petrassi. It makes a much more international atmosphere.

Much love to Marie-Claire and yourself from us both – write lots of music this summer and let's hear from you soon.

As ever
Elliott

PS: We thought of you and ΜΑΒΡΟΔΑΦΝΗ[22] on July 6 – our wedding anniversary – you remember at Chatham.

[Autograph letter; Harry Ransom Humanities Research Center, University of Texas at Austin. Reprinted by permission of Dominique Nabokov.]

Carter gave the following lecture on 13 February 1957 in Schoenberg Hall at the University of California in Los Angeles as part of a three-day event dedicated to his music (12–14 February 1957). The lecture, accompanied by a live performance of the *Piano Sonata* by the pianist James MacInnes, was the centerpiece of the event, which also included discussions with the composer of the *String Quartet No. 1* and the *Variations for Orchestra* on the day before and the day after the lecture, respectively, illustrated by recorded performances.[23] While in Los Angeles, Carter also took the opportunity to visit old friends, including Stravinsky and Robert Craft: "I saw the master while in Los Angeles and heard the *Canticum [sacrum]*, which I loved very much."[24] During this visit Carter and Stravinsky also "had a long talk about Webern apropos the Craft-Columbia records which have just appeared." (Both of the above quotations from Carter's letter to Glock, 3 May 1957, see below, p. 149.)[25] Although Webern's music had been played in the United States since before the war, these recordings unleashed a more intense interest in the composer's music than ever before.

Carter's lecture, in dealing with the most basic elements of music and their psychological and physiological implications, is his most theoretical text. In a detailed discussion of musical "first principles," Carter examines in turn the most basic elements of music: sound, silence, and time. His discussion of sound, which includes the acoustical, perceptual, and imaginative realms, is strongly influenced by consideration of a medium he never employed in his own works: electronic sound production. It is hard to avoid the conclusion that Carter's extensive rumination on silence must have had something to do with his encounter with the Webern recordings, where the sonic reality of Webern's silences is much more evident than it is in the scores alone. More importantly, the lecture contains Carter's first extended discussion of musical time as a fundamental element; this provides the theoretical

---

18 The meeting at which Mitropoulos delivered this "confession" before the New York Philharmonic's two managers, Arthur Judson and Bruno Zirato, was organized by the American Symphony Orchestra League and the League of Composers-ISCM and took place on 15 June 1956. Mitropoulos's statements created all the more puzzlement in that the object of the meeting was to place more contemporary music on the orchestra's programs. A few weeks earlier, Mitropoulos had been severely criticized in the *New York Times* for his choice of contemporary music as well as for other shortcomings; see Howard Taubman, "The Philharmonic: What's Wrong With It and Why," *The New York Times*, 29 April 1956.

19 Although Carter had turned down William Glock's invitation to teach at the Darting-

ton Summer School in 1956, he did pay the festival a short visit in August of that year. His other traveling plans were apparently dropped: there is no archival evidence to suggest that he made a trip through Spain in spring 1957, or that he attended the ISCM festival in Zurich, which took place from 31 May to 6 June 1957.

20 Samuel Barber lived in a house called "Capricorn" in Mount Kisco, NY, together with Gian Carlo Menotti and Kinch Horan; Copland resided in Ossining, NY.

21 After Carter's father died in 1955, leaving as part of his estate some residential buildings, Carter decided to sell these rather than take on time-consuming duties as landlord (Elliott Carter, personal communication to the authors, 22 April 2008). The inheritance might have also made it possible to send David to the

Brooks School, a private boarding school in North Andover, MA.

22 Mavrodaphne: a sweet red wine grown in the Patras area of Greece.

23 The *String Quartet No. 1* was heard in the recording by the Walden Quartet (Columbia ML 5104, published 1956), while the *Variations for Orchestra* were presented in a pre-release tape of the recording by the Louisville Orchestra conducted by Robert Whitney (LOU-58-3, published 1958).

24 Stravinsky's *Canticum sacrum* had been premièred in Venice five months earlier, on 13 September 1956.

25 Robert Craft's Webern recordings were made between February 1954 and May 1956 and released by Columbia Records in 1957 as *The Complete Music of Anton Webern* (K4L-232).

background to the rhythmic phenomena described in "The Rhythmic Basis of American Music" (1955).[26] Carter explores the paradoxes of time perception – "We learn about thousands of years in a few seconds and about some remarkable thing that took but a few minutes by thinking about it for many hours" – and concludes that Western music uniquely has developed a directional notion of time, which has had enormous implications for its formal designs. Carter's thinking on time and rhythm would be developed further in later essays, including "A Further Step" (1958), "The Time Dimension in Music" (1965), and "Music and the Time Screen" (1976).[27] Finally, with his suggestion that the most advanced ideas in contemporary music are necessarily difficult for audiences, and that universities should help to "protect these ideas, as they do other ideas beyond the average man's reach," Carter anticipates Milton Babbitt's more emphatic statement of this position a year later in his (in)famous essay, "Who Cares If You Listen," though Carter adds his concern that "this may be hard on the art."[28] The theoretical nature of Carter's lecture and its intentionally élitist position are consistent with other trends in musical life in the late 1950s: the *Journal of Music Theory* was founded in 1957, and *Perspectives of New Music* was to follow five years later. Although Carter himself was not associated with a university at that time, and did not contribute regularly to these journals, the new emphasis on theory and analysis did create a more favorable environment for his music.

68 Elliott Carter, "Sound and Silence in Time: A Contemporary Approach to the Elements of Music" (1957)

L[adies] & G[entlemen],

I hope that you are perfectly aware of the fact that a composer, in addressing his audience with words instead of with his customary sounds – music –, is really at a great disadvantage – the uncomfortable efforts of an American working under the weight of heavy, cumbersome winter sweaters and overcoats and woolen gloves in an unheated European apartment come to mind, or of Baudelaire's albatross, so clumsy when hobbling about the deck of a boat and so wonderful in flight. For a composer, words, especially about music itself, are bound to seem clumsy, unclear, complicated, and misleading in describing or explaining the happenings in music which, when heard, are so clear and unequivocal. As for the public, it must always bear in mind that, although one of the arts, music is not a branch of literature – that musicians talking about their art are generally not skilled word users and as such easily get tangled in a web of misunderstanding, particularly when dealing with an elusive subject about which even highly skillful writers often have trouble. I stress this point because we live in a highly verbal time, as well as a very busy one. It is a time for condensed explanations, shortcuts, and even writing which is easily written and more easily read and which, while pretending to deal with a subject, includes just enough of it to give the reader pleasure and not enough to make him think. The humble, unglib man working at his laboratory desk, the mathematician at his computers, and to a certain extent the artist in paint and music seldom come in contact with the public directly except through the results of their labours – labours that are often cryptic enough and sometimes too novel for a public that has not the time to follow the latest things. It is here that a large group of talkers and writers come in, critics and authors whose very lives depend on their ability to interest all the different levels of society they write for – and who are frequently more interested in an easily explained story than in the facts.

In our field, such a writer will express an idea about a musical work, another will argue the point, another elaborate on it, and as more and more join in, the actual work

26 Carter, "The Rhythmic Basis of American Music" (see above, p. 115, notes 73 and 74), in *CEL*, pp. 57–62.

27 Elliott Carter, "A Further Step," in *The American Composer Speaks, 1770–1965*, ed. Gilbert Chase (Baton Rouge: Lousiana State University Press, 1966), pp. 245–254; most recently reprinted in *CEL*, pp. 5–11. Idem, "The Time Dimension in Music," *Music Journal* 23/8 (November 1965), pp. 29–30; most recently reprinted in *CEL*, pp. 224–228. Idem, "Music and the Time Screen" (see above, p. 98, note 24), in *CEL*, pp. 262–280.

is lost from view. A myth grows up, only to be projected by the literary-minded listener onto the original music – where it is apt to stick for a very long time.

One of the main reasons, therefore, for a composer's belaboring his audience with words is to make an attempt to confront the verbal-minded with some bit of musical reality, however inadequately expressed – to try to sweep away the cobweb of myth, hopeful all the time that he is not substituting another of his own.

I would like to start my short sketch of musical elements by situating it in an environment which throws a new light on them. Some time ago a number of musicians fresh from a meeting of a New York society of acousticians visited me. The scientists hadn't the faintest idea of what music was about, they thought, and how were they going to explain the art in terms which the scientists would understand? These scientists seemed to be a group of those remarkable engineers who have been responsible for developing the extraordinary microphones, amplifiers, filters, analyzers, and the rest of that acoustical equipment which is bringing more and more life-like music into [our] homes. Among them were the men, I believe, who patiently had developed extremely refined machines that could imitate the sound of any musical instrument, combine them together, and finally produce the effect of a large symphonic orchestra – playing Dixie. Apparently these men themselves wished to delve further into the matter of music, especially because they had read in technical journals about the electronic music studios now set up in Germany, France, Switzerland, Italy, and Japan which are using a great deal of the very equipment they developed. They had read articles about these studios which quoted from American acoustical journals and even from our mathematical and philosophical learned papers on information theory and other new developments in thought – matters which have scarcely been heard of in our musical world, but which have evidently been carefully studied by sound engineers and a group of experimental musicians in Europe. The few Americans who know enough about all these matters – rarities, I must say –[29] feel that the Europeans and Japanese have embarked on a very interesting adventure, but that their grasp of many acoustical problems and information-theory questions is very poor and is mainly in the form of using a jargon. But our acousticians wanted the musicians to invite some Americans interested in these matters to explain. But explanation is not at all easy, for in our society, in order to bridge gaps between different fields, we are always having to go back to first principles – and even these are never agreed on. The difference between a science and a fine art is one of those standard subjects that one would imagine every educated man had ideas and even convictions about; even the justification of the existence of an art of music is apt to come into question at these moments, and after that the justification for contemporary music – all subjects that should not need to be discussed. The scientists were interested and my musician friends were put to the test of trying to explain what they would want out of electronic sound-producing machines and finally out of what and how music was put together, so that machines could be developed that would answer a composer's needs.

Before speculating on this matter, I would like you to understand how expanded this horizon of possibilities of sound the new machines can offer is. At first one is a little repulsed by the doing away of the performer and the relying entirely on mechanisms, but the wealth of possibilities is so great that it would certainly seem possible to compensate for the loss in interest due to the lack of performers. Composers in the past have faced this problem by exaggerating other kinds of musical interest to compensate for the mechanicalness of the machine – indeed one of Mozart's finest works, his late *Fantasy* in F minor for mechanical organ, does just this.

Anybody can easily imagine how exciting it is first off for a composer to realize that he could be in complete control of the entire sound world and every item in it. That every detail could be subjected to his choice and his invention. He could invent new tone colors like, somewhat like, or entirely different from, those of our live instruments. He could combine them – any number of them – in any way, separate them, and make them play with just the desired degree of loudness, expressivity, and intensity, easy or terrifically difficult passages at any speed, fast or slow. He could make up new scales with new tunings, or invent infinite numbers of scale-like gradations that would systematize other qualities besides those of pitch. In all of this, of course, he would be entirely free from our finger-operated instruments, the

---

28 Milton Babbitt, "Who Cares If You Listen?" Originally published in *High Fidelity* 8/2 (February 1958), pp. 38–40 and 126–127. (Babbitt's original title was "The Composer as Specialist.") Reprinted in *Contemporary Composers on Contemporary Music*, ed. Elliott Schwartz and Barney Childs (New York: Da Capo, 1978), pp. 243–250.

29 Here Carter originally marked an insertion: "like Professor Milton Babbitt at Princeton."

instrumentalists that play them, and their rehearsal problems. He could produce just what he wanted, directly on a recording with the help of a machine, doing away with performers, just as his wife we hope can do away with a laundry or a laundress or a bout of scrub-it-yourself by putting the dirty clothes in the washing machine.

Beside the vast world of possibilities, our present little musical world shrinks to a tiny system of timid sounds, our present instruments unresponsive, dull, and crude beside their colorful electronic counterparts, and even our best performers limited, slow to learn, and clumsy beside the nimble versatility of these electronic possibilities. In fact, the composer suddenly faced with even the thought of this world – since it is as yet far from realized – reacts in very much the same way that many have who obtain rather unexpectedly a lot of money and a lot of leisure to spend it in.

Disoriented, having to lead a life whose boundaries [they] no longer understand, we often see men confused, often almost drunk, staggering about, hitting out at random, trying one course of action after another without interest or pleasure, leading a life of complete meaninglessness. The other way that one also sees is the adoption of some arbitrary system of action completely unrelated to the situation but which cuts down on the possibilites of choice – such as one who bases his life on the lucky number five, or another who bases his actions on the advice of a numerologist or of a tax expert. Both of these are very human ways to act in an extremely confusing situation. To some extent such types of conduct can be practical enough in extreme situations, but disorientation has to be checked quickly if life is to have any interest and meaning. In the history of music, both of these methods exist – the method of utter random choice and the method of imposing some arbitrary outside order pattern on material which was too novel to be understood and dealt with effectively. A considerable amount of music of the middle ages impresses me as being this way – and also some contemporary music, as well as all present electronic music and *musique concrète*. Though I find it of considerable interest – [but] more as a catalogue of sound effects than as music.

Change, development in music is really not at all easy – for to be valid and to justify itself, a work has to be created in which all the new ideas fit together, and in which every detail adds to the total effect. Fooling around with sounds bores everyone, while the process of developing a new work with a convincing style and an order of its own must always have been the result of long, careful preparation.[30] Before the beautiful flower bursts into bloom, there has to be cross-fertilization, a crossing of strains to produce a good seed, the preparation of the ground, the planting, the gardener's careful attention, covering up the plant when it is too cold, watering it when it is too dry. Experience, reason, and a certain amount of intuition direct him. An even more elaborate preparation, obviously, goes into the composition of a great and novel work of art. *Tristan and Isolde*, for instance, is not only the product of inspiration, of a directing and unifying vision, but of a considerable effort of preparation in developing suitable techniques to realize the author's aim. The first, basic, idea was that of writing a long and far more than commonly unified work. The notion of so completely stylizing an entire work was quite new in this case and came from a combination of a poetic vision with its possible expression in chromatic harmony. But chromatic harmony had up to that time not been thoroughly explored, hence this decision involved Wagner in what must have been a great deal of work in ordering, developing a repertory of chromatic devices which could be sorted out, graded, and extended according to their own inherent logic. All this and many other methods had to be prepared before the major effort of composition took place.

Some kind of communal preparation on the part of composers, theorists, and other members of the profession and of the public must precede the individual preparation the composer makes for his own works – and in discussing electronic music, musicians find themselves suddenly in a field the full use of which would involve us in a lot of preparation.[31] It has always seemed to me that a very thoughtful and realistic consideration of the elements of music might result in ideas which could extend our world of music in many interesting ways, and now, with these infinite possibilities at hand, it might be interesting to touch on these elements briefly – pointing out their contribution to music, and suggesting how they can be extended.

From a musician's point of view, music is a succession of special kinds of sounds projected on a background of

---

30 The sentence originally continued: "with just that added touch of lively inspiration coming in at the end."

31 Handwritten note in the margin: "our types of musical skills are inadequate for the problems this music poses."

silence during a period of time. These sounds, these silences, and this time are thought of in the composer's mind and transmitted to the listener's mind through the physical sound world.

The dimensions of the physical and psychic screen of silence on which music is projected are first an extension in time and then one that extends from the highest to the lowest audible sound, and still another that extends from the softest to the loudest sound. Like all dimensions these can be divided infinitely – but, unlike ordinary physical spatial dimensions, they can never be completely filled up. There is always room for another sound, either coinciding [with] or different from the sounds already being heard. The ear can perceive very minute gradations of pitch, loudness and softness, and divisions of time; it can assemble them in groups and dissociate them according to the way the composer draws attention to them. In this silence there seems to be a limit to the amount of crowding the ear can sort out clearly into separate pitches before it begins to group them into single effects. But it is obvious that the quality of crowding sounds together, called in usual musical terms the spacing of chords, can play a much more important function in tape music, by relating this to the overtone effects which produce tone colors, for instance.

But this quality of silence itself merits a good deal of consideration. Most of you here have had the experience of visiting those remote places in deserted canyons where there is a more unusual, a more complete, silence than we are accustomed to. And you must have felt – as I have felt in this desert world where no creature seems to move, no wind blows, no water runs, where few plants grow and those that do have no leaves to rustle – a strange awe, as if your life were suddenly standing still. It is an inanimate silence, quite similar to that of a well-insulated radio or recording studio. This silence is very different from that of a concert hall even partly filled with people, although in the remote canyon one can imagine an expectancy, a waiting for a sound. Concert-hall silence is the silence of people paying attention, insulated from the noises of daily living by a building. It is the faint noise of attentiveness, if what is going on commands their silence, or the slightly louder noises of inattentiveness, which can be graded from a faint rustle through coughing up to a

snore and from there on to whispers, talking, then hissing, and finally empty silence. For anyone who has gone to concerts in other countries the question of silence becomes very intriguing, representing as it does a complex matter of each individual's ability or willingness to concentrate and – in moments when the music is not completely absorbing to many – the matter of politeness to the performers and to one's neighbors. After a number of experiences as a part of talkative Italian audiences, one comes to realize clearly how necessary the simple and violent underlining of very definite effects in Italian opera is as a way of commanding silence.

Another side of this question of silence would, of course, deal with the acoustics of halls, and point out how different kinds of echo had affected the speed and sonority of certain composers' works. Today we assume a certain standard echo – which we don't always get in a hall – but tomorrow, and even today, on recordings even this will be part of what a composer can control.

Now this physical silence naturally also assumes parallel psychic silence – that of people who have banished from their attention everything that would prevent them from following the music. But one of the devices of music which I will deal with more at length when I come to talk about time is that of starting a type of music, a rhythm, or a melody and breaking off before it comes to resolution, leaving a moment of silence in which the listener continues to imagine music – this is particularly true in rhythmic effects during which the listener tends to continue to measure the silence according to the rhythmic pattern previously heard. A similar sort of thing happens in the field of sonority. If a piece starts with a few moments of very large and widespread sonority and then immediately breaks off, leaving one instrument playing for a time alone, the listener fills in the silent spaces above and below the solo instrument with a pattern of expectation of more large sounds – a thing he would not be so likely to do (especially if he could not see an orchestra) if he heard the instrument all alone.

This establishing a musical pattern and then abandoning it inevitably leaves a kind of echo behind in the mind of the listener, a basis for comparison, an expectation for the future, and as he listens attentively this psychic silence begins to be alive with echoes which are shared with the composer and the performer but which never reach the state of physical sound. This filling of psychic silence is part of the memory process which also has to do with time. But needless to say the composer should always be controlling this inner silence in all its dimensions.

In previous times many of these techniques were very routine and required but little attention – the three- and four-part textures with their octave doublings formed the core of music and its major substance of sonority, [and] when a piece of music departed from this, it was generally expected to return to it sooner or later. Now we often establish other kinds of norms, or we go along varying density according to the needs of the moment or according to some structural pattern.

Before I deal with the dimension of time, I would like to turn to a very brief discussion of the sounds of music – although, as you know, sound is a form of fast vibrations which our ear identifies as having high and low pitches. But at a considerably slower rate of speed these are perceived as slow or fast beats of a rhythmical nature, and at still slower speeds can only be related by the intelligence, such as the sound made at noon of one day is related to that heard 24 hours later. In one sense the art of music does consist of one large continuum of vibrations, and in recent years composers have sometimes tried to bring the pitch aspect into relationship with the rhythmic aspect. As far as the present-day ear is concerned, this is purely arbitrary, although perhaps accurate mathematically, as for instance [in] the case of the B♭ in Bruno Maderna's *String Quartet,* which is below the audible range and is tapped out by the cellist's finger on the wood of his instrument at the rate of 3½ beats a second. But as you can imagine this tapping has no relation to the B flat for the listener, and even if he is told, he can only relate the two intellectually, not directly.

About musical tones, I would like first to consider one tone in itself, for in its qualities can be heard all the simple and large-scale effects of music, since in the breaking of silence by the effort of putting a sounding body into vibration the continuation of that vibration and its dying away is, after all, one of the simplest patterns of a musical piece and the simplest pattern of our emotional reaction to it. Let us start with the attack, or ictus, as di-

vorced from its continuation: the click of a woodblock, for instance. This smallest of items in music – the abrupt effort of the performer to set his instrument vibrating, the bite of the violin bow, the slap of the trumpeter's tongue – not only starts the instrument vibrating and the air around it, but is a call to attention from the composer through the performer to the listener. Once the listener is called to attention, more refinements of this attack can be exhibited – the tensing of muscles, the preparation for the plunge into sound can be presented, and in fact this lifting of the mallet, this raising of the foot, this intake of breath presenting the physical gesture of expectancy is frequently emphasized. By cutting it off from the expected following attack, or by weakening, this attack can be led to add up tension and expectancy for long stretches of time and is characteristic of many opening sections of fairly extended musical works. This effort to begin, this propelling drive, the most powerful in music, calling attention to the beginning of sound – as the three loud knocks mark the beginning of plays in France – also has the added function of setting the mood. Obviously, as time went on and performers could quiet audiences by giving them a stern look or by simply waiting, composers have tried all sorts of fanciful beginnings: lengthening the upbeat, the leading to the attack sometimes for long stretches, perhaps after starting in a tenuous way. To me the *Rite of Spring* is one long upbeat to the final crash – most other works that start tenuously or with fairly weak attacks that are constantly superseded by more forceful ones reach their culmination sooner. For it is obvious that if a composer starts a work with the most energetic attack he can produce with the instruments at his disposal, he runs the great risk that its intensity will not be grasped by his audience, who have as yet had no opportunity to see how such an attack fits into the frame of the composition. Also, since the composer cannot go on to other, stronger attacks, his composition must be largely a dying away from this attack.

After the attack has been made, most common sorts of sounds tend to die away, such as those of gongs, and even [of] many orchestral instruments which follow the normal giving out of the breath, the normal losing of energy of the bow as the hand moves further and further away from the point of contact of the bow with the string. This giving out of energy can be checked in several ways; the simplest is to cut off the sound quickly after the attack – the way jazz players choke the cymbal or others cut their tones short. The very effort of this gesture gives the succeeding silence another tension, as if we were holding our breath in expectation. Choking of sound, which tends to produce music of hard, dry texture, has to have a certain energetic aspect in order to produce the tension which composers like Stravinsky who use it frequently want. It has the remarkable effect of endowing deliberately thin, transparent textures with a great deal of life and vitality. On the other hand, the continuation of tone after the attack can take the form of remaining comparatively static in intensity and loudness or can do any number of patterns of swelling and diminishing – all of which have different kinds of connective powers, driving intensely or quietly to the next note, or dying away on it. It is on this primary level that the whole impression of cause and effect can be heard most clearly. For the joining together of one note to another, and that to the next, can only be convincing under conditions where the tension with which the first note is endowed seems to make it push with enough inner tension to the next – this inner tension may be felt within the sound of the note itself, it may be produced by endowing the note with tensions of another sort – these tensions might be considered, for want of a better term, positional tensions. When any regular pattern is established – a chord, a rhythm, or a system of high, low, or medium sounds such as any instrument possesses – then any tone can be, and is, automatically classified according to the degree with which it fits into the pre-established pattern and is experienced as having more or less tension according to its relationship to the pattern. A dissonant note in a consonant chord is felt to have tension, a note that comes in before or after a beat has more tension than one that is on the beat, a tone which is louder or suddenly softer than its predecessors is felt to have tension, a note far from the usual register of an instrument has progressively more tension – although this is not necessarily true for all instruments. As you can see, with all these various kinds of tensions possible, all types of combinations are possible; a high, soft and dissonant tone on the beat will have its special character and, like all other qualities of tones, each one of these quali-

ties must seem the result of the complex of many types of tension. In older music, the natural routines of primitive instruments were retained for a long time – high notes, especially an upward string of high notes, were usually considered as also getting louder – and also in many cases, such as in the terraced dynamics of baroque music, louds and softs were used to mark large sections of music and were not used for the intensive effects.

Besides all these inner tensions from note to note, there is the large-scale fact that in frequent repetition or too long [a] continuation of an effect, no matter how complex or simple, the tension in the effect tends to diminish as its pattern becomes too familiar. Often, for instance, Oriental music can seem to us too repetitious, and certainly it very often moves about in a very narrow scope of sounds and effects, but usually on careful hearing one is able to find that there is a continual change, if not of the notes, then [of] the way of playing them – even though of a most restricted type, from our point of view – and hence the music moves on a rather low tension. This constant tendency for the tension of a particular kind of music to dissipate is contracted in many different ways; the simplest of course is drastic change, which starts up a new wave of energy, but if the change is so great as to seem unrelated to what goes on before, then the previous tensions and qualities will be lost and will not add to the effect of the new music.

Imperceptibly, I find, I am getting around more and more to the most intriguing element of music and the one which has received far too little attention in the past: the element of time. As our lives are projected in this moving picture of eternity, we gain a very rich experience of the passage of time; our first breath starts sometimes with a slap like the attack on an instrument, and our organic clock begins ticking and beating, at the same time drawing a history of itself like a cardiogram on our memories. And then there are the vast number of things we learn, forget, dimly remember, experience, enjoy, compare, think about – all of them operating the most remarkable tricks with time. We learn about thousands of years in a few seconds and about some remarkable thing that took but a few minutes by thinking about it for many hours. We see in our imagination the flower in a rapid nervous struggle send up its seedling, grow, and bloom in a few minutes, and an athlete do a high jump that is spread out to five minutes. We are always explaining, comparing, understanding, becoming confused, but we do tend to apply to our lives the notion of cause and effect, and in fact we have a profound, almost instinctive, belief in it; no amount of data that seems to prove that causality is untrue will shake this. I imagine in other civilizations where the feeling for causality is not so strong, the sense of time is not so developed. Certainly our sense of time is a very developed one, as is indicated apparently by the differences between the tenses of our verbs and those of many Oriental languages – apparently even Russian does not make the fine temporal distinctions our Western languages do.

In listening to a number of concerts of Oriental music recently, I have been struck by the fact that one of the important differences is that of large-scale design. East Indian music, for instance, for all its delicacy of tuning, its remarkable variety of plucking, sliding, playing with a remarkable number of kinds of attack, and for all its ability to play an entertaining game around basic rhythmic patterns – *talas* – does not give, to a Westerner at least, the impression of large developments, of the weaving of tensions of different sorts together to give a pattern which is carried from beginning to end of a piece with constantly new facets being revealed. In talking to Westerners at such concerts, it is also clear, at least to me, that many apparently musical people listen to Western music as they listen to Oriental music, as a series of sound effects strung together without much connection between, giving themselves up to the delight of the moment, the theme, or the orchestral texture.

Yet to me it seems quite obvious that our music has developed in its special way, at least since the renaissance, because it has always sought to work on our time sense, on our memories, on our ability to associate ideas, to grasp degrees of similarity. For these reasons, instruments have become very straight-laced, and the classical style of playing them has stressed only the most sober characteristics, leaving to popular music all the barking, squeaking slides, and trick articulations which draw attention to the performer and to the individual moment, draw it out of its context and hinder the flow from idea to idea.

This matter of design in time, of order, is the most remarkable and distinctive quality of Western music. It is something which is bound to be difficult for inexperienced listeners to take in, especially on hearing a work but once – yet it is this quality which lends our music its real power and gives it its significance.

Let me try to describe this order by comparing it to other temporal orders. In the first place, we can consider the process of listening to, or reading, a language. Each successive word gives a more precise meaning to the one or ones that have gone before. A word, at first vague, is modified, then its signification given perhaps a location in time and space. Sentence after sentence it continues to change and mold the meaning. Sentence modifies sentence and paragraph modifies paragraph. Whole large subjects are contrasted with others – listeners' objections are considered, there is an ever widening context which can all be made to throw its light on the basic ideas.

This very same process, of course, goes on in music, except that tones, even groups of tones, do not refer to things usually, and that the interconnection of tones is a matter of the combination of many kinds of tensions. These tensions are interpreted by the listener as a web of cause and effect, of effort, energy, satisfaction, relaxation, and, as a great work of music proceeds, the wonder of a series of remarkably motivated happenings – expected, but still, when they really make their appearance, always surprising and novel.

For it is really this almost abstract activity in time, its complex interrelations and tensions, which, as we hear, we constantly relate together and compare, as we do all our lives. These systems, of course, had their origins in very simple matters, sometimes descriptive musics that remind one of human gaiety, of lamentation, or of natural sounds, or human activities. Many of these original patterns still persist in music but have been subjected to so many layers of different treatment that few of them retain their original character and most of them are more interesting because of the abstract character they suggest. There is no use denying that music has imitated everything – but there have been no successful or interesting imitative pieces that do not have a strong abstract interest also. Over the years, besides the literary patterns that formed the basis of tone poems, there have been, as you know, tone poems about machines, about the stream of consciousness, and even arithmetical tone poems. Some of these have found interesting new methods of musical organization.

The works of Debussy and the early ones of Schoenberg introduce us to a kind of lessened musical logic that is not unlike the linguistic metaphor – in which we are made to see a connection between two rather unlike things. Similarly, abrupt and frequent contrast, the developing of patterns out of bits of apparently unrelated materials, which when forcibly brought together by musical means produce very interesting new types of expression.

In this necessarily sketchy discussion of musical time I have tried to suggest how the very fact of hearing this stream of closely interrelated materials provokes in the listener many familiar patterns, emotional ones and thought ones. Certainly no piece of music interests us much unless we have some sort of a valuable feeling about it, just as nothing does in our lives, but the patterns of music do not always follow the patterns of human feelings, nor need they. Sometimes feeling is only a concomitant to a sense of logic, of a marvelous and intricately unfolding order. But just as our feelings about causality and time have tended to conform much more to a detailed knowledge and experience of the world instead of to abstract patterns, so music has followed and it too now is written by people who live today and see things in our present way.

The experience of time which music articulates is a most unique and valuable one – but it must be based on the inner experience of time. If simply a mechanical time, it becomes nearly meaningless emotionally and aesthetically, and I doubt whether this element of music can ever be projected by a machine without the intermediary of a performer [who] makes all the fine adjustments necessary to carry on the fine threads of tension, adjusting it almost unconsciously to the experience of time lapsing and to the particular conditions under which he is playing.

In conclusion let me say that our profession has inherited a very elevated and highly developed aesthetic point of view about music from Europe. One often feels that musical publics here have really very little grasp of what this point of view means and what kind of intelligence went to make it up. Perhaps the point of view is

one that will perpetually be above the head of even the average intelligent person – in which case it will cease to be of interest – or, on the other hand, our educational institutions will protect these ideas, as they do other ideas beyond the average man's reach, acting as repositories of such things – and this may be hard on the art – or better still, we hope that the quality of education will soon become such that such ideas will once more play the role among a considerable group of interested people and raise the quality of the attitudes of our present audiences to demanding really valuable and significant works of contemporary composers, even if they compose for electronic machines.

[Typescript, carbon copy with autograph corrections; Elliott Carter Collection, Paul Sacher Foundation.]

Congratulations from Nancarrow (1957)

Even after emigrating from the United States in 1940 Conlon Nancarrow remained in contact with his American friends. Among them were Copland and Carter, both of whom visited him several times in Mexico City and strove to make his music known to the American public. It was thanks to Carter's suggestion, for example, that in early 1951 – shortly after Carter had visited Nancarrow for the second time (see above, pp. 98–99) – there were plans for a performance of a Nancarrow piece by the New Music Group in New York; this performance, however, never took place.[32] Carter also arranged for Nancarrow's *Rhythm Study No. 1 for Player Piano* to appear in the *New Music Quarterly*.[33] Further evidence of his efforts to bring about greater recognition for his friend is the following exchange of letters, which arose after another meeting between the two men during which Nancarrow mentioned a possible stay in Europe.[34] (Nancarrow had obtained his long-sought Mexican citizenship in early 1956 and thus finally owned a valid passport again.) The correspondence shows Carter encouraging him to undertake such a trip. But it also intimates that Nancarrow was ultimately unwilling to emerge from his artistic isolation. Carter's suggestion to visit him in Europe and to contact the conductor Francis Travis brought only a curt thank you from Nancarrow by way of response. On the other hand, he spoke at great length – and with great appreciation – of Carter's *String Quartet No. 1*, which he had received from the composer in both the printed edition and the gramophone recording by the Walden Quartet (see above, p. 119). Nancarrow felt that in this piece the great complexity of the compositional fabric was fully justified by the music's intellectual and emotional substance, in contrast to many other contemporary compositions. Nor is it surprising that, having generally endured negative experiences with performers, he was impressed by the superb achievement of the Walden Quartet.

69 Elliott Carter to Conlon Nancarrow, 21 March 1957

Elliott C. Carter, Jr., 31 West 12th Street,
New York City II, N.Y.

Dear Conlon,

I sent off some copies of *New Music* with your piece in it and other things which I thought might be of interest to you.[35] I hope that you receive them ere long.

It was very good seeing you again – and hearing that you are about to get out of Mexico. Perhaps if you go to Europe in the fall we can meet.

I am teaching at Dartington Hall in the South of England for the last two weeks in August – Boulez is teaching there the first two – and Robert Craft will be conducting some Stravinsky concerts during my time.[36] Then Helen will come over at the end of August and we will go to Paris – and perhaps the Soviet Union – and then on October 20th, I shall be at the Donaueschingen Festival in South Germany where my Variations for orchestra will be performed.[37] We will stay on until the end of October & return here – I suppose. If you should be in Europe at any of this period be sure and let us know.

By the way, you might write to:

Mr. Francis Travis, / Gravesano, / Canton Tessin, / Switzerland, who is a young American conductor, an excellent one, who is very close to Scherchen and might be very helpful for you to know.[38] If you go to Europe before we do write and ask to see him – telling him I suggested this.

Incidentally, Igor Markevitch, I see, is giving some conducting classes in Mexico.[39] He is a very useful person to know – if you can stand him.

Anyhow – let's hear from you sometime soon. And if I can be of any help here please don't hesitate to write.

Helen joins me in sending our best.
Elliott

March 21, 1957

[Typed letter with autograph signature; Conlon Nancarrow Collection, Paul Sacher Foundation. Reprinted by permission of Yoko Sugiura Nancarrow.]

---

32 The exact reasons for the failure of this project are unclear. A letter from Minna Lederman informs us, however, that Nancarrow evidently felt under pressure: "[...] so sorry you seem 'pressed,' even harassed. I was looking forward to hearing a work of yours here this spring but I gather difficulties have arisen – Too bad you couldn't come to straighten them out." (Letter from Minna Lederman to Conlon Nancarrow, 18 March [1951], Conlon Nancarrow Collection, Paul Sacher Foundation.)

33 Conlon Nancarrow, *Rhythm Study No. 1 for Player Piano, New Music Quarterly* 25/1 (October 1951). The production master for this edition, which in fact appeared only in June 1952, was prepared by Noah Greenberg, the founder of the New York Pro Musica. A short while later Greenberg also prepared the instrumental parts for Carter's *First String Quartet.* Several years later Carter devoted a passage to the *Rhythm Study No. 1* in his essay "The Rhythmic Basis of American Music"; see above, p. 115, notes 73 and 74.

34 It is not clear where and when exactly this meeting took place.

35 By sending some printed copies of *Rhythm Study No. 1*, Carter responded to Nancarrow's complaint, expressed two years previously, that he had not received any author's copies of this publication from *New Music* (see his letter of 8 March 1955 to Eliott Carter; Elliott Carter Collection, Paul Sacher Foundation). Among the "other things" enclosed in Carter's letter were a printed edition and a recording of his *String Quartet No. 1,* both of which are now preserved in the

70   Conlon Nancarrow to Elliott Carter, 25 March [1957]

Conlon Nancarrow / Apartado 31550 / Mexico 20, D.F.
March 25

Dear Elliott:

Your comments on the Quartet (and other recent music of yours) made me expect something so complex that the best I could expect from a first hearing would be an interest in hearing it more.[40] I listened to it first without looking at the score, and it was the most impressive musical experience I have had in many years. However, when I started looking at the score I realized that it is probably the most complex piece of music ever written (or at least the most complex ever heard). But I think most complex music sounds like hell. Or maybe it is just that music written for the sake of complexity sounds that way. For example, Messiaen's music looks complex and sounds even more so, a muddy mess. In your Quartet I see that the almost impossible difficulties for the performers are the only way that the direct sounding results can be achieved. There are several sections that sound, for lack of a better word, quite jazzy. Another thing that struck me was that it seemed short. Apart from obvious subjective factors that make something seem short, such as interest, I was wondering if your whole concept of temporal organization had anything to do with that impression. I think that if you go any further along this line you are going to need some means of mechanical performance. The dedication of this group achieved the seemingly impossible, but there is a point beyond which even dedication is not enough.

Thanks for sending the *New Music* and the name of the conductor in Switzerland.

If I get to Europe it won't be until next spring.

Congratulations on the Quartet.

Regards to you and Helen.
Conlon

[Typed letter with autograph signature; Elliott Carter Collection, Paul Sacher Foundation. Reprinted by permission of Yoko Sugiura Nancarrow.]

Nancarrow Collection at the Paul Sacher Foundation.

36 For Carter's teaching activities at the Dartington Summer Music School in 1957, see below, pp. 147–149.

37 The trip to the Soviet Union never came about, but after their stay in Dartington the Carters spent some time in Paris, from where they made a side-trip to Italy and heard a performance of the *Variations for Orchestra* at the Donaueschingen Festival. This performance, with Hans Rosbaud conducting the Southwest German Radio Symphony Orchestra, took place on

19 October 1957 rather than the originally scheduled date of the 20th; see below, p. 150.

38 Francis Travis (b. 1921) was born in the US and became a Swiss citizen. After studying with Hermann Scherchen, he conducted a wide range of repertoire with a strong focus on new music. He was professor for orchestral conducting at the Staatliche Hochschule für Musik in Freiburg, Germany, for twenty-five years.

39 Igor Markevitch's "Pan-American Course of Orchestral Conducting," organized by the National Institute of Fine Arts,

took place in Mexico City from 10 May to 25 June 1957 and involved several concerts. Carter probably learned of this event from an advertisement that appeared on the inside cover page of *Tempo*, no. 42 (Winter 1956–57).

40 The sleeve of the Walden Quartet's recording of the *String Quartet No. 1* (Columbia ML 5104) contains not only Carter's own program notes (along with a few comments added from an interview), but also several excerpts from William Glock's article "A Note on Elliott Carter," (see above, p. 115, notes 73 and 75), pp. 47–52.

"Arnold Schoenberg: *Variations for Orchestra,* op. 31" (1957)

Although Carter was by neither training nor inclination aesthetically close to the music of the Second Viennese School, his interest in the music of Schoenberg, Berg, and Webern (in that order), which he first encountered in the 1920s, continued throughout his life. By the 1950s this music was hard to avoid; in Europe as well as in the US the technical achievements of all three composers were accorded increasing respect, especially in the academic circles in which Carter moved during these years (his most recent position had been at Queens College in New York, where he taught from 1955 to 1956). Carter was an autodidact as far as twelve-tone technique was concerned. Schoenberg's own essays published in the collection *Style and Idea* in 1950 probably contributed most to his understanding of the technique, though he knew René Leibowitz's books as well.[41] The text below presents Carter's only (written) analysis of a Second Viennese School work: Schoenberg's *Variations for Orchestra*, op. 31, a radio lecture written in early 1957.[42] Commissioned by the radio producer Robert Turner of CBC Vancouver, the lecture was broadcast on 24 March 1957 as part of the year-long weekly series "Twentieth-Century Masterpieces, 1900–1957."[43] Though the subject of the lecture would probably not have appealed to the casual listener, Carter makes every effort to be intelligible to the non-specialist and to illustrate his analytical remarks with taped musical examples. The first of Carter's two main points is consistent with Schoenberg's own views: that music composed by means of the twelve-tone technique is just as expressive and flexible as any other music. Many of Carter's examples emphasize how Schoenberg used the twelve-tone technique to facilitate melodic and harmonic invention. Carter also shows how the row is not a straitjacket, but allows choices at every stage of the compositional process. Carter's second main point is distinctly polemical in the context of the 1950s: he sees Schoenberg's use of classical forms (such as variation form) in an unambiguously positive light, in contrast to the position of Boulez and others that Schoenberg's musical language was far ahead of his old-fashioned formal vocabulary.

Even though Carter never used the twelve-tone technique in his music, he was clearly influenced by Schoenberg's *Variations for Orchestra*, most of all in his own piece of that name, which was completed on 14 November 1955, five months after Carter heard a performance of the Schoenberg work in Baden-Baden.[44] Carter's *Variations for Orchestra* have the same formal design as Schoenberg's – an introduction, nine variations, and a finale – and also display the same kind of symmetry around the central fifth variation that Carter describes with respect to Schoenberg's work.[45]

41 Arnold Schoenberg, *Style and Idea*, trans. Dika Newlin (New York: Philosophical Library, 1950), particularly the 1941 lecture "Composition with Twelve Tones" (pp. 102–143), in which Schoenberg discusses his op. 31. René Leibowitz, *Introduction à la musique de douze sons: Les Variations pour orchestre op. 31, d'Arnold Schoenberg* (Paris: L'Arche, 1949). Carter was probably also acquainted with Leibowitz's *Schoenberg et son école*, which was widely known in the U.S. in an English translation by Dika Newlin (*Schoenberg and His School: The Contemporary Stage of the Language of Music* (New York: Philosophical Library, [1949]), as well as the

books on twelve-tone technique by Ernst Krenek (*Studies in Counterpoint Based on the Twelve-tone Technique* [New York: Schirmer, 1940]) and Josef Rufer (*Composition With Twelve Notes Related Only to One Another*, trans. Humphrey Searle [New York: Macmillan, 1954]).

42 The series consisted of fifty-two one-hour broadcasts that continued for a year, from 6 January to 29 December 1957, always at 11:00 pm on Saturday evening and repeated the following Monday at 1:00 am.

43 Every author contacted was asked in advance to name three prospective "masterpieces" – including Carter, who proposed Stravinsky's *Symphony of Psalms*

and Bartók's *Music for Strings, Percussion, and Celesta* (see letter from Elliott Carter to Robert Turner, 31 August 1956; carbon copy in the Elliott Carter Collection, Paul Sacher Foundation). The compositions cited most often were then presented in separate broadcasts in chronological order by composer. The front-runners were Stravinsky (eight works presented), Bartók (five), and Mahler and Schoenberg (three each). One work by Carter was also discussed in this radio series, namely the *String Quartet No. 1*, presented by Richard Franko Goldman on 1 December 1957.

71 Elliott Carter, "Arnold Schoenberg: *Variations for Orchestra,* op. 31" (1957)

Ladies & Gentlemen:

The work of contemporary music which I would like to discuss with you today, Arnold Schoenberg's *Variations for Orchestra,* is that composer's opus 31 and was completed in 1928. Just as the works written by Schoenberg in 1908 and 1909 ushered in and gave validity to a new, free use of dissonance, starting a whole new period of contemporary [music], so the works written around 1925 to 1928, of which the *Variations for Orchestra* is the most important, come at the beginning of another new stage in contemporary music. For this work, written in the composer's 54th year, is the first orchestral piece to use the twelve-tone technique in a thoroughgoing way. It is also the work which, by its extraordinary musical inspiration and expression, has established this technique of composition as a significant and important means of contemporary artistic thought. Indeed as more and more works using this technique are written by composers of almost every nationality and of every succeeding generation, especially among those which have appeared since the Second War, recognition of these *Variations* has grown. A few years ago a seminar devoted an entire week of meetings to the analysis of this work by composers from all over the world coming together in Gravesano, Switzerland,[46] and recently René Leibowitz devoted a hundred pages, the major part of his book *Introduction à la musique de douze sons,* to an analysis of this work.[47] Yet in spite of this theoretical interest and in spite of the numerous performances it has received in post-war central Europe, the work remains unrecorded, perhaps because of its performance difficulty and perhaps, too, because of an unmerited reputation gained early in its existence for inexpressive, cerebral ugliness through a number of inadequate, poorly rehearsed, and artistically misleading performances. That this reputation is unfounded, and that this work is one of great beauty and expressiveness filled with the breath of life should be obvious to almost any listener familiar with contemporary music when he hears the marvelous performance presented today on this program on a tape made by the South West German Radio Orchestra directed by Hans Rosbaud.[48]

In order to give a certain perspective on this work, which is the first by Schoenberg to appear on this radio series but which during his life was preceded by quite a number which earned for him a wide international reputation, I would like to suggest very briefly the composer's artistic point of view. Actually his ideas, for one whose music sounds so unusual, are not very different from those of many a nineteenth-century composer or critic, nor indeed from many of those who condemn Schoenberg's music as meaningless. In his lectures and books he is constantly stressing the importance of inspiration, of musical feeling, and of musical order and individuality. It is very important to bear in mind that Schoenberg wished to write music that is expressive in much the same way as that of the great nineteenth-century composers, that he wanted the listener to listen to his music in much the same way as a music lover listens, say, to Brahms – whose music, too, is sometimes difficult to grasp on first hearings. It is easy to forget this when first confronted with a description of the intricacies of the twelve-tone technique used in the *Variations.* Yet this work is, in a sense, remarkable as a musical construction in very much the same way as Bach's *Art of Fugue* is remarkable, and, like Bach's great work, becomes more and more interesting both technically and expressively as we study it. However, Schoenberg was not writing this ingenious and cleverly constructed music merely to demonstrate his skill, as Bach is said to have done in the *Art of Fugue,* but to try and make his musical style clearer. He says in a lecture: "Composition with the 12 tones has no other aim than comprehensibility."[49] – I hope that by the time I have discussed this work, you will realize that he means not only comprehensibility of organization but also of expression, which in a great work such as this is indissoluble with it.

Shortly after the conclusion of the First World War, contemporary music underwent a great change, which is

---

44 The performance of Schoenberg's *Variations for Orchestra* with the Südwestfunk Orchestra conducted by Hans Rosbaud took place on 19 June 1955 during the 1955 ISCM festival. By his own account, Carter composed his *Variations for Orchestra* "during 1955 from sketches made in 1953 and 1954 at the American Academy in Rome" (quoted in Link 2000, p. 61). Detailed study of the sketches would be necessary to ascertain how far the work had progressed by the summer of 1955.

45 In Carter's work, the fourth and sixth variations – with successive ritardandos and accelerandos, respectively – correspond to each other, like Schoenberg's

fourth and sixth variations, both scored for chamber groups. In both, the fifth variation is articulated as a middle point – in Schoenberg by its emphatic gestures, in Carter by the reverse: its stillness.

46 Carter is referring to the colloquium "Die Grundlagen der neuen Musik" [The Foundations of New Music], held from 23 July to 5 August 1956 in the experimental studio founded by Hermann Scherchen in Gravesano. During the colloquium a seminar was held from 24 to 30 July 1956 on Schoenberg's *Variations for Orchestra,* op. 31, and Anton Webern's *Variations for Orchestra,* op. 30, under the direction of Luigi Nono. Another seminar was headed

by Fritz Enkel, and still another by Luigi Nono and Hermann Scherchen. Among the participants were Roberto Schnorrenberg, Claude Roland, Marc Wilkinson, and Don Banks. We are grateful to Angela De Benedictis for helping us to identify this event. (Angela De Benedictis, personal communication, 18 April 2008.)

47 See Leibowitz, *Introduction* (see above, p. 140, note 41), pp. 109–219.

48 This was the recording of the performance Carter had heard in Baden-Baden in summer 1955; see note 44.

49 Arnold Schoenberg, "Composition With Twelve Tones" (see above, p. 140, note 41), p. 103.

amusingly depicted in a witty musical joke written to his own words in 1926 by Schoenberg. This little chamber cantata, entitled "The New Classicism," begins in mock seriousness by a tenor declaiming, "I won't be a romantic any longer. I hate the romantic. From tomorrow on, I will write in the purest classic style":[50]

[Ex. 1, "The New Classicism" – Columbia ML 5099: first 40 seconds or so till end of female chorus]

Later on, after giving ample demonstration of neoclassic pedantry in a number of remarkable fugal passages during which the words state the ridiculous premise that the cadence or conclusion is the most important thing in the classical style, as a demonstration of this proposition, the little work comes to a conclusion in which the word "klassisch" is set to arpeggios of conventional triads and diatonic scales and finally a great dissonant chord which resolves to an octave on the note C:

[Ex. 2, last 42 seconds or so. Passage starts with a pause, then a rising 3-note arpeggio, soft, by alto voice, followed by descending one in tenor.]

The remarkable thing about this neoclassic-sounding satire is that it employs all the typical neoclassic devices, sometimes even in a diatonic way, and yet all is subjugated to the twelve-tone technique, which makes it a real *tour de force.*

Yet in spite of his ridicule of the classic point of view, Schoenberg's return to it is evident in all his works of this time, as can be seen even in the *Variations.* This must have constituted a very great rupture with the past. For since 1909 the composer and his two students and followers Alban Berg and Anton Webern seem to have been heading toward a style which was not only an emancipation of dissonance but also an elimination of themes and of the usual formal methods. A more fundamental, or at least more radical, notion of what constituted a musical idea seemed to lead them to scattered, fragmented motives, to ideas made up only of changes of tone color on the same notes. On a larger scale, distantly related ideas were juxtaposed in a world where tonality could no longer be felt, where rhythm was pattern after pattern of irregular, dramatic outbursts. In his vocal works, such as *Erwartung* and *Pierrot lunaire,* Schoenberg approached non-thematic

composing and gave full rein to the notion of continuous variation, in which every element of the musical dialectic was in constant change.

The possibility of form in such an apparent state of anarchy was thought about a great deal, and out of this came the system which I am about to consider, which still allows for the impression of continuous variation – avoiding literal repetition – and yet is full of suggestions of various degrees of similarity between one idea and the next.

At the time of his *Variations* in 1928, Schoenberg had already returned to many classical procedures, so that it was no surprise that he might write a work following fairly closely the traditional pattern of theme and variations, although in the years prior to 1914 such an idea probably never would have occurred to him, and, if it had, a work of entirely different and completely unusual character would have resulted. Now, in 1928, he wrote a theme as a basis for his *Variations* which has a coherent arioso-like melodic line and yet adheres to the principle of continuous variation although having the suggestion of a return of the first phrase in the last one:

[Ex. 3, *Variations:* mm. 34–57 incl.]

The first three phrases of this tender and expressive theme are played in the upper register of the 'cellos while the fourth is heard in the high violins. Each phrase is based on an order of the twelve tones of the chromatic scale. The first phrase presents the basic set order or row of twelve different tones on which the entire work is based:

[Ex. 4: mm. 34–38, incl.]

The third phrase presents the same tones backwards in so-called retrograde motion:

[Ex. 5: mm. 46–50, incl.]

The fourth phrase, played by the high muted violins, plays the row upside down or inverted. That is, for every rising interval of the original an interval of the same size is used in the inversion and vice versa. Below the violins a soft counterpoint in the 'cellos made up of the tones in their original order can be heard:

[Ex. 6: mm. 51–57, incl.]

---

50 This is the third of *Drei Satiren,* op. 28.

The second phrase uses the tones of the inversion played backward, called retrograde inversion:

[Ex. 7: mm. 39–45, incl.]

Now you have heard how all the 4 phrases of the theme are derived from one basic pattern of tones, although given much variety of emphasis, articulation, and phrasing and shading. In this technique of composing with the twelve tones continual use is made of these four forms of the row as well as their eleven possible transpositions. Thus out of a basic row, 47 other derivations are immediately considered as available. Out of these 48 patterns of tones every detail having to do with pitch, such as melody, counterpoint, harmony, [and] figurations, is constructed. In fact in these *Variations* every note in the entire work can fairly simply be shown to have a direct connection with the original pattern or its derivatives.

The particular twelve-tone row of this work exhibits a special type of construction which deeply affects the formal organization of the entire work. That is that the first 6 tones of the inversion of the row, when transposed down a minor third, constitute a new ordering of the last 6 tones of the original row. Thus out of the combination of the first half of the original row and the first half of the inversion a new 12-tone [row] can be made. The same is true of the last six tones of each.

The working out of this feature would be of interest only to puzzle solvers if it did not have a great effect on the shape of the music. Here is one of the ways it operates in the music you have just heard. Grouping by sixes is avoided in the theme, as it is very important in all other parts of the work. The first phrase of the theme is made up of motives of 5, then 4, then 3 tones. The five melodic tones are accompanied by a chord of five tones – the first five tones of the complementary inversion – [the] next four tones of the theme are accompanied by a chord of four tones made up of the next four tones of the inversion, and so forth throughout. In this way the harmony of the work is determined by the row – although the fact that this extremely schematic arrangement of tones proved to be musically satisfactory may be a matter of chance. In any case this demonstrates a principle which is adhered to most of the time during the work – for throughout the twelve-tone pattern is constantly being revolved so that

each note is separated by as many of the other eleven as possible before its return.

Now let me give a number of brief examples of the use of the row. First, listen to its first integral appearance in the first phrase of the theme; it will be followed after short pauses by examples of its melodic use in various places in the work:

[Ex. 8: mm. 34–38, incl.; pause; mm. 435–441, incl.; pause; mm. 10–13, incl.; pause; mm. 303–304, incl.; pause; mm. 100–105, incl.]

The same can be done for the inversion. First the original appearance as the fourth phrase of the theme, then in three other places:

[Ex. 9: mm. 51–57, incl.; pause; mm. 83–86, incl.; pause; mm. 441–446, incl.]

Now here are isolated motives of the theme, each played in [its] original form and then followed immediately by [its] inverted form:

[Ex. 10: mm. 472–486, incl.]

Here is an example of the original form of the row above in one rhythmic arrangement in the flute and the inversion below, divided among the trumpet and violas, and then the whole passage inverted with different instrumentation, followed by a concluding phrase in which the two forms can be clearly heard:

[Ex. 11: mm. 286–290, incl.]

Now let us listen to a few samples of new melodic possibilities derived from the basic row. Here are two examples in which new melodic shapes are made by simply changing the octave of some of the pitches:

[Ex. 12: mm. 354–362, incl.; pause; mm. 279–285, incl.]

In the next, the first six tones of the row are sounds in chords while the flute plays the last six in a rising pattern and then descends using the inversion in the same way:

[Ex. 13: mm. 24–25, incl.]

Sometimes entirely new ideas are derived from the tone row by distributing the tones over two parts of counterpoint. In the next sample, the horn plays tones 1, 4, 6, and 10 while the oboe plays 2, 3, 5, and the remaining notes of the row. This is followed by the same process using the inversion, and then in retrograde:

[Ex. 14: mm. 344–349, incl.]

The most remarkable departures from the basic row can be made that still maintain some relationship with it. Here, for instance, all twelve tones are sounded during each two beats. The high strings play first notes 7 and 8 of the inversion while 8 tones are played by inner harmonic parts and [notes] 11 and 12 are whistled by two piccolos, the next two beats repeat the same system but apply it to the original form, and so forth:

[Ex. 15: mm. 178–179, incl.]

So much for a brief survey of the twelve-tone method as exemplified in this work. As you must have noticed, it is often hard to grasp how the row is used at all times, but I think that even from these short examples it is possible to feel the strong effect of artistic unity which its use lends to a work.

The reasons which led Schoenberg to develop this particuar method and no other are stated by him in a lecture delivered in 1941: "The method of composing with twelve tones grew out of necessity. In the last hundred years, the concept of harmony has changed tremendously through the development of chromaticism."[51] After making this remark, he traces how the sense of tonality had been weakened by Wagner's chromaticism, how Debussy's coloristic harmonies weakened this feeling still further, and how this tonal dissolution led to Schoenberg's concept of the "emancipation of dissonance," in which each chord stood by itself and hung in a scheme more ordered by literary ideas than actual musical ones. This led to the kind of tonal ambiguity often called atonality, which is quite closely related to the kind of literary ambiguity found in the symbolist and expressionist poems which Schoenberg set to music. His discussion of the development of his system is concluded by these remarks: "The desire for conscious control of new means and forms will arise in every artist's mind; and he will wish to know *consciously* the laws and rules which he has conceived 'as in a dream.' Strongly convincing as this dream may have been, the conviction that these new sounds obey the laws of nature and of our manner of thinking – the conviction that

order, logic, comprehensibility and form cannot be present without the obedience to such laws – forces the composer along the road of exploration."[52]

It is clear that about 1921–1926 Schoenberg followed such a road, and bit by bit worked out this method of composing in a series of compositions. There is nothing arbitrary about it, but it comes directly out of the experience of composing in the style Schoenberg was involved with. By the time he came to the *Variations*, which involved adapting this technique to orchestral writing, Schoenberg had developed a great deal of facility and fantasy in using the method.

Before discussing the *Variations* as a whole and not just the detail of 12-tone structure, which is, in a way, a kind of brickwork out of which the large edifice is formed, it might be interesting to consider just how restricting this system is. First of all, it only controls the order of the pitches, not their length, for all rhythmic, formal, textural, and orchestral devices can be handled with the same freedom as that of any other music. Even within the controlled field of pitch, the composer has a great latitude of free choice: he can choose the octave in which the various tones of his row are sounded, he can choose between 48 aspects of the row, he can conceal or emphasize melodic motives of the row and find new melodic motives which are not made up of the straightforward order of the row. In this work, for instance, a whole section of the finale is built up on the melodic motive of B♭, A, C, B♮ (BACH in German notation), and yet these four tones are not four closely connected tones in the row of the work. In spite of this, as you will hear, this motto is heard in all sorts of different harmonic relationships, even while the order of the row is clearly being used. This gives an example of the flexibility of this technique.

In fact, its very flexibility, its being so well thought out and answering so many problems arising from the practical experience of composing in a contemporary style, [and] the authority of a considerable number of outstanding and imaginative works have made this system attractive to a great number of younger composers. It is easy to understand why. As for myself, this system does not help in the kind of problems which my style of composition involves, and so I do not use it, much as I find it interesting.

51 Schoenberg, "Composition With Twelve Tones" (see above, p. 140, note 41), p. 103.
52 Ibid., pp. 106–107.

But let us turn to the plan of the *Variations* as a musical work. The piece has a general form of three concentric arches – the introduction and theme present certain aspects of the material that find their complete emphasis in the finale, a long final movement. The first two variations present the theme clearly against backgrounds of different accompaniment figures and are paralleled by the last two variations, the 8th & 9th, which do somewhat the same thing. The intermediary variations break up the tones of the theme more and more and relegate them to a more and more secondary role until they re-emerge in the eighth variation. Besides [being used in] the theme, the motive of BACH appears momentarily in the introduction and in the second variation and then dominates whole sections of the finale. All of this is not at all [an] uncommon procedure as a plan. The detail of working out is another matter.

The introduction sets up a mysterious atmosphere of soft tremolos in which the first note of the tone row is heard four times repeated, to be answered by the first note of the complementary inversion repeated. Then tones 1 & 2 in an alternating pattern of the original [are] answered by 1 & 2 of the inversion; there is a pause on both third tones after which by the same process tones 3, 4 [and] 5 of each row are introduced. Finally all 6 notes of the inversion are heard in the bass, followed by the first six notes of the original, then the second 6 of the original are answered by the second six of the inversion – a short transition built of these two forms brings this section to a conclusion:

[Ex. 16: m. 1 – first beat of 18]

There is a very dramatic middle section which climbs rapidly upwards, using a series of transpositions of the inversion, and relaxes through other forms of the row; and this settles into a return of the mood of the beginning – below the phrases of the flute the trombone plays BACH slowly and softly, and immediately the five-note motive which forms the opening of the theme is heard in the low clarinets, and gradually the vague static mood of the opening reappears, at first built on a different part of the tone row that gives rise to semitones, and then finally coming to rest on an eight-tone chord immediately followed by a pizzicato one of the other four tones of the row:

[Ex. 17: mm. 18–33, incl.]

Then comes the theme, which you have already heard, and it is followed by the first variation, which consists of a filigree of three-tone motives thrown about through all the instruments and registers of the orchestra except for the lowest bass, where from time to time the phrases of the theme are brought out, separated by rests:

[Ex. 18: mm. 58–81, incl.]

This first variation illustrates one of the important precepts of this school during these years – the notion that the sound of the octave was to be avoided. Now all of classical orchestration, especially from the time of Haydn and Mozart, depended on octave doublings to produce richer sounds and thicker textures. The massiveness of much romantic music is produced just by playing the same thing in octaves, sometimes through three or four octaves at once – it is a commonplace device in organ and harpsichord playing to use stops that sound these octave doublings automatically. Now the notion of atonal music, and especially the twelve-tone variety, seemed to preclude such octave sounds – it was said that the octave drew too much attention to one pitch – but, for whatever reason, Schoenberg completely avoids this stock-in-trade device throughout this work.[53] When textures need thickening, he brings in new pieces of counterpoint from his row, and when he wants to produce louder, more intense effects he simply puts more instruments on a part. The orchestra of this work contains a great many wind instruments in order to balance the modern, enlarged body of strings, yet this work in many respects resembles a kind of magnified chamber music piece, although far more colorful, since a continual change of instrumental color is possible when such a large number of instruments are available. As if to prove this chamber-music side of the work, four of the variations do use a small number of instruments only. The second variation, which uses from the string section only a solo 'cello and a solo violin, is an example of this.

In this variation the entire theme is played in inversion by the solo violin, with considerable pauses between motives and phrases, and imitated by the oboe. There is a background of close canons in the other winds. Toward the end there is a moment of slowing up during which the trombone plays its BACH in the background:

[Ex. 19: mm. 82–105, incl.]

---

53 Ibid., pp. 130–131.

With the third variation the process of fragmentation of the theme becomes more apparent, for here in the background, in the middle register of the horns, the notes of the theme are sounded two or three at a time, with rests between. In the foreground is heard a vigorous march-like movement, made up also of two-note motives from the theme. Here are the few measures:

[Ex. 20: mm. 106–(116), incl.]

The fourth variation is a delicate waltz in which the notes of the theme, separated by rests, are heard in the background played by harp, celesta, and mandolin. The waltz theme comes from a motive of the main theme and develops it into a melodic line. In this variation two different tone rows are played together and gotten through about every measure and a half. Here is the first half of it:

[Ex. 21: mm. 130–153, incl.]

I have already played a sample of the vigorous fifth variation. In it the lowest bass notes, each separated by a rest, play the tones of the theme:

[Ex. 22: mm. 178–182, incl.]

The sixth variation is a delicate chamber music piece of considerable charm in which the theme is much concealed, and the seventh variation, which starts with a beautiful bassoon solo, is the last which disguises the theme – whose separate notes are played in the highest register, widely separated by short notes of the piccolo, celesta, and glockenspiel. Toward the end of this variation the last phrases of the theme begin to be more easily heard:

[Ex. 23: mm. 238–261, incl.]

The eighth variation breaks in in a vigorous way, playing answering fragments of the theme against a rhythmic background:

[Ex. 24: mm. 262–285, incl.]

The ninth and last variation is one of the most interesting because, while giving the impression of free improvisation, its little phrases are all made up of direct quotations of parts of the theme, all clearly recognizable:

[Ex. 25: mm. 286–309, incl.]

The finale is in three large parts. The first one features the BACH motive associated always with a rather noble broad treatment, the second, the main theme of the work played against a number of different countersubjects, and then, finally, the combination of the main theme with BACH and other material. In this way the relationship with J. S. Bach's *Art of Fugue*, which ends with an uncompleted fugue of which BACH is one of the subjects, is established.

BACH is first heard in the highest notes of the string tremolo at the opening of the finale, then in the upper notes of the accented chords, and then as a chorale in the horns – and so on:

[Ex. 26: mm. 310–343, incl.]

In the middle section many different interesting contrapuntal combinations are made – here is one which sounds the retrograde inversion phrase of the theme in the high trumpet against the retrograde in the trombone, against figuration made up of the BACH motive:

[Ex. 27: mm. 398–406, incl.]

Then in a series of short rushes to climaxes BACH begins to crowd in everywhere:

[Ex. 28: mm. 435–471, incl.]

This kind of pattern is repeated in another way, and just before the end, [in] a beautiful quiet passage, the English horn sounds the first two phrases of the theme while the solo violin plays the last phrase, all against a shimmering background of little trills and melodic motives:

[Ex. 29: mm. 502–507, incl.]

Abruptly cutting off these beautiful measures, the work comes to a vigorous close in a few emphatic measures.

Schoenberg, with the writing of this work, changed the course of Western music and created a new direction, which we are just now only in the process of exploring. The power of concentration, the courage, and the imagination and training as well as innate musicality that culminated in the act of creating such a work as this is something that is worth considering and revering in a time when facile, slipshod, subconscious doodlings are often the subject matter of art, and at a time when many members of the public are no longer able to discriminate between a trifler with the arts and one who has supreme mastery. Here is a work which exhibits this supreme mastery and yet puts it at the service of a purely humanly expressive goal – for such is Arnold Schoenberg's *Variations for Orchestra*.

[Typescript with autograph corrections; Elliott Carter Collection, Paul Sacher Foundation.]

Preparations for the Dartington Summer School (1957)

Because of a lack of time Carter had to turn down an offer to teach at the Dartington Summer School in 1956 (though he probably attended). He was thus all the more happy to accept William Glock's renewed invitation to take part in the 1957 festival. His interest became even keener when he learned that Igor Stravinsky and Robert Craft as well as Pierre Boulez had also agreed to participate. Indeed, the presence of Stravinsky, whose seventy-fifth birthday was celebrated with an entire series of concerts, lent special brilliance to this year's Summer School. (Boulez, in contrast, had to cancel his visit at short notice as he had fallen behind in his work on the *Third Piano Sonata*, whose première was pending at the Darmstadt Holiday Courses.) Carter later had lively recollections of his renewed encounter with Stravinsky and his meeting with such other musicians as the pianist Paul Jacobs.[54] He himself had been invited chiefly to teach an analysis course in the second half of the four-week festival; as a composer he was represented only by a performance of his *Piano Sonata*.[55] While preparing for the Summer School Carter had the following exchange of letters with Glock on the details of his visit and the subject of his planned teaching activities. The starting point was Glock's somewhat premature announcement that Carter, in his course, would discuss Arnold Schoenberg's *Variations for Orchestra*, op. 31: evidently he knew that Carter had just given a radio lecture on this very work. Glock informed him of this plan on 14 March, and Carter accepted in principle on 4 May 1957, though he stressed that he had only recently delved into the literature on twelve-tone technique and would thus have nothing fundamentally new to say about the work. In the event, he seems not to have adhered strictly to the list of works he presented to Glock for discussion. At any rate, he later recalled teaching not only the Schoenberg *Variations* at his Dartington course (with Peter Maxwell Davies being "the only one of my students interested in twelve-tone music"[56]), but another topic not originally envisaged: Stravinsky's new ballet *Agon*, whose première he had attended shortly before, on 17 June 1957.[57]

---

54 On the meeting with Stravinsky see [Sue Knussen,] "Elliott Carter in Interview," *Tempo*, no. 197 (July 1996), pp. 2–5, esp. 3–4. On his encounter with Paul Jacobs see below, p 251.

55 The performance took place during a piano-cum-harpsichord recital given by Noel Lee (piano) and George Malcolm (harpsichord) on 19 August 1957.

56 See *CC*, p. 88.

57 See [Sue Knussen,] "Carter in Inverview" (see note 54), pp. 3–4. The première of *Agon*, conducted by Robert Craft, took place at Royce Hall, University of California at Los Angeles, on 17 June 1957 during a gala concert for Stravinsky's seventy-fifth birthday. The concert also featured the American première of

Canticum sacrum and the *Symphonies of Wind Instruments* (both conducted by Craft) as well as the *Chorale Variations on the Christmas Song "Vom Himmel hoch, da komm ich her"* after Johann Sebastian Bach and the *Symphony of Psalms* (both conducted by Stravinsky).

72 William Glock to Elliott Carter, 14 March 1957

International Music Association / 14 South Audley Street / London, W. 1
14th March, 1957

Dear Elliott,

Thank you for your letter of March 12th. I did write you a letter in January which may, however, have gone astray. I am posting today, by surface mail, a few Summer School prospectuses, which will give you a rough idea of what will be going on.

As I had not heard from you, I announced – I hope not altogether irresponsibly – that you would be giving a detailed analysis of Schoenberg's *Variations Op. 31*. I do hope you'll do that; but if you would also like to take on a complete class, something can be arranged I'm sure. Boulez will be doing analysis only, and perhaps supervising a group of lively young musicians who will be preparing various performances during the first two weeks of the Summer School; Craft will be there mainly to take charge of three Stravinsky programmes, but will also give a lecture or two; your class in Weeks 3 and 4 is planned, in fact, as the counterpart to Boulez's in the first two weeks.[58] We will, of course, pay a fee, and your expenses during the fortnight from August 17th–31st.

I forgot Nabokov: he only intends to come if I can find him a room with a piano in which he can work uninterruptedly for six hours a day, in which case he will deliver some talks on the splendours and miseries of Russian music. So none of you overlaps with the other, really.

Do please let me know whether my suggestion about *Schoenberg Op. 31* is all right.

Anne joins me in sending very best wishes to you both,[59]
Yours ever,
William

[Typed letter with autograph signature; Elliott Carter Collection, Paul Sacher Foundation. Reprinted by permission of Sebastian Balfour and David Drew (William Glock Estate).]

73 Elliott Carter to William Glock, 3 May 1957

Elliott C. Carter / 31 West 12th Street / New York City 11, N.Y.

Dear William,

I was, at first, somewhat taken aback when you suggested that I lecture on the Schoenberg Variations. As you must realise, the lecture I gave over CBC[60] was one for lay listeners and explained rather simply the devices Schoenberg used in that work. Since I was very much impressed by the performance of the work we both heard in Baden-Baden,[61] I set myself the task of learning about it and amidst a rather busy season I read Leibowitz etc.[62] and learned all the pertinent information that the 12-tone school has developed about it. I am, therefore, in no sense an original or even deeply critical appreciator of the music, and had really not intended to become one, since in the context of American society the question of 12-tone music is restricted to a small [and] not influential – although interesting – group. Very few have bothered to grasp the basic principles even, since such music has been hideously unpopular among critics, performers, and college departments. The story of Krenek's long-suffering life of rejection has dramatised this point here.

Anyhow, I do not claim to have very good ideas on the 12-tone school or, for that matter, on the question of musical analysis, which in its present incarnation had its main principles laid down by Alban Berg et al.

Nevertheless your suggestion has acted as a challenge to me and I must say I welcome the stimulus to find my way around in the 12-tone literature, much of which I have enjoyed without bothering to count to a dozen. Therefore, if you don't expect too much of me, I would like to discuss the following works:

---

58 The prospectus for the 1957 Dartington Summer School of Music announced (p. 3): "Composers will be especially interested in classes in advanced analysis: by Pierre Boulez in weeks 1 and 2 (week 2 will be entirely devoted to a study of Webern's Second Cantata, Op. 31); and by Elliott Carter in weeks 3 and 4 (week 3 will be devoted to a study of Schönberg's Variations, Op. 31)."

59 Anne Glock (*née* Geoffroy-Dechaume) was William Glock's second wife; see above, p. 94, note 10.

60 See above, pp. 140–147.

61 The performance took place during the 1955 ISCM festival in Baden-Baden on 19 June 1955, with Hans Rosbaud conducting the Südwestfunk Orchestra.

62 See above, p. 140, note 41.

63 Handwritten addition in the margin of the letter.

64 The work was performed during a concert of the Chamber Music Circle at Carnegie Recital Hall on 7 April 1957. The performers on this occasion, and on the LP recording made on 16 May 1957 (Columbia ML 5576), were Anabel Brieff Hulme (flute), Josef Marx (oboe), Lorin Bernsohn (cello), and Robert Conant (harpsichord).

65 The performances of the *Holiday Overture* conducted by Dimitri Mitropoulos took place on 25, 26, and 28 April 1957 in Carnegie Hall.

66 The Juilliard Quartet's performance of the *String Quartet No. 1*, preceded by Carter's introductory talk, took place in

the Baltimore Museum of Art on 25 February 1957. Their performance at Brandeis University was held on 2 June 1957 during the Fourth Festival of the Creative Arts.

67 Richard [Franko] Goldman, "The Music of Elliott Carter," *The Musical Quarterly* 43/2 (April 1957), pp. 151–170; Robert Erich Wolf, "Elliott Carter: String Quartet, 1951," *Notes*, ser. 2, 14/2 (March 1957), pp. 198–200.

68 Hans Rosbaud's performance of the *Variations for Orchestra* at the Donaueschingen Festival finally took place on 19 rather than 20 October 1957; see below, p. 150.

69 In Paris, where they spent the time between the Dartington Summer Music School and the Donaueschingen Festival, the Carters heard the European première

- Debussy   - *Rondes de printemps*
                - (violin sonata?)
- Schoenberg   - Variations [Could a recording or
                  tape of this work be gotten for my
                  lecture?[63]]
                - Trio
- Stravinsky   - *Symphony in 3 movements*

and works of a number of young Americans.

But this is only tentative.

My little Sonata for flute, oboe, cello, & harpsichord has been beautifully played here and is being recorded next week by Columbia Records.[64] Mitropoulos played my *Holiday Overture* at the N[ew] Y[ork] Philharmonic last week,[65] and as ever my quartet keeps getting played around. The most recent performances will be a performance on May 6 by the Fine Arts Quartet in Duluth, and the Juilliard, who played it last month at a lecture I gave in Baltimore, will play it at a festival of new music at Brandeis University at the beginning of June (Waltham, Massachusetts).[66]

You have no doubt seen the *Musical Quarterly* article about my music which appeared yesterday – and the good review of my quartet in *Notes*.[67]

As you doubtless know, Rosbaud & the Südwestfunk orch[estra] are playing my *Variations* in Donaueschingen on October 20.[68] I shall stay over in Europe until that time.[69] Later, in March–April of 1958, I shall lecture in Salzburg at the Salzburg Seminar.[70]

Nicolas N[abokov], who is rushing about the States, tells me that Stravinsky will come to Dartington for his birthday festival with Craft. Naturally I should like to be there at that time – will it be while I am scheduled to be there or before? If before, please let me know at once when & if I could come for those concerts and could find a room. I saw the master while in Los Angeles and heard the *Canticum* [*sacrum*], which I loved very much.[71] We had a long talk about Webern apropos the Craft-Columbia records which have just appeared,[72] and agreed that what

you can't explain is the best part of it – and frankly I find the rather Mendelssohnian charm of W[ebern] delightful and touching, but as an analyzer of music I must say I find the part you can't explain the best part of any piece.

In a sense the musical conversational piece so glibly and amusingly established by Satie has had an interesting tradition in our time – going through V[irgil] Thomson to Cage, Leibowitz, Boulez, and Cologne.[73] The conversation has become more and more like an actuarial table, but many conversations about artistic matters have wandered in and out of philosophy, mathematics, sociology, politics and the rest in our time, leaving in their wake art works that fade when the conversationalists change the subject. I have been enjoying Roman Vlad's Italian book and find him full of imaginative conversational turns & novel points of view.[74]

I notice in the excellent March *Score* (a periodical that I find extremely absorbing) that the BBC is going to perform my old symphony[75] – a work for which I have a great deal of affection, although my friends all feel that it is completely uncharacteristic. I even had to restrain Goldman from condemning it in his article. If, by any wild chance, there were a possibility of having a tape or a record made of the broadcast I should be very happy to pay for it when I come this summer. Thank you for arranging this performance.

Helen joins me in sending you both our warmest greetings,
Elliott

May 3, 1957

[Typed letter with autograph signature; William Glock Estate, British Library. Reprinted by pemission of Sebastian Balfour and David Drew (William Glock Estate).]

---

of Stravinsky's *Agon*, conducted by the composer, on 11 October 1957 in the Salle Pleyel. Shortly before returning to the United States they also had an opportunity to attend a performance of the *String Quartet No. 1*, played by the Quatuor Parrenin at the Centre Culturel Américain on 30 October; see below, p. 151.

70 From 15 March to 15 April 1958 Carter and his wife stayed in Salzburg, where he gave a lecture on "The American Composer: His Cultural, Social, and Economic Situation Today" at the International Composers' Seminar and led a seminar on "Leading Trends in Contemporary American Music."

71 During Carter's visit to Los Angeles in February (see above, p. 129) Stravinsky probably played him a tape recording of the première of the *Canticum sacrum*, which the composer had conducted in St. Mark's Basilica, Venice, on 13 September 1956. The work was given its American première on 17 June 1957 during a concert in honor of Stravinsky's seventy-fifth birthday (see above, p. 147, note 57).

72 See above, p. 129, note 25.

73 Carter here uses "Cologne" as a shorthand term for the serially-organized electronic music being produced at the WDR studio there by Karlheinz Stockhausen and others. In his lecture "Extending the Classical Syntax" (see below, p. 165),

he makes an explicit comparison between descriptive program music such as Honegger's *Pacific 231* and total serialism, "another type of program music, one whose program is of a scientific, arithmetical nature."

74 Roman Vlad, *Modernità e tradizione nella musica contemporanea* (Milan: Einaudi, 1955).

75 The first performance in England of Carter's *Symphony No. 1*, announced for 17 May 1957 (see *The Score and I.M.A Magazine*, no. 19 [March 1957], p. 76) does not seem to have materialized; see the list of BBC premières in Nicolas Kenyon, *The BBC Symphony Orchestra: The First Fifty Years, 1930–1980* (London: British Broadcasting Corporation, 1981), p. 473.

74 Elliott Carter and Hans Rosbaud after the Donau-
    eschingen performance of the *Variations for Orchestra*
    (1957), photo by Willy Pragher

At the end of their two-and-a-half-month European tour
in fall 1957 the Carters spent several weeks in Paris, from
where, among other things, they travelled to the Donaueschingen Festival for the European première of the *Variations for Orchestra*. The performance was given on 19 October 1957 during the first of two orchestral concerts in the
Donaueschingen Stadthalle. The program also included
works by Gilbert Amy (*Cantate brève*), Michel Ciry (*Concerto for Piano, 16 Wind Instruments, and Percussion*), and
the German première of Igor Stravinsky's ballet *Agon*,
conducted by Stravinsky himself. The other works were
conducted by the orchestra's principal conductor Hans
Rosbaud, who, in this photograph, can be seen congrat-

ulating Carter on his work. Judging from the weak response in the press, the *Variations for Orchestra* did not
make an especially lasting impression in Donaueschingen – at least not on the same scale as the Stravinsky ballet, which the critics discussed all the more thoroughly.
(This was perhaps partly due to the fact that Carter's publishers, AMP, did so little for his publicity and had reissued none of his scores; see below, p. 245.) In contrast,
the conductor held the work in high esteem; to quote the
composer's letter to Kurt Stone: "[...] Rosbaud said to me
mine was the best [piece] on the two programs [...]."[76]

[Landesarchiv Baden-Württemberg, Staatsarchiv Freiburg, W 134 Nr. 50014;
Copyright Landesarchiv Baden-Württemberg.]

---

76 Letter from Elliott Carter to Kurt Stone,
    23 October [1957]; Kurt Stone Collection,
    Irving S. Gilmore Music Library, Yale
    University.

75   Nadia Boulanger and Elliott Carter during a reception
at the Centre Culturel Américain in Paris (1957)

After returning from Donaueschingen Carter again met
up with Nadia Boulanger. The occasion was a concert
sponsored by the United States Information Service
(USIS) in the theater of the Centre Culturel Américain,
where on 30 October 1957 the Quatuor Parrenin played
Carter's *String Quartet No. 1* and Darius Milhaud's *String
Quartet No. 18* (1946). This photograph was taken during
the reception after the concert. Carter recalls that Boulanger congratulated him on his work with the slightly
ambiguous words: "Je n'aurais jamais pensé que vous écri-
riez une partition pareille!" [I would never have thought
you would write such a score!][77]

---

77   This anecdote is also found in Carter's
tribute "'Elle est la musique en personne':
A Reminiscence of Nadia Boulanger"
(ca. 1985/1995), in *CEL*, pp. 281–292,
esp. 292, where, however, it is mistakenly
dated 1952.

News from Rome (1959)

Ever since his stay in Rome in 1953–54 Carter had remained in close contact with his Italian colleague Goffredo Petrassi (1904–2003), whose music he had first heard while visiting the ISCM's Amsterdam Festival in 1933[78] and whom he held in the highest esteem both as a composer and as a person. Carter had expressed interest in Petrassi's music even before they became friends (see his admiring remarks in the letter of 6 September 1950 to William Glock, above, p. 96), and he later paid tribute to his colleague both in his writings[79] and in the dedications of his *Riconoscenza per Goffredo Petrassi* for unaccompanied violin (1984) and *90+* for piano (1994). Petrassi returned Carter's interest and championed his music on a long-term basis; many performances of Carter's music in Italy came about through Petrassi's good offices. Their mutual admiration also finds expression in the following exchange of letters, in which Carter reports on a New York performance of Petrassi's *String Quartet* and Petrassi comments on a Rome performance of Carter's *Variations for Orchestra*, scheduled without the composer's knowledge.

76 Elliott Carter to Goffredo Petrassi, 6 February 1959
(English translation in Appendix 1, p. 347)

Elliott C. Carter, Mead Street, Waccabuc, New York
le 6 février, 1959

Cher ami –

Hier soir nous sommes allés à New York entendre votre quatuor merveilleux très bien joué par les Parrenin.[80] C'est une œuvre qui m'[a] impressionné beaucoup par son imagination et sa résolution des techniques dodécaphoniques dans votre style personnel. J'aime surtout cet esprit inquiet et émouvant qui ici est si personnellement exprimé.

Votre quatuor a eu un grand succès et beaucoup de personnes l'ont aimé. Ci-inclus est la critique de William Flanagan, le plus intelligent et musical de nos critiques-journalistes.[81]

J'espère que tout va bien chez vous. Votre long silence après l'annonce de l'exécution de mes *Variations* au RAI m'inquiète un peu.[82] J'espère que l'exécution de ce morceau dont je ne savais rien avant votre lettre et dont même maintenant je n'ai pas de nouvelles n'a pas été trop décevante.

Mes amitiés affectueuses,
Elliott

[Autograph letter; Fondo Goffredo Petrassi, Campus Internazionale di Musica, Latina. Reprinted by permission of Rosetta Acerbi Petrassi.]

---

78 Petrassi's *Partita* for orchestra was performed at the Eleventh ISCM Festival in Amsterdam on 13 June 1933, conducted by Alfredo Casella.

79 See especially Elliott Carter, "The Recent Works of Goffredo Petrassi" (1960) and "Some Reflections on *Tre per sette*" (1986), published as "Two Essays on Goffredo Petrassi" in *CEL*, pp. 187–197.

80 Petrassi's *String Quartet* (1958) was played by the Quatuor Parrenin on 5 February 1959 at the Rothschild Foundation (316 East 63rd Street). The program also included quartets by Anton Webern, Darius Milhaud, and Bruno Maderna, as well as Ben Weber's *Three Songs for Soprano and Strings,* sung by the soprano Patricia Neway.

81 W[illiam] F[lanagan], "Parrenin Quartet Presents 3 Premieres at Concert," *The New York Herald Tribune,* 6 February 1959.

82 Petrassi had told Carter on 15 December 1958 that RAI's third program would broadcast his *Variations for Orchestra* on January 1959 – much to the surprise of Carter, who regretted not being informed in time, because he would have considered traveling to Rome for the event. (See

77 **Goffredo Petrassi to Elliott Carter, 10 February 1959**
(English translation in Appendix 1, p. 348)

Via Germanico, 184 / Roma
Roma 10 febbraio 1959

Mio caro Elliott

il lavoro, i fastidi ed altre preoccupazioni sono stata la causa per cui non ho risposto subito alla precedente lettera. La colpa è ancora più grave perché dovevo anche ringraziarla delle gentili parole riguardo la mia Serenata. Non sempre si può fare in tempo ciò che desideriamo fare.

Les *Variations,* dunque, sono state eseguite il sabato sera ai concerti della RAI al Foro Italico;[83] il giorno dopo, domenica, sono state ritrasmesse nel pomeriggio (quindi *due* trasmissioni radio) ed è stata questa l'esecuzione che io ho ascoltato perché il sabato sera non ero potuto andare al concerto. Mi ricordavo bene dell'opera per averla ascoltata chez vous a N[ew] Y[ork] nell'esecuzione di Louisville. Ebbene, questa dell'orchestra di Roma mi è parsa dix fois meilleure que l'autre, per la sonorità generale e il livello tecnico. Non avendo sotto gli occhi la partitura non ho potuto "controllare" se tutto era a posto, come pure mi sarebbe stato difficile giudicare dell'interpretazione di Dixon; tuttavia dalla profonda impressione che ne ho riportato debbo ritenere che il direttore era all'altezza dell'opera. Se a N[ew] Y[ork] ebbi già la sensazione di trovarmi di fronte ad un lavoro di grande significato, ora la sensazione è diventata certezza perché l'esecuzione ha reso *espliciti* i valori che avevo implicitamente avvertiti. La riprova l'ho avuta il lunedì seguente al concerto della Filarmonica al Teatro Eliseo (Lei ricorderà benissimo il "rituale" della vita musicale romana) ove mi sono incontrato con alcuni giovani musicisti che avevano assistito al concerto Dixon: erano rimasti colpiti dalle *Variations* e mi domandavano notizie sull'autore.

La "trama" polifonica di questo lavoro è ammirevole e la tensione lirico-drammatica è veramente eccezionale. Sono stato felicissimo di averlo riascoltato in una ottima esecuzione. S'intende che rimane sempre valida la mia prenotazione per una copia della partitura, quando uscirà stampata. Su di essa vorrò controllare alcuni dettagli che mi hanno particolarmente colpito.

Labroca, che si occupa ora del Festivale di Venezia,[84] dovrebbe scriverle per domandarle consigli per un lavoro da eseguirsi. Siamo già d'accordo che comunque il Suo nome deve figurare nei programmi. Se in quell'occasione tutta la famiglia Carter sarà a Venezia, avremo modo di vederci, il che mi farebbe infinito piacere.

Grazie per il programma e per la critica del *N[ew] Y[ork] Herald T[ribune]*, la quale mi consola di qualche amarezza procuratami a Venezia, ove la première del mio Quartetto è stata abbastanza burrascosa. Ci vuole tempo per tutto, lo so, e noi siamo invece impazienti. I Parrenin sono sempre straordinari, non trova?

Sto partendo per Milano ove tra qualche giorno si darà la mia opera *Il cordovano* alla Piccola Scala. Dieci anni fa fu un bel fiasco alla Grande Scala: ora spero che vada un po' meglio alla Piccola.[85]

Un caro ricordo a Madame Carter e a Lei, caro Elliott, tanti saluti molto affettuosi
Goffredo

[Typed letter with autograph signature; Elliott Carter Collection, Paul Sacher Foundation. Reprinted by permission of Rosetta Acerbi Petrassi.]

---

letter from Elliott Carter to Goffredo Petrassi, 8 January 1959; Fondo Goffredo Petrassi, Campus Internazionale di Musica, Latina.)

83 The performance of the *Variations for Orchestra* took place on 3 January 1959, with Dean Dixon conducting the Orchestra Sinfonica di Roma della Radiotelevisione Italiana.

84 For Mario Labroca, see above, p. 127, note 8.

85 Petrassi's opera *Il cordovano* (1944–48) after Cervantes was premièred in its original version at La Scala, Milan, on 12 May 1949, conducted by Nino Sanzogno and staged by Giorgio Strehler. The première of the new version of 1948, with a smaller orchestra, took place at the Piccola Scala

on 18 February 1959, conducted again by Nino Sanzogno and staged by Franco Enriquez.

Success in Los Angeles (1959)

To give fresh impetus to Los Angeles's conservative concert life, with its fixation on the standard repertoire, the critic Peter Yates (1909–1976) and his wife, the pianist Frances Mullen, founded the so-called Evenings on the Roof in 1939. The concert series, devoted to unknown early works and contemporary music, became an institution of national reputation after the Second World War.[86] In 1954 Yates handed the direction of the series to Lawrence Morton but continued to follow the events, now called the Monday Evening Concerts, at close range. He was also present at the concert on 9 March 1959 when the Quatuor Parrenin played Carter's *String Quartet No. 1,* flanked by Bruno Maderna's *String Quartet* (1955) and Jean Martinon's *String Quartet No. 1,* op. 43 (1946). This performance made such a strong impression on him that he sent the composer an enthusiastic letter the very next day, freely admitting that he had previously had a rather negative view of Carter's music but would now have to change his opinion. He also asked the composer to send information on his *String Quartet No. 1.* Carter granted this request on 8 June 1959 with a letter in which he outlined the main concerns of his music and reported on the recently finished *String Quartet No. 2* and a projected "Ford Foundation Piano Concerto." The somewhat wry comments with which Yates greeted this latter item of news in his thank-you letter ("[W]hich style? [A]rchaic Model T, homely but durable Model A, or fins and quick obsolescence? Marketing a Piano Concerto poses a real marketing problem"[87]) apparently drew no response from the composer.

78 Peter Yates to Elliott Carter, 10 March 1959

Peter Yates / 1735 Micheltorena / Los Angeles 26, California
3–10–59

Dear Mr. Carter:
Last night the Parrenin Quartet projected your Quartet in all four dimensions to a chorus of Bravos! which I led. Nothing pleases me more than to have the complacency kicked out of one of my critical opinions by a renewed encounter with a work of art. If so recanting I lay a part of the blame on the not quite three-dimensional recorded performance by the Walden Quartet, which I have heard through again this evening, recantation is not excuse. I didn't like it as I heard it, and now I do. The rhinoceros may be stuffed but it is still a rhinoceros. Last night we met it live and no fence.[88]

I don't know whether the programming was expert or fortunate. The opening Maderna Quartet is one of those things between music and electronic sound-experiment that we've had so many of these last years, every timbre exploited for its own sake and no continuity so that the medium itself seems robbed. Are there only so many sounds you can make with a string quartet! So that your Quartet, instead of being the modern among classics seemed the classic.

The players were so well pleased by our receptive silence for the Maderna and our uproar of excitement for you that they apologized to me for ending with a piece as conservative as the Martinon and tried to make it up to us by playing the *Six Bagatelles* by Webern for an encore.

If you haven't heard the Parrenin play your Quartet, you should try to arrange a session with them before they leave the country. They have the true dry French style, with never a deliberately pretty tone but the utmost variety of strength and refinement, so that the conflict of viola and cello against the two violins in your second movement plays like Hamlet. Their pianissimos in the Webern are the finest and most subtly inflected I have heard from a quartet. I think it's the inflection that counts most in the playing of your Quartet.

---

86 See Dorothy Lamb Crawford, *Evenings On and Off the Roof: Pioneering Concerts in Los Angeles,* 1939–1971 (Berkeley, etc.: University of California Press, 1995).

87 Letter from Peter Yates to Elliott Carter, 14 June 1959; Elliott Carter Collection, Paul Sacher Foundation.

88 Around the same time, Yates wrote in a similar vein about the importance of music not being limited by arbitrary barriers of tradition: "A wise zoo-keeper will set his barrier according to the strength of the rhinoceros. If it is too weak, the rhinoceros will run loose; if too stringent, the rhinoceros dies." (Peter Yates, "Introductory Essay," in *Some Twentieth-Century American Composers: A Selective Bibliography,* vol. 1, ed. John Edmunds and Gordon Boelzner [New York: New York Public Library, 1959], pp. 9–22, esp. 14.

89 Performance of the *String Quartet No. 1* at Mills College, Quatuor Parrenin, 1959.

90 A reference to the *Sonata for Flute, Oboe, Cello, and Harpsichord,* performed at the Monday Evening Concerts on 27 January 1958 – the first performance of a Carter work in the series. The performers were Arthur Hoberman (flute), Donald Muggeridge (oboe), Eugene Wilson (cello) and Leonard Stein (harpsichord).

They tell me they are doing it again at Mills College.[89]

Now I must apply myself to some of your other works, trying to hear the extra non-recorded dimensions. Without these, as when we had your chamber piece with harpsichord,[90] or at least without true independent inflection in each instrument, the part-writing does not accomplish what I believe now to be your intended effect.

Within a few months I'll produce an article about you to make up for the largely negative approach in my recent series about American composers.[91] Having written it I couldn't be satisfied with my judgement, and that was why I paid you the visit. Now I am challenged.

Most of the writing about you, however devoted, does not convey so much as your few words to me about the thematic structure of the Quartet. If you can take time to write me a few ideas for my instruction, I'd be grateful. But my own writing does not hinge on that.

Yours cordially,
Peter Yates

[Typed letter with autograph signature; Elliott Carter Collection, Paul Sacher Foundation.]

79 Elliott Carter to Peter Yates, 8 June 1959

Elliott C. Carter, Mead Street, Waccabuc, New York

Dear Mr. Yates,

I have finished my 2nd Str[ing] Quartet and am coming back to earth and answering letters. It is shameful not to have answered yours before this – but you pose such a problem in it that I did not know quite what to say. The "few words" for your "instruction" are not so easy to bring out, you know, since while a composer thinks a lot about what he is going to do before he starts – once in it the music takes over, delights, amuses, horrifies, infuriates, and in general beats him about like a medium in a trance. Certainly my music has sought mainly two things – to deal with vertical and horizontal dimensions in a more varied way than is usually done – I try to find continuities that gain meaning, change, and operate in time on a level of interest that is parallel to our present experience of living. Thus there are textures and shifts of character that feature very contrasting musical behaviours, simultaneously or one after the other, but linked together by phrasing. The other aspect is an attempt to use the performing situation, the instrument, its player, and the combination of instruments as a means of individualization. To find the special music, so to speak, that needs the 'cello and the piano – which don't go together very well. To bring out their differences and make a virtue of that, even a means of expression. My new quartet treats the 4 performers with even greater individualization than did the other – and as I see it is all about the problems, the pleasures, of human cooperation. Who's to be leader, what happens when the leader goes too far, etc. This kind of thinking interests me a great deal and I try to find some kind of a system of oppositions and cooperations which gives form to the entire work –

But I leave for Italy tomorrow morning, to be back the 15th of July to start on my Ford Foundation Piano Concerto – and so I must iron my pyjamas –[92]

Best to your wife and yourself,
Elliott Carter

June 8, 1959

I have heard the Parrenins play my quartet several times – excellently.[93]

[Typed letter with autograph signature and autograph postscript; Peter Yates Papers, Mandeville Special Collections Library, University of California, San Diego.]

91 Yates's "series about American composers" could be a reference to the bibliography, cited above, of fifteen American experimental composers; this is explicitly designated as "Volume 1," indicating that it was planned as a series (but there were apparently no other volumes). Yates's introductory essay discusses most of the fifteen composers – who include Carter, Cage, Cowell, Thomson, Copland, Ives, and Varèse – at some length, but treats Carter in only a short paragraph. Although Yates praises the *String Quartet No. 1* as a "work of superb rhetoric and, when well played, almost visible action," he seems ambivalent about "the tone-row behind his melodic method" as well as about Carter's indebtedness to Ives. ("Introductory Essay" [see note 88], p. 22.)

92 During his five-week stay in Italy Carter attended the ISCM festival in Rome (10–16 June 1959), where he was elected to the jury for the 1960 ISCM festival in Cologne.

93 Carter had heard performances of the piece by the Quatuor Parrenin in Rome (11 April 1954) and Paris (30 October 1957); see above, p. 101 and p. 151.

String Quartet No. 2 (1958–59)

As shown by his letter of 8 June 1959 to Peter Yates, Carter had at this time just completed his *String Quartet No. 2*. (The final date is mistakenly given as 19 March 1959 in the printed edition, but the manuscript clearly has 3 June 1959. This latter date is also consistent with Carter's statement, in his letter of 11 May 1959 to Goffredo Petrassi, that he had "almost finished" the piece; see below, p. 158.) This work was intended for the Stanley String Quartet, an ensemble based at the University of Michigan which had commissioned it from him in August 1956. The quartet was out of its depth, however, and postponed the performance until it was finally premièred in New York by the Juilliard Quartet on 25 March 1960. The *String Quartet No. 2* marks a further way station in Carter's *volte-face* from traditional thematic-motivic organization. But most of all it bears witness, as the composer emphasized in his letter to Yates, to an even more individual treatment of the separate parts: here, in keeping with Carter's search for an "emancipated musical discourse,"[94] the instruments represent four completely distinct personalities and probe the full gamut of mutual interaction – from strict subservience to irreconcilable conflict. In order to emphasize the independence of the voices, Carter indicates in the published score that the players should be seated at a greater distance from one another than usual. (Carter remembers Walter Piston saying, on the occasion of a performance of the quartet at Harvard by the Lenox Quartet: "You know, if I had written that, I would have put each of the players in a separate room and shut the door."[95]) Yet two opposing progressions occur at the level of large-scale form. First, the four movements (Allegro fantastico, Presto scherzando, Andante espressivo, and Allegro, flanked by an Introduction and a Conclusion) reveal a tendency towards increasing cooperation among the four parts. Second, the succession of movements is interrupted by three cadenzas in which the relevant protagonist (viola, cello, violin 1) always acts more independently vis-à-vis the collective. This radical redefinition of the quartet genre, which nonetheless draws on certain historical models, such as Ives's *String Quartet No. 2* (likewise explicitly laid out as a discourse among four individuals), attracted no small amount of attention. The quartet soon became one of Carter's most frequently played works and received a Pulitzer Prize (1960), the New York Music Critics Circle Award (1960), and the UNESCO First Prize (1961).

80 *String Quartet No. 2* (1958–59), second movement, autograph draft in pencil with markings in colored pencil, p. [1]

In each movement of the *String Quartet No. 2* one instrument assumes a leadership role, thereby emphasizing the intervals, rhythmic types, and expressive gestures assigned to it. In the first movement this instrument is the first violin, in the third the viola, in the fourth the cello. In the second movement (Presto scherzando), from which we here see mm. 1–11 in Carter's penciled draft of late March 1959 (the movement heading is still missing), this instrument is the second violin. It stands out from the rest of the ensemble not only by virtue of its distinctive intervals (major third, major sixth, and major seventh) and rhythmic rigidity, but by virtue of its pizzicato attack, which is retained for the entire length of the movement. It also stands out through maintaining its own tempo: whereas the other instruments move at MM 175, the second violin obstinately remains at MM 140 and uses its more or less regular "ticks" to superpose a 4/4 meter on the 5/4 meter notated in mm. 1–6. (In the printed version Carter wrote out the 4/4 meter and the tempo mark MM 140 on a separate line for purposes of clarity.) The second violin's special role, highlighted in the printed edition by its dynamic emphasis and the term "solo," somewhat recalls the special treatment of the second violin in movement 2 of Ives's *String Quartet No. 2*, where the instrument intervenes as an "alien body" in the musical events under the name of Rollo, the eponymous hero of a popular nineteenth-century series of children's books. In the Ives piece Rollo appears as a nostalgic average guy (note his mawkish cadenzas), whereas the second violin in Carter's piece is a thoroughly unpoetic, short-spoken, mechanical time-beater. The page of music shown here, dated "Easter Monday" [1959], is still rudimentary in its handling of articulation and dynamics. That the second violin initially appears on the top staff in the lowermost system does not imply that Carter originally intended the first and second violins to switch roles. It is merely a slip of the pen that he noticed only with the entrance of the first violin in the final bar and immediately corrected by adding an appropriate arrow and the number "II."

---

94 See Carter, "A Further Step" (see above, p. 130, note 27), in *CEL*, pp. 5–11, esp. 10.
95 Interview with Felix Meyer and Anne Shreffler, 13 June 2007. The performance by the Lenox Quartet took place in Adams House on 11 March 1961.

Shoptalk with Goffredo Petrassi (1959)

In their correspondence, Carter and Goffredo Petrassi not only kept each other abreast of performances of their music and other events on the musical scene, they also discussed their creative work. Thus Petrassi, in the letter of 1 May 1959 given below, reported on the technical difficulties he encountered in conceiving his recently begun *String Trio* (1959–60), which led him to abandon the twelve-tone series on which the piece is based. Carter fully appreciated the dilemma: in his reply of 11 May 1959 he mentioned that he had encountered similar problems in his most recent work, the *String Quartet No. 2*, and found no help when he tried to apply serial technique. (The latter statement may come as a surprise, for no twelve-tone constructs have yet been discovered in the sketches.) Incidentally, Carter characterized the *String Quartet No. 2* with the same Pirandellian phrase – "four instrumentalists in search of a composer" – that David Schiff would later adopt in slightly modified form (Schiff 1983/1998, pp. 197 and 73, respectively).

81 Goffredo Petrassi to Elliott Carter, 1 May 1959
(English translation in Appendix 1, p. 348)

Via Germanico, 184 / Roma
1 Maggio 1959

Mon cher Elliott
on vous "repasse" à notre radio, ça me fait toujours plaisir.[96]

Comment-allez-vous?

Pour Venise notre ami Labroca est devenu assez mystérieux, je ne sais plus ce qu'il fabrique. On me parle d'un concert de la Philharmonie de New York sous la baguette, evidemment, de Bernstein. Composé exclusivement de musique américaine. Qui seront les compositeurs américains joués? Mystère. Le projet aboutira? Encore [un] mystère.[97]

Donnez-moi des nouvelles de vous et de votre travail. Le voyage en Europe est toujours déterminé?

Après la *Serenata* je m'acharne sur un Trio à cordes. Terribles difficultés à surmonter, la musique s'épuise subitement avec le jeu des ressources de ces trois instruments. La série ne m'est plus d'aucun secours, je l'ai abandonné; donc, un orphelin sans mère. Une espèce de pari avec moi-même.

Un saluto molto affettuoso
Goffredo

[Autograph lettter; Elliott Carter Collection, Paul Sacher Foundation. Reprinted by permission of Rosetta Acerbi Petrassi.]

82 Elliott Carter to Goffredo Petrassi, 11 May 1959
(English translation in Appendix 1, pp. 348–349)

Elliott C. Carter, Mead Street, Waccabuc, New York

Mon cher Goffredo –
Merci pour votre lettre – qui m'a fait beaucoup de bien – car moi aussi j'ai eu des difficultés avec mes compositions cet hiver. Je comprends très bien vos problèmes avec votre trio à cordes. J'ai presque fini un deuxième quatuor à cordes qui m'a coûté beaucoup de travail, de perplexité. Toujours j'ai des idées pour des moments ou des endroits dans une composition et ma technique musicale ne m'aide pas à les développer ou même à trouver d'autres choses qui vont avec les idées avec lesquelles j'ai commencé. Même la sérialisation ne m'aide pas – quoique je l'ai essayée plusieurs fois. Mon quatuor me semble un peu comme une chose pirandellienne – "4 instrumentistes cherchant un compositeur" – les pauvres.

Je viens d'entendre la nouvelle composition pour 8 instruments de Maxwell Davies – sur une commande de Dartmouth College.[98] C'est très doué – elle m'a beaucoup plu.

---

96 The recording made of Dean Dixon's performance of the *Variations for Orchestra* with the Orchestra Sinfonica di Roma on 3 January 1959 (see above, p. 153, note 83) was rebroadcast on 8 May 1959. Petrassi enclosed an announcement of the broadcast in his letter.

97 The Bernstein concert finally took place at the Venice Biennale on 26 September 1959 during the long tour of Europe and the Middle East that the New York Philharmonic undertook in the fall of 1959 (see below, note 102). The program included works by Samuel Barber (*Second Essay*), Charles Ives (*The Unanswered Question*), Bernstein (*The Age of Anxiety [Symphony No. 2]* with Seymour Lipkin as piano soloist), and Dmitry Shostakovich (*Symphony No. 5*, op. 47).

98 Peter Maxwell Davies's work, entitled *Ricercar and Doubles*, was premièred at the Dartmouth Festival in New Hampshire on 25 April 1959, conducted by David Sackson.

99 See below, p. 162.

100 Carter finally traveled to Italy in June–July 1959; see his letter of 8 June 1959 to Peter Yates, above, p. 155. It was not until a year later that he was invited to the Venice Biennale, where the Juilliard Quartet played his *String Quartet No. 2* on 15 September 1961, along with works by Gian Francesco Malipiero (*Rispetti e strambotti, Cantàri alla Madrigalesca*) and Anton Webern (*Five Movements*, op. 5).

101 In 1958–59 – his first season as sole music director of the New York Philharmonic – Leonard Bernstein presented a large-scale survey of American music from Edward

MacDowell and George Chadwick to the 1950s. Edgard Varèse's *Arcana* for orchestra (1925–27) was given on 27–30 November 1958, Roger Sessions's *Violin Concerto* (1931–35) on 19–21 February 1959 with Tossy Spivakovsky as soloist, and Kenneth Gaburo's *Elegy for Small Orchestra* (1956) on 2–5 April 1959, this being a world première. Carter devoted an extensive review to the Sessions concerto: "Current Chronicle: New York, 1959," *The Musical Quarterly* 45/3 (July 1959), pp. 375–381, reprinted as "Roger Sessions: Violin Concerto" in *CEL*, pp. 175–180.

102 The New York Philharmonic's tour under Bernstein, Thomas Schippers, and Seymour Lipkin began in Athens on 5 August 1959 and ended in London on 10 October 1959. As Carter rightly surmised, Bernstein did not conduct

Negotiating with the State Department (1960)

Nos projets de vacances sont nébuleux et je serais très reconnaissant si vous pouviez stimuler Labroca à répondre à la lettre que je lui ai écrite. Vous voyez – tout est changé car j'ai reçu une commande pour un *concerto de piano* du Ford Foundation, à laquelle il me faut travailler cet été.[99] Pour cette raison nous ne pouvons passer qu'un mois en Europe, ou mi-juin – mi-juillet, ou fin août – fin septembre, le dernier seulement si je suis invité à Venise – car nous avons déjà les billets pour le bateau de juin. Si je n'ai pas de réponse (ou une réponse négative) de Labroca en quelques semaines, je viendrai en juin.[100]

Le Philharmonique sous Leonard Bernstein n'a joué que très peu de choses intéressantes cet hiver en musique américaine – le *concerto de violon* de Sessions et une chose pas trop bien faite de Gaburo et les *Arcanes* de Varèse.[101] Sauf ceux-là c'était ou très néo-jazziste ou classiciste ou pas très professionnel. Bernstein, comme vous savez, s'intéresse à la musique avancée seulement pour faire la publicité ou scandale – il ne l'aime pas – mais plutôt les versions américaines de Prokofiev & Shostakovitch. – Je ne sais pas ce qu'il va prendre sur sa tournée avec le Philharmonique,[102] certainement très peu ou pas de musique comme on trouvera à la SIMC, dont le festival a l'air d'être très bien cette année-ci.[103] Malheureusement je ne pourrai pas venir à cause de mes travaux – nous comptons vous voir d'une manière ou d'une autre & à bientôt.

Ma femme me joint en vous envoyant nos amitiés affectueuses,
Elliott

Le 11 Mai, 1959

[Autograph letter; Fondo Goffredo Petrassi, Campus Internazionale di Musica, Latina. Reprinted by permission of Rosetta Acerbi Petrassi.]

Even as the escalating arms race increased hostility between the Soviet and American spheres of influence during the 1950s, international scientific and cultural exchanges took on a new importance. Classical music became one of the front lines in the cultural Cold War, which was waged with symphonies, composers, and concert pianists as proxies for the nuclear weapons that were too dangerous to use. In 1958 (the same year that the American pianist Van Cliburn, against all political expectations, won first prize in the First International Tchaikovsky Competition in Moscow), the Soviet Union and the US signed the Krushchev-initiated "Agreement … on Exchanges in the Cultural, Technical, and Educational Fields." The US State Department began the exchange by sending composers Roy Harris, Ulysses Kay, Peter Mennin, and Roger Sessions on an extended tour of the Soviet Union.[104] This was followed by a US tour in 1959 of a group of Soviet composers which included the prominent figures Dmitry Shostakovich and Dmitry Kabalevsky as well as the president of the Composers' Union, Tikhon Khrennikov.[105] Although the encounters were uniformly polite on both sides, a *Pravda* article published after the tour and signed by Shostakovich and Khrennikov later "disparaged the prominence of the twin evils of jazz and serialism in America" in utterances that were widely reported in the American press.[106]

Just two months after the departure of the Soviet delegation at the end of November 1959 Carter, who had already turned down one invitation from the State Department, was invited again, this time for a two-month tour of the Soviet Union (with Copland) and Eastern Europe (on his own).[107] His extended response to Frederick Colwell, Chief of the State Department's American Specialists Branch, expresses frustration and resentment about the disparity between the Soviet Union's and the US's support of their native composers. Carter, who like most of his compatriots may not have been fully aware of the suppression

---

any experimental contemporary music. American music was well represented, but Bernstein, in the thirty-six concerts he conducted, chose (neo)tonal compositions by Ives, Piston, Copland, Gershwin, and Barber as well as a work of his own, *The Age of Anxiety* (Symphony No. 2).

103 Carter wrote a detailed report on the ISCM's Rome festival from 10 to 16 June 1959, bestowing special praise on Goffredo Petrassi's *Serenata* for harpsichord, flute, viola, double bass, and percussion (1958), Pierre Boulez's *Improvisation sur Mallarmé II* for soprano and instrumental ensemble (1957), and Bo Nilsson's *Ein irrender Sohn* for alto, alto flute, and eighteen instruments (1959); see Elliott Carter, "Current Chronicle: Italy", in *The Musical Quarterly* 45/4 (October 1959),

pp. 530–541; most recently reprinted as "ISCM Festival, Rome" in *CEL*, pp. 18–28.
104 *"Aaron Copland Meets the Soviet Composers:* A Television Special," transcribed and introduced by Emily Abrams, in *Aaron Copland and His World* (see above, p. 52, note 32), pp. 379–392, esp. 380.
105 The other composers were Fikret Amirov and Kostyantyn Dankevych; the musicologist Boris Yarustovsky was also part of the group. "Touring New York, Washington, San Francisco, Los Angeles, Louisville, Philadelphia, Boston, and Chicago, they visited college campuses and attended concerts, movies, and receptions." (Abrams, *"Aaron Copland Meets the Soviet Composers"* [see note 104], pp. 380–381.)
106 Abrams, *"Aaron Copland Meets the Soviet Composers"* (see note 104), p. 381. See "Soviet Composers Describe U.S Trip:

Report in Pravda Praises Some Musicians but Scorns Twelve-Tone Technique," *The New York Times*, 18 December 1959. We are grateful to Emily Abrams Ansari for sharing her knowledge of the inner workings of the State Department cultural diplomacy programs (personal communication, 5 November 2007). Her dissertation, "Masters of the President's Music: Cold War Composers and the United States Government" (Ph.D., Harvard University), is forthcoming.
107 Carter had been invited to tour the Soviet Union from 15 October until 15 November 1959 together with Copland and Norman Dello Joio. See letter from Frederick Colwell to Elliott Carter, 12 June 1959; Elliott Carter Collection, Paul Sacher Foundation.

and persecutions that Shostakovich and other Soviet composers had suffered at the hands of their government, emphasized the asymmetry of such cultural exchanges: since Soviet music enjoyed much greater favor in the US than American music did in the Soviet Union, it was not clear what, if anything, was achieved by American composers visiting the Soviet Union. Given the limited performance opportunities granted to American composers in their own country, and to his music in particular, Carter wrote that he could not in good faith represent American culture abroad. In his letter, he explicitly employs Cold War political rhetoric: "[...] we deplore the results, while eagerly enjoying them, of Soviet musical dictatorship, and hail the results of American musical freedom without bothering to play or listen to them."[108] In place of Carter Lukas Foss, who also had mixed feelings about the effectiveness of cultural diplomacy, went on the trip, later recalling that "Aaron was the proper ambassador, and I was the enfant terrible."[109]

83 Frederick A. Colwell to Elliott Carter, 26 January 1960

Department of State / Washington
January 26, 1960

Dear Mr. Carter:
In accordance with the telephone conversation Mr. Sanchez of my office had with Mrs. Carter concerning the possibility of your going to the Soviet Union with Mr. Aaron Copland, I would like to know as soon as possible if you would be available for one but preferably two months starting March 14, 1960. As you probably know Mr. Copland has indicated his availability for this project from March 14 to April 11, 1960.

I mentioned that we would like to have you available for two months as we believe that a series of lectures could be arranged for you in other Eastern European countries immediately upon your departure from the Soviet Union. Unfortunately Mr. Copland has informed us that previous engagements prevent him from participating in this extended tour.

I hope to hear from you as soon as it may be convenient.
Sincerely yours,
Frederick A. Colwell

Chief, American Specialists Branch
International Educational Exchange Service

Mr. Elliott C. Carter, / 31 West 12th Street, / New York City, New York.

[Typed letter with autograph signature; Elliott Carter Collection, Paul Sacher Foundation.]

84 Elliott Carter to Frederick A. Colwell, 28 January 1960

Mr. Frederick A. Colwell, / IES/LSD / Chief, American Specialists Branch / International Educational Exchange Service / Department of State.

Dear Mr. Colwell:
Thank you for your letter of January 26th, 1960, concerning the possibility of my going to Russia. As was stressed in our recent 'phone conversations with Mr. Sanchez, I have many works of music I am committed to finish at this time and would not like to interrupt my composing unless I were absolutely convinced that my trip to Russia under the auspices of the Department of State would serve a useful purpose to my country. I have just returned from a trip to Cologne (which I wrote up on the music page of last Sunday's N[ew] Y[ork] Times)[110] that resulted not only in professional contact and cooperation with a number of outstanding European composers in choosing the programs for an important music festival,[111] but had the added result of the inclusion of three important American works on the festival programs – more works than any other country participating in the International Society for Contemporary Music, except those of the host – Germany.[112] Since I was invited by the ISCM and the German Radio to participate on this jury, I considered this trip very useful in terms of encouraging respect for American composers and their accomplishments – so important that I was willing to pay the trans-Atlantic airfare myself.

108 Later that year, Paul Fromm wrote to Carter, "I well understand why you hesitate to go to Russia. Touring and sightseeing is one thing; being exploited for political propaganda is another. Culture must begin at home." (Letter from Paul Fromm to Elliott Carter, 28 July 1959; Elliott Carter Collection, Paul Sacher Foundation.) In spite of Carter's emphatic refusal, half a year later he received yet another invitation, which he again turned down.

109 Copland and Perlis, Copland: Since 1943 (see above, p. 54, note 44), p. 285.

110 Carter had traveled to Cologne as a member of the ISCM jury that selected the contributions for the impending world music festival in Cologne (10–19 June 1960). See Elliott Carter, "Sixty Staves to Read: This Was One of the Problems Faced by ISCM Jury in Cologne," The New York Times, 24 January 1960, reprinted in WEC, pp. 197–199.

111 Besides Carter, the festival's jury included Wolfgang Fortner (Germany), Karl-Birger Blomdahl (Sweden), Guillaume Landré (Netherlands), and Marcel Mihalovici (France).

112 The three American works selected were Arthur Berger's String Quartet (1958), Gunther Schuller's Spectra 1958, and Roger Sessions's Symphony No. 4 (1958).

113 The amount of the fee that NBC paid for the rights of the US first performance of Shostakovich's Symphony No. 7

In talking with Mr. Sanchez, I soon realised that no assurance of accomplishing anything of similar concrete professional value could be given about my possible trip to Russia. In an attempt to clarify my position, I would like to ask a few questions:

A) The leading Soviet composers have been played more widely in the United States than any American composers. Some of them have been remunerated in a way that no American composer has ever been remunerated. Shostakovitch was paid by the NBC Symphony, during the war, $20,000 for the rights of the US first performance of his 7th Symphony.[113] Most of us were, and are, paid about $100 for NBC or other orchestral performances, and while Soviet composers can live on their commissions, we receive at most $1,000 for a large work, so that we are always being asked by the Income Tax Bureau whether our music is not really a hobby. The discrepancy between the acceptance of Soviet music right here in the United States and the acceptance of even the most frequently played Americans is ludicrous, certainly not very flattering to ourselves or our notions of freedom. For we deplore the results, while eagerly enjoying them, of Soviet musical dictatorship, and hail the results of American musical freedom without bothering to play or listen to them. I do not honestly see how any American composer can conceal this embarassing situation, or explain it away convincingly to the Russians.

B) In my particular case, no US performers or orchestras have ever played any work of mine on their trips to the Soviet Union. The N[ew] Y[ork] Philharmonic, like many other American visiting orchestras, have played a preponderance of Soviet music in the Soviet Union.[114] They play more of it when the Soviet composers visit the US. The Soviet orchestras visiting the US play Soviet music here, and when American composers go to Russia a lot more Soviet music is played for them there. – Now, my works take a good deal of rehearsal, and because I have enjoyed American liberty they are rather unusual in character and would be very perplexing to Soviet orchestras and audiences, because of their lack of experience in the newer musical techniques. There is a very good chance that

they would be played badly and misunderstood generally – if, under the circumstances, I were there and could point out that US orchestras played them better and the works had received American acceptance, there might be a point in this, but since they are not played here either, do you think it would be good propaganda to say that only in Germany and England are they played? (Which is a fact.) Therefore, as a tax payer, I am not at all convinced that I should be sent as a composer.

As my trip to Cologne shows, I am ready at any time that I possibly can arrange to do something to help in the appreciation and understanding of American culture abroad. I am not interested in going to the Soviet Union under the auspices of the State Department as a private citizen, I can do that on my own. But in going as an American composer singled out from others for this honor, I think that I have the right to be represented as an important figure in our culture – as I was in Cologne – and not as someone trying unsuccessfully to give the impression that American culture can keep up its end in the field of musical composition – a thing of which I am convinced, but which is hard to demonstrate except under proper conditions. Until I can be assured that these conditions are well understood and can be satisfactorily met by those in charge of sending American composers to Russia, I shall be very reluctant to accept your offer.

Yours sincerely,
Elliott Carter

31 West 12th Street, / New York, 11, New York.
January 28th, 1960

[Typed letter draft, carbon copy; Elliott Carter Collection, Paul Sacher Foundation.]

("Leningrad") on 19 July 1942 is unknown and was not publicized at the time. Carter could have been thinking of *Life* magazine's report on 22 November 1943 on the *Symphony No. 8:* "Shostakovich Sells Symphony for $10,000" (p. 43). According to the report, this was the highest price ever paid for a symphony's first performance rights. The Soviets had charged $5,000 for the US premiere of Shostakovich's Fifth Symphony (according to Halina Rodzinski, *Our Two Lives*

[New York: Scribner, 1976], p. 175), and the Philadelphia Orchestra had also paid a "stiff" fee for the Sixth. Carter, like most Americans, could not have known that Shostakovich himself received little if any of these fees, which were paid directly to the Soviet government. We are grateful to Laurel Fay for this information (personal communication, 6 November 2007).

114 This did not apply, however, to the New York Philharmonic's aforementioned tour of Europe and the Middle East in autumn

1959 (see above, pp. 158–159, note 102), during which the orchestra played several pieces by Barber, Bernstein, Copland, Ives, and Piston in its concerts in Moscow, Leningrad, and Kiev, but only one piece by a Soviet composer, namely, Shostakovich's *Symphony No. 5* (op. 47), as well as two early pieces by Igor Stravinsky (*Le Sacre du printemps* and the *Piano Concerto*), at that time a precarious tribute to a Russian émigré.

Disagreement with Copland (1960 or 1961)

As shown by his letter of 11 May 1959 to Goffredo Petrassi (see above, p. 159), immediately after finishing his *String Quartet No. 2* in summer 1959 Carter wanted to embark on the piano concerto commissioned by the Ford Foundation, at the recommendation of pianist Jacob Lateiner, for their newly created "Program for Concert Artists." But despite his original intentions – and in spite of the enticing terms of the commission, which among other things specified that the new works would be performed by three different orchestras[115] – he first took up a different commission that he had received as far back as 1956, and from 1959 to 1961 he wrote the *Double Concerto* at the behest of the Fromm Music Foundation (see below, pp. 167–169). The new work went yet another step beyond the level achieved in the *String Quartet No. 2* and defined Carter as a highly visible proponent of an advanced modernism whose structural complexity placed supreme demands on performers and listeners alike. This brought him widespread recognition in progressive musical circles, but it also increasingly distanced him from such earlier comrades-in-arms as Aaron Copland. When *Copland on Music*, a collection of articles dating from 1926 to 1959, appeared in 1960[116] the volume seemed to Carter like a time-capsule from a bygone age. His displeasure, which found expression in the following note, resulted partly from the fact that Copland had omitted him from earlier overviews of up-and-coming American composers – overviews that now reappeared in print. Still more serious was the fact that in Carter's opinion Copland, trapped in a retrospective mindset, was unwilling and unable to do justice to the recent currents on the music scene, and thus to Carter's leading position in that scene.

85 Elliott Carter to Aaron Copland, [late 1960 or early 1961]

Elliott Carter / Mead Street / Waccabuc, New York

Dear Aaron,
Thank you for sending me your book. Reading it was like reliving the past with the League. Now that that time is quite over, I rather appreciate never having been singled out in your articles as so many passed-up past masters and dead wood were,[117] since by this it is made more clear than ever that my music has taken an opposite direction – one that can be talked about now and not reminisced about.[118]

Your comrade,
Elliott

[Typed letter with autograph signature; Aaron Copland Collection, Music Division, Library of Congress, Washington, D.C. Reprinted by permission of the Aaron Copland Fund for Music, Inc., copyright owner.]

---

115 Besides the ten nominating soloists, ten orchestras were involved in the "Program for Concert Artists": the Atlanta Symphony, the Denver Symphony, the Detroit Symphony, the Houston Symphony, the Indianapolis Symphony, the Los Angeles Philharmonic, the New York Philharmonic, the Pittsburgh Symphony, the San Antonio Symphony, and the Seattle Symphony. See Jane Gottlieb, "Elliott Carter's Piano Concerto and the Ford Foundation's Support of American Composers and Performers,"

in *Pianist, Scholar, Connoisseur: Essays in Honor of Jacob Lateiner*, ed. Bruce Brubaker and Jane Gottlieb (Stuyvesant, NY: Pendragon, 2000), pp. 175–186.

116 [Aaron Copland,] *Copland on Music* (Garden City, NY: Doubleday, 1960).

117 Carter was probably thinking mainly of Copland's overview articles "Our Younger Generation: Ten Years Later," published in *Modern Music* 13/4 (May–June 1936), pp. 3–11, and "The 'New School' of American Composers," published in *The New York Times Magazine*, 14 March 1948,

pp. 18 and 51–54, both of which fail to mention his name. However, the *Copland on Music* collection in which these articles were reprinted mentions Carter in a positive light in a newly written article of 1959 ("Postscript for the Generation of the Fifties," pp. 175–178). Shortly after the book's publication Copland wrote an article in which he delved a little more deeply, albeit in a reserved tone, into Carter's *String Quartet No. 1*; see "America's Young Men of Music," *Music and Musicians* 9/4 (December 1960), pp. 11 and 33.

"Extending the Classical Syntax" (1961)

During his time as professor of composition at Yale University (1960–62), Carter wrote the following text for the festival and conference "East-West Music Encounter," which took place from 17 April to 6 May 1961 in Tokyo (the symposium, from 17 to 22 April 1961). This was the fourth large-scale music festival that Nicolas Nabokov had organized under the aegis of the Congress for Cultural Freedom. The members of the Music Committee included William Glock, Fred Goldbeck, Mario Labroca, Rolf Liebermann, Heinrich Strobel, Hans Heinz Stuckenschmidt, and Virgil Thomson (Leonard Bernstein was designated as a "corresponding member"). All of these were invited to Tokyo; those present (in addition to Carter) included also Luciano Berio, Boris Blacher, Henry Cowell, Lou Harrison, Colin McPhee, Leo Schrade, and Iannis Xenakis. Notably absent from the festival were left-wing Japanese musicians and critics as well as some left-wing German musicians living in Tokyo, who objected to the festival's political orientation.[119]

In his lecture, given on 21 April 1961, Carter first seeks a common ground between Western and Eastern music by pointing out that "the Western composer, like the Oriental performer, is basically an improviser, but one not caught in the chains of time." He goes on to set Western modernist music apart from Asian music, popular music, and folk music by emphasizing its abstraction, its difficulty, and its need for innovation. A modern Western artwork, in his view, sets up and resolves processes that are contained entirely within itself; a piece unfolds in a "musical dialectic," which Carter characterized elsewhere as an "audible musical order that can be distinguished, remembered, and followed."[120] Whereas the most successful new works freshen and extend the "boundaries of the musical language," another (for him less fruitful) tendency is to "dislocat[e] the musical dialectic" by imposing extra-musical programs upon it. Carter includes mathematical methods of serial patterning in this category of "program music." The lecture ends with a veiled critique of mid-1950s European serialism, which may in some cases "come perilously close to the practical joke." Carter later recalled his encounters with scores of the "Darmstadt school," which "then [in the 1950s] seemed to

me appallingly systematized and dry."[121] Carter's critique recognizes a fundamental difference between European and American serialism (broadly construed): the former seeks to break up continuities (musical and historical), whereas the latter values coherence and builds upon previous musical languages. The festival also featured a performance of Carter's *String Quartet No. 2* by the Juilliard Quartet on 23 April 1961.

86 Elliott Carter, "Extending the Classical Syntax" (1961)

In the discussions carried on at this conference, a constantly recurring theme has been a concern with the danger that each type of music today might lose its unique character and consequently its power to give us important artistic experiences. Certainly, one of the main activities of Western aesthetics and art, especially in recent centuries, has been to draw attention to, and emphasize, differences of artistic character, and so it is not surprising that we of the West should be so concerned with the matter. The Western composer, himself, has long considered an important side of his activity to be the creation and vivid presentation of differing musical characters and expressions. So Western musicians are particularly distressed when the traditional techniques are used as a matter of routine, so as to weaken rather than strengthen the definiteness of musical characterization. This is true, whether within their own type of music or when these techniques are used by other cultures, for Western techniques were developed certainly partly to enhance musical characterization and expression. The notion of characterization itself is a way of directing the mind to hear a group of notes as one unit and to follow the growth, expansion, and change of this unit according to some perceptible intention or plan.

In fact, the very question of improvisation, so much discussed here, involves this notion [of] characterization deeply. The Western composer, like the Oriental performer, is basically an improviser, but one not caught in the chains of time. His compositions are basically a choice

---

118 In his autobiography, Copland quoted Carter's critique (beginning at "I rather appreciate") but preceded it, surely not by coincidence, with the following comment on his "Postscript for the Generation of the Fifties" (see note 117): "In the article I wrote: 'The young composer of today seems to be fighting hard to stay abreast of a fast-moving post-World War II European musical scene.' By this I meant Pierre Boulez, Karlheinz Stockhausen, and Luigi Nono. I mentioned Elliott Carter as an honorable exception to this trend."

(Copland and Perlis, *Copland: Since 1943* [see above, p. 54, note 44], p. 296.)

119 See Hans Heinz Stuckenschmidt, *Zum Hören geboren: Ein Leben mit der Musik unserer Zeit* (Munich and Zurich: Piper, 1979), p. 283: "Schon im Winter, Monate vor dem Start, hatte ein Teil der linken Intelligenz gegen das East–West Encounter gestichelt. Der Kritiker Yamané, stark Moskau-gebunden, denunzierte das Ganze als eine Form des Kalten Kriegs." [Already in the winter, months before the opening, part of the left-wing intel-

ligentsia had made stabs at the East–West Encounter. The critic Yamané, strongly Moscow-inclined, denounced the enterprise as a form of cold war.]

120 Carter, "A Further Step" (see above, p. 130, note 27), in *WEC*, p. 191.

121 Carter, funeral oration for Paul Jacobs; see below, p. 251.

from among many imagined improvisations rather than the first that occurs to him. Thus he is able to choose, before the performance, the particular patterns of notes that will give the highest degree of characterization and from which the most interesting results can be drawn. He is, therefore, able to emphasize character and variety of character strongly, in many ways that the improviser cannot on the spur of the moment. The same is true of the control of the large pattern.

For the most striking characteristic of Western art music is that it makes its appeal to a special aspect of the listener's intelligence and memory. The composer assumes that the listener will carry out a creative task analogous to his [own], that is, to the act of composition proper – that he will organize notes into groups and these groups in turn into larger units, that he will perceive the relationship of these building blocks to one another and apprehend the similarities and differences that exist in diverse elements or, indeed, in various placings or occurrences of the same element. That is the dialectic method of Western art music. It is by using this method that it is able to express such a variety of interrelated thoughts and feelings and give a remarkable experience of living time.

In making such a demand on the attention, art music sets itself apart from popular music, for example, or folk music, which are quite different in their aims and achievements. For this reason, the qualities of concert music are often not self-evident to most persons when they first hear it. No other art has striven so persistently for a self-contained dialectic and is therefore so untranslatable. One thinks of Mallarmé's making a life-work out of the search for the perfect poem, the one that would be as little like prose as possible, and far removed from "making sense" in the prosaic meaning of that phrase. One can say of music that its masterworks have come closest to partaking of the essential perfection of the art in proportion to the degree in which the musical argument was a self-sufficient thing, developed within the music itself, on its own terms.

The history of Western music is a sequence of particular examples, which notoriously have defied rational description. Critics and historians have in general failed to draw an abstract system of syntax or rhetoric from these examples. Indeed, they, with the general public, have tended to forget that the compositions themselves are irreducible, concrete matter. No summary of them is possible, but they can only be grasped as they are heard,

in time. To say that there is a classical syntax is to mistake the unconvincing generalizations of music theorists for the musical dialectic itself, each time different in each outstanding work. What is significant is the special use of musical resources rather than their conventional or syntactical use.

The Western musical dialectic represents many centuries of trial and error, all directed by the apparent intention of finding ever greater co-ordination between the musical elements – the stressing of their ability to be heard in groups and in temporal patterns. For instance, tuning by equal temperament had to be developed when musical concepts became large enough in scale to require extensive modulation – when, in other words, the need to produce big architecture and the *grande ligne* outweighed any pedantic considerations concerning intervals slightly out of tune. By the same token, brilliant performing techniques and special sound effects were subordinated to the general pattern in order not to distract the listener from following the more interesting large design of the music.

Although constantly preoccupied with musical dialectic, composers have often felt [the] need of preventing it from becoming a meaningless routine, and have searched in many directions for new freshness. Indeed, the public itself, when it seeks justification for the existence of any work of art, looks for those qualities that make it fresh, new, different, irreplaceable, and that give it something, perhaps some one thing only, that is unduplicated in other, comparable works. And of the artists it expects the conscious and purposeful intention of presenting the valuable and the new.

The means of freshening and extending the boundaries of the musical language, its vocabulary, grammar, rhetoric, and syntax, have been of two kinds. One might be described as a logical projection of already existing technical patterns. To the triad, two superimposed thirds, was added still another third to make a seventh chord. And with the seventh once accepted, one could continue the process by creating and establishing the ninth, and the eleventh and the thirteenth. In analogy with this stacking of thirds, Schoenberg and Scriabin could base some of their harmonic theory and practice on pile-ups of fourths. Likewise, Wagner with methodical logic elaborated an entire work, *Tristan and Isolde*, out of a consideration of the uses of one single chord. Such a method of developing ideas from one single musical feature is of course characteristic of many important contemporary works. To mention a few, *The Rite of Spring* deals among other things with patterns of irregular scansion, the Webern *Bagatelles* deal with the intervals of the seventh and the ninth, and the third of the Schoenberg *Five Pieces for Orchestra* deals with sonority.

This kind of freshening consists essentially of an internal operation performed upon the language itself. The other kind is achieved by dislocating the musical dialectic by imposing on it programs derived from non-musical experience and non-musical thought. The phrase "program music" of course suggests primarily such things as the *Iron Foundry, Pacific 231, Ionisation,* or, to the more musicological, Marain Marais describing his gallstone operation in a sonata for viola da gamba with basso continuo.[122] Natural sounds and human feelings and actions have been the most exploited source for such program music, and, through opera particularly, have had a great effect on concert music. One might characterize these programs with the word "random," being careful, however, to explain that the word is used not with any pretension to scientific or mathematical usage, but simply to denote the familiar, everyday phenomenon of experiential random. Thunderstorms inspired the "random music" of the nineteenth century.

There is also another type of program music, one whose program is of a scientific, arithmetical nature, such as the isorhythms, mensuration canons, and the other fantastic integrative devices of fourteenth- and fifteenth-century music. The parallel between the medieval and renaissance compositions of that sort and certain twentieth-century trends has been too often drawn to need further elaboration here, except to stress the point that while many of the methods of serialization are a type of program that can be described apart from the music, this program should not be mistaken for musical dialectic itself, which cannot be so described.[123]

Both programmatic methods have led to many uninteresting and a few good results and much wasted effort. Ultimately, the composer who uses them is experimenting with a new approach that may not prove valuable. In the long run it is only works of a preponderantly dialectical interest that continue to be heard – those whose concern is mainly programmatic fade very soon.

It is interesting to point out also the appeal that program music has always had for non-musical persons. Sometimes the public is deceived into believing that those factors that can be verbalized are the essentials of the music. It is obvious to the musically experienced that this is not so. On the other hand, we have seen the tendency to believe that merely mapping out the technical devices constitutes a justification and sufficient defense of a composition. But ultimately this is a reversion to a traditional way of enlivening musical order: that of applying an arithmetical order literally, as literally as Strauss dealt with his programs. Such efforts may be of speculative or entertainment value. Whether they are of musical value seems to be a matter of chance.

There is a more intelligent and less wasteful way of dealing with the question of musical syntax. How do we understand the music we hear? How has the training provided by the finest of Western music shaped listeners' expectations, abilities, and perceptions? There have been composers who have understood these matters very well indeed, and who have made successful and interesting attempts to discover new methods of musical dialectic: for example, the later Debussy etudes and sonatas, the pre-12-tone Schoenberg, and some early Bartók and Stravinsky works. In many different places today there exist composers who are contributing in this way to [the] extension of specifically musical ways of thinking. Our interest leads us to avoid the cynicism and contempt [of] some music so perilously close to the practical joke. In avoiding the distracting temptation of sensationalism for its own tedious sake, we are seeking new kinds of musical thought patterns, new formations of ideas, and new methods of continuity that make use of the special faculty of musical understanding that has been developed so extensively by Western art music already.

[Published in *Music – East and West: Report on [the] 1961 Tokyo East-West Music Encounter Conference*, ed. Executive Committee for [the] 1961 Tokyo East-West Music Encounter, n.p., n.d., pp. 126–129. In his lecture notes, which are preserved in the Paul Sacher Foundation, Carter consistently used the title "The Extension of the Classical Syntax."]

---

122 Carter is referring to Alexander Mosolov's *Zavod* [The Foundry] (1926–28), Arthur Honegger's *Pacific 231: Mouvement symphonique No. 1* (1923), Edgard Varèse's *Ionisation* for 13 percussion players (1931), and Marin Marais's *Tableau de l'opération de la taille*, from *La gamme et autres morceaux de symphonie* for violin, viol, and harpsichord (1723).

123 American composers were well informed about recent developments in European serialism from their visits to European music festivals and also from the publication in English translation of *Die Reihe* starting in 1958: *Die Reihe: A Periodical Devoted to Developments in Contemporary Music* (Bryn Mawr, PA: Presser; Vienna: Universal, 1958–68).

87 Elliott and Helen Carter with Luciano Berio
    (Hong Kong, 1961)

On their return from Tokyo the Carters also visited Bang-
kok and Hong Kong (at that time, being American citizens, they were not allowed to enter mainland China).
They were joined along the way by Luciano Berio, who
had likewise attended the 1961 Tokyo East-West Music Encounter. This photograph shows Berio and the Carters
in a relaxed mood while visiting a floating restaurant in
Hong Kong.

87

Double Concerto (1959–61)

The history of the *Double Concerto* dates back to 1956, when the harpsichordist Ralph Kirkpatrick asked Carter to write a work for harpsichord and piano. In the winter of 1956–57 Carter worked intensively on the new piece, expanding its scoring so that each solo instrument was supported by a carefully selected instrumental ensemble, including percussion. But Carter soon encountered severe conceptual difficulties that caused him to interrupt the piece in order to work on another project, namely, the *String Quartet No. 2* for the Stanley Quartet. It was not until 1959, once the string quartet was completed and the Fromm Music Foundation had agreed to commission the piece for Kirkpatrick, that he resumed work on the *Double Concerto*. Ultimately the work took more than two years to finish, reaching completion only in August 1961, a few weeks before its première. As with his later *Concerto for Orchestra* and *A Symphony of Three Orchestras*, Carter took literary models as his guide for the *Double Concerto*, namely, Lucretius's philosophical epic poem *De rerum natura* and Alexander Pope's satire *The Dunciad*. The origins of the cosmos from random collisions of atoms, as described by Lucretius, was meant to function in particular as a point of departure for the beginning of the work, while the annihilation and return to a state of chaos, as described by both writers, served the same function for the ending. (As always in such cases, Carter made use of these analogies only after the fact, as creative aids that helped lend shape to a pre-existing musical idea.) The result was a work with a symmetrical series of movements (Introduction, Allegro scherzando, Adagio, Presto, Coda) expanded by means of three cadenzas, one for the harpsichord towards the end of the Introduction, and two for the piano in the Presto. Superposed on this basic architectural plan, however, are a great many subliminal continuities. As a result it merely offers a rough guide to following the music, which again and again, despite its extreme technical complexity and multi-tiered construction, conveys an impression of quasi-rhapsodic spontaneity.

88 *Double Concerto,* for harpsichord and piano with two chamber orchestras (1959–61), rhythm chart ("Rhythmic Basis of Introduction"), 1 p.

While conceiving the Introduction to his *Double Concerto*, Carter was guided by the notion of "organized chaos" (see *CC*, p. 64) and tried to implement it with an extreme form of musical stratification. Beginning with noise-like percussion sounds from which specific pitches gradually emerge, the Introduction is based on the superposition of ten rhythmically divergent textural layers. Carter's analytical diagram, shown here, reveals that at first two rhythms appear in a ratio of 49:50 (from mm. 6 and 7, respectively). Others are added in mm. 13, 16, 20, 31, and 36, each in antiphonal interplay between the first and second orchestras. (The underscored numbers at the beginning of the staves indicate the metronomic speeds of the associated pulses, the preceding fractions the type and number of rhythmic durations relative to the half-note beat, e.g. 10/21 = 21 sixteenth-note quintuplets.) The superpositions give rise to a dense polyrhythmic texture moving toward two points of partial intersection in mm. 45 and 46 – one in layers 5 through 10 (m. 45) and the other in layers 1 through 6 (m. 46). The patterns of acceleration and deceleration moving toward or away from these points are indicated in the diagram by turquoise and violet crayon. Moreover, the chart indicates that Carter, adopting an idea from Henry Cowell's *New Musical Resources*,[124] also coordinated the tempo and the intervallic size in this movement: each rhythmic pulse is assigned a particular interval, as notated at the opening of the diagram, e.g. MM 24.5 is assigned the minor second, and MM 25 the major second (only the minor sixth is omitted). It is safe to assume that Carter used a similar diagram while working out the score. However, the document displayed here seems to have been made after the fact for explanatory purposes. Carter may conceivably have prepared it for his article "The Orchestral Composer's Point of View" (1970), which reproduces an excerpt from it in simplified form (mm. 44–46).[125]

---

124 See Cowell, *New Musical Resources* (see above, p. 14, note 42), part 2 ("Rhythm"), esp. pp. 90–98 and 104–108.

125 Carter, "The Orchestral Composer's Point of View" (see above, p. 63, note 64), in *CEL*, p. 245.

88 *Double Concerto*

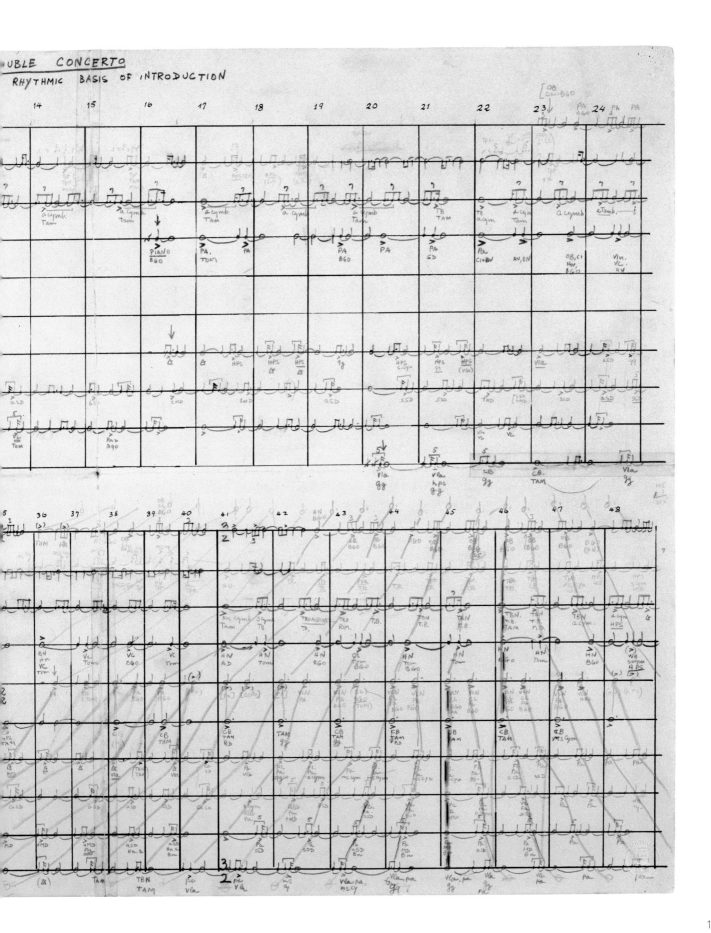

Gratitude to Paul Fromm (1961)

Paul Fromm, a musical amateur deeply devoted to contemporary music and a successful wine merchant, was born in 1906 in Kitzingen, Germany, into the fifth generation of a Jewish family of vintners.[126] Forced to emigrate in 1938, Fromm settled in Chicago and quickly established himself in business, becoming an American citizen in 1944. The Fromm Music Foundation, launched in 1952, was of far more modest dimensions than the Rockefeller or Ford Foundations; its annual budget at first was a mere $50,000, and even in the 1980s it had grown only to $150,000.[127] In his hands-on, unbureaucratic way, Fromm ran the foundation on a shoestring, commissioning new works (often unsolicited) from composers including Babbitt, Berio, Carter, Krenek, Sessions, Shapey, Wuorinen, and many others. Recognizing the limits of a typical commission, he was equally keen to support performances and recordings of those works.[128] The Fromm Music Foundation also supported larger projects such as the Seminar in Advanced Musical Studies at Princeton University, the journal *Perspectives of New Music*, the Contemporary Chamber Players at the University of Chicago, the Festival of Contemporary Music at Tanglewood (later at the Aspen Festival), and the large-scale commissioning project and festival of American music for the US Bicentennial in 1976. The Fromm Music Foundation, based since 1972 at Harvard University, continues its activities in support of new music.

The première of the *Double Concerto*, given by Ralph Kirkpatrick (harpsichord), Charles Rosen (piano), and a chamber orchestra conducted by Gustav Meier, took place in Grace Rainey Rogers Auditorium at New York's Metropolitan Museum on 6 September 1961. It formed the centerpiece of a concert mounted by the Fromm Music Foundation for the Eighth Congress of the International Musicological Society, and was followed over the next two days by a gramophone recording for the Epic label (7–8 September 1961).[129] The choice of venue itself proved beneficial, for it ensured that the *Double Concerto* would attract great attention. Still more important from Carter's viewpoint was the fact that he was able to rehearse the work at leisure and with great care with his performers. He specially emphasized this point in the following letter of thanks to Paul Fromm, who had made it

all possible. The patron for his part was especially proud of the success of Carter's *Double Concerto*, often referring to it as the Foundation's *Firebird*.[130]

89 Elliott Carter to Paul Fromm, 11 (?) September 1961[131]

Mr. Paul Fromm, / The Fromm Foundation, /
1028 West Van Buren Street / Chicago
September 21, 1961

Dear Paul,
This is to thank you for everything you did for my *Double Concerto* last week. First and foremost, in giving me the reassurance that I could follow my own ideas and write a piece that might take time and patience at rehearsal and present problems of a purely technical kind – and yet have it taken seriously and be rehearsed enough to have it played well by enterprising and skillful performers. The prospect of such an opportunity, as you know, practically never comes to an American composer, who is always being told how limited the resources are going to be if he writes anything requiring larger groups than a string quartet. For this prospect I am truly grateful, for, of course, it allowed me to try new methods and new conceptions and then, when once written, not to have them kept from being heard live even by me through bad performance or neglect. Here, for once, I was able to get the practical experience of careful rehearsals, which is invaluable in helping to predict the degree of difficulty and of effectiveness of unusual passages in future works – as you can imagine, a most important kind of experience for a composer and yet one that rarely comes to an American composer here. Likewise the careful rehearsals gave an opportunity to find out which of the thousands of indications to the performers were foolproof and which were unclear and needed to be made more precise, and in thus testing the indications in the score under careful conditions it was possible to make markings more self-evident that would produce more easily rehearsed and more immediately effective future performances. This opportunity, too, I have never had with my orchestral scores, which usually have been hurried through at re-

---

126 See David Gable, "Paul Fromm in American Musical Life," introduction to *A Life for New Music: Selected Papers of Paul Fromm*, ed. David Gable and Christoph Wolff (Cambridge, MA: Department of Music, Harvard University, 1988), pp. ix–xviii.

127 John Rockwell, "Paul Fromm, Classical-Music Patron, Is Dead," *The New York Times*, 6 July 1987. The Foundation's income, Rockwell explains, did not come from interest on capital, but rather from yearly inputs taken out of Fromm's business profits. Fromm also received third-party donations; Carter in particular often donated money to the Fromm Foundation to support performers and

composers from his circle of friends, including Charles Rosen, Paul Jacobs, David Diamond, and Stefan Wolpe.

128 Works commissioned by the Fromm Music Foundation include (in addition to Carter's *Double Concerto*) Luciano Berio's *Circles* (1960), Milton Babbitt's *Vision and Prayer* (1961), George Rochberg's *Music for the Magic Theater* (1965), and Steve Reich's *New York Counterpoint* (1985).

hearsals, allowing the more unusual and difficult places to be relegated to the category of "ineffective" before any effort had been made to find out what was intended. Thus, as a practising composer who is always seeking for new knowledge and experience with his medium, and for opportunities to bring into practical realization ideas often untried or unusual, the experiences which your foundation afforded me at the rehearsals, performance, and recording were of utmost importance and value. I do not expect ever again to have such an opportunity in this country, as it not merely involves a wise patron, aware of the professional problems of music, but one who can realize that when such professionalism is treated with understanding and respect, there are chances of a good result.

Of course, the public aspect of the concert was gratifying. The performance and reception of the work, its being surrounded by two other works of caliber,[132] and its recording will help, I hope, to make the cause of new music and particularly of new American music seem an important and valid one that cannot be neglected by our culture as it usually is. I am particularly grateful [for] your efforts to present contemporary music as if it were of real importance and value, and to support enthusiastically what seems to you good. It is only in this way that some interest will be aroused – usually the presentation of new music is done as an empty gesture without real knowledge or interest and results in even more apathy and estrangement of the public.

Helen joins me in sending our warmest regards to Mrs. Fromm and yourself,
Elliott

[Typed letter, carbon copy with autograph signature and corrections; Elliott Carter Collection, Paul Sacher Foundation. Reprinted by permission of Michael Greenstone.]

---

129 Elliott Carter, *Double Concerto*, performed by Ralph Kirkpatrick (harpsichord), Charles Rosen (piano), and a chamber orchestra conducted by Gustav Meier; and Leon Kirchner, *Concerto for Violin, Cello, Ten Winds, and Percussion*, performed by Tossy Spivakovsky (violin), Aldo Parisot (cello), and a chamber orchestra conducted by Leon Kirchner; Epic LC 3830.

130 See Gable, "Paul Fromm," (see note 126), p. xiv.

131 The reference to "last week" in the first sentence of this letter, meaning the première of the *Double Concerto* on 6 September 1961 and the gramophone recording on the two days thereafter, strongly suggests that the date "21 September," given on the letter, is a typographical error.

132 Besides Carter's *Double Concerto*, the program of the Metropolitan Museum concert also featured Milton Babbitt's *Vision and Prayer* for soprano and pre-recorded tape (likewise a world première) and Leon Kirchner's *Concerto for Violin, Cello, Ten Winds, and Percussion* (a New York première).

90 Robert Craft and Elliott Carter in a rehearsal of the
Double Concerto (Los Angeles, 1962)

This photograph was taken at a rehearsal for the second performance of the *Double Concerto*, conducted by Robert Craft with Leonard Stein and Pearl Kaufman as soloists. Presented by the Fromm Music Foundation, the performance took place at the Monday Evening Concerts in Los Angeles on 19 February 1962 and featured, in addition to the *Double Concerto*, Bach's *Wedding Cantata*, Schoenberg's *Chamber Symphony No. 1* (op. 9), and the world première of Stravinsky's *Anthem* ("The Dove Descending Breaks the Air"). In a letter of thanks to Paul Fromm for his renewed support, Carter emphasized how important it was for him to experience a second performance of a new work shortly after the première, this being the only way "to get all the 'bugs' out of the score, make it practical to play in all its details, and to have its effect as clearly indicated in the notation as possible." He also praised Craft and the other performers for their efforts: "The performance went well with far fewer rehearsals than we had in New York, and was more emphatic, vivid and meaningful." He then added an amusing observation: "Everybody I met outside of music was a psychoanalyst – and these enjoyed that the man, Leonard Stein, played the soft harpsichord while the woman played the loud and vigorous piano in my piece – You see." [133]

---

[133] Letter from Elliott Carter to Paul Fromm, 22 February 1962; carbon copy in the Elliott Carter Collection, Paul Sacher Foundation. In a letter of 6 March 1962 to Lawrence Morton, the director of the Monday Evening Concerts, Carter added a few reservations: "[...] naturally its [the *Double Concerto*'s] many problems can seldom be expected to be solved at every performance." Quoted from Crawford, *Evenings On and Off the Roof* (see above, p. 154, not 86), p. 199.

91 Igor Stravinsky and Elliott Carter (New York, 1962),
photo by Don Hunstein (Columbia Records)

To pay respects to Igor Stravinsky's wife, Vera Soudeikina
Stravinsky, Carter attended the opening night of her exhibition at New York's Galerie Internationale on 1 May
1962. Stravinsky, seen here in conversation with Carter,
had arrived a day earlier from Toronto, where he had
given the première of his *Eight Instrumental Miniatures*
on 29 April. According to Vera's diary, several prominent visitors to the exhibition decided to buy paintings,
among them Leonard Bernstein, the violinist Samuel
Dushkin, Robert Graff (the producer of Stravinsky's recently recorded "musical play" *The Flood*), Robert Craft,
and – Elliott Carter.[134]

[Reprinted by permission of Don Hunstein and Sony BMG Music Entertainment.]

---

134 See *Dearest Bubushkin: The Correspondence
of Vera and Igor Stravinsky, 1921–1954,
with Excerpts from Vera Stravinsky's Diaries,
1922–1971*, ed. Robert Craft, trans.
Lucia Davidova (London: Thames and
Hudson, 1985), p. 210 (diary entry of
8 May 1962).

"A Very Isolating Effort"

1962–1973

Forging Plans with Nabokov (1962)

A snapshot of Carter's travels in 1962 and 1963 gives an impression of the peripatetic quality of the last five decades of his life. In February and June 1962, he attended performances of the *Double Concerto* in Los Angeles and London, respectively. From London, he went on to Paris and then to Rome, where he again stayed at the American Academy, this time as composer-in-residence (until July 1963). In September 1962 he traveled for the first time to the Warsaw Autumn festival; and the following spring he went to Berlin as a guest of the Berliner Begegnungen. Shortly before the letter exchange below, the Carters had seen the Nabokovs in Paris, where Nabokov was based in the main office of the Congress for Cultural Freedom. Nabokov organized a party for his friend on 12 June 1962 at the home of the noted Parisian patroness Suzanne Tézenas, who also supported Boulez's concert series, Domaine Musical. A French woodwind ensemble played Carter's *Eight Etudes and a Fantasy* on this occasion.[1] Although the timing of this party coincided with a meeting of the Music Committee of the CCF, which would be attended by "500 Strobels and 21,567 Labrocas,"[2] Carter was not a member of the committee and was not invited to attend the meeting. Five years earlier, Nabokov had discussed with CCF board member Virgil Thomson whether they should invite Carter, who had "seemed very much interested," to join the committee.[3] For whatever reason, nothing came of this.

During his Rome residency, Carter worked on his Ford Foundation commission, the *Piano Concerto*, attended the ISCM festival in Amsterdam in June 1963 (where he was a member of the jury), and also began to prepare for the family's extended stay in Berlin in 1964. Nabokov, who was an advisor to the Ford Foundation's Berlin program and who would take over the directorship of the Berliner Festwochen in 1963, offered his assistance in matters large and small, including plans for a year of study abroad in Berlin for the Carters' nineteen-year-old son, David, who in July 1962 had just finished his freshman year at Yale. Carter also sought his friend's advice about hosting the annual ISCM festival in New York in 1967 or 1968. These ambitious and expensive plans (which Carter estimates at $200,000 – well over a million 2007 dollars) were however not realized. Apparently the CCF did not ever support the ISCM's activities (although

Carter had indirectly sounded Nabokov out about this years earlier in his letter of 9 July 1956, see above, p. 128), and subsequent festivals all took place outside of the United States, in Stockholm (1966), Prague (1967), Warsaw (1968), and Hamburg (1969).

92   Nicolas Nabokov to Elliott Carter, 22 July 1962

Verderonne, 22nd July 1962

Dearest Elliott,
Unfortunately I was not able to go from Venice to Rome. Instead I had to go to Geneva and Berlin and hence had to forego the pleasure of visiting you and Helen in Rom[e]. Then, after returning from Berlin, I was again completely tired out, my doctor got cross with me and put me in gaol in Verderonne, surrounded by my family. Here I will stay until I have to leave for Brazil on the 17th of August.[4]

I am afraid that I was not able to do anything so far either about the ISCM Festival in New York nor about your trip to Israel.[5] Both these problems will have to await my return from America. But if you give me a typed-out memorandum about the needs of the ISCM Festival, I will take up this matter in New York with some friends of mine.

As for David, I have asked my assistant Ruby d'Arschot to inquire at the German cultural relations attaché's office, whether the German House of the Cité Universitaire still takes foreigners. As soon as I know something, I will write you.

Meanwhile I send you and Helen and David all my love, and my family joins me.

Yours ever
[Nicolas]

Mr. Elliott Carter / American Academy in Rome / Via Angelo Masina, 5 / ROME

[Typed letter, carbon copy; Harry Ransom Humanities Research Center, University of Texas, Austin. Reprinted by permission of Dominique Nabokov.]

---

1   See letter from Elliott Carter to William Glock, 23 June 1962; William Glock Estate, British Library.
2   Letter from Nicolas Nabokov to Elliott Carter, 18 April 1962; Elliott Carter Collection, Paul Sacher Foundation.
3   Letter from Nicolas Nabokov to Virgil Thomson, 26 February 1957; Virgil

Thomson Papers, Irving S. Gilmore Music Library, Yale University: MSS 29/29A.
4   Nabokov had been planning another international music festival for the Congress for Cultural Freedom, which was to take place in Rio de Janeiro in August–September 1963, but he was no longer involved in the preparations after he moved to Berlin (see letter from

Nicolas Nabokov to Virgil Thomson, 6 March 1962; Virgil Thomson Papers, Irving S. Gilmore Music Library, Yale University: MSS 29, Box 69, folder 18). It is not clear whether this festival took place.
5   Carter's planned trip to Israel, for which Nabokov had apparently tried to pave the way when he traveled there in April 1962, did not come about.

93   Elliott Carter to Nicolas Nabokov, 31 July 1962

American Academy in Rome / Via Angelo Masina, 5 /
(Porta S. Pancrazio) / Rome
July 31, 1962

Dear Nicolas,
As you must have learned, I have tried fairly frequently
to 'phone you in the past few days, after learning of your
return to Paris through Mlle d'Arschot's telegram about
David's année scolaire.[6] I appreciate very much your bothering with this at [a] time when you must be very tired.
As indicated by your letter that arrived today.

Please take care of yourself, we need you very much
and we hate the idea of you wasting yourself on too many
things. Be prudent, please, because your real work is so important and necessary, to so many people, and to us musicians in particular, since so few people anywhere who deal
with large-scale affairs have the faintest idea about music
and do all sorts of foolish, wasteful and destructive things
in the name of helping.

Let me know whether it is possible to 'phone to Verderonne and when it is convenient – if you have a moment.
(Is it still 'le cinq à Verderonne, Seine et Oise'?)

The idea of the German House for David next year is
excellent – I hope that it can be arranged. He is no whizz
at German, but he has worked hard at it and should have a
chance to use it –

The Amacadmy [sic; cable address] is odd as usual. I
felt the need of pictures in this white-walled house you
used to live in and asked to borrow some from the fellow painters, and now we have some weird nightmares
– people, indistinctly doing things to each other and to
dogs in dark brown and violet – and we wish we had
never thought of being loyal, since everybody that comes
in (including J. J. Sweeney[7]) says the pictures are God-aw-
ful. The Am[erican] Ac[ademy] seems gifted at turning up
artists and composers nobody else wants. We have the
Ohio Prokofieff and the Iowa Apostel and the Kansas
Zimmermann and the 21st-Street Messiaen, not to speak
of yours truly, whom I see Stravinsky has called the Berg
of Waccabuc.[8]

Helen and I go to Warsaw to the festival next month
and back here for something odd that Jack Bornoff seems
to have cooked up in Rome with Labroca – some talk fest
about in-concrete music.

As I work at my *Piano Concerto*, I can see that I am in
for a long and troubled siege – and will probably have to
lay aside all trips and distractions – Tiresome –

Helen joins in sending you & Marie-Claire our love –
Elliott
get well soon –

[Typed letter with autograph date, signature, greetings, and postscript;
Harry Ransom Humanities Research Center, University of Texas at Austin,
Nicolas Nabokov Papers.]

94   Elliott Carter to Nicolas Nabokov, 5 August 1962

American Academy, / Via Angelo Masina, 5 / Rome, Italy
Rome, le 5 Août, 1962

Dear Nicolas,
In answering your letter of July 22nd, I omitted to talk
about the ISCM (possible) New York Festival which you
so kindly have taken an interest in.

Unfortunately from here – and with my general
lack of [knowledge of] such things – I cannot make very
much sense and can hardly send you a satisfactory memorandum before your departure for America and Brazil,
on the 17th.

What seem to be the principal items are:
1) Round trip air-fare for about 20 delegates
2) Their living expenses for a week in N[ew] Y[ork]
3) Their "entertainment" such as tourist visits – outside
of the concerts.
4) The giving of, at least, one large, well-rehearsed orchestral concert (chosen by the international jury, and hence
very difficult avant-garde music)
5) at least one smaller orchestral concert
6) 2 chamber music concerts
7) and, usually, another concert of music of the inviting
nation (the US, in this case) not chosen by the jury.
8) Money for the arrangement of the jury meeting in
the previous January (the ISCM Fests usually take place
in June). This would consist of 5 men who have all the

---

6   Ruby d'Arschot was Nabokov's assistant at
the Congrès pour la Liberté de la Culture.

7   James Johnson Sweeney (1900–1986) was
an art historian and critic who headed the
Guggenheim Museum from 1951 to 1960
and became director of the Museum of
Fine Arts in Houston in 1961.

8   See Igor Strawinsky, "Some Composers"
[interview with Robert Craft], *Musical
America* 82/6 (June 1962), pp. 6–11, esp. 6:

"That the *Double Concerto* should suggest
Berg's towering example in general
ways is not surprising, but I hear direct
references to the Berg in it, too. (Carter is
certainly not a naïve composer, but I
think these Berg bits are unknowing.) The
passage from 432 (the piano entrance here
is one of the finest things in the piece)
to 460, and especially the flute at 436 and
the bassoon at 441 remind me of the Berg,

but the architectural plot of the solo instruments – their roles as separate soloists,
duo-soloists, parts of ensemble groups – is
also reminiscent of the Berg." Reprinted
in Igor Stravinsky and Robert Craft,
Dialogues and a Diary (Garden City, NY:
Doubleday, 1963), pp. 46–62, esp. 48, and
in Igor Strawinsky and Robert Craft,
Dialogues and a Diary (London: Faber and
Faber, 1968), pp. 99–112, esp. 100.

expenses paid and meet for about a week – preferably in the inviting country (the US) – but they could meet in Europe to save expense.

9) The setting up of an office to take care of the many different arrangements connected with all this – possibly a year in advance.

Strobel suggested that the Festival be in 1967 or '68.

I have in my inexperience imagined all this might cost about $ 200,000, but this is probably conservative – certainly not carefully thought out. In any case Mr. Felix Greissle is the active head of the US Section (address: 340 East 80th Street, New York 21, Telephone: UN-1-6380), and I have just written him asking him to write you for an appointment, while you are in New York.[9]

We are going off to Warsaw for the festival in a few weeks. Is there anything I can do for you there?

I hope that your resting is producing very good results.

Helen & David join in sending our affectionate wishes to you, Marie-Claire, Alexandre et Caroline[10]
Elliott

[Typed letter with autograph signature and greetings; Harry Ransom Humanities Research Center, University of Texas at Austin, Nicolas Nabokov Papers.]

Impressions from Warsaw (1962)

Leaving Rome in September 1962, the Carters traveled via Vienna and Berlin to Warsaw in order to visit the sixth annual Warsaw Autumn Festival of Contemporary Music (15–23 September 1962). Among the many events they attended was a performance of *Eight Etudes and a Fantasy* given by the Dorian Quintet in the Chamber Music Hall of the National Philharmonic on 21 September 1962. They also came into contact with many composers and performers from the countries of Eastern Europe. For musicians on the other side of the Iron Curtain, the Warsaw Autumn Festival, founded in 1956 during a period of political thaw, was an important window to the West and one of the few places where they had an opportunity to exchange thoughts and information freely with their western colleagues. It also served many younger Polish composers (from Witold Lutosławski, Kazimierz Serocki, and Tadeusz Baird to Henryk Gorecki and Krzysztof Penderecki) as a springboard for their careers, securing performances of their music at festivals in Western Europe. The following letter to Kurt Stone, written on his return from Warsaw, shows that Carter was actively involved in these exchanges and tried to have scores of his music sent to several interested parties via the editor of his publishing house. (Stone's reply shows that he satisfied this request immediately.) At the same time, however, he let it be known that he viewed the avantgardist trends he encountered in Warsaw with a skeptical eye. The fact that he enclosed the terms "advanced" and "old-fashionedness" in quotation marks bears witness to this skepticism, as does his surprising reference to Penderecki, Gorecki, Serocki, and Wojciech Kilar as "Darmstadt composers" – by which, of course, he merely singled out the radicality of the Polish "sonorists" rather than suggesting any deeper ties to the methods of Darmstadt serialism. A short while later, in an article for *Perspectives of New Music*, he reported on the Warsaw Autumn Festival and explained precisely what he found troublesome about the music of the Darmstadters and the Polish avant-garde: the former, he felt (despite his admiration for the constructive ingenuity of many of their works), neglected "the listener's psychology," while the latter all too often allowed the sonic events to unfold on a "simple sensuous level" without being anchored in higher principles of construction.[11]

---

9   Felix Greissle (1894–1982), a pupil and son-in-law of Schoenberg, emigrated in 1938 to America, where he worked as an editor for G. Schirmer and E. B. Marx Music Corporation.

10 Marie-Claire and Alexandre Nabokov: see above, p. 126, note 5. Caroline Corre was Marie-Claire's daughter from her first marriage.

11 Elliott Carter, "Letter from Europe," *Perspectives of New Music* 1/2 (Spring 1963), pp. 195–205, esp. 197 and 201; most recently reprinted in *CEL*, pp. 31–40, esp. 33 and 37.

95 Elliott Carter to Kurt Stone, 23 September [1962]

September 23. Airplane = Warsaw–Vienna

Dear Kurt –

There are a number of scores I promised to send to friends in the Iron-Curtain countries who were interested in my music. Naturally there can be no question of their paying – but I, in return, have gotten a (small) list of Czech, Russian "advanced" composers & will write for their music later.

So would you please be so kind as to send (at my expense) score[s] of

1. *Woodwind Quintet*
2. *2nd String Quartet*
3. *Holiday Overture*
4. *Sonata for Fl[ute,] Ob[oe,] Cell[o,] Harps[ichord]*
5. *First Symphony* (if out)

to: Alexei Machavariani / Union of Composers and Musicologists / Tbilissi / USSR

– –

1. *8 Etudes & Fantasy*
2. *1st String Quartet*
3. *2 R[o]b[er]t Frost Songs*
4. *Variations*
5. *Cello Sonata*

to: Felix Glonti / (same address as above)

– –

Also a string quartet from Bratislava, who played me excellent recordings of wonderful performances of Czech works and heard my 1st Quartet in Warsaw a few years ago,[12] is very anxious to learn both quartets – I gave them the record of the 2nd & the miniature score. So would you please send them the *parts* of both I & II and the score of I. The address is: (They would like these right away as they want to play the 2nd on tour in Czechoslovakia in November)

Alojz (ALOJZ) Nemec / Bartoňova 14 / Bratislava / Czechoslovakia

Also at the Composers Union in Warsaw I left scores of 2nd Qu[arte]t, Sonata for Fl[ute], Ob[oe], etc., 8 Etudes. Would you please send scores of *Variations* and (later)

of *Double Concerto* – I think they will do an important work of mine at next year's festival – probably the *D[ouble] C[oncerto]*, of which I left a recording.[13] With this you might include some "advanced" American works [inserted:] / *Babbitt, Kirchner, Brown* (?) / orchestra & ch[amber] music – the Poles are very interested in the USA and know very little of our music. They have a whole group of advanced Darmstadt composers – Penderecki, Gorecki, Serocki, Kilar, that make the efforts of Shapey et al. seem very tame – These pieces are very much liked & play to full (symphony-hall sized) houses. So anything th[at] we can dig up that would not sound too old-fashioned & was really interesting would be appreciated & performed. Kirchner would be the limit of "old-fashionedness" I should think –

Address:
Stefan Śledziński / Warszawa, / Rynek St. Miasta 27 / (ZKP) / Poland

The whole Polish business is extraordinary – to have rebuilt, according to the paintings of Canaletto & others,[14] a section of Warsaw as it was in the XVIIth century & very convincingly too – and very expensive & beautifully done – is odd & fascinating beyond words. There is a whole "old city," much of which had ceased to exist before the destruction of 1944–5.

Best to you & Elsa[15]
Will write soon from Rome –
Elliott

[Autograph letter; Kurt Stone Collection, Irving S. Gilmore Music Library, Yale University.]

---

12 Carter's *String Quartet No. 1* had been performed by the Quatuor Parrenin on 19 September 1960, likewise during the Warsaw Autumn Festival. This was its Polish première.

13 It was not until three years later, on 26 September 1965, that the *Double Concerto* was performed at the Warsaw Autumn Festival, with the Great Polish Radio Symphony Orchestra conducted by Ernest

Bour and the solo parts taken by Mariolina de Robertis (harpsichord) and Aleksandra Utrecht (piano).

14 The painter Bernardo Bellotto, alias Canaletto (1722–1780), spent the 1770s at the court of the Polish king Stanislaw II August, where he created a famous series of cityscapes displayed today in the reconstructed rooms of the Warsaw Palace.

15 Kurt Stone's wife Else was a translator and editor. In the 1970s she and her husband edited the volume *The Writings of Elliott Carter* (WEC).

96 Kurt Stone to Helen and Elliott Carter, 1 October 1962

Associated Music Publishers, Inc. / One West 47th Street, New York 36, N.Y.

Mr. [and] Mrs. Elliott Carter / American Academy in Rome / Via Angelo Masina, 5 / Rome, Italy
October 1, 1962

Dear Helen and Elliott:
Thank you both for keeping me posted through pretty picture postcards.[16] What a fascinating experience! Especially the pictures of Warsaw, and your description of the Warsaw Festival makes me drool.

We have sent all the music you asked for to the various Iron-Curtain people. In order to make sure that nothing will be lost I have also sent letters separately to all the recipients telling them that the music is being sent at your request and under separate cover. We will charge you for the blueprint set of parts for your First Quartet because this is an outright expense, and also for the air-mail postage. All the printed scores we will send as promotional material without any charge to you.

Milton Babbitt's music will have to be sent by Mr. Boelke because our agency for his catalogue does not extend to Europe. I have written to him about your request.

The autographing of the Double Concerto score is almost finished; 150 pages have been done, and we have begun to proofread them. In order to waste as little time as possible we decided to ask the autographer to correct batches of about 25 pages at a time, as they get proofread. Then, as they get corrected, we'll send them to you for your perusal. I do not think that you should feel obligated to do a thorough proofreading job, but, of course, there will be a number of questions for you, and a critical glance at everything will no doubt result in finding a few more errors. In such a complex piece it is impossible to catch absolutely everything, no matter how hard we try.

I just learned that the BSO is definitely interested in doing the première of your as yet presumably unborn piano concerto. Sounds great! How's it coming?

New York now has Philharmonic Hall in full operation.[17] The opening night, a week ago yesterday, was very, very gala with red carpet, flashbulbs, television, and movie cameras, and with thousands of beautiful dresses, mink and ermine stoles, monumental coiffures, etc., on the glamorous ladies, and ill-fitting rented dress suits and white ties on their impoverished males. The music wasn't half as pretty, neither the program of chunks of larger works, nor their execution. Nor were the hall's acoustical qualities satisfactory, although this aspect is being improved by way of the acoustical clouds which clutter up the ceiling.[18] I find the audience's part of the hall very beautiful and the stage part much too gaudy and busy – they don't go together. And then there are those clouds!

Meanwhile, the sound engineers have been busy, and when Szell conducted the Clevelanders the acoustics were quite satisfactory.[19] Last Friday the Juilliard Quartet gave their first concert there: your Second Quartet framed by Schubert's *Quartettsatz* and Beethoven's Opus 59 No. 2.[20] Your Quartet sounded remarkably well: the individual parts came out extremely clear although the players sat quite close together. On the other hand, there was very little depth and warmth in the ensemble sound, and the cello sounded thin and wiry, which is of course not at all representative of Claus Adam's actual playing. I understand, though, that in most seats in the hall all seemed to be well.

We had a very nice vacation trip all through the north and north-east of the province of Québec. Unlike your summer, ours was totally a-cultural (except for some excellent food in Québec city), but it was most exciting and a complete change from routine. Nothing compared to your adventures, though.

Best to both of you.
Yours,
Associated Music Publishers, Inc.
Kurt Stone
KS/cf

Else sends her love.

[Typed letter with autograph signature and postscript; Elliott Carter Collection, Paul Sacher Foundation.]

---

16 The Kurt Stone Collection (Irving S. Gilmore Music Library, Yale University) contains two such postcards: one from Helen Carter (16 September 1962) and another from Elliott Carter (undated, probably 23 September 1962).

17 Philharmonic Hall (or Avery Fisher Hall, as it has been known since 1973), was the first part of the Lincoln Center for the Performing Arts, then currently under construction, to be finished. It opened on 23 September 1962 with a gala concert by the New York Philharmonic, conducted by Leonard Bernstein. To inaugurate their new home the orchestra joined by the Schola Cantorum of New York, the Columbia Boychoir, the Juilliard Chorus, and several leading vocal soloists, performed the "Gloria" from Ludwig van Beethoven's *Missa solemnis*, Aaron Copland's *Connotations* (a world première), the serenade *To Music* by Ralph Vaughan Williams, and the first movement of Gustav Mahler's *Symphony No. 8.*

18 Many improvements on both a larger and a smaller scale had to be made to counteract the universally lamented acoustical imbalances in the Philharmonic. At the end of its first week the chief acoustical engineer, Leo Beranek,

97 Carl Ruggles showing his paintings to Elliott Carter
(Arlington, VT, 1963)

During a two-week tenure as composer-in-residence at the Dartmouth Summer School (from 5 to 18 August 1963) Carter made a side-trip to Arlington, VT, in order to visit Carl Ruggles, now eighty-seven years old. Having virtually given up composition in his old age, Ruggles was more concerned with his paintings and took the opportunity to show them to his visitor. Carter recalled the event two years later in a newspaper interview: "I saw him [Ruggles] recently. He told me that a New York gallery is willing to pay his price for any of his pictures. He won't part with them, but he does lend them to the motel for wall decoration." He also mentioned an earlier encounter with Ruggles's paintings: "Years ago my wife Helen and I were in Vermont and saw some of Ruggles' paintings there. I wanted to buy one; I thought they had something, some value, but Helen said no. Now we can't get any at all."[21]

---

stated "that it would take a year before the hall could be brought into its ultimate condition." See Ross Parmenter, "Music World: The New Acoustics," in *The New York Times*, 30 September 1962.

19   Four of America's "big five" orchestras made guest appearances in Philharmonic Hall during the opening-week festivities. The last was the Cleveland Orchestra, which, on 27 September 1962, performed

Alvin Etler's *Concerto in One Movement*, Franz Schubert's *Symphony No. 8* in C major ("The Great"), and the Brahms *Violin Concerto* (with Isaac Stern) under the direction of George Szell.

20   This concert took place on 28 September 1962, one day after the guest appearance of the Cleveland Orchestra.

21   George Gelles, "As Seen By Elliott Carter: Orchestra, Audience, Musical Problems"

[interview with Elliott Carter], *The Boston Sunday Globe*, 12 September 1965. The second statement refers to an exhibition mounted at the Southern Vermont Art Center (Manchester, VT) from 5 to 24 July 1953. Several dozen paintings by Ruggles were shown in that exhibition, along with portraits of the artist by John Atherton, Thomas Hart Benton, and Boardman Robinson.

Thoughts on Expressionism (1964)

From January to mid-November 1964 Carter was invited by the Ford Foundation and the Berlin Senate to join a newly created artists-in-residence program in Berlin. This was certainly facilitated by Nicolas Nabokov, who, in addition to his duties with the Berlin Festival, was involved with setting up the new program.[22] It allowed practitioners of a wide range of arts – sculpture, painting, literature, music – to spend a year in this "outpost" of the western world, now even more isolated by the Berlin Wall. The local cultural scene, it was hoped, would thereby obtain important international contacts and artistic impetus. The first visitors – the writer Ingeborg Bachmann and her Argentina-based Polish colleague Witold Gombrowicz – arrived in Berlin in May 1963. They were later joined by, among others, the poets W. H. Auden and Michel Butor, the painters Ruth Franken, Frédéric Benrath, and William Scott, and the sculptor Mário Cravo. Music was represented by Carter, Gilbert Amy, Hans Werner Henze, Peter Heyworth, Roger Sessions, Isang Yun, Iannis Xenakis, and, at Carter's instigation, his two former students Alvin Curran and Joel Chadabe as well as Frederic Rzewski. Although the artists-in-residence program failed to meet Carter's expectations (see below, pp. 187–188), his stay in Berlin turned out to be creatively productive through his work on the *Piano Concerto*. He was also stimulated by several shorter and longer side-trips from Berlin, including visits to the Bach memorials in Leipzig (March 1964) and the Bayreuth Festival (August 1964). Between these two trips he attended the Convegno Internazionale di Studi sull'Espressionismo (18–23 May 1964), organized by Roman Vlad for the twenty-seventh Maggio Musicale Fiorentino, where Carter gave a lecture, "On the Borders of Expressionism," on 20 May 1964.[23] While preparing for this symposium he asked his colleague Benjamin Boretz (b. 1934), the editor of *Perspectives of New Music* (Carter belonged to its editorial board from its foundation in 1961 until 1972) to commission several articles on this subject and to publish them together with a revised version of his lecture. The following exchange of letters documents Boretz's enthusiastic response and his many follow-up questions, which Carter answered at length immediately after his return from Florence. Although the planned topic did not materialize in *Perspectives* in the form discussed here, the journal did carry a completely reworded and much longer article on "Expressionism and American Music" in 1965. This article, based on Carter's Florence paper, also covered in greater detail a number of ideas expressed in the letter, such as the "expressionist" proclivities among American ultra-modernists for the *Gesamtkunstwerk* (or for spontaneous interdisciplinary expression) and their seemingly opposite tendency towards rationally grounded, geometrical forms of presentation.[24]

22 See letter from Nicolas Nabokov to Virgil Thomson, [April 1963]: "My (part-time) job is a) to advise the Mayor of Berlin on music and the arts 'internationalwise'; b) to prepare the 1964 Berlin Festival, c) *indirectly* to help the concretization of the Ford Berlin program." (Virgil Thomson Papers, Irving S. Gilmore Music Library, Yale University: MSS 29, Box 69, folder 18.)

23 A typescript of this lecture, with handwritten annotations, is preserved in the Elliott Carter Collection, Paul Sacher Foundation. Until now this lecture has been noted only in the two lists of writings prepared by Henning Eisenlohr, where it is inaccurately dated "1961" and "after 1961," respectively. See Henning Eisenlohr, *Komponieren als Entscheidungsprozeß: Studien zur Problematik von Form und Gehalt, dargestellt am Beispiel von Elliott Carters "Trilogy for oboe and harp"* (1992), Kölner Beiträge zur Musikforschung 206 (Kassel: Gustav Bosse,

1999), p. 457; and idem, "Elliott Carter," in *Komponisten der Gegenwart*, ed. Hanns-Werner Heister and Walter-Wolfgang Sparrer (Munich: Text und Kritik, 1992ff.), bibliography, p. xi.

24 Elliott Carter, "Expressionism and American Music," *Perspectives of New Music* 4/1 (Autumn–Winter 1965), pp. 1–13; reprinted several times, most recently in *CEL*, pp. 72–83.

25 To commemorate the journal *Modern Music*, the relevant issue of *Perspectives*

98 Benjamin Boretz to Elliott Carter, 26 May 1964

26 May 1964

Dear Elliott:

I hope I didn't goof in contacting Vlad about doing the Maggio Musicale – I had his name from you as someone you trusted, and thought you would like the idea. In any case, I've gotten all excited about your proposal about a group of articles dealing with pre-1930 American avant-gardism. What you propose sounds like a terrific, really major, article, certainly one of the [most] important things *P[erspectives of] N[ew] M[usic]*'s ever likely to be able to publish in its lifetime. Can I say more, except, do you think you could find time to do it soon? In the "cracks" of the Piano Concerto, perhaps? But I've already taken several more steps – and want to ask your advice on several others – how would you feel about something on Ruggles by Charlie Seeger, something on Ives – as a companion to what you might do later, as you mention, on him – by a younger-generation composer interested in his work – Bob Cogan, for example, comes to mind (did you know that we are reprinting your old Ives essay from *M[odern] M[usic]* in our spring-issue *M[odern] M[usic]* anthology, in connection with the 40th anniversary of the magazine's birth?)[25] – and how about something on the "forgotten" composers of the time – Gruenberg, Ornstein, Ruth Crawford, Antheil – Gunther [Schuller] was going to be doing an interview with Varèse anyway[26] – seems appropriate in this context, no? – I certainly would want to invite Henry Cowell to contribute – what would you suggest as a good topic for him? – and perhaps Boatwright has done some work on Ives that would shed some light – or is he too pedantic and musicological for us? – of course John Kirkpatrick, as you suggest. The whole thing strikes me as a wonderful way for *Perspectives* to give real context and background to a lot of the most important contemporary American music that is entirely independent of Paris–Vienna – our own peculiar tradition that somehow permeates even the most evidently Europe-derived music composed here, but especially that which has a quite different attitude.

If you have a moment – I really hate to encroach on your composing time – any, every, and all ideas will be much appreciated, and especially some notion of when you would like to do your piece so that we could schedule a whole group of articles for the same issue.

Deeply sorry we won't see you in Salzburg – any chance of seeing you elsewhere during August?

Best from everyone to all.
Ben

[Typed letter with autograph signature; Elliott Carter Collection, Paul Sacher Foundation. Reprinted by permission of Benjamin Boretz.]

99 Elliott Carter to Benjamin Boretz, 30 May 1964

Dear Ben,

I did not mean to give the impression that Vlad would review the Maggio Fiorentino ineffectively, on the contrary, since he is its main organizer both from an intellectual (it is a new kind of "thematic" festival) and artistic (in all the arts) point of view; it is only that he is an interested party – which could produce a very good result. Certainly, in spite of the German domination, the whole thing *was* fascinating and will continue to be all through next month.[27] *The Nose* of Shostakovitch is a scream – like an old Keystone Kops Komedy, and surprisingly pointillistic, tone-clusterish, atonal and dissonant here and there – even a total percussion interlude (while the fish of the Neva eat up the nose that the barber who cut it off has tried to dispose of). Very funny timing, some scenes one minute long – the fish scene only a backdrop – and others very extended and filled with contretemps. It's the best opera buffa since Rossini – not a shred of "human" feeling but more than enough slapstick both on the stage and in the orchestra pit. Half the cast sings *above* high C it seems, which makes it hard to cast, as you can imagine.[28] Saw also a rehearsal of *Glückliche Hand* with Schoenberg's own sets, costumes, and complex lighting cues all carried out with religious accuracy – and it was much more effective than the Hannover performance

carried an article by Eric Salzman ("*Modern Music* in Retrospect," *Perspectives of New Music* 2/2 [Spring–Summer 1964], pp. 14–20) as well as an anthology "From *Modern Music*: Some Representative Passages" (ibid., pp. 21–34), in which Carter's review of Ives ("The Case of Mr. Ives," *Modern Music* 16/3 [March–April 1939], pp. 172–176) was reprinted on pp. 27–29.

26 See Gunther Schuller, "Conversation with Varèse," *Perspectives of New Music* 3/2 (Spring–Summer 1965), pp. 32–37;

reprinted in Benjamin Boretz and Edward T. Cone, *Perspectives on American Composers* (New York: W.W. Norton, 1971), pp. 35–36 and 39.

27 The festival had begun on 2 May and lasted until 23 June 1964.

28 Shostakovich's opera *The Nose* (1927–28), conducted by Bruno Bartoletti and staged by Eduardo De Filippo, was given in the Teatro della Pergola on 23, 26 and 30 May 1964. In all likelihood Carter attended the performance on 23 May. His enthusiasm

for this work stands in glaring contrast to his opinion of Shostakovich's symphonies. He reaffirmed it three years later: "[...] it is one of the funniest operas I have ever seen in my life – like an old Mack Sennett comedy – and of a musical brilliance which perhaps makes it difficult for the typical opera house to produce" (Elliott Carter, lecture delivered at Sarah Lawrence College on 24 May 1967, reprinted in revised form as "Soviet Music" in *CEL*, pp. 331–335, esp. 332).

we saw in Venice last year.[29] It is the most total Gesamt-kunstwerk ever done – it's a pity it does not have a less banal plot, but nevertheless the whole is really fascinating.

We all received a book-sized (printed) bibliography of Espressionismo, *Caos e geometria*, by P. Chiarini, with quotes from all the important texts and their dates of printing – and summaries.[30] This is most helpful, for now I shall try and relate the American school more precisely, ideologically, with the middle European, Italian, French, and English currents of the time.

The ideas I have about this project we discussed and which seems to interest you: I do not think that, besides the composers you have mentioned, minor ones like Charles Griffes (whose Gesamt?kunstwerk based on Walt Whitman's *Salut au monde* – with very fancy lighting by Thomas Wilfred and his *clavilux* – made a distinct impression in its day at the Grand Street Theatre[31]) or Emerson Whithorne, or John Becker, or especially Dane Rudhyar (and Nicolas Slonimsky) and Carlos Salzedo should be entirely overlooked. Nor should the influence of the Cuban avant-garde, in the quarter-tone composer Julián Carillo, or the primitivist Amadeo Roldán – nor the early Villa-Lobos or Chávez or Revueltas – or Adolph Weiss. – There is a small subject on ¼-tone music, some of which Ives wrote, some of which a man named Hans Barth (an American) wrote, as well as Carillo (see Cowell's Ives book, p. 101 – also in Boatwright's ed[ition] of Ives['s] *Essays* – p. 112 – Mehlin Piano Co. N[ew] Y[ork]).[32] I myself remember very distinctly going over to Jersey City around 1924 or '[2]5 and fooling around with the 2-keyboard ¼-tone piano for a whole day at the factory of the piano co[mpany]. Perhaps someone could find out something about all of this – and include too something about Yasser's theory of evolving tonality.[33]

Another kind of thing ought to be brought out of Slonimsky's reminiscences – in fact he might be the one to write on the "*geometria*" side of this whole movement and include not only all these theoretical subjects but also those posed in Cowell's 1930 book, *New Musical Resources*,[34] and the point of view of Schillinger, who, after all, lived for many years in the US and had an in-

fluence on many composers – The whole "*geometria*" side (prior to the promulgation of the 12-tone system) is most interesting. The Eaglefield Hull *Modern Harmony*, the Lenormand *Modern Harmony* deserve to be looked at in connection with the dating of all of this[35] – as do the programs of contemporary European music that was heard in the US in the early years.

In any case, Henry Cowell could write a history of his *New Music Edition* or about his book *New Musical Resources*.

Another who may still be alive and contacted was the pianist E. Robert Schmitz, who was a friend of all of these, particularly Ives, for many years. Too, Chávez might be interested in writing about the American avant-garde since he lived in N[ew] Y[ork] during those early years. Also a pianist, Richard Buhlig – Perhaps, if you want to keep up with Antheil (who really was not a part of this) you could write to Ezra Pound and ask him for some reminiscences of Antheil from the old times.

Personally, I would like to see *Perspectives* publish a few of the better paintings of Carl Ruggles in good color reproductions – and would be glad to foot the bill – In fact, an article on his paintings, even very brief, by someone respected in the art world, especially among the new abstract expressionists (since some of R[uggles]'s early pictures resemble this movement a great deal) would be very interesting (perhaps even James Sweeney, if he would like them). Of course, some claim Ruggles was very amateurish as a painter, and this is partly true (but not as bad as Schoenberg, who was really awful), but both a short article on the painting itself and another relating the music and painting would be interesting if you could find someone capable of doing this. Also, as I said in my last, someone should try to get Ruggles into the hands of a proper publisher and get a performance of *Angels* with the old set-up of 6 trumpets – as well as his *Vox Clamans*, his song *Toys*, as well as the more known works on a good recording.

There is still another side to all of this – the influence of Russian avant-garde music and thought here. Schillinger is one case, of course, but many refugees came

---

29 Schoenberg's *Die glückliche Hand* (staged by Walter Boccaccini) stood alongside Gian Francesco Malipiero's *Pantea* (staged by Beppe Menegatti) and Richard Strauss's *Salome* (staged by Erwin Piscator) on a triple bill conducted by Bruno Maderna at the Teatro Comunale on 29 and 31 May and 3 June 1964.

30 Paolo Chiarini, *Caos e geometria: Per un regesto delle poetiche espressioniste* (Florence: La Nuova Italia, 1964). The volume contains summaries of a total of 205 source texts on German Expressionism

(pp. 3–139) and a brief anthology of nine unabridged texts (pp. 143–224).

31 Charles Griffes's *Salut au monde*, a three-act "festival-drama" after Walt Whitman's like-named poem, consists of music, singing, spoken words, dance, and lighting effects. Composed in 1919, it was left incomplete by the mortally ill composer. A performance version prepared by Edmond Rickett was premièred on 22 April 1922 under the baton of Georges Barrère in the Neighborhood Playhouse, an off-Broadway theater in Grand Street.

32 Henry and Sidney Cowell, *Charles Ives and His Music* (New York: Oxford University Press, 1955); Charles Ives, *Essays Before a Sonata, The Majority, and Other Writings*, ed. Howard Boatwright (New York: W.W. Norton, 1962). The reference to the Mehlin Piano Company of New York, which built an instrument with two manuals tuned a quarter-tone apart, is found in Ives (on p. 112, as Carter indicated).

33 See Joseph Yasser, *A Theory of Evolving Tonality* (New York: American Library of Musicology, 1932).

bring[ing] an interest in Skriabin (of whom an American pianist, the late Katherine Ruth Heyman, was an especial advocate – playing the music, I remember, for Ives in her studio on Cooper Union Square one afternoon in about 1924).[36] Then there were influences of all the extremists from Russian painters, like David Burliuk (who is still alive, I think), Arshile Gorky, and a man named Narodny, who organized avant-garde literary and musical evenings somewhere on East 17th Street – and who published a magazine (?).[37] The continual show of Roerich's paintings at the Roerich Museum on Riverside Drive and 102 (?) St., which I think still exists, is one of the left-overs from this time. Perhaps someone there would know more about this aspect. Certainly, we were all very interested in the Scriabinists, Roslavetz, Gnessin, Protopopov, etc. at one time –

You might have Kurt Stone or Howard Boatwright discuss the problems of the Ives manuscripts. Howard is so violently anti-present-day-modern that he might be hard to direct in a non-polemic direction. Stone, who has fussed over the 4th Symphony for years, is filled with ideas and information and could tell a very interesting story that would have a direct bearing on the score which will come very soon –[38]

Hope to see you while you are on this side – Will probably go to Bayreuth in August and Venice in Sept. –[39]

Best to all from Helen and me –
[Elliott]

1, Berlin 33 / Kudowastrasse 12A / Germany
May 30, 1964

[Typed letter, carbon copy; Elliott Carter Collection, Paul Sacher Foundation. Reprinted by permission of Benjamin Boretz.]

34 Cowell, *New Musical Resources* (see above, p. 14, note 42).

35 Arthur Eaglefield Hull, *Modern Harmony: Its Explanation and Application* (London: Augener, 1914); René Lenormand, *Etude sur l'harmonie moderne* (Paris: Le Monde Musical, 1912), trans. into English as *A Study of Modern Harmony* (Boston: Boston Music Co., ca. 1915).

36 Katherine Ruth Heyman (1877–1944) was a California-born pianist and Skryabin devotée who championed his music both in her piano recitals and in her book *The Relation of Ultramodern to Archaic Music* (Boston: Small, Maynard, 1921). Carter came into contact with Skryabin's music through Heyman, who also maintained relations with Ives and Clifton Furness.

37 David Davidovic Burliuk (1882–1967) was a Russian painter and journalist who lived in the United States from 1922; Arshile Gorky (ca. 1904–1948) was an Armenian-American painter who prepared the ground for abstract expressionism; Ivan Narodny (1874–1953) was a Russian-American artist and critic who edited the journal *The Pilgrims Almanach* along with David Burliuk and Robert Chanler in 1925–26.

38 Charles E. Ives, *Symphony No. 4*, preface by John Kirkpatrick (New York: Associated Music Publishers, 1965).

39 In late July 1964 the Carters, at the invitation of Wieland Wagner, visited the Bayreuth Festival. They returned to Berlin by car via Prague and Dresden.

100 Fedele d'Amico, Elliott Carter, and Nicolas Nabokov
at a reception in the Berlin Philharmonie (1964), photo by
Harry Croner

This photograph was taken at a reception following the
concert that Igor Stravinsky and Robert Craft gave in
the Berlin Philharmonie on 22 September 1964 – one of
the highlights of Nicolas Nabokov's first year as head of
the Berlin Festival. The composer himself led the Berlin Philharmonic and the chorus of the Deutsche Oper
in his burlesque *Renard* and his *Capriccio* for piano and
orchestra (with Nikita Magaloff as soloist), while Craft
conducted the Russian ballet *Les Noces* and the European
première of the cantata *Abraham and Isaac* (1962–63), with
the baritone Dietrich Fischer-Dieskau. At the left, alongside Carter and Nabokov, is Fedele d'Amico, the music
critic of the Roman daily newspaper *Espresso*.

[Reprinted by permission of the Stiftung Stadtmuseum Berlin.]

100

"Statement on the Artists-in-Residence Project" (1964)

The Ford Foundation's artists-in-residence program invited leading artists to Berlin with the aim of preventing the city from slipping into provinciality. Nonetheless, the hoped-for close interchange between the visitors and local artists failed to come about: the organizers were too late in providing their guests with the necessary means to present their works and did too little to prepare local artists for encounters with the visiting fellows. Often enough the Berlin artists felt slighted by the Foundation, while many of the visitors viewed their stay in Berlin with disappointment. Among the latter was Carter, who regarded the project as a wasted opportunity. As early as March 1964 he gave vent to his skepticism in a newspaper interview: "[...] das Musikleben einer Stadt wie Berlin ist natürlich fest gegründet. Da kann man als Gast schwer einbrechen. Das ist der Nachteil dieser Art von Einladungen." [The musical life of a city like Berlin is, of course, firmly rooted. It is hard to break into it as an outside visitor. That's the drawback to this type of invitation.][40] Towards the end of his residency, in an interview with Cornelia Jacobsen, he drew a sobering conclusion that the journalist reported as follows: "[...] er selber habe fünfzehn Jahre eine Organisation geleitet, die jedesmal, wenn ein angesehener ausländischer Komponist in die Stadt kam, ein Konzert mit dessen Werken arrangierte. Er sei in dem Glauben nach Berlin gekommen, daß hier ähnliche Usancen herrschten. So wie die Dinge lägen, hätte er es lieber gesehen, man hätte seine Werke in Berlin aufgeführt und ihn selber in New York gelassen." [For fifteen years, Carter points out, he himself headed an organization that arranged a special concert every time an esteemed foreign composer came to the city. He came to Berlin believing that similar customs reigned here. As things stand, he would have preferred to have his music performed in Berlin while he stayed in New York.][41] Indeed, Carter had to wait four months before Berlin was given a hearing of one of his works (the *String Quartet No. 2*),[42] followed towards the end of his stay by a performance of the *Double Concerto*.[43] His feeling of having been insufficiently noticed by Berlin's cultural élite and the broader public also found expression in a final report to his hosts, in which he continued as ever to praise the idea of the project while expressing the hope that the proper lessons would be drawn from his experiences. (Indeed, this is exactly what happened when the artists-in-residence program was superseded in 1965 by the "Berlin Artists Program" of the German Academic Exchange Service [DAAD].) The Paul Sacher Foundation preserves not only the original English version of this final report (reproduced below) but also the German translation submitted by Carter, who was helped at the final editing stage by Kurt Stone.

101 Elliott Carter, "Statement on the Artists-in-Residence Project" (1964)

Berlin, October 18th, 1964

The Berlin program for "artists-in-residence" promised much to those of us who accepted the invitation of the Berlin *Senat* and the Ford Foundation. It proposed an important, new, and exciting experiment in city planning with a cultural goal. Instead of lavishing more money and effort on the resurrection of art of the past and encouraging those skilled undertakers – museum directors, famous musical conductors and performers – to re-embalm our cultural heritage in ever more brilliant falsifications of life, this program proposed to go to the heart of the artistic situation and invite the creators themselves to come and live in this city and from their relations with its society help it live again, as it had in the 1920s, a more intense and lively contemporary artistic life. It was and still is a stimulating idea, this new concept of city development and artistic encouragement, and made many of us eager to participate.

Obviously such an idea requires, even for a measure of success, much more than a sketched-out plan and a stated goal, more than a group of international artists living and working in the city, more than money; it requires, above all, intelligent direction that keeps the ultimate intention clearly in mind, a direction with a vision consistent with the broadness of scope of the original conception. During the first year of the operation of this plan, which was my period of tenure, this vision was either entirely lacking or else lost in a maze of small problems. Consequently, the presence of "artists-in-residence" in Berlin seemed pointless. Those of us who had

---

40 Klaus Geitel, "'Berlin ist ein Ort für Inspiration': Besuch bei sechs Komponisten aus fünf Ländern – Gäste der Ford Foundation," *Die Welt*, 12 March 1964.

41 Cornelia Jacobsen, "Halbzeit bei der Ford-Stiftung: Warum viele der eingeladenen Künstler in Berlin unzufrieden sind," *Die Zeit*, 2 October 1964, p. 17.

42 This performance, supported by the Ford Foundation, was given by the Quatuor Parrenin on 9 May 1964 in the auditorium of the Amerika-Gedenkbibliothek, in a recital mounted jointly by Berlin's Amerika-Haus and the Amerika-Gedenkbibliothek.

43 The piece was performed at the Berlin Musikhochschule during a Berlin Festival concert on 1 October 1964. Bruno Maderna conducted the Ensemble Instrumental de Musique Contemporaine with Mariolina de Robertis (harpsichord) and Frederic Rzewski (piano) on the solo parts.

Piano Concerto (1961–65)

accepted to participate at considerable personal sacrifice, exchanging cultural milieux where an active interest in our work is taken for one in which we were scarcely known, receiving less financial return and less comfortable living quarters than we are accustomed to at home, did so because of our enthusiasm for the idea and were deeply disappointed. Instead of cultural participation, we found ourselves living in agreeable surroundings, paid, and left alone, entirely unconnected with the activities of Berlin's cultural life in spite of our wishes. Aware of this problem, the managers of the project made occasional misguided efforts to secure feeble and often embarrassing newspaper publicity for us – of the kind useful for bureaucratic reports but hardly useful for true cultural exchange.

In spite of all of this, I would like to thank the Berlin *Senat* and the Ford Foundation for making it possible for me to live and work in this pleasant city and to renew my acquaintance with some German colleagues whom I have always respected. It is to be hoped that, although this project appears to have been almost totally unsuccessful in achieving its goals so far, perhaps this year's experience will produce better results later. For experiments, like dreams, have a way of revealing unexpectedly important information even when they seem least promising.

[Typescript, carbon copy with autograph corrections; Elliott Carter Collection, Paul Sacher Foundation.]

For Carter, the lack of interaction between the Ford fellows and Berlin artists had at least one benefit: as with his stay in Rome the previous year, he could immerse himself in his *Piano Concerto*. Admittedly, the work reached completion only in autumn 1965, long after his return to the United States, where he took over a chair in composition at Juilliard towards the end of 1964. But something of the tense and gloomy atmosphere that reigned in Berlin in the early 1960s apparently left a mark on it. The thought even arises that the relationship between piano and orchestra, more one of antagonism than cooperation, may have served as an expressive vehicle for his personal experiences. It would be a gross simplification, though, to think of the *Piano Concerto* as an "autobiography" in notes. For one thing, Carter's contrast between a sensitive, imaginative soloist and a massive, forcefully aggressive orchestra draws on the old idea of the concerto as a contest or allegorical embodiment of individual and collective. In this case, however, Carter lent this idea a "timely" political dimension by conceiving the soloist as an anti-hero and the orchestra as an ominous mass: "The piano is born, then the orchestra teaches it what to say. The piano learns. Then it learns the orchestra is wrong. They fight and the piano wins – not triumphantly, but with a few, weak, sad notes – sort of Charlie Chaplin humorous."[44] For another thing, the opposition between solo and tutti is by no means absolute: for large stretches at a time Carter augments the piano soloist with a seven-piece concertino (flute, English horn, bass clarinet, violin, viola, cello, and double bass) that supports, sustains, and elaborates his music. Equally multifarious is the texture of this extraordinarily complex two-movement concerto, which places utmost demands not only on the pianist but on the members of the orchestra, especially its soloists. To be sure, Carter did not have to worry much about problems of execution, for as early as 1961 he had arranged with the Ford Foundation to have the première given by an orchestra of his choice. Instead of the Denver Symphony Orchestra, as originally planned, the *Piano Concerto* was premièred on 6–7 January 1967 by the Boston Symphony Orchestra under the baton of its music director, Erich Leinsdorf. Similarly, the two follow-up performances assured by the Ford Foundation were given, not

---

44 Carter, in Kurt Stone, "Treat Worth the Travail," *Time* 89/2 (13 January 1967), p. 44.

by the Indianapolis Symphony and the Pittsburgh Symphony, but by the symphony orchestras of Chicago and Minneapolis (see below, p. 193, note 54). In all of these performances the solo part was taken by Jacob Lateiner, who had commissioned the work.

102 a *Piano Concerto*, verbal notes

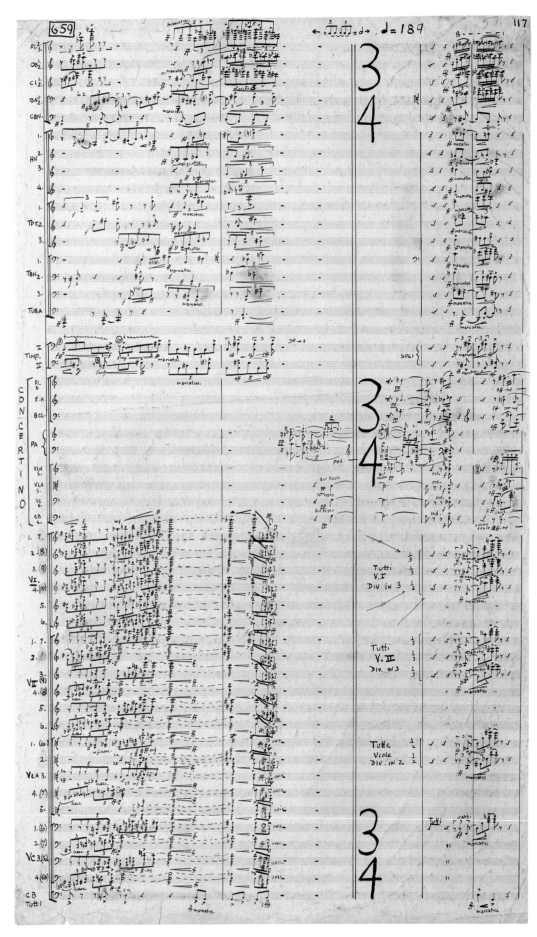

102 b *Piano Concerto*, full score

102 *Piano Concerto* (1961–65)
a   verbal notes in notebook
b   autograph full score in ink, p. 117 (mm. 659–663)

The very first jottings for the *Piano Concerto*, in a notebook dating from winter 1961–62, reveal the importance that Carter attached to the contrast between piano and orchestra (see p. 189): the first three sets of antonyms defining the musical characters of solo and tutti read "soft, restrained, delicate" vs. "violent, loud", "brilliant" vs. "dull," and "expressive" vs. "mechanical." (To avoid the danger of a too narrowly defined dichotomy, however, two later pairs of terms – "slow"/"fast" and "comic"/ "serious" – are assigned to both piano and orchestra.) This notion of an antithetical relationship between orchestra and soloist governs the entire piece, especially its second movement, where it takes the form of an implacable antagonism, with the soloist increasingly assuming the role of "victim" while the all-powerful orchestral apparatus acts as "perpetrator." Thus, in a long passage of escalation, the piano is virtually smothered by coagulating string chords and increasingly fast staccato pulses. In the bars that follow (mm. 608 ff.) it can for the moment only manage to bring forth the reiterated pitch F. (It is tempting to see this pitch as a symbol for "freedom," one of the keywords in the Iron-Curtain era.) The conflict culminates shortly before the transition to the coda, shown on p. 190 in Carter's calligraphic fair copy of the score. Here we see mm. 659–663, in which the orchestra attempts to "muzzle" the soloist completely with the last of several violent tutti attacks. As shown by the (minimum) response of the piano in m. 660 and thereafter, the attempt is not entirely successful: even after this massive outburst of violence the soloist, soon surrounded only by the concertino, raises his voice. He is even allowed to have the "last word" at the end of the coda. But his concluding utterances lack any sense of affirmation. It is therefore not surprising that at least one commentator, Joseph Kerman, should have interpreted the ending of the concerto in an entirely pessimistic light: "The victim dies and then refuses to die, dies and is not suffered to die, survives to take new punishment. Coming after this, the second ending (it does not reclaim the pitch F) sounds to me [...] like a second dying."[45]

---

45 Joseph Kerman, *Concerto Conversations* (Cambridge, MA, and London: Harvard University Press, 1999), pp. 120 and 122.

Dedication to Igor Stravinsky (1968)

If the première of the *Piano Concerto* (in Boston on 6–7 January 1967) and the follow-up performances in Chicago and Minneapolis gave Carter considerable publicity, no less interest was kindled by the recording of the première released in early 1968.[46] When the first reviews of the recording began to appear even Igor Stravinsky became curious: on 2 April 1968 he penned a letter asking Carter to send him both the score and the recording of the new work. Carter, who, in addition to his duties at Juilliard, had accepted the position of professor-at-large at Cornell University in autumn 1967, felt honored and responded on 7 June 1968 with a detailed reply. Not only did he express his gratitude for the permission, conveyed by Robert Craft a few months earlier, to dedicate his *Piano Concerto* to Stravinsky,[47] he also thanked Stravinsky for the interest he had shown in his music previously. Indeed, Stravinsky had praised Carter in public on several occasions, in particular expressing his admiration for the *Double Concerto* in an interview with Craft, concluding that it was "a masterpiece, and by an American composer."[48] It was probably not least his memory of this interview that prompted Carter, in his letter of thanks, to mention his preparations for a second and, in his opinion, more successful recording of the *Double Concerto*, for Stravinsky (or Craft) had complained of certain problems of balance in the début recording of 1961 and especially of the over-amplification of the naturally delicate sound of the harpsichord.[49] Carter's letter also alludes to the dramatic political events of spring 1968 – the murder of Martin Luther King in Memphis on 4 April, and the assassination of Robert Kennedy in Los Angeles on 5 June.

103 Igor Stravinsky to Elliott Carter, 2 April 1968

1218 North Wetherly Drive / Hollywood 69, California

Dear Elliott,

The reviews of the Piano Concerto recording[50] remind me that I haven't heard from you in a half-year and haven't even heard the piece yet. Could you call Richard Mohr[51] and ask him to send me a copy and also could you send me a copy of the score, perhaps a proof copy which I would be glad to return. I am very eager to hear it.

My own travels have been restricted to short trips to San Francisco and Arizona, but we are expecting to come east and go to Europe in a month or so.[52]

Wishing you and Helen all best,
I. Stravinsky
IS:ms

[Typed letter with autograph signature; Elliott Carter Collection, Paul Sacher Foundation. Reprinted by permission of John Stravinsky.]

---

46 Elliott Carter, *Piano Concerto*, and Michael Colgrass, *As Quiet As;* Boston Symphony Orchestra, conducted by Erich Leinsdorf (RCA Victor LM 3001).

47 The dedication ultimately read "To Igor Stravinsky on his 85th birthday, with great admiration and friendship."

48 Stravinsky, "Some Composers" (see above, p. 177, note 8), pp. 6 (*Musical America*), 49 (*Dialogues and a Diary*, 1963), and 101 (*Dialogues and a Diary*, 1968), respectively.

49 Ibid.

50 Howard Klein, "It's Great But Will It Sell?" *The New York Times*, 17 March 1968; Moses Hager, "Mr. Carter and the Electric Guitar," *The New York Times*, 31 March

1968. The latter article, a response to Klein's review, bemoans the "sterile academism blighting contemporary music" and goes so far as to suggest that "rock 'n roll, as an example, offers to an Elliott Carter a rhythmic framework within which he could order a viable musical statement." It quickly prompted two outraged letters to the editor from Carter's circle of friends: Paul Jacobs, "Bagpipes Don't Help," *The New York Times*, 14 April 1968; and Frederik Prausnitz, "Like Mozart," *The New York Times*, 5 May 1968.

51 Richard Mohr (1919–2002) had worked as a record producer for RCA Victor since the 1940s, in which capacity he was

responsible not only for several Stravinsky recordings but for the 1966 recording of Carter's *Woodwind Quintet* with the Boston Chamber Players, alongside works by Mozart, Brahms, Beethoven, Fine, Copland, and Piston on three LPs (RCA Victor LM 6167).

52 Despite his poor health, Stravinsky traveled to Oakland from 10 to 15 February 1968 to hear three concerts of the local symphony orchestra, conducted by Robert Craft. Roughly a month later he also boarded an airplane to attend a production of *The Rake's Progress*, again under Craft's direction, which was mounted by the American National Opera Company in

104 Elliott Carter to Igor Stravinsky, 7 June 1968

Elliott Carter / Mead Street / Waccabuc, New York
June 7, 1968

Cher maître,

I was very much touched by your letter asking about my Piano Concerto – and flattered that you were interested. In fact your previous interest in it & my music encouraged me to dedicate the score to you – I mean, in print – for your 85th birthday. I wrote to find out from Bob whether you would take it amiss. Word was you would be touched – so I dared.[53]

It's a shame you did not receive the blueprint copy I sent for your last birthday. I hope by now you have it with the record. Unfortunately the printed score – just finished being autographed this week – is still uncorrected so the dedication is not visible. It is also being made visible in the piano-reduction, printed in Feb[ruary] 1967 with many less important errors than the omission of the dedication.

There is much good BSO playing on the record, but it [is], shall we say, not altogether accurate, especially in the bagarre at the end. Performances at Minneapolis & Chicago were clearer but the soloists were never as good as in Boston.[54] I hope you will like the piece – it's a little forbidding and "expressionist" (after all it was written in Berlin) and not so whimsical as my Double Concerto.

We spent yesterday picking out "takes" at *Columbia Records* for the *Double C[oncerto]* from an English Chamber Orchestra recording – which [will] be livelier, clearer and, on the whole, more accurate than the old one.[55]

We have hoped that, as you said in your letter, you would soon come East, and have looked forward to seeing you. Natasha Nabokov says that your trip to San Francisco was pleasant – but I can imagine that with the heat – and now the frightful Kennedy disaster – in L.A. you would want to go to a quieter, cooler place.[56] However, these signs of your recovering health make us happy and hope that the amelioration will continue.

I have been much away from New York. I was professor-(not dog-)-at-large for my annual month at Cornell[57] – very much at large as the students, etc. demonstrated over the M[artin] L[uther] King assassination during a good part of my stay.

Helen, and I to a less[er] extent, have been busy through these trying months making an effort to help my former Berlin student Isang Yun – the kidnapped South Korean composer on whose behalf you signed a petition for clemency in October published in *Die Zeit*.[58] Fortunately his second trial has changed his life sentence to fifteen years' imprisonment and his wife was released to return to Berlin and their adolescent children. Just now she has returned to Seoul to take care of her husband, who has been transferred from prison to a Seoul hospital (surrounded by guards) – being ill with a cardiac condition and TB – all this at the expense of his publishers and friends since beds, heat, etc., and hospitalization for grave illness are not included in the amenities of a South Korean prison.

Helen joins in sending our love and warmest wishes (in this hot weather) for your complete and rapid recovery and a very happy 86th birthday. We hope your work goes well & will continue to do so –

Love too to Vera and Bob.
Elliott

[Autograph letter; Igor Stravinsky Collection, Paul Sacher Foundation. Reprinted by permission of John Stravinsky.]

Gray Gammage Auditorium (near Phoenix, AZ) on 21 March 1968. It was thus not until autumn 1968 that he was able to embark on the planned trip to the East Coast and Europe, among other things with the purpose of settling several important matters with regard to his estate.

53 Carter's inquiry to Robert Craft is dated 24 September 1967. Craft's announcement that Stravinsky would gladly accept the dedication followed on 3 October 1967.

54 These performances, all with Jacob Lateiner (piano), took place on 24 and 25 May 1968, with the Chicago Symphony Orchestra conducted by Jean Martinon, and on 5 July 1968, with Stanislaw

Skrowaczewski conducting the Minneapolis Symphony Orchestra.

55 This new recording, with Paul Jacobs (harpsichord), Charles Rosen (piano), and the English Chamber Orchestra conducted by Frederik Prausnitz, was released as Columbia MS 7191, coupled with a recording of the *Variations for Orchestra* by the New Philharmonia Orchestra under Frederik Prausnitz. For the début recording see above, p. 171, note 129.

56 In May 1968 Stravinsky had travelled to Berkeley to take part in the concerts that opened the Zellerbach Auditorium. On his return he dislocated a vertebra and had to spend a month lying in bed.

57 Carter's term at Cornell University (as Andrew D. White Professor-at-Large) lasted from 3 to 15 April 1968. It was his only such visit, for he stepped down from this position in the same year.

58 For the Isang Yun affair, see below, pp. 194–195. The petition mentioned by Carter was signed by 160 leading composers, musicians, and scholars in addition to Stravinsky and published in the German weekly *Die Zeit* on 20 October 1967 to accompany an article by H. Hannover, "Die Entführung des Isang Yun: Ein Plädoyer für die Freilassung des koreanischen Komponisten" (p. 7).

Speaking Up for Isang Yun (1967–69)

In June 1967, seventeen Koreans living in West Germany were abducted to Seoul by South Korean secret service agents owing to alleged treasonous contacts with communist North Korea. The incident shocked the world of music, for among the abductees were the distinguished composer Isang Yun, a West German resident since 1956, and his wife. Given that the suspects were threatened with long prison sentences, and in some cases even execution, many intellectuals stood up in their defence. Among them was Carter, who had met and taught Yun during his stay in Berlin in 1964. On 9 October 1967, even before Yun was sentenced to lifelong imprisonment by a trial court on 13 December 1967, Carter sent a letter of request (which went unanswered) to the American Secretary of State Dean Rusk, followed by further letters to George McGhee (the American ambassador in Germany) and McGeorge Bundy (the president of the Ford Foundation). Later it transpired that there was not enough evidence to convict Yun of spying, but only of visiting the North Korean capital of Pyong-yang in 1963, and the sentence was reduced by a court of appeal to fifteen years. Joined by Hall Overton and Harvey Sollberger, Carter then signed a letter to the editor of the *New York Times* (9 April 1968), became involved in a political action committee, and, not least of all, made several donations in support of his colleague. It was only as a result of continued international protest that the verdict, reduced to ten years in January 1969 by another court of appeal, was finally annulled. Yun, who was in poor health, suffering from chronic tuberculosis, spent a large part of this year and a half under guard in a hospital. After his release in February 1969 he returned to the German Federal Republic, where he obtained citizenship in 1971. On 29 May 1969, having recovered from the privations of his imprisonment, he sent the Carters a letter of thanks. Carter later remained in contact with Yun, but when he heard a concert of the Pyong-yang National Symphony Orchestra playing works by Yun at the 1986 Warsaw Autumn Festival and encountered the composer traveling with the North Korean orchestra, the apparent alliance left him with ambivalent feelings.[59]

105 Elliott Carter to David Dean Rusk, 9 October 1967

From Elliott Carter / Villa Serbelloni / Bellagio, Lago di Como / Italy

The Honorable Dean Rusk, / Secretary of State, / Department of State, / Washington, D.C.
October 9, 1967

Dear Sir:
I am writing to find out if there is anything that can be done to help the unfortunate situation of the South Korean composer of music, Mr. Isang Yun, who was kidnapped with his wife from West Berlin this mid-July by the South Korean government and imprisoned in Seoul. Mr. Yun was my student in Berlin in 1964, where I participated in a Ford Foundation project that brought a number of the world's leading artists there. As a winner of the Pulitzer Prize, a member of the Institute of Arts and Letters, of the Academy of Arts and Sciences, a former professor at Yale, a present one at Cornell and at the Juilliard School in New York, my musical compositions had attracted enough attention for me to be asked to take part in this project. (Just to acquaint you with who I am.)

By 1964, Mr. Yun had himself gained considerable reputation in Europe. His music was played at many festivals and was published by Bote und Bock, an important Berlin firm. Up to that time he had been earning a precarious living teaching in various German cities, but then he came to Berlin to get a scholarship and study with me. I asked the Ford Foundation for a stipend for him, and he settled in Berlin with his wife, continually writing music, getting new commissions from the German radio, which helped to meet his modest needs. Saving on these two small sources of income, he was finally able to bring his two children to Berlin from Korea, where they had been living with their grandparents.

During the summer of 1966, the International Institute of Education sponsored a tour of the United States for him, and he made many friends in the United States.[60]

Continuing to live in Berlin from 1964 until this summer, his reputation as a composer grew. But during the summer of 1967, suddenly he and his wife disappeared, leaving his two childern alone in Berlin. His publishers

---

59 Interview with Felix Meyer and Anne Shreffler, 11 June 2007. The Warsaw concert took place on 20 September 1986. The orchestra, called the Korean People's Democratic Republic Philharmonic Orchestra and conducted by Kim Byung Hwa, played Yun's *Clarinet Concerto* (with Eduard Brunner as soloist) and *Symphony No. 1* as well as Kazimierz Serocki's *Symphonic Frescoes*.

60 This two-month study and lecture tour took Yun to the Tanglewood and Aspen festivals as well as San Francisco, Los Angeles, Chicago, and New York.

and friends have done what they could for the children since their parents' disappearance.

When I read this story, first in the French newspapers around July 15th, then more briefly in the *New York Times,* and later at great length in *Der Spiegel,* I was shocked that a so-called friendly government could violate international law in this fashion, and so pointlessly.[61] Mr. Yun was a very busy musician in Germany, very prolific, and apparently entirely uninterested in politics, much respected by his colleagues, all of whom are very indignant over the injustice and inhumanity of this kidnapping.

Since he was sponsored by several American organizations to carry on his studies and his composing, and was not only one of my more talented students but a composer I respect, I feel called upon to ask if something can be done to right this glaring wrong.

Yours sincerely,
Elliott Carter

After October 20, 1967: / 31 West 12th Street, /
New York, 10011, New York

[Typewritten letter with autograph address ("From Elliott Carter [...]"), carbon copy; Elliott Carter Collection, Paul Sacher Foundation. Reprinted by permission of Walter-Wolfgang Sparrer (Internationale Isang Yun Gesellschaft).]

106 Isang Yun to Elliott and Helen Carter, 29 May 1969
(English translation in Appendix 1, p. 349)

Isang Yun / Berlin 20, Steigerwaldstr. 13
d. 29. 5. 1969

Herrn u. Frau / Elliott Carter / 31 West 12th Street /
New York, N.Y. 10011 / USA

Meine lieben Freunde!
In den sehr traurigen langen Monaten in Seoul habe ich, durch heimliche Wege, oft gehört, wie sehr Sie [an meinem] Schicksal Anteil genommen und jede Gelegenheit entschieden wahrgenommen [haben], um mich zu retten, befreien zu lassen. In Seoul, im Krankenbett, habe ich erfahren, daß Sie mit einigen anderen bekannten Musikern über mich und über meine Musik im Radio gesprochen haben, um Gutes zu plädieren, für mich Vorteil zu gewinnen.[62] Man erzählte mir, daß Sie mehrmals Artikel geschrieben und in die Öffentlichkeit gebracht haben, für den gleichen Zweck. Sie haben mit wirkungsvollem Mittel die Musikwelt und das öffentliche Leben in [den] USA auf[ge]rufen, mich zu retten. Sie haben resonanzvollen Einfluß auf höherer Ebene der Politik Amerikas [ausgeübt], wodurch sicher, so möchte ich meinen, der koreanischen Regierung nicht wenig Achtung [auf]gezwungen wurde. Sie haben hohe Summen mir spendiert, um meine Krankenhauskosten zu begleichen. Ich erfuhr noch mehr, was Sie für mich getan haben, durch Dr. Kunz,[63] auch durch Herrn Nabokov u.a. –

Liebe Freunde! Womit und wie kann ich Ihnen alles erwidern, was ich [Ihnen schulde]? Die Asiaten schweigen lieber, wenn sie sehr ergriffen oder sehr dankbar sind. So möchte ich auch lieber schweigen, [als] mein Herzensgefühl der Dankbarkeit an Sie mit Worten auszudrücken. [An] meinem Leben und meiner Freiheit, die ich jetzt wiedergewonnen habe, haben Sie auch viel Verdienst!

In der Hoffnung, bald uns wiederzusehen, möchte ich dieses Schreiben [be]schließen

mit sehr herzlichen Wünschen und Grüßen, Ihr
Isang Yun

[Typed letter with autograph signature; Elliott Carter Collection, Paul Sacher Foundation. Reprinted by permission of Walter-Wolfgang Sparrer (Internationale Isang Yun Gesellschaft).]

---

61 The first report of the abductions (and similar cases in France) appeared in *Le Monde* on 5 July 1967. Two days later the same newspaper mentioned Isang Yun in this context: "En Corée du Sud: La détention d'étudiants en provenance d'Allemagne occidentale est confirmée. une cinquième disparition signalée à Paris," *Le Monde,* 7 July 1967. See also "South Korea Holds 70 in Red Spy Ring,"

The New York Times, 9 July 1967, and "'Ich möchte nach Deutschland zurück': *Spiegel*-Redakteur Manfred Hentschel beim südkoreanischen Geheimdienst," *Der Spiegel* (28 August 1967), pp. 24–26.

62 Carter, together with Chou Wen-chung and Eric Salzman, had taken part in an hour-long radio program entitled "The Strange Case of Isang Yun," broadcast by WRVR on 4 April 1968.

63 From 1963 to 1994 Harald Kunz was head of the Berlin music publishers Bote & Bock, who published Yun's music. Being personally close to the composer, he took care of Yun's two children during his imprisonment.

107 b *Concerto for Orchestra*, full score

Concerto for Orchestra (1967–69)

As earlier with the *Piano Concerto*, work proceeded slowly on the *Concerto for Orchestra*. Though the work was commissioned by the New York Philharmonic Society in August 1966 to celebrate its 150th anniversary in the 1967–68 season, the première did not take place until two years after the orchestra's jubilee. Once again Carter wrote large parts of the score in Europe, this time during a one-month residency at the Villa Serbelloni in Bellagio (September–October 1967), made possible by the Rockefeller Foundation, and during another term as composer-in-residence at the American Academy in Rome (mid-October 1968 to mid-April 1969). He finally completed the score on 25 November 1969. This time his source of inspiration was a poem of 1946 entitled *Vents* [Winds] by the French poet and diplomat Saint-John Perse (Alexis Léger, 1887–1975).[64] The depiction of wind as a mighty force of nature, at once destructive and rejuvenating, had both political and artistic significance for Carter – political in that Perse's "winds of change" could be taken as a symbol of the social unrest and turmoil of the age (he alluded to this himself in a text written in 1974 for an "Informal Evening" of the New York Philharmonic[65]), and artistic in that Perse, using literary means, worked towards a complex treatment of time similar to what Carter envisaged in music. (On the other hand, as we know from several later comments, Carter never warmed to the bombastic, emotionally overblown inflection of *Vents*.[66]) Especially significant was the poetic device of forward and backward reference, which Carter transferred to music by working with contrasting layers of material. Each of these layers has its "main theater of action" in one of the four elided movements (Allegro, Presto volando, Maestoso, Allegro agitato) while remaining present in reduced form from the beginning to the end of the score: "[...] the poem, like the music, seems to me to center around four main ideas, which fade in and out [...], although all four (and many others in the poem) are constantly referred to."[67] This tight dovetailing of linear progression and cyclic cross-reference is one of the most striking features of the *Concerto for Orchestra*, whose formal polyvalence can be seen as a radical redefinition of the nineteenth century's "four movements in one" principle.

107 *Concerto for Orchestra* (1967–69)
a   analytical chart (photostat with autograph annotations), p. 2
b   autograph full score in pencil, p. 10 (mm. 37–40)

Several thousand pages of sketches exist for the *Concerto for Orchestra*, proving how meticulously Carter thought out every compositional aspect of this highly complex score.[68] They include not only rhythmic sketches, chord charts, and short-score elaborations of passages of various length, but several schematic diagrams of the work's overall structure. Especially well-known, and frequently reproduced in the Carter literature, is an analytical chart made probably shortly after completing the composition.[69] The document shown here (see p. 198) is a preliminary version of that chart. Not its least interesting aspect is the title he considered at the end: "possible title[:] 'Concerto dei Quattro Venti.'" This chart shows that each movement is based on a particular set of chords (the list includes chords of two, three, four, and five notes, but the seven-note chords which, along with five-note chords, are central to the entire work are implicit as well).[70] It also reveals that Carter set the movements apart by assigning each movement a different tempo design (e.g. a series of increasingly frequent *ritardandos* for movement 1, or a continuous *ritardando* for movement 2) and a characteristic sub-orchestra. The work's underlying conception lies in the fading-in and fading-out of these contrasting layers. As a result, the four sub-orchestras, and the materials associated with them, are tightly interwoven over large expanses of the music. In the passage from the full score shown on p. 196, excerpted from the first movement (pp. 14–15 in the printed edition of 1972 [AMP 7011]), the main musical argument is entrusted to the cellos, piano, harp, and metallic percussion instruments (i.e. to the ensemble specially assigned to this movement). At the same time, however, elements from the other movements constantly crop up in the orchestral writing: note, for example, the sustained sonorities for muted trumpets in mm. 37–38, which point to movement 4, or the quintuplet figures in the first violins and piccolos in mm. 38–39, which belong to movement 2. Here these cross-relations

64   Saint-John Perse, *Vents* (Paris: Gallimard NRF, 1946); bilingual French-English edition as *Winds*, trans. Hugh Chisholm, Bollingen Series 34 (New York: Pantheon Books, 1953).

65   On this "Informal Evening," see below, p. 221. The text for this occasion was published as "On Saint-John Perse and the Concerto for Orchestra," in *CEL*, pp. 250–256, esp. p. 252.

66   See below, p. 221, as well as Carter's remarks in *ML*, p. 42: "The general plan and the general conception of the poem

were a help, but I began to dislike the details and the false primitiveness."

67   Ibid., p. 253. A detailed study of the relationship between the music and the text was published by Jonathan W. Bernard as "Poem as Non-Verbal Text: Elliott Carter's Concerto for Orchestra and Saint-John Perse's Winds," in *Analytical Strategies and Musical Interpretation: Essays on Nineteenth- and Twentieth-Century Music*, ed. Craig Ayrey and Mark Everist (Cambridge: Cambridge University Press, 1996), pp. 169–204.

68   Insight into the compositional process can be found in Jonathan W. Bernard, "Elliott

Carter: Concerto for Orchestra (1965–1969)," in *Settling New Scores: Music Manuscripts from the Paul Sacher Foundation*, ed. Felix Meyer (Mainz : Schott, 1998), pp. 121–126.

69   See especially Schiff 1983/1998, pp. 244–45 and 294–95, respectively; and Bernard, "Poem as Non-Verbal Text" (see note 67), pp. 176–177.

70   The seven-note sonorities result from the superposition of smaller chords (e.g. three- and four-note chords) or from the complementation of the five-note sonorities to form the chromatic total.

are kept at a subdued dynamic level, making them sound like a distant anticipation before gaining increasingly in significance as the movement progresses. The excerpt also illustrates Carter's treatment of the orchestra as a group of soloists. In fact, several instrumental parts in the *Concerto for Orchestra* were specifically tailored for musicians he knew personally in the New Philharmonic. This applies in particular to the sometimes highly virtuosic piano part (designed for the pianist Paul Jacobs), which also has to negotiate several especially tricky metrical modulations. In these passages, contrary to the usual practice, the conductor may take his bearings from the pianist.

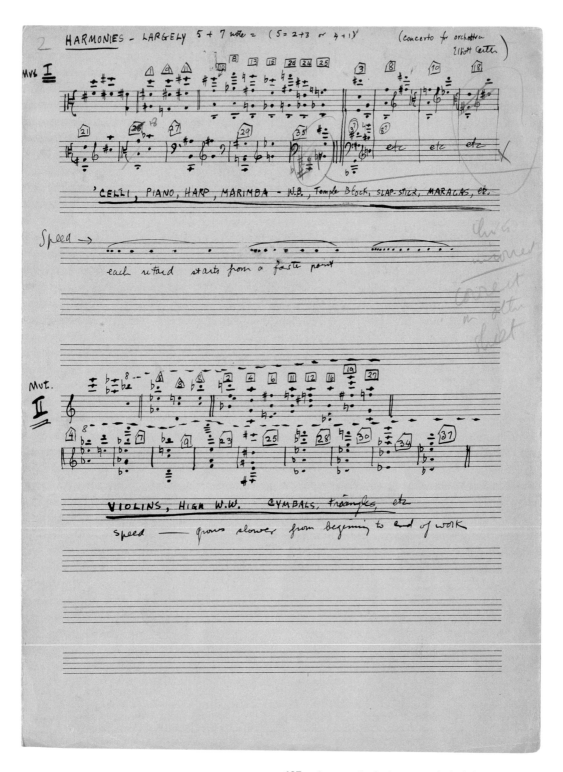

107 a *Concerto for Orchestra*, analytical chart

108 Aaron Copland, Elliott Carter, and Leonard Bernstein (from
    left to right) listening to the recording of Carter's *Con-
    certo for Orchestra* in New York's Philharmonic Hall (1970)

The *Concerto for Orchestra* was premièred by the New
York Philharmonic in Philharmonic Hall on 5–7 and
9 February 1970. The conductor was Leonard Bernstein,
who handled the difficult task to Carter's evident satisfaction: "He [Bernstein] conducted my *Concerto for Orchestra* very well – without that marvelous attention to detail that Boulez gave it later, but he did succeed perfectly
in capturing its broad line, that long breath running
through the piece."[71] Immediately after the première, on
11 February 1970, the concerto was recorded by Columbia
Records in a three-hour recording session, again in Phil-

harmonic Hall. This recording, released in early 1971,[72]
was not originally planned: the idea arose only during
the preparations for the première, and its realization was
made possible on short notice by a grant from the Ford
Foundation. The photograph reproduced here was taken
during the recording session, with Aaron Copland joining as a surprise guest.[73] Partly visibly on the right, yet
easily recognizable, is the then pianist of the New York
Philharmonic, Paul Jacobs.

---

71 CC, p. 72.
72 Elliott Carter, *Concerto for Orchestra*,
    and William Schuman, *In Praise
    of Shahn*; New York Philharmonic,
    conducted by Leonard Bernstein
    (Columbia Masterworks M 30112).

73 See David Hamilton, "Behind the Scenes:
    Carter's Virtuoso Concerto," *High Fidelity*
    (May 1970), p. 22.

Interest in Nancarrow (1970)

After visiting Conlon Nancarrow in Mexico City in the 1940s and 1950s Carter continued to maintain a regular correspondence with him in the 1960s and 1970s. Though he could not always understand Nancarrow's maverick attitude and his refusal to propagate his music in public, he followed his friend's creative work with interest, feeling an affinity with his polytemporal explorations, and was grateful for the tape recordings that Nancarrow sent him from time to time. (Conversely, he kept Nancarrow up to date on his own creative work with reports, scores, and LPs.) This letter, written on 20 February 1970, shortly after the première and recording of the *Concerto for Orchestra*, reveals that Carter was so taken by Nancarrow's music that he wanted to discuss it with his students at Juilliard. Nancarrow, in a typically terse reply of 17 March 1970, unhesitatingly agreed to Carter's request for tape recordings of his earlier pieces. The two men's correspondence also reveals that the interest was mutual: Nancarrow's early letters contain appreciative comments on Carter's *Sonata for Violoncello and Piano*[74] and *String Quartet No. 1* (see above, p. 139), and a letter of 1968 expresses his admiration for the *Double Concerto*.[75]

109 **Elliott Carter to Conlon Nancarrow, 20 February 1970**

Elliott Carter / 31 West 12th Street / New York, N.Y. 10011

Dear Conlon,

I am sorry not to have been in touch with you while we were in Italy, but the year was hectic in many different ways and, indeed, for the most part I simply stayed indoors and composed my Concerto for Orchestra, which has just recently been played by the N[ew] Y[ork] [Philharmonic] and recorded by Columbia (when it will come out I don't know).

Of course, we often talk of you with Minna & Mell Daniel and Aaron [Copland] and play over the record of your Studies with a great deal of pleasure[76] – as well as the other pieces you sent me on tape.

Now I find that I have a lot of students who are interested in polyrhythms, etc., and have decided to give a lecture on your music – mainly by playing examples of it. I remember long ago I used to have tapes of some other pieces, in particular a Boogie-Woogie piece, other than the Studies you sent me. (I still have an old paper tape of this that is very scratchy.) Would it be possible for me to get some of the other pieces beside[s] the St[u]dies – I would be very glad to pay for having the tapes copied.

We are at the present time overwhelmed by some of my former students whom we like well enough but who are living in Rome concocting live electronic music in shows something like a musical "living theatre"[77] – it is pretty hard to have them around, and I look forward to next week when I can settle down and start on another string quartet commissioned by the Juilliard Quartet for next year.[78] We are staying here for the year.

Send us some news of yourself, and if possible the tape – Of course, if you want to come up here on a visit and give the lecture yourself (it won't pay very much) we would be more than glad to put you up – and all of your old friends w[ould] be overjoyed to see you.

Affectionate regards, from Helen & myself,
Elliott

February 20, 1970

[Typed letter with autograph signature; Conlon Nancarrow Collection, Paul Sacher Foundation. Reprinted by permission of Yoko Sugiura Nancarrow.]

---

74 See letter from Conlon Nancarrow to Elliott Carter, 13 May [1952]; Elliott Carter Collection, Paul Sacher Foundation.

75 See letter from Conlon Nancarrow to Elliott Carter, 6 November [1968]; Elliott Carter Collection, Paul Sacher Foundation.

76 A short while earlier Minna Lederman had told Nancarrow about these conversations, which besides Carter and Copland also involved John Cage: "I heard it [i.e. the 1968 LP *Conlon Nancarrow: Studies for Player Piano*, Columbia Masterworks, MS 7222] discussed here by Aaron and Elliott and John C." (Letter from Minna Lederman Daniel to Conlon Nancarrow, 19 January 1970; Conlon Nancarrow Collection, Paul Sacher Foundation.) Mell Daniel, a painter, was Minna Lederman's husband.

77 The former students Carter refers to were probably Alvin Curran and Frederic Rzewski, who were both living in Rome at that time as co-founders of the live-electronics improvisation group Musica Elettronica Viva. They had also worked with the Living Theatre, a radical experimental group from New York that had relocated to Italy in 1964 after several controversial productions and the political persecution of their directors, Judith Malina and Julian Beck.

Canon for 3 (1971)

110 Conlon Nancarrow to Elliott Carter, 17 March [1970]

Conlon Nancarrow / Apartado postal 20–550 /
Mexico 20, D.F.
March 17

Dear Elliott:

I just sent you some tapes. I dumped those old pieces you wanted into #3, which I had discarded, in order to give them an identity.[79] I also found a tape piece from the same period.[80] The paper tape was falling apart, but I had it re-recorded and the volume level raised. It is incomplete, and I don't know whether this was all I could find or I simply got tired of it and stopped. Probably the latter. In any case it has only curiosity interest.

I once sent some tapes by air and they arrived ruined, but I suppose tapes could be exposed to a magnetic field anywhere. Anyhow please let me know if they are playable. The recording is not too good to begin with.

Best regards,
Conlon

[Typed letter with autograph signature; Elliott Carter Collection, Paul Sacher Foundation. Reprinted by permission of Yoko Sugiura Nancarrow.]

Following Igor Stravinsky's death on 6 April 1971, the English music periodical *Tempo* decided to devote a memorial issue to the great composer containing a number of short "in memoriam" pieces as well as several articles. The issue eventually appeared as the fourth and final number of the 1971 volume (*Tempo* no. 97), but because several of the invited composers (including Carter) fell behind schedule, it contained only the first ten musical items (by Luciano Berio, Lennox Berkeley, Harrison Birtwistle, Boris Blacher, Peter Maxwell Davies, Edison Denisov, Nicolas Maw, Alfred Schnittke, Michael Tippett, and Hugh Wood). Seven further compositions (by Pierre Boulez, Elliott Carter, Aaron Copland, Alexander Goehr, Elisabeth Lutyens, Darius Milhaud, and Roger Sessions) did not appear until early the following year, in *Tempo* no. 98 (1972). At the request of the journal's editor, David Drew, the submitted homages were to form a series of "canons and epitaphs" using some or all of the instruments that Stravinsky himself employed in two memorial compositions of 1959: flute, clarinet, and harp (in his *Epitaphium*) and string quartet (in *Double Canon [In Memory of Raoul Dufy]*). Carter, however, seems to have forgotten this stipulation, for the publication in *Tempo* (a facsimile of his fair manuscript) calls for an ideal scoring of "3 muted trumpets." A good month after the première of *Canon for 3* on 23 January 1972,[81] Carter touched on this point in a letter to Drew: "As I may have written, it was performed at a concert last month for: 1) muted trumpet, 2) clarinet, 3) oboe, and came out well. Unfortunately, I did not make my intentions clear as to performance of the piece – I simply listed the optimum performers (3 muted trumpets, preferably with different mutes), but the instrumental group you had envisioned could also be used: 1) flute, 2) viola, 3) clarinet."[82] The separate printed edition, published in early 1972 (AMP 7203), gives more neutral scoring instructions "for three equal instrumental voices." In the preface, however, Carter continued to recommend the use of three trumpets with different mutes or, alternatively, muted trumpet, clarinet, and oboe.

78 For Carter's *String Quartet No. 3*, see below, pp. 204–206.

79 The five movements of the (definitive) *Study No. 3 for Player Piano* – including two boogie-woogie movements – originally formed two unnumbered suites in combination with another number, later withdrawn; see Felix Meyer, "Auf Spurensuche im Nachlaß Conlon Nancarrows: Zur Geschichte der Study No. 3d," *Mitteilungen der Paul Sacher*

Stiftung 13 (April 2000), pp. 19–25. The original *Rhythm Study No. 3*, likewise withdrawn, was unexpectedly revived in 1988 when Nancarrow sent a slightly revised version of it, now called *For György Ligeti*, to his friend György Ligeti on his sixty-fifth birthday.

80 This item from the incomplete *Piece for Tape*, dating from ca. 1950 (like the two Boogie-Woogie movements), was released three years after Nancarrow's death on

the CD *Conlon Nancarrow: Lost Works, Last Works* (Other Minds, OM 1002-2).

81 This première took place during a concert in Alice Tully Hall with Joel Timm (oboe), Alan Blustine (clarinet), and James Stubb (trumpet).

82 Letter from Elliott Carter to David Drew, 3 March 1972; carbon copy in the Elliott Carter Collection, Paul Sacher Foundation.

111 a *Canon for 3*, full score

111 *Canon for 3: Igor Stravinsky in Memoriam,*
  for three equal instrumental voices (1971)
a autograph full score in pencil, 1 p.
b notated as a single voice, 1 p.

As unassuming as the twenty-six-bar *Canon for 3* may seem at first glance, its contrapuntal structure is highly sophisticated. The piece, whose pitch sequence Carter later wrote out in a single voice (a whole tone higher than the original and with minor slips –[83]), is based on a thirty-two-note melody opening with a twelve-note rhythmic palindrome. Once this is stated by the first voice, the second and third voices enter, each at a distance of five 6/8 bars, the former in inversion transposed upward by a tritone, the latter playing the prime form at the original pitch level. The further course of the melody is no longer dodecaphonic, and Carter designed it diastematically and rhythmically so as to produce an ingenious and effective combinatorial conclusion. Starting in m. 17, the compositional fabric "freezes" in a polymetric stratification in which each voice, by its pulse (of six, nine, or ten eighth notes), defines its own tempo (MM 28, 18.67, and 16.8). At the same time the three voices, with their pitches of entry, combine to create a two-fold recapitulation of the opening of the theme, once in inversion transposed by a tritone (mm. 17–21, as in the entry of the second voice in m. 6), and again in its prime form (mm. 22–26, as at the opening and the entry of the third voice in m. 11). This culminating *Klangfarbenmelodie,* which Carter highlighted in his fair copy of the score by drawing lines connecting notes of the three voices, generates a sort of echo chamber through the sustaining of its constituent pitches.

111 **b** *Canon for 3*, notated as a single voice

83 The dotted quarter notes in mm. 9 and 22
  are incorrectly given as dotted eighths.

112 *String Quartet No. 3*

String Quartet No. 3 (1970–71)

Carter composed only thirteen major works between 1950 and 1980.[84] There were no fallow periods during these thirty years; rather, the composer needed time to develop innovative temporal, structural, and harmonic designs, sometimes sketching over a thousand pages for each piece. These large-scale compositions retrace and reformulate the most significant genres of Western music: the string quartet (three), symphony and concerto (five major orchestral works), violin and piano sonatas (*Duo for Violin and Piano, Night Fantasies*), and song cycle (*A Mirror on Which to Dwell*). Even the *Brass Quintet* and the *Sonata for Flute, Oboe, Cello, and Harpsichord* refer to traditional ensemble groupings, however much they may be transformed. The works from this period form a kind of core repertory in Carter's output, and are among his most ambitious, with the *Concerto for Orchestra*, the *String Quartet No. 3*, and *A Symphony of Three Orchestras* reaching an apex of complexity that would not be equalled in his more streamlined later music. This period also witnessed the composer's rise to prominence. By the 1960s Carter was able to compose exclusively for first-class ensembles and performers, such as the Juilliard String Quartet, which commissioned the *String Quartet No. 3* and premièred it in Alice Tully Hall on 23 January 1973. Like the *String Quartet No. 2* thirteen years earlier, it was awarded the Pulitzer Prize. This is Carter's most difficult string quartet to play; the Composers Quartet prepared a taped click track to help them coordinate the different rhythmic layers, a practice which the Arditti Quartet also engaged in until recently. The *String Quartet No. 3* takes the idea of counterpoint (so crucial in all of Carter's music) further than ever before: there is counterpoint not only between the individual lines, but also between the two duos into which the ensemble is divided (duo I: violin I and cello; duo II: violin II and viola); there is also structural counterpoint between movements played simultaneously. The form is the quartet's most innovative feature. The four "movements" assigned to duo I, each with its own character and primary intervals, are combined in various ways with the six of duo II. Because of the limited number of movement types, the fact that Carter combines them in thirty-five ways does not lead to confusion, but rather to a kaleidoscopic play of familiar colors and textures.[85] Sometimes the juxtaposed movements are contrasting and therefore easily distinguishable, but at other times they have a similar character and blend together. The alternation between "sounding together" and "sounding apart" (to use Charles Seeger's terms) recalls the concerto idea, which was so fruitful for Carter during these years. Max Noubel suggests that the movements in this work seem to evolve even when they are not heard, resulting in a limitlessly self-referential structure conjured up in the mind of the listener and creating a veritable "*mise en abyme du temps*".[86] The sonic result of this study in contrasts is the kind of rhetorical grandeur and power more often found in orchestral than in chamber music.

112 *String Quartet No. 3* (1970–71), autograph full score in pencil, p. 12 (mm. 89–94)

The score layout of the work is unusual: the second violin and viola occupy the first two staves (duo II), while the first violin and cello are notated in the bottom two (duo I); this notation is used throughout the piece. The passage shown contains the continuation of the movement "Giusto, meccanico" for duo II and the beginning of "Giocoso" for duo I. This is one of the most striking passages in the piece. All four instruments play pizzicato, and because of the rapid tempos and the double stops, it sounds rather like an explosion in a popcorn factory. In spite of the common tone color, the two duos are clearly distinguishable from one another, because each duo employs characteristic intervals. In the slower-moving duo II, both instruments play (predominantly) dyads made up of the interval of a tritone; duo I emphasizes minor thirds, though there are also major thirds and sixths. (Here also, as throughout the piece, duo I uses seconds and sevenths.) There are four distinct rhythmic layers, which overlap within each duo but not between them. duo II's rhythms are embedded within three half notes (divided into quarter-note triplets) per measure: in the top staff the second violin's chords occur regularly every fourteenth eighth-note triplet (at a speed of 23.14 beats per minute). Its companion, the viola, articulates its chords five eighth notes apart (at a speed almost twice as fast, at MM 43.2; after the introduction of quintuplets in m. 91,

84 Not including the unfinished *Sonata for Two Pianos*, "Adagio" and "Canto" from *Eight Pieces for Four Timpani, Canon for 3*, or *A Fantasy about Purcell's "Fantasia upon One Note."*

85 See the chart of the piece's structure in Noubel 2000, p. 167.

86 Ibid., p. 168. Carter expressed a similar idea in his unpublished lecture "Sound and Silence in Time" (see above,

pp. 133–134): "This establishing a musical pattern and then abandoning it inevitably leaves a kind of echo behind in the mind of the listener, a basis for comparison, an expectation for the future, and as he listens attentively this psychic silence begins to be alive with echoes which are shared with the composer and the performer but which never reach the state of physical sound."

An Exchange about Charles Ives (1973)

the viola speeds up slightly, to MM 45). Duo I moves much faster, in a measure divided into eight dotted eighth notes. The first violin subdivides the basic MM 96 pulse into four (MM 384), while the cello subdivides the same unit into three (MM 288). As has been the case in Carter's music for some time, the notated measures do not have any metrical meaning (such as strong or weak beats); they are used merely as conveniences for the performer. A kind of graphic notation showing the events unfolding regularly at different speeds (like a Nancarrow piano roll) would look much simpler than this score and would correspond more closely to the listener's perception, but would of course be less practical to play from.

Ives's music seemed to anticipate a great many technical advances of European modernism. Carter brought up the problem of its precise dating as early as 1939 in his review of John Kirkpatrick's New York première of the *Concord Sonata*: "The fuss that critics make about Ives's innovations is, I think, greatly exaggerated, for he has rewritten his works so many times, adding dissonances and polyrhythms, that it is probably impossible to tell just at what date the works assumed the surprising form we now know."[87] At the time, Kirkpatrick must certainly have been puzzled by Carter's doubts. Yet it was not until more than thirty years later, shortly before the centennial of Ives's birth, by which time the composer had become a permanent fixture in America's musical life, that the following exchange between Kirkpatrick and Carter took place. Exactly what prompted Kirkpatrick in late May or early June of 1973 to write his open letter to Carter ("Ives – How Modern, How Soon") is unknown, but it is safe to assume that he was responding not only to a discussion with Carter in the fairly distant past (as suggested by the first sentence of the letter), but also to Carter's statements in a 1969 interview with Vivian Perlis that she was preparing for publication in her book *Charles Ives Remembered*. Here Carter again cast doubt on the standard image of Ives as an isolated, visionary innovator and drew the conclusion: "[...] one could wonder whether he was as early a precursor of 'modern' music as is sometimes made out."[88] Kirkpatrick, the curator of Ives's posthumous papers and the executive editor of the Charles Ives Society, briskly countered this skeptical verdict in his open letter, attempting to demonstrate, from his intimate knowledge of the sources, that even in his early years Ives was very free in his treatment of dissonance and thus composed in a "modern" spirit. Carter immediately responded in turn with a reply in which he gratefully noted Kirkpatrick's discoveries and placed them in a larger historical context: Ives's treatment of dissonance, he argued, ultimately derives from a centuries-old, originally unnotated tradition of "subversive" utilitarian music with a strongly experimental bent, and this tradition had an impact not only on Ives but on the roughly contemporary expansion of harmony in the music of such composers as Strauss, Skryabin, and Schoenberg. Carter's interpretation neutralized the question of "priority" and placed Ives, a com-

---

87 Carter, "The Case of Mr. Ives" (see above, p. 70, note 86), in *CEL*, p. 89.

88 Carter, interview with Vivian Perlis, 20 June 1969; first published in Vivian Perlis, *Charles Ives Remembered: An Oral History* (New Haven: Yale University Press, 1974), pp. 131–145, esp. 238; frequently reprinted in excerpt, most recently in Vivian Perlis and Libby Van Cleve, *Composers' Voices from Ives to Ellington: An Oral History of American Music* (New Haven and London: Yale University Press, 2005), pp. 33–34.

poser fondly lauded as an iconic, fundamentally American maverick, into a European musical context. He by no means questioned Ives's "modernity," but found it less in his treatment of dissonance than in his innovations in structure, form, and acoustical space – innovations that he ascribed to Ives's need for enhanced "acoustical realism," another feature typical of his age.

Carter was in agreement with the publication of Kirkpatrick's letter and likewise wrote his reply with an eye to its possible publication (the Paul Sacher Foundation also preserves a draft with a much different wording).[89] But, although the journal *Parnassus* showed interest, the publication never materialized; the two documents lay fallow and were only recently made accessible to a larger readership in an essay by Drew Massey.[90] In the narrow world of Ives scholarship, however, Kirkpatrick's and Carter's exchange of views added fuel to a debate on the chronology of Ives's works and the status of their subsequent revisions – a debate that was impending in any case in relation to the editorial projects of the Charles Ives Society. The debate finally culminated in 1987 with the publication of Maynard Solomon's essay "Charles Ives: Some Questions of Veracity," which claimed to descry "a systematic pattern of falsification" in the manner in which Ives reordered and redated his manuscripts. Solomon's essay triggered an occasionally vitriolic public debate in which Carter was time and again invoked as a witness for the prosecution or as an *agent provocateur*, depending on the debater's point of view.[91] Carter himself refused to take part in these polemics: not only did he feel misunderstood by those who cast doubt on his memories of Ives's revisions, he was equally nonplussed to find his statements quoted in the context of an issue which, as he had already stressed in his 1969 interview with Vivian Perlis and reiterated in his letter to Kirkpatrick, he regarded as secondary. Years later, in another interview with Vivian Perlis, he gave vent to his discontent: "I felt that I would never talk about Ives again because I didn't like to be treated as if I was either not telling the truth or misunderstanding what Mr. Ives said. [...] what made me quite cross was that all these people who didn't know anything about him or were not interested, even during the time when he was alive, as I was, were suddenly proving that I was wrong about almost everything."[92]

113 John Kirkpatrick: "Ives – How Modern How Soon? An Open Letter to Elliott Carter" (1973)

Dear Elliott,

Some years ago you told me that, when you knew Ives in 1924–26, you occasionally saw him take up old sketches and make them more dissonant than they had been – and that this memory made you skeptical of the degree to which he was really a precursor.

In telling me this, you awoke my own memories of a strange conversation I had with him around 1939. He had given me photostats of the last few pages of the ink manuscript of *Hawthorne*, and I was delighted to find that, at the moment where both editions have a♯' against a♮" (revised edition, p. 49, 2nd brace, 3rd beat), the old manuscript of 1911 made the melodic sequences unfold naturally into a♯' against a♯". But when I faced him with this, he first tried to deny that both were sharp, and finally burst out with "I couldn't possibly have written that – it makes an octave!" Evidently, between 1911 and the engraving of *Concord* in 1920, his inner necessity for more dissonance had found the octave unacceptable, and he had changed the a♯" to a♮".

How much else did he change? How sure can anyone be how early his music was how dissonant? How literally can we believe his own datings of his music?

Having had the privilege of cataloguing his music manuscripts, I feel I owe you some account of evidences that bear on these questions, which are of concern not only to those who knew and loved him, but to the many more who have come to love his music.

It would be logical to start with manuscripts known to have been out of his hands by a certain time, or which he seems not to have altered. First we must note sadly that all the pieces that were "lost" in his youth remain lost. But when he went to New Haven early in 1893, he apparently left his father's music copybook behind in Danbury, also after his father died in 1894. Among his many sketches in this book, the most amazing is the *Song for Harvest Season*, probably the most important single item for our inquiry. A later copy of it bears a memo: "From old study Mother found in Danbury house – copybook, about in middle (board-cover 8-line blank book) – has exercises, pieces, fugues by Father – and I used it when studying counterpoint etc. with him.

89 Carter, in his cover letter of 16 June 1973 (John Kirkpatrick Papers, Irving S. Gilmore Music Library, Yale University), pointed out that if the exchange was to be published he wanted to rework a few passages and include such compositions as Scarlatti's "Cat's Fugue" and Alkan's "tone-cluster pieces" in his observations.

90 Drew Massey, "The Problem of Ives's Revisions, 1973–1987," *Journal of the American Musicological Society* 60/3 (Fall 2007), pp. 599–645, esp. 631–638.

91 Maynard Solomon, "Charles Ives: Some Questions of Veracity," *Journal of the American Musicological Society* 40/3 (Fall 1987), pp. 443–470, esp. 465–466. The resultant debate is discussed in

Massey, "The Problem of Ives's Revisions" (see note 90), pp. 599–601.

92 Elliott Carter, interview with Vivian Perlis, 8 November 1999, published in Perlis/Van Cleve, *Composers' Voices* (see note 88), p. 34.

This piece was played about when the new Baptist Ch[urch] in Danbury was opened, either in summer of 1893 or 1894. Father played the cornet, Mrs. Smyth tried to sing, and I played [the] lower parts [on the organ]."[93]

This sounds as if Ives had not seen the book for a long time before his mother found it (she died in 1929), and as if he had not sketched in it since leaving Danbury – also as if he remembered it more as a book than as separate leaves (of its 96 leaves, 36 were torn or cut out, of which 10 are missing). Though this memo implies some well-behaved counterpoint, the only exercises on the extant pages are take-offs, polytonal harmonizations, and a couple of tiny fugues in four keys (in C-G-D-A), each voice keeping doggedly to its own key, come what may.

The *Song for Harvest Season* is also a fugue in four keys (in C-F-B♭-E♭), but freely expressive, with the four scales often altered to make a rhapsodic, dissonant polyphony. It was published in the *34 Songs* (*New Music* 1933, now Merion), and the later copy mentioned above is from that time, betraying weak eyes and shaky hand. But in changing a few notes, Ives did so only in the new copy, not on the old copybook pages. Comparison of the two texts shows that the older is no less dissonant than the newer.

Ives's dating also rings true, since the church was dedicated on Sunday 16 April 1893, and Ives, being the regular organist, was one of those who played at the dedication service. He had been at Hopkins Grammar School, New Haven, since the beginning of the spring term, but came back to the Danbury Baptist Church every Sunday through 30 April. Mrs. Smyth was the choir director, a person of some pretension (her husband was born Smith), and she would have relished being asked to try her organist's experiment, especially since she knew at first hand the expert beauty of his conventional anthems. Perhaps parts were copied for this run-through, which have not survived, or maybe they looked over Charlie's shoulder at the sketch. If this piece were a sample of the future, she must have felt relieved when he became organist at a New Haven church.

Any way you look at it, this is remarkable music, especially for 1893, age 18. Though short and concise, the melodic phrases are as long and sure as in *Lincoln* (1912). The most dissonant moments are the most polytonally pure, and are identical in the two versions.

Also in the copybook are two examples of the kind of interlude Ives used to play in church between hymn stanzas, one of them (for *Bethany* – "Nearer, my God, to Thee...") reprinted in the Cowell biography, page 35.[94] The basic chord form is two dominant 7ths, their roots separated by a minor 9th, the lower root outlining the melodic phrase with the chords (*pp* on the salicional stop) strictly parallel. These also show no sign of any later change. Ives continued using such interludes at Center Church, New Haven, where our good friend Harmony Twichell and her roommate Sally Whitney heard them and rather liked them.

In 1895 Ives orchestrated his own *Postlude in F* (an organ piece of 1892), and in 1897 he used the blank outside page of this score for the beginning of a *Thanksgiving Postlude* for organ, which he played in Center Church, presumably on Thursday, 25 November 1897. This opening page is all that survives; it became the opening of the orchestral *Thanksgiving* in 1904. Here too, Ives seems not to have touched up the organ piece when he made the orchestra score-sketch, and his account, in the *Memos*, of how the polytonal dissonances were to express the rather harsh, uncompromising Puritan integrity is fully borne out in the 1897 version. Unfortunately New Haven's newspaper coverage of church music was almost non-existent – which I am sure you regret as much as I do – any reaction would be interesting.

It was probably shortly after graduation in 1898 that he transformed a vivid memory into the orchestral take-off, *Yale-Princeton Football Game*. The pencil sketch is complete (mostly atonal except for the tunes quoted), but the full score was lost (Ives lent it to his classmate Huntington Mason who died in 1914). His failure to recover it probably discouraged him from further elaboration of the sketch, which seems unchanged. Among various memos, one toward the end says: "When Trumpet (= running halfback, Charley Desaulles) reaches this meas[ure], every other instrument must make a hell of a noise and stop." – that is, Charles A.H. des Saulles (1876–1962), Yale '99, who wrote me in 1961: "I knew Ives [...] never saw him after graduation. Yale 6 – Princeton 0, played Nov. [20], 1897 (Princeton was 5 to 1 favorite). I was on Walter Camp's All-American team that year."

---

93 See Charles E. Ives, *Memos*, ed. John Kirkpatrick (New York: W.W. Norton, 1972), p. 176.

94 Cowell, *Charles Ives* (see above, p. 14, note 42).

In 1904, shortly after the explosion of the steamboat General Slocum, Ives sketched a short tone poem about this tragedy. Later, in the *Memos* of 1932, he dictated: "I don't believe I had a serious intention of finishing it. This awful catastrophe got on everybody's nerves. I can give no other reason for attempting to put it to music, and I'm glad to look back and see the sketch is hardly more than a page."[95] In view of his regretting the whole idea, one can safely assume that he never retouched this sketch after 1904. The background engine noises are atonal, the three little deck orchestras play simultaneously in E♭, A and B♭, the explosion is an atonal build-up of different-intervalled scales rising at different speeds, and the final phrases of *Bethany* are heard against an atonal background.

The sketch of *Halloween* is dated: "*Halloween* (on the 1st of April!) – Pine Mt." With his full business life, Ives could have been composing at the shack on Pine Mountain only on a Sunday, and April 1 was Sunday in 1900, 1906, and 1917, not in between. In 1900 the shack was not yet built, 1917 was too late for the Poverty Flat address on the manuscript, so [this] amazing polytonal study must have been written in 1906. Its hair-raising effect depends in no degree on added dissonance but on the relations of the purely diatonic scales.

In view of these datable manuscripts, one can hardly question his seniority in the use of various types of dissonance. The "spiking" of certain moments is another story, ranging all the way from touches of genius (like the later a♯' in *Mists* at "days") to mere avoidance (like the above-mentioned a♮" in *Hawthorne*). But these moments hardly made his music any more dissonant as a whole.

All these pieces antedate your friendship with him even longer than yours antedates mine. But no one can ever blame you (seeing what you saw) for wondering how recently he had become how dissonant.

With many thanks for the wonderful experiences you have given me both as composer and as friend,

Ever yours,
John.

[Typescript with autograph corrections; Elliott Carter Collection, Paul Sacher Foundation. Reprinted by permission of Daisy Kirkpatrick. Published in Drew Massey, "The Problem of Ives's Revisions, 1973–1987," *Journal of the American Musicological Society* 60/3 (Fall 2007), pp. 599–646, esp. 631–635.]

114 Elliott Carter to John Kirkpatrick, 16 June 1973

(a possible "open" answer to John Kirkpatrick from Elliott Carter)

Waccabuc, New York / 10597
June 16, 1973

Dear John,
Thank you very much for your interesting yet flattering letter. Now I have a clearer idea about Ives' historical position as a forerunner, a matter I have always been uncertain about. As always I am deeply impressed and moved by your careful, loving concern for the matter of music itself and the precise facts relating to it. Your *Ives Mss.* volume,[96] your edition of the *Memos*[97] down to this letter to me impress as the outward manifestation of an attitude, infinitely valuable and as worthy as it is rare.

The subject of your letter has often been thought about, since I heard and saw Ives play for me the 3 "transcriptions" from *Emerson* at Redding during the mid-'20s and especially when I recall the vivid memory of a visit to the top-floor of 164 E. 74 Street, with him sitting at a small upright in a little attic room lit with a bridge lamp, score paper strewn around the room, playing bits on the piano as he "prepared" the score of (if my memory serves me correctly) *Three Places in New England* for publication (it must have been around '30), trying out the effect of "diminishing" or "augmenting" what were previously octaves in the old score and strengthening the older chords with a shot of dissonance. It was primarily these two sessions, and the revisions in the copy of the *Concord Sonata* he gave me in '25 (and which I once lent you) that made me wonder just how dissonant earlier versions of the pieces were, as if that really mattered.

But it did then, of course, because in the '20s and '30s many were still acutely interested in the degrees of dissonance and the, so to speak, "originality" or "courage" it took to include extremes of this in scores. Today, naturally, this is of less concern, because it begins to seem that dissonance must have existed ever since it was separated from consonance in Western music, if not elsewhere. Yet as the negative image of consonance, it must have long played a part in musical "take-offs," in "lunatic," or "wild," diabolic, devilish music, even though this music

---

95 Ibid., p. 105.
96 John Kirkpatrick, "A Temporary Mimeographed Catalogue of the Music Manuscripts and Related Materials of Charles Edward Ives, 1874–1954" (New Haven: Yale School of Music, 1960).
97 Ives, *Memos* (see note 93).

was seldom granted the honor of being written down, because its improvisers seemed like clowns or freaks. There are a few written-out examples, of course, such as Hans Newsidler's lute piece *Der Juden Tanz*, of around 1550,[98] and the mixed-up ending of Mozart's *Musical Joke* – both using polytonality as a means of producing a dissonant but still "logical" effect[99] – then there is, of course, all that unfairness to Beckmesser done in perfect 4ths.

Along the same lines, there is the old French custom, sometimes banned, of banging out noisy serenades with pots and pans and other special instruments at weddings that gave the neighbors Greek headaches, leading them to name these "charivari," creolized as "shivaree." (*Les Noces* as a charivari is intriguing to think of.) Certainly when serious musicians began to pay attention to dissonances they remained very close to the types of expression that had always been associated with it – Strauss with the lunatic and insane, Scriabin with the weird and strange, as also Schoenberg, Stravinsky with the primitive and diabolic, and Ives with the parodistic or "take-off," although there was an element of "take-off" in almost all early XXth-century composers.

(Pursuing what may be my own fantasy:) Just how much this dissonant but largely unwritten music had a codification and a method (as clowning has a system), and how much of it arose from the familiar mistakes made by musicians (misreading key-signatures, "quacking," etc.), is, of course, impossible to tell. Certainly in the cases mentioned above, polytonality was a specific method of producing "harsh" but somehow reasonable dissonance. What is interesting about Ives, today, are the many different procedures he thought up, so it seems, to produce his polyrhythmic and dissonant textures. It seems as though these were his own invention and not derived from the "dissonant tradition" – although the fact that about the same time Bartók, Schoenberg, and others were arriving at similar results without contact with Ives or he with them lends some credence to the "tradition" having certain methods. A clear example of one of his techniques of handling dissonance can be found in his building of chords on the analogy of triadic harmony which builds up 7th, 9th, [and] 11th chords by adding 3rds, but substituting other intervals. In the *Fourth of July,* the background

harmonies of measures 4–50 demonstrate this very clearly: in m. 8 the string chord is built on 4ths; m. 9, on major 2nds; m. 10, on perfect 5ths; m. 11, on minor 7ths; m. 16, on major and minor 3rds; m. 38, the first chord is built on minor 7ths, the second on major 7ths. As for measure 20, the strings play in 16th-note motion a converging series of 4 5-note chords that is continued as the parts close in in 4-note chords. This passage starts with a vertical chord of 4 major 7ths, this is followed by one of 4 major 6ths, then by one of 4 perfect 5ths, then 4 perfect 4ths, then, continuing in 4 parts, there is an augmented triad with an added note, followed by a chord of two major 2nds and finally converging on one of 3 minor 2nds.

Whether this is the first example of such a strict working-out of intervallic chords by Ives or anyone else, I leave to those who occupy themselves with such matters. But it is obvious [that] intervallic insistence comes by way of Chopin's Etudes in 3rds and 6ths, through similar ones by Debussy stressing also 4ths, and Scriabin stressing 5ths, major 7ths and major 9ths, although these composers did not take the final step but integrated the intervals into their own harmonic style. It was Bartók, apparently, in the *Bagatelles* of 1908, [who] began building chords as Ives did (Rebikov had done this for 4ths earlier),[100] and this was taken up by the Viennese (Schoenberg discusses it in the *Harmonielehre*) and *Le Sacre du printemps*, and then more crudely in the '20s by Hindemith and Milhaud, whose *Saudades do Brasil* dances a tango on each of the interval-chords.

Another matter for speculation, which you, too, must have thought about, is what led Ives to be so "iconoclastic" musically when his outlook on life and society was so conservative, harking back, as he did, to the transcendentalists of an earlier generation. To me one reason was his methodological, almost pragmatic, progressiveness characteristic of the business man and multifaceted person. Another reason is that as a man living in his period, he was concerned, as many writers like Frank Norris, William Dean Howells, Henry Adams, Stephen Crane, and Edward Arlington Robinson were, in artistic "realism." This seems to have been his predominant aesthetic outlook, and many of his later works, especially, were written with the idea of presenting a human situation as it

---

98 In the draft of this letter Carter added the source "Harvard Anthology" in brackets. See Archibald T. Davison and Willi Apel, *Historical Anthology of Music: Oriental, Medieval, and Renaissance Music* (Cambridge, MA: Harvard University Press, 1946), p. 108.

99 As it turned out, the "shrill dissonances" that Willi Apel observed in *Der Juden Tanz*

(*Historical Anthology*, [see note 99], p. 227) were merely the result of a misinterpretation of the composer's tuning directions; see Michael Morrow, "Ayre on the F♯ String," *The Lute Society Journal*, no. 1 (1959), pp. 9–12.

100 Though practically forgotten today, the Russian composer Vladimir Ivanovich Rebikov (1866–1920) wrote a number of

whole-tone piano pieces around the turn of the century and experimented with harmonies based on seconds, fourths, sevenths, and so forth, as well as bitonal key schemes. He was also a pioneer of rhythmic *Sprechgesang* and the combination of pantomine and music. See Larry Sitsky, *Music of the Repressed Russian Avant-garde, 1909–1929* (Westport, CT, and London: Greenwood, 1994), pp. 10–26.

actually sounded – a roaring crowd, a jolly dancing party, determined pilgrims forging ahead through a swamp, singing hymns. With this attitude came a desire for what Lionel Trilling calls "authenticity"[101] that led him to re-produce exactly how improvising musicians played at a given scene, in their impromptu, comic "take-offs," or to present how marching bands playing different music actually sounded. A very up-to-date view at the time, as is exhibited by the conversation of Mahler about simi-lar situations and for similar reasons I quoted in *Flawed Words and Stubborn Sounds*.[102] Yet "realistic" music pre-sents troubling problems when you think of the double bass's grinding squeak on its high B♭ when Jochanaan's head is cut off, or the prolonged loud tape of many people screaming that is the hair-raising (the first time) conclu-sion of Zimmermann's *Die Soldaten*.

These random thoughts, provoked by your letter, would be even less coherent if I had not read through your wonderful efforts at bringing order out of the confusing Ives collection of manuscripts, memos, and thoughts. Thank you for sending these, and your letter. The *Memos* are illuminating and fascinating and I would like some day to have the time to really think and write about them. If no one has ever thanked you for your devotion to and effort for American composers and their music, they should have. It is, in one way, what one expects from our culture, an intelligent, penetrating, serious concern, yet in music we almost never get it. Just to have your careful, in-tense concern monitoring the scene is profoundly heart-ening and makes one forget the superficial lip-service that so many – not interested enough to find out what really goes on and what needs to be done – reveal and therefore act destructively by trying [to] mold and influence a pro-fession by ignorance and wishful thinking.

Thanks,
Elliott

Do print your letter –
Love to you both from Helen & me
hope to see you this summer –

PS. If you are interested in the enclosed BBC talk[103] please xerox it & return it as I don't have a xerox machine near-by –

Do you want the xerox copy of your letter back or may I keep it?

[Typescript with autograph corrections, signature, and postscript. Original in the John Kirkpatrick Papers, Irving S. Gilmore Music Library, Yale University; photocopy in the Elliott Carter Collection, Paul Sacher Foundation. Reprinted by permission of Daisy Kirkpatrick. Published in Drew Massey, "The Problem of Ives's Revisions, 1973–1987," *Journal of the American Musicological Society* 60/3 (Fall 2007), pp. 599–646, esp. 635–638.]

---

101 See Lionel Trilling, *Sincerity and Authenticity* (Cambridge, MA: Harvard University Press, 1972).

102 In a footnote to *FW*, p. 102, Carter referred to Mahler's remarks on "true polyphony" handed down in Natalie Bauer-Lechner's *Erinnerungen an Gustav Mahler* (Leipzig: E. P. Tal, 1923), p. 147. Among other things he wrote: "Frau Bauer-Lechner describes a *Festtag* when she and Mahler climbed a mountain together: when they were at a certain height, he stopped, hearing the festive sounds, bands, and a men's chorus coming from different directions, and exclaimed, 'Das ist die eigentliche Polyphonie!' ('That is the true polyphony!'), enjoying both the disconnectedness of the different musical materials and also the fact that they were metrically uncoordinated. It reminded him of treasured childhood experiences, just as similar situations did Ives."

103 Here Carter is referring to "Music Criticism," a lecture recorded by the BBC on 11 August 1972 for the series "Com-posers and Criticism." Reprinted in *WEC*, pp. 310–318, and most recently in *CEL*, pp. 335–342.

**115 Isang Yun and Elliott Carter (Aspen, August 1973),
photo by Ferenc Berko**

Carter visited the Aspen Festival for the first time in 1958 and again several times in the 1960s and 70s. Here, in summer 1973, he again encountered his colleague and former pupil Isang Yun, who joined Carter, Gilbert Amy, and Nicolas Nabokov as one of four composers-in-residence at the Conference on Contemporary Music (23 July – 6 August 1973). Among the works performed were Carter's *Sonata for Violoncello and Piano* and *The Harmony of Morning* (both on 23 July 1973), the *String Quartet No. 2* (30 July), and the *Double Concerto* (6 August). Further, his *Piano Concerto* was performed outside the contemporary programs on 12 August 1973, with Samuel Lipman as soloist and the Aspen Festival Orchestra conducted by Gerard Schwarz, who deputized for the ailing Eleazar de Carvalho. The program also included Yun's *Glissées* for unaccompanied cello (23 July), *Loyang* for chamber ensemble (30 July), and the duo compositions *Riul*, *Gasa*, and *Garak* (6 August).

[Reprinted by permission of Ferenc Berko.]

An Interview with Stuart Liebman (1973)

A few weeks before Carter's sixty-fifth birthday the *Boston Phoenix*, an alternative newspaper akin to New York's *Village Voice*, published an interview entitled "Elliott Carter: Champion of a Neglected Art," which appeared in its edition of 12 November 1973. As Carter admitted to the interviewer Stuart Liebman at the very beginning, he distrusted interviews as a form of communication: to avoid the dangers of disjointedness and superficiality, he preferred to present his thoughts at length and well-considered in writing. Indeed, probably because of these reservations (and aware of the possibility of editorial distortion), Carter had given relatively few interviews for many years and had heavily rewritten the transcripts of his more formal discussions, such as the one he conducted with Benjamin Boretz.[104] (Even the book *Flawed Words and Stubborn Sounds [SS]*, though touted as "a conversation with Elliott Carter," had been heavily revised at the editing stage and was partly based on pre-existing lecture notes.[105]) Despite such misgivings, which gradually gave way in his later years to great equanimity and aplomb in his dealings with interviewers, Carter responded to Liebman's questions with a candor that makes this little-known interview (it is omitted in John Link's bibliography [Link 2000]), still worth reading today. Here, as in many of his writings, Carter again takes up the subject of the troubled position of contemporary music in America's culture and society, casting a comparative eye not only at Europe, where he notes the much more generous support of new music by the state, but at the visual arts, which enjoy far greater public prestige in Europe and America alike. Yet his conclusion is not overly pessimistic: "I believe the power of music is strong enough on enough people for them to find a way of solving whatever kind of physical problems there are."

116 Elliott Carter, Interview with Stuart Liebman (1973)

[Biographical introduction by Stuart Liebman]

SL Mr. Carter, you were somewhat reluctant to give this interview. Was it that you are besieged by interviewers, or do you find this format inappropriate for serious discussion of your music?

EC Well, I find that it is difficult for me to formulate in an interview serious thoughts that require some kind of elaborate exposition. It is impossible to get a sufficiently dense discussion of any important matter going because there are always all sorts of extraneous things that keep coming in during an interview which would not if I were writing. I find that I can give a much more ordered and understandable presentation in writing on a subject that I am interested in than in an interview, which is so much a matter of random thoughts – on a rather superficial level of random.

SL Your own creative life has spanned two eras of American music, the early modern period of Varèse, Ruggles, and Ives – people you knew – and the period after World War II, when the United States emerged as the focal point for contemporary music. How has the situation and role of the composer in American life changed?

EC There were really at least three periods of American music that I have survived. One that I was only slightly aware of furnishes the background of my work. Before the Great Depression the composer seems to have been – at least as Charles Ives described himself in his *Memos* – somebody quite apart from this country's musical life. For a composer of any originality here at that time tended to be sidetracked. Our musical life was dominated by the European view expounded by European musicians. This was also, of course, the period when the European "avant-garde," Stravinsky, Bartók, Prokofiev, and many others were being played rather frequently here while American composers were treated as dilettantes.

When the Depression came, there was a great struggle to establish the American composer as a professional. There were even what now seem like comic efforts by American artists to establish their professional status, such as demonstrations against the Metropolitan Museum

---

104 Benjamin Boretz, "Conversation with Elliott Carter," *Contemporary Music Newsletter* 2/8 (November–December 1968), pp. 1–4; reprinted in revised form in *Perspectives of New Music* 8/2 (Spring–Summer 1970), pp. 1–22.

105 See the preface by Allen Edwards in *FW*, pp. 9–10.

for favoring Europeans over Americans. During these years many of us were involved in forming a union of American composers in order to establish the point that we were worthy of professional consideration and hence of being paid for our work.[106] Before this, when an American had a work performed, he invariably had to sign his copyright away (thus losing all future rights) and didn't get paid for the performance. The assumption was that the orchestra was doing him a favor by playing his work and investing so much expensive rehearsal time. Our union established the principle that the composer would not give away his rights and must be paid performance and radio-broadcast royalties. Even today these sums are appallingly small, but at least the principle of professionalism was established.

Since that period, which led to the post-Second-War era, music departments sprang up in colleges all over the U.S., many more composers were produced, and a group of musical works came into existence that established the importance of our music. But problems persist, for attitudes that are a hangover from previous periods continue to play an important role in musical society. Certainly a very large proportion of the musical world is still very Europe-oriented.

SL Why is that?

EC One of the reasons is that European societies and their governments believe in the importance of their own musical artists in a way we still do not believe in ours. We have enough faith in the future to spend lavishly on education and scholarships for beginners, but nothing after that, so it seems. European societies continue to be structured according to an inherited aristocratic point of view. Germans, for instance, believe that their society should continue to produce great composers today as they have in the past, and make every effort to make this come true. The government-subsidized radio, opera houses, and concert organizations play their works to the accompaniment of a lot of publicity – even sent by German government agencies abroad so that the chosen composers soon reach world-wide recognition. They don't have much competition from similar American agencies. For our cultural agency in London or wherever has so small a budget that hardly anything can be done, and what little is done is under constant pressure to be distributed equally among each of our few thousand composers, which means nobody gets to be known.[107] In my case, one of the oddities of this is that many of my works are performed over the American radio from tapes made at performances for European radio and hence become part of European cultural propaganda.

SL You've written before how pitiful the remuneration is even when one receives a foundation grant. There must always be a great deal of political infighting surrounding these awards.

EC I really don't have any sense of that at all. It seems to me that people in my generation who serve on juries for awards and fellowships do everything we can to help those with talent even if we disagree with what they are trying to do. If a composer is a difficult person, he can have a hard time, because like most of us, he, too, has to make his living elsewhere than in composition. He is, therefore, judged not by his music but by his teaching or other work. Yet, composers who have the ability to fit into the university situation have the opportunity to make quite considerable salaries. They're not having as tough a time now as they did. Why do you think all the Europeans come over here looking for jobs? Because they can't make enough money at home, though the opportunity to make money out of compositions is greater there. In any case, the activity of composing concert music (except for the most "popular" kind) seems to be, you might say, an un-American activity since it doesn't pay, unlike painting, sculpture, or writing. Recently, when I was discussing a commission with the New York Philharmonic,[108] I pointed out the window of its Lincoln Center office and said: "There is a work of Alexander Calder, who was awarded the highest award for American artists, the Gold Medal of the Institute of Arts and Letters, at the same time as I. He was paid, I understand, $300,000 for it. This was apparently only for a little sketch, and the donor also had to pay for the casting, transportation and for setting it up.[109] If you would pay me 1/10 of that – and it takes me about a year to write out the thousands of notes that make up an orchestra score – I would feel happy.

106 A reference to the American Composers Alliance (ACA), founded in 1938 and headed by Aaron Copland until 1945. Carter was a member of the ACA from its inception until 1961, when he joined Broadcast Music Incorporated (BMI).

107 Carter is referring to the (now defunct) US Information Agency, a sort of successor organization to the OWI whose goal was to promote "mutual understanding between the United States and other nations by conducting educational and cultural activities." (Quoted from the "Fact Sheet" on the USIA website: http://dosfan.lib.uic.edu/usia/usiahome/factshe.htm.)

108 In August 1973 Carter had met with Carlos Moseley, the president of the New York Philharmonic, to discuss this commission, which eventually led to the composition of *A Symphony of Three Orchestras* (see below, pp. 225–227). The exchange that follows regarding composers' fees was already touched on in the draft of Carter's thank-you letter of 26 August 1973, but he declined to remind Mosely of it in the version he finally posted. Both documents are preserved in Elliott Carter Collection, Paul Sacher Foundation, the latter as a carbon copy.

This did not produce the desired [result, however, since it was believed that the visual][110] arts were an entirely different matter from music.[111]

SL I know that you have been affiliated with various schools for many years, but in a university context aren't you a teacher first, an administrator second, and a composer only third?

EC I have the impression that universities are generous with absences, vacations, and sabbaticals as well as with salaries, teaching hours, and subsidies for performances of faculty works. I would think that teaching in a university was less demanding of time and effort away from creation than a conducting career, like that of Mahler, Bernstein, Boulez, and Maderna.

SL Getting back to the musical situation. Is there an American tradition which contemporary composers work within or against?

EC There were periods in which composers were influenced by jazz or popular music or American folksongs, but like all [such] tendencies, these were merely transitional. It seems to me that America is a culture that is constantly being created out of the acts, intentions, and visions of our people. This very process gives a special character to all of our art. But we don't have a homogeneous public which can be expected to share in the cultural norms that a European expects of his public. So we have to invent what we think would be important for our public. This can be a very isolating effort. It's certainly that way here in poetry and even in painting. Our public may have some knowledge of a European artistic past, but our past does not furnish a basis for cultural attitudes – certainly not in music.

SL It's almost as if each piece presented a new language or some unfamiliar dialect of an old one. Isn't this asking more of an audience than [has] ever been asked before – even more than by Wagner or Brahms in their day?

EC I have had this kind of feedback all my life. Yet when I hear the music many European composers have written since the War, I find American music is comparatively easy to understand. Certain works by Boulez or

Stockhausen or others written in the 60s are much harder to play than anything American composers have written, especially for orchestra. To play them precisely and musically – Stockhausen's *Gruppen*, for example – takes months of rehearsal, which would be out of the question here. One of our problems results directly from the fact that musical institutions are supported by relatively small private donations and therefore must cater to the present, actual tastes of the musical public in order to continue to receive donations. This means that music played before the general public tends to be conservative.

SL You wrote several years ago that a composer who wanted to write for orchestra was really a masochist looking for a great deal of self-punishment. Yet you have continued to write for what you called a "brontosaurus,"[112] and your works have been increasingly performed, better played and more widely applauded. Is the situation for the orchestral composer changing for the better?

EC I've lots of ideas about writing for the orchestra and do like to have time and the incentive to put them down, but it's a terrible lot of thought, imaginative effort and just plain note-writing. I limit myself to a small number of orchestra pieces just because the effort often hardly seems justified when I hear some of the performances (not all) that I get and see the long faces of musicians and public at poorly rehearsed performances. At the present time, it isn't a very hopeful picture. But I must say that I have always regretted losing faith in a musical situation. I lost faith in the orchestra after my Variations (and even after my ballets), but after a while these works began to be played well and some listeners even thought they were remarkable, and then, of course, I wished I had written more. The same goes for the string quartet, although that medium was always hospitable to me and performers played my works well from their very beginnings.

SL In describing your own work, you fairly consistently use two types of metaphors: that of films and dreams. Why?

EC It's partly due to the fact that when I was a student of about 25 I was very interested in films, particularly those of Eisenstein, who was a remarkable director.

---

109 Alexander Calder's *Le guichet* [The Ticket Window] (1963), erected near the entrance to the New York Public Library at Lincoln Center, was unveiled on 15 November 1965. It had made headlines in early 1965 because the Commissioner of Parks was unwilling to place it on public property, though eventually the city's Art Commission voted in favor of it. *Le guichet* was

donated to Lincoln Center by the stockbroker Howard Lipman and his wife Jean.

110 Here the printed version inadvertently skips a line; our attempted reconstruction appears in square brackets.

111 In the end Carter's fee for the commission of *A Symphony of Three Orchestras,* including performance rights, amounted to $10,000.

112 Among other places, Carter had used this metaphor in his essay of 1970, "The

Orchestral Composer's Point of View," where he described the sclerotic institution of the symphony orchestra as follows: "The orchestral brontosaur staggers with inertia and ossification; its very complexity resists change" (Elliott Carter, "The Orchestral Composer's Point of View" [see above, p. 63, note 64], in *CEL*, pp. 235–250, esp. 238).

I was a friend of James Agee and we used to discuss the films a great deal together. The film world was part of one's experience from the 20s on.

SL Does your music attempt to mime certain processes suggested by film techniques, for example, the "close-up," the "dissolve," or "coming into focus"? Your *Double Concerto* seems to offer some interesting analogies.

EC Sometimes, yes. There are different ways of making sequences of shots by cutting them in different ways. A shot stops in the middle of an action and leaves its "hangover," so to speak, through the next shot where, perhaps, it is picked up to be completed or continued in an unexpected way. This is particularly true of the Eisenstein films which interested me a great deal as a concept.

SL Have you ever considered writing film music, like Copland or Virgil Thomson?

EC I used to consider it, but not recently at all. Only in the period that Virgil and Copland worked in films were directors willing to accept some feed-in from outside. The underground film might be more receptive today. But I don't think my music is pictorial, it doesn't suggest enough visual character. Copland's suggests specific locations and characters, as did Virgil Thomson's. So does Hans Werner Henze's score for *Muriel* by [Alain] Resnais.[113]

SL Yet most commentators resort to terms derived from the graphic arts to describe your work. But the other metaphors you prefer to use, especially for the First Quartet, are taken from the vocabulary of dreams.

EC I see the motion of music as a kind of analogue to the processes of our inner life. It must present not merely the patterns of feeling, but also the patterns of logical thought and of the stream-of-consciousness. I've tried to develop patterns which include all these ways of thinking in any given work and which also attempt to motivate these types of thought. For instance, the dreams of systematic logical thought as opposed to the flux of the dream world.

SL Your emphasis on contrasting characters of thought as a structure as well as your long-time interest in the idiomatic natures of individual instruments seems characteristic of other "modernist" arts' investigation and affirmation of their media of expression. Do you see analogies between your work and the other "modernist" arts?

EC Only superficially. Sound for its own sake is of very limited interest to me. Human beings, I think, come to expect more from music than entertaining patterns of tone-colors. Mine uses a large variety of these but, I hope, always to transcend the medium of sound completely and present a more significant human message.

SL Charles Rosen said about your *Double Concerto* that it was music without a central rhythmic pulse.[114] That must pose enormous difficulties for performers as well as for listeners.

EC This does not mean that it has no pulse as, for instance, most of the music of Boulez and Stockhausen, but that there are superimposed pulses, each having its own life, and kept in relationship by a conductor's beat, which does not correspond to the rhythms that are played and heard. At first, performers were so busy keeping off the conductor's beat and made so nervous by this that the musical sense was lost. Gradually, with experience, they've learned to keep together (apart?) very musically. After all, such staggering of pulse was characteristic of certain styles of jazz. My music is unusual, though it obviously makes sense to me as I write it. It's filled with events some find so confusing that they play in a disturbed way. The technical effort is so much in the foreground that performers can't pay attention to what the message of the music is. After a first performance, especially one that is recorded, players and listeners know what a piece is going to sound like, and this can lay the groundwork for a better performance. If these pieces didn't have any substance and were only difficult to perform, they would have fallen by the wayside long before any of this could happen.

SL Then recordings of new pieces have really changed the structure of contemporary music. Without them there could be no easy communication of stan-

---

113 *Muriel ou Le temps d'un retour* (1963) by Alain Resnais (director) and Jean Cayrol (screenplay). The music to this film was partly by Georges Delerue and partly by Hans Werner Henze.

114 Charles Rosen, "One Easy Piece," *The New York Review of Books* 20/2 (22 February 1973), pp. 25–29, esp. 26; most recently reprinted in *ML*, pp. 21–31, esp. 26–27. Rosen's actual words read: "No central beat can be heard: the rhythms therefore do not cross but proceed independently. They are, in fact, cross-tempi or cross-speeds, if you like. The occasional coincidence of accent in two parts no longer refers to the existence of a slower and all-governing beat, but to periodic movements which have momentarily come together and are about to spread apart once again."

dards of excellence. But what about bad recorded performances? Do composers have any control on the quality of performance their works receive?

EC You know, there is a technical matter connected with the recording industry, that is, the composer has the right to prevent a first recording if he doesn't think it any good, but once recorded he has no subsequent right and anybody can record it and play it badly or well. A composer tries to get a good performance at first, but a lot of the time he wants to get it on a record anyhow, hoping that it will encourage other people to learn the piece and play it. But to decide between a poor performance on record or no recording at all can be very perplexing. On the whole, I've been lucky and had pretty good performances on first recordings. They're getting better.

SL Do you supervise or try to supervise recordings?

EC Yes, but there's very little I can do. Either the performers get it or they don't and there's very little I can say. I can suggest "a little louder or softer" here or there, but with some performers it's like trying to plug a hole in a leaky pot. With others who give a convincing performance, I hate to hamstring their spirit by being fussy about details.

SL Do you believe that there is a large potential audience among young people who will support serious contemporary music?

EC Yes, it seems so. Of course, in America, the popularity of popular things is appalling by comparison, and it grows more and more every year. It tends to overshadow things that are not very widely appreciated. But this doesn't mean that these things aren't growing also. It's just that attention is being drawn away from them more and more. It's being drawn away from them in the newspapers because there's less and less space devoted to serious music and more to popular music. At one time there was no coverage of popular music at all.

SL To sum up then: given the relative reluctance of the American government to pay much attention to music, given the economically insubstantial product of composers' efforts, given the increasingly high costs of performances and recordings, and the uncertainty of a future audience, what are the prospects for American musical life in the next 30 years or so?

EC It has survived this far. If the costs go up, there will be a new way of funding. I believe that the power of music is strong enough on enough people for them to find a way of solving whatever kind of physical problems there are.

[Stuart Liebman, "Elliott Carter: Champion of a Neglected Art," *The Boston Phoenix*, 12 November 1973, Section 2, pp. 10, 12, and 36.]

"Honors, Well Deserved"

1974–1988

117 Elliott Carter at the exhibition devoted to him by the
New York Public Library (Lincoln Center, Library
of Performing Arts, 1974), photo by Nancy Crampton

In winter 1973–74, in honor of Carter's sixty-fifth birthday, the New York Public Library mounted an exhibition entitled "Elliott Carter: Sketches and Scores in Manuscript." It opened on 12 December 1973, one day after
his birthday, and ended, after an extension, on 10 March
1974. This photograph shows the composer in the exhibition room in the Library of Performing Arts in front of
a large-scale portrait by William Gedney (the same that
has been used for the cover of the present publication)
and a glass showcase with further photographs. The exhibition marked the outset of Carter's relatively long connection with the library, in which, from 1975, he placed a
substantial number of his music manuscripts on loan.

[Reprinted by permission of Nancy Crampton.]

118 Pierre Boulez taking a break from the rehearsals
for the *Concerto for Orchestra* (New York, 1974),
photo by Henry Grossman

Hardly a year after its première under Leonard Bernstein, the *Concerto for Orchestra* was taken up by Pierre Boulez, first in Cleveland with the Cleveland Orchestra (21–23 January 1971) and later in Graz and Vienna, where he introduced it to European audiences during a tour of the BBC Symphony Orchestra (18 and 20 October 1971). Once he had become music director of the New York Philharmonic in autumn 1971, Boulez also conducted the piece in New York, along with many other Carter compositions. This photograph shows him taking a break while rehearsing the *Concerto for Orchestra* in Avery Fisher Hall, where it was scheduled for performance in the New York Philharmonic's subscription series (7–8 and 12 February 1974) and during an "informal evening" with explanations by the composer and conductor (11 February 1974).[1] (Boulez and Carter also recited, in French and English, excerpts from Saint-John Perse's *Vents*, the poem to which the work relates.) Carter mentioned this "informal evening" and the concert performances in a letter to William Glock: "I made a lot more of Perse's windy bombast than I would have liked to keep the whole thing from being too dry – We had some wonderful performances – Pierre worked very hard with the orchestra & got beautiful results & was very charming & interesting during the talking."[2] In autumn 1975 Boulez again conducted the *Concerto for Orchestra* on a European tour with the New York Philharmonic, in Edinburgh (28 August 1975), London (30 August 1975), Ghent (31 August 1975), and Paris (18 September 1975).

[Reprinted by permission of Henry Grossman.]

1   The date 5 February 1974 given for
this occasion in *CL*, p. 50, stands in need
of correction.
2   Letter from Elliott Carter to William
Glock, 15 February 1974; William Glock
Estate, British Library.

119 Susan Davenny Wyner and Richard Dufallo in rehearsal at the Aspen Festival (1974), photo by Yehudi Wyner

The summer after visiting the Carters in Waccabuc, on 8 August 1974 at the Aspen Music Festival, Susan Davenny Wyner sang the newly-orchestrated version of *Voyage*, *Warble for Lilac Time* (in an orchestration from 1955), and Aribert Reimann's *Inane* for soprano and orchestra (1968) with the Aspen Festival Orchestra conducted by Richard Dufallo, who later also conducted the Rome première of *A Mirror on Which to Dwell*. This photograph shows the artists in rehearsal; according to Ms. Wyner, Carter was sitting in the front row, out of view, when this picture was taken. Already thinking about composing a song cycle, Carter expressed interest in the Reimann work and asked Ms. Wyner to send him a copy of the score.[3]

[Reprinted by permission of Yehudi Wyner and Susan Davenny Wyner.]

---

3   Susan Davenny Wyner, personal communication, 9 May 2008.

A Mirror on Which to Dwell (1974–75)

The song cycle *A Mirror on Which to Dwell*, for soprano and chamber orchestra, was Carter's first composition for solo voice in over thirty years. While composing it he consciously reconnected with some of his earlier solo vocal music by orchestrating the *Three Poems of Robert Frost* (1942) and *Voyage* (1943) for Susan Davenny Wyner in 1974.[4] In preparation for composing *Mirror*, Carter sought texts by a woman poet, because he intended the songs to be sung by a soprano. Robert Lowell recommended Elizabeth Bishop (1911–1979), who was already in the public eye at the time, as her *Complete Poems* had won the National Book Award in 1970.[5] *Mirror* was commissioned by the new music ensemble Speculum Musicae in 1973 in celebration of the US Bicentennial, and was dedicated to Speculum and Susan Davenny Wyner, who premièred the work under the direction of Richard Fitz on 24 February 1976 at the Hunter College Playhouse in New York. The group, which was founded in 1971, had explicitly requested a vocal piece with ensemble, knowing that Carter was interested in writing for voice again.[6] Donal Henahan of the *New York Times* commented on the song cycle's "directness and accessibility as compared with [Carter's] string quartets, his *Piano Concerto* or his *Concerto for Orchestra*" and praised the "dramatic intensity" of the "splendid soprano soloist."[7] A few days later, in the same newspaper, Harold Schonberg complained (about the music of Sessions, Carter, Babbitt, and others) that "This 'Modern' Music is Out of Touch With Today."[8] Actually *Mirror*, in its wry, often ironic, but deeply sympathetic look at the human condition, is very much a product of its time, and has become one of Carter's best-known works. The fifth song, Carter's Ivesian setting of "A View of the Capitol from the Library of Congress," alludes ironically to the current politics of the post-Vietnam age.[9]

Mirror was followed by five other major song cycles on texts of American poets, which together with the earlier vocal music (including choral works) bear witness to Carter's life-long dedication to American literature. Carter's poets read like a "Who's Who" in American letters: Walt Whitman, Emily Dickinson, Hart Crane, Robert Frost, Allen Tate, Elizabeth Bishop, Robert Lowell, John Ashbery, Wallace Stevens, William Carlos Williams, and John Hollander (to name only some). Carter, who made his reputation in the 1950s and 1960s composing large-scale and ambitious works for orchestra and string quartet, has turned out to be one of the twentieth century's leading American composers of song.

120 *A Mirror on Which to Dwell*, six poems of Elizabeth Bishop for soprano and chamber orchestra (1974–75), sketches in pencil for an unrealized setting of "Conversation", p. [1]

Many of Carter's sketches for vocal works resemble this one: sketched vocal lines over a line-by-line paste-up of a text, in this case one that was ultimately not included in the finished piece.[10] This page represents the second step in the text-setting process. First Carter chose the poems – he originally selected thirteen – and analyzed each one in detail, sketching its main images, its tensions, and its dramatic structure in verbal notes. Then he typed out the poem, and cut out each line and pasted it onto staff paper. Some (unnotated) musical ideas must have preceded even this step, since he divided some words into syllables with spaces between them, implying that he had already decided on a melismatic treatment. In fact the syllables "tu-mult," "ask-ing," and "ques-[t-ions]" are set with two eighth notes each; this insistent rhythmic repetition (presumably at a quick tempo) in addition to the extremely high register of the vocal line at "ask-ing" reflects the "tumult" described in the poem's first line. While it is not always possible to tell which of the sketches in the staves above the text was written first, a top-to-bottom order seems likely here, as the second staff varies the music above it slightly, adding more rhythmic complexity. One of Carter's main ideas was finding musical equivalents for the "questions" and "answers" that make up the inner "conversation" of the poem. At the beginning of the fourth and fifth systems of this sketch page, he has notated "A" (for "Answer") and "A [arrow] Q" (for "Answer leading to Question") (these abbreviations are clear from the following sketch page, not shown). These musical equivalents would have operated on different levels, but the ascending direction of the vocal lines on "questions" in the first system and the descending lines on

4   Carter had given Susan Davenny Wyner the scores of his old songs during a visit to Waccabuc on 14 June 1973. That fall the soprano and her husband Yehudi Wyner played through the songs at his home in New York and urged Carter to orchestrate them. Personal communication from Susan Davenny Wyner, 9 May 2008.

5   Elizabeth Bishop, *Complete Poems* (New York: Farrar, Straus, and Giroux, 1969).

6   Personal communication from Virgil Blackwell, one of the founding members of Speculum Musicae, 14 November 2007.

7   Donal Henahan, "Carter's 'A Mirror' Given Premiere by a New Group," *The New York Times*, 26 February 1976.

8   Ibid., 29 February 1976.

9   See Anne C. Shreffler, "'Give the Music Room': Elliott Carters 'View of the Capitol from the Library of Congress' aus *A Mirror on Which to Dwell*," trans. Felix Meyer, in *Quellenstudien II: Zwölf Komponisten des 20. Jahrhunderts*, ed. Felix Meyer (Winterthur: Amadeus, 1993), pp. 255–283.

10 "Conversation" is the first of "Four Poems" originally from the volume *North and South* (1946); see Elizabeth Bishop, *The Complete Poems 1927–1979* (New York: Farrar, Straus and Giroux, 1983), p. 76.

A Symphony of Three Orchestras (1976)

"answer" in the second are surely part of this scheme. These settings would also reflect the tone of the voice in normal conversational speaking, which characterizes the decidedly non-operatic vocal writing of *Mirror* in general. Carter found Bishop's poetry very conducive to musical setting: "[Her poems] impressed me because of their clear verbal coherence as well as their imaginative use of syllabic sounds that suggest the singing voice. I was very much in sympathy with their point of view, for there is almost always a secondary layer of meaning, sometimes ironic, sometimes passionate, that gives a special ambience, often contradictory, to what the words say."[11] Bishop's poetry shares with Carter's music a lucidity of structure, subtle irony, flashes of wit, and formidable craftsmanship disguised as free association.

Carter's long-cherished but unrealized plan to compose a cantata on Hart Crane's cycle of poems *The Bridge* was ultimately subsumed in *A Symphony of Three Orchestras*, composed between June and late December 1976 and premièred on 17–19 and 22 February 1977 by the New York Philharmonic under Pierre Boulez. This work owes its existence to a commission granted by the New York Philharmonic in August 1973. The funding was ultimately made possible by a commissioning grant awarded by the National Endowment for the Arts to six major orchestras in celebration of the US Bicentennial. (Besides the New York Philharmonic, these included the Boston, Chicago, Cleveland, Los Angeles, and Philadelphia symphony orchestras.[12]) As could only be expected, however, Carter's Bicentennial piece was by no means mindlessly celebratory; on the contrary, it casts an ambivalent, sometimes gloomy, light on American reality, mediated by Crane's literary perspective. In particular the subject of "the world's fall from natural beauty to mechanical terror,"[13] which plays a central role in Crane's poetry (and to a certain extent reflects the career of the poet himself), finds a vivid analogy in *A Symphony of Three Orchestras*. The "fall" is suggested by a gradual descent from the uppermost to the lowermost register, from the radiant sounds of the introduction (an auroral image of the great city of New York wakening to life) to the muffled concluding gestures from the bass instruments at the end of the coda (which Carter himself interpreted as a symbol of Crane's suicide).[14] Similarly, the transition from the organic to the mechanical is implied by the work's main section culminating in a series of massive *tutti* chords after which, in the coda, all that remains are static reiterations of ostinato-like figures. In between, the composition unfolds as a highly complex, collage-like sequence of twelve overlapping sections, with four movements being assigned to each of the three orchestral groups mentioned in the title, each with its associated intervals, tempos, and expressive moods. Once again, as in the *Concerto for Orchestra*, the fact that the openings and the endings of the movements elide in time-honored Carterian fashion conveys an impression of continuous emergence and retreat among the various layers of texture subliminally present throughout the piece.

---

11 Elliott Carter, liner notes to the LP recording of *A Symphony of Three Orchestras* (New York Philharmonic, conducted by Pierre Boulez) and *A Mirror on Which to Dwell* (Susan Davenny Wyner [soprano], Speculum Musicae, conducted by Richard Fitz); Columbia Masterworks M 35171.

12 In fact the commissioned works were meant to be performed by all these orchestras, which did not happen. On the Harvard Library copy of the Columbia recording (which is inscribed "for Erika and Paul [Fromm]/Elliott/Sept. 17, 1980"),

Carter has circled Chicago, Los Angeles, and Philadelphia in this list and noted "have not played this."

13 Schiff 1983/1998, pp. 297 and 302, respectively.

14 *ML*, p. 42. Admittedly in this case, too, Carter stressed that the literary analogy occurred to him only after the fact: "[...] that is the way I saw it *after* I had the conception of the music." (Ibid.) Accordingly, he explained the overall descending gesture of the *Symphony of Three Orchestras* elsewhere without

mentioning Crane's poem at all: "[...] the musical origin of *A Symphony* came from a remark by Aaron Copland, who once commented that my works always seemed to progress with an upward inflection and so frequently ended in an upward direction. So I decided to try to write a work which would feature constant downward movement, both in the large form and in many of the small details." (Bernard, "Interview with Elliott Carter" [see above, p. 101, note 41], pp. 182–183.)

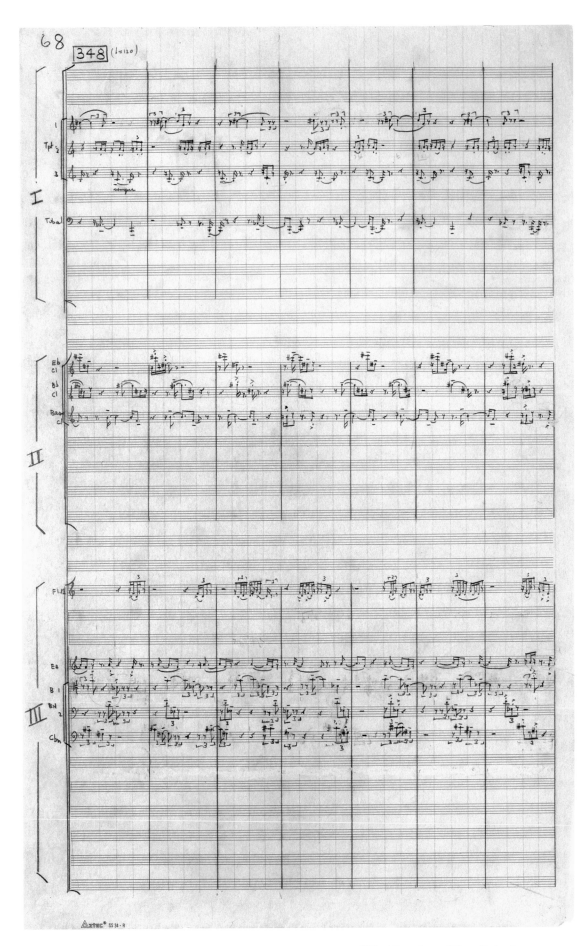

121 *A Symphony of Three Orchestras*

121 *A Symphony of Three Orchestras* (1976),
autograph full score in pencil, p. 68 (mm. 348–354)

This passage from the coda to *A Symphony of Three Orchestras* marks the antithesis of the work's opening. If the symphony's beginning, with its rhapsodic, virtuoso trumpet solo offset by glittering sheets of sound (Carter specially tailored this solo for the New York Philharmonic's solo trumpeter Gerard Schwarz), suggests the free flight of a seagull (see *ML*, p. 42), the superposed ostinatos shown here evoke an aura of mechanical compulsion. (David Schiff even spoke specifically in this connection of "factory-noise ostinati"; Schiff 1983/1998, pp. 200 and 306, respectively.) Each of the twelve (wind) instruments employed in this passage is limited to more or less rigid repetitions of a single two-note figure, with each figure being assigned one of the eleven intervals within the span of an octave, from the minor second to the major seventh, including two occurrences of the tritone (trumpet 3: minor second; trumpet 2: major second; flute: minor third; English horn: major third; contrabassoon: fourth; trumpet 1 / bass clarinet: tritone; B♭ clarinet: fifth; tuba: minor sixth; bassoon 1: major sixth; E♭ clarinet: minor seventh; bassoon 2: major seventh).[15] This passage is unique in Carter's music, both for its repetitiveness and for its harmonic stasis. Its motivation in the work's overall dramatic design is both structural and poetic. In technical terms it can be viewed as a sort of horizontal flattening of the powerful *tutti* chords that had just brought the staggered polyrhythmic cycles of the main section to a point of convergence (mm. 318ff.), thereby signaling an abrupt end to the previous course of the music. On the literary and programmatic level – i.e. in relation to Crane's life and poetry – it represents what Carter himself has called "the cessation of poetic impulse."[16] Finally, it may perhaps also be regarded as Carter's critique of minimalism, which had brought forth such emblematic works as Steve Reich's *Music for 18 Musicians* (1974–76) and Philip Glass's *Einstein on the Beach* (1975–76) at exactly the time that *A Symphony of Three Orchestras* was being composed. In any event, Carter made no secret of his rejection of this style of music, which he considered no less "mechanical" than much pop music: "[...] music that is mechanically ordered like some minimalist music or some popular music seems to me pointless as it does not give any sense of being alive."[17]

---

15 See the chart in Noubel 2000, p. 186, which lists the various lengths and "intervallic rhythms" of the rhythmic cycles.

16 See "Elliott Carter in conversation with Robert Johnston, Michael Century, Robert Rosen, and Don Stein," below, p. 258.

17 Ibid., see below, p. 256.

"France – America Ltd." (1976)

Carter wrote the following essay for the catalogue of the exhibition "Paris – New York" (1 June – 19 September 1977), a broad survey of the artistic interaction between these two metropolises held in the newly founded Centre Pompidou, which was inaugurated on 31 January 1977.[18] Choosing the title "France–America Ltd.," Carter touched on the musical relations between France and the United States in the nineteenth and twentieth centuries, especially emphasizing the role of his former teacher Nadia Boulanger, who had taught several generations of American students beginning in the 1920s. Indeed, Carter's now elderly but still active teacher was second to none in personifying the musical rapport between these two countries, a rapport that witnessed a significant upsurge in the first half of the twentieth century. If young American composers of the nineteenth century had been spellbound by the German tradition (America's "highbrow music" was largely dominated by German émigrés, and German conservatories were the preferred European centers of learning), those of the turn of the century turned increasingly to French music. The catastrophe brought about by Germany in the First World War obviously contributed to this change of orientation. Still, the *volte face* had its roots not only in the political denigration of German cultural values, but in an aesthetic realignment that had begun much earlier: as Carter notes in his essay, not the least significant factor was the interest shown by modern French composers in America's popular music, especially the nascent forms of jazz. Whatever the case, there is no denying that young Americans received important impetus from French culture for developing a contemporary music of their own, and that they found in Nadia Boulanger an important teacher who constantly promoted their efforts towards musical independence by inculcating not so much a particular musical style as rigorous compositional craftsmanship, thereby enabling them to express themselves in a very wide range of idioms. (For this reason the composers she taught were soon able to grow beyond the narrow confines of nationalist "Americanism.") Carter's essay was published only in French; the original version in English appears here for the first time.

122 Elliott Carter, "France–America Ltd." (1976)

Among the arts imported from Europe during the 18th and 19th centuries, concert music has had a very special problem of acculturation to American society. Always facing the threat of extinction by the spectacular successes of popular music, by the constantly increasing expenses of concert-giving, it has never had the benefit of the continuous pressure from a respected élite that could convince the public of its value. The cultural pattern that encouraged the development of the repertory and performance methods that constitute the familiar musical world could never have existed without such an élite in Europe, and it is surprising that America has been able to develop so far musically virtually without one. This situation has been particularly difficult for musical composition, since the repertory of concert music is that of the familiar European classics, [which] establish[ed] on the part of audiences many kinds of expectations which, particularly at present, do not interest composers. Yet it was inevitable that, in spite of great difficulties, our composers would attempt to find their own way, a way that would reflect their personal experiences. Of course, the European musical aesthetic itself prompted all composers, especially during the 19th century, to find a national style, to be original within very strict limitations, and hence to search their surroundings for distinctive material, which for American settlers was the music of the blacks and the Indians.

Of the three important musical cultures of the 19th century, the German and Italian were brought to our main cities and towns by masses of immigrants from every class of society of Europe. These made a determined effort to continue their former styles of life, founding *Sängervereine*, symphony orchestras, and opera houses. The French settlers, on the other hand, did not have the same influence, since they were few in the important centers, although active on the periphery, in Louisiana and Québec. This is unlikely to change, although the English historian Arnold Toynbee, writing in the '30s, predicted that French culture would soon spread into the United States in a new wave of migration coming down from Canada and up from Louisiana to meet in Washington. The French culture we do know, and have known, has

18 Carter was present at the opening of the Centre Pompidou. He had traveled to Paris on 19 January 1977 to attend the events devoted to him in the "Passage du XXe siècle" cycle by Pierre Boulez's newly founded IRCAM, the research center attached to the Centre Pompidou, and its associated Ensemble InterCon-

temporain. (At this point, however, IRCAM had not entered its new premises, for the construction work was not yet finished.) His *Eight Etudes and a Fantasy*, *String Quartet No. 2*, *Eight Pieces for Four Timpani*, and *Duo for Violin and Piano* were presented in the "Atelier Carter" (29 January 1977), while the *Sonata for

Violoncello and Piano*, the *Double Concerto*, *String Quartet No. 3*, and *A Mirror on Which to Dwell* were heard in the concert "Autour de Carter" (30 January 1977). As Boulez was in America at this time, the *Double Concerto* and *A Mirror on Which to Dwell* were conducted by Michel Tabachnik.

always been widely, if thinly, disseminated here, since the ideas of Rousseau, Montesquieu, and de Tocqueville are embedded in our political structures.

So, except in Louisiana, French culture has had little popular basis, being the concern of the educated and/or the wealthy, who looked to aristocratic and bourgeois France as exemplars of elegant, luxurious living. Concert music, which used to – and probably still does – serve to conjure up a vision of refinement and gentility for Americans, as did art collecting, has always used the important works of the French repertory for this. For the same reasons, the larger public welcomed French performers and French conductors, who were often encouraged to import the highly trained instrumentalists of the Conservatoire for their orchestras. It is not surprising that any American seriously wishing to be a musician should have wanted to study in Paris, impressed by the skill, authority, and respect French musicians command.

Such study was encouraged for musicians in the 20th century after both wars by the French and American governments with generous scholarships. The Conservatoire Américain was founded in 1921 for these students in the palace of Fontainebleau. Also, after the First War, the devaluation of the franc made it possible for many American artists who loved France to live in Paris – Ezra Pound, Gertrude Stein, Ernest Hemingway, Man Ray, Virgil Thomson, and George Antheil – and their presence brought many others, especially those interested in contemporary art, which then flourished there. It was during these years that the example of French and Russian music being written in Paris suggested a new and important direction for American music.

French composers, throughout the 19th century, and even before, had been dealing with the problem of using folk and popular music in their compositions. The treatment of Spanish music, for instance by Bizet, Lalo, and Chabrier – not to mention Debussy and Ravel – involved adding an element of drama, of gestural excitement, of colorfulness, or of nostalgia, as well as of expanded musical continuity to folk material when introduced into the "high" style of the concert hall. This reconciliation of the two by the French was soon to give rise to national schools, especially that of Spain, where composers adapted the French example to their own uses, and

also partly to that of Russia, where the brilliance and picturesque qualities of Berlioz and others suggested useful ideas. This example even spread to New Orleans, where Berlioz's student Louis Moreau Gottschalk wrote his charmingly Creole pieces *Le Bananier* and *La Bamboula.*

The relation of concert music to popular music went though many different phases, relating to the political scene in Europe. The Russians began emphasizing the primitive and elemental aspects in their concert music, and finally, in a reaction to the older "high" style of the concert hall, popular music (very often the music of fairs and circuses) was distorted to emphasize its coarseness, its repetitiousness, and its almost pathetic emptiness, as in the music of Satie and some of *Les Six*. With Stravinsky's *Renard* and *Histoire du soldat* a new, convincing way of combining these two styles, partly suggested by his contact with French musicians and partly highly original, was to lead to important developments in other cultures.

This music written during and right after the First War in France was watched by young American composers of that time with growing interest, especially since it frequently used their own popular music as a basis – the cake-walk (as in Debussy), ragtime, and jazz. They soon saw this as a direction out of which they could develop a new American school more vital than the older American attempts to treat their folklore in the romantic style, which, except for Charles Ives, had been unconvincing.

To encourage this tendency, the conductor of the Boston Symphony during the '20s and '30s, Serge Koussevitzky, who had been the champion of contemporary music from Russia and France, decided to stimulate American composers to form a nationalist school like that of the Russian "Five" and commissioned and performed American works that followed this trend. His advisor on the contemporary repertory was said to have been Mlle Nadia Boulanger in Paris, who by that time was already attracting many American students.

In fact right after the First War, a great deal of contemporary music was performed in the United States. This was due, at first, to the efforts of French musicians who had come to live here at that time. Robert Schmitz, the French pianist, for example, with money from the French government and the organization of the Alliance Française offices around the country, started modern-music concerts given by what was first called the Franco-American and later the Pro Musica Society (on whose Board of Directors were Charles Ives, Edgard Varèse, and Carlos Salzedo). Besides concerts containing much new French music, this group sponsored tours of the American continent by Bartók, Prokofiev, Stravinsky, Milhaud, and Honegger. In 1927 it introduced some movements of Ives's Fourth Symphony on the same program with Milhaud conducting his *Malheurs d'Orphée* in New York.[19] At the same period, the French harpist-composer Carlos Salzedo and Edgard Varèse started a similar society, the International Composers' Guild, devoted to more extreme music, including performances of their own works. The initiative for both of these, at a time when no other modern music groups existed in the United States, was taken by French musicians, although very soon after them, Americans formed the League of Composers, which featured music of their own country.[20] For by this time many American musicians had already begun to resent the constant emphasis on European musicians at the expense of Americans, feeling, as did Debussy, about the Germans: "Il est bien évident que nous avons été plus qu'accueillants envers les musiciens allemands. Dans cinquante ans, on saura ce qui doit rester de nos engouements actuels. Nous aimons tout ce qui vient du dehors. Comme des enfants, nous battons des mains devant une œuvre qui vient de loin [...], sans nous rendre compte de la valeur réelle et de la solidité de cette œuvre, sans nous demander si nous pouvons éprouver une émotion sincère au frisson d'âmes étrangères aux nôtres." [It is quite clear that we have been more than generous towards German musicians. In fifty years' time we will know what should remain of our current enthusiasms. We appreciate everything that comes from abroad. We clap our hands like children at any piece hailing from far and wide (...), without considering the real value and soundness of the work, or stopping to think whether one can in fact be genuinely moved by what is spine-tingling for other backs than ours.][21]

What attracted many young American students of composition to Paris after the First World War was the awareness that the contemporary movement could head to a new and more individual, maybe even more American, style than was possible to the romantics. Contemporary music, however, was only just beginning to be known in the United States, and there seemed to be no teacher [who] took it seriously enough to have any knowledge or judgement about it. In Europe only two such teachers were talked about, Arnold Schoenberg and Nadia Boulanger, and given the feeling about Germany after the First War, most Americans interested in new music went to Paris. This was the beginning [of] Mlle Boulanger's career as a teacher and an influence which continues to the present. It is primarily through her that French culture has had an influence on American music.

This remarkable teacher, who met her first students at the Conservatoire Américain in Fontainebleau in the early '20s and taught later at the Ecole Normale and gave the *cours d'accompagnement* at the Conservatoire, could be said to be the teacher of the Stravinskian aesthetic. For not only did she constantly hold up his works (and of each new period) as models of completely realized contemporary music, her tastes in musical [composition] developed parallel to his. When he was interested in Beethoven quartets, Bach cantatas, renaissance or medieval music, or later in Webern and twelve-tone music, she soon was drawing her students' attention to these works and analyzing them in detail. Thus the anti-Wagnerian, anti-Straussian tastes of the Russian composer were reflected in Nadia Boulanger's own taste. This is not to say that she slavishly followed the master, but in following Stravinsky's production year by year, she also followed his views about older music. This meant that the musical tradition was seen as new and fresh and stimulating because Bach [and] Mozart were made to illuminate Stravinsky. This was accepted by students very gratefully because of what seemed its great cogency. In any case, her teaching had an intuitive grasp of many sides of musical composition ([there were] enormous numbers [of] examples [from] which she could quote from memory at the piano) and an ability to show by example how the student might have solved a certain problem in his own work. Her remarkable intensity of attention and musical awareness and her personal concern for her students [were] something that all of them remain deeply grateful for.

Her many decades of teaching reveal a constant evolution, changing with the times, in ways most musicians did, including Stravinsky. The group of students from the '20s, which included Aaron Copland, Walter Piston,

---

19 Carter is referring to the Sunday matinée concert of the New York Pro Musica on 29 January 1927. In addition to two movements ("Prelude" and "Comedy") from Ives's *Symphony No. 4* (ca. 1910–16), the program of this concert, performed by members of the New York Philharmonic, also included Darius Milhaud's chamber opera *Les Malheurs d'Orphée* (1924) and several fragments from Claude

Debussy's incidental music to *Le Roi Lear* (1904–06). Milhaud's opera was conducted by the composer himself, the other works by Eugene Goossens.

20 The Franco-American (Pro Musica) Society, the International Composers' Guild, the League of Composers, and other New York composer societies of the 1920s are discussed in Oja, *Making Music Modern* (see above, pp. 8–9, note 20),

chap. 11 ("Organizing the Moderns"), pp. 177–200.

21 Claude Debussy, "Une semaine de musique française à Munich," *Paris-Journal*, 21 August 1910; quoted from idem, *Monsieur Croche et autres écrits: Edition complète de son œuvre critique, avec une introduction et des notes par François Lesure* (Paris: Gallimard, 1971), pp. 286-87, esp. 286. See the revised and enlarged new

and Roy Harris, the founders of a new Americanism, found her open to all new music. She would read over the score of Berg's *Wozzeck* at the piano with the students filling what her hands could not reach, or the *Sacre du printemps,* discussing their wonderful, imaginative writing, as if it were Beethoven. Such was her penetration and judgement that many other composers, like Roger Sessions and Virgil Thomson, who were not her students, brought scores for her criticism. It was said that even Honegger and Stravinsky did this.

In the '30s, she became much less receptive to the Viennese School and to Bartók, for like many young musicians of the time – Hindemith, Milhaud, or Copland – she, too, had gradually turned against what then began to seem like "old-fashioned modernism." For some who were just catching up with this earlier period this was disappointing, especially when such a work as Stravinsky's *Perséphone* was held up as a model.

At that time Nadia Boulanger was not enthusiastic about the new French music except that of Poulenc, but it was another story with old composers like Fauré, Debussy, and Ravel, whose music she loved and discussed with intimate knowledge. During all of this time she was constantly reading over the scores of early music being resurrected by musicologists. At lessons she would draw our attention to a *ballade* of Guillaume de Machaut or of a French madrigalist, or of Monteverdi, whose music she recorded, leaving a vivid reminder of her penetration into these works. Even though the students were being constantly presented with many new things, still Mlle Boulanger is basically a traditional teacher in demanding thorough training in harmony and counterpoint, solfège, and orchestration, although when she teaches any of these the illumination that she brings even to the simplest harmony exercise makes even this usually dull routine exciting and rewarding.

In more recent years, her interest in the late Stravinsky and Webern has led her on to a knowledge of the work of Boulez, and when her present students try to write in this style they find her criticisms very helpful.

For a while, the special taste of the '30s dominated her students and gave rise to what was called the style of the "Boulangerie," a light, charming kind of music that Nadia Boulanger encouraged in students who seemed to have a talent for this. But it was characteristic of only a few, while the many others attest to the very broad vision which helped all kinds of different young composers find their own way. Reflecting the devotion of so many students Saint-John Perse wrote this of her on her 80th birthday: "Nadia, les Siècles changent de visage et changent de langage, mais la Musique, votre Siècle, n'a point de masques à dépouiller, étant plus qu'aucun art et plus qu'aucune science du langage, connaissance de l'Etre. / A vous, Nadia, libre et vassale dans a grande famille musicale, mais à cette seule divination soumise, qui n'est d'aucun servage, d'aucune école et d'aucun rite, / A Celle qu'entre deux guerres Paul Valéry m'adressait un jour avec ces simples mots: 'Elle est la Musique en personne' (et la Musique pour lui se couronnait toujours d''intelligence'), / A Celle qu'en Amérique, aux heures les plus sombres du drame occidental, j'ai vue vivre parmi nous sa vie d'apôtre et de sibylle: animatrice, instigatrice, éducatrice et libératrice, l'oreille à toutes sources et l'âme à tous les souffles, feuille elle-même frémissante dans l'immense feuillage, / Honneur et grâces soient rendus, au nom et la Musique même." [Nadia, the Centuries change their look and change their language, but Music, your domain, has no masks to peel off, being – more than any other art or science of expression – knowledge of the Self. / To you Nadia, free spirit and vassal in the great family of music, subject to this one divination alone, which requires no subservience, no school, no rite. / To the One whom Paul Valéry once addressed in the twenties with the simple words: 'She is Music in person' (and for him Music was always crowned with 'intelligence'), / To the One whom I saw in America, in the darkest hours of the West's travail, going about her life of apostle and sybil amongst us: animating, instigating, educating, and liberating, a sympathetic ear for all sources, a kindred soul for all inspirations, herself one more leaf quivering in the immense canopy, Honor and gratitude be rendered, to the name and to Music herself.][22]

Finally, the troubling thing about the influence of French culture, indeed that of any other culture on another, is that only certain aspects of it are useful, and it is extremely difficult to clarify which ones these are. First of all, America, having no respected group of leaders in shaping the public's artistic taste, especially in music,

---

edition: Claude Debussy, *Monsieur Croche et autres écrits,* ed. François Lesure (Paris: Gallimard, 1987), pp. 305–306, esp. 305.

22 This text ("Pour Nadia Boulanger") was written by Saint-John Perse for the eightieth-birthday celebrations of Nadia Boulanger, which took place in the Opéra de Monte-Carlo on 30 September 1967 under the patronage of the Prince and Princess of Monaco. The text was re-produced in facsimile in the program booklet (no page number). The gala event focused on a concert of the Orchestre National de Monte-Carlo under Igor Markevitch and was attended by distinguished guests from all over the world, including several of her former pupils, among them Aaron Copland, Virgil Thomson, Jean Françaix, and Elliott Carter.

Syringa (1977–78)

where there is no possibility of economic benefit from influencing the public taste, the structure of the music profession is built on a very different basis from that of Europe, which means that the public for concert music, which is very large and enthusiastic, is, in large part, conservative, although it is not opposed to contemporary work, but rather mystified by it. Similarly in a culture where there is not state-institutionalized schooling like the Conservatoire, through which almost all aspiring professionals must go, the education of musicians, reflecting almost every aspect of American culture, is extremely varied in quality, sometimes of an extremely high level and at others very low. This, of course, does not help to develop a clear-cut public opinion about American artists and, in general, makes them prefer Europeans, whose standards can be depended upon. All of this makes artistic judgements in composition like "conservative" or "avant-garde" have an entirely different meaning from that of more homogeneous artistic societies. In fact, such terms, like so many others, are not really applicable to American music in the way they were used by Europeans. For the one thing that can be said of American composers is that they form no school, although they have tried to, and that their work is, on the whole, anarchic in the light of European judgement. In fact our whole cultural life is very incoherent, and, in spite of a recent tendency to have the government partially support the arts, as has been happening in Europe for generations, it is very unlikely that any agreement to organize and build something like the Centre [Pompidou] could ever be [reached] by American public officials. All of our museums were financed and built by private individuals – and this illustrates the fundamental difference between French and American culture.

[Typescript, photocopy (later inaccurately dated "1975"); Elliott Carter Collection, Paul Sacher Foundation. Published in a French trans-lation in the catalogue for the exhibition held in the Centre Pompidou from 1 June to 19 September 1977: *Paris – New York,* ed. Pontus Hulten (Paris: Centre Pompidou, 1977), pp. 7–11; reprinted in the new edition *Paris – New York,* 1908–1968, ed. Pontus Hulten (Paris: Centre Pompidou/Gallimard, 1991), pp. 21–26.]

Carter did not approach a writer for his next vocal work, *Syringa,* as he had done for *A Mirror on Which to Dwell.* Instead John Ashbery (b. 1927), at that time a professor at Brooklyn College, took the initiative in early 1975 by asking the composer to consider the possibility of a collaboration.[23] In his reply Carter, who had long held Ashbery in high esteem, expressed his interest in principle but was unable to be specific because of other commitments (among other things he had not yet begun work on *A Symphony of Three Orchestras* commissioned by the New York Philharmonic). Instead, he proposed getting together to discuss the matter.[24] Over the next few years he made a deep study of Ashbery's poetry. Finally in 1977–78, he went to work on the long-cherished project. Not only did he set the book's title-poem *Syringa,* a profoundly ironic reflection on the ancient Orpheus myth (the title refers to the flower saxifrage which grows in limestone fissures),[25] he also lent a voice to the myth's "subtext" in the form of passages which he selected from such ancient Greek writers as Aeschylus, Archilochus, Hesiod, and Homer.[26] It was not least in this double perspective – the use of two simultaneous, mutually interacting textual layers – that Carter struck new ground with his treatment of poetry in this generically hybrid work, "a polytextual motet, a cantata, a chamber opera, a vocal double concerto – all in one" (Schiff 1983/1998, pp. 302–303 and 179, respectively). In retrospect, however, he emphasized that his bi- or polytextual approach had been inspired by such venerable models as the multi-lingual isothythmic motets of the late middle ages, Emilio de Cavalieri's *Rappresentazione di anima e di corpo,* and the two-voice madrigals of Claudio Monteverdi.[27] *Syringa* was premièred on 10 December 1978 by Jan DeGaetani (mezzo-soprano), Thomas Paul (bass), and Speculum Musicae, conducted by Harvey Sollberger at a New York concert in honor of Carter's seventieth birthday.

23 See letter from John Ashbery to Elliott Carter, 2 March 1975; Elliott Carter Collection, Paul Sacher Foundation.

24 See letter from Elliott Carter to John Ashbery, 30 March 1975; Elliott Carter Collection, Paul Sacher Foundation.

25 John Ashbery, "Syringa," in *Houseboat Days: Poems by John Ashbery* (Harmondsworth: Penguin Books; New York: Viking Press, 1977), pp. 69–71.

26 The sources of the Greek texts are identified in Schiff 1983/1998, pp. 312 and 188, respectively.

27 See Bernard, "Interview with Elliott Carter" (see above, p. 101, note 41), esp. p. 187, and Schiff 1983/1998, pp. 302 and 179, respectively. Carter evinced astonishment at the fact that Lawrence Kramer, in an essay, stressed the novelty of his "polyvocal" approach; see Lawrence Kramer, "'Syringa': John Ashbery and Elliott Carter," in *Beyond Amazement: New Essays on*

John Ashbery, ed. David Lehman (Ithaca and London: Cornell University Press, 1980), pp. 255–71, reprinted in revised form as "Song As Insight – John Ashbery, Elliott Carter, and Orpheus," in Lawrence Kramer, *Music and Poetry: The Nineteenth Century and After* (Berkeley and Los Angeles: University of California Press, 1984), pp. 203–221. Kramer, for his part, felt misunderstood and reaffirmed his position in a letter to the editor of *Perspectives of New Music* 29/1 (Winter 1991), p. 335.

Praise from John Hollander (1978)

123 *Syringa,* for mezzo-soprano, bass, guitar, and ten instrumentalists (1977–78), on texts by John Ashbery and ancient Greek authors, short score draft in pencil with markings in colored pencil (mm. "43"–"52" [= mm. 54–65 of the final score])

In *Syringa,* as in his other vocal works, Carter set down the course of the two vocal parts very precisely at an early stage of the compositional process before advancing on the elaboration of the instrumental part. The result of this working out of the vocal lines is documented in the draft shown here, written in August–September 1977, in which the instrumental part is at times only jotted down in skeletal form. Here we see mm. "43"–"52" from this draft, corresponding to mm. 54–65 in the finished score and equipped with the Greek and English text in the bottom two staves. (The textual underlay is still missing in the upper two staves, where the rhythm of the female voice also occurs in an alternative notation that was later reproduced in the printed score.) The visible continuity of the vocal layer at this point is typical of large parts of the work: the bass and mezzo-soprano either overlap, as at the beginning of our example, or alternate, as they do in the third system. Only rarely is the flow of the words interrupted by relatively long passages of purely instrumental music. Equally characteristic is the fact that on the whole the bass voice, in keeping with the "elevated" tone of the Greek texts, moves in larger intervals and more complex rhythms than the mezzo-soprano, which responds in fairly plain fashion to the deliberately sober language of Ashbery's poem. Moreover in m. "48," after the Euripides quotation "moros gar apotomos plathé" ["for doom, fathomless, approaches"], Carter has inserted a bold vertical line and added the time of the preceding and the following sections (5" and 33", respectively) in order to indicate the change of emotional perspective at this point. This change occurs in the form of the entrance of Ashbery's Apollo, who dismisses Orpheus's laments for Eurydice as futile. In the fully worked-out score, Apollo's words are ultimately introduced by a brief solo for English horn (mm. 60–61) and an instrumental movement that assigns an especially prominent role to the guitar, the modern equivalent of the god's emblematic instrument, the lyre.

The publication of Allen Edwards's book-length interview with Carter in 1971, *Flawed Words and Stubborn Sounds* (*FW*), marked the beginning of a steady increase in literature about the composer and his music. There had already been significant discussions of Carter's music by Richard Franko Goldman, William Glock, George Rochberg, Joseph Kerman, Martin Boykan, Arnold Whittall, Richard Kostelanetz, and others, but the vast majority of articles on Carter (and all the subsequent books) were to follow the Edwards monograph.[28] The publication of *The Writings of Elliott Carter* (*WEC*) in 1977 (a year before Carter's seventieth birthday) was the second major milestone in the Carter literature and elicited widespread interest. Edited and compiled by Else Stone and Kurt Stone (Carter's former music editor at Associated Music Publishers), the 390-page volume presents a large selection of Carter's writings in chronological order, ranging from his earliest reviews for *Modern Music* in the 1930s to his program note for *A Symphony of Three Orchestras* (1976). Several reviewers were impressed by the "extensive humane learning" that lay behind Carter's reviews and descriptive texts on his own and others' music.[29] Robert Morgan, in a little-known review in *The Nation,* pointed out that Carter's evolving views on Ives tell us more about Carter's music and aesthetic position than they do about Ives, whose music was at that time in the middle of a major revival. Morgan also noted that "Carter conceives of musical events in essentially dramatic terms," a critical trope that would become standard in the later literature on Carter's music.[30]

Carter had known John Hollander (b. 1929) since the early 1950s, when the young poet was living in New York writing liner notes for classical music albums to support himself after graduating from Columbia University. The contact could have come about through Carter's friend Mark Van Doren, who had taught Hollander at Columbia. The musically-inclined Hollander wrote texts for composers including Milton Babbitt (*Philomel* and other works), Alexander Goehr, and Hugo Weisgall. Much later (in 1994), Carter set five of Hollander's poems under the title *Of Challenge and of Love.* Not wanting simply to acknowledge receipt of the book, Hollander waited to respond until he had read it through. His answer to Carter is thoughtful and affectionate.

---

28 See entries 667, 663, 749, 686, 624, 810, and 691 in Link 2000.

29 Barney Childs, review of *WEC, Notes* 35/1 (September 1978), pp. 69–70, esp. 70.

30 Robert Morgan, "The Musician's Dialogue," *The Nation* 225/20 (10 December 1977), pp. 630–632 (not listed in Link 2000).

124 John Hollander to Elliott Carter, 11 (1?) January 1978

Yale University / New Haven, Connecticut 06520 /
Department of English / Linsly-Chittenden Hall /
Box 3545 / (203) 432-4454

Dear Elliott,

The excessive lateness of this communication (your *Writings* arrived nearly two months ago) is I hope excusable because of the very nature of the acknowledgment, given the book in question. In a case like this, acknowledgment of receipt is not enough, and I couldn't bear merely to thank you and to express my eager anticipation of "getting down to" (*down*?!?) reading it soon. I wanted to say I had read you, and I'm sorry that it took so long before there was any time. But there has been – most recently – and the time surrendered itself almost immediately, totally giving in to your pages. Some pieces I had seen, others (early ones in particular) never. I loved reading you on ballet, and your youthful reviewing was moving and exciting – it conjured up so much of the musical scene of the period that the official reviewing, read in retrospect, seldom does for me: the commitment, the enthusiasm, the impatience, of a serious and important composer comes through even in the brief pieces, even through the decorum.

All the rest of the chronicles and the theoretical writings are equally moving and impressive – so free of narrow polemic, so full of the sense – even the *insistence* – that musical knowledge is part of, as well as representative of, humane knowledge generally. The authority of the voice of the later pieces, particularly when you are deploring the departure of meaning from some newer music (the example of the palindrome that doesn't *say* anything is wonderfully resonant),[31] is one for which all artists of any kind can be grateful. What you say comes not from petulance nor impatience but from – and how awkward the archaic word seems to our fallen pens – wisdom.

Your editors have done you well, I suppose; but it seems more than possible that whatever selection they had made, the effect of energy, seriousness, a relevant and cogent presence of literary and artistic culture, and the kind of stylistic clarity that is always more than clarity of surface, would all have made themselves known. Your thought about music, and your music about thought, seem more closely connected than are left and right hands.

The book is handsome as well as virtuous. Thank you so much for thinking of me. My friend Natalie joins me in New Year greetings to you and Helen.[32]

As ever,
John

[Autograph letter; Elliott Carter Collection, Paul Sacher Foundation. Reprinted by permission of John Hollander.]

---

31 See Elliott Carter, "A Further Step" (see above, p. 130, note 27), in *WEC*, pp. 185–191, esp. 191; reprinted in *CEL*, pp. 5–11, esp. 10. Carter refers in this passage to the expansion of the serial principle, in integral serial music, to include parameters other than pitch. He goes on to comment: "The real problem of such music-puzzles is illustrated simply by the verbal palindrome ('able was I ere I saw Elba'), which has to obey both a strict patterning of letters and has to make sense into the bargain. A palindrome of random letters is a bit pointless in itself. Although musical meaning is not quite so easy to establish, still up to the end of Webern's life this double standard of order and of meaning applied to all such types of musical ingenuity, with the exception perhaps of certain medieval and early renaissance works. But the recent European school seems to have become occupied with pattern alone, hoping somehow that interest and meaning would emerge."

32 The Philadelphia-born artist Natalie Charkow became Hollander's wife a short while later.

A Letter from Oliver Knussen (1978)

Few musicians have done as much for the dissemination of Carter's music in recent decades as has the English composer and conductor Oliver Knussen (b. 1952). Knussen began to take an interest in Carter's music already as a teenager; indeed, his encounter with the *Piano Concerto* and the *Double Concerto* in 1968 was a sort of musical rite of passage. In 1970 he met Carter personally while studying in Tanglewood with Gunther Schuller. On 1 March 1978, ten years after his initial acquaintance, he again heard a performance of the *Piano Concerto*, this time in London's Royal Festival Hall.[33] The concert prompted him to write the following letter, in which he recalls his early encounters with Carter's music and expresses his unstinting admiration. It was the beginning of an ever-closer relationship which, among other things, left its mark in Knussen's many performances and recordings of Carter's works and Carter's dedication to Knussen of the *Allegro scorrevole* (1996–97) and the duo *Au Quai* for viola and bassoon (2002). The latter work, a present to Knussen on his fiftieth birthday, led Carter to write the following words of appreciation for the occasion: "As modernism seemed headed for shipwreck, Olly Knussen, treasuring the wonderful works that that movement produced and still does, stepped into the breach and with extraordinary musicianship, artistic awareness, and great care not only brought these works to a vivid, enthusiastic life which had long been concealed, but also added significant works of his own."[34]

125 **Oliver Knussen to Elliott Carter, 2 March 1978**

Cholesbury Road Nursery / Tring. / Herts. HP236PD
March 2nd, 1978

Dear Mr. Carter –
Sometimes it is impossible to express what one feels vocally, especially to someone one admires – one flounders around hopelessly for words, & they come out sounding sycophantic & wrong to an embarrassing extent. That was what I felt happened to me last night after the performance of the *Piano Concerto*, so I'm sitting down to try & write it out.

When I was about 14 I bought a 2nd-hand copy of the record (but not a score) of your *Double Concerto*, which I liked a lot on my level then but, I know now, didn't "get" at all. When I first came to New York a few years later in April 1968 I bought as many new records of American music as I could (I already loved Ives, Copland, & late Irving Fine) – the record of your *Piano Conc[erto]* had just come out, so I bought it. A few days later (before I had heard it), I saw the 2-piano score in the Schirmer showroom, opened it, realized this was something quite new for me in terms of musical content (& notation!), & bought that too, ordering the score of the *Double [Concerto]* while I was at it. The next few months I was holed up in my grandmother's apartment in Chicago & I listened to the record of the *P[iano] C[oncerto]* with the score, also bashing out what bits I could on the piano, every day of that time. In May (I think) I found out that it was being played in Chicago and went along to all the rehearsals and the concert.[35] Despite the fact that people had told me that you were a good person I didn't have the courage to go up and say anything to you – the truth was that I couldn't express verbally what that music meant & *still* means to me – so you might now understand a little bit why I couldn't stop talking when I finally met you at Tanglewood!

Although it was underplayed in Chicago, or "boring" as you said last night, that experience did at least prove to me that it was possible for such complex music to work "live" (I was even more naïve then). But the music itself taught me much more: it was the first really advanced music I could respond to emotionally, because I found the lines beautiful (damn that programme-note man and his "[t]waddle") and memorable, the temporal juxtaposition

---

33 The performers were Charles Rosen (piano) and the BBC Symphony Orchestra conducted by Charles Mackerras.

34 Program booklet for the concerts on 12 June 2002 in Queen Elizabeth Hall, London ("Knussen at 50: A Celebration"), no page number.

35 The *Piano Concerto* was performed in Chicago on 24–25 May 1968 by Jacob Lateiner (piano) and the Chicago Symphony Orchestra under Jean Martinon.

of those lines so free & yet controlled, the large form so clear & directional, the details so rewarding & mind-tickling, and the orchestral "realization" of them so successful. It was the first advanced music I had heard in which everything was heard, expressive (even the "pointillism", as I then thought it, was linear) & expansive but paced with a Stravinsky-like concision in its own terms. This was the embodiment of a music I had hitherto only dreamt could exist. I did *not* find it "intellectually pugilistic" even if I knew what that meant, & have never understood why people refer to the piece which knocked me for six on a gut level as "forbidding" – *formidable* maybe. In any case, literally the first thing I did after walking in the door (after 24 sleepless hours) on my return home to England was at long last to listen to the *Double Conc[erto]* with the score, twice in succession!

For the following year (a long time to me then) everything I wrote was inept imitation Carter in one way or another. A bit later Michael Steinberg heard something of mine for the first time, & when he wrote that my music showed obvious traces of your influence I could not have been happier. Since then I have listened to your *Variations* & *Concerto for Orchestra* more than practically any other post-1920 pieces except *Lulu*, whose composer holds about the same position in my musical hierarchy as you do – that is, as one of the half-dozen composers of any time whose standards I try to keep in mind when I compose & who are, in a sense, "responsible" for the very notes I write. Finally, a large part of my "growing up" as a composer has been in coming to terms with what you can do technically that I just can't, and finding alternative ways of dealing with these deficiencies of mine.

I hope you aren't annoyed by this outpouring, but the shattering experience of hearing the *Piano Concerto* "live" again after 10 years, whatever the performance, has brought it all home to me as it was the first time I ever heard any of your music –

With best wishes,
Oliver Knussen

P.S. May I dedicate something to you on your 70th birthday? (It won't be finished for a while, but...)[36]

[Autograph letter; Elliott Carter Collection, Paul Sacher Foundation. Reprinted by permission of Oliver Knussen.]

A Late Exchange with Nadia Boulanger (1978)

For decades Carter sent Nadia Boulanger birthday greetings every 16th of September – as in 1978, when his former teacher was approaching her ninety-first birthday. Though ill and infirm (she had been forced the previous summer to give up her courses at the Conservatoire Américain and to abandon or delegate her private lessons, and had just returned from hospital), she thanked Carter in the following letter, written on her birthday. Carter responded on 9 November 1978 with a letter in which he alluded, not without pride, to the many concerts devoted to him in honor of his seventieth birthday. Hardly a week later Boulanger expressed her admiration, adding a note of regret that her frail health prohibited her from taking part in musical life. A year after this exchange of letters, on 22 October 1979, Nadia Boulanger died at the age of ninety-two.

126 Nadia Boulanger to Elliott and Helen Carter, 16 September 1978
(English translation in Appendix 1, p. 349)

Le Directeur / Conservatoire Américain /
77305 Palais de Fontainebleau
16 septembre 1978

Chère Helen et cher Elliott,
Par votre vue si noble de la vie, vous représentez ce qui nous dirige tous.[37] Je vous remercie mal, car je suis encore en grande déficience, mais vous sentirez probablement tout ce que je ne puis exprimer. Je me croyais à l'entrée même de l'inconnu, puis toutes ces fleurs, tous ces télégrammes, toutes ces lettres représentant une si grande tendresse, vous forcent à essayer de vous reprendre et de retrouver un semblant de force. Vous parlez du mois de mars,[38] mais la semaine dernière je croyais encore que je ne vivrais pas jusqu'au 16, et maintenant, n'étant pas mieux, je brûle d'impatience à l'attente de vos dernières œuvres. Pardonnez-moi de vous le dire si mal, mais de tout cœur, en toute fidélité – votre

[N. B.]

[Autograph letter; Elliott Carter Collection, Paul Sacher Foundation. Reprinted by permission of the Fondation Internationale Nadia et Lili Boulanger.]

---

36 The piece that Knussen dedicated to Carter on his seventieth birthday was *Coursing (Etude 1)*, op.17, for chamber orchestra (1978–79, rev. 1981).

37 Carter, in his greeting on Boulanger's ninety-first birthday, had expressed his thanks "pour tout ce que vous avez fait pour nous, pour la musique [...] et pour tout ce que vous représentez humaine-ment de courage, de noblesse, de sérieux et de dévouement" [for everything you have done for us, for music (...) and for everything you represent in terms of human courage, *noblesse*, seriousness and dedication]. (Letter from Elliott Carter to Nadia Boulanger, 11 September 1978, Fonds Nadia Boulanger, Bibliothèque Nationale de France.)

38 Carter had written the following in his letter (ibid.): "Nous espérons pouvoir venir à Paris au mois de mars pour le plaisir de vous revoir." [We hope to be able to come to Paris in March and look forward to the pleasure of seeing you again.]

127 Elliott Carter to Nadia Boulanger, 9 November 1978
(English translation in Appendix 1, p. 350)

Le 9 novembre 1978
Waccabuc, New York, / 10597

Chère Mademoiselle,
Mille remerciements pour la lettre, si émouvante, que vous m'avez écrite après votre anniversaire, qui m'a profondément touché. J'espère qu'en recevant celle-ci vous allez mieux et que vous avez pu reprendre un peu cette vie musicale qui nous est toujours et a toujours été une inspiration très importante.

Cette année, ma 70ème, se célèbre par des concerts de ma musique à New York, Los Angeles, Washington, Hartford.[39] Ici on a déjà donné un concert de mes œuvres des années 30–40,[40] et le Juilliard Quartet a joué ma sonate pour violoncelle, mon *Duo*, mon 2ème quatuor[41] et le New York Philharmonic joue mon *Piano Concerto* à la fin du mois[42] et puis on donne mon *Double Concerto* et deux cycles de chants avec orchestre de chambre le 10 décembre.[43] Le 11, mon anniversaire, on joue mes *Variations*.[44] Les répétitions commencent déjà à être un peu désœuvrantes –

Je vous envoie la brochure que mes éditeurs anglais ont fait paraître pour cette occasion, espérant que cela vous donnerait plaisir.

Affectueusement
Elliott

[Autograph letter; Fonds Nadia Boulanger, Bibliothèque Nationale de France. Reprinted by permission of the Fondation Internationale Nadia et Lili Boulanger.]

128 Nadia Boulanger to Elliott Carter, 14 November 1978
(English translation in Appendix 1, p. 350)

Paris, ce 14 novembre 1978

Quelle lettre, cher Elliott! Qui vous apporte, vous le musicien, vous l'ami, vous mon cher Elliott.

Devez-vous venir en Europe au mois de juillet ou d'août? J'aimerais beaucoup le savoir prochainement.

Sentez avec quelle sincérité et quelle confiance je vous suis toujours. Sentez que je rêve de vous revoir, mais cela est imprudent, car je ne sais trop combien de temps je serai là, plus ou moins à végeter, mais après tout c'est avec la même passion que je donne mon attention, alors peut-être, vaut-il mieux pas stipuler avec le temps.

Je regrette de n'être pas parmi ceux qui entendront celles de vos œuvres qui vont être présentées, comme un faisceau vous entourant et vous éclairant.

A vous deux toute ma tendre et profonde affection,
N. B.

[Typed letter with autograph signature; Elliott Carter Collection, Paul Sacher Foundation. Reprinted by permission of the Fondation Internationale Nadia et Lili Boulanger.]

---

39 On the New York concerts, see notes 41–45. An "Elliott Carter Day" was proclaimed by the Mayor of the City of Los Angeles on 27 April 1979. The Washington tribute was arranged by the Library of Congress, which, on 7 October 1978, held a lecture-recital with Charles Rosen (on the *Piano Sonata*) and a chamber recital with Paul Zukofsky, Gilbert Kalish, and members of the Juilliard String Quartet (*Elegy*, *Pastoral*, *Sonata for Violoncello and Piano*, *Duo for Violin and Piano*, and *String Quartet No. 2*). Finally, on 1 and 3 February 1979, the Hartt College of Music in Hartford, CT, held two concerts entitled "An Elliott Carter

Retrospective on the Composer's 70th Birthday." The first featured *The Harmony of Morning*, the *Sonata for Violoncello and Piano*, the *Duo for Violin and Piano*, and the *Variations for Orchestra*, the second consisted of *String Quartets Nos. 1, 2,* and *3,* played by the Composers String Quartet.

40 On 26 October 1978 the League of Composers and the ISCM held a concert in the Carnegie Recital Hall entitled "Carter and the Previous Generation." In addition to works by Walter Piston and Leo Ornstein, it included Carter's *Elegy*, the piano songs *Warble for Lilac Time*, *Voyage* and *Three Poems of Robert Frost*, and the *Sonata for Flute, Oboe, Cello, and Harpsichord*.

41 This recital took place in the Juilliard School on 7 November 1978. In addition to the *Sonata for Violoncello and Piano* (played by Joel Krosnick and Gilbert Kalish), the *Duo for Violin and Piano* (Robert Mann, Gilbert Kalish), and *String Quartet No. 2* (Juilliard String Quartet), the program also included the *Eight Etudes and a Fantasy* performed by the Atlantic Woodwind Quartet.

42 Carter's *Piano Concerto* was performed by Ursula Oppens (piano) and the New York Philharmonic under Zubin Mehta in Alice Tully Hall on 30 November and 1–2 December 1978.

Night Fantasies (1978–80)

With *Night Fantasies*, written in Waccabuc and Rome and completed on 12 April 1980, Carter produced his first solo piano work since the *Piano Sonata* more than thirty years earlier.[45] But he had never stopped composing for piano; in addition to the two concertos (*Double Concerto* and *Piano Concerto*), other works, including the *Cello Sonata*, the *Concerto for Orchestra, A Symphony of Three Orchestras, A Mirror on Which to Dwell*, and the *Duo for Violin and Piano*, contain prominent piano parts. Even though Carter has rediscovered the solo piano in recent years, the *Piano Sonata* and *Night Fantasies* (both about twenty minutes long) remain his only large-scale solo works for the instrument.[46] The four pianists who commissioned *Night Fantasies* – Paul Jacobs (who organized the project), Gilbert Kalish, Ursula Oppens, and Charles Rosen – were experienced performers of Carter's music and greatly esteemed by him. The composer acknowledged: "The step-by-step change from the *Piano Sonata* to the *Fantasies* is […] not only the result of a personal development but also of the collaborative encouragement these pianists gave."[47] The piece is ferociously difficult, even by Carter's standards. Ursula Oppens, a passionately engaged virtuoso of a wide range of modern idioms, played the première of *Night Fantasies* on 2 June 1980, less than two months after it had been completed.[48] Identifying specific passages of *Night Fantasies* that might have been composed with the playing styles and personalities of each of the four performers in mind, as Carter has hinted, has become a kind of musicological parlor game (which will be briefly engaged in below). But more significant than any kind of secret code – if there is one – is the sheer variety of the piano writing. David Schiff, who studied with Carter at the time, relates: "Quite early in the course of composing the work he told me that he had already written fifty different kinds of piano music, and was now looking for ways to bring them together."[49] In this work Carter continues to explore the limits of disjunct and nonlinear musical structure. Whereas in previous works (such as the *String Quartet No. 3* and *A Symphony of Three Orchestras*) discrete sections of music with a particular character were still identifiable (even if these overlapped or were heard simultaneously), in *Night Fantasies* the rates of change between different textures and characters are so rapid, and the links between them so smooth, that the form has become more processual than architectonic in nature.

129 *Night Fantasies,* for piano (1978–80), autograph draft in pencil with markings in colored pencil (mm. "278"–"296" [= mm. 316–334 of the final score])

The passage from the first complete draft, dating from February–March 1980, shows how Carter literally assembled the score from short fragments of music. John Link describes how Carter numbered the different sketches (with the numbers circled in purple) and "simply pinned them to the wall of his studio and rearranged them until he found an ordering he liked."[50] Then he would write (or paste) the passage into the draft score, sometimes altering the notation so that it would fit into the rhythmic scheme. On this page four distinct piano idioms can be heard in sequence: 1) a partly imitative, two-part texture (the first two measures of the page [= mm. 316–317 of the final score]) that began a few measures earlier, 2) faster *leggero* writing in the right hand, both against steady eighth notes (second system) and 3) alone (end of the second system and beginning of the third), and 4) slow-moving staggered chords with moving inner voices (end of the third system to the bottom of the page). (The latter texture continues until m. "309" [347], creating one of the most extended continuous sections in the piece.) At the top of the page the pulse is quarter = 94.5 (or half = 47.25), which is also the pulse of the beginning of the piece. Carter calculated the polyrhythm using fractional metronome markings (which are indicated in the final score) because he wanted to use "only those tempi that would allow every pulse to be precisely notated." (Schiff 1983/1998, 321 and 218, respectively.) The pulse of quarter = 94.5 in

43 This recital, held in Alice Tully Hall, was given by Speculum Musicae together with the guest performers Susan Davenny Wyner (soprano), Jan DeGaetani (mezzo-soprano), Thomas Paul (bass), Paul Jacobs (harpsichord), Harvey Sollberger (conductor), and the American Brass Quintet. In addition to the *Double Concerto* and the song cycles *A Mirror on Which to Dwell* and *Syringa,* the program also included the *Brass Quintet.*

44 The *Variations for Orchestra* were performed in Alice Tully Hall on 11 December 1978 during a concert of the American Composers Orchestra, conducted by Dennis Russell Davies.

45 From the beginning of November 1979 until the end of February 1980 Carter was again in residence at the American Academy in Rome.

46 Carter's recent solo piano music includes *90+* (1994), *Two Diversions* (2000), *Retrouvailles* (2000), *Intermittences* (2006), *Caténaires* (2006), and *Matribute* (2007). The longest of these (*Two Diversions*) lasts eight minutes.

47 Elliott Carter, liner notes to Paul Jacobs's 1982 recording of *Night Fantasies* and *Piano Sonata,* Paul Jacobs, piano (Nonesuch 79047-1).

48 She received the score in three installments; see John Link, "The Composition of Carter's *Night Fantasies," Sonus* 14/2 (Spring 1994), pp. 67–89, esp. 84. The numerous works written for Oppens, who was also a founding member of Speculum Musicae, include Frederic Rzewski's *The People United Will Never Be Defeated* (1975).

49 Schiff 1983/1998, pp. 316 and 214, respectively.

50 Link, "The Composition of Carter's *Night Fantasies*" (see note 49), pp. 79–80.

129 *Night Fantasies*

Prizewinner in Munich (1981)

fact contains within it both of the slower pulses that make up the large-scale polyrhythm: MM 8.75 (here, 54 sixteenth-note quintuplets) and MM 10.8 (here, 35 normal sixteenths). The right hand has the quintuplet values and the left has the sixteenths. The right and left hands in mm. "276"–"279" play five against four – there are no simultaneities, but many of the notes come very close. While all four pianists for whom the work was written could handle this passage, it demands the extraordinary rhythmic precision for which Paul Jacobs was justifiably famous. In the second system the texture shifts to a faster, *leggero* music, the kind of rapid virtuoso figuration that Oppens could toss off with aplomb. Finally, the low-register passage in the lower half of the page is similar to the "recitativo collerico" earlier in the work (mm. 235ff. in the final score). Many have associated this "hot-tempered recitative" with Charles Rosen, because of his legendary rhetorical brilliance and eagerness to argue.[51] These passages, if they have any connection to the musicians, are not portraits, but brief homages to their special strengths.

The chord that begins in the left hand in the first measure of the third system has the duration of MM 21.6, as does the following chord in the left hand: these are "eighth notes" in the basic 10.8 pulse. The pitches unfold an all-interval twelve-note sonority, using common tones to shift slowly from chord to chord. Some years earlier, Carter had read with great enthusiasm an article by Stefan Bauer-Mengelberg and Melvin Ferentz that listed some all-interval twelve-tone rows.[52] Carter had already used similar collections himself. The authors offered to send a printout of all 1,928 such rows upon request. Since Bauer-Mengelberg lived nearby, Carter asked him for a copy, and consulted this chart regularly for many years.[53]

Among the many awards Carter has received is one of the most prestigious, the Ernst von Siemens Prize (1981). Carter was the first American to win this award. He owed his nomination to his friend Pierre Boulez, who wrote to him in May 1980: "[...] I was very happy that my proposition was taken up unanimously, and I hope that you will be able to make the trip to Munich in April 81 (more or less) to receive it officially. Practise your German in the meantime!"[54] By then Carter had already received the following official notification from Paul Sacher, the chairman of the Board of Trustees, and formally accepted the award. This was the beginning of his contact with Sacher, which would later become important in another way: not only did the famous Basel conductor and arts patron commission him to write an oboe concerto for Heinz Holliger in summer 1985, he also invited Carter, in early 1986, to entrust all his music manuscripts and other working materials to the Paul Sacher Foundation (see below, p. 283). The official awards ceremony of the Ernst von Siemens Prize took place in the Bavarian Academy of Fine Arts, Munich, on 8 April 1981. The laudatory address was delivered in German by William Glock,[55] and Carter expressed his gratitude, likewise in German, in the speech reproduced here for the first time in the original English. The ceremony was rounded off by a performance of the *Sonata for Violoncello and Piano* by Jan Polasek (cello) and Barbara Korn (piano). The award certificate reads as follows: "Die Ernst von Siemens Stiftung verleiht Elliott Carter den Ernst-von-Siemens-Musikpreis in Würdigung seiner großen Verdienste um die Erschließung neuer musikalischer Dimensionen, die ihn in zahlreichen Werken voller Originalität zu einem der führenden Komponisten der Gegenwart geprägt haben." [The Ernst von Siemens Foundation awards Elliott Carter the Ernst von Siemens Music Prize in appreciation of his meritorious achievements in the opening up of new musical dimensions, which, in works abounding with originality, have made him a leading composer of the present day.]

51 Will Crutchfield, "Paul Jacobs Talks About Carter and Messiaen," *Keynote: A Magazine for the Musical Arts (WNCN Program Guide)* 7/10 (December 1983), pp. 18–24, esp. 23.

52 Stefan Bauer-Mengelberg and Melvin Ferentz, "On Eleven-Interval Twelve-Tone Rows," *Perspectives of New Music*, 3/2 (Spring–Summer 1965), pp. 93–103. We are grateful to John Link for identifying this article and for providing information about Carter and Bauer-

Mengelberg (personal communications, 28 November and 4 December 2007).

53 John Link has identified a further grouping of all-interval 12-tone chords: those that have the all-trichord hexachord 012478 as a contiguous subset. Carter used these in *Symphonia* and other works; they have become known as "Link" chords, and are listed in Schiff 1998, pp. 325–327.

54 Letter from Pierre Boulez to Elliott Carter, 22 May 1980; Elliott Carter Collection, Paul Sacher Foundation.

55 Glock's appreciation was published in German translation both in a private print of the Ernst von Siemens Music Foundation and in the collection *Die Musik und ihr Preis: Die internationale Ernst von Siemens Stiftung: Eine Dokumentation über 20 Jahre Ernst von Siemens Musikpreis (1973–1993)*, ed. Rüdiger von Canal and Günther Weiss (Regensburg: ConBrio, 1994), pp. 142–150. The original English version appeared as "'Greatness in Our Time Can Only Be Solitary': An Appreciation," *Sonus* 19/1 (Fall 1998), pp. 3–11.

130 **Paul Sacher to Elliott Carter, 18 April 1980**

Ernst von Siemens Stiftung / Das Kuratorium
Paul Sacher / Schönenberg / CH-4133 Pratteln BL
April 18th, 1980

Dear Mr. Carter,

I have the great pleasure to inform you that the Ernst von Siemens Foundation decided to award next year the Ernst von Siemens Prize to you. If you are ready to accept it, it will be presented to you in Munich on April 9th, 1981, or some date nearby.[56]

It is the custom that on this occasion a *Laudatio* on the prizewinner should be read, and if you agree we would like to ask Sir William Glock to do so.

The prize consists in a sum of Sfr. 150,000.—
The precedent prizewinners are:

1973 Benjamin Britten
1975 Olivier Messiaen
1976 Mstislav Rostropovitch
1977 Herbert von Karajan
1978 Rudolf Serkin
1979 Pierre Boulez
1980 Dietrich Fischer-Dieskau.

I hope to hear from you soon and would be very happy about your consent.

I remain, with best wishes and kind regards,
Sincerely yours,

The President of the Kuratorium
Ernst von Siemens Stiftung
Paul Sacher

Mr. Elliott Carter / 31 West 12th Street, / New York /
N.Y. 10011

[Typed letter with autograph signature; Elliott Carter Collection, Paul Sacher Foundation.]

131 **Elliott Carter to Paul Sacher, 27 April 1980**

Dr. Paul Sacher / Schönenberg / CH-4133 Pratteln BL
April 27, 1980

Dear Dr. Sacher:

I am greatly honored and pleased that the Ernst von Siemens Foundation has decided to award the Ernst von Siemens Prize to me next year. To be the fourth composer among such eminent musicians to be so chosen is highly flattering to me, and I proudly accept. I will be glad to come to Munich at whatever date is decided upon in April, 1981, and receive the prize. To have Sir William Glock read the Laudatio will add to the honor of the occasion.

Being most grateful that the Siemens Foundation wishes to give me this award, I would like to thank its advisors. Indeed, to read your name, Paul Sacher, on a letter to me has made me very happy, for I have often read it on dedications of musical scores that I admire very much, and have always had the greatest respect for your musical judgment.

Yours sincerely,
[Elliott Carter]

[Typed letter, carbon copy; Paul Sacher Collection, Paul Sacher Foundation.]

---

56 As mentioned above, the awards ceremony ultimately took place on 8 April 1981.

132 Elliott Carter, acceptance speech for the Ernst von Siemens Music Prize (1981)

[Dear Dr. von Siemens, ladies and gentlemen:]
When asked to make a personal appearance on public occasions, and especially this most important one, I see myself as an impostor, drawing attention to my person rather than to the compositions which in many ways have created me, not I them. If it were not for them, my presence would be of little interest. Certainly it is they who are really awarded this prize, and if they could speak the language of everyday life, they would, I am sure, be extremely grateful for being considered so significant by the advisors of the Foundation, and grateful to Herr Ernst von Siemens for having set up this generous award, and for the wonderful talk about them by Sir William Glock. Besides, if these compositions could speak, they would, I imagine, also express their surprise at being singled out from among the many musical works of our time, and could consider this recognition largely a matter of good fortune. For their reputation, such as it is, is probably more the result of many factors other than their intrinsic merit. For, certainly, they have become known through the efforts of a number of excellent performers who have spent much time, skill, and imagination in presenting them publicly. Without such committed instrumentalists and singers, general understanding and appreciation even of the best of musical works is hardly possible, while with such good performers even inferior ones can be persuasive. So a good share of the honor of this prize should go to performers.

Another share should go to the long-suffering, patient audiences made up of a small group of adventurous music lovers who, since the rise of public concerts, have courageously listened to so many relatively uninteresting works of newly composed music in the hope of finding a few scores that made the trial worthwhile. Surely these deserve honor, because their faith that some really good scores would eventually appear has been a great stimulus to performers' and composers' efforts, including my own. It is this group that has been so lavish in its support of the entire musical life as we know it, not only encouraging composers in each generation, but creating a situation that allowed the development of a background of musical skill, aesthetic vision, and artistic standards of many contrasting types.

Finally, in listing the various things to which contemporary compositions owe a debt, and perhaps the most important, are the human feelings and thoughts new music evokes that are only partially unique to their composer, being mainly made up of the experiences all of us have had living in this very turbulent century, trying to understand it, trying to find a way of living in the midst of its appalling problems and its over-publicized consumerist hedonism.

If the music honored here today gives the kind of pleasure gotten from important artistic accomplishments and rises above the level of transitory novelty, it is because of this rich background that my country shares with Europe. That music composed so far away from this artistic milieu physically and culturally finds a response here is a heart-warming sign of the brotherhood of artists and music lovers that transcends international boundaries and cultural barriers.

It is, therefore, on behalf of my compositions that I thank the Ernst von Siemens Foundation for this wonderful prize. With it, I shall be able to help many devoted, selfless performers of contemporary music to present worthy new works, hoping that some of these, in their turn, will become important to musical audiences and be honored here.

[Typescript, carbon copy; archive of the Ernst von Siemens Music Foundation, Munich. Carter's speech was published in German translation, along with William Glock's appreciation, in a private publication of the Siemens Foundation as "Dankesworte von Elliott Carter," *Ernst-von-Siemens-Musikpreis 1981, Sir William Glock, Laudatio auf Elliott Carter*, pp. 19–22.]

A Recommendation for Leonard Bernstein (1981)

Although Carter's musical interests were vastly different from those of Leonard Bernstein (1918–1990), and although he knew that he was far from being Bernstein's preferred composer, he always bore respect and admiration for the achievements of his famous colleague. His appreciation also applied to Bernstein's compositions, as became apparent when he nominated Bernstein for membership in the American Academy of Arts and Letters in early 1981 – a gesture for which the great conductor briefly but warmly thanked him after his election. Carter, a member of the Academy from 1956, later recalled his acquaintance with Bernstein: "I've known Bernstein ever since he was a student at Harvard. At that time Aaron Copland gave a party for him. That was where I met him, and I was very much taken by this young man who sat down at the piano as soon as he arrived and went on playing passionately for the rest of the evening. It was clear he had a lot of talent and would have a great career, and I felt an immediate liking for him that has lasted through time." (CC, p. 72.)

133 Elliott Carter, nomination of Leonard Bernstein for induction into the American Academy of Arts and Letters (1981)

Nomination for Membership in the American Academy of Arts and Letters
Date: Academy meeting, 5/20/81

We have the honor to nominate
LEONARD BERNSTEIN
for membership in the American Academy of Arts and Letters.

(Signatures of five or more Members of the Academy)
1. Elliott Carter
2. Malcolm Cowley
3. Jack Levine
4. John Updike
5. Richard Wilbur

Citation:
Leonard Bernstein is America's most renowned musician because he has gained a universal reputation as conductor of classical music, as pedagogue, and as composer of outstanding scores of concert music and of music for the theatre. His concern with broad communication has led him to write very telling, highly imaginative works for Broadway that have freshness and newness and yet wide appeal. His concert works of wide variety have captured musical audiences everywhere.

Elliott Carter

[Typescript, photocopy; Elliott Carter Collection, Paul Sacher Foundation.]

134 Leonard Bernstein to Elliott Carter, 14 December 1981

Leonard Bernstein

Mr. Elliott Carter / 31 West 12th Street /New York, NY 10003
December 14, 1981

Dear Elliott:
My election to the Academy has touched me deeply, and my thanks go to you, dear Elliott, for having initiated this honor. That I occupy dear Sam Barber's chair is especially moving for me, and I will strive to be worthy of it.[57]

Please accept my best wishes for the holiday season, and again, my thanks.

With affection and esteem,
Your old friend
Lenny

[Typed letter with autograph salutation, greetings, and signature; Elliott Carter Collection, Paul Sacher Foundation. © Amberson Holdings LLC. Reprinted by permission of the Leonard Bernstein Office, Inc.]

---

57 Samuel Barber, a member of the American Academy of Arts and Letters since 1958, had died on 23 January 1981.

In Sleep, in Thunder (1980–81)

Although Carter's music – the string quartets and the *Double Concerto* in particular – had long been played in Europe, the song cycle *In Sleep, in Thunder* was his first work to be commissioned by an ensemble outside of the United States. Completed on 11 December 1981 (Carter's seventy-third birthday) in Waccabuc, these settings of poems by Robert Lowell for tenor and ensemble were commissioned and premièred by the London Sinfonietta and Oliver Knussen, already a longtime admirer of Carter's music (see above, pp. 236–237). (The première took place on 26 October 1982 in London, with the tenor soloist Martyn Hill.) From this point on, Carter's music became increasingly recognized in Europe. The same year that he composed the Lowell songs he became the first American composer to win the prestigious Ernst von Siemens Music Prize, awarded in Munich (see above, pp. 241–243). In 1982 he left Associated Music Publishers, whose catalogue consisted mainly of American composers, and switched to Boosey and Hawkes, an international firm based in London; *In Sleep, in Thunder* was the first work to be published under the new contract. Commissions by other European ensembles and performers followed: *Triple Duo* (The Fires of London), *Penthode* (Ensemble InterContemporain), *Oboe Concerto* (Paul Sacher), *Adagio tenebroso* from *Symphonia* (BBC Symphony Orchestra), *What Next?* (Staatsoper Berlin), and many others. While this enthusiasm for Carter's music in Europe was not sudden or unprecedented, it was qualitatively different from the occasionally condescending treatment that he and his music had received earlier. In 1955, for example, he had written to Kurt Stone that "Mr. Heinrich Strobel told me that my quartet [the *String Quartet No. 1*] is a little too conservative for his Donaueschingen Festival."[58] Two years later, a successful performance of Carter's *Variations for Orchestra* at the Donaueschingen Festival was overshadowed by his and Helen's sense of "having been outsiders for two days among highly publicized jazz bands and composers & performers – outsiders in a small town where the 'insiders' [i.e. Willy Strecker, Strobel and their protégés Nono, Henze, and Boulez] had reserved all the tables at meals and sat at them interminably – outsiders in that not one word of information or publicity, not one score of my music [was] available among thousands of available scores [...]."[59] By 1980, Boulez, Knussen, and

other performers, supported by the eloquent advocacy of the British musicologist Arnold Whittall, were at the forefront of Carter's new European prominence.

For *In Sleep, in Thunder* Carter appropriately enough selected poems that Lowell had written while living in London. Carter knew and genuinely admired the controversial poet: "I liked his work and I was very fond of him, so when he died unexpectedly here in New York [in 1977] I decided to compose a sort of portrait of him. I chose certain of his poems that illustrated different aspects of his character [...] I wanted my music to bring out the tragic contradictions of his personality." (*CC*, 86.)

135 *In Sleep, in Thunder,* six poems of Robert Lowell for tenor and 14 instruments (1980–81), No. 2: "Across the Yard: La Ignota," short score draft in pencil ("second version"), p. [1] (discarded)

This draft of the second song in the cycle, dated 3–10 October 1980 (and ultimately rejected with a large X), shows that the main idea of the obbligato trumpet line as a counterpart to the voice was already present in the early stages of composition. The poem recounts, from the perspective of a male narrator, his keen and not entirely disinterested observance of an aging and out-of-work soprano who indefatigably keeps up her daily vocalizing. Since the actual singer is a man, Carter portrays the soprano's practicing with a florid solo trumpet line. The draft consists almost entirely of the tenor's vocal line (setting the whole poem) and the trumpet part. The opening bars introduce the solo trumpet over sustained chords. The vocal line, setting the text, "The soprano's bosom breathes the [joy of God]," is very similar to that of the final version, except it is a semitone higher and the 3/2 bars are notated as alternating 4/4 and 2/4. The trumpet line is quite different, however; Carter changes its triplet note values to quintuplets in the final version, and in general makes it more extravagant. But even in this early draft, there is a clear contrast between a vocal line that is not very idiomatically "vocal" and a trumpet line that is; we hear it imitating a singer warming up, improvising, and doing vocalises (see for example the rising and falling figures at the bottom of the page). As in the final version, the

---

58 Letter from Elliott Carter to Kurt Stone, undated [summer 1955]; Kurt Stone Collection, Irving S. Gilmore Music Library, Yale University.

59 Letter from Elliott Carter to Kurt Stone, 23 October [1957]; Kurt Stone Collection, Irving S. Gilmore Music Library, Yale University.

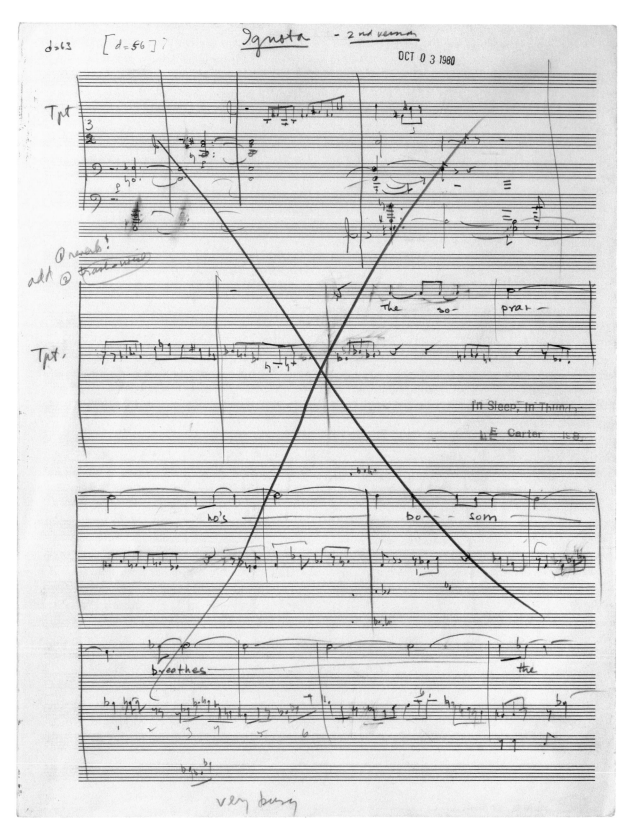

135 *In Sleep, in Thunder*

Triple Duo (1982–83)

trumpet part is here fragmentary and sporadic, as the voice of the soprano is heard only in snatches from behind the "besmirched gauze" curtains in her apartment across the yard. The draft also shows that Carter sometimes jotted down verbal notes along with the musical ones, for example the words "very busy" written under the trumpet line at the bottom of the page. The two remarks "add (1) reverb! and (2) trash-noise" are intriguing. The first probably refers to the echo-like impression that results in the final version when the alto flute continues after the trumpet has stopped. In the draft, Carter notates only one continuous instrumental line, but in the final version, he divides it up between the trumpet and the much softer alto flute. The second is likely to indicate Carter's idea for setting the line "She flings her high aria to the trash like roses." While the draft shows just some curvy lines at this point, in the final version a sudden barrage of percussion including tenor drum, sizzle cymbal, cowbell, side drum, tamtam, woodblock, suspended cymbal, and bottle comes to the fore, the "trash-noises" contrasting ironically with her imagined "roses." Both verbal notes indicate that Carter's intention was to represent, and not just describe, the soprano's singing as vividly and concretely as possible; in this way the musical setting goes beyond what the poem alone can do.

Triple Duo, commissioned by the Fires of London and premièred in New York by them on 23 April 1983 (and completed on 7 February of that year), was part of the festival "Britain Salutes New York," which honored the bicentennial of the treaty by which Britain acknowledged the independence of the thirteen colonies. *Triple Duo* continues the Carterian preoccupation with dividing instrumental ensembles into smaller groups that squabble, spar, and at times become reconciled with each other. This kind of "polyphony squared" – a counterpoint not just of lines, but of groups – can be heard in Carter's works since the *Sonata for Violoncello and Piano* and the *String Quartet No. 1*, but becomes especially prevalent in the large-scale orchestral works of the 1960s and reached its apex with the *String Quartet No. 3* and *A Symphony of Three Orchestras*. After *Triple Duo*, Carter again used dramatic counterpoint as a structural feature in *Penthode*, which Paul Griffiths described as a "Quintuple Quartet."[60] *Triple Duo* divides its *Pierrot* ensemble plus percussion – the instrumentation of the commissioning ensemble – into timbrally related groups of winds (piccolo doubling flute and E♭ and bass clarinets doubling B♭ clarinet), strings (violin and cello), and the "percussive" instruments (piano and percussion, including the crotales for which the Fires of London were famous). The relationships among these duos are not confrontational, but (as in Goethe's famous aphorism about the string quartet) conversational; *Triple Duo* is an elegant, light-hearted work that has been aptly described as Mozartian.[61] Andrew Porter has likened the work to a "'play' for enactment by six instruments, its score a 'scenario' in which three couples [...] are the characters."[62] Peter Maxwell Davies, who founded the Fires of London in 1971, had studied with Carter at the Dartington Summer School in 1957, where he participated in Carter's course on Schoenberg's *Variations for Orchestra*; Carter remembered him "as an intelligent, musical young man who "at that time [...] was the only one of my students interested in twelve-tone music" (*CC*, 88). The spontaneity and charm of *Triple Duo* are intentionally in the same spirit as the *Woodwind Quintet*: "I wanted each duo to have its own music, and the others to make short commentaries on it. In that way the writing would be more sharply defined, and at the same time I would be able to achieve a more agile, more sprightly articulation." (*CC*, 89.)

60 Paul Griffiths, "US Tour 1986: A commemorative program book," p. 65 (for the 1986 tour of Pierre Boulez and the Ensemble InterContemporain).

61 David Schiff, liner notes to the Wergo recording (WER 60124).

62 Andrew Porter, "Thought-Executing Fires," *New Yorker* (9 May 1983), pp. 114–118, esp. 114; reprinted in idem, *Musical Events: A Chronicle: 1980–1983* (New York etc.: Summit Books, 1987), pp. 435–440, esp. 436.

136 *Triple Duo,* for flute (piccolo), clarinet in B-flat (clarinet in E-flat, bass clarinet), percussion, piano, violin, and violoncello (1982–83), autograph full score in pencil, p. 62 (mm. 440–444)

The three duos are here, as elsewhere, clearly distinguished from one another by timbre, predominant rhythmic values, and characteristic intervals. As in the rest of the piece, the two woodwinds, the violin and cello, and the piano and percussion are grouped together into three distinct timbral layers. Their rhythms reinforce this: the woodwinds move in eighth-note triplet subdivisions, the percussion and piano in sixteenth-note quintuplets, and the strings in regular sixteenths, producing a rhythmic counterpoint of 3 against 4 against 5. After the *fortefortissimo* and *fortissimo* outburst in mm. 440–441, in a development familiar to anyone who has ever attended a dinner party, the three duos cease conversing among themselves and converge into a single "discussion" (starting in m. 442).[63] All six parts share the same quarter-note pulse of 100, which results in a fairly high degree of rhythmic congruence, even if there are few actual simultaneities. The metrical unity allows something seldom found in Carter's music of this time: a melodic main voice, here in the violin (marked in mm. 442 and 443 with brackets), which is then shared by the different instruments. This melodic *Hauptstimme*, here marked "legato espr[essivo]," is accompanied by interjections (clarinet, snare drums, and tomtoms), imitative flourishes (piano), and dyspeptic remarks (cello). (The cello starting in mm. 442–444 and the violin in m. 444 move in rhythmic units of three sixteenth notes, articulating a faster alternative pulse.) After m. 442 the violin's and cello's characteristic major sixths and perfect fifths are clearly audible; the flute and clarinet share a vocabulary of major and minor thirds and major sevenths, while the piano focuses on minor sevenths, perfect fourths, and minor seconds / minor ninths. (All groups use tritones.) In a letter to Oliver Knussen, Carter wrote about this passage: "[...] the part marked Hauptstimme should be brought out very prominently, and the switch from one instrument to another [...] should give the impression of complete continuity – one leading to the next."[64] This exuberant line is passed from the violin to the clarinet (mm. 443–445), whose arch-shaped melody and opening rhythm – a longer duration followed by three shorter notes of equal length, ascending – echoes the shape and rhythm of its antecedent. Then (on the following page) the cello joins the discussion, "rephrasing" the statement yet again and varying its basic rhythmic profile. This *Hauptstimme* continues to be exchanged among the instruments, varied each time and steadily increasing in intensity. The conversation begins (on the page shown) in a fairly reasoned manner and becomes more vehement and strident until shortly before the end of the piece, where the *Hauptstimme* moves into the highest register and the dynamics increase to *fff*. Just as in a real conversation, the six protagonists discuss the same subject while still maintaining their characteristic identities.

63 "'It's like three couples at a dinner party,'" said Ursula Oppens about *Triple Duo*. Quoted in David Schiff, "A Composer Finds His Muses in the Here and Now: Performers," *The New York Times,* 17 March 1996.

64 Letter from Elliott Carter to Oliver Knussen, 24 October 1984; carbon copy in the Elliott Carter Collection, Paul Sacher Foundation.

137 **Charles Rosen and Elliott Carter at the Arnold Schoenberg Institute (Los Angeles, 1983)**

Carter's seventy-fifth year was again marked by many honors. Among them was the "Elliott Carter Festival" mounted by the Arnold Schoenberg Institute in Los Angeles from 12 to 14 April 1983, accompanied by an exhibition. Among other things the festival included a talk by David Schiff on "Elliott Carter's American Vision" (12 April), a chamber music recital with the Kronos Quartet, the Fine Arts Woodwind Quintet, the percussionist Kenneth Watson, and several other musicians (14 April), and three events featuring the pianist Charles Rosen: a

panel discussion with Carter and a piano recital (both 13 April) as well as a master class (14 April). Besides works by Chopin and Schumann, Rosen's recital included *Night Fantasies*, which he had recorded the year before.[65] This recital marked the end of a remarkable series of four performances of this work at the Arnold Schoenberg Institute, for within the space of ten months it had also been played there by the other three pianists who commissioned it: Paul Jacobs (7 June 1982), Ursula Oppens (26 January 1983), and Gilbert Kalish (16 March 1983).

65 Elliott Carter, *Piano Sonata, Night Fantasies;* Charles Rosen (piano); Etcetera ETC 1008.
66 Will Crutchfield, "Paul Jacobs Talks About Carter and Messiaen" (see above, p. 241, note 52), p. 24.
67 Many musicians from Jacobs's circle of friends took part in this concert, including Bethany Beardslee, William Bolcom, Gilbert Kalish, James Levine, Ned Rorem, and Ursula Oppens. The program ranged from Paolo da Firenze and Josquin Desprez to Bolcom and Carter, whose *Sonata for Flute, Oboe, Cello, and Harpsichord* was performed by Harvey Sollberger (flute), Stephen Taylor (oboe), Fred Sherry (cello), and Martin Goldray (harpsichord).

Remembering Paul Jacobs (1983)

Born in 1930 and educated at Juilliard, the pianist Paul Jacobs was one of Carter's closest musical associates. In the 1950s he lived in Europe, where he developed ties with the post-war avant-garde, performing for example in the Domaine Musical concert series founded by Pierre Boulez. After returning to New York in 1960 he became a leading figure on the contemporary music scene as a soloist, teacher, and official pianist of the New York Philharmonic. His association with Carter began when he turned pages for the harpsichordist Ralph Kirkpatrick at the première of the *Double Concerto* on 6 September 1961. A short while later Jacobs himself played the harpsichord in the same work, and over the next twenty years he became one of the staunchest advocates of Carter's music. The closeness of their relationship found expression in his final interview: "[...] I feel about him and his wife almost as though they were my parents. I think of him as my father. He is a wonderful man in private – we share ideas, we're on the same wavelength. She has a backbone of steel, but can be extraordinarily sensitive and considerate. I can't put into words how fond I am of them."[66] Jacobs died of AIDS on 25 September 1983. At his burial services on 27 September 1983 Carter gave the following funeral oration, in which he praised Jacobs's tireless commitment to contemporary music and outlined the major stages of their friendship. The other speakers were the composer William Bolcom, Albert K. Webster (the managing director of the New York Philharmonic), and the cellist Lorin Bernsohn (a longstanding member of the orchestra). All four speeches were subsequently printed in the program booklet for a memorial concert given in New York's Symphony Space five months later, on 24 February 1984.[67] Carter again delivered an address at this concert, having already published a brief appreciation of Jacobs in the periodical *Keynote* in December 1983.[68]

138 **Elliott Carter, funeral oration for Paul Jacobs (1983)**

Paul Jacobs,

Still before us is the image of your lively, fascinating presence, so human, so sensitive, so dedicated. We are here to express our thanks for the generous gift of life that you brought to everything you did that meant so much to us and will continue to do so. This gift of life, still so vivid in our minds, is prime in our communications not only with you but with each other. It is the most important quality which a performer and teacher such as yourself has to give. While a composer such as myself wants a performer to play his music as he has written it, as you did most conscientiously, he wants even more to have the performer understand why his notes seemed worth writing – how he thought they were [to be] handled in a fresh and imaginative way and permeated with expressive content. These you were deeply aware of, and [you] brought before the public in concerts, recordings and lectures what you found in the scores with unique perceptiveness and focused enthusiasm. There was a memorable distinctiveness about your performances and, above all, that extraordinary gift of human liveliness that makes these events forever fresh, even in retrospect.

I was first aware of this wonderful quality at a concert in an overcrowded art gallery in Paris in the mid-fifties at which Paul played some scores of the Darmstadt School that I had never heard – scores that then seemed to me appallingly systematized and dry – to which he brought a concentrated, striking intensity that made them very telling.[69] A year or two later we came to know each other at the English Dartington Hall Summer Music School, at which he performed, among other things, one of the pianos of Stravinsky's two-piano *Concerto* with a verve that brought forth praise from the composer, who was present.[70]

Then when Paul came to live in New York and had difficulty in getting established, he used to come and practise at our house and we saw each other often. Our relationship deepened, artistically, when Paul took over the harpsichord part of my *Double Concerto* from Ralph Kirkpatrick, whose deteriorating eyesight prevented him from performing it in 1962. Paul's numerous performances of this work, about once or twice a year for about a decade,

68 Elliott Carter, untitled contribution to "Paul Jacobs (June 22, 1930 – September 25, 1983)," *Keynote* 7/10 (December 1983), p. 21; reprinted in the program booklet for the memorial concert for Paul Jacobs, 24 February 1984, Symphony Space, New York, no page number (not listed in Link 2000). The speech that Carter gave at this concert is unpublished but preserved

in typescript in the Paul Sacher Foundation.
69 Paul Jacobs's concert may have taken place during an exhibition of paintings by his friend Bernard Saby at the Galerie du Dragon in 1955, 1956, or perhaps early 1957.
70 Carter is referring to the 1957 Dartington Summer School. The concert in which Jacobs joined Noel Lee in the Stravinsky

Concerto took place on 14 August 1957; it consisted entirely of works by Stravinsky and also included his *Deux poèmes de Balmont*, *Trois poésies de la lyrique japonaise*, the *Concertino* for string quartet, the *Septet*, and the *Cantata*, with the latter two works conducted by Robert Craft.

An Interview at the Banff Centre (1984)

and his two recordings of the work remain memorable to many.[71] From that time [on], Paul became deeply involved with the harpsichord, although continuing to play the piano, and collected various types of keyboard instruments, finally having a special harpsichord built that would meet the specifications of the two works of mine that used it, since makers of old instruments had progressed toward producing more and more archaic (authentic) ones that no longer had the variety of color for which I wrote.[72]

Meanwhile he had become the pianist of the New York Philharmonic, and when that orchestra commissioned two works from me I thought of him and wrote important piano parts as an homage to his remarkable abilites. Fortunately for me, Paul played and recorded, during the sixties and seventies, most of my works using keyboard, and then got together three other pianists to commission my *Night Fantasies*, which he recorded in a most beautiful performance, [together] with the *Piano Sonata*, the summer before last, when his disease was already weakening him so that he had to rest frequently during the recording sessions.[73] Even then, his intense concentration, focusing his characteristic, vibrant living power, was extraordinary and the artistic results better than ever.

His generous, selfless dedication to contemporary music, making it live for so many, both among professionals and public, is surely one of [the] important contributions to this particular period of music in America.

Paul, you remain with us, not only as an example of an artist more dedicated to his art than to himself, and through that art making our lives more fascinating and valuable, but as one with whom we will always be in dialogue, asking you what you think of some piece or other, what you value most in it, enjoying, cherishing, and loving every moment of your presence.

[Published in the program booklet of the memorial concert for Paul Jacobs on 24 February 1984, Symphony Space, New York, no page number. We reproduce the original version of this address from the photocopy of a typescript preserved in the Paul Sacher Foundation. It differs in minor details from the slightly more formal printed version.]

The following interview was given on 8 February 1984 in the Banff Centre for the Arts (Alberta, Canada), where Carter spent a week from 6 to 10 February 1984 as a visiting lecturer in the Advanced Music Studies Program and supervised students in preparing a concert of his music.[74] The interviewers were Robert Johnston (RJ), Michael Century (MC), Robert J. Rosen (RR), and Don Stein (DS). A printed version of the interview was published in the Banff Centre's house organ, the *Banff Letters*, in spring 1985. The much different version reproduced below is based on a typescript with handwritten corrections located in the Elliott Carter Collection of the Paul Sacher Foundation. Evidently Carter had taken the trouble to edit the interview himself, cutting a few (negative) opinions of his fellow-composers, e.g. Krzysztof Penderecki's *Violin Concerto* (No. 1): ("[...] that's like a Liszt tone-poem. It's all diminished sevenths and chromatic scales") and John Cage's aesthetic ("To me he is cynical about nature. He believes in its confusion").[75] On the other hand he retained a few statements that were shortened or expurgated in the printed version, e.g. on his formative impressions of Sergey Eisenstein's films, the far-reaching impact of William Glock at the BBC, and the specific requirements placed on composers in the twentieth century as compared to the eighteenth, using the example of Haydn. Either way, whether in the printed version or the typescript version, with its seemingly more "authentic" voice, the Banff interview conveys a vivid impression of Carter's thought in the early 1980s. Not least interesting, besides the information on his artistic development and his compositional methods, are his critical comments on several recent developments in music. In particular he has little good to say of young composers attempting to write simple music with a neo-romantic tinge. In the final analysis, as shown by his drastic comparison with "populist" music written by decree in Nazi Germany and the Soviet Union, he viewed such music as succumbing to the dictates of the market – dictates profoundly at odds with his (politically allusive) modernist notion of individual freedom in musical expression. In later interviews, too, Carter clearly parted ways from what he suspected to be "post-modern" trends. Usually, however, he worded his reservations more cautiously than in this interview, which may reflect the fact that at the time of

---

71 Elliott Carter, *Double Concerto* and *Variations for Orchestra*, Paul Jacobs (harpsichord), Charles Rosen (piano), English Chamber Orchestra, conducted by Frederik Prausnitz, and New Philharmonia Orchestra, conducted by Frederik Prausnitz (Columbia MS 7191), recorded in January 1968 and March 1967, respectively. Elliott Carter, *Double Concerto* and *Duo for Violin and Piano;*

Paul Jacobs (harpsichord), Gilbert Kalish (piano), Contemporary Chamber Ensemble, conducted by Arthur Weisberg, and Paul Zukofsky (violin), Gilbert Kalish (piano) (Nonesuch H 71314), recorded in September 1973 and March 1975, respectively.

72 Jacobs left this instrument, a Dowd harpsichord, to the Yale School of Music with the proviso that it should be made

available for performances of the *Double Concerto;* see Schiff 1998, p. 237.

73 Elliott Carter, *Piano Sonata, Night Fantasies,* Paul Jacobs (piano) (Nonesuch 79047-1), recorded in August 1982.

74 This "Young Artists' Recital" took place in Margaret Greenham Theatre on 10 February 1984 – the final day of Carter's stay – and included the *Woodwind Quintet, Pastoral* (transcribed for clarinet

the Banff interview he was still a professor at Juilliard and thus in direct contact with the changing attitudes of a young generation of composers.

139 Elliott Carter in conversation with Robert Johnston, Michael Century, Robert Rosen, and Don Stein (1984)

RJ   What are conditions like for composers today?

EC   We are living through one of the most remarkable and richest periods that the history of music has ever seen. New possibilities of every sort have opened up to composers and have made musical composition a fascinating adventure. However, for these very reasons, it's a hard job being a composer for many. To be a young composer must be especially so, because the enormous range of possibilities makes it difficult to decide what to do, especially when other members of the profession and the public are so uncertain about what they expect. The section of our society interested in so-called serious music has, in recent times, seldom been presented in a strongly convincing way with the important works of new music, as societies of the 18th and 19th centuries were – in fact these older societies, during which our present "classical" repertoire was written (and could hardly have been written without its enthusiastic support), were primarily interested in their contemporaries' music. Today we live in a state of confusion and uncertainty about new music which is very disturbing. One year composers write the kind of music that seemed very advanced in the early part of this century, and the next [they] imitate romantic music in a less interesting way than composers of the '30s and '40s did. Frankly I am disturbed to find so many young composers embracing of their own free will the type of reactionary music imposed by Hitler's *Reichsmusikkammer* on German composers or by the Soviet Composers Union during Stalin's time. Along with all the remarkable advances that many composers are making with deep conviction, I find there is what Adorno called "a regression of listening ability," even a loss of the wish to pay attention to music, but only to use it as a background for other activities. It is hard not to feel that this is one of many types of breakdown of communication we are faced with at a time when focused attention [is] needed more than ever in our democratic and highly complex society, where choices of citizens are so important even for their own welfare.

New music, it seems, has been reduced to a second-class art as far as the general public is concerned. This does not mean that no striking and important works are being written, there certainly are. Nor does it mean that there is a gap between them and the public that can never be bridged, for wherever an intensive effort to interest the public has been made, as in Paris with IRCAM or in London by the BBC, there is a large and enthusiastic audience.[76]

This reduction of new music to an inferior status was made clear to me in a conversation I had here in Banff with Roald Nasgaard, chief curator of the Art Gallery [of Ontario] in Toronto.[77] We talked of the music of Philip Glass and he said: "Oh, I like it because it is so accessible." And I asked: "Is that a judgment you would make about a painter – that you like his work because it is so accessible?" Then he gave me the impression that paintings that were judged solely on their accessibility almost invariably lose interest in a few years, so I said: "Then you are telling me that Glass's music is not likely to have a lasting interest." And he replied: "But I don't like music that is not accessible."

Most composers were taught – until very recently, I imagine – to write what [were] at one time considered to be important works expected to last, music that dealt with the many aspects of composition in an imaginative, original, and interesting way. Yet such an attitude now often seems to lead composers to write music only appreciated by [their] colleagues. But who can say. It is nearly impossible to assess the judgment of public or critics.

When you get to be my age, not to be arrogant, I get a great many reviews, and when I bother to read them, I have come to realize that they very nearly mean nothing whatever, because, say, out [of] 25 reviews of the same piece there will be every shade of possible opinion: that it's incompetent, that it's so skillful it means nothing, and so forth.

RR   What I admire about your music is your conviction about your own personal language. Each piece grows on the strengths of the previous ones without

---

and piano), the *Sonata for Violoncello and Piano, Eight Etudes and a Fantasy*, and the *Sonata for Flute, Oboe, Cello, and Harpsichord*.

75 "Elliott Carter, "The Art is Knowing What to Leave Out," *Banff Letters* (Spring 1985), pp. 22–27, esp. 25 and 26, respectively.

76 IRCAM (Institut de Recherche et de Coordination Acoustique/Musique),

located in the Centre Pompidou in Paris, supports the composition and performance of contemporary music as well as research about electronic and computer music. It was conceived and founded by Pierre Boulez and opened its doors in 1977. See above, p. 228.

77 The art historian Roald Nasgaard, who later moved to Florida State University, gave a talk at the Banff Centre on

10 February 1984, the final day of Carter's stay in Alberta. The Centre's archives do not reveal the topic of his lecture. Personal communication from Jane Parkinson (Paul D. Fleck Library and Archives, Banff Centre), 18 December 2007.

attempts to appease anyone else's wishes. There is a strong progression.

EC Some have thought adhering so much to one's own style was like the shell a turtle builds to protect himself from the world.

RR Isn't that due to your own belief in your own language?

CC I suppose so, but it is also a sort of self-protection. If one were to follow the feedback from public and press and be affected by it, it would be so disturbing… Besides you can never make up your mind what it really means. For we often don't know how informed critics are in the first place, so we have no basis on which to assess their feedback. When you think of the extremely wide variety of types of composers and compositions being written or improvised today, it's really difficult for anyone to judge what is good and what is bad. I usually know what I think, but realize that it's my own prejudiced point of view.

RJ It's difficult to know what kind of education is most beneficial to someone who wants to compose.

EC Oh, it's very perplexing, especially if you really want to be helpful. How do you think composers should be educated?

RJ So many people are now bringing disciplines to music that weren't previously related to composition: for instance, mathematics and architecture in the case of Xenakis, and serious consideration of non-Western ways of making music. There are so many different musical languages.

EC You can have the dog that howls, he is a pretty good composer, too.

RJ How can someone teach all the possibilites?

EC Every teacher must invent his own way of dealing with this problem. For a long time we had Luciano Berio at the Juilliard School.[78] His composition students were horrified to learn that he demanded that they all must do strict counterpoint in the most academic fashion. None of them could believe that he would insist on that. But he was very serious and anybody who wouldn't do it had to change teachers.

Now the question is, in what way could such strict counterpoint relate to Luciano's compositional outlook? That's puzzling. I decided in the end it was really a test of the students' devotion to music and probably to Berio himself, and as far as this situation was concerned not really a training in anything else, since these were all graduate students who presumably had already done such exercises in their earlier studies. It is also true that at that time strict counterpoint had not been taught at the Juilliard School for many years. The students learned counterpoint by trying to imitate examples drawn from the scores of Bach and others, which I myself never had thought was very effective.

There are many strange things about education in these years. Graduate students from other schools take entrance exams for advanced study at Juilliard and we find that many can hardly recognize one piece of older music. They have never heard the opening of *Tristan* before, for example. Or they have such poorly trained ears they can't tell one note from another, and yet such students sometimes produce quite interesting pieces. As teachers we are very perplexed as to what to do. The Juilliard [School] will not accept graduate students with poor ears or with a weak knowledge of musical literature, even though they show talent as composers. But in such cases we suggest that the student apply again after having remedied the deficienies.

It's a peculiar time. Not very long ago there were very clearly defined requirements for a composer. If one didn't know counterpoint, it would be obvious, to professionals at least, in one's compositions. But if someone who doesn't know counterpoint today comes up with a piece that looks like Xenakis and is not bad for what it is, you wonder if he wouldn't be better as a student than someone who can do counterpoint well but who writes in a dreary old style. So, the teaching profession is in as much confusion as the composing profession. Both are becoming more and more a very personal, individual matter.

RJ Can you think of any teacher today who might be as influential as Nadia Boulanger was when you were a student?

EC I must say that all my life I never felt I learned anything from anybody; it seemed to me I always learned

---

78 Luciano Berio taught from autumn 1965 to spring 1971 at the Juilliard School, where he also founded and headed the Juilliard Ensemble.

what I wanted to know by myself. Nadia Boulanger was very helpful, but at the time I studied with her, she no longer liked the music of the Viennese composers or Bartók. She only liked Stravinsky, and I was a great fan of Bartók and Varèse, and, of course, Ives. She used to say that if you write string quartets with minor seconds or major sevenths, they will be played out of tune, so don't write them. 15 or 20 years before she had felt quite differently. But like many people in the '30s she gradually came to think that earlier twentieth-century music, except for Stravinsky, was dead and no longer interesting. She discouraged students during my time from writing what had been called "advanced music," that is, music that seemed exaggeratedly dissonant during the '30s.

RJ   Do you think that had something to do with political and social problems – possibly a connection with Expressionism?

EC   Well, yes, the coming of the Nazi regime seemed to many to be the final extravagance of the madness of Expressionism. The cultivation of irrationality was exemplified right there in front of you with Hitler talking on the radio or in newsreels. And that was frightening.

RJ   Later, your reassessment of that time led [you] to the ideas of Freud and psychoanalysis.

EC   Well, as one lived through these changing times during and after the Second War, it became obvious that there was a permanent extravagant part of people's experiences and actions that had to be faced. We don't want to run around like wild people and hurt each other at every turn, but on the other hand we do have that wild side and it has to be fitted into a socially effective situation if we are going to live together and profit by it. It seems to me that this could be part of the message of my music. It could be seen as a way of trying to deal with this irrational, rather extravagant, and violent side of ourselves. I did feel at the time I studied and since that the musical neo-classicists, Stravinsky excepted, begged the issue; that much of Hindemith and some of the earlier twelve-tone works of Schoenberg were a little too cut and dried and not very meaningful.

RJ   How do you distinguish the strong expressive gestures in your music from more common expressionism?

EC   Oh, you've got me there. It's hard for me to talk about that. You know, one writes one's music and one doesn't think about these things until one is questioned about them. I do what I think sounds right or fits into the piece, but I must say that I would never allow anything to get into a work that didn't have an expressive value, at least to me. I don't think about whether my music can be considered expressionist or anything else.

RJ   Your concept of time is unique. You talk about pieces with all four movements unfolding at the same time.

EC   Yes, this is something I got very interested in: the idea that we are constantly experiencing moments in our lives in the context of other moments, previous or anticipated experiences. This idea came from reading Joyce and Proust. We are all partially aware of our own past, of the world around us, as we focus on present actions, like a movie camera paying attention to things of immediate concern while giving a background of other events. There always is something going on in the background – in the subconscious or peripheral world – of our attention. To me, this is a very vivid realization. We have so many experiences with repercussions beyond what is happening at the moment, and I want to express this situation in my music. That is why it seems complicated to some, I think.

RJ   In the romantic era, music unfolded like theatrical time, whereas now we jump between extreme expressive gestures in a short span of time.

EC   Yes, movies have changed all that a great deal. Our perception of time sequences visually has been very strongly influenced by this medium. Of course, poetry and prose in the past have always treated time descriptively and seldom have tried to present the "real" flow of time. The movies have at times produced remarkable sequential effects that were quite new. I remember very vividly seeing the movie *Potemkin* when I was 15 or 16 years old.[79] I don't know if any of you know this or any other of Eisenstein's old movies, but they were extraordinary examples of [the] cross-cutting of sequences that presented the kind of foreground-background idea that I am discussing. For instance, there was a scene, of the begin-

---

79 Sergey Eisenstein's silent film *Battleship Potemkin* originated in 1925 and was first released in New York City on 5 December 1926. Therefore Carter must have been at least eighteen years old when he became acquainted with it.

ning of the Russian Revolution, of boats coming into the waterways of a city, with drawbridges rising one after the other. This was shown in a sequence of many shots of rising drawbridges, each cut before each motion was concluded, and gave a sense of an entire city rising to a moment of great intensity.

Another scene – very famous – [showed] Tsarist soldiers shooting revolutionaries on a huge flight of steps. The entire scene was cut around a constantly interrupted shot of an abandoned baby carriage rolling uncontrollably down the steps, while on every side of it brief shots of the terrible massacre were focused on. These and many more uses of sequential effects in the movies have suggested many ideas of musical shape to me.

MC I wanted to ask you about the effects of using tape, radio, the rise of phonographs, and other technical sources of sound that have increased the amount of music around us.

EC I can't think of music as a mechanical phenomenon; it is a human one. Recordings are like photographs, they recall live performance. There is no doubt that the extreme accessibility of music through Walkmans and the like tends to reduce the attentiveness of listeners and discourages attentive listening – providing a sonic wallpaper to other, non-musical activities. Music is treated as mechanically stamped out and as low in content as most wallpaper designs. To me this has little direct human meaning, for music that is mechanically produced at its sound source already has lost much of the human touch, and music that is mechanically ordered like some minimalist music or some popular music seems to me pointless as it does not give any sense of being alive. When both the sound source and the presentation are mechanical, as is true of much electronic music, I find it nearly impossible to find anything in it except perhaps a momentary entertainment. Even amplified sounds bother me, for I like the sense that music is being performed by people. Indeed, my own music dramatizes this performing situation. You see I'm old-fashioned in the sense that much modern mechanization disturbs me – Mozart's piece for the mechanical organ is, however, a great work in spite of this.

RJ You have expressed the view that there is more of a sense of convention among composers in Europe.

EC I find Europe in some ways old-fashioned. It seems Europeans tend to respect the educated and the opinions of educated and trained professionals. For instance, when someone is appointed director of music at the BBC, it is highly unlikely that it will be a person who has never showed any interest in music before, which could easily happen in the US – if we had a public radio that had a sizeable budget for serious music. In the case of England, there was a remarkable man, Sir William Glock, [who was] appointed to take charge of the BBC Third Program music. He had Boulez hired to run the London BBC orchestra for many years.[80] Then Sir William commissioned a large group of English composers to write for the orchestra: Peter Maxwell Davies, Harrison Birtwistle, Cornelius Cardew, Susan Bradshaw, and a dozen others, all of whose works were championed by the BBC. A whole important school of English composers emerged because of this intelligent sponsorship that changed the entire face of British music. In this atmosphere even performers became more skillful. For English music had tended to be a culture of amateur performers before Sir William appeared, but [thanks to] his enthusiastic efforts there [are now] a vast number of very good performers, even percussionists. This is all the result of having one highly intelligent, energetic, forward-looking man occupy a key position.

RJ As we look back at American art of the 1950s and 60s, particularly the visual arts, we are beginning to see that it was culturally conditioned, even though we may not have thought so at the time. For instance, the exportation of the abstract painting of the 60s…

EC You mean the Abstract Expressionist School? Of course, that partly came out of the influence of Hans Hofmann and a number of other German refugees who were teaching in New York at the time. When you compare music and painting there is one fundamental difference as far as reaching the public is concerned. Paintings are objects that people can buy and own. Therefore they become investments – bought for a sum of money, often with the hope that their value will go up before they are sold or do-

---

80 Pierre Boulez was chief conductor of the BBC Symphony Orchestra from 1971 to 1974.

nated to a museum. Inevitably, there is much behind-the-scenes activity to keep the investment from deteriorating in value. While dealers and collectors profit by this most, painters too can at times command very high prices.

Composers, on the other hand, perhaps mercifully, are confronted with the fact that we are, you might say, protected from making money with our works, which can never be investments since they are not objects that can be bought and sold. The scores we write, nowadays, are usually very hard for anyone but a professional to read and cannot be expected to sell, nor can they be expected to be performed so frequently that they earn sums commensurate with what a painter of importance receives for one single painting. It must be remembered that Stravinsky had to take up conducting to pay the bills, and Bartók had to give two-piano recitals with his wife, because he would not teach as most composers must.

DS   Do you find external sources of inspiration, for instance in poetry?

EC   Sometimes, yes, although I am not sure what you mean by inspiration. I am continually thinking of musical possibilites, of short motivic figures, chord progressions, trying over in my head all sorts of musical textures and colors. Sometimes one of these seems particularly interesting, and then I begin to think of how it could be led into and away from, and soon a whole section of a piece begins to form itself. This very often suggests some section of a poem or an event, movie, or painting that seems parallel to the musical idea. Is that what you call being inspired?

I find that I tend to do this more with orchestral pieces than with chamber music. I really don't know why that is. Perhaps it is because in orchestral music, what with the problems of dealing with large masses of sound and all the instrumental paraphernalia, you have to have a fairly good guide of some kind. So I often end up choosing some poetic text, after having had the initial musical idea, that would help me continue.

Often there is an idea of constructing a musical world, operating in it, and then leaving it in one way or another, perhaps having it disintegrate. Such an idea, for instance, didn't occur to me until after I had started writing the *Double Concerto* for harpsichord, piano, and two cham-

ber orchestras, and I could take account of where the music was leading me. Then I began to read poems that had to do with creation, with the formation of things. Lucretius's *De rerum natura* describes the world as being created by falling atoms that swerve and hit each other, producing bits of material more and more complex, until finally human beings result. It ends with a plague at Athens in which there is a great destruction. This vision was very helpful in writing my piece, [as] I discovered after I had completed many parts of it. I began to see that the *Double Concerto* could follow a pattern similar to that of Lucretius's poem. The introduction presented bits of musical material that, when combined and elaborated, would open up into various movements with different characters.

Sometimes, however, I like to give the impression of plunging into the middle of a piece, as in my Third String Quartet, and then sort out the various strands of material which at first are being presented at the same time. In fact, with each piece I try to do something different because I like to be involved in the piece and take chances with it, not knowing at first where it will lead or how it will turn out. To me it's like going on an expedition to a place where I have not been. I enjoy this challenge. When I don't follow such a path and find that I'm writing something I already know about, I get bored and stop.

In the old days, obviously, Haydn could turn out six quartets all approximately the same in a large number of respects. It is true each has its own theme and character, but he liked the same old forms, textures, harmonies, scale figures, arpeggios, and used a great deal of this material over and over again. I find that for myself I get very impatient with such an approach and have to invent new harmonies, textures, figurations, and the rest for each piece. So I can't write many pieces. It takes a lot of thought and effort – inspiration, if you like – to avoid prefabricated material (even your own) [in favor of material] that also has a real cogent musical point within the context of any given piece. I often think that with the very small demand there is nowadays for the kind of music I am interested in, there is little reason to write a lot, and a good deal of reason to take a lot of effort and write what you really think worthwhile.

RJ Do you think that a consistency of form, as in Haydn's work, reflects a kind of social contract?

EC What do you mean by social contract?

RJ That the audience knew something about Haydn's work and assumed it was going to follow a certain form and unfold in a certain way – the same way that language is a social contract.

EC There certainly was a social contract in this sense. After the drastic change that occurred between Bach and his sons – which must have violated many tenets of the musical social contract of the baroque – musical language again began to be shared. But, of course, Haydn was very inventive. In spite of the fact that he used sonata form over and over again, he seldom repeated himself. Every single one of those more than 100 symphonies deals with the form in an original, usually different, way. He seldom, if ever, was routine about such matters. He did have large amounts of what I called prefabricated material at his disposal which no longer seems useful to most present composers. He had a whole field of systematized harmony, of standardized four-part writing, which, when departed from even slightly, could be very surprising.

You see, Haydn lived in a small, highly cultivated portion of society that really knew a lot about music. Some members of it were composers of considerable skill, many amateur performers. These were the ones that supported and appreciated him. One of our dilemmas today is that we have this extraordinary legacy of classical music produced under conditions which cannot now be duplicated. Music in Haydn's time was encouraged and supported by the musical members of an educated aristocracy and leisured members of the upper bourgeousie. In the 19th century many such people had a lot of time to practise the piano, learn music and about it, as servants took care of so many practical problems, and the fading aristocracy established the idea of what a cultivated life should consist in. Now all this is past, although we still have the musical repertory from that time setting a high standard of accomplishment for composers, a standard that one often feels the present-day listener is hardly aware of. As composers many of us try to carry on on this old level of musical skill and imagination and this poses very serious prob-

lem, since only a very small part of the public is likely to treasure such skills, at least at first, and this small part seldom has much say in the larger musical world.

MC As a final question, could you tell me what is going on in that extraordinary part near the end of *A Symphony of Three Orchestras* – those enormous *tutti* chords?

EC What do you mean, what's going on? There are several big, loud chords, as you said. Of course, this short section is the only time when the entire orchestra attacks all together. It's a great surprise. You bet.

MC It's like the creation of the world; it can only happen once. I can never imagine you doing this kind of gesture again.

EC You may be right. Throughout the work three different orchestras play contrasting sorts of music, often against each other, in many different layers of speeds which, like polyrhythms, finally come to a rhythmic unison. One main beat takes over and wipes out the others, and after that the music disintegrates for the last part of the piece, recalling fragments of what had been heard previously.

MC Was there a poetic connection with Hart Crane, whose poetry inspired you to write this work?

EC Yes, sure. After all, Hart Crane committed suicide, having become a drunkard, having [had] a terrible time trying to write always with greater and greater difficulty, finally being unable to. I wanted to give the impression of the cessation of poetic impulse and then the awful realization of his own self-destruction from which he could not recover. My idea of awful is, you might say, when everybody plays together. I guess that I'm just joking in that last remark.

[Typescript with autograph annotations; Elliott Carter Collection, Paul Sacher Foundation. A different version of this conversation was published as "Elliott Carter: The Art is Knowing What to Leave Out," *Banff Letters* (Spring 1985), pp. 22–27.]

140 Elliott Carter at the University of California in
Los Angeles (May 1984)

On 6, 13, and 20 May 1984 the Los Angeles Philharmonic
Orchestra, conducted by Pierre Boulez, presented three
concerts in Royce Hall (University of California in Los
Angeles), followed by two more at the Ojai Festival on
2 and 3 June. To hear Boulez conduct *A Symphony of Three
Orchestras* in the 13 May concert, Carter traveled to Los
Angeles, where on 15 May 1984 he also took part in a panel
discussion with Boulez, moderated by the orchestra's
executive director, Ernest Fleischmann. He also agreed
to answer questions from students in the university's music department, where this photograph was taken.

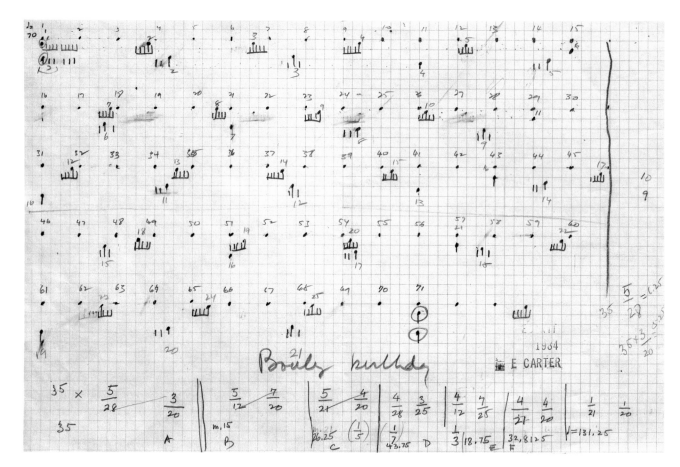

141 a *Esprit rude / Esprit doux I*, polyrhythmic graph

Esprit rude / Esprit doux I (1984)

Carter wrote the duo *Esprit rude / Esprit doux I* for flute and clarinet in autumn 1984 as a tribute to Pierre Boulez on his sixtieth birthday. It was premièred in Baden-Baden on Boulez's birthday, 31 March 1985, by Lawrence Beauregard (flute) and Alain Damiens (clarinet) during a four-day festival entitled "Hommage à Pierre Boulez" (29 March – 1 April 1985).[81] The title refers to the two ways of pronouncing ancient Greek words beginning with a vowel or the letter ρ ("rough breathing" = with preceding *h*, "smooth breathing" = without *h*), both of which occur in the expression *hexēkoston etos* (sixtieth year). It also indicates the two forms of musical expression that collide, complement, and intermingle in this piece, with each instrument being made to play both "rough" and "smooth" music. And finally, the two words may also be taken to allude to two contradictory aspects of Boulez's personality, all the more so as the piece relates to the dedicatee in yet another way, namely by beginning and ending with the motto B♭–C–A–E in reference to Boulez's name, where B♭ is written "B" in German letter notation, C functions as the equivalent of *ut*, and A as the equivalent of l[a]. In any event Boulez, who thanked Carter in writing for the birthday present after the festival (Carter had been unable to attend), allowed for this possibility himself, saying of the piece that "*Esprit rude / Esprit doux* [...] est à la fois une référence à la langue grècque et peut-être aussi à mon caractère..." [*Esprit rude / Esprit doux* refers to the Greek language and perhaps also to my character].[82]

141 *Esprit rude / Esprit doux I,* for flute and clarinet (1984)
a   polyrhythmic graph, 1 p.
b   autograph draft in pencil, p. [7]
     (mm. "41"–"57" [= mm. 51–67 of the final score])

Esprit rude / Esprit doux I is a prime example of Carter's interest, beginning in the mid-1970s, in large-scale polyrhythms underlying a full movement or work. Indeed, starting at m. 6, this entire eighty-eight-bar piece is based on the simultaneous progress of two rhythmic pulses in a ratio of 21 : 25, with the slower pulse given to the flute and the faster one to the clarinet. At an early stage of the compositional process Carter wrote down this polyrhythm on the graph shown on p. 260, in which the proportion 21 : 25 – at the specified tempo of quarter-note = 70 – is expressed by the superposition of two rhythmic periods spanning, respectively, twenty quarter-note triplets (lower voice = flute) and twenty-eight eighth-note quintuplets (upper voice = clarinet). Accordingly, the cycle is seventy bars long, and at no point within it do the two periods coincide. (The only two points of convergence, at the beginnings of m. 1 and m. 71, are indicated on the graph by placing the notes in circles.) While working out the piece Carter used three tempos instead of a single unified tempo, thereby increasing the number of bars. Nevertheless, he adhered basically to this polyrhythmic ground plan. Thus, even in the slightly incomplete draft of 27 October 1984, which comes very close to the final version (see p. 262), all the note values derive from the two basic tempos of MM 5.25 and MM 6.25 (articulating the ratio 21 : 25), which themselves appear only at a single place, namely, in mm. 51–61 (mm. 41–51 in the draft), a moment of repose in this otherwise primarily lively and scherzo-like piece. Here, after a time span of twenty quarter-note triplets (flute) or twenty-eight eighth-note triplets (clarinet), the pitches interchange, and the basic 21 : 25 polyrhythm finds its simplest form of expression. We can also clearly notice in this passage the division of the intervallic repertoire which is characteristic of the entire piece: the flute moves entirely in minor and major thirds, perfect fourths, and major and minor sevenths, whereas the clarinet plays minor and major seconds, perfect fifths, and minor and major sixths. (Both instruments make use of the tritone.)

---

81 This première was given at the Baden-Baden Kurhaus on 31 March 1985 during a matinée concert announced as a surprise event. Clytus Gottwald gave a laudatory address, and the Ensemble InterContemporain (conducted by Peter Eötvös) presented a large number of dedicatory pieces including, besides Carter's *Esprit rude/Esprit doux I,* compositions by Gilbert Amy, Luciano Berio, Sylvano Bussotti, Edison Denisov, Peter Eötvös, York Höller, Heinz Holliger, Philippe Manoury, Luigi Nono, Wolfgang Rihm, and Karlheinz Stockhausen.

82 K[laus] S[tichweh], "Entretien avec Pierre Boulez," program booklet of the concert "Elliott Carter: A l'occasion de son 80e anniversaire," Théâtre Renaud-Barrault, Paris, 19 December 1988, pp. 4–6, esp. 4.

141 b *Esprit rude / Esprit doux I*, autograph draft

142 Pierre Boulez to Elliott Carter, 24 April 1985
(English translation in Appendix 1, pp. 350)

25, Quai André Citroën / 75015 Paris

Mon cher Elliott,

Ce fut une grande joie d'entendre votre musique au cours du concert "surprise – hommage" de Baden-Baden le 31 mars dernier. Vous voyez, j'ai à peine récupéré de ce festival!... c'est pourquoi je vous écris aussi tardivement.

Je vous remercie de l'intention, de la dédicace, et de la pièce elle-même, qui fut excellemment jouée. Et j'espère que nous aurons bien d'autres occasions de l'entendre, désormais. Comme toujours dans votre musique, il y a une admirable écriture, très fouillée, et une grande invention dont j'ai fait plus d'une fois mon profit. Nous avons tous regretté votre absence, seul point noir de ce tableau, très idyllique!

Je viens d'apprendre par Brigitte Marger que vous avez fini *Penthode* pour l'Ensemble, et je m'en réjouis vivement.[83] Nous l'avons gardé dans un programme des Proms pour le 26 juillet et je compte bien sur votre présence pour nous suivre dans les répétitions et assister à l'exécution.[84]

Merci encore, chaleureusement, de votre pièce, et aussi du texte pour le Festschrift.[85] Il m'a remis en mémoire une anecdote (le programme brûlé) dont je ne me souvenais absolument plus.[86] Il faut sans doute mettre cela sur le compte de l'arrosage des fins de banquet... Mais enfin un acte révélateur est un acte révélateur, le "tonus" des circonstances enlevant toute limite à la bienséance.

A vous et à Helen, mes très amicales pensées,
PB

[Autograph letter; Elliott Carter Collection, Paul Sacher Foundation.
Reprinted by permission of Pierre Boulez.]

---

83 *Penthode* for five instrumental groups was written in 1984–85 in response to a commission from the Ensemble Inter-Contemporain. Brigitte Marger was the ensemble's managing director.

84 The première of *Penthode* took place as scheduled – and in Carter's presence – in London's Royal Albert Hall on 26 July 1985; see below, p. 265.

85 Elliott Carter, "For Pierre on his Sixtieth," in *Pierre Boulez: Eine Festschrift zum 60. Geburtstag am 26. März 1985*, ed. Josef Häusler (Vienna: Universal Edition, 1985), pp. 12–13, reprinted in *CEL*, pp. 199–200. Besides this festschrift, Boulez was also honored in Baden-Baden with an exhibition in the Staatliche Kunsthalle entitled "Hommage à Pierre Boulez" (24 March – 14 April 1985).

86 Carter, in his article, recalled the following occurrence during the concluding celebrations of the 1955 ISCM festival in Baden-Baden (where he had first met Boulez): "Boulez jumped up on a table and with quite a flourish burned the festival program, pronouncing that most of the music played at such festivals was 'caduc.'" (Elliott Carter, "For Pierre on his Sixtieth" [see note 86], pp. 13 and 200, respectively.)

143 Elliott Carter and Goffredo Petrassi with Dorothy Dorow
(Rome, 1985)

From early January to mid-March 1985 Carter again resided at the American Academy in Rome. This time his
hosts decided to join forces with the Aspen Institute Italy
and devote two events to Carter and his friend Goffredo
Petrassi: a panel discussion moderated by Roman Vlad
(Villa Aurelia, 20 February 1985)[87] and a concert entitled
"Un piccolo omaggio a Goffredo Petrassi ed Elliott Carter" (Teatro Ghione, 24 February 1985). The photograph
shown here was taken at this concert, which featured
three works by Petrassi – *Sestina d'autunno* (*"Veni, creator
Igor"*) (1981–82), *Grand Septuor* with concertante clarinet

(1977–78), and *Elogio per un'ombra* for solo violin (1971) –
as well as Carter's *Riconoscenza per Goffredo Petrassi* for
solo violin (1984) and the Italian première of the song
cycle *A Mirror on Which to Dwell.* The performers were
Georg Mönch (violin), Franco Ferranti (clarinet), Dorothy Dorow (soprano), and the Musica d'Oggi ensemble
conducted by Richard Dufallo. A few weeks earlier Carter had also been honored in Milan, in the form of a public
masterclass entitled "Incontro con Elliott Carter" (Civi-
ca Scuola di Musica, 5–6 February 1985) and a recital of
his chamber music.

87 The discussion, edited by Raffaele Pozzi,
was published as "Goffredo Petrassi –
Elliott Carter: Cronaca di un'amicizia"
in *Piano Time,* no. 30 (September 1985),
pp. 32–37.

144 William Glock and Elliott Carter at the back entrance
to Royal Albert Hall (London, 1985)

When Carter traveled to London to hear the world première of *Penthode* at the Proms (26 July 1985) he got together not only with Pierre Boulez, who had commissioned the piece for the Ensemble InterContemporain and conducted the première, but with the Proms' former director William Glock. Performed by the Ensemble InterContemporain, *Penthode* achieved a noteworthy success in the company of works by York Höller (*Resonance*), Luciano Berio (*Corale*), and Boulez himself (*Eclat/Multiples*). The critic Peter Heyworth was especially taken by Carter's "brilliant use of instrumental colour" and imaginative "play of ideas," which in his opinion placed the work in the proximity of a sophisticated divertimento. At the same time, however, Heyworth confessed that he had difficulty discerning the three formal divisions that Carter had mentioned in his pre-concert talk.[88]

---

88 Peter Heyworth, "Pioneers from the
New World," *The Observer*, 28 July 1985.

String Quartet No. 4 (1985–86)

If Carter emphasized the centrifugal forces in his preceding three string quartets, his concern in the *String Quartet No. 4* – written in 1985–86 to satisfy a joint commission from the Composers String Quartet, the Sequoia String Quartet, and the Thouvenel String Quartet – tended to stress the juxtaposition of disparate elements. Once again the four instruments are conceived as independent personalities, but their individual efforts are ultimately, Carter insisted, subsumed in a higher commonality: "In the Fourth Quartet I've been more concerned with making them all join together; they're all playing different things but somehow they're all interconnected with each other."[89] To put it another way, this piece, like the *String Quartet No. 2,* can be viewed as a conversation among four individuals characterized by particular intervals, tempos, and expressive gestures, but the participants are much more mellow, or less antagonistic, than in the earlier quartet. Accordingly Carter, although he again divided the score into four overlapping movements (Appassionato, Scherzando, Lento, Presto), avoided relatively long solo episodes or cadenzas of the sort found in the *String Quartet No. 2.* Like most of his compositions from this period, the *String Quartet No. 4* is based on an underlying polyrhythm (more specifically it extends from m. 3 to the conclusion in m. 464) which can be expressed in the ratio 120 : 126 : 175 : 98. Carter also used this polyrhythm to measure off the four equally long movements: the decisive changes of direction for the transitions from one movement to another occur on the thirty-first, sixty-first, and ninety-first of the 120 pulsation points in the first violin. Yet, in typically Carterian fashion, the "official" openings of these movements, as opposed to their initial events, are slightly shifted.[90] The work was completed in June 1986 and premièred in Miami on 17 September 1986 by the Composers String Quartet, to whom it is dedicated.

In addition to the more cooperative than combative stance of its four instrumentalists, one of the main features of the *String Quartet No. 4* is the more discontinuous flux of its musical discourse compared to other works. Carter himself singled out this feature for comment: "My earlier music is similar to Bach's in which there's a continuous stream of music, whilst this Fourth Quartet is more like Mozart or Haydn or Beethoven in which the music is broken up into various phrases punctuated with pauses. Sometimes the pause comes in as a dramatic effect."[91] Nowhere does this find clearer expression than in the alternation of *pianissimo* and *tranquillo* sections and the violent *fortissimo* hammerblows in the quartet's concluding passage, from which mm. 434–444 are shown here from Carter's fair copy of the score. Admittedly, the four instruments go their own ways, each emphasizing a different subset of the intervallic repertoire (violin 1: major second and major sixth; violin 2: minor third, tritone, and major seventh; viola: major third, perfect fifth, and minor seventh; cello: minor second, perfect fourth, and minor sixth). Further, each moves at a different speed, as can be seen in the unequal subdivisions of the beat. As a result, only twice in the entire excerpt do attacks coincide: on beat 2 of m. 438 (violin 2 and cello) and beat 4 of m. 442 (violins 1 and 2).[92] Yet all instruments participate equally in the section's predominant characteristic: the abrupt change from muted sustained sonorities harking back to the slow movement (here mm. [431]–435, 437–441, and 443–[445]) to violent interjections (mm. 436–437 and 442). The glaring contrast thus results not from the superposition of conflicting materials, but from their successive juxtaposition. The short pauses in which the players place and remove their mutes have the added dramatic function of heightening the contrast.[93] This passage is of such great urgency that one reviewer of the New York première, Leighton Kerner, called it an "echo of the Orpheus-and-Furies evocation in [the slow movement of] Beethoven's G-major piano concerto," the more so as "the appeasingly soft-voice Orpheus, the hero of *Syringa,* prevails at the end, as he does in Beethoven."[94]

89 "Elliott Carter's New String Quartet – An Interview with the Composer" [interview with Robert Matthew-Walker], *Music and Musicians* (September 1986), pp. 10–12, esp. 12.

90 See John Link, "Long-Range Polyrhythms in Elliott Carter's Recent Music" (Ph. D. diss., City University of New York, 1994), pp. 63–64.

91 "Elliott Carter's New String Quartet" (see note 90), p. 12.

92 The former passage (m. 438, beat 2) is also the penultimate of a total of twenty-one points of partial intersection in the structural polyrhythm, i.e. those formed by the coincident pulse of two or three instruments.

93 In the printed score, published in 1989 by Hendon Music/Boosey & Hawkes

(M051211302/HPS 1130), Carter proposed an alternative if the placement or removal of the mutes should take too long: namely, to switch from *sul tasto* to normal bowing.

94 Leighton Kerner, "Elliott Carter: Gang of Four," *Village Voice,* 30 December 1986, p. 90. The New York première was given by the Composers String Quartet in Merkin Hall on 13 December 1986.

145 *String Quartet No. 4*

A View on Counterpoint (1986)

The following letter is Carter's response to the outline of a course on counterpoint that his fellow-composer William Bergsma (1921–1994) planned to hold at the University of Washington in Seattle in the winter semester 1986–87. Bergsma had sent the outline with the note "Dear Elliott: /??/ Best ever / BB," and Carter felt called upon to write a critique of Bergsma's ideas. He found fault especially with the latter's attempt to describe such phenomena as collages of heterogeneous materials or minimalist layering techniques as continuations of traditional contrapuntal practices, i.e., as "extended counterpoint" under the conditions of a modern "hypotactic" concept of time. Among other things, Bergsma had written: "We are linear; twentieth-century harmony is defined and dead; motor rhythm out-of-fashion; texture commands. We enter the theater of the absurd, the theater of cruelty. [...] But the general acceptance of current practice has not brought forth a body of criticism and analysis equal to the scope of what seems to me a new procedure: extended counterpoint, counterpoint out of joint, so to speak; asymmetrical, nonsynchronous; not smooth and joined, but jagged, superimposed." In contrast Carter, pointing to Mahler, insisted on distinguishing between the generic term of polyphony and the craft of counterpoint, with its aim of precise vertical combinations of sound. Disappointed by the *al fresco* effects of many post-modern collage compositions, he was more than ever willing to stand up for this craft.

146 **Elliott Carter to William Bergsma, 7 August 1986**

Dear Bill,

I am not sure whether your syllabus of counterpoint is asking for a serious or a comic rebuttal. In either case, I am not endowed with enough leisure now to answer more than briefly and dully. To me counterpoint as it came to be practised in [the] XVIIIth & XIXth centuries involved, as you know only too well, a very careful vertical control of the coincidences of the various parts. Even from the time of Josquin, whose work is more often called polyphonic, there is a very careful systematization of how the parts sounded together according to accepted consonances and dissonant resolution. But by Mahler's time things began to change – Mahler is quoted by Natalie Bauer-Lechner as saying: "[...] da ich seltsamerweise von jeher nicht anders [musikalisch] denken konnte als polyphon. Hier aber fehlt mir wahrscheinlich heute noch der Kontrapunkt, der reine Satz, welcher da für jeden Schüler, der ihn geübt hat, spielend eingreifen müßte." [...] "Jetzt begreife ich, daß Schubert, wie man erzählt, noch kurz vor seinem Ende Kontrapunkt studieren wollte. Er empfand, wie der ihm fehlte. Und ich kann ihm das nachfühlen, weil mir selbst dieses Können und ein richtiges, hundertfältiges Üben in Kontrapunkt aus der Lernzeit so abgeht." [(...) since as far back as I can remember my musical thinking was, oddly enough, never anything but polyphonic. But here I'm probably still suffering from lack of strict counterpoint, which every student who has been trained in it would use at this point with the greatest of ease. (...) Now I can understand why, as we are told, Schubert still wanted to study counterpoint even shortly before his death. He was aware of what he lacked. And I can feel for him in this, as I myself am deficient in this technique, having missed a really thorough grounding in counterpoint in my student years.][95]

So Mahler was making a distinction between polyphony (which he later mentions as existing between various distant musics heard from the top of a mountain)[96] and the vertically controlled counterpoint. Now, of course, we also know about heterophony used in so many kinds of oriental music. To my mind, most of the examples you give[97] are primarily heterophonic, i.e., canonic, without much concern for the vertical effect – a tiresome

---

95 Natalie Bauer-Lechner, *Erinnerungen an Gustav Mahler* (Leipzig etc.: E. P. Tal, 1923), pp. 154 and 138. The English translation is quoted from Natalie Bauer-Lechner, *Recollections of Gustav Mahler*, trans. Dika Newlin, ed. Peter Franklin (Cambridge etc.: Cambridge University Press, 1980), p. 162 and 147.

96 Ibid., p. 147.

97 Among his examples Bergsma had listed Henry Brant's *Grand Universal Circus* ("polychoral collage"), John Corigliano's *Concerto for Clarinet and Orchestra* (movement three: "spatial counterpoint, disjunct counterpoint, collage canon"), Gunther Schuller's *Seven Studies on Themes of Paul Klee* ("superimposed ostinati, in canon"), and Terry Riley's *In C* ("canon").

procedure that has been so frequently used to fill up orchestral sound and which I parodied in my old *Holiday Overture*. Various attempts to "verticalize" simultaneously sounding lines have been tried by many, including myself (as described in David Schiff's book), but as this takes a lot of time and effort (and is seldom noticed or is meaningful to anyone but the analyst), composers most sensibly avoid anything so publicly useless.

It surprised many students at Juilliard in the old days when Berio was teaching there that he made them do strict counterpoint, although nothing like that was to be used in composition. There is no doubt that such exercises focus the young composer's attention on careful choice of notes, on following a preestablished pattern, and making a musical effect within a very limited frame. This habit of close application to the compositional process, [which] seems to be very essential to some, if more widely adhered to would cut down on the amount of thoughtless junk we have to hear nowadays in concerts.

Sorry not to offer more illuminating and more amusing ideas.

Best,
[Elliott]

August 7, 1986

[Typed letter, carbon copy with autograph corrections; Elliott Carter Collection, Paul Sacher Foundation. Reprinted by permission of Anne Rose Bergsma.]

147 Conlon Nancarrow and Elliott Carter during a
panel discussion with Roeland Hazendonk at the
Holland Festival (Amsterdam 1987), photo by
Irene de Groot (Holland Festival)

From 26 to 28 June 1987 the Amsterdam contemporary music organizer De Ijsbreker presented three concerts at the Thirty-Ninth Holland Festival under the heading "Van en voor Nancarrow, Carter, Cage, Crawford." Here Carter again met up with his old friend Conlon Nancarrow, whom he had not seen for many years (John Cage was unable to attend). On 27 June he also joined Nancarrow in a panel discussion moderated by the music critic Roeland Hazendonk in the arts center De Balie, where the photograph shown here was taken. The concert on that same evening contained works which the three partici-pating composers considered seminal to their own music. Carter proposed Goffredo Petrassi's wind trio *Tre per sette*, Mozart's Quintet in E-flat major for piano, oboe, clarinet, horn, and bassoon (K. 452), and Igor Stravinsky's *Octuor* (a work likewise requested by Nancarrow). Nancarrow asked for excerpts from Bach's *Goldberg Variations* and György Ligeti's *String Quartet No. 1*, while Cage wished for works by Erik Satie (*Trois poèmes d'amour*) and Anton Webern (*Rondo* for string quartet). The program also included one work each by the guests of honor: Carter's *Riconoscenza per Goffredo Petrassi*, Nancarrow's *Study No. 21 for Player Piano*, and Cage's *Winter Music*. Among the performers were the Netherlands Wind Ensemble, the Arditti Quartet, Ronald Brautigam (piano), and Glen Wilson (harpsichord).

147

Oboe Concerto (1986–87)

The *Oboe Concerto*, commissioned by Paul Sacher, marks the beginning of a long artistic collaboration with the oboist, composer, and conductor Heinz Holliger (b. 1939); the resulting "Basel connection" would be played out on the international stages of Holliger's performing tours, as the correspondence below indicates. Even before they met in 1985[98] Carter knew of Holliger's reputation as the foremost oboe soloist of his time, and also of the major works written for him and his wife, the harpist Ursula Holliger (including Luciano Berio's *Sequenza VII* for oboe and Witold Lutosławski's *Double Concerto for Oboe and Harp*). Carter was interested in Holliger's own compositions as well, as his mention of Holliger's *Gesänge der Frühe* in the letters of 5 November and 4 December 1987 indicates (see below, pp. 273 and 275). His collaboration with Holliger continued with the arrangement of *Pastoral* for English horn, marimba, and string orchestra (1943/1988), made at Holliger's request immediately after the work on the *Oboe Concerto* was finished on 10 October 1987, and was followed by *Trilogy* for oboe and harp (1991–92), the *Quintet for Piano and Winds* (1992), *A Six Letter Letter* for English horn (1996), the *Oboe Quartet* (2001), and most recently, the birthday tribute *HBHH* for oboe solo (2007). During the composition of the *Oboe Concerto*, his first solo concerto since the *Piano Concerto*, Carter carried on an extensive correspondence with Holliger about the technical possibilities of the oboe.[99] Holliger's mastery of a large vocabulary of extended techniques for his instrument, many of which he pioneered himself, led Carter to venture further afield in terms of instrumental timbre than was his habit, employing multiphonics (including some multiphonic fluttertongued trills), harmonics, double-key trills, and an extended range; the first note in the oboe part is a high A, a whole step higher than the usual upper limit. As in the *Piano Concerto*, the soloist's relationship with the orchestra is one of contrast, conflict, and misunderstanding. The oboe's more lyrical, impulsive, and thoroughly witty character – like that of the original soloist! – is set against the orchestra's more brash, crude gestures, led by the trombone as a kind of anti-hero. The soloist is supported by a discrete concertino group of percussion and four violas. But the dramaturgy of the *Oboe Concerto* differs from that of the *Piano Concerto* in that the *tutti* group confronts and harangues the oboe without ever managing to subdue it; in the slow, lyrical section with which the piece ends (whose final oboe gesture reverses the contour of the opening one), a kind of reconciliation – or perhaps even a victory for the oboe – has been achieved.[100] At the première in Zürich on 17 June 1988, with Heinz Holliger and the Collegium Musicum conducted by John Carewe, the work was played twice, with remarks from the stage by the composer and the soloist.

148 *Oboe Concerto* (1986–87), short score draft in pencil with markings in colored pencil (mm. "350"–"361" [= mm. 360–371 of the final score])

The dramatic shaping of Carter's concertos evokes the historical concerto principle in a general sense – by vividly representing different kinds of encounters between individuals and groups – but has little in common with any specific concerto form. Even the seemingly traditional solo cadenza, as in the passage shown, has less to do with convention than with its role within the piece's internal drama. In this draft, which Carter completed in July 1987, the cadenza for the concertino group begins after three quarter notes on the beat (which are filled out as chords in the final version), analogous perhaps to the cadential 6/4. The oboe line itself is divided into two distinct voices (indicated by the direction of the stems), the upper one soft and sustained, and the lower one loud, staccato, and accented. This (for the oboe) natural dynamic profile is reversed as the voices cross: the *piano* upper voice descends and the *forte* lower one ascends, both having adopted the monosyllabic utterances characteristic of the previous "lower" voice (mm. 358–360). This means that the short notes in the oboe's low register now have to be played more softly than the higher notes, which is very difficult to achieve on the oboe and which allows the soloist to show off his outstanding control of dynamics. Given a tempo of quarter = 93, the oboe's two parts articulate the two main tempos of the piece: the upper voice in mm. 352–358 moves at MM 70, the tempo of the beginning and end of the piece; and the

98 The meeting took place only after Sacher had commissioned the *Oboe Concerto*, at a Carnegie Hall concert of 8 November 1985 in which Holliger played Richard Strauss's *Oboe Concerto* with the Orchestre de la Suisse Romande under Armin Jordan. Holliger recalls that Carter carried the Strauss score in one pocket of his jacket and Friedrich Dürrenmatt's *Der Tunnel* in the other, saying that he wanted to brush up on his German (personal communication from Heinz Holliger, 18 January 2008).

99 For a discussion of Heinz and Ursula Holliger's collaborations with Carter (in *Trilogy*), see Anne C. Shreffler, "Netzwerke der Zusammenarbeit – Heinz und Ursula Holliger," trans. Ulrich Mosch, in "*Entre Denges et Denezy...*": *Dokumente zur Schweizer Musikgeschichte 1900–2000*, ed. Ulrich Mosch in collaboration with Matthias Kassel (Mainz, London etc.: Schott, 2000), pp. 106–116, esp. 113–115.

100 Arnold Whittall gives a compelling reading of the piece's dramaturgy in an untitled review of the *Oboe Concerto* score, *Music and Letters* 73/2 (May 1992), pp. 339–340.

lower one at MM 93+ (actually 93.333 etc.; Carter no longer notates fractional tempos). (The oboe's upper voice moves in units of eight sixteenth-note triplets, which creates the duration of MM 35, or "half notes" in the tempo MM 70, while the lower one clearly articulates the beats in the notated tempo MM 93+.) In the oboe's polyphonic lines two of the contrasting types of oboe writing heard throughout the piece are juxtaposed: lyrical, legato melodic lines and "rude," staccato single notes. The latter are of course more typical of the *tutti* group, especially of the trombone, the oboe's main antagonist. In this brief cadenza, then, the oboe solo part re-enacts the central dramatic conflict of the piece. Here too, as at the end of the piece, the confrontation is resolved in favor of the lyrical voice (mm. 361–363, not shown). In this draft, Carter notates only the oboe's part of the cadenza. In the final version, he adds unobtrusive support for the solo instrument from the concertino group.

149 Elliott Carter to Heinz Holliger, 5 November 1987

Dear Heinz,

Here is a copy of the score of the orchestration of the *Pastoral*.[101] As I took it to be reproduced, I met Angie Marx,[102] who is renting space in the office of my printer and asks to be remembered to you.

As yet the parts have not been extracted, and, since the piano version is printed now by Merion Music, Inc. (Theodore Presser, sole representative, Bryn Mawr, Pennsylvania, 19010), the parts and other copies of the score will have to be rented through them (or their European representative?). We do hope to have the parts ready by the 1st of the year. If you should need them before please let me know *at once.* I am eager to hear this arrangement, as the problem of reducing piano music to strings is not something I am accustomed to do.

I hope that you have had a chance to look a the Oboe Concerto score. I have been looking at it myself and find a number of small omissions (like changes from pizz[icato] to arco, and dynamics not clearly indicated). These will all be taken care of when the parts are extracted. As you see in mm. 380–384, I decided, for the moment, to have the conductor beat a measure or two of quintuplets, but I may decide to write these out as five against the conductor's three in syncopations?

I am busy, now, writing a little flute & cello duet and a 4-minute orchestra piece, before I start on a violin concerto.[103]

I hope this finds you well and Ursula too. How did you ever find time to write your big Schumannerei?[104]

Best from us both
Elliott

31 West 12 Street, NY, NY 10011, November 5, 1987

[Typed letter with autograph signature; private collection of Heinz Holliger (carbon copy in the Elliott Carter Collection, Paul Sacher Foundation). Reprinted by permission of Heinz Holliger.]

---

101 In the program notes to his orchestration of *Pastoral*, Carter wrote: "*Pastoral* for English Horn and Piano was composed in 1940 for the late Josef Marx, who interested me in the instrument. At the request of Heinz Holliger I arranged the score for string orchestra and marimba in October of 1987."

102 Angelina Marx was the second wife of 102 oboist and publisher Josef Marx (1913–1978), who was a friend of Carter's from at least 1944, when the two men premièred the *Pastoral* in its original version for English horn and piano. Holliger, for his part, was in contact with Marx from the early 1960s; they met on 17 March 1963 at a concert in New York's Town Hall, where Holliger appeared with the Lucerne Festival Strings.

103 The duo for flute and cello refers to *Enchanted Preludes* (1987–88), a piece written at the request of Harry Santen for the fiftieth birthday of his wife, the radio producer Anne Santen. The orchestral piece, which was ultimately a good seven minutes longer in performance, was *Remembrance* (1987–88), a memorial piece for Paul Fromm (see below, p. 282). For the *Violin Concerto,* see below, pp. 286–287.

104 Holliger had just finished his *Gesänge der Frühe* after Schumann and Hölderlin, a work commissioned by the Westdeutscher Rundfunk in Cologne and premièred on 4 March 1988 under Matthias Bamert.

150 Heinz Holliger to Elliott Carter, 22 November 1987

Vienna, Nov. 22 1987

Dear Elliott,

I am completely overwhelmed by your marvelous double gift. First, the absolutely fascinating complete score of the Concerto, and now this refined orchestration of *Pastoral*. I admire so much how you achieved to integrate the oboe solo part so completely in[to] the orchestral discourse and yet to have written a very brilliant and prominent solo concerto. I can't wait to hear the piece together.

In the *Pastoral* I admire how you achieved the difficult task to be faithful to a music written 45 years ago, and to give this music wholly new dimensions and perspectives by writing out all the resonances and shadows of the harmonies, and to bring out so clearly the rhythmical shape by the marimba and the pizz[icati]. As the orchestration asks for quite a large string section I am not sure whether we could already play it in Japan (end of January) with the Orpheus Orchestra, New York. I [will] let you know very soon.[105]

After June '88 the Concerto is now scheduled in Geneva (Aug 10) with David Atherton, whom I like very much.[106]

And the German première will very probably be on October 16, '88 in Donaueschingen, with Michael Gielen and [the] SWF Orchestra. I think this is about the best possible solution.[107]

Whether the London première will be on Dec[ember] 12 (with Boulez) or on Sept[ember] 10 (Proms) is not yet decided. But Boulez wants to do an Erato recording after the Paris performance (19 Dec[ember]).[108]

You will soon get more news!

Tonight I have to conduct here at the Vienna Konzerthaus an early Mozart "azione teatrale": *Il sogno di Scipione* (5 singers, chorus, orchestra). 2 hours of mostly very beautiful but delicate music.[109] I hope all goes well...

Best wishes to Helen and you
Yours,
Heinz

[Autograph letter; Elliott Carter Collection, Paul Sacher Foundation. Reprinted by permission of Heinz Holliger.]

151 Elliott Carter to Heinz Holliger, 4 December 1987

Elliott Carter / 31 West 12th Street / New York, N.Y. 10011

Dear Heinz

Thank you for your enthusiastic letter from the middle of the *Sogno di Scipione*. It meant a great deal more than I can express to have you write about my two scores with such approval and appreciation. The parts for the Oboe Concerto are being copied and will be ready – because Paul Sacher asked for them soon – in January.[110] However, the parts for the *Pastoral* have not yet been started, and we are having trouble finding someone to do them very soon, as all copyists here are very booked up.

As soon as I received your letter about the possibility of performing the *Pastoral* in Japan, end of January, with the Orpheus Ensemble, I called the publisher of the *Pastoral*, and we both agreed that it was just barely possible that we could get [the] parts in time. Then I called the manager of Orpheus and found that the strings were less than the score calls for and that there would be no marimba on the tour, but he said he would call you. I also felt that with the restricted rehearsal time you will have in New York it might be hard to get the work in shape for Japan.

Also Howard Hartog called and said that the *Pastoral* might be substituted for the Oboe Concerto at the Proms in September.[111] Apparently the London Sinfonietta has few strings. I looked over my score of the *P[astoral]* and thought it might be possible with 6.5(4).3.3.1. A few changes would have to be made for the contrabass & cello parts, in this case.

Please forgive all this lengthy practicality.

I wonder how you could get that delicate Mozart score to sound in that big Konzerthaus. It is a score I would like to know – even early Mozart is beginning to fascinate me now, as I am commissioned to write a violin concerto[112] and have been studying the Mozart 5 concerti. He was so aware of how to deal with the medium even in those young days! It must be wonderful to be in

---

105 In the end, the première of *Pastoral* in its orchestral version for English horn, marimba, and strings was given by Heinz Holliger and the Orpheus Chamber Orchestra in New York's Carnegie Hall on 25 April 1988.

106 The Geneva performance of the *Oboe Concerto* – with the Orchestre de la Suisse Romande – took place two days later on 12 August 1988 and was conducted by Matthias Bamert rather than David Atherton.

107 This performance at the 1988 Donaueschingen Festival was issued on the CD documentation *40 Jahre Donaueschinger Musiktage 1950–1990*, Col legno AU 318000 (4 CDs, released 1991).

108 The English première of the *Oboe Concerto* took place on 12 December 1988 at London's South Bank Centre during the first of two concerts entitled "Elliott Carter at 80." The French première was given in the Théâtre Renaud-Barrault on 19 December 1988. In both performances

Holliger was joined by the Ensemble InterContemporain and Pierre Boulez. The Erato recording made after the Paris concert is the CD Elliott Carter, *Oboe Concerto; A Mirror on Which to Dwell; Penthode; Esprit rude/Esprit doux I*, with Phyllis Bryn-Julson (soprano), Heinz Holliger (oboe), Sophie Cherrier (flute), André Trouttet (clarinet), and the Ensemble InterContemporain conducted by Pierre Boulez; Erato ECD 75553 (released 1990).

such close contact with Mozart's music for the time it takes to rehearse and perform such a work.

How is your big piece coming along, the one to be performed in March?[113] I don't see how you can get anything composed and also perform, conduct, and travel so much. Just thinking about it makes me feel confused!

From what Orpheus tells me, you will be here in January to rehearse for Japan. I suppose that you will be so busy that we won't see each other. But if you have a moment, give us a ring and maybe something can be arranged.

Helen joins me in sending Ursula and you our love,
Elliott

December 4, 1987

PS: Just before mailing this letter the publisher of the *Pastoral* 'phoned to say he found a copyist who will have the parts ready at the end of the 1st week in January. Also one of the players in Orpheus thinks it might be possible to pick up a marimba player in Japan, if you really want to do the work. Best, E.

[Typed letter with autograph signature; private collection of Heinz Holliger (carbon copy in the Elliott Carter Collection, Paul Sacher Foundation). Reprinted by permission of Heinz Holliger.]

---

109 Holliger conducted Mozart's *Il sogno di Scipione* during the Second Vienna Mozart Festival with the ORF Symphony Orchestra, the Chorus of Vienna University of Economics, Robert Gambill (Scipione), Pamela Coburn (Costanza), Adelina Scarabelli (Fortuna), and other solo vocalists.

110 Paul Sacher had planned to conduct the *Oboe Concerto* himself on 17 June 1988 during a subscription concert of his Collegium Musicum Zurich, but was forced by family concerns to delegate this task to John Carewe. The solo part was taken, as planned, by Heinz Holliger.

111 At that time the Dutch-born English musical organizer Howard Hartog, who had supervised the music program of Northwest German Radio in Hamburg after World War II and later worked for Schott in London, was the head of the concert agents Ingpen & Williams. In this capacity he was also responsible for Heinz Holliger's performances in England.

112 See below, pp. 286–287.

113 A reference to Holliger's *Gesänge der Frühe*; see above, p. 273, note 105.

Apologies from Goffredo Petrassi (1988)

Even in advanced age Carter and Goffredo Petrassi continued to correspond on a regular basis, and Carter visited his Italian colleague whenever the opportunity presented itself. One such opportunity arose when the Twenty-Fourth Pontino di Musica Festival planned a tribute to Carter on his eightieth birthday for the summer of 1988 and asked its honorary president, Petrassi, and several other composers to submit birthday pieces for the event. To his regret Petrassi, who was now almost blind and could neither read nor write, had to turn down this and a similar request from the New York ensemble Speculum Musicae, which likewise planned to mount a tribute to Carter on 1 December 1988 (see below, p. 277). In the following letter he told Carter of his plight and apologized for being unable to present a "Riconoscenza per Elliott Carter" (an allusion to Carter's *Riconoscenza per Goffredo Petrassi* of 1984 for Petrassi's eightieth birthday). Carter replied with great understanding and sympathy. In the end, the Pontino Festival's four-day tribute to Carter (22–25 June 1988) featured birthday pieces by Gérard Grisey (*Accords perdus* for two horns, premièred on 23 June), Henri Pousseur (*Litanie du miel matinal* for high melody instrument, 23 June), Aldo Clementi (*Tribute* for string quartet, 24 June), and Louis de Pablo (*Scherzo* for unaccompanied violin, 24 June), among others, and performed several of Carter's own orchestral and chamber works.[114]

152 Goffredo Petrassi to Elliott Carter, 28 January 1988
(English translation in Appendix 1, pp. 350–351)

Goffredo Petrassi / Via F. di Savoia, 3 / 00196 Roma
Roma, 28 gennaio 1988

Caro Elliott,
con molto ritardo ringrazio te ed Hélène degli auguri per il nuovo anno. Insieme a Rosetta[115] ne ricambiamo a voi due una grande quantità e tutti con grandissimo affetto.

Gli auguri per questo 1988 sono particolarmente calorosi per te, carissimo Amico, perché è l'anno del tuo 80° anniversario che verrà giustamente celebrato in tutto il mondo. Nel mio animo lo celebrerò intimamente con fervore, reso ancora più intenso dalla circostanza in cui mi trovo.

Non so se saprai che da circa due anni ho dei problemi di vista con il mio unico occhio. All'inizio sembrava che il processo dovesse essere non del tutto negativo e che il disturbo si fosse potuto arrestare. Purtroppo non è stato così ed ora la situazione è tale – la dieu mercie [sic] non definitiva – per cui non posso leggere e non posso scrivere.

Avrai solo un'idea del mio dispiacere quando ti dico che ho dovuto rinunciare dolorosamente a scrivere un pezzo in tuo onore che mi è stato richiesto da varie parti, dagli Stati Uniti e dall'Italia. Non mi sarà possibile scrivere a mia volta la "Riconoscenza per Elliott Carter" che mi ripromettevo di ricambiarti proprio in questo solenne anniversario.

Ho voluto darti notizia sulle ragioni della mia assenza tra gli autori da cui riceverai gli omaggi. La carta da musica mi è diventata ostile e la mia fantasia si è oscurata ma io cerco di rimediare come posso alle varie limitazioni a cui sono costretto.

Lo spirito, per fortuna, è forte e la salute è buona. Della tua eccellente forma ho avuto un esempio dalla fotografia che ti ritrae felicemente riposato dopo un bagno nel lago; ne ho avuto molto piacere e me ne rallegro.

Ho appreso dal nostro eccellente amico architetto [Riccardo] Cerocchi, che al prossimo Festival Pontino, ove sarai doverosamente festeggiato, hai promesso di rimanere una settimana intera a S. Felice Circeo. In quel periodo io spero di avere la mia casa aperta e di poter passare qualche ora insieme.

Mi scuso di averti recato disturbo con le mie traversie private, le quali spiegano anche perchè ricorro alla macchina da scrivere per questa lettera amichevole: è una "impolitesse" che in altri tempi mi sarei ben guardato di commettere.

Rosetta vi ricorda teneramente ed io vi abbraccio con la stessa tenerezza.
Goffredo

[Typed letter with autograph signature; Elliott Carter Collection, Paul Sacher Foundation. Reprinted by permission of Rosetta Acerbi Petrassi.]

---

114 The tribute to Carter formed the opening of a roughly six-week festival. It included three evening concerts dedicated to Carter, with works by various composers (22–24 June 1988), as well as a matinée and an evening concert of Carter's own works (25 June 1988). The matinée on 25 June featured the Arditti String Quartet and Luigi Sini playing *String Quartets Nos. 2 and 4* and *Changes.* In contrast, the evening concert on 25 June, given by the Orchestra Sinfonica di Roma della RAI under Eberhard Kloke, included not only Carter's *Symphony No. 1* and the *Suite from "The Minotaur,"* but two compositions by Petrassi: *Frammento per orchestra* (from an incomplete composition of 1983) and *Poema* for strings and trumpet (1977–80). There was also a seminar and a round-table discussion on 24 and 25 June 1988, respectively, involving Carter, Petrassi, and other musicians and critics.

115 Petrassi was married to the painter Rosetta Acerbi from 1961.

153 Elliott Carter to Goffredo Petrassi, 14 March 1988
(English translation in Appendix 1, p. 351)

Elliott Carter / 31 West 12th Street / New York, N.Y. 10011
le 14 mars 1988

Carissimo Goffredo,
Je suis vraiment très triste de savoir que ton bon œil ne
fonctionne pas bien et qu'il te faut écrire à la machine.
Cette détérioration de ta vue doit être épouvantablement
pénible et je te plains de tout mon cœur.

D'autre part j'étais très flatté que tu as même pensé
d'écrire quelque chose pour mon anniversaire, et je te remercie vivement.

Heureusement nous aurons le grand plaisir de vous
voir tous les deux à San Felice du 22 au (?) 28 juin. Une première présentation d'un film TV sur John Cage (!) et moi-
même le 21 juin à Amsterdam,[116] à laquelle j'ai promis
d'assister, nous fait manquer le début du Festival Pontino.[117]
Mais nous nous réjouissons, Hélène et moi, du prospect
de la rencontre avec Rosette et toi et de recommencer ce
bavardage si cher à moi qui a commencé en 1954.

Hélène me joint en vous envoyant tous les deux nos amitiés très affectueuses,
Elliott

Excuse écriture illisible – j'ai l'habitude de la machine.

[Autograph letter; Fondo Goffredo Petrassi, Campus Internazionale di Musica,
Latina. Reprinted by permission of Rosetta Acerbi Petrassi.]

A Birthday Gift from Witold Lutosławski (1988)

Witold Lutosławski (1913–1994), the leading Polish composer of his generation, had met Carter in 1962 during
the latter's first visit to the Warsaw Autumn Festival of
Contemporary Music (see above, p. 178). Thereafter the
two composers remained in regular contact. It was therefore only fitting that the New York ensemble Speculum
Musicae should invite Lutosławski to submit a congrat-
ulatory piece for the concert it was planning in honor
of Carter's eightieth birthday. The result, *Slides*, was premièred by Speculum Musicae in Merkin Hall on 1 December 1988 during a concert entitled "An 80th Birthday
Tribute to Elliott Carter." Two weeks later Carter, who
was honored with many other New York performances
in December 1988,[118] expressed his thanks in a letter. Five
years later he took the opportunity to reciprocate this
friendly gesture with his *Gra* for unaccompanied clarinet (1993), commissioned by the Pontino di Musica Festival for Lutosławski's eightieth birthday.

**154 Witold Lutosławski, *Slides* [Przezrocza], for 11 soloists
(1988), autograph full score in ink, p. 4**

Written between 4 and 13 September 1988, Lutosławski's
birthday present for Carter, *Slides*, is conceived as a sort
of "slide show." The short, highly contrasting episodes
recall isolated memories (perhaps scenes from the two
men's friendship), while the interpolated percussion flourishes imitate the noise produced by a slide projector when
changing slides. The percussionist, stationed in the middle with his back to the audience, has to play six instruments (gran cassa, three tom-toms, two bongos) and function as a conductor. Rather than giving signs, however,
he marks the beginnings and endings of the episodes
with his entrances. Within these episodes the other ten
instrumentalists must play their parts, whose pitch content is precisely defined but whose rhythmic execution
is left uncoordinated. Such passages of "limited aleatori-
cism" are a typical feature of Lutosławski's mature style
and are easy to recognize in the musical notation – as illustrated by the page shown here, written entirely without bar lines. Here we see the short passage following the
second percussion flourish, in which the woodwinds and

---

116 A reference to the film *Time is Music:
Elliott Carter and John Cage*, directed
by Frank Scheffer and produced by
Henk Pauwls (Amsterdam: Sine Film/
Video, 1988).

117 Carter ultimately managed to catch the
opening of the Pontino di Musica Festival:
he flew from Amsterdam to Rome on
22 June and was present at the very first of

the concerts dedicated to him (in Latina
that very evening).

118 On 3–4 December 1988 the New York
Chamber Symphony, conducted by
Gerald Schwarz, gave the first concert
performance of the complete ballet score
for *The Minotaur* at the 92nd Street Y.
On 4 December 1988 Ursula Oppens
(piano) and the American Composers
Orchestra gave an afternoon performance

of the *Piano Concerto* in Carnegie Hall.
That evening, likewise in Carnegie
Hall, Herbert Blomstedt conducted the
San Francisco Symphony in the New York
première of the *Oboe Concerto*, with
Heinz Holliger as soloist. The latter
concert also included *Birthday Flourish*
for five trumpets, a short birthday present
for Helen Carter composed on 4 July
1988.

154 Witold Lutosławski, *Slides*

strings (except for the double bass) play rapid chromatic arabesques during a predefined period of ten to twenty seconds. These figures of varying length are repeated *ad libitum* until the next flourish from the percussionist. The opening of this flourish, indicated by the broken vertical line on the right-hand side of the page, causes the collective to fall abruptly silent.

[Witold Lutosławski Collection, Paul Sacher Foundation.]

155 Elliott Carter to Witold Lutosławski, 15 December 1988

Elliott Carter / 31 West 12th Street / New York, N.Y. 10011
December 15, 1988

Dear Witold,
Slides! Thank you very much for such a fascinating and so Lutosławskiesque birthday present. Full of charm and delight, your lovely piece was directed by Joe Passaro, the fantastic percussionist, who stunned us with his fanciful explosions that punctuated marvelous soft music, each a gem in itself – Your *Slides* gave the birthday concert a lively brightness that it otherwise would have lacked[119] –

On top of that we heard your evocative *Piano Concerto* with its enchanting stillnesses so effectively presented by [Krystian] Zimerman.[120] It was a great hit with the Philharmonic (N[ew] Y[ork]) public –

Helen joins me in sending Danuta & you our love[121] & wishes for a Merry Christmas & Happy New Year – & much, much gratitude
Elliott

[Autograph letter; Witold Lutosławski Collection, Paul Sacher Foundation. Reprinted by permission.]

---

119 The program of Speculum Musicae's tribute on 1 December 1988 included three compositions by Carter (the *Sonata for Flute, Oboe, Cello, and Harpsichord* and the vocal pieces *Syringa* and *A Mirror on Which to Dwell*) as well as Lutosławski's birthday present and a dedicatory piece by Milton Babbitt (*The Crowded Air* for eleven instruments). A compositional tribute from Pierre Boulez, though announced, had to be cancelled as the composer was unable to complete the piece on schedule. He completed the piece, *Dérive II*, fifteen years later, in time for Carter's ninety-fifth birthday.

120 Krystian Zimerman played the Lutosławski *Piano Concerto* in Avery Fisher Hall on 1–3 and 6 December 1988 during a concert of the New York Philharmonic conducted by Zubin Mehta.

121 Lutosławski was married to Maria Danuta Bogusławska (*née* Dygat) from 1946.

"... immer neu ..."

1988–1998

156 Oliver Knussen and Elliott Carter at the
      Tanglewood Festival (Lenox, MA, 1988), photo by Walter
      Scott (Boosey & Hawkes Collection/ArenaPAL)

Among the institutions that paid tribute to Carter in the year of his eightieth birthday was the Tanglewood Festival. On 9 August 1988 it mounted a chamber music recital with works by David Schiff, Bayan Northcott, and Peter Lieberson as well as Carter's *Canon for 4, Riconoscenza per Goffredo Petrassi, Esprit rude / Esprit doux I, Enchanted Preludes, Brass Quintet,* and *Triple Duo;* and the next day Oliver Knussen conducted the Tanglewood Music Center Orchestra in *A Celebration of Some 100 × 150 Notes* and *Remembrance,* the memorial piece that Carter was commissioned by the Fromm Music Foundation to write for Paul Fromm, who had died on 4 July 1987. This marked the première of the latter piece, which was immediately encored.[1] (The two works were later combined with *Anniversary* to form the *Three Occasions for Orchestra;* see below, p. 284). These two concerts were relatively modest affairs compared to the lavish tribute to Leonard Bernstein for his seventieth birthday (the critic Leighton

Kerner even spoke of an "economy-size salute"[2]), but the balance was to a certain extent restored by the fact that, after the concert of 10 August, Carter received the Boston Symphony's Mark M. Horblit Award. The driving force behind the Carter performances was Oliver Knussen, who headed the Tanglewood Festival of Contemporary Music from 1986 to 1988. In his birthday greetings published shortly thereafter, Knussen stressed Carter's importance to his own evolution as a composer and called it a privilege to have been associated with his music as a conductor for so long. He also emphasized the special significance various Carter concerts at the Tanglewood Festival had had for him, "beginning with our attempt at the extraordinary, craggy single-movement mountain that is *Penthode,* and culminating this year in the first performance of *Remembrance,* his magnificent, stark and moving elegy for Paul Fromm."[3]

1   The concert also included works by
     Hans Werner Henze (his cello concerto
     Sieben Liebeslieder, conducted by the
     composer with Yo-Yo Ma as soloist),
     Jorge Liderman (*For Orchestra*), and Colin
     Matthews (*Fourth Sonata for Orchestra*).
     Knussen had also conducted the
     Brass Quintet and the *Triple Duo* the
     previous day.

2   Leighton Kerner, "Toward the Sun,"
     Village Voice, 27 September 1988,
     p. 94.

3   Oliver Knussen, untitled contribution
     to "Carter at 80," *Quarternotes* (Boosey
     & Hawkes, November 1988), p. [3].
     The Tanglewood performance of
     Penthode, mentioned by Knussen, took
     place on 3 August 1986.

157 Helen and Elliott Carter with Heinz Holliger at
the Paul Sacher Foundation (Basel, 1988), photo by
Lukas Handschin (Paul Sacher Foundation)

On 4 November 1988 the Carters took advantage of their stay at the Römerbad Hotel in the South German town of Badenweiler – the scene of a Carter festival from 9 to 13 November 1988[4]– to make a side trip to the Paul Sacher Foundation in Basel, where they also met up with Heinz Holliger. Carter had been present at the opening of the Foundation on 28 April 1986, and had since accepted Sacher's offer to place the bulk of his music manuscripts, letters, and other documents on his life and work in the Foundation's care. This offer had caused him a certain amount of headache, for it involved retrieving all the documents that he had placed on deposit years earlier in the Library of Congress and the New York Public Library. Nonetheless, Carter ultimately consented to the proposal, and in December 1987 he signed a contract that led to the transfer of his papers to Basel in February 1988.[5] His decision was received in America with a mixture of admiration and disappointment. Characteristic of the reactions from Carter's circle of friends were the following words

from Minna Lederman: "It's a great honor, of course, to be in [Sacher's] famous collection, and well deserved. [...] But you, Elliott, I can only think of as deeply American, and – though without deserved honor in your own country – still an integral part of it."[6] Carter himself took the nationalistic argument seriously, but gave it a different turn: "I regretted, of course, that my material would leave America, but I also realized that the payment I received could be more useful to American contemporary music than the presence of my manuscripts on this side of the Atlantic."[7] This comment was an allusion to the fact that the proceeds from the sale were earmarked for the Amphion Foundation he had founded in summer 1987. Since then the foundation has helped to advance a great many music projects, lending its support to concerts, CD productions, and music festivals in accordance with its stated purpose "to foster and promote excellence in, and public appreciation of, contemporary concert music, particularly by American composers."[8]

4   Besides works by various composers, the festival presented performances of Carter's *Piano Sonata* (by Noel Lee, 9 November), *Sonata for Violoncello and Piano* (with Frances-Marie Uitti and Ursula Oppens, 10 November), *Night Fantasies* (Charles Rosen, 11 November), *String Quartet No. 1* (Arditti Quartet, 12 November), and *A Mirror on Which to Dwell* and

Triple Duo (with Phyllis Bryn-Julson and Ensemble Modern, conducted by Heinz Holliger, 13 November).

5   See Felix Meyer, "Die Sammlung Elliott Carter in der Sacher-Stiftung," *Neue Zürcher Zeitung*, 10–11 December 1988, p. 65, supplement "Literatur und Kunst."

6   Letter from Minna Lederman to Elliott Carter, 5 February 1988; carbon copy

in the Estate of Minna Lederman Daniel, private collection.

7   Bernard, "Interview with Elliott Carter" (see above, p. 101, note 41), p. 206.

8   Quoted from the official "Guidelines" of the Amphion Foundation (15th floor, 254 West 31st Street, New York, NY 10001).

Anniversary (1989),
from *Three Occasions* (1986–89)

Although Carter generally conceived his works as unified wholes, in a few cases he combined pieces that were originally unrelated. One example is *Three Occasions for Orchestra* (1986–89), which received its full title only *ex post facto* and accordingly more closely resembles a loose gathering akin to Ives's "orchestral sets" than a holistic unity. The first piece, *A Celebration of Some 100×150 Notes*, was written in 1986 in response to a commission from the Houston Symphony Orchestra for its approaching 150th anniversary in 1987, whereas the second, *Remembrance*, originated in 1988 in commemoration of the arts patron Paul Fromm, with whom Carter had been closely associated for more than three decades. (The piece was commissioned by the Fromm Music Foundation for the Tanglewood Festival of Contemporary Music.) Still more personal were the circumstances surrounding the third piece, *Anniversary*, which Carter dedicated to his wife Helen in 1989 in honor of their fiftieth wedding anniversary. It bears a fitting quotation from a poem by John Donne: "Only our love hath no decay; / This, no to morrow hath, nor yesterday, / Running it never runs from us away, / But truly keepes his first, last, everlasting day."[9] By then Carter was well aware that the three pieces could be combined in performance, for Oliver Knussen, having already conducted both *Celebration* and *Remembrance*, asked him for a new work to form a "triptych." Carter took this into account by brightening the orchestral writing vis-à-vis the two preceding pieces and avoiding certain instrumental effects he had employed there. *Anniversary* was premièred on 5 October 1989 in London's Royal Festival Hall during the first complete performance of *Three Occasions*, with Oliver Knussen conducting the BBC Symphony Orchestra.

158 *Three Occasions*, for orchestra (1986–89); no. 3, *Anniversary* (1989), short score draft in pencil with corrections in colored pencil, p. [9] (mm. 96–114)

It is with good reason that David Schiff has referred to the orchestral piece *Anniversary*, completed on 25 May 1989, as "Carter's tongue-in-cheek *Sinfonia domestica*" (Schiff 1998, p. 314), for the piece is based on an underlying structure of two interwoven contrapuntal lines joined later by a third, all of which can be readily construed as depicting the life-lines of the Carters and their son. Here we see the "birth" of the third line in a twenty-three-page short-score draft of March–April 1989 labeled "new version." This refers to the penultimate bar of the first system (m. 99), where a long instrumental solo (later assigned to the horn) enters on the final beat, starting on a tied-over B♮ in the second staff from the top. This added melodic line is easily visible on the page, as the skeletal texture, starting from the second system, now appears on three staves rather than two. Thereafter every top staff of the score contains the "second" voice that entered the piece in m. 6 (Carter marked this voice "X" in the published score), every second staff the newly added "third" voice ("Z"), and every third staff the "first" voice ("Y"), initially heard in m. 3 of *Anniversary*. (The lower systems of the staves contain all the other elements in the compositional fabric, such as chords, long sustained notes, and rapid figuration.) In keeping with the work's "program," the final word is ultimately given to the third of the three voices with their contrasting intervallic material (the third voice emphasizes the minor second and tritone), and the piece ends *mezzo-forte* with an ascending gesture on the tuba and bass clarinet while X and Y fade away in *piano* and *pianissimo*.

---

9 John Donne, "The Anniversarie"; quoted from idem, *Selected Poems*, ed. John Haward (Harmondsworth: Penguin Books, 1950), p. 37.

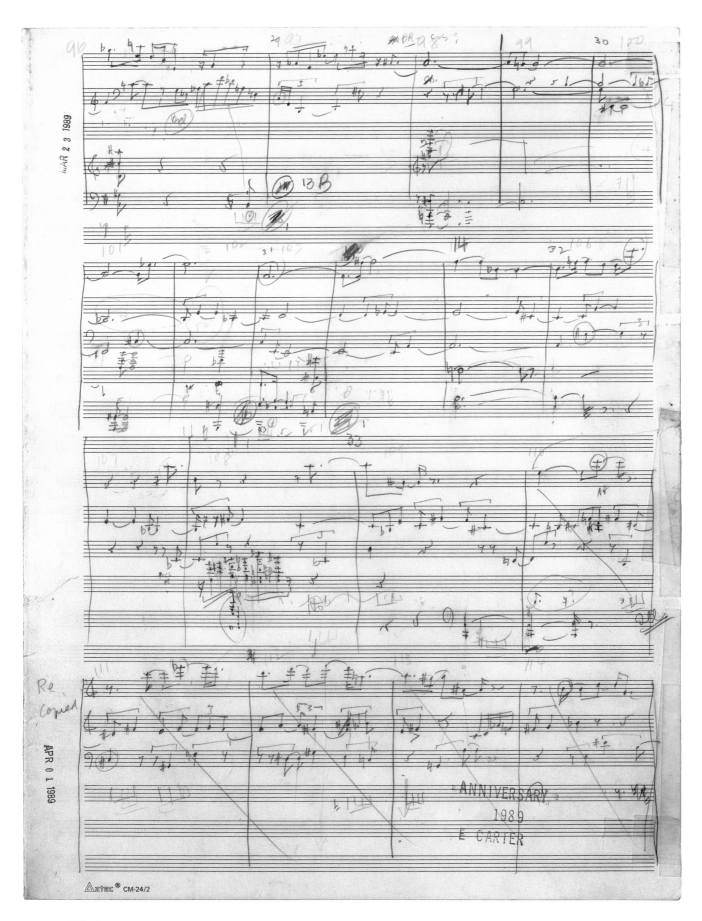

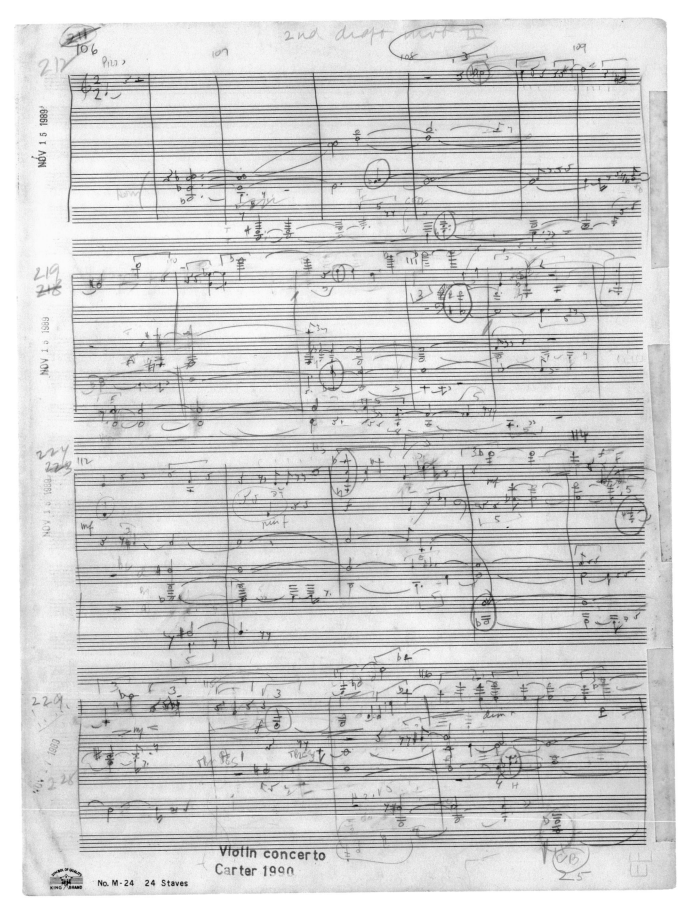

Violin concerto
Carter 1990

Violin Concerto (1988–90)

Although the violinist Ole Böhn (b. 1945) had long urged Carter to compose a violin concerto, it was only when his request coincided with a commission from the San Francisco Symphony Orchestra ("through the generosity of Mrs. Ralph I. Dorfman") that Carter finally brought the project to fruition in 1988–90. The conception and drafting of the work, which was completed in late February 1990, were subject to delays, not least owing to Carter's extensive travels in the year of his eightieth birthday and his ensuing health problems. While working on the piece, Carter immersed himself in scores and recordings of the concerto literature for violin, as can be seen, for example, in the reference to his perusal of Mozart's concertos in his letter of 4 December 1987 to Heinz Holliger (see above, pp. 274–275). From this study he resolved, first of all, to avoid any form of stereotyped "violinistic" figuration, and, second, to help the soloist to stand out more conspicuously than is the case in many works of his predecessors and contemporaries. Consequently the relationship between soloist and orchestra in the *Violin Concerto* is far less confrontational than in his earlier concertos: the soloist, rather than being surrounded by a concertino and given an almost uninterrupted solo line, functions as the uncontested protagonist for long stretches at a time, and the orchestra, to quote David Schiff, is "no longer a threatening adversary, but a scattered landscape brought together and redeemed by the solo protagonist's lyrical propositions."[10] Still, Schiff's description is far more applicable to the first two movements ("Impulsivo" and "Tranquillo/Angosciato") than to the finale ("Scherzando"), whose tarantella rhythms and jazz sounds markedly intensify the interaction between soloist and orchestra, only to cast them asunder in the solo cadenza shortly before the end. The three movements are separated by written-out pauses, including the soloist's simulated "tuning" of the open strings. The *Violin Concerto* was premièred on 2–5 May 1990 by Ole Böhn and the San Francisco Symphony Orchestra, conducted by Herbert Blomstedt.

159 *Violin Concerto* (1988–90), second moement, short score draft in pencil with markings in colored pencil, p. [1] (mm. "212"–"233" [= mm. 213–234 of the final score])

The center of gravity in the *Violin Concerto* is its second movement, whose dual heading "Tranquillo/Angosciato" refers to a simultaneous rather than consecutive expressive contrast between the orchestra and the solo part. This contrast is clearly visible in the second short-score draft of the movement, written in November 1989. Here we see the first page with mm. "212"–"233" (mm. 213–234 in the definitive score). The solo part is kept in a free style akin to recitative and almost exhausts its full ambitus, whereas the orchestral writing consists almost entirely of sustained low-register sonorities involving, as a few instrument cues reveal, mainly the brass and double basses. Referring to this movement Carter one spoke of the "struggles of a lone swimmer at sea."[11] The image is readily comprehensible: the violin's utterances – now tentative, now agitated, always interspersed with short pauses for breath – do indeed suggest the tense predicament of a man left entirely to his own devices, while the slowly changing chordal surfaces of the orchestra evoke an image of a tranquil but threatening sea. The final score, unlike the draft, contains meticulously assigned crescendo and diminuendo marks to these orchestral chords, which add further emphasis to the "wave-like" ebb and flow of the music. In contrast, the draft makes another aspect of the work visible: its overriding polyrhythm, which Carter, as so often in his working manuscripts, has marked by encircling particular notes and chords. The markings in purple, green, and brown crayon indicate that the pulses of the solo violin (in mm. "216," "221," "226," and "230") occur at intervals of twenty-eight quarter-note triplets, and that the orchestral part contains two superposed rhythmic layers: a "fast" layer with pulses in mm. "215," "221," "227," and "232" (at intervals of forty-five eighth notes) and a "slow" one with pulses at mm. "216," "222," and "228" (at intervals of sixty-three eighth-note quintuplets). However, this three-tiered structure can be felt only subliminally: what one hears is mainly the dualism between soloist and orchestra, not only in the rhythm and the level of gesture and expression, but also in the typically Carterian assignment of complementary intervals (violin: minor second, minor third, perfect fifth, minor sixth, and minor seventh; orchestra: major second, major third, perfect fourth, major sixth, major seventh).

---

10 David Schiff, "Carter's Violin Concerto,"
Tempo, no. 174 (September 1990),
pp. 22–24, esp. 24.

11 Ibid., p. 23.

Inner Song, from *Trilogy* (1991–92)

In 1991 Heinz Holliger asked Carter to write a work for un-accompanied oboe, to be performed during a memorial concert for Stefan Wolpe at the Witten Festival of New Chamber Music (the year 1992 marked both the composer's ninetieth birthday and the twentieth anniversary of his death). Carter was very happy to comply with the request, since he had friendly connections with both Holliger and Wolpe. He began work in November 1991, and, since at this time he was already composing a harp piece for Ursula Holliger (commissioned for the Geneva-based ensemble Contrechamps), he soon decided to expand the two solo pieces into a trilogy by adding a final duo for both instruments (*Immer neu*), with each item preceded by a quotation from Rainer Maria Rilke's *Sonette an Orpheus* and their connection further strengthened by the appearance of three sustained notes on the oboe in the introductory harp piece (*Bariolage*) and three chordal interpolations by the harp in the central oboe piece (*Inner Song*). These interjections are nonetheless *ad libitum* addenda intended to be played only when all three are performed by a duo, because even after having completed the third piece Carter still considered the performance of *Bariolage* and *Inner Song* alone to be a valid possibility. In accordance with their ambivalent status, the two solo items were published both separately and as parts of the complete *Trilogy*.

160 *Trilogy,* for oboe and harp (1991–92); no. 2: *Inner Song,* for oboe solo (1991–92), draft in pencil, p. [3] (mm. 69–133 [132])

In keeping with the occasion to which it owed its existence, *Inner Song* is a dual tribute: first to Heinz Holliger, who gave the piece its première in Witten on 25 April 1992, and then to Stefan Wolpe, drawing on the chromatic hexachord G, G♯, A, B♭, B, C (= G–C) that forms the basis of Wolpe's *Suite im Hexachord* for oboe and clarinet, op. 24b (1936). In his earliest drafts of November 1991 Carter limited himself to the prime form of this hexachord, just as Wolpe had done in the first three movements of his four-movement *Suite*, but he included its transpositions when he resumed work in January 1992. Here we see the final page of a draft, dated 12–16 January 1992, that departs markedly from the 115-bar final version both in its underlying hexachordal structure and in its length (132 mm.). Interestingly, in this version Carter set aside the complementary hexachord C♯–F♯ for the very end of the piece, where he presents it in direct confrontation with the basic hexachord G–C, first consecutively (G–C: mm. "117"–"119",[12] C♯–F♯: mm. "119"–"122"), then simultaneously or intermittently (mm. "122"–"127"), and finally once again consecutively (mm. "127"–"130" and "130"–"133"), with the two phrases ending in the dyads G–C and F♯–C♯ from the "outside notes" of the hexachords. The final version largely retains this final turn of phrase, with its deliberate saturation of the chromatic total, but treats the hexachordal structure with greater flexibility. It also adds a similar juxtaposition of the two complementary hexachords at the end of the first third of the piece, thereby anticipating the final effect.

---

12 As Carter apparently counted m. 90 twice, the measure numbers marked in the left-hand margin should be lowered by one, beginning in the middle of the page ("96" = 95, "99" = 98, etc.). The passage described here starts in the penultimate bar on the sixth staff from the bottom. A transcription can be found in Henning Eisenlohr, *Komponieren als Entscheidungsprozeß* (see above, p. 182, note 23), pp. 423–424.

A List of Films for Frank Scheffer (1992)

No sooner had the Rotterdam Conservatory invited Carter to be its composer-in-residence in spring 1993 than the composer Martijn Padding was commissioned to organize a festival around Carter's music.[13] Padding contacted the composer's friend Frank Scheffer (b. 1956), who asked Carter which films had left a special impression on him and might be screened as part of such a festival. Carter sent Scheffer his suggestions in the following letter, proposing no fewer than twenty-eight titles ranging from experimental films to Hollywood comedies, and from chamber dramas to historical epics. Given the limited budget, however, a large-scale film retrospective was out of the question, and it was agreed that a small selection of film clips on the subject of time should be presented instead. Carter himself proposed the "Odessa steps" sequence from Eisenstein's *Battleship Potemkin* (1925), the framing sections of Jean Cocteau's *Le sang d'un poète* (1930), and the final scene of Michelangelo Antonioni's *The Passenger* (1975); Scheffer suggested including the Einstein scene from Nicolas Roeg's *Insignificance* (1985), Shōhei Imamura's *Black Rain* (1989), and a scene from the material he himself shot on Carter in Breukelen, Netherlands, in 1982. In the end these six excerpts were screened at the Rotterdam Conservatory on 30 March 1993 during an event that also included a lecture on the abstraction of time by the philosopher Jos de Mul, a performance of *Pastoral* by Arno Bornkamp (alto saxophone) and Ivo Janssen (piano), and an interview of Carter by the musicologist Frans van Rossum. The event underscored the important artistic impetus that Carter owed to the cinema, especially in the presentation of contrasting temporal levels.[14] (Particularly telling was the inclusion of Cocteau's *Le sang d'un poète*, which Carter himself had singled out as a model for his *String Quartet No. 1*:[15] in both works an initial event measured in "chronometric" time – the collapse of an exploding chimney in Cocteau's film – is prematurely interrupted and completed only at the end, so that it appears extremely drawn out in "psychological" time. In contrast, the long "objective" events lying in between seem no less drastically shortened in "subjective" time.[16]) The event also showed how intensively Carter could respond to the message of a film, especially in the case of *Battleship Potemkin*. In the words of Frank Scheffer: "He was sitting on the stage together with Frans van Rossum looking at the baby carriage from Potemkin. When it was finished and the light went on, Elliott was in tears. And he said to the audience: 'Excuse me, but it [i. e. the social utopia presented in the film] meant such a lot to me at that time, and look what's happened to it.'"[17]

---

161 Elliott Carter to Frank Scheffer, 30 September 1992

September 30, 1992

Dear Frank,

I see that we are listed as choosing my favorite films for the Rotterdam Festival. I have been thinking about them and would like to send you a list, more or less in order of what I like most:

1) Buster Keaton – *Seven Days* (the film about the prefabricated house)
1a) Buster Keaton – *Cops*
2) *Reds* – Warren Beatty's film about John Reed
3) [Sergey] Eisenstein's *October* (or *Potemkin*)
[3a] [Vsevolod] Pudovkin – *End of St. Petersburg*
4) [Luis] Buñuel – [*The*] *Exterminating Angel* (or *Simon of the Desert*)
5) [Vittorio] de Sica's *Bicycle Thief* (or [Roberto Rossellini's] *Rome, Open City*)
6) [F. W. Murnau's] *The Last Laugh* (with Emil Jannings) or [Josef von Sternberg's] *The Blue Angel* with Marlene Dietrich
7) [François] Truffaut – *The Wild Child*
8) [Michelangelo] Antonioni – *Blow-up*
9) [Yasujiro] Ozu – *Tokyo Story*
10) [Federico] Fellini – *8½*
11) [Erich von] Stroheim – *Greed*
12) [Orson] Welles – *Citizen Kane*
13) [Charles] Chaplin – *Monsieur Verdoux* (or *The Great Dictator*)
14) [Billy Wilder –] *Some Like it Hot* (Marilyn Monroe)
15) [Susan Seidelman –] *Desperately Seeking Susan*
16) [Louis Malle –] *Lacombe Lucien*
17) [Jim Jarmusch –] *Down By Law* (or *Mystery Train*)
18) [François Truffaut –] *The Last Metro*

---

13 The festival, co-sponsored by several institutions (including the Rotterdam Philharmonic), lasted from 29 March to 4 April 1993 and featured not only concerts but lectures, film screenings, and other events.

14 See Jonathan W. Bernard, "Elliott Carter and the Modern Meaning of Time," *The Musical Quarterly* 79/4 (Winter 1995), pp. 644–682.

15 See Elliott Carter, introduction to the Nonesuch recording of *String Quartets Nos. 1 and 2* by the Composers String Quartet (NON 32803), most recently reprinted in *CEL*, pp. 231–235, esp. 233.

16 See Judy Lochhead, "On the 'Framing Music' of Elliott Carter's First String Quartet," in *Musical Transformation and Musical Intuition: Essays in Honor of David Lewin*, ed. Raphael Atlas and Michael Cherlin (Roxbury, MA: Ovenbird Press, 1994), pp. 179–198.

17 Personal communication from Frank Scheffer, 2 December 2007. We wish to thank Frank Scheffer for the detailed background information he provided on this event.

Esprit rude / Esprit doux II (1994)

I can think of a lot more – but it would make it even harder to make a program.

I hope your work on the new film goes well –[18]

Helen joins me in sending Niki, Allegri, and you[19] our warmest greetings,
[Elliott]

P. S. Of course, [Max] Ophüls – *The Sorrow & the Pity*, and any Hitchcock film!
[Alain] Resnais – *Last Year in Marienbad*
[Ingmar] Bergman – *Wild Strawberries*, etc.

[Typed letter with autograph signature, carbon copy; Elliott Carter Collection, Paul Sacher Foundation. Reprinted by permission of Frank Scheffer.]

To honor Boulez on his seventieth birthday Carter took a leaf out of his dedicatee's book and wrote a sequel to the work he had written for Boulez's sixtieth. In a nod to how Boulez often expands existing compositions, Carter constructed *Esprit rude / Esprit doux II* in such a way that it can be played as a literal continuation of the first piece, with the first measure of *II* substituting for the last measure of *I*. The two works may also be played one after the other, or separately. Even the addition of the marimba to the original duo of flute and clarinet alludes to the Boulezian procedure of adding voices to pre-existing music, though Carter's *Esprit rude / Esprit doux I* and *II* do not share material other than the B(b) (O) U[t] L[a] E (Z) motto. This can be clearly heard at the end of *II*, and it is also woven into the first six measures (in reverse). The dichotomy between aspirated and unaspirated vowels, here as before inspired by the Greek words for Boulez's age – in this case seventieth year, or *hebdomēkoston etos* – finds a musical counterpart in the juxtaposition of quick, staccato figures made up of large intervals ("*rude*") and sustained single notes, melodic gestures, or ostinato-like oscillations between two notes or chords ("*doux*"). Carter also makes several structural references to the number seventy: in the metronome mark, the number of measures, and even in the number of notes, for the flute and clarinet each play seventy notes (counting repeated notes or oscillations only once) up to the midpoint of the piece (m. 35), and the marimba plays twice seventy by this point (with the second seventy beginning in the middle of m. 17, which is halfway to m. 35). Just before the midpoint, the texture becomes very sparse and pointillistic. Here (mm. 27–35) the flute and clarinet have the last ten notes of their seventy for the first half. Setting apart the ten from the preceding sixty notes illustrates the French word for seventy: *soixante-dix*. The three instruments are rhythmically differentiated: the flute moves in quintuple sixteenth values (and their multiples) throughout, the clarinet in triplet eighths, and the marimba in sixteenths. The work was premièred on 30–31 March 1995 in Chicago by three members of the Chicago Symphony Orchestra: Richard Graef (flute), John Bruce Yeh (clarinet), and Patricia Dash (marimba). In addition to *Esprit rude / Esprit doux II* pieces written in honor of Boulez's seventieth birthday by Bernard Rands, Harrison Birtwistle,

---

18 After completing his film *Time is Music: Elliott Carter and John Cage* of 1988 (see above, p. 277, note 117), Scheffer worked on another documentary on Carter which eventually resulted in the two-part TV film *A Labyrinth of Memory* (2003) and the film *A Labyrinth of Time* (Allegri Films, 2005).

19 Veronica (Niki) Scheffer Block was Frank Scheffer's then wife. Allegri was the name of Scheffer's film company.

This piece may be played:
1) by itself
2) following ESPRIT (I) after a pause
3) or as a continuation of ESPRIT (I)
   by substituting measure 1 of ESPRIT, II
   for the last measure of ESPRIT (I)

MARIMBA
HARD / SOFT
STICKS MAY
BE USED
THROUGHOUT.

and Franco Donatoni were also performed. Boulez was touched by Carter's gesture, as his warm and witty thank-you letter shows.

162 *Esprit rude / Esprit doux II,* **for flute, clarinet, and marimba (1994), autograph full score in pencil, p. 1**

The opening gesture is a good example of the *"esprit rude"*: the *fortissimo,* accented, and flutter-tongued attacks in flute and clarinet are noisy and aspirated, and abruptly cut short by the marimba's sixteenth-note chord, played with hard sticks, in m. 3. This is followed immediately by its opposite, the *"esprit doux,"* marked by softer dynamics, normal tone production, tenuto attacks and longer sustained notes in the flute and clarinet. (The marimba continues to interject its chords, which try to fit in at first – witness the softer dynamics in mm. 5 and 6 – but become steadily more active and disruptive by m. 9.) The tremolo figures in flute (mm. 8–9), marimba (mm. 8–9), and clarinet (m. 9) are very prominent in the piece, resulting in fairly long stretches of a rather un-Carterian stasis. These slow, quiet tremolos represent another face of the *"esprit doux"*; moreover, they allow Carter to vary the rate of pitch circulation, so that he can place the right number of notes in each section for each instrument. Rather than dividing up the interval collection, as in *Esprit rude / Esprit doux I,* in *II* the three instruments share the all-triad (and all-interval) hexachord 012478. As in all of Carter's music, instrumental color and the exact registral placement of the pitch are just as important as the underlying harmony. For example, in the first 012478 hexachord, which is made up of the six pitches in mm. 1–3 (after the first note, E, which is not part of the hexachord), the flute and clarinet articulate the highest and lowest notes, respectively (F6 and D3), and the marimba fills in the four "inner voices." The situation is completely reversed in the next hexachord, which unfolds from the end of m. 3 to the first half of m. 5. (This hexachord shares the pitches D♭4 and G5 with the first one.) Here the marimba sounds the outer voices (D♭4 and C7), while the woodwinds have the inner parts. The third hexachord, which starts with the F♯4 in the flute in m. 5 and ends with the marimba's chord in m. 6, has a blended sound: the clarinet returns

to its low D, the top note (A♯) is played by the marimba, marking also the twelfth pitch of the total chromatic. Continuity between the hexachords is provided by two pitches (in the same register) carrying over into the next one. Sometimes (though not on the page shown) a hexachord is repeated with the same pitches in the same registers, but scored differently. By constantly varying the pitch content, registral placement, and instrumental timbre of the 012478 hexachord, in a manner quite different from twelve-tone practice, Carter ensures that there is still a great deal of variety in spite of the relatively homogenous harmonic content. *Esprit rude / Esprit doux I* had ended with a statement of the "Boulez" motto; *II* begins with the last note of the motto, E (first note in flute and clarinet), and continues in retrograde with A (marimba, m. 3), C (marimba, m. 5), and B♭ (marimba, m. 6).

163 **Pierre Boulez to Elliott Carter, 18 January 1995**
(English translation in Appendix 1, p. 351)

Pierre Boulez

Cher Elliott,
Voici trois semaines que je suis rentré de Chicago, et trois semaines (les mêmes!) que je veux vous écrire. John Bruce Yeh m'a communiqué, malgré le secret – mais il m'a dit vous avoir prévenu – qui doit être gardé jusqu'au 26 mars, votre pierre miliaire pour mon futur et très proche 70ᵉ anniversaire, la deuxième dix ans après sur ma trajectoire.

Merci infiniment de ce témoignage à la fois fidèle et affectueux que j'apprécie très vivement. C'est un plaisir de savoir qu'il existe des amis comme vous, et des musiciens de votre type qui sont rares, refusant le compromis et "suivant leur pente, pourvu qu'elle monte". (Ce mot est de Gide, je crois – et, pour une fois, j'adhère totalement à une de ses définitions.[20])

J'espère vous voir peut-être à Chicago le jour de l'exécution, ou plus probablement à New-York lorsque j'y viens avec le LSO au mois d'avril prochain.[21]

Je vous envoie à vous et Helen toutes mes amitiés
P. Boulez

[Autograph card; Elliott Carter Collection, Paul Sacher Foundation. Reprinted by permission of Pierre Boulez.]

---

20 This phrase is taken from Part 3 of André Gide's novel *Les Faux-monnayeurs,* where the writer Edouard gives the following piece of advice to the schoolboy Bernard, whom he has hired as secretary: "Il est bon de suivre sa pente, pourvu que ce soit en montant."
[It's a good thing to follow one's inclination, provided it leads upwards.]
Quoted from André Gide, *Les Faux-*

monnayeurs (Paris: Gallimard, 1925; paperback edn. 1972), p. 340.

21 Boulez's guest appearance in New York with the London Symphony Orchestra consisted of three concerts in Carnegie Hall from 22 to 24 April 1995. The program included works by Ravel, Boulez, Webern, and Berg (on 22 April), Boulez, Messiaen, and Stravinsky (23 April), and Ravel, Berg, Stravinsky, and Boulez (24 April).

String Quartet No. 5 (1995)

Carter composed his *String Quartet No. 5* in 1995 to satisfy a request from the Arditti Quartet, which had championed his music for more than a decade and made a highly acclaimed recording of the first four quartets in June 1988.[22] Completed on 30 July 1995 and premièred in Antwerp by the Arditti Quartet on 19 September 1995, Carter's *Fifth Quartet* was made possible by a joint commission from the City of Antwerp; the Witten Festival of New Chamber Music; the Festival d'Automne, Paris; and Lincoln Center, New York. The work consists of six contrasting "main movements" plus a prelude and five interludes. On the surface it seems to be patterned after a suite, but, unlike the historical form of the suite, the progress of the music is based on a typically Carterian and highly self-reflective idea: its alternation between seemingly improvised interludes of a solo character and more compact ensemble numbers might be construed as a written-out presentation of a quartet at rehearsal. (This reading, suggested by Carter himself in his introductory text, has the quartet members rehearsing various things in the interludes, joining forces to play through the music, and then discussing or analyzing what they have just played in the interlude that follows.) At the same time the resultant process of shaping and ordering may be regarded as a metaphor for the act of composition itself (see Schiff 1998, p. 92). Another aspect of the piece's self-reflective character is the fact that Carter frequently reverts to typical gestures from *String Quartets Nos. 1* through *4*, thereby imparting an element of retrospection to the work despite its novel dramatic structure. This may be one reason why Carter, after completing this work, regarded his series of string quartets as finished. True, in 1999, again for the Arditti Quartet, he added the brief *Fragment No. 2*, a successor to his *Fragment No. 1* of 1994, which was itself a sort of preliminary study for the "Adagio sereno" of *String Quartet No. 5*. But since then he has refrained from making another full-scale contribution to the genre – much to the regret of Irvine Arditti, who wrote Carter while rehearsing *Fragment No. 2:* "The piece sounds great and again different. If you ever wanted to expand it into a 6th Quartet... (I could arrange something tomorrow morning – or even tonight!)"[23]

164 *String Quartet No. 5* (1995), autograph full score in pencil, p. 35 (mm. 305–313)

The transition from the last interlude to the finale ("Capriccioso") illustrates how seamlessly the movements of the *String Quartet No. 5* interweave without losing their individual characters. Here we see this transition from the fair copy in full score, in which each page bears in work's date of completion. To begin with, the interlude has its own distinctive identity: the first violin assumes a leading role for large stretches at a time, lending the movement, to a certain extent, the flavor of melody and accompaniment. On the other hand it also has the function of preparing the finale, which begins in m. 309, by foreshadowing its rhythmic stratification – the characteristic superposition of sixteenth notes and sixteenth-note quintuplets, sextuplets, and septuplets – and by the gradual introduction of pizzicato. Towards the end of the interlude (just before the excerpt shown here) the pizzicato is added to the ascending, ever-faster cantilena of the violin in three steps: first in the second violin (m. 302), then in the viola (m. 303), and finally in the cello (m. 304). It then becomes the predominant timbre (or mode of attack) in the "Capriccioso," which is set apart from the interlude also by its tempo, i. e. by the metrical modulation in m. 309. This movement is played entirely pizzicato, sometimes with chordal pizzicato (as on the page shown here) and later with pizzicato harmonics and "snap" pizzicato. In this way Carter hearkens back to a fairly long pizzicato passage in *String Quartet No. 3* (albeit only with respect to sound production), perhaps in a desire to have the work end as weightlessly as possible. Indeed, undramatic, "anti-heroic" endings are virtually a defining feature of Carter's late music. (In the final measures of the *String Quartet No. 5* this effect is given an almost ironic, quasi-tonal hue by the return to *ordinario* bowing and the fade-out of the *pianissimo* double-stop A♯3–F♯4 in the first violin). A similarly expansive use of pizzicato, now applied to an orchestral *tutti*, occurs a few years later in the ritornellos of Carter's *Boston Concerto* (2004).

22 Elliott Carter, *The Works for String Quartet*, vol. 1 (*String Quartets Nos. 1 and 4*), vol. 2 (*String Quartets Nos. 2* and *3* plus *Elegy for String Quartet*); Arditti String Quartet (Etcetera KTC 1065 and 1066); released in 1989.

23 Letter from Irvine Arditti to Elliott Carter, 10 June 1999; Elliott Carter Collection, Paul Sacher Foundation. *Fragment No. 2* was premièred by the Arditti Quartet in Munich on 23 June 1999.

Allegro scorrevole (1996), from *Symphonia* (1993–96)

With *Symphonia*, Carter returned to the venerable genre of the symphony after more than half a century. If the large-scale orchestral works of the 1950s, 60s, and 70s redefined the symphonic tradition in their emphasis on the concerto principle and their chamber music-like complexity, *Symphonia* wholeheartedly embraces symphonic vocabularies, gestures, and dimensions, but without retrospection or classicism. Whereas Carter often collected smaller pieces, conceived individually, into a single opus (such as the orchestral triptych of the 1980s, *Three Occasions for Orchestra*), with *Symphonia* he intended a single three-movement work from the beginning. Its three movements, composed for three separate commissions and performed separately before the whole piece was premièred by the BBC Symphony Orchestra under the direction of Oliver Knussen on 25 April 1998 in Manchester, UK, are interrelated and create a coherent whole. At the instigation of Knussen, three orchestras jointly commissioned the work: the Chicago Symphony, the BBC Symphony, and the New York Philharmonic. The first movement, *Partita*, was premièred by the Chicago Symphony and Daniel Barenboim on 17–19 February 1994. Andrew Davis conducted the BBC Symphony in the première of the second movement, *Adagio tenebroso*, on 13 September 1995. In 1996, the New York Philharmonic placed additional and prohibitive conditions upon the commission – in the meantime Kurt Masur had replaced Zubin Mehta, who had made the original contract – so Christoph von Dohnányi and the Cleveland Orchestra took over the commission, premièring the third movement, *Allegro scorrevole*, on 22 and 24 May 1997.[24]

The full title, *Symphonia: Sum Fluxae Pretium Spei* ("I am the prize of vacillating hope"), refers to the Latin poem *Bulla* [Bubble] by the seventeenth-century English poet Richard Crashaw. Carter's use of a motto from the poem for each of the three movements provides a unifying idea for pieces with otherwise quite different characters. The image of the bubble – light, transparent, beautiful, yet fragile and evanescent – provides an apt analogy, especially to the two fast movements, *Partita* and *Allegro scorrevole*. It also signals to the listener that the symphony, in spite of its eighteenth-century fast-slow-fast form, its brass tuttis, its long Mahlerian melo-

dies, and its Mozartian woodwind figuration, will have a dramaturgy fundamentally different from the traditional one.

Symphonia outwardly resembles a truncated classical-romantic symphonic form: there is an allegro first movement, an adagio second movement, and a scherzo third movement, but no finale. If Carter had been writing in the 1890s instead of the 1990s, we could speculate that he was anxious about writing a fourth movement in the wake of Beethoven's colossal example in the *Ninth Symphony* (a parallel, perhaps, with the absent finale of Bruckner's *Ninth Symphony*). But Carter, who has always kept his distance from the Germanic tradition, has a fundamentally different conception of what a symphony should be, one redefined in terms of the narrative strategies that he has developed over a lifetime of finding new ways to organize musical time. His intentional avoidance of an emphatic fourth movement and the evanescent close of the third movement are consistent with the "bubble" theme of the poem, but also have a broader social and even political dimension. If the symphony of the nineteenth and early twentieth centuries aimed to represent an entire world view, the confidence of an all-encompassing perspective would seem like hubris at the end of the twentieth. "I couldn't write a grand finale after the manner of Bruckner or Mahler," Carter said to Richard Dyer in an interview just before the US presidential elections in 2004, "– that kind of grandiose thing seems to me a little hard to do – and it would be even harder now, especially right before this election. I ended the symphony on a high piccolo note, which seems to me more fitting for our time than a military peroration."[25]

---

24 The events that led to the cancellation of the New York Philharmonic's commission are recorded in Schiff 1998, pp. 321–322, and in Paul Griffiths, "A Prophet Finds Honor in Cleveland," *The New York Times*, 29 June 1997.

25 Richard Dyer, "Inside His Compositions, Life's Complexities Take Shape," *Boston Sunday Globe*, 7 November 2004.

Clarinet Concerto (1996)

165 *Symphonia: Sum Fluxae Pretium Spei,* **for orchestra (1993–97); no.3:** *Allegro scorrevole* **(1996), autograph full score in pencil, p. 60 (mm. 235–239)**

This page shows the striking, intentionally un-grandiose ending of the third and final movement of *Symphonia.* Low-register instruments are almost entirely absent; with the exception of the piano's low A in mm. 236–237 (which articulates a slow pulse begun earlier), the texture is dominated by high strings (*divisi*), harp, and woodwinds. The piccolo's solo gesture that ends the piece on a high G♯, marked *pianissimo possibile,* may be extended with string harmonics on the same pitch, in order to produce a softer dynamic level than is normally possible on the piccolo in that register. (In the recording by the BBC Symphony Orchestra and Oliver Knussen, the superb piccolo player manages it alone.) On this page one can also see the two main types of motion in the piece: a rapid, flickering, "Queen Mab scherzo" kind of music (as in the first two measures), and sustained lyrical melodic music (as in the piccolo solo in the last three measures). These two layers continue simultaneously throughout the movement. Whereas in a traditional texture the melodic lines would form the main idea and the fast music the accompaniment, here the two parts are equally balanced. Moreover, in keeping with the meaning of the typically Carterian designation "scorrevole", they are transformed seamlessly into one another with the multilayered fluidity of an *opera buffa* ensemble. Another remarkable feature of *Allegro scorrevole* is its almost complete lack of cadences or resting points. The music proceeds for almost twelve minutes in an uninterrupted flow of sound, yet it articulates a distinct shape. The music builds to a climax just before the end, then all the energy of the piece seems to evaporate as everything sinks into the bottom register, after which, for the last two minutes of the piece, the high-register instruments essay a tentative reawakening, marked by fast music and tremolos. This does not come to a culmination, however, as the instruments simply drop out one by one, until the piccolo is left alone in its highest register. The page is dated 18 May 1996, a little over four months after Carter had begun sketching the piece, on 8 January 1996.

The *Clarinet Concerto* was the second work (after *Penthode*) commissioned from Carter by Boulez and the Ensemble InterContemporain, IRCAM's "house orchestra." The ensemble, one of the major forces in contemporary music since its founding in 1976, has a huge repertory of twentieth- and twenty-first-century music and has commissioned hundreds of works. Fully supported by the French government, the group is made up of thirty-one highly skilled musicians who are employed full time.[26] The ensemble had suggested to Carter that the piece be playable by its tour configuration of eighteen solo instruments, made up of thirteen winds and percussion and five solo strings. Carter decided to write a clarinet concerto because of his admiration for the ensemble's clarinettist, Alain Damiens.

The concerto is an ideal form to embody Carter's aesthetic of dramatized polyphony, and he has turned to it many times. The social dynamic expressed in Carter's concertos uses the traditional struggle between the persona of the soloist (representing the individual) and that of the orchestra (representing the anonymous crowd) only as a starting point. Carter's instrumental soloists are dramatic personae who express a wide range of attitudes and situations in their virtuosic monologues. In many of his concertos, Carter complicates the traditional concerto dynamic by giving the soloist an accompanying concertino group. Whereas in both the *Piano Concerto* and the *Oboe Concerto* the concertino group is made up of a fixed group of instruments, in the *Double Concerto* the orchestra is divided into two timbrally distinct groups, one for each of the solo instruments (harpsichord and piano). The *Clarinet Concerto* extends this principle by pairing the solo instrument with a series of sonically homogeneous ensembles in turn. (In some performances, the clarinettist moves from group to group, visually emphasizing the shifting configurations.) Here the traditional concerto principle of soloist vs. *tutti* has been erased, as the soloist elicits support and even imitation from the groups with which he or she interacts. Seven short *tutti* passages – like ritornelli in a baroque concerto – are interspersed between the six solo/concertino sections. The clarinet never becomes submerged into the ensemble – its part is too exposed and virtuosic for that – but

---

26 Alan Riding reported in 1997 that the ensemble received $4 million, and IRCAM $7 million, in yearly subsidies; see "Maestro on a Mission: Sell Modern Music," *The New York Times,* 22 January 1997.

by changing its "personality" in accordance with each group it encounters it serves as peacekeeper rather than antagonist. The *Clarinet Concerto,* composed during the summer of 1996 and completed on 6 November 1996, was premièred on 10–11 January 1997 by Damiens and the Ensemble InterContemporain, conducted by Pierre Boulez. Clarinettists including Michael Collins, Charles Neidich, John Bruce Yeh, Thomas Martin, and Ismail Lumanovski (a Juilliard undergraduate and a student of Neidich) have become advocates for the piece.

166 *Clarinet Concerto* (1996), short score draft in pencil with markings in colored pencil, 1 p. (mm. "389"–"409" [= mm. 387–407 of the final version])

This page from the short score draft contains the completely notated clarinet part, a rhythmic grid indicating the three main temporal layers, and fragmentary orchestra parts. The measures have been renumbered (see the crossed out "363" over the third measure), because Carter had added about thirty measures to a previous passage. As in the sketches for many other works, this one shows how Carter began composing with the leading melodic part. The clarinet line, here notated in C, moves in the wide range characteristic of the solo part as a whole: on this page it traverses the entire range of the instrument, from the high F♯ in m. "390" (= m. 388 of the final score) to the low Ds in m. "403" (401). Major seconds, major thirds, perfect fifths, and major sixths are the clarinet's main intervals (in addition to the minor seconds common to all instruments). The other parts will concentrate on different intervals: the sixteenth-note figure in m. "391" (389), read in bass clef (it will later be designated for cellos and violas), contains the minor seventh, perfect fourth, minor third, and tritone. Among the few precisely notated figures on the page (aside from the clarinet part) are several chords, in mm. "394" (392), "398–99" (396–97), "403" (401), and the last measure on the page; these imply that Carter is working with pitches drawn from a fixed-register twelve-tone chord, and indicate that even at this early stage he is concerned with the overall harmonic structure of the passage. A similarly "global" view is implied by the rhythmic sketches. The solo part moves in multiples of sixteenth-note quintuplets, while the rhythmic notations in the staves beneath it move in eighth-note triplets and sixteenth notes, respectively. Although the three layers move in subdivisions of 5, 4, and 3 of a common notated beat, they actually articulate different pulses: the short score draft (especially in the first system) shows that beats fall on every fourth triplet and every third sixteenth note. The clarinet part shows a decided tendency to move in dotted eighths ($^3/_4$ of a quarter note). The page reproduced here, marked "Conclusion," shows the beginning of the seventh and final section of the concerto. Whereas earlier sections had focused on different instrumental families, the whole ensemble plays here. Carter dated the page 27 June 1996 with his customary date stamp; he also habitually used another stamp designating the composition's title, his name, and the year on every page. He drafted this short score between June and August 1996.

---

27 The recording was made in Purchase, NY, on 7 December 1998 in Carter's presence and released in 1999 along with recordings of *Fragment II, Syringa, Tempo e tempi,* the *Quintet for Piano and Winds,* and *Retrouvailles* on the CD "Elliott Carter: Quintets and Voices" (Mode Records 128).

167 Elliott Carter with Ursula Oppens and the Arditti Quartet (from left to right: Dov Scheindlin, Irvine Arditti, Graeme Jennings, and Rohan de Saram) at the Huddersfield Contemporary Music Festival (1998), photo by the Huddersfield Contemporary Music Festival

On 27 November 1998 the Twenty-First Huddersfield Contemporary Music Festival (18–29 November 1998) mounted a tribute to Carter in honor of his approaching ninetieth birthday. Besides a performance of the *Oboe Concerto* with Gareth Hulse (during a matinée concert of the Vaganza ensemble conducted by Thierry Fischer), the tribute included an evening recital with the Arditti Quartet and the pianist Ursula Oppens, preceded by a conversation between Carter and the festival's then director, Richard Steinitz. The recital featured the *Sonata for Violoncello and Piano*, the *String Quartet No. 5*, the *Duo for Violin and Piano*, and the European première of the *Quintet for Piano and String Quartet*. Both the Arditti Quartet and Oppens had been Carter's friends for many years and had ardently championed his music on a long-term basis in their concerts and recordings. Not the least of their achievements were Oppens's première of *Night Fantasies* (see above, p. 239) and the Arditti's première of the *String Quartet No. 5* (see above, p. 294). On 18 November 1998 they joined forces in the Library of Congress, Washington DC, to première the *Quintet for Piano and String Quartet*, which they then performed in close succession in twelve American and European cities. They also released the work on CD.[27]

167

What Next? (1997–98)

The news in 1997 that Carter had begun his first opera – at the age of 88 – was greeted with joyful if incredulous astonishment.[28] After all, Rossini was a relatively youthful 65 when he began his *Péchés de vieillesse* [Sins of Old Age], and Verdi had finished his last opera, *Falstaff*, by the age of 80. It seemed that Carter, like Brahms, would be one of those composers who did not write operas. In fact Carter, a life-long opera-goer, had turned down several other requests, including an invitation from the San Francisco Opera in 1961. At that time he wrote: "Since America is so diverse culturally, with little agreement except on the mass-entertainment level, it seems to me highly unlikely that an opera of any real value can be written, because opera – at least as we know it – is a big enterprise and must reach a large public and must be intended to do so, and yet that public must be assumed to be [...] cultured enough to receive important experiences from new music – a fact we know is not so here."[29] It was Daniel Barenboim, music director of the Staatsoper Unter den Linden in Berlin, who finally got Carter to take the step. Barenboim recalled: "I always admired his music, and one time when we met, we talked about what he liked in opera. And he said that he liked this phrase or that phrase in *Siegfried*, and he had the whole text in his memory. [...]. So I said, 'If you know so much about opera, why don't you write one?' 'I don't like violence,' he said.' 'You don't have to write *Elektra*,' I told him. 'You could write a comedy.' And that's what he did."[30]

Carter considered several possible librettos before turning to the writer and music critic Paul Griffiths (b. 1947), who had written several books on twentieth-century music and was at the time enjoying critical acclaim for his libretto for Tan Dun's opera *Marco Polo* (premièred in 1996).[31] In his capacity as music critic of *The New Yorker*, Griffiths had often written sympathetically about Carter's music, most recently in an extended article and interview published in August 1996.[32] The letter exchange below marks the beginning of their collaboration; the first letter was written the day after their first meeting on 19 March 1997.[33] The opera takes Jacques Tati's film *Trafic* (1971) as a starting point: six people, disoriented and confused after an accident, try to clarify their identities and their relationships to each other. Griffiths credits that starting point as well as the title *What Next?* to the composer.[34] From this idea Griffiths developed a modern comedy whose richly polyphonic text, full of irony and word play, is very much in the spirit of Carter's music.[35] Griffiths's intriguing suggestion to create "a unique bridge between the orchestra and the singing characters" by having an instrumentalist, Horn, as one of the characters resonates with Carter's own practice of instrumental drama. While this idea was not ultimately realized in this form, live percussionists do take the stage as the rescue squad, measuring and photographing the scene of the accident but paying no attention to the victims (libretto, nos. 32–36); this scene was inspired by Carter's description of an automobile accident he had observed in Rome (see his letter to Griffiths of 20 March 1997, below, p. 304). Carter also created the specific realization of Rose as an opera singer who sings throughout (with vocalises where there is no text). As he explained to the dramaturg Micaela von Marcard (see his fax of 19 March 1999, below, p. 307), Rose's utterances are not signs of psychosis or derangement, but are literal musical sounds (diegetic music). *What Next?* was premièred on 16 September 1999 in Berlin, a few months before Carter's ninety-first birthday. Originally planned "as a curtain-raiser for *Salome*," it was ultimately paired with Schoenberg's *Von heute auf morgen*.[36] The work received its American stage première on 27–28 July 2006 at the Tanglewood Music Center, conducted by James Levine.

28 Arnold Whittall even (apparently coincidentally) anticipated the opera's title: "What next? Did I hear talk of an opera for Barenboim to conduct?" (Arnold Whittall, "Summer's Long Shadows," *The Musical Times*, vol. 138, no. 1850 [April 1997], pp. 14–22, esp. 22.)

29 Elliott Carter, letter to Kurt Herbert Adler, 26 June 1961; carbon copy in the Elliott Carter Collection, Paul Sacher Foundation. Adler, the then director of the San Francisco Opera, had made his request on 19 June 1961.

30 "Quizzing the Maestro" [interview with Daniel Barenboim], *Opera News* 64/11 (May 2000), p. 45.

31 See in particular Paul Griffiths, *Modern Music: The Avant-garde since 1945* (New York: G. Braziller, 1981), and its revised edition, *Modern Music and After* (Oxford and New York: Oxford University Press, 1995).

32 Paul Griffiths, "Paying Attention," *The New Yorker*, 26 August 1996, p. 59 (in column "The Talk of the Town"). Griffiths wrote for *The New Yorker* from 1992 to 1996.

33 Griffiths's work on the libretto for Carter from February to July 1997 is documented in his published account "What Next? –

168 Paul Griffiths to Elliott Carter, 20 March 1997

from Paul Griffiths, The New York Times,
229 West 43rd Street, NYC, NY 10036
March 20, 1997

Dear Mr. Carter,
Goodness. I'm a bit bewildered by the course events are taking, but hope my sense of responsibility to you will direct and hone my work rather than inhibit it utterly. About that I'm optimistic: ideas are beginning to form. And I hope I needn't say that I find the project immensely exciting.

It's an excellent idea of yours to have two of the characters as bride and bridegroom in wedding clothes: that will take some of the heat out of establishing right away who these people are. My initial thought is that there should be seven characters altogether: three male, three female, one instrumental.

The three male characters might be Bridegroom, Old Man, and Boy. (I like the boy soprano voice. If you don't, or don't trust it, this role could be imagined for a countertenor or lyric tenor.) The audience should feel that these are independent people, but also at times that they represent the same figure at different ages. For instance, I thought the Old Man could spend almost the whole opera in reflective mood, going backwards through his life, and that at certain points his recollections could be mirrored by what the Bridegroom and later the Boy are doing.

The instrumental character could be Horn. The horn is something more than a modern-day machine, can easily "sing," and has poetic qualities that might be useful (shades of the hunting horn, *Des Knaben Wunderhorn*). The six other characters see and hear the horn (probably they see and hear it as horn rather than hornist), but they don't make any such acknowledgement of the orchestra, whether this is on stage or in the pit. The horn is therefore a unique bridge between the orchestra and the singing characters. If we get going you might, of course, prefer another instrument to have this role. Trumpet might be a possibility, if you don't think Stockhausen has copyright.

The three female characters, who would remain distinct from each other, might be Bride, Mother, and Chauffeuse. The Mother, in a fantastic situation, tries to retain a totally realistic viewpoint: for instance, she interprets the horn as a motor horn. The Chauffeuse I feel as rather sinister.

There really have to be two cars in the initial crash to account for seven characters. Part of the drama will come – apart from out of the developing and changing relationships – from the question of who was in which car and who was driving. Bride, Bridegroom and Chauffeuse make one obvious set, but really any combination makes some kind of sense. (Sorry, this is beginning to sound like pitch-class talk.) Maybe the title could be in the form of a [question]: "Who's Driving?" (except that it properly ought to be "Who Drove?," which isn't as good). A questioning title would be good for setting the ambiguous light / serious, comic / tragic tone.

I have some thoughts about the first words (after the car crash in the music), but would like to explore further before saying anything more. For the moment I just wanted you to know that my mind is in action, and that I'm profoundly grateful to you for even the possibility of maybe working with you.

With all best wishes, also to Mrs. Carter –
Paul

[Typed letter with autograph greetings and signature; Elliott Carter Collection, Paul Sacher Foundation. Reprinted by permission of Paul Griffiths.]

169 Elliott Carter to Paul Griffiths, 20 March 1997

Elliott Carter / 31 West 12th Street / New York,
N.Y. 10011-8545
March 20, 1997

Dear Paul Griffiths,
Thank you for your letter. I, too, have been thinking and have some possible thoughts that might be useful:

1) Cause of accident – a deer crossing the road; a cyclist making a turn; a witless pedestrian – all of whom were unscathed (deer excepted?) and do not appear except in discussions. Arguments about who is to blame!

A Journal," in the CD booklet for Elliott Carter/Paul Griffiths, *What Next?* (ECM New Series 1817, 472 1882 [2003]), pp. 24–33.

34 Ibid., p. 30.

35 See Anne C. Shreffler, "Instrumental Dramaturgy as Humane Comedy: *What Next?* by Elliott Carter and Paul Griffiths," in *Musiktheater heute: Internationales Symposion der Paul Sacher Stiftung*, ed. Hermann Danuser in collaboration with Matthias Kassel, Veröffentlichungen der Paul Sacher Stiftung 9 (Mainz, London, etc.: Schott, 2003), pp. 147–171. As the libretto indicates, the event that has taken place immediately before the opera begins does not have to be a car accident, but can be any kind of catastrophe or natural disaster.

36 Griffiths, "What Next? – A Journal" (see note 33), p. 25.

2) Sociological differences between bride & groom – *bride* from wealthy family, but very whimsical, and accident makes her almost schizoid – sings all the time, finally consults her shrink by portable 'phone and is somewhat cured. Her father has been eager to find a groom that would accept her flighty character, but is aware that the groom is poor and may be marrying for money. She is dressed in a very extreme way for the prospective wedding...

(Tattered?) *groom*, deeply in love, does not realize how problematic she would be as wife – and after the accident fears that he may be marrying a mad woman, but will go through with it anyway. His mother has been against the marriage, because of the money-class problem and the bride's character.

3) The bride does something appalling, smashes the car window or tears up her dress or...

4) I would like one character, maybe the chauffeuse, to sing in very short snippets, with long or short rests in between, while the bride (or the groom) sings in long lyrical lines – a mad scene? and love scene? The boy might carry on quite separately, playing a game?

In Rome one year I witnessed an auto accident and was profoundly shocked to see the police come with measuring tapes to try and find out what had happened and who was to blame – while the injured young man lay on the pavement, not being attended to or being paid attention to. In Mexico I was in a bus that knocked a boy down, and the passengers all yelled at him for getting in the way! Indifference may be part of this affair?

Anyhow, ideas, for what they are worth – Incidentally I don't know about accident insurance and how this might affect this story.

Eagerly looking forward
Elliott

[Typed letter with autograph date, greetings, and signature, photocopy; Elliott Carter Collection, Paul Sacher Foundation. Reprinted by permission of Paul Griffiths.]

170 *What Next?*, opera to a libretto by Paul Griffiths (1997–98)
a sketches in pencil ("ideas for soprano, July 12, 1997"), 1 p.
b short score draft in pencil of the beginning, p. [1]

That Carter started sketching *What Next?* with Rose's music indicates the importance of the character, especially in her vocally expanded new role as singer. (The date on the sketch page, 12 July 1997, is consistent with Griffiths's note on 14 July that Carter had "begun making sketches."[37]) Apart from a setting of "starlings" – Rose's first word in the opera – on the right side of the page, the vocal lines are sketched without words. Carter's aim was to compose music illustrating a wide variety of different moods and emotions: from the top of the page to the bottom, he indicated "anger," "lyrical," "ecstatic," [illegible], "tender," "ironic," "comic," and "tragic/heroic." Although Carter had not yet settled on Rose's final inventory of intervals – major third, perfect fifth, and minor seventh – the fifth is prominent in these sketches (see for example the opening E–B at the top left, and the first interval of "starlings" at left), as are major and minor sixths and tritones. Rhythms are indicated partially or not at all: the "ecstatic" vocal line (third line), which also features the fifth E–B, is notated in whole notes. Both the "angry" and the "lyrical" vocalises (the first two lines) end on high C, which ultimately became Rose's last note in the opera. The "tragic" line (at the bottom of the page) also spans a wide vocal range, in this case striding in fourths and sevenths from middle C to a high A♭. The page provides the background for the statement that Paul Griffiths reported three days later, on 15 July: "[Carter said,] Rose will sing throughout, in her role as performer: the whole thing will be, for her, a performance in which she tries out various parts – in vocalise except when she has to take part in the verbal drama."[38] It also shows how Carter took care to ensure variety in Rose's vocal utterances from the very beginning of the compositional process. He describes this emotional world in detail with regard to the finished opera in his fax of 29 March to Micaela von Marcard (see below, pp. 307–308). Here Carter also instructs the dramaturg in detail about Rose's entire part, indicating where Rose's vocalizing is in the background and where it should be brought to the fore.

---

37 Ibid., p. 33.
38 Ibid.
39 See Dörte Schmidt, "What Next? oder: Ein Porträt des Künstlers als 'grand old man'," in program book *Arnold Schönberg: Von heute auf morgen; Elliott Carter: What Next? Zwei Einakter*, ed. Staatsoper Unter den Linden Berlin (Frankfurt am Main; Leipzig: Insel, 1999), pp. 168–171.

A few days after sketching this page, Carter sketched the beginning of the piece, also shown here (and marked "Anfang," possibly because he was thinking about the place of the upcoming première), where each singer's "s," "sh," or "st" sound comes directly out of the unpitched percussion (see p. 306). Since the first sounds are meant to depict the car accident, Carter draws on automotive-related percussion sounds, such as brake drum in addition to bass drum, cymbal ("rim"), whip, guiro, tamtam, ratchet, and piano. (In the final version a large washboard and a trash can are also included.) On this sketch page, the progression from unpitched percussion to pitched vocal sounds occurs very quickly: already at the beginning of the third system Rose's sustained F to F♯ sets up a clear pitch orientation. (Carter changed this designation to Kid, as he deemed it "too low" for Rose.) In the final version, the gradual emergence of pitched from unpitched sounds,

and the dynamic shape of *fortissimo* fading to *pianissimo* is, apart from its programmatic function, also a musical process that governs the first forty-eight measures of the opera. (A similar transformation from "noise" to pitch, or more metaphorically, from chaos to order, is heard at the beginning of the *Double Concerto*.[39]) The singers' unpitched sibilants gradually turn into words, each of which already gives some hint of the character's background: for example, the astronomer Stella, who utters the first complete word, thinks first of "Star," which is then picked up by the other characters in turn. On this page Carter splits the word by having Zen say "sss" and Mama finishing the "tar." In the final version, other words appear out of the unformed "sss" sounds: "starts" (Zen), "startle" (Harry or Larry), "starlings" (Rose), "starch" (Mama), "starkest" (Stella). The introductory episode is brought to a close with Kid's comic punch line: "Starve. I'm starving."

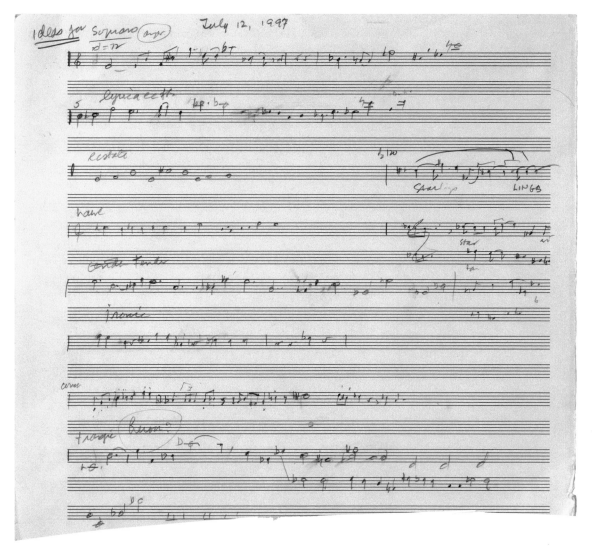

170 b *What Next?*, short score draft

171 **Micaela von Marcard to Elliott Carter, 29 March 1999**

Micaela v. Marcard / Dahlmannstr. 11 / 10629 Berlin
Berlin, 29th March

Dear Elliott Carter,
It was so nice to stay with you at the end of January, and I enjoyed very much discussing with you *What Next?* and possibilities to combine your opera with another Einakter. Unfortunately there was no possibility anymore to change the piece and so we are doing the Schoenberg *Von heute auf morgen.*

Meanwhile we are [working hard] on a conception for both operas, and we have one little question to ask you concerning Rose: she is singing nearly permanently very strange things [of] which we don't quite understand the sense. Is she citing something (I remember vaguely a Poulenc piece [using] an imaginary language[40]), is it some language which we don't know, is it just a combination of sounds, is it an expression of pain?

Could you perhaps help us [in] finding an interpretation for the Rose part?

And do you already know whether the little concert you planned in May in the Guggenheim Museum is going to be realized?[41] We are desperately longing for some examples of the music so that we get an [idea of] the sound of the notes. It would be highly helpful to hear the music, the realized score.

So many questions, and I am really curious for your answers. Thank you in advance for your response.

Many, many greetings, also to your wife, from
Micaela

[Typed fax with autograph signature; Elliott Carter Collection, Paul Sacher Foundation. Reprinted by permission of Micaela von Marcard.]

172 **Elliott Carter to Micaela von Marcard, 29 March 1999**

March 29, 1999

Dear Micaela von Marcard,
Thank you for your fax. I did enjoy meeting you in January, and am most delighted that your group has been working on *What Next?* As for *Rose* – here are some thoughts about her part...

Rose is a lieder singer and so is often accompanied by the piano as she attempts to recall her concert of the previous night. As a singer she is constantly recalling bits of her repertoire, often substituting vocal syllables for the words which she cannot remember. There should be many changes of vocal character during these asides, and in most cases they should be sung as a background to the parts of other singers and sung quite far away from the other singers. She is always sunk in the world of her music, except for a few moments when she becomes aware of what is going on. Thus her role is often a comment on the parts of the other singers and actors. After all, her big moment after her child-like narration is when she thinks she is losing her voice! After saying she feels sick, she must burst very soon into a grand flight of intense singing! at the end.

Suggestions:
measure

34–:	Rose, no vibrato
36–:	slight vibr[ato]
43–:	as written
58–59:	Rose in background, quietly lyrical
73–80:	Rose, as written
81–125:	Rose has forgotten her words and invents syllables.
82–86:	Rose is in background
88–90:	[same]
91–92:	same
93–94:	Rose very lyrically
95–115:	Rose background
116–119:	Rose more lightly, humorous
119–125:	same, but in background
130–160:	Rose, as written
161–162:	Rose in background

---

40 Probably a reference to Poulenc's *Rapsodie nègre* for baritone, flute, clarinet, string quartet, and piano (1917), a setting of nonsense syllables attributed to "Makoko Kangourou."

41 See Carter's reply, below, p. 308.

163–194: Rose in background but in a lighter character
204–221: Rose background, dolce (crescendo on 221)
222–223: Rose, bursts of humor
228–239: Rose, as written
273–274: *mistake in score, "Hush" is to be sung by MAMA*
308–310: Rose, warmly but quietly in background
332: Rose starts out very lyrically
333–335: Rose then turns to light comedy
392–397, Rose starts warmly and then lightens up
407,
420–421: Rose sings lightly
422–428: Rose warmly lyrical at end of 428 to 430, then becomes comic.
433–: continues 430
436–437: Rose, as previous[ly]
449–450: Rose marks each note
463–464: Rose, humorous
468–470: Rose, as previous[ly] (background)
474–475: Rose lyrically, background
476–480: Rose in foreground
489–493: Rose, nervously
537–: Rose returns to stage and sings as indicated
546–547: Rose, at each statement of "listen" the second note should have a slight crescendo after it is sung.

Lis ten

559–560: Rose leading voice
560 (end): Zen leading voice, Rose & Mama in background to 564
564–565: Stella leads.
574–587: Rose, very dramatically
591: Rose: "is she your mother," should be like a parenthesis
597–601: Rose, *dolce*
602–604: quasi parlando
605–621: as if practising (more or less neutral inflection)
623–659: Rose, dolce; from 626–677: Rose dolce in background

677 (end)
–713: Rose sings more and more dramatically
756–765: duet sung ironically?
779–789: Rose sings quietly, espressivo
792–793: Rose becomes more emphatic
794–799: Rose returns to quiet lyricism
828–832: Rose with growing intensity
863–867: *mistake* in first edition of score; top line is to be sung by *Rose* and not by *Mama*
863–870: Rose, lyrically to comic – this continues lightly in 866–870
879–966: Rose leads whenever she sings
968–971: Rose expressive but in background
975–977
(middle): nervously
977 (second half): Rose starts softly, in background, and, gaining confidence, sings more and more lyrically and "operatically" to end – last note of opera should have much vibrato – maybe even a trill.

I hope this helps. I will be glad to answer anything you want to know about the opera. We are going to have a performance of excerpts on May 16, probably at the Guggenheim Museum.[42] I will let you know around April 15 more precisely about this. As for *Von heute auf morgen*, several good friends [including] Oliver Knussen, conductor, and Steve Pruslin, répétiteur, were involved in a performance at the Netherlands Opera last year,[43] and after much effort in learning the score they found it a very effective and humorous opera, liking it very much. Knussen has made a recording for Deutsche G[rammophon].[44]

We all send our greetings and very best wishes,
Elliott Carter

March 29, 1999

[Typed fax with autograph date and signature; Elliott Carter Collection, Paul Sacher Foundation. Reproduced by permission of Micaela von Marcard.]

---

42 This tryout performance of *What Next?*, funded by various foundations and private patrons, was organized by Virgil Blackwell and Mary Cronson. Owing to the contract with the Staatsoper Unter den Linden, it could be neither staged nor held in a public venue. And contrary to the original intention, it did not take place in the Guggenheim Museum's "Works in Process" series, but was presented in Kaplan Penthouse of the Rose Building, Lincoln Center, on 16 May 1999 as a private event before some 200 invited guests, without the press. The performance was uncut and used the full instrumental forces. The hand-selected orchestra was conducted by Brad Lubman, augmented by the vocalists Elizabeth Keusch (Rose), Patrick Mason (Harry or Larry), Lucy Shelton (Mama), Mark Showalter (Zen), Elaine Bonazzi (Stella), and Holly Mentzer (Kid).

43 The production of Schoenberg's *Von heute auf morgen* at the Netherlands Opera (conducted by Oliver Knussen and staged by Pierre Audi) formed part of a triple bill with his *Die glückliche Hand* and *Erwartung*. It took place somewhat earlier than Carter assumed, being

173 Elliott Carter and Daniel Barenboim with Anne Griffiths,
Paul Griffiths (in the back row), and others during the
preparations for *What Next?* at the Staatsoper Unter den
Linden, Berlin (1999), photo by Hans Pölkow

The première of *What Next?* took place on 16 September
1999, and Carter traveled to Berlin a few days beforehand.
This photograph, taken in the Staatsoper Unter den Linden, shows him during the final preparations. The piece
created a considerable stir among the audience and the
international press. The fact that Daniel Barenboim had
taken up the cause of a contemporary work at a time when
Berlin's three opera houses were under great financial
pressure was praised almost as highly as the production's
artistic quality. Particularly well received was Carter's
music, to which the critic Simone Mahrenholz ascribed
"great transparency, economy of sound and structure, and
a vibrant sonic poetry."[45] (This economy of means was noticed by many others; only Kyle Gann expressed the astonishing view that "90 percent of *What Next?* harked back to
Mr. Carter's ultracomplex style of the 1960's and 70's."[46])
Something less than unity reigned, however, regarding
the opera's theatrical viability. Not every reviewer could
warm to the deliberate paucity of stage action in a work
whose figures, still dazed by the automobile accident, are
mainly concerned with reconstructing their identities
and tend to communicate at cross purposes rather than
with each other. Several critics appreciated that Carter's
and Griffiths's conception drew on the Theater of the Absurd of Ionesco and Beckett, while others tended to measure the work against the conventional opera aesthetic
and found interiorization of the plot "undramatic." One
of them, Klaus Geitel, went so far as to conclude that
Carter, in *What Next?*, had inadvertently "written an oratorio instead of his first opera."[47]

premièred on 11 March 1995 and
running only in spring 1995.

44 This recording, made in June 1995,
was never published.

45 Simone Mahrenholz, "Einsamkeit in
Eigenzeit," *Der Tagesspiegel* (Berlin),
18 September 1999.

46 Kyle Gann, "'What Next?': Place Opera
on Life's To-Do List," *The New York
Times*, 7 March 2000. Gann's review was

of the New York concert première that
Barenboim conducted in Carnegie
Hall on 5 March 2000 with the Chicago
Symphony Orchestra. The cast was
virtually the same as in Berlin, except that
the Kid was now sung by the thirteen-
year-old John Devine.

47 Klaus Geitel, "Katastrophen mit
Augenmusik," *Die Welt*, 18 September
1999.

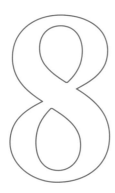

"Fons juventatis"

1998–2008

Tempo e tempi (1998–99)

The initial impetus for *Tempo e tempi* came from Raffaele Pozzi, one of the directors of the Pontino festival and a professor of music at Roma Tre University, who sent Carter two poems by Eugenio Montale (1896–1981), knowing that they would interest him. One was "Tempo e tempi," which deals with the very Carterian subject of time and how we perceive it. Carter immediately responded with a setting of this poem for soprano, violin, English horn, and bass clarinet. The song, completed on 14 June 1998 and first performed (by Victoria Schneider, Isabelle Magnenat, Heinz Holliger, and René Meyer) on 1 July 1998 at the Pontino Festival, "pleased its Italian audience so much that I was encouraged to set others," the composer recalled.[1] After completing his opera, Carter returned to the more intimate vocal form of the song cycle. Using the instrumentation oboe / English horn, clarinet / bass clarinet, violin, and cello, he added settings of the second Montale poem, "L'Arno a Rovezzano," and six other Italian poems, two by Salvatore Quasimodo (1901–1968) and four by Giuseppe Ungaretti (1888–1970). So it happened that in his ninetieth year, after four major song cycles on American poetry (of Bishop, Ashbery, Lowell, and Hollander), he produced his first songs based entirely on foreign-language texts. (Two more American song cycles, on poems of William Carlos Williams and Wallace Stevens, respectively, would follow in 2003 and 2006.) *Tempo e tempi*, first performed in its entirety on 24 May 2000 in London (by Lucy Shelton and the London Sinfonietta under Oliver Knussen), reaches new extremes of textural transparency and intense lyricism. There is a very sparing use of instruments; three of the eight songs are scored as duets between the voice and a solo instrument, and one uses three instruments. No two songs are scored in exactly the same way. The brevity of the songs – four take a minute and a half or less each – contributes to their lucid intelligibility and directness of expression; Paul Griffiths has suggested a convincing parallel between these songs and the miniatures of György Kurtág.[2] Finally, *Tempo e tempi* is a testament to Carter's lifelong love for Italy, which he first visited with his mother around 1924. Extended residencies at the American Academy in Rome, visits to the Pontino Festival, friendships with Petrassi, Dallapiccola, Roman Vlad, and others,

as well as numerous Italian performances of his music would follow in the decades to come. Carter wrote, "This song-cycle is a small gesture of gratitude to Italian culture and its musicians that have shown such an interest in my work."[3]

174 *Tempo e tempi,* for soprano, oboe (English horn), clarinet (bass clarinet), violin, and cello (1998–99), on texts by Eugenio Montale, Giuseppe Ungaretti, and Salvatore Quasimodo, no. 4: "Una colomba", draft in pencil, 1 p.

This pencil draft, dated 28 April 1999, sets Ungaretti's brief poem in its entirety, and has every appearance of having been written in one sitting. Carter seems to have conceived the clarinet and voice parts at the same time, rather than beginning with the vocal line alone, as had been his usual habit. The draft begins with a soft sustained A♭ in the solo clarinet (marked "Tranquillo" at quarter = 54), which gradually creeps upward in tremolo in half and whole steps. The voice joins in, extending the clarinet's chromatic ascent with its top notes A♯ and B. In the second system, which has been crossed out and rewritten in the third, the voice part already takes its final shape: a simple rising and falling line with strong E minor associations. The clarinet part is still indistinct, but Carter's choice of a low-register accompaniment as well as his decision to end on the same A♭ with which the clarinet began (shown precisely notated in the third system) are already in place. The entire range of the voice spans only a minor ninth, and the clarinet is also confined to the lower half of its range. The layout of the music on the page may reflect an implicit line break in this tiny poem, which in its entirety reads: "D'altri diluvi / una colomba ascolto" (literally, "from other floods / a dove I hear," and in Carter's more grammatically correct English translation, "I hear a dove from other floods").[4] The allusion to the doves released by the biblical Noah after the flood implies a shimmer of hope after a great catastrophe. Carter's setting, which is *piano* throughout, seems to illuminate a single moment of hushed expectancy rather than evoking the previous disaster. In a stroke of subtle resonance with the text, the clarinet's quiet flutterings may evoke

---

1 Quoted from Joel Sachs's notes in "All About Elliott: Honoring Elliott Carter's 100th Year," program booklet for the 2008 "Focus!" festival, p. 22.

2 Paul Griffiths, liner notes to the CD "Elliott Carter: Quintets and Voices," Mode Records 128 (2003), p. [3].

3 Quoted from Sachs, "All About Elliott" (see note 1), p. 22.

4 "Una colomba" comes from the collection *Sentimento del tempo* (Florence: Vallecchi, 1933) and has been reprinted many times since then.

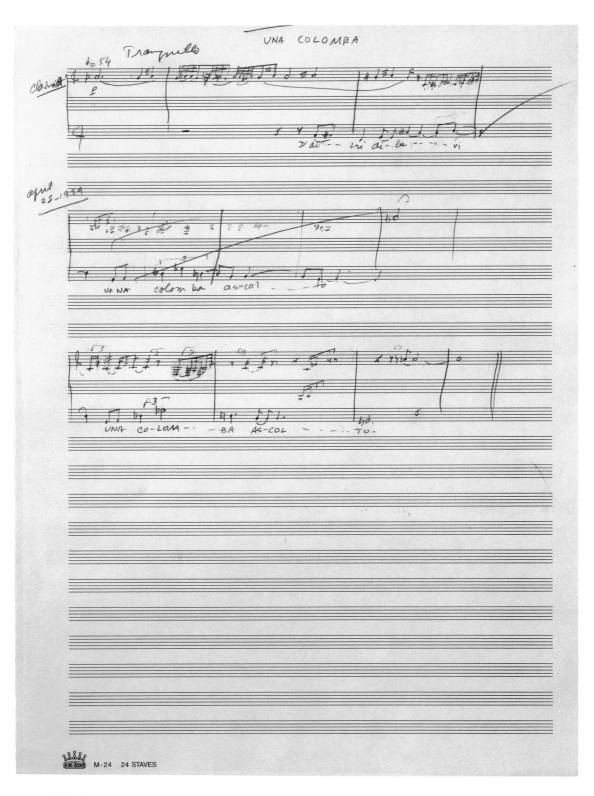

Oboe Quartet (2000–01)

the heard dove's cooing. The counterparts to this song are no. 7, "Uno," scored for voice and cello, which sets another very brief poem by Ungaretti, and the shortest, no. 2, "Ed è subito sera," which in the performance with Lucy Shelton and the Ensemble Sospeso lasts only forty-one seconds.[5] The brevity, simplicity, and emotional directness of this song cycle are worlds away from the multilayered complexity typical of much of Carter's previous music. *Tempo e tempi* anticipates several features of Carter's more recent music and may even mark the point at which one could say that his "late style" begins.

In late 1994 Heinz Holliger asked Carter whether he might write a piece for him to perform alongside Mozart's *Oboe Quartet:* "I am looking for new pieces for oboe, violin, viola, and cello (as Mozart KV 370) with Thomas Zehetmair, Tabea Zimmermann and Thomas Demenga. Would this be a combination for you?"[6] But it was not until 2000, when Carter was invited to the 2001 Lucerne Festival as composer-in-residence and received a corresponding commission, that he took up the idea and wrote his *Oboe Quartet* in winter 2000–01. Unlike the first work he had written for Holliger, the *Oboe Concerto,* this one did not require a bulky exchange of ideas on technical matters during the compositional process: not only was the composer aware of how intimately Holliger knew his music, he largely dispensed with special instrumental effects in the *Oboe Quartet.* He finished the fair copy of the full score on 15 April 2001 and sent it to the dedicatee, who was so taken with it that he promptly proposed two further works from the composer: a *sinfonia concertante* with winds in the manner of Mozart or Haydn, and a work for chorus (see Holliger's postcard of 2 July 2001, below, p. 316). The *Oboe Quartet* was premièred in Lucerne's Church of St. Matthew on 2 September 2001 by Thomas Zehetmair (violin), Ruth Killius (viola), Thomas Demenga (cello), and the work's dedicatee, Heinz Holliger, who also played several other Carter works at the Festival.[7] A short while later the same ensemble recorded the piece for ECM along with Isang Yun's *Quartet for Oboe and String Trio* (1994) – a work likewise written for Holliger – and other pieces by Carter and Yun.[8]

5 CD "Elliott Carter, Quintets and Voices," Mode 128 (2003).

6 Letter from Heinz Holliger to Elliott Carter, 6 December 1994; Elliott Carter Collection, Paul Sacher Foundation.

7 In the concert on 2 September 2001 he also played *A Six Letter Letter* and *Trilogy,* while Thomas Zehetmair presented *Four Lauds* and Thomas Demenga

Figment I. Before then, on 25 August 2001, Holliger had given the *ASKO Concerto* and *A Mirror on Which to Dwell* with the Ensemble Contrechamps and the soprano Juliane Banse. On 9 September 2001 he again appeared as a soloist in the *Oboe Concerto,* this time with the Southwest German Symphony Orchestra conducted by Sylvain Cambreling.

8 Elliott Carter: *Oboe Quartet, 4 Lauds, A 6 Letter Letter, Figment I, Figment II,* and Isang Yun: *Piri, Quartet for Oboe and String Trio;* Heinz Holliger (oboe), Thomas Zehetmair (volin), Ruth Killius (viola), and Thomas Demenga (cello); ECM New Series 1848/1849, 472 787-2 (recorded in September 2001 and February 2002, released in 2003).

175 *Oboe Quartet,* for oboe, violin, viola, and cello (2000–01), short score draft in pencil with markings in colored pencil, p. [15]

Proceeding from the notion that four instruments can be grouped into six possible sets of two, Carter designed his *Oboe Quartet* as a series of six short duos differing markedly in tempo and expression. He took into account that the oboe stands out against the strings by assigning it a special role. Although it cooperates closely with its counterparts in its three duos (with viola, cello, and violin, in that order), it goes its own way elsewhere: "[...] I made the oboe seem like a character that does not quite fit in," Carter explained, pointing out that outside the duo context the oboe is often a bit "obstreperous and difficult."[9] The oboe's special role is visible in the excerpt from the twenty-two-page short-score draft shown here, produced between December 2000 and February 2001. Here we see the end of the duo for viola and cello in the top system (mm. 190–194 of the final version) and, set clearly apart, the opening of the duo for violin and cello in the second system (mm. 210ff.), here numbered "6" although it later wound up as No. 5. In the final version these two duo passages were joined by a fifteen-bar intervening section missing in the draft (also missing are the chordal interpolations from the violin later added to the viola / cello duo, and the viola pizzicatos in the violin / cello duo). Still, the final three bars of the first system and the inserted line thereafter contain the solo oboe line with which this intervening section begins and ends as well as its rhythmically flexible, melodically expansive figures, setting it sharply apart from the string writing. (The first bar of the insert corresponds to m. 194 in the definitive score, the second and third to mm. 208–209. In between, i.e. in the bars not shown here [mm. 195–207], the oboe offsets the solid string chords with an obsessively repeated sustained g^1, again completely contrary to the other instruments.)

176 Heinz Holliger to Elliott Carter, [2 July 2001]

Dear Elliott,
It was so good to hear you on the phone! Sorry that Helen isn't so well. I hope she will recover in Connecticut. I have so much pleasure with your beautiful *Oboe Quartet.* I hope we can present you a good performance! Please don't spend much time on the new libretto when you feel it isn't the thing you need.[10] Did you ever consider writing a "Sinfonia concertante": 4 winds like Mozart, or V[iolin,] V[iolon]c[ello,] Ob[oe,] B[a]s[soo]n like Haydn (for instance for Boston...)? I still dream of a work for a cappella chorus (the fantastic Stuttgart Radio Chorus would be overhappy to commission such a work).

You do know so much about chorus, and there are your early works which would need a counterpart! Europe is full of very good choruses.

Much love, also from Ursula
Yours
Heinz

[Autograph postcard; Elliott Carter Collection, Paul Sacher Foundation. Reprinted by permission of Heinz Holliger.]

---

9 Elliott Carter, interview with Felix Meyer, 20 April 2001; published in German in the program book for the 2001 Lucerne Festival, pp. 61–76, esp. 63, and in abridged form in the CD booklet for the première recording of the work for ECM (see above, p. 314, note 8), p. 27.

10 In spring 2001 Carter had begun work on a second opera, again to a libretto by Paul Griffiths (see below, pp. 320–322). This project did not, however, come to fruition; in fact, by the time he received Holliger's message Carter had abandoned it.

**177 Elliott and Helen Carter with Felix Meyer
(New York, 2001), photo by Erich Singer (Lucerne)**

This photograph was taken on 20 April 2001, a few days after Carter finished the *Oboe Quartet* commissioned by the Lucerne Festival. On this afternoon he made himself available not only for an interview about his new composition, but for a series of photographs that the Festival's delegate, Erich Singer, took with an eye to the publication he supervised on the Festival's two composers-in-residence in 2001, Carter and Hanspeter Kyburz.[11] Eventually, however, Carter was unable to travel to Lucerne that summer, as his wife's delicate health would not allow long periods of absence.

11 *Composers-in-Residence: Elliott Carter,
Hanspeter Kyburz,* program book
for the 2001 Lucerne Festival,
ed. Erich Singer and Basil Rogger
(Lucerne: Lucerne Festival, 2001).

Steep Steps (2001)

Carter wrote *Steep Steps* for "the greatly admired clarinettist and friend Virgil Blackwell during the summer of 2001." Blackwell (b. 1942), a Juilliard graduate and founding member of Speculum Musicae, first encountered the composer during preparations for a performance of the *Double Concerto* in 1974,[12] and worked closely with him during the preparations for the première of *A Mirror on Which to Dwell* (24 February 1976). Blackwell became Carter's assistant in 1988, managing all matters regarding Carter's professional life and becoming especially indispensable after Helen's death in 2003. *Steep Steps* belongs to a group of recent solo (or small-scale) instrumental works dedicated to specific performers. After decades of producing only major works, Carter's 1983 solo guitar piece *Changes* for David Starobin seemed like an exception. But in the 1990s and 2000s pieces for the flutist Robert Aitken (*Scrivo in vento*), the oboist-harpist duo Heinz and Ursula Holliger (*Trilogy*), the cellists Thomas Demenga and Fred Sherry (*Figment I* and *II*, respectively), and another for Starobin (*Shard*) showed Carter's renewed enthusiasm for small forms. In recent years, Carter has continued to write solo pieces for some of the most prominent performers of contemporary music, including Pierre-Laurent Aimard, Ayako and Charles Neidich, and Samuel Rhodes. Instrumental virtuosity is the main feature of all these works; written in close collaboration with their dedicatees, each one is completely idiomatic for the instrument and moreover matches the personality and performing style of its soloist.

The title *Steep Steps*, the composer explains in a note to the score, "comes from the fact that, unlike the other woodwind instruments, the clarinet overblows at the twelfth, a large interval that forms the basis of much of this composition." The twelfth is indeed a prominent interval in the piece, locally as well as structurally (the range of many phrases, for example, is a twelfth or an octave plus a twelfth). Carter takes advantage of the bass clarinet's enormous range and flexibility, writing large leaps and extended passages in each of the instrument's main registers. The pitch material is based on the all-triad 012478 hexachord (one of Carter's favorites), with its subset 0146 (the all-interval tetrachord) featured prominently. There are two main rhythmic layers: a slow one,

moving in dotted quarters (or multiples), and a faster one moving in sixteenth-note triplets. Blackwell premièred *Steep Steps* in New York on 17 October 2001.

178 *Steep Steps*, for bass clarinet in B flat (2001), revised version of mm. 63–65, photocopy with handwritten additions, 1 p.

This page shows an early version of the ending of *Steep Steps*. Like many other pages of drafts, this one was sent by fax to the clarinettist. Blackwell recalls that he first learned of the piece's existence after the unexpected arrival of a draft page in his fax machine on 22 May 2001. A week later, a sketch of a difficult passage in the high register appeared (corresponding to mm. 46–48 of the final version), accompanied by the query: "Virgil – is this too impossible for bass cl.?" A complete draft was faxed on 1 June. On the page shown – faxed to Blackwell on 5 October 2001 with the note, "Virgil, how about this?" – the end of the piece features the sudden introduction of sixteenth-note triplets in m. 65, contrasting with the eighth-note triplets in the previous two measures. The last note (a stratospheric F♯5, written G♯6), is accented and off the beat. Two pitches were changed: E3–B3 (written G♭4–D♭5) in m. 64 had been A3–D♭4 (written B4–E♭5) in an earlier draft. In changing a major third to a perfect fifth, the revised interval matches the many other fifths and twelfths in the passage. After faxing the page to Blackwell, Carter added the markings "Ritard. poco" at m. 64 and "sub[ito] più mosso" at m. 65. Then the clarinettist suggested that Carter change the triplet sixteenths to eighths (marked "più mosso") and place the final note on the beat. This would accomplish Carter's desired result – a surge of forward motion at the very end – more reliably and more emphatically, and Carter immediately agreed to the change. (The revised ending first appears in the Boosey & Hawkes score dated 2001/2005.)

The first six pitches in the passage shown belong to hexachord 012478. The rest of the passage elaborates on the characteristic interval of the twelfth. For example, the descending twelfths E♭5–A♭3 (written F6–B♭4) and A3–D2 (written B4–E3) in m. 63 taken together span the

---

12 The *Double Concerto* was conducted by Gerard Schwarz with the soloists Paul Jacobs (harpsichord) and Ursula Oppens (piano) at a tribute concert for Carter's sixty-fifth birthday on 30 October 1974; also on the program of this concert, which took place at the Whitney Museum, were the *Sonata for Violoncello and Piano* (played by Michael Rudiakov and Ursula Oppens) and the *String Quartet No. 3* (played by the Composers String Quartet).

entire normal range of the bass clarinet. (The lowest note in the piece is a B1 – written D♭3 – in mm. 45; the special key needed to produce this note is not found on all instruments.) The prominent twelfth between F2 and C4 (written G3–D5) is heard twice in m. 65 in literal form, and, with the upper note "ornamented" by neighbor notes, throughout the last two measures. The final leap, which takes the bass clarinet up to F♯5 (written G♯6), is also a twelfth. The total range of the piece is therefore three octaves plus a fifth, or a "super twelfth" reaching from B1 to F♯5.

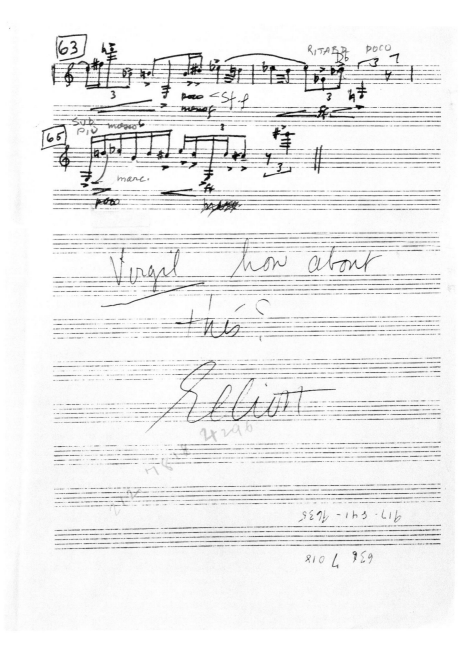

Prequel to *What Next?* (2001)

1: The Beginning of the End

(The temple of the sect. Joseph is standing on a dais or enthroned, addressing his followers: Amy, Harry or Larry, Kid, Rose, Stella, Troy and Zen, all of them robed and seated. Rose and Kid are near Joseph, who wields a book as he preaches. There is a vacant chair. At one side, behind a screen or wall, is a booth in which there is a control panel. A chant, which goes right through the opera, is shown in uppercase type: it continues seamlessly, so that when one character moves out of it, it is taken up by another. The chant text generally underlays the other text above it, if any.)

JOSEPH: AND THE FIRST VOICE
               What will it be, that first voice of heaven?
               That trumpet in your ear, what will it be?
               It will be the voice you thought you'd forgotten,
               The voice you had as a baby child,
               Only wailing now constantly for joy
               As you draw as if through many waters
               Into the region of light forever.

STELLA: WHICH I HEARD WAS AS IT WERE OF A TRUMPET TALKING
               WITH ME WHICH SAID

ROSE: COME UP HITHER

ZEN: *(He begins simultaneously with Rose, but breaks away from the temple to move downstage and address the audience directly. Crescendo on his first word as he does so?)*

               COME up here if you dare!
               Are you ready for this?
               We will show you things.
               But you don't have to be shown.

1

179 a Prequel to *What Next?*, libretto

During the reception after the 1999 première of *What Next?* in Berlin, Daniel Barenboim toasted the composer and librettist on their success, and then called for a second opera to go with it ("What first?"). About a month later Carter mentioned to Griffiths that "I suppose an American *Khovanshchina* would be Waco."[13] Mussorgsky's opera, whose characters include members of a religious cult who commit mass suicide by burning, offered obvious parallels to the death by fire of about eighty members of the Branch Dravidian cult in their compound near Waco, TX, after an attack by US federal agents and the Texas National Guard on 19 April 1993.[14] Nothing more came of this idea until the second half of April 2001, when Carter asked Griffiths to work out a libretto based on the apocalyptic suicide cult idea.[15] Composer and librettist worked together on the text, as they had done with *What Next?*, throughout May, and the new libretto was completed on 6 June.[16] Carter made a few sketches in June of that year before the project was discontinued. In the untitled libretto, a prequel to *What Next?*, the action clearly takes place before the initial catastophe of the earlier opera, and it features the same six characters in addition to three new ones. The two operas together would have created a single full-length two-act opera, resolving the programming difficulties posed by all one-acters. Notes on the libretto in the composer's hand show Carter's involvement in conceiving the plot.[17] The characters of *What Next?* are here imagined to be part of an apocalyptic suicide sect, led by a charismatic guru, Joseph, who controls every aspect of their lives. Through prayers and exhortations they prepare for the final reckoning, when they will cast off their "leaden, suffocating physical bodies" and begin a transit to the "promised place," Sirius. (The two librettos are linked through a number of prominent common keywords; "Sirius" also figures in *What Next?*, as the name of a star and as a pun on "serious.") While Carter's notes indicate that the group suicide would be stopped by the arrival of the police, the final version of the libretto had a more violent conclusion, in keeping with the *Khovanshchina* idea. As the guns with which they will commit suicide are distributed, it is discovered that Joseph has been trafficking in weapons for a terrorist group. Rose, the soprano in *What Next?*, kills Joseph and escapes with her four *What Next?* compatriots.[18] The

13 Paul Griffiths, personal communication, 23 May 2008.

14 The Metropolitan Opera's 1985 production of *Khovanshchina* (in the Shostakovich version) was revived in 1999. The Waco events were again in the news in November 2000, when the results of a federal investigation were released (which largely confirmed the government's original interpretation of the death by fire as collective suicide).

15 The present authors remember Carter talking about suicide cults during a visit to New York on 20 April 2001.

16 Paul Griffiths, personal communication, 23 May 2008.

17 These consist of a) two pages of handwritten notes on lined paper entitled "OPERA (II)"; b) two pages of handwritten notes on unlined paper entitled "STARRY – WAY";

and c) one typed page, entitled "Cult opera –? Order of the Astral templ[e]?," dated 25 April 2001, apparently a draft of a letter to Griffiths. (Elliott Carter Collection, Paul Sacher Foundation.)

18 Carter's notes (b) had suggested that "Zen" shoot the guru, "or prepares to and loses heart." There is no mention of gun-running or terrorism in Carter's notes or scenario.

179 b Prequel to *What Next?*, sketch page

new characters Amy and Troy choose to die with their leader. The survivors presumably then go off in a car (or two cars?), and experience the accident with which *What Next?* begins, or perhaps the mass suicide itelf represents the catastophe. According to Carter's scenario of 25 April 2001, they "invent the parts they play in *What Next?* in order to conceal their horror at what they, as former cultists, have witnessed." The prequel's dramatic arch is the opposite to that of the first opera: if all the energies in *What Next?* are generated by the opening cataclysm, the prequel starts very slowly and culminates in a scene of violence at the end. This would have created a potentially very satisfying shape for the whole evening. Moreover, the prequel would have revealed the exact nature of the past trauma as well as the characters' former identities, both of which in *What Next?* are not completely known even to the characters themselves. But even as Carter set out to sketch the music, he began to have doubts about the topic of this project, and in mid-June 2001 he stopped work on the opera.

179 Prequel to *What Next?,* opera project to a libretto by Paul Griffiths (2001)
a libretto, computer printout, p. 1
b sketches in pencil, 1 p.

In keeping with the cult depicted in the plot, a continuous "chant" setting texts from the Book of Revelation is passed from character to character and projected onto a screen throughout the opera. This text layer, printed in upper case type, is described in the stage directions on the libretto page shown (a). The rest of the dialogue takes place over the chant's cantus firmus. The result of this two-layered libretto would be a polyphonic vocal texture throughout; at least two voices would always be singing, even during the "arias." On this page both layers of text allude to the "last trumpet" of the apocalypse; the chant, sung by Joseph, Stella, and Rose in sequence, sets Revelation 4:1–3 and 5, and the sect leader, Joseph, refers to "that trumpet in your ear." On the stage are all the characters of *What Next?* except Mama, who is inducted into the sect in the next scene, and the new characters Joseph, Amy (a mezzo-soprano), and Troy (a baritone). At the bottom of

the page, Zen offers a Brechtian comment directly to the audience (a perspective which is however never repeated). Carter began sketching on 2 June 2001 with twelve-note chords, searching for the ones that would include the primarily diatonic intervals he desired for the chant. Then he set the chant for the entire first scene in a narrow-ranged, almost modal melody that features many fifths and other diatonic intervals. On the page shown (b), he added the second layer of text for the first time. The page begins with Joseph singing the chant's beginning, "And the first voice," to a diatonic C–G–A figure in measured dotted halves and quarters in an implied 6/8 meter. Stella picks up the chant, "which I heard was as it were of a trumpet," overlapping with Joseph's A and continuing with an emphatic reiteration of the C and G from Joseph's chant ("as it were of"). This was apparently too much pitch repetition, as Carter changed the Cs to Bs in an alternative version sketched underneath (see arrow), but the falling fifth D–G, which echoes in inversion Joseph's starting interval, remained. Joseph's shift from the chant to his own words is marked by a faster surface rhythm and a 3/4 division of the bar, with his quarter notes subdivided into triplets. The contrasting meters between the chant line and the other vocal line in this sketch imply that Carter would have used the dual text layers to create a (very Carterian) polyrhythmic texture throughout.

Boston Concerto (2001–02)

In summer 2001 Carter embarked on a new orchestral work, the *Boston Concerto,* in response to a commission from the Boston Symphony Orchestra made possible by the New Works Fund of the Massachusetts Cultural Council. In his program notes for the première Carter himself referred to the work as a " 'Thank you' piece" for the orchestra, a token of his gratitude for the formative musical experiences he had received from its concerts during his years as a Harvard student and a member of the Harvard Glee Club. Yet he also wanted to express, one last time, his deep attachment to his wife Helen, now aged and infirm. Accordingly the score, which he finished on 7 May 2002 and prefixed with a quotation from William Carlos Williams's poem "Rain" (see below, p. 325), is dedicated to her, as was his *Symphony No. 1* sixty years previously and several other works since then. The *Boston Concerto* draws on the form of the baroque *concerto grosso,* being a series of tutti sections resembling ritornellos or refrains, and episodes dominated by solo playing. (A similar formal design is found in the *ASKO Concerto* of 1999–2000 for small orchestra.) But unlike the ritornellos in a *concerto grosso* (or the *ASKO Concerto*), here they are characterized by a delicately filigreed texture, while the lyric solo episodes unfold in large arcs of tension, sometimes reaching high levels of emotional intensity. In this sense the work might be said to be a psychological inversion of its historical model. The *Boston Concerto* was premièred on 3–5 April 2003 by the Boston Symphony Orchestra, conducted by Ingo Metzmacher. Later the orchestra played the piece under James Levine, who became its new music director in 2004 with the declared goal of elevating the status of contemporary music in its programs.

180 *Boston Concerto,* for orchestra (2001–02), autograph full score in pencil, p. 6 (mm. 24–28)

For the ritornellos of the *Boston Concerto* Carter drew on the extended pizzicato passages of *String Quartet No. 3* and the final movement of *String Quartet No. 5,* transferring this timbral effect for the first time on a large scale to a full string section. The tutti pizzicato in the strings also lends the relevant sections a specific "pointillist" sound readily associated with the image of rain evoked in William Carlos Williams's poem. All in all, there are seven such "rain" ritornellos framing six solo episodes: one for flutes and clarinets; another for vibraphone, piano, and harp; one for violas and double basses; one for horns, trumpets, trombones, and tuba; one for oboes and bassoons; and finally one for violins and cellos. The ritornellos, marked "Allegro staccatissimo," are all in the same tempo (quarter note = 90), whereas each episode moves at its own, usually slower, speed. Here we see the ending of the first ritornello (mm. 24–28) in Carter's fair copy of the full score (a dual dedication in pencil "To Helen and the members of the Boston Symphony" can be faintly descried through the erasure). It reveals that Carter wrote out what might be called a deliberate element of soft focus in the strings: the rapid chordal pizzicatos, when executed with the oscillating finger movement indicated by the arrows, unavoidably lead to minor shifts of coordination that blur the rhythmic contours. No less noticeable is the fact that the *staccatissimo* effect involves not only the strings but the other instruments as well, in this case mainly the brass, which is employed with staccato figures and repeated tones in the manner of pizzicato. Finally we should mention an orchestration strategy employed later in the work: each tutti section omits the instruments emphasized in the episode that follows. Here the instruments left out are the flutes and clarinets, which enter all the more conspicuously on the next page of the score with a slow, almost unaccompanied sextet marked "Lento, teneramente."

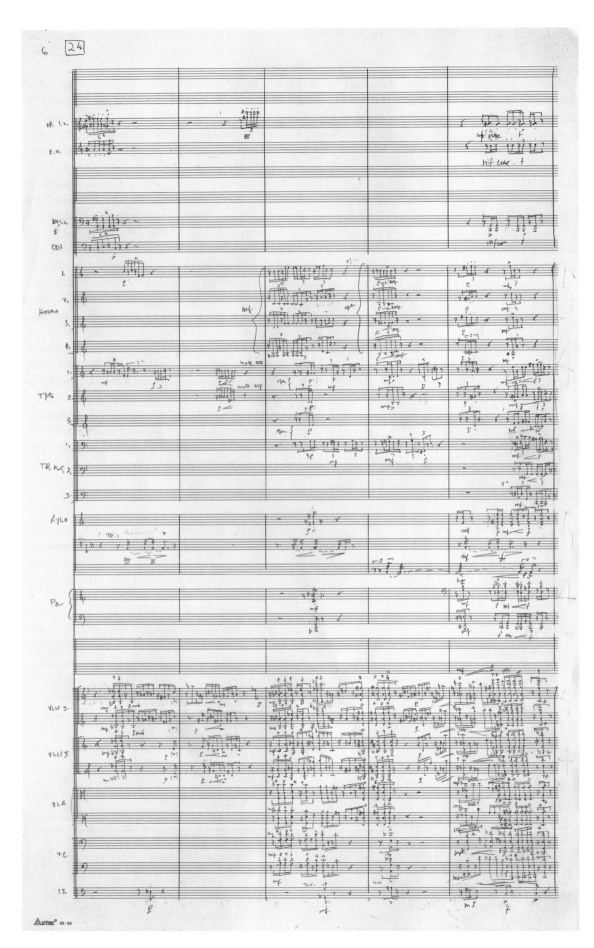

Robert Craft's Tribute to Helen Carter (2003)

Helen Carter passed away on 17 May 2003 at the age of ninety-five. On 15 September of the same year friends and acquaintances gathered together to pay homage to the deceased in a memorial ceremony at New York's Century Club. The ceremony consisted of appreciations by Charles Rosen, Lucy Shelton, Robert Craft, Ursula Oppens, and Elizabeth Hardwick as well as film excerpts by Frank Scheffer and a performance by Rolf Schulte of Stravinsky's *Elegy* for unaccompanied violin. Below we reproduce the address given by Robert Craft, who had belonged to the Carters' intimate circle of friends for decades and had done yeoman's duty with his performances of the *Double Concerto* (see above, p. 172).

181   Robert Craft, "For Helen Jones Carter" (2003)

As we all know, Elliott dedicated his *Boston Concerto* to Helen, choosing the perfect epigraph for it from William Carlos Williams:

"As the rain falls / so does / your love
bathe every / open / object of the world –"[19]

The ovation that greeted Elliott and the new concerto at the Proms last month acclaimed him, in the words of the *Times Literary Supplement,* "the world's greatest living composer."[20] This has been recognized by the musical élite since the death of the preceding titleholder in April 1971, who had himself been among the first to perceive the stature of his successor.

*   *   *

On July 15, 1966, the Lincoln Center Stravinsky Festival presented a staged performance of *Histoire du soldat*, with Elliott as the Soldier, Aaron Copland as the Narrator, and – typecasting a bit – John Cage as the Devil.[21] Three days later, Helen and Elliott dined with the Stravinskys at La Côte Basque. As always with this combination, the two composers talked about music, and so intently that neither of them noticed the famous face, better known as "the voice," approaching their table. Helen, the first to identify the intruder, nudged Elliott, but Stravinsky saw

only that a piece of paper and a pen, with which to inscribe his name on it, had been placed next to him on the table – by no means the first time this had happened to him. When he endorsed the paper without bothering to look up, Helen and Elliott were shocked. Frankie, unaccustomed to this newfound anonymity, retreated to his secluded table and rejoined Mia Farrow, who would fly with him the next day to Honolulu and become Mrs. Sinatra.[22] Situations of this kind were not new to Helen and Elliott, who had witnessed many equally curious incidents in their adventures with Stravinsky.

But then, Helen and Elliott were the closest long-time friends of the Stravinskys in the American musical world, especially during the last years of the older composer's life, after his move from California to New York. Vera Stravinsky's diaries are the source of an extensive but far from complete agenda of visits, dinners, concerts, ballets, *vernissages*, experienced together with Helen and Elliott in Rome, Berlin, Dartington, et al. I should add that George Balanchine and Nicolas and Dominique Nabokov[23] were also frequent companions during his last years. Helen and Elliott, along with Balanchine, were among the very few who attended the private funeral service for Stravinsky on the day of his death.

*   *   *

"Call Helen" was Elliott's response when a difficulty of any kind arose, and call Helen we did. When Alva[24] and I were negotiating to purchase an apartment in Venice, Helen returned us to reality with an inimitable remark: "Just try to have a light bulb changed!"

When the tenor selected for our performance and recording of *The Rake's Progress* in New York[25] proved incapable of learning some of the rhythmically intricate passages, and clearly had to be replaced – two days before the dress rehearsal – we turned to Helen in despair. "Get Jon Garrison," she said, knowing that he was familiar with the role. We explained to her that Garrison was vexed with us since we had chosen him for the Shepherd's part in *Oedipus Rex*, instead of the title role. Helen volunteered to arrange the matter herself, and within a half hour we had an excellent as well as bonhomous "Tom Rakewell, Esquire" for the part.

---

19   William Carlos Williams, "Rain" (1930), *The Collected Poems of William Carlos Williams*, vol. 1: *1909–1939*, ed. A. Walton Litz and Christopher MacCowan (New York: New Directions, 1986), pp. 343–346, esp. 343.

20   Andrew Porter, "Many Happy Refrains," *Times Literary Supplement*, no. 5238 (22 August 2003), p. 16.

21   The performance took place during the New York Philharmonic's second summer festival ("A Festival of Stravinsky: His Heritage and His Legacy"), conducted by Lukas Foss.

22   Carter's own version of this anecdote is recounted in *CC*, pp. 24–25.

23   Nabokov married his fifth wife, the French-born photographer Dominique Cibiel, in 1970.

24   Alva Minoff Craft, Robert Craft's wife.

25   Robert Craft's recording of Stravinsky's opera *The Rake's Progress* (with the Orchestra of St. Luke's and the Gregg Smith Singers) was made at the State University of New York at Purchase from 10 to 18 May 1993 and released on the Music Masters label (01612-67131-2). It was preceded by a concert performance in Avery Fisher Hall, New York, on 9 May 1993.

182   Helen and Elliott Carter (Waccabuc, 1977)

The very next day our Ann Truelove developed laryngitis, or said she did. Again, we called Helen. She proposed Lucy Shelton, but unfortunately, and much to our chagrin, Lucy had a previous engagement. A substitute was found, and though she was no Lucy, achieved a creditable performance.

Needless to say, Helen and Elliott were there encouraging us throughout the opera. Later, Elliott wrote praising our recording of it, and adding with his habitual perception: "The *Rake* is wonderful. It avoids the dragging gait of Stravinsky's recording, which hurts the Third Act especially [...]. I had forgotten that pervasive melancholy that surrounds the whole in some strange way, but adds a beauty [...]. Perhaps Bedlam is the true artist's place in capitalist society."[26]

* * *

One day Alva was lamenting her inability to lure me out of the house for some exercise. She called Helen for advice, and was told: "That's simple. Just open the door and *push* him out. I do that every day with Elliott."

Helen's spunkiness was one of her most endearing qualities. One evening at a Fifty-Eighth Street bistro, Elliott must have sensed that Helen was on the verge of mentioning someone whose name he apparently thought impolitic to pronounce in the present company. Then suddenly Helen said to her beloved husband *sotto voce*, but distinctly: "Don't you *dare* kick me under the table again."

* * *

I think of Helen and Elliott as a French poet, Charles Maray, in the 1970s, thought of the Stravinskys:

"Un Couple de Légende...

Depuis 1971, dès que les premiers jours du printemps arrivent à Venise, on voit débarquer une grande dame distinguée, qui aussitôt descendue sur les quais, se dirige vers San Michele...

Madame Véra STRAVINSKY vient régulièrement se recueillir sur la tombe de son mari...

Dans les allées, sous les cyprès, se perpétue une belle légende d'un couple hors de destin, d'un couple qui a trouvé son oasis, sa paix sous le ciel de Venise, d'un couple de créateurs; lui[,] musicien, et elle, peintre, dont toutes les œuvres sont inspirées d'un air étrange, féérique, d'une Venise d'un autre monde..."

[A Couple from Legend...

Each year since 1971, as the first days of spring come to Venice, a highly distinguished lady is seen to disembark; no sooner does she set foot on the quayside than she makes her way to San Michele...

Madame Véra STRAVINSKY comes regularly to pay her respects at the tomb of her husband...

In the alleys, beneath the cypresses, a wonderful legend is perpetuated, involving a couple truly set apart, who found an oasis for themselves, a haven of peace beneath the sky of Venice, creators both; he, a musician, and she, a painter, whose works are all filled with a strange, fairylike quality, a Venice of another world...][27]

* * *

In 1922, a few weeks after his arrival in Taos, New Mexico, D. H. Lawrence wrote to the widower of a recently deceased friend: "[...] I knew Sallie was turning away to go. And what can one do. Only it hurts, the inevitable hurt [...]. And if Sallie had to go to sleep, being really tired, having gone a long way [...] well, the rest of the journey she goes with us, but as a passenger now, instead of a traveller. Nevertheless, one uses words to cover up a crying inside one."[28]

A few weeks later the same writer, on hearing the news of Katherine Mansfield's death, wrote to her husband: "I had sent a new book I wanted Katherine to read. She'll know, though. The dead don't die. They look on and help."[29]

[Published as „Remembering Helen Carter" in Robert Craft, *Down a Path of Wonder* (n.p.: Naxos Books, 2006), pp. 414–417. Reproduced here from the typescript in the Elliott Carter Collection, Paul Sacher Foundation. Reprinted by permission of Robert Craft.]

---

26 Letter from Elliott Carter to Robert Craft, 22 August 1994, draft in the Elliott Carter Collection, Paul Sacher Foundation. The beginning reads: "The Craft *Rake* is wonderful. It avoids the dragging gait of the Stravinsky one, which hurts the 3rd act especially. [...] I had forgotten that a pervasive melancholy surrounds the whole in some strange way, but adds a beauty, unexpected." The final sentence comes at the end of the following sentences by Carter: "Of course, Nick Shadow is the vile Public Relations expert that artists should be wary of. This is obviously in Auden's view of things. A case could be made that Baba is Karl Marx in disguise? That Bedlam is the true artist's place in capitalist society."

27 Charles D. Maray, *San Michele: Le cimetière flottant de Venise* (Paris: private publication), 1979, p. 77; English translation by Mark Weir.

28 Letter from D.H. Lawrence to William Hopkin, 25 October 1922; quoted freely from *The Letters of D.H. Lawrence*, vol. 4: *June 1921 – March 1924*, ed. Warren Roberts, James T. Boulton, and Elizabeth Mansfield (Cambridge: Cambridge University Press, 1987), p. 327.

29 Letter from D.H. Lawrence to John Middleton Murry, 2 February 1923; quoted freely from ibid., p. 375.

Mosaic (2004)

Many of Carter's recent works pay tribute to admired composers and musicians; the *Four Lauds* for violin solo, for example, memorialize the composers Copland, Petrassi, and Sessions, as well as the former first violinist of the Juilliard String Quartet, Robert Mann, as *Figment II* for cello (which is subtitled "Remembering Mr. Ives") does for Carter's erstwhile mentor. These memorial compositions are much more than occasional pieces. In his tenth decade Carter often draws upon his rich store of memories to kindle ideas for major compositions. *Mosaic* recalls Carter's old friend Carlos Salzedo (1885–1961), the French-American harpist, pianist, and composer who had been active in Varèse's International Composers' Guild, and whom Carter had known in the 1930s. Scored for a small ensemble of winds, strings, and harp, *Mosaic* also pays homage to Salzedo's exploration of advanced playing techniques, which helped to bring the harp, a structurally diatonic instrument, into the world of twentieth-century music. While Carter had already written ambitious harp parts in his earlier orchestral music, his work with the harpist Ursula Holliger in preparing *Bariolage*, the first piece of *Trilogy* for oboe and harp (1992), helped him to gain further mastery over the fine points of pedaling and notation for the instrument.[30] A commission from the Nash Ensemble of London, which includes the Philharmonia Orchestra's principal harpist Lucy Wakeford as a standing member, again presented the opportunity to write a challenging piece for harp. In *Mosaic*, Carter uses Salzedo's techniques of timpanic sounds (striking the sounding-board with the finger or knuckle), Aeolian rustling (a glissando played with the open hand), snare drum effect (muting lower strings and allowing the upper ones to "rattle"), whistling sounds (sliding the hand rapidly along the string), xylophonic sounds (plucking strings muted with the other hand), and many other effects.[31] The score is dated 22 August 2004, and the first performance – by the Nash Ensemble – took place in London on 16 March 2005.

183 *Mosaic,* **for chamber ensemble (2004),**
autograph full score in pencil, p. 26 (mm.197–203)

Although the harp part in *Mosaic* is prominent, the piece is by no means a harp concerto. Carter explained that to balance the sections where "the harp played elaborately alone," he "wanted to give the other musicians something interesting to play."[32] This passage, which occurs about forty measures from the end, is the climax of the piece. Its repetitive double stops in the strings with off-beat accents recall a famous passage from Stravinsky's *Le Sacre du printemps*, which exerted a particularly strong influence on Varèse. Both of these composers moved in Salzedo's circle, and were of course also revered by Carter. The harp plays overlapping glissandi in both hands, *fortissimo*, in the upper register. These are punctuated by two "thunder effect" chords in the low register, produced (according to Salzedo's manual) by sliding "violently" with the forefinger of the left hand in the direction of the arrow, allowing the strings intentionally to strike against each other (Carter's indication "l. v." means *"laissez vibrer"*). The wire strings in this register of the harp make a thunder-like, metallic noise when they collide. The pedal markings here and in the preceding measures indicate that the notes of this glissando are G♭, F♯ (the same pitch on another string), E♯, D♭, C, B, and A, which produce the all-triad hexachord, one of Carter's favorites. The woodwinds, which had been prominently featured in the preceding section, join the other instruments in m. 203, at the loudest part of the climax. In his introduction to the score Carter writes of the "many short mosaic-like tessera[e]" [stones or tiles] that make up the piece's form. The juxtaposition of distinct sections, such as the one of the extended woodwind trio at the center of the piece and the texturally contrasting sections that surround it, is reminiscent of Carter's earlier formal experiments, but here the form is more spontaneous – and mosaic-like – since the "movements" do not recur.

30 This is shown in his extensive correspondence with Ursula Holliger, described in Anne C. Shreffler, "Netzwerke der Zusammenarbeit – Heinz und Ursula Holliger," trans. Ulrich Mosch, in *"Entre Denges et Denezy...": Dokumente zur Schweizer Musikgeschichte*

1900–2000, ed. Ulrich Mosch in collaboration with Matthias Kassel (Mainz, London, etc.: Schott, 2000), pp. 106–116, esp. 113.

31 These effects are explained in Salzedo's book, *Modern Study of the Harp / L'Etude moderne de la harpe* (New York: Schirmer, 1921).

32 Conversation with Robert Aitken, 28 May 2006, at the Glenn Gould Studio of the CBC, on the occasion of performances of Mosaic at the New Music Concerts' presentation of "Elliott Carter at 97." (Private recording; Elliott Carter Collection, Paul Sacher Foundation.)

184 Elliott Carter and Virgil Blackwell, in the back row
(from left to right:) Anne Shreffler, John Link,
and Frank Scheffer (Boston, 2004), photo by Phoebe
Sexton (Harvard News Office)

This photo was taken on 9 November 2004 at the symposium "Elliott Carter's Orchestral Music," organized jointly by the Boston Symphony Orchestra, the Harvard University Department of Music, and the Minda de Gunzburg Center for European Studies, on the occasion of performances of *Symphonia* and *Micomicón* by the Boston Symphony Orchestra conducted by James Levine, 11–13 November 2004. The conference, whose aim was to honor and reflect upon Carter's achievements in orchestral composition, featured scholarly papers by Daniel Albright, Anne Shreffler, and David Schiff; a panel discussion with John Link, Charles Rosen, and the speakers; and a screening of Frank Scheffer's film on the composer, *A Labyrinth of Time.* The not-quite-ninety-six-year-old guest of honor had not been scheduled to speak, but much to the audience's delight, he rose at the beginning of the conference and spontaneously delivered some remarks about his student years at Harvard, his compositions *Symphonia* and *Micomicón,* and his admiration for James Levine and the Boston Symphony Orchestra. The conductor was also present in the hall and contributed actively to the panel discussion.

33 Telegram from Elliott Carter to James Levine, 6 July 1990; Elliott Carter Collection, Paul Sacher Foundation. Levine's recording of the *Variations for Orchestra* was made in July 1990, along with works by Gunther Schuller (*Spectra*), Milton Babbitt (*Correspondences*), and John Cage (*Atlas eclipticalis*), but not released until 1994 (Deutsche Grammophon (431 698-2).

34 A reference to John Harbison's opera *The Great Gatsby* (after the novel by F. Scott Fitzgerald), premièred on 20 December 1999 under Levine's direction with staging by Mark Lamos. The official wording of the commission reads: "commissioned by the Metropolitan Opera to commemorate the 25th anniversary of the début of James Levine."

In Praise of James Levine (2005)

Joining the company of Pierre Boulez, Heinz Holliger, Oliver Knussen, and Daniel Barenboim, the longstanding music director of the Metropolitan Opera and (from 2004) also of the Boston Symphony Orchestra, James Levine (b. 1943), has been an ardent champion of Carter's music from the 1990s on. Levine's close ties with Carter began in summer 1990, when he called the composer unexpectedly to inform him that he would be performing and recording the *Variations for Orchestra* with the Chicago Symphony Orchestra. Carter immediately thanked him by telegram: "I am very delighted that you, whom I so admire, are conducting my Variations and, what a wonderful surprise, recording them."[33] Later Levine conducted many other works by Carter, especially in Boston, where he gave the world premières of *Micomicón* (15–17 January 2004), the complete set of *Three Illusions* (6–8 October 2005), and the *Horn Concerto* (15, 17, and 20 November 2007), and at the Tanglewood Festival, where he gave the first staged performance in America of Carter's opera *What Next?* (27–28 July 2006). It was thus only appropriate that Carter should have been asked to give a speech on 18 May 2005, when Levine was handed the Award for Distinguished Service to the Arts by the American Academy of Arts and Letters. In his address Carter lauded the conductor's achievements on behalf of contemporary music. With good reason he drew a connection with Arnold Schoenberg: not only had Levine presented a highly regarded production of the unfinished opera *Moses und Aron* at the Met in 1999, he was also about to undertake an ambitious large-scale comparison of Schoenberg's and Beethoven's orchestral music in his second and third seasons in Boston (2005–06 and 2006–07), a project he had already tried out in the 2002–03 season in his capacity as music director of the Munich Philharmonic. Levine's tireless commitment to Carter's music has culminated in a series of ten concerts entitled "Elliott Carter Centennial Celebration" at the Tanglewood Festival (20–24 July 2008). In 2007, as a token of his gratitude, Carter wrote *Matribute*, a piano miniature that also served as a tribute to the conductor's mother and thus bore the dual dedication: "To Helen Levine for James Levine."

185 Elliott Carter, address for James Levine (2005)

[Ladies and gentlemen,]
To stand here and do verbal justice to James Levine, once a child prodigy and now an adult prodigy, to one of the most remarkable musicians that ever existed, seems impossible.

Mr. Levine, please forgive what is inevitably superficial. You are a musician who has thrown a shining light on every aspect of the musical world.

For instance, the Metropolitan Opera Orchestra, once somewhat mediocre, has become, under your 33 years as music director, one of our leading orchestras. The [fact that you have brought to life] more than 2000 performances of operas there is truly astonishing. From those of Handel and Mozart to the present of Arnold Schoenberg and John Harbison, the last of which you commissioned,[34] you have grasped with great conviction each style and made it speak to us. For an outsider it's hard to imagine the planning that went into these [productions]; choosing which operas to do, finding singers, stage designers, sometimes far in advance, and having to deal with stage problems like those of Arnold Schoenberg, the great Viennese composer, who came to the US in 1933. His *Moses and Aron* asks for 70 elders and 4 naked virgins and has all those on stage tearing off all their clothes in the worship of the golden calf. This opera you did with such devotion [that] it is hard to forget its end when Moses half sings: "Oh word, thou word that fails me."[35]

Since we are here in the American Academy of Arts and Letters, I would like to recall that [in 1947] this institution gave Schoenberg $1000, the sum then given to young composers; and he wrote in a thank-you letter, in English: "That all I have endeavored to accomplish during these fifty years is now by you evaluated as an achievement seems in some respects to be an overestimation. [...] Personally, I had the feeling as if I had fallen into an ocean of boiling water, [...] not knowing how to swim [...]."[36]

You have made the large, hostile or indifferent American public realize his greatness, which a few of us have never doubted. Your present music directorship of the Boston Symphony has presented for each of the season's concerts one contemporary work, many of which have been considered too difficult for an American orchestra's

---

35 The Met production of *Moses und Aron*, conducted by Levine (and staged by Graham Vick), went on the boards for the first time on 8 February 1999. The "Dance of the Golden Calf" was not quite as explicit in this production as Carter suggests: to quote a press report, "the binocular crowd [had] to make do with writhing sports bras and white cotton underpants." (Bernard Holland, "Fake

Nudity With Real Angst," *The New York Times*, 10 February 1999.)
36 Carter's wording departs slightly from Schoenberg's original, which we quote here from "Schoenberg's Reply to the National Institute of Arts and Letters, June 1947," in Joseph Auner, *A Schoenberg Reader: Documents of a Life* (New Haven and London: Yale University Press, 2003), pp. 317–319, esp. 318. Schoenberg

expressed his gratitude to the National Institute of Arts and Letters not only with this letter of thanks, but with his own spoken recording of the text. At the same time this statement, with added commentary by Virgil Thomson, appeared in the *New York Herald Tribune* on 1 June 1947.

allotted rehearsal time and too difficult for the usual concert audience.[37] With great conviction you have convinced the audience and even aroused its enthusiasm. Many of these works were commissioned by the Boston Symphony, and proposed by you. Under your great care and belief, you have shown how vivid and meaningful contemporary and older music can be today.

Now I would like to read the citation that a non-musician but wonderful literary scholar, Helen Vendler, has written: "Inspiring musician, inspired conductor, James Levine, rejuvenator of the Metropolitan [Opera] Orchestra and supporter of notable singers, has now become as well the conductor of the Boston Symphony Orchestra, where he has daringly programmed experimental 20th-century music as well as classics of the symphonic and operatic traditions."[38]

[Computer printout; Elliott Carter Collection, Paul Sacher Foundation.]

186 James Levine and Elliott Carter backstage after the première of *Three Illusions* (Boston, 2005), photo by Michael Lutch

In 2002 Carter dedicated a short orchestral piece to James Levine: *Micomicón*, based on an episode from Cervantes's *Don Quixote*. Two years later he augmented it with another two miniatures likewise inspired by literary fantasies: *Fons juventatis* (after the Roman legend of the Fountain of Youth) and *More's Utopia* (after the like-named book by Thomas More). The resultant triptych, barely ten minutes long, was given the title *Three Illusions* and premièred by the Boston Symphony Orchestra under James Levine on 6–8 October 2005. This first complete performance of all three pieces (*Micomicón* had already been premièred in January 2004) unhappily coincided with the première of *Soundings* in Chicago on 6–7 October 2005. Carter decided to hear the two works in their order of origin, attending the première of *Three Illusions* in Boston on 6 October 2005 (when this photograph was taken) and traveling to Chicago for the second performance of *Soundings* on 7 October.

186

Soundings (2004–05)

For the final season of his fifteen-year tenure as music director of the Chicago Symphony Orchestra, Daniel Barenboim sought a work from Carter that would give him an opportunity to appear in a dual capacity as conductor and pianist. Carter solved this ticklish problem in *Soundings* by having the pianist play, not simultaneously, but in alternation with the orchestra, and by giving the piano a much-reduced role: it has only two brief solo passages at the opening (mm. 1–6 and 19–26), after which it remains silent until the end of the piece, when it reappears, first with isolated pitches (mm. 144, 145, and 149), then with a concluding nine-bar solo (mm. 150–157). *Soundings* is thus not a piano concerto but rather a *concertante* ensemble piece bookended by piano solos. As in the *Boston Concerto*, this diaphanous, airily orchestrated ten-minute composition is a sort of *concerto grosso* whose string ritornellos (occasionally augmented to an orchestral tutti) alternate with episodes dominated by solo players: one for oboe, bassoon, and horn (mm. 25–34), another for English horn and three clarinets (mm. 48–67), one for three piccolos (mm. 91–103), and finally one for tuba and percussion (mm. 120–137). By highlighting particular instruments, Carter paid homage to the members of an orchestra that he knew intimately, as it had played his music regularly ever since the première of *Partita* and had commissioned several of his works. *Soundings* was premièred in Chicago on 6–7 October 2005 and also joined Mahler's *Ninth* on 15 June 2006 in the first of Barenboim's three farewell concerts in Chicago (15–17 June 2006).

187 *Soundings*, for orchestra (2004–05), autograph full score in pencil, p. 32 (mm. 142–146)

Carter's *Soundings* not only carries a verbal dedication to Daniel Barenboim but refers to him in the framing piano solos by employing his initials D and B♭ as a musical monogram. The very first piano solo opens with these two pitches, and the monogram appears no less clearly in the transition to the final passage. Here we can see mm. 142–146 from this passage in Carter's still precise, if occasionally slightly shaky, hand. In m. 144 the piano responds unexpectedly to the preceding massive tutti chord with a staccato D, followed after a gentler and shorter woodwind chord by an equally isolated B♭. These two pitches, rising dynamically from *mezzo-forte* to *forte* while the orchestra recedes step by step, form the most terse and economical preparation imaginable for the final piano solo that follows shortly thereafter. All that comes after the tutti and woodwind chords before the piano speaks its final word is a short passage for the two percussionists (mm. 145–147), further ebbing away, and a four-voice phrase in the strings in contrary motion (mm. 144–146). This terse reappearance of the piano not only presages the conclusion, but is structurally related to the two orchestral chords that surround it (mm. 142–143 and 144–145), as the piano provides the very two pitches missing from these chords: the dyad B♭–D. This example illustrates just how much attention Carter paid to the balance between continuity and discontinuity in this seemingly kaleidoscopic piece, and how carefully he integrated even as whimsical a detail as the unanticipated entrance of the piano in m. 144 into the overriding dramatic structure.

---

37 In the 2004–05 season Levine had conducted three world premières of works by Milton Babbitt, John Harbison, and Charles Wuorinen, all commissioned by the BSO, as well as performances of Carter's *Micomión* and *Symphonia* on 11–13 November 2004. In the same season he also conducted works by Bartók, Ives, Ligeti, Lutosławski, Messiaen, Schoenberg, Stravinsky, and Varèse.

38 The Harvard literary scholar Helen Vendler (b. 1933) has been a member of the American Academy of Arts and Letters since 1993.

Admiration for Daniel Barenboim (2006)

In the 1980s the pianist and conductor Daniel Barenboim, then still principal conductor of the Orchestre de Paris, began to take a strong interest in present-day music. During his tenures as music director of the Chicago Symphony Orchestra (1991–2006) and as general music director of the Staatsoper Unter den Linden in Berlin (from 1992), Barenboim numbered Carter alongside Pierre Boulez and Harrison Birtwistle among his preferred contemporary composers, not least because Carter's music represented an organic outgrowth of traditional values. (As Barenboim once put it in a film interview, "[Carter] is one of the last properly classically-trained composers, and he is a composer who doesn't feel that Mozart is old-fashioned, or that Schubert is *passé*, but that there is a continuity."[39]) In February 1994 Barenboim gave the world première of *Partita* in Chicago, followed in 2001, 2003, and 2005 by the *Cello Concerto*, the song cycle *Of Rewaking*, and *Soundings*, all of which were commissioned at his instigation. In Berlin, in October 1999, he also premièred Carter's opera *What Next?* – another work composed at his suggestion (see above, p. 309). This and many other performances, both as a conductor and as a pianist, made this versatile musician one of the composer's staunchest advocates. As a small token of the gratitude he feels towards Barenboim, Carter wrote the following letter at the behest of the Chicago Symphony Orchestra. It was handed to Barenboim in a bound volume of letters, program pages, and other memorabilia on 17 June 2006 following the last of his three farewell concerts in Chicago.

188 Elliott Carter to Daniel Barenboim, 22 April 2006

Elliott Carter / 31 West 12th Street / New York, N.Y. 10011-8545
April 22, 2006

Dear Daniel,
We owe you such a deep appreciation for your inspiring talks, your amazing performances with orchestra and with piano and your caring and enthusiastic presence that it is impossible to put it into words.

Music comes alive under your baton and under your hands, as all agree.

Your courageous commissioning and performances of new music reveal a profound belief in the future.

I remember so vividly your performance of *La Mer* in Cologne,[40] and so many others, including my own works.

Affectionately,
Elliott

[Autograph letter, photocopy; Elliott Carter Collection, Paul Sacher Foundation. By permission of Daniel Barenboim.]

---

39 Interview with Daniel Barenboim, in Frank Scheffer, *A Labyrinth of Time* (see above, p. 291, note 18).
40 On 31 May and 1 June 1994 the first Cologne Music Triennale featured two guest appearances of the Chicago Symphony Orchestra, which Barenboim opened with Carter's *Partita* in the composer's presence. It was followed by Debussy's "symphonic sketches" *La Mer* and Stravinsky's ballet *Le sacre du printemps*.

In the Distances of Sleep (2006)

For his seventh song cycle, Carter turned to the poetry of Wallace Stevens, a poet whom he has long admired. The composer and poet are parallel spirits in many ways, sharing a clear-eyed, unvarnished rhetoric and a delight in the contrasts and ironic undertones of everyday life. Stevens, whose first book of poetry was published when he was forty-four and who brought out his first major collection at the age of seventy-five, was, like the composer, a late bloomer.[41] Perhaps Carter hesitated to set his poetry precisely because they are so close aesthetically; also, Stevens's "quick changes of character, irony, and unusual use of words [...] seemed hard to deal with musically," as the composer put it in a note to the score. A commission from the Carnegie Hall Corporation (on the recommendation of James Levine) led him to take the plunge. Carter chose six poems from various stages in Stevens's output: "Puella Parvula" (published in 1950), "Metamorphosis" (1942), "Re-statement of Romance" (1936), "The Wind Shifts" (1923), "To the Roaring Wind" (1923), and "God is Good. It Is a Beautiful Night" (1947).[42] The settings, for mezzo-soprano and an ensemble of woodwinds, percussion, and *tutti* strings, are grouped into a cycle framed on each end by the two longest and most thickly scored songs (nos. 1 and 6). In the middle is the remarkable third song, a serene love poem accompanied by a single melodic line passed from one string section to another. Between these pillars are the second song, the quick, thirty-three-measure "Metamorphosis," and the brief fourth and fifth songs, whose texts are both about the wind and which follow one another *attacca* as if they were a single piece. The score is dated 19 March 2006; the piece was premièred on 15 October of that year in Zankel Hall, New York, by Michelle DeYoung (mezzo-soprano) and the Met Chamber Ensemble conducted by James Levine.

189 *In the Distances of Sleep,* for mezzo-soprano and ensemble (2006), on texts by Wallace Stevens, no. 3: "Re-statement of Romance," sketches in pencil, p. [1]

This sketch page, the first of three for this song, suggests that Carter had already decided before he started that the voice would be accompanied by a single wide-ranging line in the strings. The opening words, "The night knows nothing of the chants of night" (third staff), are set to the fifth D–A, which returns at the end of the phrase, giving the melody a static, circular quality that exactly parallels the words. (The pitches D, A, G, E♭, A♭, and B, transposed down a half step in the final version, form the all-interval hexachord; the top three staves show Carter working this out.) Two notes of the accompanying line – F♯ and C – are already faintly visible in this sketch of the opening line (fifth continuing onto the fourth staves, top middle of page). On the second try (sixth, seventh, and eighth staves), the previously indistinct rhythms have been blocked out into 4/4 bars, and the instrumental line plunges from F♯6 to E3 in its typically wide intervals (possibly illustrating the "chants of night" of the first line). The scoring is never explicitly indicated, but it was probably meant for strings from the beginning. Carter writes out the next few lines of text in block letters, but the musical setting breaks off and is continued on the next page. The eleventh line (of twelve), "supremely true each to its separate self," expresses the crux of the poem's meaning: that a lasting union of two people is achieved only if each is secure in him- or herself. Before sketching this line where it belongs on the second page, Carter returned to the first page (ninth staff from the bottom, right, continuing onto the last three notated staves, left) to work out a preliminary draft of this crucial passage, which is remarkable for several reasons. First, the vocal line reaches its high point, F♯, for the first and only time in the piece (on the word "[sup]rem[ely]"). Secondly, the string line, in which leaps of more than an octave are common, uncharacteristically plays small intervals; the semitone, for example, is heard here – between A♭ and G – for the only time. Finally, the two parts momentarily switch rhythmic roles here; the strings move faster, and the voice has long sustained notes. The two musical lines, by sharing, intensifying, and exchanging the music that they had before, embody both the "separate sel[ves]" and the union of the two lovers.

41 David Schiff has drawn astute comparisons between the aesthetic positions of Carter and the writers Henry James and Wallace Stevens, "Carter's spiritual forbears" (Schiff 1998, pp. 2–8, esp. 4).

42 These poems were also published in Wallace Stevens, *Collected Poems* (New York: Knopf, 1954), for which the poet won the 1955 Pulitzer Prize.

189 *In the Distances of Sleep*

190 Milton Babbitt, Elliott Carter, and John Harbison (from left to right) in a performance of Igor Stravinsky's *Histoire du soldat* at the Tanglewood Festival (2006), photo by Hilary Scott

The cast of the performance of Stravinsky's *Histoire du soldat* presented at Tanglewood on 25 July 2006 could hardly have been more unusual: a young ensemble conducted by Tomasz Golka was joined by none other than Elliott Carter (as the Soldier), Milton Babbitt (the Devil), and John Harbison (the Narrator). The idea of assembling these three illustrious composers, whose combined ages totaled 254 years, came from James Levine, who also adapted the text in conjunction with Harbison (head of the Composition Department) and Ellen Highstein (director of the Tanglewood Music Center). (They radically abridged the original, shifted the action from *"entre Denges et Denezy"* to "between Lenox and Back Bay," and addressed the Soldier and the Devil as, respectively, "Elliott" and "Milton.") If the rehearsals already proceeded in high spirits, this applied all the more to the performance itself, at which the audience went along enthusiastically even when the two nonagenarians suffered slight lapses of concentration. As the *New York Times* reported: "Mr. Babbitt handled the 'Devil's Song' fairly well but came in early with the line 'Give me your fiddle.' Mr. Carter was thrown off. He looked flummoxed, searching for his line. The audience murmured as the discomforting silence dragged on. He found his place, and yelled out a triumphant response: 'No!' The audience exploded with laughter."[43] Incidentally, this was not the first time that Carter took part in a performance of *Histoire du soldat:* as early as 1966 he had presented Stravinsky's work in public together with John Cage as the Devil and Aaron Copland as the Narrator (see above, p. 325). Nor was it to be the last: a good year later, on 28 October 2007, the Carter-Babbitt-Harbison triumvirate repeated their performance in a concert of the Met Chamber Ensemble conducted by James Levine in New York's Weill Recital Hall. The program also included Carter's *Tempo e tempi*, Harbison's *North and South* (1995–99), and Babbitt's *The Head of the Bed* (1982) sung by Susan Narucki (soprano), Sasha Cooke (mezzo-soprano), and Judith Bettina (soprano).

Homage to Charles Rosen (2006)

Hardly any musician can look back on such a long and intimate artistic friendship with Carter as the pianist Charles Rosen (b. 1927), who first met the composer in autumn 1956 during an ISCM concert in Carnegie Recital Hall.[44] The very next year, in autumn 1957, Rosen played Carter's *Piano Sonata* in various cities of Germany and, in the composer's presence, in Brussels. Later he not only took part in the première of the *Double Concerto* but co-commissioned – together with Paul Jacobs, Gilbert Kalish, and Ursula Oppens – *Night Fantasies* (see above, pp. 170 and 239). Rosen has performed these three works, as well as the *Piano Concerto,* time and again in the course of his long career, during which he has achieved equal distinction as a musicologist (his writings include various essays on Carter as well as *The Classical Style,* which is dedicated to Helen and Elliott Carter[45]). He has also recorded the solo pieces and the *Double Concerto* – twice in the case of the latter and the *Piano Sonata.*[46] Carter has appreciated, no less than Rosen's commitment to his music, his broad intellectual horizons and his love of France (Rosen has a doctorate in French literature and has spent many periods living in France), and he has supported his friend whenever the opportunity arose, notably in the form of grants from the Fromm Music Foundation. It was thus only natural that he would accept the request from the musicologists David Gable and Robert Curry for a tribute article for their prospective festschrift in honor of Rosen's eightieth birthday on 5 May 2007.

191 Elliott Carter, "Charles Rosen for His Eightieth Birthday" (2006)

I believe I first met Charles Rosen after the war in 1949 at an ISCM concert in New York, where Aaron Copland introduced us.[47] A few years later I was fascinated by remarks he made at Milton Babbitt's apartment in New York City. It must have been when I was in Paris around 1951 that the American Consul told me of a performance of my *Piano Sonata* in Brussels; arriving there I was amazed at how wonderfully in command of my work Charles was, both technically and expressively. This performance was certainly the best I had heard up to that time.

Since then I have frequently enjoyed his company and consider him one of my best friends. Early on we usually talked about French literature – his Ph.D. at Princeton on the seventeenth-century poet La Fontaine had made him extremely well informed on the subject[48] – but our conversations over the years have covered an extraordinary range: music, literature, art, and many other topics including gastronomy. (We have had long and penetrating discussions of wine, French cheese, and cooking!) Always apparent has been his awareness of people and their special characteristics and the sources of some of their remarkable contributions.

As for his invaluable devotion to music, I must say that piano recitals of most other performers leave me disturbed by their lack of understanding of phrasing, of character or expressivity, and even of form; but when I hear a recital by Charles I am completely convinced and carried away. He not only has a complete command of technique but also of color, which is rare; and he puts this all to use in bringing out not only a vision of the period in which the music was composed but in making it a present, vivid experience. It is astonishing how he plays Mozart as compared to Beethoven or each of these as compared to Chopin or Schumann or Stravinsky or Schoenberg; this highly imaginative awareness of the distinctions among styles makes him one of the most engaging performers I have ever heard; and his many recordings from Haydn to Schoenberg and of my own *Piano Sonata, Double Concerto,* and *Night Fantasies* bear witness to this.

43 Daniel J. Wakin, "With a Nod to Stravinsky, Three Composers Become Stars of the Stage at Tanglewood," *The New York Times,* 27 July 2006.

44 Rosen reported on this first meeting in a newspaper article for Carter's ninety-ninth birthday: "An Old Master Still in Development," *The New York Times,* 9 December 2007.

45 Charles Rosen, *The Classical Style: Haydn, Mozart, Beethoven* (London: Faber and Faber, 1971). Some of Rosen's writings on

Carter are collected in idem, *The Musical Languages of Elliott Carter,* ed. Jon Newsom (Washington, DC: Library of Congress, 1984) (*ML*).

46 Rosen's first recording of the *Piano Sonata,* made in 1961, appeared in 1962 on the Epic label (LC 3850), together with the *Suite from "Pocahontas"* performed by the Zurich Radio Orchestra under Jacques Monod. His second recording (Etcetera Records) dates from 1982; see above, p. 250, note 66.

47 Carter seems to have misremembered the year of this meeting, which – in accordance with Rosen's birthday tribute (see note 44) – is likely to have taken place in 1956. Similarly the date given in the following sentence needs to be corrected: Rosen's performance of Carter's *Piano Sonata* in Brussels took place not "around 1951," but on 14 October 1957.

48 Charles Welles Rosen, "Style and Morality in La Fontaine" (Ph. D. Diss. Princeton University, 1951).

Mad Regales (2007)

His memory astonishes. Once he was invited to play my *Night Fantasies* as part of a festival of my work in Turin, Italy.[49] When he arrived, the presenters of the festival asked him if he could play my *Piano Sonata* as well. He explained that he did not have the music with him and had not performed the work in over two years; so a musician in New York was contacted, the score was faxed two days before the intended performance, and, to everyone's delight, Charles came forth with a brilliant, captivating performance.

Another remarkable side of Charles, of course, is his writing, beginning with *The Classical Style* – which means so much to me, since it is dedicated to my wife and me – and then a series of books, including especially *The Romantic Generation* and the little one on Schoenberg.[50] His essays in *The New York Review of Books*, covering not only the German philosopher Walter Benjamin but many diverse subjects, are well worth reading, as is his charming interview in French, *Plaisir de jouer – plaisir de penser*.[51] In this interview he says that, viewed from the perspective of musical history, the so-called modernist movement is being carried on in a way that makes "neoromanticism" and repetitive music seem like a step backward[52] – which seems a very reasonable point of view to me.

In writing this I feel I cannot express how grateful I am for all that Charles has done, not only for my work and for my imagination, but for music in general. Many more wonderful birthdays!

November 29, 2006

[Published in *Variations on the Canon: Essays on Music from Bach to Boulez*, ed. David Gable and Robert Curry (Rochester, N.Y.: University of Rochester Press, in press). Reproduced with the kind permission of David Gable and Robert Curry from their edited version of Carter's text. A photocopy of the typescript of this article, entitled "For Charles Rosen on his 80th Birthday," is preserved in the Elliott Carter Collection, Paul Sacher Foundation.]

With this piece for six solo voices *a cappella*, Carter returned to composing for vocal groups for the first time since *Emblems*, which had been completed sixty years earlier. Carter's punning title alludes to madrigals as well as to the idea of telling crazy tales (mad regaling). Indeed there is a playful quality to the music, which unselfconsciously draws on a harmonic and rhythmic simplicity that would not have been out of place in Carter's earlier music. He again turned to the poetry of John Ashbery, as he had done with *Syringa* thirty years before, completing his setting of the three poems, "8 Haiku" (from "37 Haiku"), "Meditations of a Parrot," and "At North Farm" before even contacting the poet. The correspondence below reflects their mutual esteem; they also "commiserate" with each other on the trials and joys of big birthday celebrations (Ashbery celebrated his eightieth birthday on 28 July 2007). The eight haiku of Carter's first piece range from the whimsical to the poetic; some strike an intentionally colloquial tone, as Ashbery describes in his letter to the composer. The individual haiku texts are presented by one solo singer at a time. These rhythmically lively solos (reminiscent of passages in *Heart Not So Heavy as Mine*) emerge from a texture of sustained chords with staggered entrances, which Carter described as "exclamations while the 'orchestra' plays in the background."[53] Setting apart the haiku texts ensures that they will be understood; this is why he avoided the contrapuntal texture typical of madrigals.[54] The third piece, "At North Farm," whose text is more serious in tone, similarly juxtaposes different layers of text. Two features of this piece are quite atypical of Carter's music since the late 1940s: first, the high degree of rhythmic homophony, and second, the striking number of major, minor, diminished, and augmented triads. The triads are not functional in a tonal sense, but by evoking an older vocabulary, they do give the piece a fresh and unusual sound. *Mad Regales* is dedicated to Ellen Highstein, the director of the Tanglewood Music Center, which commissioned the work. It received its première on 22 July 2008, during the "Elliott Carter Centennial Celebration" of the Festival of Contemporary Music at Tanglewood.[55]

49 The Settembre Musica festival in Turin devoted several concerts and a panel dis-cussion to Carter between 17 and 23 September 1989. Rosen's concert took place on 22 September 1989; besides *Night Fantasies* (and the unscheduled *Piano Sonata*), it featured Rosen in a performance of the *Piano Concerto* with the Orchestra Sinfonica dell'Emilia Romagna "Arturo Toscanini" conducted by Giam-piero Taverna. The same orchestra also played *A Symphony of Three Orchestras*.

50 Charles Rosen, *The Classical Style* (see above, p. 339, note 45); idem., *The Romantic Generation* (Cambridge, MA: Harvard University Press, 1995); idem, *Schoenberg* (Baltimore: Penguin USA, 1975).

51 Charles Rosen, *Plaisir de jouer [–] plaisir de penser: Conversation avec Cartherine Temerson* (Paris: Editions Eshel, 1993).

52 Ibid., pp. 39–40.

53 Interview with Felix Meyer and Anne Shreffler, 11 June 2007.

54 Carter told us, "If you have counterpoint in a chorus, you can't understand what anybody's saying." (Interview with Felix Meyer and Anne Shreffler, 11 June 2007.)

55 Carter wrote *Mad Regales* for a program of his choral music that was planned for the festival but not realized; ibid.

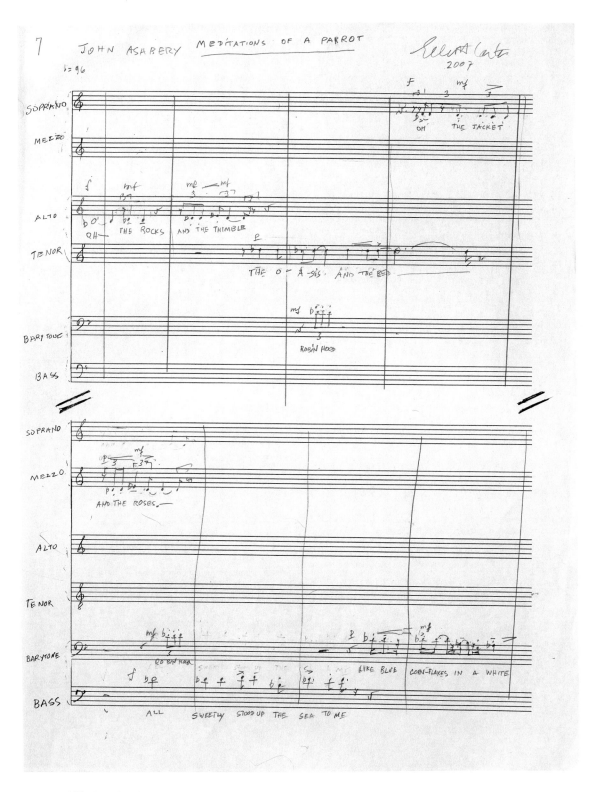

192 *Mad Regales*, for six solo voices (2007), on texts by John Ashbery, autograph full score in pencil, p. 7 (no. 2: "Meditations of a Parrot," mm. 1–9)

193 Elliott Carter to John Ashbery, 17 May 2007

The second piece of *Mad Regales* was completed on 26 April 2007, a couple of weeks before Carter wrote to Ashbery, initiating the correspondence given below. On the page shown, the spare monophonic texture and the extreme prominence of the pitch D♭4 catch the eye immediately. Indeed this pitch, which represents the "talking" of the parrot, is heard in every single bar. There are two levels of the parrot's thoughts: first, an internal monologue whose playful juxtapositions of the sublime with the mundane somehow seem appropriate for the consciousness of a bird ("Oh, the rocks and the thimble / The oasis and the bed / Oh the jacket and the roses / All sweetly stood up the sea to me / Like blue cornflakes in a white bowl," etc.). The second level consists of the parrot's actual speech as he repeats, all day long, the words "Robin Hood." While these two levels are presented sequentially in the poem (with "Robin Hood" coming at the very end), Carter puts them together, repeating "Robin Hood," always on D♭4, several times, just as the bird is said to do. (There is a third level, as another protagonist – a girl – enters the picture and begins to speak.) All this is set to music that is practically a monotone; a greater contrast with Carter's typically labyrinthine style can hardly be imagined. Other pitches are used, all within the narrow range of a major seventh above and a minor ninth below the D♭, but D♭ is by far the most prominent. Still there is timbral variation, as the same pitch sung by an alto (as in the beginning) naturally sounds different when sung by the other voice types. Moreover, the different vowel sounds lend further variety. The piece recalls (but does not quite belong to) the category of "one-note pieces," to which Carter himself contributed in Etude No. 7 of his *Eight Etudes and a Fantasy*. "Meditations of a Parrot" is the oldest of the three Ashbery poems; as the poet explains in his letter to Carter, it was written in 1949–50 as a whimsical misreading of the title of a patriotic Scottish poem called "Meditation of a Patriot."[56] The music aptly reflects – and augments – the humor of the poem, which can be read as a loopy (parrot-inspired?) take on the hoary genre of patriotic poetry.

Elliott Carter / 31 West 12th Street / N.Y., N.Y. 10011
5/17/07

Dear John,
The complexit[ies] of living have kept me from you for much too long.

I think of you often, often through your fascinating poems.

Now, I have composed three short pieces on these poems:
"Meditations of a Parrot"
"At North Farm"
and 8 of your *Haiku*
and would think (but not definitively) of calling them *Madregales*, possibly with a hyphen here [arrow pointing to "*Mad-regales*"].[57] Let me know if you approve – & with or without hyphen.

Also "Meditations of a Parrot" presents to me a problem of quotation marks: when the poem is printed as text should the present marks be as they are in *Some Trees*, or is there a misprint?

Since my 100th birthday is beginning to bother me too much and Tanglewood is planning a 2008 summer festival including the above I need guidance –

With delight & admiration,
Elliott

P. S. The "*Mad*" of *Regales* refers to my ... music, of course, as the performers will realize (6 solo voices). *Parrot* sings only one note.

[Autograph letter, photocopy; Elliott Carter Collection, Paul Sacher Foundation. Reprinted by permission of John Ashbery.]

---

56 Ashbery's "Meditations of a Parrot" was published in his collection *Some Trees*, with a foreword by W.H. Auden (New Haven: Yale University Press, 1956), p. 73. "37 Haiku" and "At North Farm" are from *A Wave* (Manchester: Carcanet, 1984), pp. 37–38 and p. 1, respectively.

57 In autumn 2007 Carter decided definitively in favor of two words without hyphen: *Mad Regales*.

58 A reference to the poem "Meditation of a Patriot" (in the singular!) by the Scottish poet and critic G.S. Fraser (1915–1980), first published in his collection *Home Town Elegy* (London: Poetry London, 1944), pp. 21–22. The anthology in which Ashbery found the poem has eluded

194 John Ashbery to Elliott Carter, 23 May 2007

John Ashbery

Mr. Elliott Carter / 31 West 12th Street / New York,
New York 10011-8545
May 23, 2007

Dear Elliott,

I was thrilled to get your letter. You are my favorite living composer, and to have you set my words to music (again) is a tremendous honor. Also the fact that you are continuing to produce profound, exciting music is wonderfully encouraging to a somewhat younger but still senior poet like me. I'll be eighty this year, but every time I think of hanging up my lyre your example comes to mind and I continue to plug away.

The poem "Meditations of a Parrot" I wrote in the winter of 1949–50 when I was going to graduate school at Columbia and living just down the street from you at 60 West 12th. The title came about from misreading a title in an anthology of British war poetry, "Meditations of a Patriot."[58] The quotation marks are confusing, though correct I think. The fourth stanza is part of the girl's speech that begins in the previous stanza, as is the first line of the fifth stanza. If these are printed as prose, the quotation marks at the beginning of the fourth and the fifth stanzas could be omitted. If they are printed as poetry they are probably correct as they are in the book. I've found similar examples printed thus in *Some Trees* (the last two stanzas of the poem "He," for instance). Whether this is correct or just proves I'm consistent I don't know. (Unfortunately I also found an example which is printed differently, but let's not worry about that.)

The haiku and "At North Farm" were written in 1981. For the former I used examples of haiku in an anthology of Japanese poetry called *From the Country of Eight Islands*.[59] The translator, Hiroaki Sato, who lives in New York, renders haiku throughout as a single unpunctuated line with a varying number of syllables, and it struck me that this must be closer to the way a Japanese reader would experience the haiku than the rather precious syllable counting of most English versions. Nonetheless, after reading them at a university in Tokyo and carefully explaining that they weren't intended to be "real" haiku,

I was taken to task afterwards by a professor who said he found them "plozaic." I'd be interested to know which ones you are setting. I love your title for the group of poems as a whole, by the way.

I can well understand how your 100th birthday is "beginning to bother you too much," if bruited preparations for my eightieth are any indication.[60] It would be nice if one could be both fussed over and left completely alone at the same time.

I saw Richard and Dee Wilson recently[61] and Dee said you are interested in the new Gehry building, which I can see from my window in New York.[62] She thought you might like to come over with them some time for a viewing. I could even get my windows washed for the occasion. Actually one can't see it too well from my place but perhaps that is best; at any rate I like it from a distance and have yet to see it up close.

With affectionate admiration,
John

[Typed letter with autograph signature, followed by handwritten address, photocopy; Elliott Carter Collection, Paul Sacher Foundation. Reprinted by permission of John Ashbery.]

---

discovery; when asked, not even Ashbery himself could identify the source (personal communication from John Ashbery, 11 January 2008).

59 *From the Country of Eight Islands: An Anthology of Japanese Poetry*, ed. and trans. Hiroaki Sato and Burton Watson (Seattle: University of Washington Press, 1981; New York: Doubleday Anchor, 1981).

60 Ashbery's eightieth birthday (on 28 July 2007) was celebrated not least with a three-day event consisting of readings, panel discussions, and music under the title "The Feeling of Exaltation." This event took place from 14 to 16 September 2007 at Bard College, where he had been professor of languages and literature since 1990.

61 A reference to the composer Richard Wilson (b. 1942) and his wife. Wilson, a professor at Vassar College, had likewise set poems by Ashbery (*Three Songs on Poems by John Ashbery*, 2000).

62 The "new Gehry building" refers to Frank Gehry's IAC Headquarters on the West Side Highway in Chelsea, New York City.

Sound Fields (2007)

Sound Fields, like *Mad Regales*, was commissioned by the Tanglewood Music Center and was premièred on 20 July 2008 during the "Carter Centennial Festival." With this piece, Carter ventured further away from his hallmark style than ever before. Rhythmic motion and formal contrast, the two most typical features of Carter's music, are completely absent. (The score's serene stasis seems more typical of Morton Feldman.) Scored for strings divided into twelve parts playing quietly and *non vibrato* throughout, *Sound Fields* moves very slowly in tied whole and half note values. The sustained tones, whose pitches are drawn from a single twelve-note chord, create constantly fluctuating sonories of varying densities, ranging from a single note to twelve. Many of the durations are extremely long; in 2/2 time, with a slow tempo of half note = 54, a note may be held for ten measures or more. This means that no sense of pulse emerges. Each sonority seamlessly overlaps with the next. The extreme reduction of the musical material focuses the listener's attention on small changes in texture and the constant variety of timbres that results from the different densities, registers, and combinations of notes. Carter thought "it would be interesting to write a piece that had no changes of color, no changes of dynamic, but that had different kinds of texture."[63] He explains in the preface to the score that the impulse for the piece came from "color field" painting as practiced by Helen Frankenthaler (b. 1928). Commonly seen as a less overtly subjective, "cooler" alternative to the abstract expressionism of Jackson Pollock, color-field painting draws the viewer into the subtle play of light, shadow, and texture.

195 *Sound Fields,* **for strings (2007), autograph full score in pencil, p. 12 (mm. 100–108)**

The last page of the score, like all the others, has nine measures; the appearance of the barlines (ruled and in part hastily applied) indicates that Carter pre-barred the twelve pages in advance. The strings are divided here, as they are throughout the piece, into three groups of first violins, two of second violins, two of violas, three of cellos, and two of basses (twelve groups in all). The division into twelve groups allows Carter to distribute the pitches of an all-interval twelve-note chord among them. On this page, all twelve notes of the source chord are heard; in ascending order, they are G1 and D#2 in the basses, C3 and Bb3 in the third cellos, D4 in the second violas, E4 in the third group of first violins (in m. 4 of this page), B4 in the second group of second violins, E#5 (tied over from the previous page) in the first violas, F#5 in the first group of second violins, and A5, G#6, and C#7 (the 8va sign is obviously missing) in the first violins. Here, at the end of the piece, the pitches are again sounded in their original registers. These fixed registers distinguish the outer sections of the piece; a "contrasting" middle section (after letter F) redistributes the pitch classes into different registers. Further timbral nuance is achieved within the fixed-register portions of the piece by shifting the same pitch to different instruments, as for example on this page when the B4 of the second group of second violins is taken over by the first cellos in the third measure. (The technique is similar to that of the repeated Db4 in "Meditations of a Parrot" sung by different voice types, but the effect is very different.) This page also shows the fluctuation in density that is characteristic of the piece; it begins with a sonority of three notes, then eleven, then closes with a succession of three-note chords. Except for the moments when two sonorities briefly overlap, there are no doublings. The last sonority is a Bb-major triad. Even though all three of the pitches (and their registers) come from the twelve-tone source chord, Carter's re-spelling of the E#5 as F (for the only time in the piece) indicates his acknowledgment of the chord's tonal quality. The score was completed on 16 May 2007.

63 Interview with Felix Meyer and Anne Shreffler, 11 June 2007.

195 *Sound Fields*

Appendices

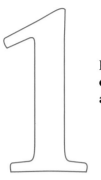

English Translations
of Letters in French, Italian,
and German

45 Elliott Carter to Nadia Boulanger, 31 August [1949]

Paris, 31 August

Chère Mademoiselle,
I am truly sorry not to have seen you in Paris, but we had to leave suddenly for America on account of an annoying change of dates by Cunard, and this prevented me from arranging to see you as I should have done. I do hope that next time we will be able to meet up and have a chat as I have been wanting to do for so long.

Our visit to France, although so short, was full of charming and enjoyable things. Once again we were deeply moved by the cathedrals, the castles, and the landscape, and how we should have liked to share our impressions with you!

By way of a little souvenir I am sending you a copy of the quintet I've been so bold as to dedicate to you, which I hope will give you as much pleasure to read through as it gave me to compose. If ever I were lucky enough to have it played here, it would give me great pleasure, for I have always admired the refinement of French performers.

We wish you a very happy year here – and how could it be otherwise? Helen joins me in sending you our most affectionate greetings,
Elliott

[Original in French, see pp. 90–91; English translation by Mark Weir.]

76 Elliott Carter to Goffredo Petrassi, 6 February 1959

Elliott Carter, Mead Street, Waccabuc, New York
6 February 1959

Dear friend –
We went to New York last night to hear your wonderful quartet, which was very well played by the Parrenins. The work impressed me a lot, on account of its inventiveness as well as its successful integration of serial technique into your personal style. I especially like its restless and moving mood, which is so personally expressed here.

Your quartet enjoyed a great success, and many people liked it. I enclose the review by William Flanagan, the most intelligent and musical of our music critics.

I hope that things are going well with you. Your long silence after your announcement of the performance of my *Variations* at the RAI worries me a little. I hope that this performance, about which I knew nothing before your letter and about which I have no news even now, did not disappoint you too much.

With my best wishes,
Elliott

[Original in French, see p. 152; English translation by Mark Weir.]

77   Goffredo Petrassi to Elliott Carter, 10 February 1959

Via Germanico, 184 / Roma
Rome, 10 February 1959

My dear Elliott

Work, my troubles, and other problems have prevented me from replying at once to your previous letter. I am all the more to blame because I had to thank you for your kind words about my Serenata. We cannot always do what we want to do when we should.

So the *Variations* were performed that Saturday evening at the RAI concerts in Foro Italico; the next day, Sunday, they were rebroadcast in the afternoon (thus *two* radio broadcasts), and it was this performance I heard, because on the Saturday evening I couldn't go to the concert. I remembered the work very well, having listened to it *chez vous* in N[ew] Y[ork] in the Louisville performance. Well, this one by the Rome orchestra seemed to me *dix fois meilleure que l'autre*, both for the overall sound and the level of performance. Since I did not have the score in front of me I couldn't "check" whether everything was as written, and likewise I can hardly express an opinion on Dixon's interpretation; nonetheless, since it made a profound impression on me, I can only think that the conductor was up to the task. If in N[ew] Y[ork] I already had the impression that I was in the presence of a work of great significance, now the impression has become a certainty, because this performance made *explicit* the values I had sensed implicitly. I had proof the following Monday in the Filarmonica concert at the Teatro Eliseo (you will remember the "ritual" of Roman musical life), where I met some young musicians who had been at Dixon's concert: they had been struck by the *Variations* and asked me to tell them about its author.

The polyphonic "plot" of this work is admirable, and its lyrical-dramatic tension is truly outstanding. I was really delighted to have heard it again in a fine performance. Naturally I am still relying on receiving the copy of the score I reserved once it is out in print. I want it to check up on some details which struck me in particular.

Labroca, who is now responsible for the Venice Festival, is supposed to write to you to ask for some advice about a work to be performed. In any case we have already agreed that your name is to figure in the programmes. If the whole of the Carter family should come to Venice for the occasion, we will be able to see each other, which would give me infinite pleasure.

Thank you for the programme and for the review from the *N[ew] Y[ork] Herald T[ribune]*, which consoles me for some unpleasantness I suffered in Venice, where the première of my quartet got a pretty rough ride. Everything takes time, I know, whereas we are impatient. The Parrenins are always extraordinary, don't you think?

I am off to Milan, where in a few days my opera *Il cordovano* is being given at the Piccola Scala. Ten years ago it was quite a fiasco at the Grande Scala: now I hope it will go a bit better at the Piccola.

Give my kindest regards to Madame Carter, and my most affectionate wishes to you, dear Elliott,
Goffredo

[Original in Italian, see p. 153; English translation by Mark Weir.]

81   Goffredo Petrassi to Elliott Carter, 1 May 1959

Via Germanico, 184 / Roma
1 May 1959

My dear Elliott

They are giving a repeat broadcast of you on the radio here, which always makes me happy.

How are you?

Concerning Venice our friend Labroca has become quite mysterious. I really don't know any more what he's up to. I hear tell of a concert by the New York Philharmonic under the baton, of course, of Bernstein. Consisting exclusively of American music. Who are the American composers to be performed? No idea. Will anything come of the project? Again, no idea.

Give me news of yourself and your work. Is your trip to Europe still going ahead?

After the *Serenata* I am struggling with a string trio. There are terrible difficulties to be overcome; the music runs out immediately once I've exploited the resources of these three instruments. The row is no longer any help to me, I've abandoned it; thus, a motherless orphan. It's a sort of challenge I've set myself.

With my most affectionate greetings
Goffredo

[Original in French, see p. 158; English translation by Mark Weir.]

82   Elliott Carter to Goffredo Petrassi, 11 May 1959

Elliott C. Carter, Mead Street, Waccabuc, New York

My dear Goffredo –

Thank you for your letter – which did me a lot of good – since I too have had difficulties composing this winter. I can well understand your problems with your string trio. I have almost finished a second string quartet which has cost me a lot of work and worry. I always have ideas for certain moments or places in a composition, but my musical technique can't help me develop them or indeed find other things to go with the ideas I started out with. Even serialization isn't any help – even though I've tried it several times. My quartet seems to me a bit like something out of Pirandello – "4 instrumentalists in search of a composer" – poor things.

I have just heard the new work for eight instruments by Maxwell Davies – to a commission by Dartmouth College. It shows great talent – I liked it a lot.

Our holiday plans are hazy and I should be very grateful if you could urge Labroca to reply to the letter I wrote him. You see, everything has changed because I have received a commission for a *piano concerto* from the Ford Foundation which I'll have to work on this summer. So we'll only be able to spend a month in Europe, either mid-June – mid-July, or end of August – end of September, the latter only if I am invited to Venice – because we already have the tickets for the crossing in June. If I have no answer (or a negative one) from Labroca in a few weeks, I'll come in June.

The Philharmonic under Leonard Bernstein played very few things of interest this winter in terms of American music – the *Violin Concerto* by Sessions, something not very good by Gaburo and Varèse's *Arcana*. Apart from these works it was all in a neo-jazz or neo-classical style or just not very professional. Bernstein, as you know, shows an interest in progressive music only for the sake of publicity or scandal – he doesn't like it – what he likes is American versions of Prokofiev and Shostakovich. – I don't know what he is going to take on his Philharmonic tour, but certainly very little or no music of the sort you find at the ISCM, whose festival promises to be very good this year. Unfortunately I won't be able to come on account of my work – anyhow, we are counting on seeing you one way or another, soon.

My wife joins me in sending you our fondest wishes, Elliott

11 May 1959

[Original in French, see pp. 158–159; English translation by Mark Weir.]

106 Isang Yun to Elliott and Helen Carter, 29 May 1969

Isang Yun / Berlin 20, Steigerwaldstr. 13
29 May 1969

Herrn u. Frau / Elliott Carter / 31 West 12th Street / New York, N.Y. 10101 / USA

My dear friends!
During my long, very sad months in Seoul, I often heard, by roundabout paths, how much sympathy you showed for my fate, and how you decisively took every opportunity to rescue me and have me set free. In Seoul, while in my sick bed, I often learned that you and a few other well-known musicians had spoken about me and my music on the radio, speaking well of me and working for my benefit. I was told that you wrote several articles and placed them before the public for the same purpose. With effective methods, you appealed to the world of music and the public life of the United States in order to rescue me. You exercised a resonant influence on a higher level of America's politics, which certainly, I should say, forced not a little respect upon the Korean government. You donated large amounts of money to me to cover my hospital costs. I learned of still more things you did for me from Dr. Kunz and also from Mr. Nabokov and others. –

Dear friends! How and with what can I repay everything I owe you? Asians prefer to be silent when they are deeply moved or very grateful. So I would rather be silent than express in words the gratitude I feel in my heart. So very much of my life and liberty that I have now regained is your doing!

In the hope that we shall soon meet again, I wish to conclude this letter

with very warm wishes and greetings, your
Isang Yun

[Original in German, see p. 195; English translation by J. Bradford Robinson.]

126 Nadia Boulanger to Elliott and Helen Carter, 16 September 1978

Le Directeur / Conservatoire Américain /
77305 Palais de Fontainebleau
16 September 1978

Dear Helen and dear Elliott,
The truly noble outlook you have on life means that you stand for what guides us all. I am not thanking you properly, for I am still very weak, but you will surely be able to sense everything I am unable to express. I thought I was on the threshold of the great unknown, but then all these flowers, telegrams, letters represent such loving care that it makes you try to recover and regain some sort of strength. You talk about the month of March, but last week I still thought I wouldn't live until the 16th, and now, being no better, I'm consumed by impatience to see your last compositions. Forgive me for putting it so badly, but with all my heart, in all sincerity – your

[N. B.]

[Original in French, see p. 237; English translation by Mark Weir.]

127 Elliott Carter to Nadia Boulanger, 9 November 1978

9 November 1978
Waccabuc, New York, / 10597

Chère Mademoiselle,
A thousand thanks for the truly touching letter you wrote after your birthday, which moved me greatly. I hope that on receiving this you are in better health and have been able to resume some part of that musical life which is, and has always been, a major inspiration for us.

This year, my 70th, is being celebrated with concerts of my music in New York, Los Angeles, Washington, Hartford. Here there has already been a concert of works of mine from the 30s and 40s, and the Juilliard Quartet played my *cello sonata*, my *Duo*, my *2nd quartet*, and the New York Philharmonic plays my *Piano Concerto* at the end of the month and then there will be my *Double Concerto* and two song cycles with chamber orchestra on 10 December. On the 11th, my birthday, my *Variations* are to be performed. The rehearsals are already beginning to make my head spin.

I send you the brochure which my English publishers have brought out for the occasion, hoping that it will give you some pleasure.

Affectionately,
Elliott

[Original in French, see p. 238; English translation by Mark Weir.]

128 Nadia Boulanger to Elliott Carter, 14 November 1978

Paris, 14 November 1978

What a letter, dear Elliott! Bringing you to me, you the musician, the friend, you, my dear Elliott.

Are you coming to Europe in July or August? I would very much like to know soon.

Make no mistake as to the sincerity and confidence with which I follow you always. Make no mistake about how I long to see you again, but that is imprudent, because I don't now how much longer I shall still be here, merely vegetating more or less, but after all here I am taking an interest with all the old passion, so perhaps it's better not to commit oneself regarding time.

I am sorry not to be among those who will hear those works of yours that are to be performed, enveloping you like a spotlight and making you shine and scintillate.

To both of you my fondest and most heartfelt wishes,
N. B.

[Original in French, see p. 238; English translation by Mark Weir.]

142 Pierre Boulez to Elliott Carter, 24 April 1985

25, Quai André Citroën / 75015 Paris

My dear Elliott,
It was a great joy to hear your music during the concert "Surprise – Hommage" in Baden-Baden on 31 March last. You see, I have only just recovered from the festival!... that's why I'm so late writing to you.

I thank you for the thought, for the dedication and for the piece itself, which was played superbly. And I hope we shall have plenty of other occasions to hear it from now on. As always in your music there is an admirable technique, very accomplished, and a great inventiveness which I have profited from on more than one occasion. We were all sorry for you absence, the only dark spot in a truly idyllic experience!

I have just learnt from Brigitte Marger that you have finished *Penthode* for the Ensemble, and I am truly delighted. We have kept it in a program for the Proms on 26 July and I am of course counting on having you there to assist us in the rehearsals and being present at the performance.

Thank you once again with all my heart for your piece, and also for the text for the festschrift. It brought back to me an anecdote (the program that was set alight) which I had completely forgotten. No doubt we'll have to put that on the account of the after-dinner drinks... But after all a revealing action is a revealing action, the spirit of the circumstances loosening dispenses with all constraints of propriety.

To you and to Helen my warmest sentiments,
PB

[Original in French, see p. 263; English translation by Mark Weir.]

152 Goffredo Petrassi to Elliott Carter, 28 January 1988

Goffredo Petrassi / Via F. di Savoia, 3 / 00196 Roma
Rome, 28 January 1988

Dear Elliott,
I am very late in thanking you and Helen for your New Year's wishes. I and Rosetta reciprocate, wishing you both all the very best from the bottom of our hearts.

Wishes for this 1988 are all the more warm-hearted, dearest friend, because it's the year of your 80th birthday, which will quite rightly be celebrated all over the world. I shall celebrate it fervently in my heart of hearts, all the more so for the circumstances in which I find myself.

I don't know whether you have heard that for the last two years or so I have had problems with the sight in my one remaining eye. At the beginning it seemed that the process might not be entirely without hope and that the trouble might clear up. Unfortunately this has not proved to be the case, and now the situation is such – but *dieu merci* not definitive – that I cannot read and cannot write.

You will have only some idea of my distress when I tell you that I have dolefully had to forgo writing a piece in your honor that I had been asked for from various quarters, both in the United States and in Italy. It will not be possible for me to write that "Riconoscenza per Elliott Carter" with which I had intended to honor you in my turn on this solemn anniversary.

I wanted to tell you the reasons why I shall be missing from the authors whose tributes you will receive. Manuscript paper has become inimical to me and my fantasy has clouded over, but I try to compensate as best I can for the various constrictions to which I am subjected.

Fortunately the spirit is strong, and my health good. I have a token of your own excellent form in the photograph showing you happily rested after a swim in the lake; it filled me with happiness and I congratulate you.

I have heard from our excellent friend, the architect [Riccardo] Cerocchi, that for the next Pontino Festival, where you are to be properly celebrated, you have promised to stay for a whole week at San Felice Circeo. I hope to hold open house in that period, and for us to be able to spend a few hours together.

I am sorry to have troubled you with my personal trials, which also explain why I resort to the typewriter for this affectionate letter: indeed an *impolitesse* which in the past I would have been sure to avoid.

Rosetta remembers you tenderly and I embrace you with no less tenderness.
Goffredo

[Original in Italian, see p. 276; English translation by Mark Weir.]

153 Elliott Carter to Goffredo Petrassi, 14 March 1988

Elliott Carter / 31 West 12th Street/New York, N.Y. 10011
14 March 1988

Dearest Goffredo,
It saddens me very much to hear that your good eye does not function properly and that you are forced to use a typewriter. This deterioration of your eyesight must be terribly distressing, and I feel deeply sorry for you.

At the same time I was very flattered that you even considered writing something for my birthday. Thank you very much indeed.

Fortunately we will have the great pleasure of seeing both of you in San Felice from 22 to (?) 28 June. The première screening of a TV film on John Cage (!) and myself, which I have promised to attend in Amsterdam on 21 June, will cause us to miss the beginning of the Pontino Festival. But it is with all the more joy that Helen and I are looking forward to seeing you and Rosetta again and to resuming our dialogue, so dear to me, which began in 1954.

Helen joins me in sending both of you our kindest regards,
Elliott

Excuse illegible handwriting – I'm used to the typewriter.

[Original in French, see p. 277; English translation by Mark Weir]

163 Pierre Boulez to Elliott Carter, 18 January 1995

Pierre Boulez

Dear Elliott,
It's been three weeks since I got back from Chicago and three weeks (the same!) that I have been intending to write to you. John Bruce Yeh told me, in spite of the secret which has to be kept until 26 March (but he said he'd informed you in advance), about your milestone for my future, fast approaching 70th birthday – the second one, ten years later in my progress.

I thank you most warmly for a testimony which is both loyal and affectionate, and which I greatly appreciate. It is a pleasure to know that friends like you exist, and musicians of your kind, a rarity in refusing all compromise and "following their inclination, provided it leads upward." (The expression is Gide's, I think – and for once I am fully in agreement with a definition of his.)

I hope to see you perhaps in Chicago on the day of the performance, or more probably in New York when I come with the LSO next April.

I send you and Helen my very best wishes,
P. Boulez

[Original in French, see p. 293; English translation by Mark Weir.]

List of Published Works

1936   ***Tarantella,*** on a text by Ovid
a) for men's chorus and piano four hands (1936).
Première: 5 March 1937, Milton Academy, Boston
(Harvard Glee Club; G. Wallace Woodworth, conductor).
b) for men's chorus and orchestra (1937, revised 1971).
Première: 17 May 1937, Symphony Hall, Boston
(Harvard Glee Club; Boston Pops Orchestra;
G. Wallace Woodworth, conductor).

1937   ***Let's Be Gay,*** for women's chorus and two pianos,
on a text by John Gay (1937). Première: spring 1938,
Wells College, Aurora, NY (Wells College Glee Club;
Nicolas Nabokov, conductor).

Harvest Home, for mixed chorus *a cappella,* on a text
by Robert Herrick (1937). Première: spring 1938,
New York (Lehman Engel Madrigal Singers; Lehman
Engel, conductor).

To Music, for mixed chorus *a cappella* with soprano
solo, on a text by Robert Herrick (1937). Première:
16 March 1938, Federal Music Theatre, New York
(Lehman Engel Madrigal Singers; Lehman Engel,
conductor).

1938   ***Tell Me Where is Fancy Bred,*** for alto voice and guitar,
on a text by William Shakespeare (*The Merchant
of Venice,* Act III, Scene 2) (1938). Première (recording,
part of the recording of the Orson Welles Mercury
Theatre production of *The Merchant of Venice*):
1938, Columbia MC 6-1 (Adelyn Colla-Negri, alto;
Julius Wexler, guitar).

Heart Not So Heavy As Mine, mixed chorus *a cappella,*
on a text by Emily Dickinson (1938). Completed
December 1938. Première: 31 March 1939, Temple
Emanu-El, New York (Temple Emanu-El Choir; Lazare
Saminsky, conductor).

1939   ***Pocahontas*** (Ballet Legend in One Act), for orchestra
(1936–39). Première: 24 May 1939, Martin Beck
Theatre, New York (Ballet Caravan; Fritz Kitzinger,
conductor).

Suite from "Pocahontas," for orchestra (1939, revised
1960).

[***Canonic Suite***]
a) ***Musical Studies Nos. 1–4*** (1939?).
b) ***Suite for Quartet of Alto Saxophones***
(revision of *a,* 1944).
c) ***Canonic Suite for Four Clarinets in B flat*** (1955).
d) ***Canonic Suite for Quartet of Alto Saxophones***
(revision of *b,* 1981).

1940   ***Pastoral***
a) for English horn or viola and piano (1940).
Première: 12 November 1944, New York
(Joseph Marx, English horn; Elliott Carter, piano).
b) for clarinet or viola and piano (1942). Première:
1942, New York (Ralph Hersh, viola; Elliott Carter,
piano).
c) for English horn or alto saxophone in E flat,
marimba, and string orchestra (1987). Completed
31 October 1987. Première: 25 April 1988,
Carnegie Hall, New York (Orpheus Chamber Orchestra;
Heinz Holliger, English horn).

1941 ***The Defense of Corinth,*** for speaker, men's chorus and piano four hands, on a text by François Rabelais (*Pantagruel,* prologue to Book III, translated by Urquhart and Motteux) (1940–41). Première: 12 March 1942, Sanders Theatre, Harvard University, Cambridge, MA (Harvard Glee Club; G. Wallace Woodworth, conductor).

1942 ***Three Poems of Robert Frost***
a) for voice and piano (1942).
b) for voice and chamber orchestra (1974) (withdrawn).
c) for voice and chamber orchestra (1980).

Symphony No. 1 (1942). Completed 19 December 1942. Première: 27 April 1944, Eastman Theatre, Eastman School of Music, Rochester (Eastman-Rochester Symphony Orchestra; Howard Hanson, conductor).

1943 ***Warble for Lilac Time,*** on a text by Walt Whitman
a) for soprano or tenor and piano (1943?, rev. 1954). Première: 16 March 1947, Museum of Modern Art, New York (Helen Boatwright, soprano; Helmut Baerwald, piano).
b) for soprano and chamber orchestra (orchestration of *a,* 1946?, rev. 1955). Première: 14 September 1946, Yaddo, Saratoga Springs, NY (Helen Boatwright, soprano; Music Group Chamber Orchestra; Frederick Fennell, conductor).

Voyage, on a text by Hart Crane
a) for medium voice and piano (1943?). Première: 16 March 1947, Museum of Modern Art, New York (Helen Boatwright, soprano; Helmut Baerwald, piano).
b) for medium voice and orchestra (1974, revised 1979). Première: 8 August 1974, Aspen (Susan Davenny Wyner, soprano; Aspen Festival Orchestra; Richard Dufallo, conductor).

[*Elegy*]
a) ***Adagio,*** for cello and piano (1943?, unpublished).
b) ***Adagio,*** for viola and piano (transcription of *a,* 1943?).
c) ***Elegy,*** for string quartet (arrangement of *a,* 1946). Première: 21–22 August 1946, Eliot, ME (Lanier String Quartet: Frances Brockman Lanier, violin I; Marilyn Olson, violin II; Anna Golden, viola; Hazel Theodorowicz, cello).
d) ***Elegy,*** for string orchestra (arrangement of *c,* 1952). Première: 1 March 1953, Great Hall, Cooper Union, New York (orchestra of the American Federation of Musicians; David Boekman, conductor).
e) ***Elegy,*** for viola and piano (revision of *b,* 1961). Première: 16 April 1963, Cambridge, MA (George Humphrey, viola; Alice Canady, piano).
f) ***Elegy*** for cello and piano (arrangement of *c,* 2007). Completed 12 October 2007. Première: 14 January 2008, Auditorium RAI Arturo Toscanini, Turin (Fred Sherry, cello; Charles Rosen, piano).

1944 ***Holiday Overture,*** for orchestra (1944, revised 1960). Completed August 1944. Première (?): 1946, Frankfurt (Frankfurt Radio Symphony Orchestra; Hans Blümer, conductor).

The Harmony of Morning, for women's chorus and chamber orchestra, on a text by Mark Van Doren (1944). Completed November 1944. Première: 25 February 1945, Temple Emanu-El, New York (Temple Emanu-El Choir; Lazare Saminsky, conductor).

1945 ***Musicians Wrestle Everywhere,*** for mixed chorus *a cappella* or with string accompaniment, on a text by Emily Dickinson (1945). Broadcast première: 20 December 1945, WNBC Radio, New York; concert première: 12 February 1946, New York Times Hall, New York (Randolph Singers; David Randolph, conductor).

1946 ***Piano Sonata*** (1945–46, revised 1982). Completed January 1946. Broadcast première: 16 February 1947, Frick Museum, New York (Webster Aitken, piano); concert première: 5 March 1947, New York Times Hall, New York (James Sykes, piano).

1947 ***The Minotaur*** (Ballet in One Act), for orchestra (1946–47). Completed 13 March 1947. Première: 26 March 1947, Central High School of Needle Trades, New York (Ballet Society; Leon Barzin, conductor).

Suite from "The Minotaur", for orchestra (1947).

Emblems, for men's chorus and piano, on a text by Allen Tate (1946–47). Completed September 1947. Première of Part II only: 18 March 1951, Harvard University, Cambridge, MA (Harvard Glee Club; G. Wallace Woodworth, conductor); première of complete work: summer 1952 (Colgate College Singers; Bernard Weiser, piano; James Sykes, conductor).

1948 ***Woodwind Quintet*** (1948). Broadcast première: 21 February 1949; concert première: 27 February 1949, New York Times Hall, New York (for both: Martin Oberstein, flute; David Abosch, oboe; Louis Paul, clarinet; Mark Popkin, bassoon; Pinson Bobo, horn).

Sonata for Violoncello and Piano (1948). Completed 11 December 1948. Première: 27 February 1950, Town Hall, New York (Bernard Greenhouse, cello; Anthony Makas, piano).

1950 ***Eight Etudes and a Fantasy,*** for flute, oboe, clarinet, and bassoon (1949–50). Première: 28 October 1952, Museum of Modern Art, New York (New York Woodwind Quintet: Murray Panitz, flute; Jerome Roth, oboe; David Glazer, clarinet; Bernard Garfield, bassoon).

[*Eight Pieces for Four Timpani* (1950/1966)]
a) ***Six Pieces for Kettledrums:*** 1. *Saëta,* 2. *Moto Perpetuo,* 3. *Recitative,* 4. *Improvisation,* 5. *Canaries,* 6. *March* (1950, unpublished). Première: 6 May 1952, Museum of Modern Art, New York (Al Howard, timpani). (Premièred under the title *Suite for Timpani*)
b) ***Eight Pieces for Four Timpani*** (1950/1966) (revision of *a,* plus *Adagio* and *Canto.* New order: 1. *Saëta,* 2. *Moto Perpetuo,* 3. *Adagio,* 4. *Recitative,* 5. *Improvisation,* 6. *Canto,* 7. *Canaries,* 8. *March*). Première of *Adagio* and *Canto:* 29 April 1967, Albright-Knox Art Gallery, Buffalo (Jan Williams, timpani).

1951   ***String Quartet No. 1*** (1950–51). Completed September 1951. Première: 26 February 1953, McMillin Theatre, Columbia University, New York (Walden String Quartet: Homer Schmitt, violin I; Bernard Goodman, violin II; John Garvey, viola; Robert Swenson, cello).

1952   ***Sonata for Flute, Oboe, Cello and Harpsichord*** (1952). Première: 10 November 1953, Carnegie Hall, New York (Harpsichord Quartet of New York: Claude Monteux, flute; Harry Shulman, oboe; Bernard Greenhouse, cello; Sylvia Marlowe, harpsichord).

1955   ***Variations for Orchestra*** (1953–55). Completed 14 November 1955. Première: 21 April 1956, Columbia Auditorium, Louisville (Louisville Orchestra; Robert Whitney, conductor).

1959   ***String Quartet No. 2*** (1958–59). Completed 3 June 1959. Première: 25 March 1960, Juilliard School, New York (Juilliard String Quartet: Robert Mann, violin I; Isidore Cohen, violin II; Raphael Hillyer, viola; Claus Adam, cello).

1961   ***Double Concerto,*** for harpsichord and piano with two chamber orchestras (1959–61). Completed August 1961. Première: 6 September 1961, Grace Rainey Rogers Auditorium, Metropolitan Museum of Art, New York (Ralph Kirkpatrick, harpsichord; Charles Rosen, piano; chamber orchestra; Gustav Meier, conductor).

1965   ***Piano Concerto*** (1961–65). Completed summer 1965. Première: 6–7 January 1967, Symphony Hall, Boston (Jacob Lateiner, piano; Boston Symphony Orchestra; Erich Leinsdorf, conductor).

1966   ***Adagio*** and ***Canto,*** for four timpani. (See *Eight Pieces for Four Timpani,* 1950/1966.)

1969   ***Concerto for Orchestra*** (1967–69). Completed 25 November 1969. Première: 5–7 and 9 February 1970, Philharmonic Hall, New York (New York Philharmonic; Leonard Bernstein, conductor).

1971   ***String Quartet No. 3*** (1970–71). Première: 23 January 1973, Alice Tully Hall, Lincoln Center, New York (Juilliard String Quartet: Robert Mann, violin I; Earl Carlyss, violin II; Samuel Rhodes, viola; Claus Adam, cello).

      Canon for 3: In Memoriam Igor Stravinsky, for three equal instrumental voices (1971). Première: 23 January 1972, Alice Tully Hall, Lincoln Center, New York (Joel Timm, oboe; Allen Blustine, clarinet; James Stubb, trumpet).

1974   ***Duo for Violin and Piano*** (1972–74). Completed 27 April 1974. Première: 21 March 1975, Great Hall, Cooper Union, New York (Paul Zukofsky, violin; Gilbert Kalish, piano).

Brass Quintet (1974). Completed 29 August 1974. Broadcast première: 20 October 1974, BBC, London; concert première: 15 November 1974, Coolidge Auditorium, Washington, D.C. (both by the American Brass Quintet: Raymond Mase, trumpet; Louis Ranger, trumpet; Edward Birdwell, horn; Herbert Rankin, trombone; Robert Bidlecombe, trombone).

A Fantasy about Purcell's "Fantasia upon One Note," for brass quintet (1974). Completed 1 September 1974. Première: 13 January 1975, Carnegie Recital Hall, New York (American Brass Quintet, see above).

1975   ***Voyage,*** for medium voice and orchestra (1974–75, revised 1979). (See *Voyage,* 1943.)

      A Mirror on Which to Dwell, for soprano and chamber orchestra, six poems of Elizabeth Bishop (1974–75). Completed 31 December 1975. Première: 24 February 1976, Hunter College Playhouse, New York (Susan Davenny Wyner, soprano; Speculum Musicae; Richard Fitz, conductor).

1976   ***A Symphony of Three Orchestras*** (1976). Completed 31 December 1976. Première: 17–19 and 22 February 1977, Avery Fisher Hall, Lincoln Center, New York (New York Philharmonic; Pierre Boulez, conductor).

1978   ***Syringa,*** for mezzo-soprano, bass, guitar, and ten instrumentalists, on texts by John Ashbery and ancient Greek authors (1977–78). Completed 1 September 1978. Première: 10 December 1978, Alice Tully Hall, Lincoln Center, New York (Jan DeGaetani, mezzo-soprano; Thomas Paul, bass; Speculum Musicae; Harvey Sollberger, conductor).

1980   ***Night Fantasies,*** for piano (1978–80). Completed 12 April 1980. Première: 2 June 1980, Assembly Rooms, Bath (Ursula Oppens, piano).

      Three Poems of Robert Frost, for voice and chamber orchestra (1980). (See *Three Poems of Robert Frost,* 1942.)

1981   ***In Sleep, in Thunder,*** for tenor and 14 instruments, six poems of Robert Lowell (1981). Completed 11 December 1981. Première: 26 October 1982, St. John's Smith Square, London (Martyn Hill, tenor; London Sinfonietta; Oliver Knussen, conductor).

1983   ***Triple Duo,*** for flute (piccolo), clarinet in B flat (clarinet in E flat, bass clarinet), violin, cello, percussion, and piano (1982–83). Completed 7 February 1983. Première: 23 April 1983, Symphony Space, New York (The Fires of London: Philippa Davies, flute [piccolo]; David Campbell, clarinets; Rosemary Furniss, violin; Jonathan Williams, cello; Gregory Knowles, percussion; Stephen Pruslin, piano).

      Changes, for guitar (1983). Completed 8 September 1983. Première: 11 December 1983, Theresa L. Kaufman Concert Hall, 92nd Street Y, New York (David Starobin, guitar).

1984   **Canon for 4 – Homage to William,** for flute, bass clarinet in B flat, violin, and cello (1984). Completed 19 April 1984. Première: 8 June 1984, Pump Room, Bath (members of the London Sinfonietta).

Riconoscenza per Goffredo Petrassi, for violin (1984). (See *Four Lauds,* 1984–2000.)

Esprit rude/Esprit doux I, for flute and clarinet (1984). Completed 2 November 1984. Première: 31 March 1985, Weinbrenner-Saal, Kurhaus, Baden-Baden (members of the Ensemble InterContemporain: Lawrence Beauregard, flute; Alain Damiens, clarinet).

1985   **Penthode,** for five groups of four instrumentalists (1984–85). Completed 9 June 1985. Première: 26 July 1985, Royal Albert Hall, London (Ensemble InterContemporain; Pierre Boulez, conductor).

1986   **String Quartet No. 4** (1985–86). Completed June 1986. Première: 17 September 1986, Festival Miami, Gusman Concert Hall, University of Miami, Miami (Composers Quartet: Matthew Raimondi, violin I; Anahid Ajemian, violin II; Jean Dane, viola; Mark Shuman, cello).

A Celebration of Some 100 x 150 Notes, for orchestra (1986). (See *Three Occasions,* 1989.)

1987   **Oboe Concerto** (1986–87). Completed 10 October 1987. Première: 17 June 1988, Großer Tonhallesaal, Zurich (Heinz Holliger, oboe; Collegium Musicum Zurich; John Carewe, conductor).

Pastoral, for English horn, marimba, and string orchestra (1987). (See *Pastoral,* 1940.)

1988   **Enchanted Preludes,** for flute and cello (1988). Completed 13 February 1988. Première: 16 May 1988, Merkin Concert Hall, New York (members of the Da Capo Chamber Players: Patricia Spencer, flute; André Emelianoff, cello).

Remembrance, for orchestra (1988). (See *Three Occasions,* 1986–89.)

Birthday Flourish, completed 4 July 1988
a) for five trumpets in C (1988). Première: 14 and 16–17 September 1988, Davies Symphony Hall, San Francisco (members of the San Francisco Symphony Orchestra; Herbert Blomstedt, conductor).
b) for two trumpets, horn, and two trombones (1988). Première: 20–21 January 1989, Music Hall, Cincinnati, OH (members of the Cincinnati Symphony Orchestra; Jesús López-Cobos, conductor).

1989   **Anniversary,** for orchestra (1989). (See *Three Occasions,* 1986–89.)

Three Occasions, for orchestra (1986–89).
1. **A Celebration of Some 100 x 150 Notes,** for orchestra (1986). Completed 28 December 1986. Première: 10–12 April 1987, Jones Hall, Houston (Houston Symphony Orchestra; Sergiu Commissiona, conductor).
2. **Remembrance,** for orchestra (1988). Completed 8 March 1988. Première: 10 August 1988, Theatre-Concert Hall, Tanglewood, Lenox, MA (Tanglewood Music Center Orchestra; Oliver Knussen, conductor).
3. **Anniversary,** for orchestra (1989). Completed 25 May 1989.
Première of complete work: 5 October 1989, Royal Festival Hall, Southbank Centre, London (BBC Symphony Orchestra; Oliver Knussen, conductor).

1990   **Violin Concerto** (1988–90). Completed end of February 1990. Première: 2–5 May 1990, Davies Symphony Hall, San Francisco (Ole Böhn, violin; San Francisco Symphony Orchestra; Herbert Blomstedt, conductor).

Con leggerezza pensosa, for clarinet in B flat, violin, and cello (1990). Completed 10 July 1990. Première: 29 September 1990, Istituto di Studi Musicali, Latina, Italy (Ciro Scarponi, clarinet; Jorge Risi, violin; Luigi Lanzillotta, cello).

1991   **Scrivo in vento,** for flute (1991). Completed 22 June 1991. Première: 20 July 1991, Centre Acanthes, Avignon (Robert Aitken, flute).

Quintet for Piano and Winds (1991). Completed summer 1991. Première: 13 September 1992, Kölner Philharmonie, Cologne (Heinz Holliger, oboe; Elmar Schmid, clarinet; Klaus Thunemann, bassoon; Radovan Vlatković, horn; András Schiff, piano).

1992   **Trilogy,** for oboe and harp (1991–92).
1. **Bariolage,** for harp. Completed 3 January 1992. Première: 23 March 1992, Salle Patino, Geneva (Ursula Holliger, harp).
2. **Inner Song,** for oboe. Completed 18 January 1992. Première: 25 April 1992, Theatersaal, Witten, Germany (Heinz Holliger, oboe).
3. **Immer neu,** for oboe and harp. Completed 5 February 1992.
Première of complete work: 30 June 1992, Pontino Festival, Castello Caetani, Sermoneta, Italy (Heinz Holliger, oboe; Ursula Holliger, harp).

1993   **Gra,** for clarinet in B flat (1993). Completed 7 March 1993. Première: 4 June 1993, Pontino Festival, Castello Caetani, Sermoneta, Italy (Roland Diry, clarinet). (Arrangement for trombone by Benny Sluchin, 1996).

Partita, for orchestra (1993). (See *Symphonia: Sum Fluxae Pretium Spei,* 1993–96.)

1994   ***90+,*** for piano (1994). Completed 16 April 1994. Première: 11 June 1994, Pontino Festival, Castello Caetani, Sermoneta, Italy (Giuseppe Scotese, piano).

      Adagio tenebroso, for orchestra (1994). (See *Symphonia: Sum Fluxae Pretium Spei, 1993–96.*)

      Figment I, for cello (1994). Completed 20 June 1994. Première: 8 May 1995, Merkin Concert Hall, New York (Thomas Demenga, cello).

      Fragment No. 1, for string quartet (1994). Completed 30 August 1994. Première: 13 October 1994, Merkin Concert Hall, New York (Kronos Quartet: David Harrington, violin I; John Sherba, violin II; Hank Dutt, viola; Joan Jeanrenaud, cello).

      Esprit rude/Esprit doux II, for flute, clarinet, and marimba (1994). Completed 11 December 1994. Première: 30–31 March 1995, Grainger Ballroom, Orchestra Hall, Symphony Center, Chicago (members of Chicago Pro Musica: Richard Graef, flute; John Bruce Yeh, clarinet; Patricia Dash, marimba).

      Of Challenge and of Love, for soprano and piano, five poems of John Hollander (1994). Completed 31 December 1994. Première: 23 June 1995, Aldeburgh Festival, The Rookery, Eyke, UK (Lucy Shelton, soprano; John Constable, piano).

1995   ***String Quartet No. 5*** (1994–95). Completed 30 July 1995. Première: 19 September 1995, De Singel, Antwerp (Arditti Quartet: Irvine Arditti, violin I; Graeme Jennings, violin II; Garth Knox, viola; Rohan de Saram, cello).

1996   ***Allegro scorrevole,*** for orchestra (1996). (See *Symphonia: Sum Fluxae Pretium Spei, 1993–96.*)

      Symphonia: Sum Fluxae Pretium Spei, for orchestra (1993–96).
      1. ***Partita,*** for orchestra (1993). Completed 12 June 1993. Première: 17–19 February 1994, Orchestra Hall, Symphony Center, Chicago (Chicago Symphony Orchestra, Daniel Barenboim, conductor).
      2. ***Adagio tenebroso,*** for orchestra (1994). Completed 10 June 1994. Première: 13 September 1995, Royal Albert Hall, London (BBC Symphony Orchestra; Andrew Davis, conductor).
      3. ***Allegro scorrevole,*** for orchestra (1996). Completed 18 May 1996. Première: 22 and 24 May 1997, Severance Hall, Cleveland (Cleveland Orchestra; Christoph von Dohnányi, conductor).
      Première of complete work: 25 April 1998, Bridgewater Hall, Manchester (BBC Symphony Orchestra; Oliver Knussen, conductor).

      A Six Letter Letter, for English horn (1996). Completed 6 February 1996. Première: 27 April 1996, Stadtcasino, Basel (Heinz Holliger, English horn).

      Clarinet Concerto (1996). Completed 6 November 1996. Première: 10–11 January 1997, Salle des Concerts, Cité de la Musique, Paris (Alain Damiens, clarinet; Ensemble InterContemporain; Pierre Boulez, conductor).

1997   ***Quintet for Piano and String Quartet*** (1997). Completed 14 April 1997. Première: 18 November 1998, Coolidge Auditorium, Library of Congress, Washington, D.C. (Ursula Oppens, piano; Arditti Quartet: Irvine Arditti, violin I; Graeme Jennings, violin II; Dov Scheindlin, viola; Rohan de Saram, cello).

      Shard, for guitar (1997). Completed 23 April 1997. Première: 11 June 1997, Louisiana Concert Hall, Louisiana Museum of Modern Art, Humlebæk, Denmark (David Starobin, guitar). (Incorporated into *Luimen,* 1997.)

      Luimen, for trumpet, trombone, harp, vibraphone, mandolin, and guitar (1997). Completed 7 July 1997. Première: 31 March 1998, Paradiso, Amsterdam (Nieuw Ensemble; Ed Spanjaard, conductor).

1998   ***What Next?,*** opera to a libretto by Paul Griffiths (1997–98). Completed December 1998. Première: 16 September 1999, Deutsche Staatsoper Unter den Linden, Berlin (staged by Nicholas Brieger; Simone Nold [Rose]; Hanno Müller-Brachmann [Harry or Larry]; Lynne Dawson [Mama]; William Joyner [Zen]; Hilary Summers [Stella]; Ian Antal [Kid]; Staatskapelle Berlin; Daniel Barenboim, conductor).

1999   ***Two Diversions,*** for piano (1999). Completed 14 March 1999. Première: 2 March 2000, Weill Recital Hall, Carnegie Hall, New York (Kirill Gerstein, piano).

      Fragment No. 2, for string quartet (1999). Completed 17 March 1999. Première: 23 June 1999, Cuvilliés-Theater, Munich (Arditti Quartet: Irvine Arditti, violin I; Graeme Jennings, violin II; Dov Scheindlin, viola; Rohan de Saram, cello).

      Tempo e tempi, for soprano, oboe (English horn), clarinet (bass clarinet), violin, and cello, on texts by Eugenio Montale, Giuseppe Ungaretti, and Salvatore Quasimodo (1998–99).
      1. "Tempo e tempi," completed 14 June 1998. Première: 1 July 1998, Pontino Festival, Castello Caetani, Sermoneta, Italy (Victoria Schneider, soprano; Heinz Holliger, English horn; and members of the Ensemble Contrehamps: René Meyer, bass clarinet; Isabelle Magnenat, violin).
      2.–8. completed 16 August 1999.
      Première of complete work: 24 May 2000, Queen Elizabeth Hall, Southbank Centre, London (Lucy Shelton, soprano; members of the London Sinfonietta; Oliver Knussen, conductor).

      Statement – Remembering Aaron, for violin (1999). (See *Four Lauds, 1984–2000.*)

      Fantasy – Remembering Roger, for violin (1999). (See *Four Lauds, 1984–2000.*)

2000   **ASKO Concerto,** for ensemble (1999–2000). Completed 15 January 2000. Première: 26 April 2000, Concertgebouw, Amsterdam (ASKO Ensemble; Oliver Knussen, conductor).

Retrouvailles, for piano (2000). Completed 20 January 2000. Première: 26 March 2000, Queen Elizabeth Hall, South Bank Centre, London (Rolf Hind, piano).

Cello Concerto (2000). Completed 11 November 2000. Première: 27–29 September 2001, Symphony Hall, Chicago (Yo-Yo Ma, cello; Chicago Symphony Orchestra; Daniel Barenboim, conductor).

Rhapsodic Musings (for Robert Mann), for violin (2000). (See *Four Lauds,* 1984–2000.)

Four Lauds, for violin (1984–2000).
1. **Statement – Remembering Aaron,** for violin (1999). Completed 30 March 1999. Première: 22 May 1999, Peer Gynt Saalen, Grieghallen, Bergen (Ole Böhn, violin).
2. **Riconoscenza per Goffredo Petrassi,** for violin (1984). Completed 30 April 1984. Première: 15 June 1984, Pontino Festival, Abbey of Fossanova, Priverno, Italy (Georg Mönch, violin).
3. **Rhapsodic Musings (for Robert Mann),** for violin (2000). Completed 18 June 2000. Première: 28 March 2001, Merkin Concert Hall, New York (Robert Mann, violin).
4. **Fantasy – Remembering Roger,** for violin (1999). Completed 25 April 1999. Première: 18 November 1999, John Knowles Paine Concert Hall, Harvard University, Cambridge, MA (Rolf Schulte, violin). Première of whole set: 17 October 2001, Weill Recital Hall, Carnegie Hall, New York (Rolf Schulte, violin) (1., 2., and 4. originally grouped as *Three Recollections*.)

2001   **Figment II: Remembering Mr. Ives,** for cello (2000–01). Completed March 2001. Première: 2 December 2001, Alice Tully Hall, Lincoln Center, New York (Fred Sherry, cello).

Oboe Quartet, for oboe, violin, viola, and cello. Completed 15 April 2001. Première: 2 September 2001, Matthäuskirche, Lucerne (Heinz Holliger, oboe; Thomas Zehetmair, violin; Ruth Killius, viola; Thomas Demenga, cello).

Hiyoku, for two clarinets in B flat (2001). Completed 11 May 2001. Première: 9 December 2001, Kleine Zaal, Concertgebouw, Amsterdam (Charles Neidich, clarinet; Ayako Oshima, clarinet).

Steep Steps, for bass clarinet in B flat (2001). Completed summer 2001. Première: 17 October 2001, Weill Recital Hall, Carnegie Hall, New York (Virgil Blackwell, bass clarinet).

2002   **Au Quai,** for bassoon and viola (2002). Completed 19 January 2002. Première: 12 June 2002, Queen Elizabeth Hall, Southbank Centre, London (members of the London Sinfonietta: John Orford, bassoon; Paul Silverthorne, viola).

Retracing, for bassoon (2002). Première: 3 December 2002, Weill Recital Hall, Carnegie Hall, New York (Peter Kolkay, bassoon). (Extracted from *ASKO Concerto,* 1999–2000)

Boston Concerto, for orchestra (2001–02). Completed 7 May 2002. Première: 3–5 April 2003, Symphony Hall, Boston (Boston Symphony Orchestra; Ingo Metzmacher, conductor).

Of Rewaking, for mezzo-soprano and orchestra, on a text by William Carlos Williams (2002). Completed October 2002. Première: 29–31 May 2003, Orchestra Hall, Symphony Center, Chicago (Michelle DeYoung, mezzo-soprano; Chicago Symphony Orchestra; Daniel Barenboim, conductor).

Micomicón, for orchestra (2002). (See *Three Illusions,* 2002–04.)

2003   **Dialogues,** for piano and large ensemble (2003). Completed 15 July 2003. Première: 23 January 2004, Queen Elizabeth Hall, Southbank Centre, London (Nicolas Hodges, piano; London Sinfonietta; Oliver Knussen, conductor).

Call, for two trumpets and horn (2003). Completed 6 October 2003. Première: 5 May 2004, United Artists Battery Park Theater, New York (Kevin Cobb, trumpet; Mark Gould, trumpet; William Purvis, horn). (Incorporated into *Réflexions,* 2004.)

2004   **Réflexions,** for ensemble (2004). Completed 12 May 2004. Première: 15 February 2005, Salle des Concerts, Cité de la Musique, Paris (Ensemble InterContemporain; Pierre Boulez, conductor).

Mosaic, for chamber ensemble (2004). Completed 22 August 2004. Première: 16 March 2005, Purcell Room, Southbank Centre, London (Nash Ensemble).

More's Utopia, for orchestra (2004). (See *Three Illusions,* 2002–04.)

Fons juventatis, for orchestra (2004). (See *Three Illusions,* 2002–04.)

Three Illusions, for orchestra (2002–04).
1. **Micomicón,** for orchestra (2002). Completed 4 December 2002. Première: 15–17 January 2004, Symphony Hall, Boston (Boston Symphony Orchestra; James Levine, conductor).
2. **Fons juventatis,** for orchestra (2004). Completed 6 October 2004.
3. **More's Utopia,** for orchestra (2004). Completed 15 September 2004.
Première of complete work: 6–8 October 2005, Symphony Hall, Boston (Boston Symphony Orchestra; James Levine, conductor).

2005   **Soundings,** for orchestra (2004–05). Completed 23 June 2005. Première: 6–7 October 2005, Orchestra Hall, Symphony Center, Chicago (Chicago Symphony Orchestra; Daniel Barenboim, pianist and conductor).

Intermittences, for piano (2005). (See *Two Thoughts about the Piano,* 2005–06.)

2006   ***In the Distances of Sleep,*** for mezzo-soprano and ensemble, on texts by Wallace Stevens (2006). Completed 19 March 2006. Première: 15 October 2006, Zankel Hall, Carnegie Hall, New York (Michelle DeYoung, mezzo-soprano; MET Chamber Ensemble; James Levine, conductor).

Horn Concerto (2006). Completed 19 August 2006. Première: 15, 17, and 20 November 2007, Symphony Hall, Boston (James Sommerville, horn; Boston Symphony Orchestra; James Levine, conductor).

Caténaires, for piano (2006). (See *Two Thoughts about the Piano,* 2005–06.)

Two Thoughts about the Piano (2005–06).
1. ***Intermittences,*** for piano (2005). Completed 1 4 August 2005. Première: 3 May 2006, Miller Auditorium, Kalamazoo, MI (Peter Serkin, piano).
2. ***Caténaires,*** for piano (2006). Completed 23 September 2006. Première: 11 December 2006, Zankel Hall, Carnegie Hall, New York (Pierre-Laurent Aimard, piano).

2007   ***Interventions,*** for piano and orchestra (2007). Completed 16 April 2007. Forthcoming première: 4–6 December 2008, Symphony Hall, Boston, (Daniel Barenboim, piano; Boston Symphony Orchestra; James Levine, conductor).

Mad Regales, for six solo voices, on texts by John Ashbery (2007). Completed 9 May 2007. Forthcoming première: 22 July 2008, Seiji Ozawa Hall, Lenox, MA (Tanglewood Center Music Fellows; James Levine, conductor).

HBHH, for oboe (2007). Completed 11 May 2007. Première: 27 May 2007, Remise, Karthause Ittingen, Warth, Switzerland (Heinz Holliger, oboe).

Sound Fields, for strings (2007). Completed 16 May 2007. Première: 20 July 2008, Seiji Ozawa Hall, Tanglewood, Lenox, MA (Tanglewood Center Music Fellows; Stefan Asbury, conductor).

Matribute, for piano (2007). Completed 27 May 2007. Première: 27 August 2007, Konzertsaal, Kultur- und Kongreßzentrum, Lucerne (James Levine, piano).

Figment III, for contrabass (2007). Completed 4 June 2007, revised 18 July 2007. Première: 7 April 2008, Jordan Hall, New England Conservatory, Boston, MA (Donald Palma, contrabass).

Figment IV, for viola (2007). Completed 23 June 2007, revised 18 July 2007. Première: 22 January 2008, Salle des Concerts, Cité de la Musique, Paris (Samuel Rhodes, viola).

La Musique, for solo voice, on a text by Charles Baudelaire (2007). Completed 24 June 2007. Première: 19 October 2007, Brown University, Providence, RI (Lucy Shelton, soprano).

Clarinet Quintet, for clarinet and string quartet (2007). Completed 7 October 2007. Première: 29 April 2008, Peter Jay Sharp Theater, Juilliard School, New York (Charles Neidich, clarinet; Juilliard String Quartet: Joel Smirnoff, violin I; Ronald Copes, violin II; Samuel Rhodes, viola; Joel Krosnick, cello).

Elegy, for string quartet, arrangement for cello and piano (2007). (See *Elegy,* 1943 or 1944.)

2008   ***Flute Concerto*** (2007–08). Completed 25 February 2008. Première: 9 September 2008, YMCA, Jerusalem (Emmanuel Pahud, flute; Jerusalem International Chamber Music Festival Ensemble; Daniel Barenboim, conductor).

Tintinnabulation, for percussion sextet (2008). Completed 19 April 2008. Forthcoming première: 2 December 2008, Jordan Hall, New England Conservatory, Boston (New England Conservatory Percussion Ensemble; Frank Epstein, conductor).

Duettino, for violin and cello (2008). Completed 11 May 2008. Forthcoming première: 14 December 2008, Zankel Hall, Carnegie Hall, New York (Rolf Schulte, violin; Fred Sherry, cello).

Fratribute, for piano (2008). Completed 23 May 2008.

Sistribute, for piano (2008). Completed 28 May 2008.

Wind Rose, for 24 woodwinds. Completed 8 August 2008. Forthcoming première: 16 December 2008, Barbican Centre, London (BBC Symphony Orchestra; Oliver Knussen, conductor).

On Conversing with Paradise, for baritone and chamber orchestra, on texts by Ezra Pound (2008). In progress as of 29 September 2008. Forthcoming première: June 2009, Aldeburgh (Oliver Knussen, conductor).

Index

The following index contains all names mentioned in
the main text and footnotes except for simple bibliographical
references. In the case of Carter, we have chosen to list
the works and documents rather than the myriad occurrences
of his name. Page numbers in boldface type refer to
letters, texts, and music manuscripts reproduced in this book.